STRAIGHT AND LEVEL: PRACTICAL AIRLINE ECONOMICS

Aldershot: Ashgate
Publishing, 2003

0754619303

For Captain David Holloway
and in memory of Squadron Leader Richard Holloway

Straight and Level:
Practical Airline Economics

STEPHEN HOLLOWAY

ASHGATE

Published by
Ashgate Publishing Limited
Gower House
Croft Road
Aldershot
Hampshire GU11 3HR
England

Ashgate Publishing Company
Suite 420
101 Cherry Street
Burlington, VT 05401-4405 USA

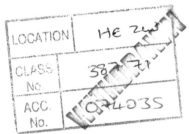

Ashgate website: http://www.ashgate.com

British Library Cataloguing in Publication Data
Holloway, S. (Stephen) , 1952-
    Straight and level : practical airline economics. - 2nd ed.
    1.Aeronautics, Commercial - Finance
    I.Title
    387.7'1

Library of Congress Cataloging-in-Publication Data
Holloway, Stephen, 1952-
    Straight and level : practical airline economics / Stephen Holloway.-- 2nd ed.
        p. cm.
    Includes bibliographical references and index.
    ISBN 0-7546-1929-X (alk. paper) -- ISBN 0-7546-1930-3 (pbk. : alk. paper)
    1. Aeronautics, Commercial--Finance. I. Title.

    HE9782.H65 2003
    387.7'1--dc21

                                                                                2002043970

ISBN 0 7546 1929 X (HBK)
ISBN 0 7546 1930 3 (PBK)

Printed and bound in Great Britain by MPG Books Ltd, Bodmin, Cornwall

Contents

v

Figures and Tables

xi

Foreword

When we started Emirates in 1985 we decided we would create a standard of service in the air and on the ground which would be unbeatable – but we also made a promise to our customers and ourselves that we wouldn't introduce a new service unless we could maintain it and never reduce or drop it. This commitment to customer service underlines the very essence of quality which depends on uniformity and continuity, but most of all a philosophy that the customer always comes first. It sounds easy but it's not, for airlines have to juggle scores of aircraft across scores of destinations to please their clients. This becomes a nightmare in keeping promises. How can one remain profitable by providing the businessperson with an 8 a.m. morning departure when the plane for economic reasons should be thousands of miles away at another destination? It sounds easy, too, to offer services on the ground which ease the First and Business Class passenger through check-in, customs and immigration....but it requires enormous investments in special check-in lounges and extraordinary relations with the airport and government authorities to achieve such seamless travel. In the good old days friends could wave goodbye to you on the tarmac, but in the security-conscious 21st century such personal gestures have been replaced by metal detectors and body searches changing not only the relationship of a passenger with travel but with the airline too. Today ground-handling staff and flight-crews need to be chosen for their understanding of passengers' psychology and their relationship with new and changing technology. It is no longer just a question of picking people for their qualifications. It is important to use a whole range of psychometric tests and in-depth interviews to find team members who can relate to today's business and leisure travel experience. With all these hindrances and obstacles to achieving passenger appeal, it is amazing that any airline can make a profit. Sometimes in the aviation business, we wishfully wonder whether we should just concentrate on freight (which can't complain) rather than the millions of personable individuals who all require their own special treatment. Not that I am complaining, because the success of my own airline has come as a result of fulfilling these myriad wishes.

It is always a salutary lesson to newcomers to the airline industry that in order to maintain standards and keep our promises to customers, we have to invest in modern and sophisticated equipment, ranging from a fully operational cabin crew simulator which looks like and costs almost as much as an average jetliner, to the less expensive but still vital defibrillators to complement our medical equipment on board. At one time customers expected a meal and a beverage (which they often had to pay for) and a pretty hostess to turn off the lights so they could sleep on long-distance flights. Today they expect their own lounge before they board and in the sky a telephone, fax, multi-channel television service, five-course meal, etc. while at the same time insisting that airfares go down.

The question in everyone's mind at the moment is whether airlines will use the A380 for moving passenger service to an entirely different level or whether they will, as I predict, use the Super Jumbos to keep costs down and to enable them to maintain the low level of fares to which the travelling public seem to think they are entitled. It would be ludicrous to suggest that this mammoth aircraft can be used for introducing shops, restaurants, nurseries, hair salons, and the like. Let's admit it: they will be used for putting more people into the air and enabling us to maintain the number of slots, which we have grandfathered at various airports around the world. Running an airline in the 21st century is one of the most perilous jobs for ambitious executives wanting to satisfy the share- and stake-holders of their company, yet at the same time trying to achieve the quality of service that is now desired and expected by the customer. Steve Holloway's book amply explains the complexity and scale of the challenge.

Maurice Flanagan
Group Managing Director
Emirates.

Preface

This book says little about the past evolution of the air transport industry, and neither does it forecast the future. Its sole objective is to describe in a practical way the fundamental economic forces that underlie the business. Unlike the industry itself, these fundamental forces change only slowly.

The book is divided into four parts. Part 1 provides a strategic context within which to consider the industry's economics. Part 2 is structured around a relationship that lies at the heart of the business:

$$\text{TRAFFIC x YIELD} > < \text{OUTPUT x UNIT COST}$$
$$= \text{OPERATING PERFORMANCE (i.e., PROFIT or LOSS)}$$

Capacity management is clearly central to airline economics, and Part 3 looks at topics critical to capacity management: network design and scheduling; fleet management; and revenue management. Part 4 closes the book with a review of several macro-level metrics of operating performance.

The book has been written primarily for masters-level students on aviation management courses; it should also be useful to advanced undergraduates. Amongst practitioners, it will appeal in particular to managers at the beginning of their careers and to established managers moving from functional posts into general management. More broadly, anyone wanting to gain an understanding of the economics of the airline industry at a practical level and an insight into the reasons for its financial volatility should find the book of interest.

Acknowledgements

I should first like to thank Maurice Flanagan for contributing the Foreword. Its insightfulness will come as no surprise to anybody who has watched the carefully crafted rise of Emirates since launch in the mid-1980s.

The following people have been exceptionally generous with their time, making observations and suggestions that have contributed substantially to the 'finished product': Bryson Monteleone (Morten Beyer & Agnew); Rodger Robertson (University of New South Wales); and Simon Walker (Virtual Aviation College). Two anonymous reviewers have also provided helpful comments. The usual caveat applies. Thanks are due in addition to Bridget Dooling (Air Transport Association), Steve Double (British Airways), Richard Lonsdale (Boeing), and Mike Simon (Emirates).

John Hindley at Ashgate Publishing provided encouragement from the inception of this second edition, and Pauline Beavers guided it through the final stages of publication. Thanks are once again owed to my wife Paula for her forbearance throughout yet another lengthy project.

Abbreviations and Definitions

ABC	Activity-based costing.
ACMI	Aircraft, crew, maintenance, and insurance (a form of wet-leasing).
AD	Airworthiness directive.
AOC	Air operator's certificate.
AOCC	Airline operations control centre.
AOG	Aircraft-on-the-ground (i.e., unserviceable).
APU	Auxiliary power unit.
APV	Acceptable perceived value.
ASA	Air services agreement.
ASK	Available seat-kilometre: one seat flown one kilometre, whether occupied or not. A measure of output.
ASM	Available seat-mile: one seat flown one mile.
ATK	Available tonne-kilometre: one tonne of payload capacity flown one kilometre, whether sold or not.
ATM	Available ton-mile: one ton of payload capacity flown one mile. ('ATM' is also a widely used abbreviation for 'air traffic management', but is not used as such in the present book.)
ATPCO	Airline Tariff Publishing Company.
ATS	Air traffic services.
AVC	Average variable cost.
BELF	Break-even load factor.
BFE	Buyer-furnished equipment.
BIDT	Billing information data tape.
CAB	Civil Aeronautics Board (US).
CASM	Cost per available seat-mile ('unit cost').
CCQ	Cross-crew qualification.
CEO	Chief executive officer.

CNS	Communication, navigation, and surveillance.
CRS	Computer reservation system.
D^3	Demand-driven despatch.
DFM	Dynamic fleet management.
DOC	Direct operating cost.
DOJ	Department of Justice (US).
DOT	Department of Transportation (US).
ECAA	European Common Aviation Area.
EDI	Electronic data interchange.
ETOPS	Extended-range twin-engine operations.
EU	European Union.
FAA	Federal Aviation Administration (US).
FAK	Freight-all-kinds (rate).
FFP	Frequent flyer programme.
FOD	Fuel over destination.
FTK	Freight tonne-kilometre.
FTM	Freight ton-mile.
GAAP	Generally accepted accounting principles.
GDP	Gross domestic product.
GDS	Global distribution system.
GIT	Group inclusive tour.
GNP	Gross national product.
GSA	General sales agent.
GSE	Ground support equipment.
HUD	Head-up display.
IATA	International Air Transport Association.
ICAO	International Civil Aviation Organization.
IFC	Inflight communications.
IFE	Inflight entertainment.
IO	Industrial organization (economics).
IOC	Indirect operating cost.
IP	Initial provisioning.
IPO	Initial public offering.
IRR	Internal rate of return.
IT	Information technology.
JIT	Just-in-time (inventory management).
LRAC	Long-run average cost.
LRMC	Long-run marginal cost.
LROPS	Long-range operations.

LRU	Line-replaceable unit.
MAF	Minimum acceptable fare.
MCT	Minimum connecting time.
MEL	Minimum equipment list.
MES	Minimum efficient scale.
MFF	Mixed fleet flying.
MIDT	Marketing information data tape.
MTOW	Maximum take-off weight.
NPV	Net present value.
O & D	Origin and destination (markets).
OEM	Original equipment manufacturer.
PMA	Parts manufacturing approval.
PNR	Passenger name record.
PR	Public relations.
QC	Quick-change.
QSI	Quality of service index.
RASM	Revenue per available seat-mile.
RATM	Revenue per available ton-mile.
RBT	Resource-based theory of competitive advantage/ strategy.
RJ	Regional jet.
RMS	Revenue management system.
Rotables	'Rotables' are high-value components that are either returned to service – not necessarily on the same aircraft – or held in inventory after repair or overhaul, rather than being consumed in use or discarded after use.
RPK	Revenue passenger-kilometre: one revenue passenger flown one kilometre. (A measure of sold output.)
RPM	Revenue passenger-mile: one revenue passenger flown one mile.
RTK	Revenue tonne-kilometre: one tonne of payload flown one kilometre.
RTM	Revenue ton-mile: one ton of payload flown one mile.
RV	Residual value.
SB	Service bulletin.

SCP	Structure-conduct-performance approach to competitive advantage/strategy.
Seat pitch	The distance from the point where the back and pan of a seat join, to the same point on the seat in front.
SFE	Seller-furnished equipment.
SRAC	Short-run average cost.
SRMC	Short-run marginal cost.
TACO	Travel agency commission override.
TOC	Total operating cost.
TTL	Ticketing time limit.
ULD	Unit load device.
Unit cost	Operating cost per ASK, ASM, ATK or ATM.
Unit revenue	Operating revenue per ASK, ASM, ATK or ATM.
VFR	Visiting friends and relatives/relations.
Yield	Revenue per RPK/RPM or RTK/RTM.

Additional comments on definitions and usages adopted in the book

This book is consistent in its use of words or expressions that might be considered technical or terms of art. The following paragraphs clarify some of the usages adopted that might be considered open to debate.

Units of measurement Miles and tons have generally been adopted rather than kilometres and tonnes, simply because the majority of sales of the first edition were made in the United States.

Capacity and output Although the words 'capacity' and 'output' tend to be used interchangeably in the airline industry, they are not in fact synonymous. Assume an airline has one 300-mile route on which it operates a single 100-seat aircraft on one rotation (i.e., round-trip) each day. It is generating $(300 \times 2) \times 100 = 60,000$ ASMs per day. This is its *output* (although, as we will see in chapter 4, output can also be measured using other metrics). If we further assume that the aircraft could feasibly be operated on as many as four rotations when fully utilised, it has the *capacity* to produce $60,000 \times 4 = 240,000$ ASMs each day. Its output is therefore currently well below capacity; in other words, its capacity is not being fully utilised.

It is of course very difficult – often impossible – for an airline to put a precise figure on the potential capacity of its fleet, and it is industry practice to refer to ASMs and ASKs actually produced as 'capacity' rather than 'output'. This book does not follow industry convention because it is analytically useful to retain a distinction between capacity (i.e., maximum potential output) and actual output.

Demand and traffic Demand is a measure of potential customers willing and able to purchase air transport services in a market or group of markets given assumed price levels. Some of that demand will be unsatisfied because seats are not available and potential customers choose not to travel on alternative flights. Demand that is satisfied results in 'traffic' being carried.

Traffic as 'sold output' As we will see in chapter 2, traffic can be measured in terms of passenger enplanements or on a distance-weighted basis in terms of RPMs. Given that output is measured in ASMs, we can treat traffic expressed in RPMs as 'sold output'. The reason for adopting the expression 'sold output' will be made clear in chapter 10; in the rest of the book, the word 'traffic' is used.

Unit cost, unit revenue, and yield Unit cost is operating cost per ASM or ATM; unit revenue is operating revenue per ASM or ATM; and yield is operating revenue per RPM or RTM. Whilst unit cost and unit revenue are standard definitions, yield can be defined in other ways; none of the other definitions of yield is used in this book.

Revenue management versus yield management The expression 'revenue management' has come to displace 'yield management' in recent years, although not universally. This book uses 'revenue management'. (In fact, as we will see in chapter 9, some observers define 'revenue management' as an umbrella term encompassing both pricing and yield management; that is not the approach used here.)

GDS versus CRS The abbreviation 'GDS' has come to displace 'CRS' – although, once again, not universally. This book actually uses the terms somewhat differently. 'CRS' here refers to an individual airline's internal reservation system – whether maintained inhouse, co-hosted in another airline's CRS or in a GDS, or maintained by a supplier such as IBM or EDS. 'GDS' here refers to industry-wide systems such as Amadeus and Sabre –

systems which have until recently themselves been widely referred to as CRSs but whose expanding scope as travel service distributors for a range of companies and industries makes the expression 'GDS' more appropriate. The essence of this distinction is that a GDS is an industry-wide distribution system, whereas a CRS is a single-airline inventory management system.

Flight-legs, routes, and markets A flight-leg is a nonstop flight; it might be synonymous with a route and a market, or it might not. Orlando–Dallas nonstop is a flight-leg serving the Orlando–Dallas market; if it is part of an Orlando–Dallas-Salt Lake City (SLC) through-service, we can say that the Orlando–SLC route has two flight-legs (Orlando–Dallas and Dallas–SLC) and directly serves three origin and destination (O & D) markets (Orlando–Dallas, Orlando–SLC, and Dallas–SLC), together with a large number of connecting markets involving origins and destinations behind and/or beyond these three cities.

Nonstop, through-plane, direct, and connecting service Staying with the same example, Orlando–Dallas and Dallas–SLC are both 'nonstops', whilst Orlando–SLC is a through-plane service. According to different definitions encountered in the industry, the word 'direct' could be synonymous with either 'nonstop' or 'through-plane' service; this book adopts the latter approach, treating direct service as service on a one-stop or multi-stop route using the same aircraft (and generally the same flight number). Both nonstop and direct or through-plane services are distinct from connecting itineraries, which serve an O & D market with one or more change of planes (e.g., Dallas–Boise connecting at SLC).

Network carriers This expression is used here to distinguish airlines which primarily operate hub-and-spoke networks (generally full-service carriers) from others which primarily operate only point-to-point services (often, but not invariably, low-fare carriers). Most network carriers also offer point-to-point services in addition to hub connections, but their distinguishing characteristic is the centrality of hub operations to their strategic positions.

Low-fare carriers This expression is used to describe airlines which have sufficiently low costs to sustain a low-fare price platform in all their markets and which make low fares a major part of their brand positioning. The more widely adopted expression 'low-cost' is not used to describe these carriers in the present book, because customers do not care about an airline's costs – they do care about fares, and it is as well to remember this. Full-service network carriers also offer low fares in many of their markets, of course. However, they tend to do this only where they have to – in order to match competitors, offload distressed inventory, compensate for some market-specific source of competitive weakness such as unattractive routings or frequencies, or to respond to an industry-wide circumstance such as the Gulf War; low fares are not, and are unlikely ever to be, as central to the brand identities, market positioning, and operating economics of American and British Airways as they are to Southwest and Ryanair.

Start-ups and new entrants 'Start-up' is used to refer to a newly launched carrier. 'New entrant' or 'entrant' refers to a carrier entering a market to challenge one or more incumbents; a new entrant might be a start-up, or it might be an established airline.

Cargo and freight Some definitions treat these as synonymous, whereas others define freight as a subset of cargo (albeit by far the major subset in volume and revenue terms for the industry as a whole) alongside mail and unaccompanied baggage. This book takes the second approach.

Product 'Product' is an umbrella term which encompasses tangible goods (e.g., automobiles) and intangible services (e.g., life insurance). Airlines offer products that are primarily intangible services (i.e., the transportation of people and goods), but which nonetheless have significant tangible attributes (e.g., lounges, aircraft cabins, food, cargo documentation, etc.). This book generally refers to airline 'services', but the word 'product' is also used and can be treated in this case as synonymous with 'service'.

Fleets and sub-fleets A 'fleet' is the aggregate of all aircraft operated by an airline, whereas a 'sub-fleet' is comprised of one particular type (including variants). In the case of a single-type operator, the words are synonymous; a carrier operating more than one distinct type, on the other hand, has a number of sub-fleets.

9/11 As readers from the United States will recognise but others might not, '9/11' is used as shorthand for the events in New York, Washington DC, and Pennsylvania on 11 September, 2001.

Part 1
Strategic Context

One point of view is that industry economics are our master, determining what can and cannot be done. Less deterministically, we can take the view that an understanding of industry economics is a tool which allows managers to work towards the vision they have for their airline's future and to meet the more explicit objectives established by stakeholders such as customers, employees, alliance partners, shareholders, and members of the wider community. This book takes the latter approach. The single chapter in the opening part of the book outlines a customer-oriented strategic framework within which the understanding of industry economics developed in subsequent chapters can be applied. Holloway (2002) provides a more comprehensive treatment of the themes introduced in the first chapter, and is in many respects complementary to the present book.

1 Economics and Strategy

> Two balloonists, after drifting for days in stormy weather, saw a house.
> They descended over it and noticed a man who came out to see what they wanted.
> 'Where are we?', they asked. 'In a balloon', replied the man.
> 'He must be an economist', remarked one of the balloonists.
> 'Totally rigorous and utterly useless.'
> Apocryphal story quoted in Varoufakis (1998: 370)

Chapter overview

Most airlines have a competitive strategy embodying the type of value they intend delivering to targeted customers. This choice of competitive strategy is reflected in each carrier's operating strategy. The performance associated with any operating strategy is driven by the revenues earned from delivering expected benefits to targeted customers and the costs incurred delivering those benefits. Part 2 of the book will look at airline revenues (traffic x yield) and costs (output x unit cost). Part 3 will focus on key aspects of capacity management, which is in many respects the critical operations management challenge because it lies at the interface between cost and revenue streams. Part 4 looks at several key macro-level metrics of operating performance. What this opening chapter does is outline the strategic context within which costs and revenues are generated. It begins by making the point that although economists have made major contributions to the study of both organizations and their strategies, they do not provide the only valid perspective on either.

i. Alternative perspectives on the nature of organizations

Consider how three different baseball umpires might call balls and strikes.

- **Umpire 1** 'I call them as they are.' (i.e., They are 'out there' and I observe them.)
- **Umpire 2** 'I call them as I see them.' (i.e., I construct reality by interpreting what I perceive.)
- **Umpire 3** 'They're nothing until I call them.' (i.e., Balls and strikes are not real things, just labels applied to give meaning to passing baseballs.)

These explanations are respectively representative of the positivist/modernist, interpretivist/constructivist, and postmodern paradigms which frame the worldviews of academic researchers and managers. Economics is an overwhelmingly positivist/modernist discipline. Reducing to numbers all the most critical variables used to understand and manage an airline, or indeed any other organization, is not without its dangers, however.

The purpose here is not to judge this debate, but to stress that although the present book adopts the positivist leanings common to most economics texts, the fact that there are alternative ways of looking at organizations and how they behave needs to be borne in mind. This can be seen particularly clearly in three topics that lie at the heart of organization studies: external environments, objectives, and decision-making processes. We will look briefly at each of these.

Representing the external environment

From a positivist/modernist perspective, the environment exists and can be observed – perhaps by breaking it down into its constituent elements, as when a strategic planner conducts a PEST analysis (of an organization's political, economic, social, and technological environments) or a network theorist identifies external actors in the networks within which each organization is embedded. The environment lies outside the boundaries of the organization (itself a definable 'thing'), and imposes: demands (e.g., for specific types of adaptive behaviour as the 'price' for survival); and uncertainty (e.g., the unpredictability of future environmental demands).

The environment as seen from an interpretivist perspective, on the other hand, imposes itself on organizations less through the 'real' impact of 'real' events than through the interpretations people place on what they perceive to be happening. For example, one manager's threat is another's opportunity. Neither the environment nor its supposed constituent elements are objective facts; pressures, influences, complexity, change, instability, turbulence, and other 'qualities' are in the eye – or, more correctly, the mind – of the beholder. In other words, it is people who are uncertain, not environments. From this perspective, environments do not control people or organizations by enforcing certain types of response, as positivists might argue; instead, what happens is that people construct images of their environments and then respond to those images as though they were a controlling influence. A back-firing car does not *make* a passer-by jump or duck, but that person's image of a bullet or a bomb certainly might. Interpretivist theories of organization-environment relations have been slower developing and less influential overall than positivist/modernist theories.

Finally, many postmodernists would argue that the distinction between organization and environment is the child not of reality, but of the use of language such as 'internal', 'boundary', and 'external'. Similarly the growing use of new concepts invoking recognition of 'virtual', 'network', or 'boundary-less' organizations is less a reflection of the sudden appearance of these new forms than a comment on the power of language to use metaphors in the construction of 'reality'. Whilst postmodernist concerns with issues such as environmental sustainability, ethics, and social responsibility have begun to introduce themselves into discourse on organization-environment relations, their impact on mainstream debate and theorising in the field has been limited.

Does any of this matter in practice? If we bear in mind that several generations of airline managers have been schooled in the use of strategic management techniques designed to 'fit' their (unitary) organizations to their (objectively identifiable) external environments, the answer is that it probably does.

Organizational objectives

Although conflict and political processes are not ignored, the 'organization-as-individual' metaphor – the notion that each organization acts in a unitary way as though it were a single individual with rationally chosen and clearly articulated objectives – is implicit in much of the academic literature and most college-level textbooks (particularly economics textbooks). In practice, each organization is influenced by external and internal stakeholders who have different expectations about its performance – about what it should achieve; different expectations about performance will often mask different assumptions with regard to purpose. Despite the fact that most people working inside airlines and other organizations are well aware of this, the 'organization-as-individual' metaphor remains pervasive. Indeed, neoclassical microeconomics assumes that each firm – whether a sole trader or a global corporation – has only a single objective function, almost invariably profit maximisation.

Profit maximisation is not an unproblematic purpose, however.

1. As an espoused objective, it has flaws.
    - There is no way of knowing whether profit has 'really' been max-imised. As we will see, economics gives us marginal analysis to help maximise profits by continuing to produce output until marg-inal revenue equates exactly to marginal cost. Fine in theory, nob-ody has yet figured out to everybody else's satisfaction how to measure (as opposed to how to define) marginal revenue or marg-inal cost in highly complex and dynamic multi-product organizat-ions (rather than simple textbook examples).
    - Steps taken to maximise short-run profits (e.g., trimming the curr-ent advertising or training budget) might damage long-run profits (e.g., by weakening the brand).
    - Accounting practices, particularly in respect of aircraft depreciation and the recognition of foreign exchange gains and losses, make att-ainment of earnings per share and other profit objectives as much a matter of opinion as of fact (something that cash flow-based share-holder value metrics are now addressing).
2. The chosen route to profit maximisation can be as important as the obj-ective itself. Many airlines (e.g., American and United in the 1980s) have pursued growth in market share on the mistaken assumption that dominant share inevitably brings with it pricing power and higher earn-ings (Damodaran, 2001).
3. There are viable alternatives even within economics to the neoclassical assumption that profit maximisation is the sole objective function.
    - Simon (1960) and Cyert and March (1963) argued that objectives arise not from rational planning but out of negotiations between shifting coalitions.
    - Baumol (1959) proposed a model based on revenue-maximisation subject to a 'minimum profit' constraint. The argument is that ex-ternal and internal stakeholders pay more attention to – and reward – steady sales growth (subject to earnings above some minimum level) than to inherently less stable earnings gyrations.
4. There is an influential stream within the recently developed services management literature that characterises profit not as an objective to be maximised, but as a by-product of the satisfaction and loyalty of both employees and customers (Heskett et al, 1994; Holloway, 2002).
5. Airlines, like most other organizations, are socially complex phenom-ena comprised of individuals who either singly or in a coalition with others might be willing superficially to accept profit maximisation or shareholder value enhancement as a dominant purpose, but whose real

agendas are likely to have several other items of business on them. Some economists refer to this as the 'maximisation of managerial utility', arguing that managers pursue their own personal objectives (e.g., compensation, power, aggrandisement) but subject to some minimum profit sufficient to keep shareholders and analysts satisfied.

The dominant paradigm in textbooks and amongst practitioners nonetheless makes a fundamental assumption that organizations are unitary entities, inevitably goal-seeking, and driven fundamentally by pursuit of profit. An alternative view is that behaviour has at least as much to do with individual and group survival and betterment as with pursuit of espoused organizational objectives. It is fair to say that whilst economic considerations are rarely unimportant, neither are they always the sole driving force behind action and performance.

Organizational decision-making

Managerial decision-making can be studied from either a prescriptive or descriptive perspective (Bazerman, 1998). Prescriptive approaches try to establish how decisions should be made; they are often referred to as 'rational choice' models, and both economics and quantitative decision sciences fall into this camp. Descriptive approaches examine not how decisions *should* be made, but how in practice they *are* made. The message, again, is that economics is not the only discipline with views on the matter.

Economists generally see economic action as:

- arising from the application of rational choice models to decisions regarding the allocation of resources that are scarce and have alternative uses (and therefore carry opportunity costs);
- being driven by a hierarchy of preferences held by utility-maximising individuals, households, and firms; and
- starting and ending at points of equilibrium (although there are traditions within economics away from the neoclassical mainstream – one of which, 'evolutionary economics', we will meet shortly – that see competition as dynamic and disequilibrating).

Economists holding these perspectives broadly take the view that market mechanisms are the preferred means through which to allocate resources, and they assume in most cases that market participants carry no histories (personal, organizational, cultural or political) into the making of rational, goal-oriented decisions. Mainstream neoclassical microeconomics pays no attention to the impact of social relations and social structures on production, distribution, or consumption.

Sociologists, on the other hand, tend to see economic acts as socially constructed, because economic action is just one part of a much broader flow of social relations between individual actors both inside and outside organizations. Apparently rational economic decisions might be taken, for example, as a result of considerations which do not figure in the supposedly acontextual models that economists like to argue are universal in their application. A seminal contribution from Granovetter (1985) argued that economic decision-making must be looked at not in isolation, but as purposive action that is *embedded* in ongoing systems of social relations.

As with much else in this chapter, we will hear echoes of these ideas later in the book.

Conclusion

Neither economics nor any other discipline has comprehensive insight into all organizational problems; each has only partial insight into what is a complex social reality. However, the more that the solution to a given problem turns upon arriving at an optimal allocation of scarce resources, the greater the contribution that economic approaches to understanding organizations can make. Many strategic decisions essentially address resource allocation problems; the next section looks at the relationship between economics and strategy.

ii. Economics and strategy

If there is active debate about the nature of organizations and the manner in which we should treat their environments, objectives, and decision-making processes, there is also active debate in the field which tries to explain why firms exist and behave in the ways they do and why some outperform others. This field – variously referred to as strategy, strategic management or business policy – is covered in detail by a large number of texts. The purpose of the present section is to briefly contextualise the field and highlight the contribution of economics, so laying the foundations for consideration of competitive strategy and customer value later in the chapter.

What is a strategy?

There are several possible answers to this seemingly simple question.

- **Strategy as a plan** Until relatively recently, strategy has been thought of as just another type of plan, albeit a significant variety of the species. This is a positivist/modernist standpoint which peddles images of top managers marshalling the resources of an inherently controllable organization so that it can plot a determinate course through a knowable, albeit perhaps uncertain, environment. The reified organization is implicitly a production facility that can be 'tooled-up' in order to get it to objectives pre-established by strategic managers.
- **Strategy as a pattern** Instead of being a plan, a deliberate course of action intended to take an organization from here to there, strategy can be characterised as a pattern of decisions. Sometimes a pattern emerges unplanned and can only be labelled as strategy in hindsight. The strategy-as-pattern metaphor is pithily summarised by Mintzberg (1989), who observed that life might be lived forwards but it can only be understood by looking back. In other words, people make sense of their experiences and actions by declaring *ex post* that they were following a strategy. Strategy is seen not as an *ex ante* creation, but as an *ex post* construction of meaning.
- **Strategy as a theme** According to Grant (1998: 3), 'Strategy is not a detailed plan or programme of instructions; it is a unifying theme that gives coherence and direction to the actions and decisions of an individual or organization'. Porter (1996: 71) argues that, 'In companies with a clear strategic position, a number of higher-order themes can be identified and implemented through clusters of tightly linked activities'. We will return to this idea later in the chapter and at several other points in the book.
- **Strategy as a narrative** From a postmodern perspective, strategy is simply a narrative comprising socially constructed 'entities' such as formulation, implementation, organization, and environment. It has its own heroes and villains, and story-tellers (called 'strategists') able to put their own slant on proceedings. Strategy is here represented as fiction – not in the sense that it is a falsehood, but in the sense that it is something made up in much the same way that a novel is created. Somebody has to choose the theme, decide who the key characters are to be and what roles they will play, orchestrate the sub-plots, and present the work in such a way that the audience finds it credible and willingly becomes immersed in – rather than turned-off or alienated by – what is taking place. Strategic managers are characterised as using

narrative techniques to interpret, make sense of, and create meaning out of the path taken in the past, being taken at present, or to be taken in future; they are participants in multi-faceted discourses or dialogues rather than just reciters of sequenced check-lists.

The 'strategist as story-teller' approach might not appeal to managers schooled in SWOT analyses, directional policy matrices, and generic competitive strategies. It does, nonetheless, highlight the fact that strategy is more than a written plan; strategy embodies the mindsets, authority structures, and political pressures which shape the analyses underlying any plan, the final form of that plan, its interpretation, and the myriad verbal communications which actually determine strategic behaviour. It also underlines the truism that just as different people may interpret a book or movie in different ways, so might the audience for a strategic narrative have different perceptions of its theme, characters, and sub-plots.

The field of strategy

At the heart of any discussion of strategy lie three fundamental issues: the boundaries of the firm; the position it will occupy within its markets, together with the resources available to support that position; and the design of the organization. We will look at each in turn.

The field of strategy 1: Boundaries of the firm

Boundaries define the scope and scale of a firm's activities. There are three types: corporate; horizontal; and vertical.

Corporate boundaries: the industrial scope decision This decision addresses which businesses a corporation should be investing its resources in. It is the heart of 'corporate' – as opposed to 'competitive' – strategy. During the 1970s and early 1980s, portfolio planning matrices such as the Boston Box, the McKinsey Directional Policy Matrix, and the Arthur D. Little Life-Cycle Matrix were widely used to help structure industrial scope decisions (Bowman and Faulkner, 1997). Since the late 1980s the emphasis has shifted towards analysis of shared competencies and the search for a better understanding of how it is that aggregating different businesses within the same corporate group actually creates more shareholder value than would be created were each independent; this has contributed to a shift away from conglomerate diversification.

In the context of the airline industry, the industrial scope decision is a matter of whether and, if so, how far to diversify away from the core air transport business. The decision might result in one of three group structures for an airline or its holding company (Holloway, 2002).

1. **Single business** This is the model adopted by carriers concentrating on air transportation as their core business and outsourcing all activities considered 'non-core' relative to the carriage of passengers and cargo.
2. **Portfolio of related businesses** This model includes in addition to air transport operations a number of divisions, subsidiaries, and/or joint ventures in fields related to air transport. How to define 'relatedness' is an open question, but generally we would expect 'related' operations to share inputs, technology, competencies, and/or markets and to reap economic benefits from this sharing. Whilst some airlines (e.g., British Airways) have over the last decade been focusing increasingly on air transport operations, others (e.g., Lufthansa and Singapore Airlines) have been developing activities related to air transport into significant independent revenue-generators.
3. **Portfolio of unrelated businesses** Most airlines and airline holding companies are now less inclined than some have been in the past to involve themselves in activities only tenuously related to air transport. There are exceptions, of course, notably in respect of hotels (e.g., All Nippon Airways, Royal Air Maroc, and SAS), whilst a number of carriers are endeavouring to deepen relationships with high-value customers by using external partners to provide such 'value-added' extras as financial services and wine clubs to members of their frequent flyer programmes (FFPs). A few carriers are themselves part of diversified industrial portfolios (e.g., Asiana, Cathay Pacific, Dragonair, and EVA Air).

The corporate strategies of different airlines or airline holding companies can be outlined by using comparative bar-charts to map the percentages of total revenue attributable to different businesses within their portfolios. Our interest in this book is limited to the economics of air transport operations.

Vertical boundaries: the 'make or buy' decision Having decided which businesses they want to invest in, strategic managers next have to choose the extent to which they intend to be involved in the various activities that together contribute to the final service output delivered to customers of each of these businesses. Vertical integration may be 'backward' if control over the supply of inputs is sought, or 'forward' if control over distribution channels is acquired. The difference between vertical integration and related diversification is open to debate, but can for practical purposes be described as follows: an airline which performs, for example, its own heavy maintenance and (at least at major stations) its own ground-handling and catering but does not generate significant revenue by selling these services to other carriers can be considered vertically integrated; if an airline's maintenance, catering, and other support operations are significant revenue generators in their own right because substantial third-party business is actively sought, the airline is pursuing a corporate strategy of related diversification.

There are basically five vertical scope options, with the word 'vertical' here being loosely defined to apply to any activity or process contributing ultimately to the delivery of customer value (Holloway, 1998b, 2002).

1. **Inhouse supply by an internal department/cost centre** This has been the traditional approach in large, highly integrated airlines.
2. **Inhouse supply by an internal profit centre** Some carriers that are prepared neither to spin internal service suppliers off into separate subsidiaries nor to outsource the services they supply, have instead tried to instil a more entrepreneurial and bottom-line oriented culture by enforcing greater cost transparency and expectations of profitability on what were previously accepted simply as necessary cost centres. How successful this approach will be might depend upon whether or not the core air transport operation remains a captive purchaser compelled to buy inhouse (Doganis, 2001).
3. **Inhouse supply by a subsidiary or joint venture** The objectives here are to cut costs by removing the 'monopoly supplier' mentality and to earn incremental revenues by competing more aggressively for third-party work; in the case of joint ventures (which might be with alliance partners or external suppliers), motives can extend to the realisation of cash from partial sale of existing assets or expertise, access to a 'captive' source of external skills, or the sharing of future investment costs. Going a step further than a joint venture with one or more external parties, some airlines began in the 1990s considering public flotations for subsidiaries. As well as raising cash, an additional motive for a listing might be to realise shareholder value in that subsidiary not currently reflected in the parent's balance sheet or market rating.
4. **Tapered integration** This mixture of vertical integration and market exchange involves retaining inhouse some of the work done in respect of a certain activity or process, and outsourcing the rest. One advantage is that tapered integration allows expansion of supply without having to invest in additional inhouse capacity. Another is that retaining an inhouse capability gives the airline concerned a first-hand knowledge

of costs and achievable efficiency levels against which to benchmark outsourced work. This assumes that the inhouse supplier represents an efficiency benchmark; one potential disadvantage of tapered integration is in fact that it might deprive inhouse suppliers of sufficient scale and scope to optimise their cost-effectiveness.

5. **External supply** This is the antithesis of integrative growth; where the external supplier was previously an inhouse unit we can refer to the arrangement as 'outsourcing', although in practice the word has come to encompass all forms of external supply. Cost savings and a preference for redirecting investment into core activities in which sources of real competitive advantage can be found are the most frequently cited motivations for outsourcing. The close monitoring of quality is particularly vital when safety or key operational and business processes are involved, and also when corporate reputation and brand integrity are at risk. Whatever the work being outsourced, however, somebody somewhere in the airline concerned has to be sufficiently qualified and knowledgeable to evaluate the quality of that work. (It is not only vertical transactions that can be outsourced; we will see in chapter 6 that airlines now commonly outsource capacity provision to franchisees and other code-share partners.)

Arguments in favour of vertical integration have generally included reliability of supply, better control over performance, and the economies of scale available to large inhouse operations; other considerations might be the influence of trades unions wanting to retain work inhouse or, particularly in developing countries, politicians wanting to build a local skills base. Arguments against vertical integration frequently include the opportunity costs involved, the lack of competitive advantage that airlines sometimes face in respect of activities peripheral to their core air transport operations, the need to focus scarce management time on those core operations, and the fact that inhouse suppliers bring with them fixed costs that can be difficult to shrink rapidly in response to a market downturn, whilst external suppliers largely represent a variable cost.

Because airlines in various parts of the world function in supplier markets having very different levels of sophistication (distribution tending to be more uniform in nature), and also because each carrier has its own financial and emotional investment sunk into existing organizational architecture, there is little prescriptive that can be said about vertical integration in the industry. Airlines vary widely with regard to the choices they make in respect of vertical integration. Large, long-established carriers frequently perform inhouse many functions ancillary to the actual transportation of passengers and cargo that smaller, newer airlines prefer in most cases to outsource. However, airlines as a whole have been taking a closer look at which activities need to be inhouse, and which could be outsourced – along with their overheads. The outcome has been a range of different decisions, reflecting divergent strategic perspectives with regard to what it is that constitutes a core activity for each carrier. Every management team must ultimately come to its own conclusion on whether retaining particular activities inhouse builds or destroys shareholder value.

Horizontal boundaries: the competitive scope decision Having decided in which businesses they want to invest and how much of the value chain of each they prefer to retain inhouse, the next decision facing strategists is which product and geographical markets to compete in. This is the essence of the competitive scope decision.

A customer purchasing air transportation is simultaneously participating in both a service market and a geographical market (Holloway, 2002).

- **Service scope** can be:
  - *Wide-market* A portfolio of passenger and cargo transport services is offered by a single carrier, either under its sole corporate brand or using a mixture of mainline, divisional, subsidiary, and/or franchised sub-brands (in addition to a corporate masterbrand) to target distinct segments of demand.
  - *Niche* A single service concept is offered. A typical example of this would be a low-fare carrier offering single-class service to one or a relatively narrow range of segments. Midwest provides another example at the opposite end of the service-price spectrum.
- **Geographical scope** can be:
  - *Wide-market* There are several large international airlines, but no truly global carriers. Alliances are intended in part to broaden geographical scope within the constraints of both industry economics and the prevailing international aeropolitical regime – a regime which, as we will see in chapter 4, is still on the whole relatively restrictive.
  - *Niche* This involves offering either a wide or a narrow range of services into a small number of geographical markets. What constitutes a geographical niche and what represents a geographical wide-market strategy is obvious at the extremes (e.g., regional carriers on the one hand, and the US 'Big Three' on the other), but unclear in the middle-ground. A large number of the world's international airlines make wide-market service offers into a relatively limited range of geographical markets, and are in this sense 'geographical niche carriers' – although they might not think

of themselves as such. Some are moving out of niches by joining global alliances; those that choose not to make this move will need confidence that they have distinctive and sustainable cost and/or service advantages with which to defend their niches.

Box 1.1 takes a closer look at the 'niche' concept.

Box 1.1: Niches within niches

Significant variations in focus can occur even within an apparently homogenous niche. Looking at European low-fare airlines, Ryanair tends to target leisure and VFR (visiting friends and relatives) traffic whilst easyJet has a stronger orientation towards the price-sensitive end of the business segment, and this is reflected in their different networks. Whereas Ryanair focuses to a considerable degree on secondary cities and airports, easyJet is more inclined to serve primary cities and major airports. (Neither carrier is entirely focused on one segment, however.) Staying in Europe, some charter carriers serving price-sensitive inclusive tour markets now also offer a premium cabin, and several operate almost as many scheduled as charter services (at least in the off-season).

Although positioned as a low-fare carrier, jetBlue launched from New York JFK with a brand-new fleet and a single-class inflight product offering advance seat selection, generous 32-inch seat-pitch, leather seats, free 24-channel seat-back satellite television, and catering that is limited but reasonable in quality. AirTran with its two classes and Frontier with its full-service approach were positioned to pitch low-fare products to the Atlanta and Denver business communities very different from Spirit's more basic service in leisure-oriented Midwest-Florida markets. The point is that even relatively narrow niches and approaches to serving them are not necessarily homogeneous.

That said, gradually evolving changes in the structure of the industry, particularly in North America and Europe, are in the process of transforming several 'niches' into mainstream markets. The industry is becoming steadily more polarised between low-fare and full-service carriers, and between point-to-point operations and hub-and-spoke networks.

Geographical and service scope are distinct but closely linked choices. Indeed, in a network industry such as commercial air transportation these two scope decisions are fundamentally symbiotic: every departure is in itself a product offered to one or more geographical markets, and different levels of ground and onboard amenities provided to customers travelling in whatever separate classes are available on each departure can be character-ised as product attributes offered to different segments of those markets. An airline's network is, in fact, now widely perceived as a core attribute of its service – hence the rush, amongst full-service carriers, to build alliances (Holloway, 2002).

Field of strategy 2: Strategic position and resources

The last section addressed one of the central issues in strategy: the setting of a firm's corporate, vertical, and horizontal boundaries. We moved from the question of how many distinct businesses should be in the corporate portfolio to consideration of how much of each business's value chain should be vertically integrated, and finally to identification of the horizont-al scope of each business. Figure 1.1 summarises the choices.

The focus in this book is on the air transport business. We are not concerned with decision 1 in figure 1.1, and our concern with decision 2 is limited to its impact on the cost of air transport operations (discussed in chapter 5). Horizontal scope – decision 3 – is a topic that will resurface at several points in the book. Competitive advantage and positioning provide a vital context for what follows in the rest of the book, and it is to these that we turn next.

Each airline participating in air transport markets needs to consider the manner in which it will position itself in the markets it chooses to enter, and the resources required to sustain the chosen position. These choices underlie another central issue in strategy: how some firms are able to build competitive advantage and outperform their competitors.

Competitive advantage Anything that allows one firm to earn and sustain higher profitability than the average for its industry can be considered a source of competitive advantage. However, because the airline industry is a network business, each carrier can potentially face a wide range of different competitors depending upon which city-pair market is analysed; what gives an airline an advantage over competitors in one city-pair market might be insufficient to give it an advantage over competitors in another. Competit-ive advantage is therefore better characterised as a useful concept than a precise number. Its sources do nonetheless need to be understood and, where possible, proactively managed; it is the recognition and management of sources of competitive advantage that underpin a sound competitive strategy.

Although academics in the fields of individual cognition, social cognit-ion, organizational culture, and political science have gained wider audien-ces for their contributions to research into competitive advantage and

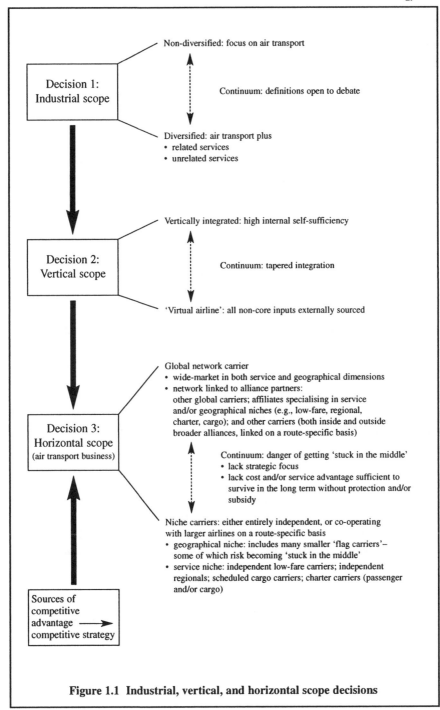

Figure 1.1 Industrial, vertical, and horizontal scope decisions

competitive strategy since the early 1980s, economists have ensconced themselves at the heart of the field. Two streams of work in particular have made noteworthy contributions to the understanding of potential sources of competitive advantage: strategic positioning and resource-based theory. Both are more fully summarised in Holloway (2002), and explained at length in most strategic management texts (e.g., Grant, 1998).

Strategic positioning   Neoclassical microeconomics proposes a rather deterministic model which attributes a firm's conduct and performance to the structure of the market in which it competes. This structure-conduct-performance (SCP) approach has been developed by a branch of the discipline known as industrial organization (IO) economics – which is, in essence, a field concerned with applied microeconomic analysis. Although IO economics has become inextricably linked with the name of Michael Porter since the late 1970s, its origins date back much further and some of its key concepts – such as product differentiation, for example – can be traced to the 1930s (Mason, 1939). Whilst the roots of IO analysis lie in analysing industry concentration, barriers to entry, collusion, and other sources of supernormal profits that make particular industries good candidates for regulatory or antitrust action on public policy grounds (Bain, 1956, 1968), Porter's industry-based theory of strategy turns the analysis 'upside down' by explicitly searching out industry structures that make superior returns feasible on a sustainable basis (Barney and Ouchi, 1986).

The unit of analysis is the industry of competing firms, rather than firms themselves. Heterogeneous performance amongst firms is attributed to industry structure, and to different conduct in response to structure.

- **Structure** An industry's structure is defined by variables such as the number and size distribution of sellers and buyers, the relative sizes of firms and concentration of output, the presence of barriers to entry and exit, levels of vertical integration, the scope for product differentiation, the nature of cost structures, and the price-elasticity of demand.
- **Conduct** Firms' conduct covers choices with regard to product and pricing strategies, advertising, and collusion amongst competitors.
- **Performance** Performance refers not just to the earnings and market share of any one firm, but to profitability, output growth, employment trends, and technological progress in the industry as a whole (Douma and Schreuder, 1998).

Structure, conduct, and performance variables can be analysed across one or more markets, or across all of the markets served by an industry.

A firm's strategic conduct – that is whether, in Porter's (1980) terms, it pursues a wide-market or niche product differentiation or cost leadership strategy – should essentially be shaped by industry structure, and its success in adapting to these environmental circumstances will determine performance relative to the rest of the industry. In other words, firms must 'fit' competitive strategies to their environments. Outperformance relative to competitors happens when a firm's conduct in response to industry structure exploits or creates, and then leverages, one or more sources of competitive advantage.

Porter's pursuit of the sources of sustainable competitive advantage using analytical concepts imported from IO economics in the late 1970s and early 1980s sensitised practitioners to the concepts of competitive advantage and competitive strategy. Economists began to dominate the sub-field of competitive strategy from the early 1980s onwards, arguing a pre-eminent role in strategy-making for rational economic choices under strong environmental influence. The environment – notably a firm's ability to 'fit' itself into the environment – took pride of place, with internal processes (conceptualised as a 'value chain') considered important to the achievement of 'fit' but nonetheless left largely unexplored. It was not until the early 1990s that momentum began to build behind the alternative perspective offered by resource-based theory (itself dating back to the 1950s), and the gaze of strategy researchers turned more consistently inwards into the firm.

Resource-based theory Resource-based theory (RBT) – which is in fact a stream of research rather than a single coherent body of theory – argues that competitive advantage lies not in positioning *per se*, because returns to position can be appropriated by others, but in the relevance of a particular firm's resource endowment to the current needs of the marketplace(s) it is able to serve and to the strategic position it wants to carve for itself. Encompassed within most definitions of 'resources' are 'capabilities'; whereas a resource is something tangible or intangible that an airline *has* and which allows it to do certain things, a capability is something an airline actually *does* (Besanko et al, 2000). Capabilities might reside within a business function such as revenue management, or they might be cross-functional – as when an airline has a brand management capability (e.g., British Airways) or a rapid aircraft turnaround capability (e.g., Southwest).

In contrast to the neoclassical tradition which views firms as time- and place-independent mathematical abstractions, RBT sees them as historically situated in time and space (Hunt, 2000). Neoclassical microeconomics has typically held that because firms combine homogeneous, perfectly mobile resources in an industry-standard production function and intra-industry demand and supply are homogeneous (i.e., products are not differentiated), any variance in financial performance across firms must result in large measure from 'industry effects' – including, notably, collusion and barriers to entry (Schmalensee, 1985). The potency of industry effects has also long been central to IO economics (Bain, 1956). On the other hand, if firms are viewed as combiners of heterogeneous, imperfectly mobile resources and intra-industry demand and supply are considered heterogeneous (i.e., what is essentially the same product can nonetheless be differentiated by individual producers), then 'firm effects' should dominate 'industry effects'.

According to RBT, a firm is indeed comprised of an integrated bundle of resources – tangible (human and physical) and intangible (e.g., hubs, networks, systems, practices, culture, cost structure, and reputation) (Selznick, 1957; Penrose, 1959; Rumelt, 1984; Wernerfelt, 1984; Barney, 1991). Intangible resources might be further divided into those that are protected by property rights (e.g., brand names, service marks, and patented innovations) and those that are not (e.g., organizational routines and general knowhow, market presence, and a retained base of brand-loyal customers); slots at capacity-controlled airports are an interesting hybrid insofar as they are in many cases strategically critical and are treated by grandfathered carriers as though they are owned, yet there is a strong argument that they are in fact a public good whose ownership is seldom clearly established. In a service business such as the airline industry, intangible resources – notably corporate culture and its impact on the style and tone of service delivery – are likely to be particularly important sources of competitive advantage (Holloway, 2002).

The specialised linkages which integrate a firm's resources imbue them with more 'value in use' to the airline concerned than their individual 'exchange value' in factor markets; some, such as organizational routines (Nelson and Winter, 1982) and unarticulated 'know-how', might be impossible to value outside the context of a particular firm. The way in which linkages within a vertically integrated airline and relationships with external parties such as alliance partners are co-ordinated can also be important resources that competitors might find difficult to imitate.

Although rooted in microeconomics, RBT has a distinct heritage (having emerged from a tradition within the discipline known as 'evolutionary economics'), and it differs greatly from the neoclassical tradition in the way firms are characterised. RBT identifies a much broader range of resources than does neoclassical theory, and uses their heterogeneity to distinguish between different firms. In neoclassical theory, resources are embodied as homogeneous factors of production – land, labour, and capital (i.e., production facilities); these are tangible and exist only in the context of production functions. There are, for example, no neoclassical factor markets – no demand or supply curves – for brand image, reputation, corporate culture, or relationships with suppliers, alliance partners, or customers (i.e., for 'reputational' and 'relational' resources). Neither, incidentally, do these resources often appear in balance sheets, even though they are a primary source of wealth creation (Falkenburg, 1996).

Some firms have resources that give them an advantage over others in producing certain types of output. However, it is not resources themselves that matter, but how they are put to use in order to effectively and efficiently produce output for one or more segments of demand (Penrose, 1959). Competitive strategy is a conscious attempt to build and capitalise on the firm's endowment of strategic resources (Zou and Cavusgil, 1996). This is done by matching resources to available opportunities that can be exploited at an acceptable level of risk, and by using them wherever possible to neutralise threats (Foss, 1997).

If a resource is to be a source of competitive advantage, it must contribute to something valuable that an airline can do for its targeted customers but competitors cannot, or to something that enables the airline to provide a given level of customer value at a lower cost than competitors (Barney, 1986a). In other words, it must yield positional advantage whether in terms of differentiation, price or both – *as perceived by customers*. If a resource is to be a *sustainable* source of competitive advantage, it must be difficult for competitors to acquire, imitate, or substitute (Bogner and Thomas, 1994).

Synthesis In the strategic management literature competitive advantage is widely accepted as being derived from an ability to provide better customer value for equivalent cost, or equivalent customer value at lower cost than competitors (Porter, 1985). To achieve either of these advantageous positions, a firm chooses to perform particular activities, to perform activities in a certain way, not to perform particular activities, or to link activities (internally or across organizational boundaries) in a particular manner; from this choice flows an advantage over competitors serving the same customers but making different choices (Porter, 1991, 1996). Strategic positions, whether based on differentiation or cost leadership, are underpinned by relevant resources (including capabilities) which allow the firm to distinguish itself from competitors in respect of what it can do and how it can do it. Resources, brought together in the context of particular activities, are the foundation of an airline's relative cost position and the ability to differentiate its service(s).

In the language of microeconomics, we can say that an airline having one or more sources of competitive advantage is able to earn 'economic rent' from the activities its resources and capabilities allow it to undertake and the manner in which it chooses to undertake them – in other words, from the configuration of its value chain. We will return to this shortly.

Field of strategy 3: Internal organization

The third of the three fundamental issues we identified as confronting strategists (alongside establishment of the boundaries of the firm, and of the strategic position it will occupy within its markets) is the design of the organization. This is important because it affects the implementation of strategies – how resources are distributed, work is done, information is transmitted, and learning takes place. Indeed, the question of whether in practice structure follows strategy (as in principle it should) or strategy is shaped by organizational structure (as politics dictate it often is) preoccupied business strategy researchers for several decades after the birth of the field in the early 1960s (Chandler, 1962). Four basic types of organizational structure are: unitary/functional ('U-form'); multi-divisional ('M-form'); matrix; and network (or 'virtual'). (There are, of course, many hybrid forms.) Most airlines retain functional structures, although larger carriers tend to organise marketing and sales functions in particular into separate divisions based on geography or, less frequently, products; some small carriers, particularly recent start-ups, have outsourced so many of their activities that they approximate a network structure.

Economics has not been silent on the structuring debate, and in particular has contributed agency theory. Comprehensive coverage of both agency theory and the wider field of organizational structuring can be found in Besanko et al (2000).

Summary

Economics remains deeply influential in the endeavour to understand competitive strategy – that is, behaviour in pursuit of (and pursuant to the possession of) sustainable competitive advantage. It is, however, open to the accusation that individuals and groups, and their values and conflicts, receive only 'bit parts' in the unfolding strategic narrative. Whilst not ignored, these actors are generally subordinated to the overarching – and often distinctly rational – dictates of economic efficiency.

Neoclassical microeconomics – still the core of many 'business economics' courses and liberally sampled in the present book – is arguably ill at ease with the concept of the firm, preferring instead to frame all economic problems in a market setting and treat organizations as black boxes that costlessly make optimal decisions in response to price signals from the marketplace (Penrose, 1959). The position taken by neoclassical theory is that performance will tend to converge over time to a 'normal' level of economic profit that is just sufficient to cover costs (including the cost of capital) and keep resources from being redeployed to their next best alternative uses; only with the assistance of artificial barriers to competition can this normal profit be sustainably bettered.

Industrial organization economics is also fundamentally an equilibrium-oriented, comparative statics approach – although Porter (1985, 1991, 1996) does move inside the organization with his attention to value chains and activities; this edges him towards RBT. The latter takes an evolutionary perspective, seeing competition as an innovation-inducing, disequilibrating process fuelled by the efforts of organizations to develop strategically valuable resources, routines, and capabilities that can help build and sustain competitive advantage.

This second section of the chapter has introduced the concept of strategy and identified three fundamental issues that strategists must address: the boundaries of the firm; the position it will occupy within its markets and the resources available to support that position; and the design of the organization. Concepts introduced here will resurface at various points in subsequent chapters. What we will do in the next section is develop the second of those issues – positioning and resources – to provide a strategic context for the discussion of industry economics that follows in Parts 2 and 3 of the book.

iii. Cost advantage, benefit advantage, and customer value

Porter's 'five-forces' framework for industry analysis (threat of substitutes and new entrants, bargaining power of buyers and suppliers, and intensity of inter-firm rivalry) and the strategic positioning advice that flows from it (wide-market or niche differentiation or cost leadership) are consistent with the perspective of IO economics that industry conditions are the primary determinant of a firm's performance. That there is truth in this is borne out by the persistently miserable financial performance of the airline industry as a whole relative to, say, the pharmaceutical industry. However, profitability varies not only across industries but also within them – as the long-term performances of carriers such as Southwest and Singapore Airlines relative to most others bear out. The perspective taken in this section of the chapter is that intra-industry performance variations can be traced to whether or not individual airlines possess the resources (including capabilities) required to deliver the type of value expected by the particular customers each has positioned itself to serve, whether those resources are protected by 'isolating mechanisms' (Rumelt, 1984) such as uniqueness and inimitability, and how effectively and efficiently they are managed.

Airline managers do not confront the economics of the industry in a vacuum, but within the context of a particular competitive strategy. Competitive strategy is behaviour intended to build and/or leverage a competitive advantage. Below competitive strategy in the 'strategy hierarchy' are functional strategies – marketing, operations, human resources, finance, and so on – that need to be integrated in support of competitive strategy. The purpose of each is to deliver customer value.

Customer value

Utility and customer value

The concept of utility underlies neoclassical demand theory. Exchange takes place when two parties each give up something that provides them with less utility than what they receive in return (Fabrycky et al, 1998). The utility of a product is not intrinsic to the product itself, but is reflected in its ability to satisfy a particular consumer's needs and wants. Evaluation of utility might lead a consumer to hold a level of desire for a product somewhere between abhorrence and 'must have'.

Utility and customer value are closely related. Whereas utility (at least according to one definition) is the satisfaction a particular person derives from using a product, value is that person's appraisal of the worth of utility received net of any disutility – such as price paid, requirement to book in advance, having to change planes at a congested hub, or minimum and maximum stay restrictions. Value is neither the cost of a product nor its price, but a consumer's appraisal of what is to be gained from acquiring that product net of what has to be given up to acquire it.

The question of who decides what amounts to value has been answered somewhat differently within the different traditions of economics. The Austrian-subjectivist tradition places great store in the subjective opinions of individual actors; as Rothbard (1962: 19) puts it from this perspective, '....physically, there may be no discernible difference between one pound of butter and another. But if the actor chooses to evaluate them differently, they are no longer part of the supply of the same good'. Similarly, the services management literature also takes the view that perception *is* reality as far as consumers are concerned (Holloway, 2002). This view is followed here.

A closer look at customer value

Figure 1.2 proposes the following definitions.

1. A customer's **perceived benefit** from using a service is equivalent to the gross benefits (or 'utility') offered by that particular service (e.g., safety, schedule convenience, ontime performance, inflight comfort, enhanced self-image through brand association, frequent flyer miles, etc.) less non-monetary costs (e.g., ticket conditionality, queues at various points in the service delivery system, elapsed journey time lengthened by having to connect at a hub, crowded airports and airplanes, etc.). This concept could in principle be monetised by equating it to the maximum price the customer is prepared to pay.

   It is important to stress that we are talking about benefits as perceived by customers rather than by airline managers. Mid-90s UK start-up Debonair tried to distinguish its low-fare product by adding a few minor cabin service benefits not offered by competitors such as Ryanair and easyJet. Unfortunately, most potential customers were either unaware of the incremental benefits or failed to perceive them as meaningful to the purchase decision. These benefits therefore generated costs uncompensated by incremental revenues, and were one factor (among several) contributing to Debonair's subsequent failure. In contrast, jetBlue was launched out of New York with benefits that were well-communicated to target customers and favourably received.

2. **Value created** by a service is the customer-perceived benefit as just defined, less all the input costs that have been spent right along the 'value chain' in order to create the service and deliver value to the customer.

3. **Consumer surplus** is perceived benefit less the monetary price paid by the customer. This is widely referred to as 'customer-perceived value' or simply 'customer value'; although the terms are not always used synonymously, they can be treated as such for our purposes here. In effect this is the part of 'value created' that the customer is capturing. Because each customer is likely to place a different value on any particular service, the amount of consumer surplus will vary between individuals; we will revisit this idea in chapters 3 and 9, because it is the foundation of price discrimination and therefore of revenue management. Consumers are generally assumed, certainly by most economists, to make purchase decisions that maximise consumer surplus (Bowman and Ambrosini, 1998). Sometimes there might be no consumer surplus: the price paid in this case equates exactly to the value placed by the consumer on perceived benefits; this is likely only

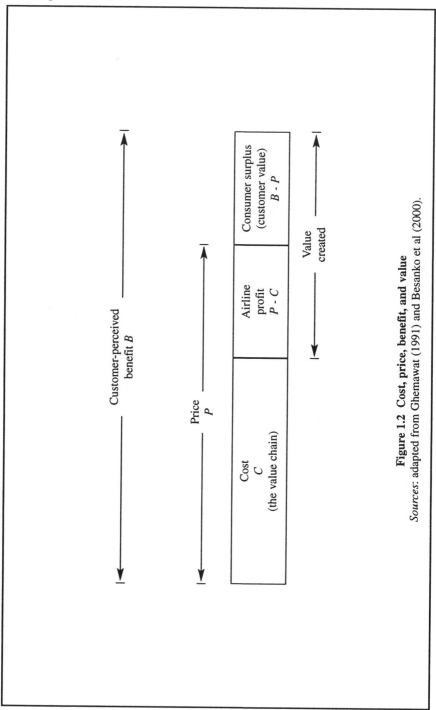

Figure 1.2 Cost, price, benefit, and value
Sources: adapted from Ghemawat (1991) and Besanko et al (2000).

where there is a monopoly supplier who knows each customer's valuation of the service and is able to price-discriminate accordingly (ibid). (Note that in principle there can never be a negative consumer surplus insofar as nobody is likely to pay for a service from which they derive no value.)

4. **Seller's profit** is the monetary price paid by the customer less the cost of inputs. This is the portion of 'value created' that the airline – the final seller of the service fashioned out of all the inputs that went into creating and delivering it – is capturing. In terms of Porter's five-forces model, we could characterise this as the proportion of whatever value has been created that the airline is able to appropriate for itself given the bargaining power of customers and suppliers (including suppliers of labour), the intensity of competitive rivalry, and inroads being made by substitutes and new entrants. The effect of a fare war, for example, would be to put downward pressure on P and result in reduced profit (lower, or perhaps even negative, P-C) and increased consumer surplus (higher B-P).

What airlines are, in principle, doing in the marketplace is trying to win business by manipulating service-price offers – that is, by managing gross benefits, non-monetary costs, and price. Box 1.2 illustrates the point.

Box 1.2: Southwest and Midwest: different types of customer value

When demand evaporated from low-fare carriers in the US domestic market during the summer of 1996 after a fatal accident involving one of their number, this was because the core benefit they were perceived to be delivering in respect of safety was being reassessed by customers. Despite the low prices they continued to offer, the value propositions put forward by these carriers (with the exception of long-established and highly regarded Southwest) had been unbalanced by changed consumer perceptions in respect of that key service attribute. Not even the most price-sensitive end of the US domestic market, it seems, is driven entirely by price; customer-perceived value is driven by both sides of the service-price offer, rather than by price alone. Customers may well buy into tight seat pitches and an absence of 'frills', but this does not mean that those service attributes that are in fact offered will necessarily be acceptable irrespective of quality; safety is perhaps the attribute which most strongly demonstrates this fact.

It is missing the point to assume that, say, Southwest sells on price alone. Southwest sells on value for money – on the right service-price offer. It has targeted customers who prefer not to pay as much as other carriers want them to pay, and it gives them good value. Many of the 'hard' service attributes offered by 'full-service' airlines, such as lounges, meals, seat assignment, and other amenities, are not a feature of Southwest's value proposition; but value is embodied in emotional benefits derived from using the brand (e.g., the corporate ethos of 'fun') and from a culture supporting consistent standards of personal service, as well as in high frequencies, punctuality, and low prices.

Were a new competitor to undercut Southwest's fares but in the process offer low frequencies, patchy schedule reliability, and surly service, it is doubtful that more than a small percentage of demand would be attracted: the reason is that many customers are looking not just at price, but at the overall service-price offer. What is beyond doubt is that whenever two competitors match each other's prices, consumers need to be given a reason to buy from one rather than the other. Observers who talk about the 'commoditisation' of the industry, because so many consumers are price-sensitive, and who dismiss branding as an irrelevant luxury miss this point. Southwest, on the other hand, proves it: low costs and strong branding are not incompatible, and together they help provide value that competitors cannot match as readily as they can match prices.

Midwest, a very different airline with a very different approach to its markets built around high standards of inflight service, also sells on value for money. Different though their value propositions are, these two carriers share one thing in common: clearly defined service concepts that have been effectively translated into service packages designed to deliver the value expected by targeted customers and supported by appropriate cost structures (Holloway, 2002).

A brand offers good value relative to competitors when it provides one or more of:

- fewer benefits, sufficiently compensated by lower prices;
- similar benefits of similar quality at lower prices;
- unique benefits at the same price;
- unique benefits which justify premium pricing.

The fundamental objective is to pitch a better bid for customers' business than competitors are pitching, by offering perceptibly more customer value to targeted segments; the ultimate objective, of course, should be to do this and at the same time keep the price element of the service-price offer above input costs and ensure acceptable earnings. The critical point to remember is that customer value is defined by customers – not by airline employees; the 'value game' is played by the customers' rules, and in this game perception *is* reality. If customers perceive a service attribute to provide a benefit that adds value, it adds value – and if they don't, it doesn't.

Figures 1.3 and 1.4 illustrate some of these ideas. With reference to figure 1.3:

- the 'acceptable perceived value' (APV) curve is the theoretical indifference curve of a single consumer. In principle, a service-price offer positioned anywhere on this curve should be acceptable to the consumer. Bowman and Faulkner (1997) refer to this as a 'consumer surplus isoquant'. A service-price offer positioned off the curve has the potential to provide higher value (if to the left) or lower value (if to the right);
- there are two ways customer-perceived value could be improved relative to an existing value proposition on the indifference curve: by reducing price whilst maintaining or improving perceived benefits, or by improving benefits whilst maintaining or reducing price. Either would result in a new proposition located to the left of the indifference curve. Conversely, a reduction in benefits without downward adjustment in price, or an increase in price without an improvement in perceived benefits, would shift a proposition to the right of the curve;
- a segment of demand is comprised of customers whose similarly shaped APV curves imply broadly-shared service expectations, attribute weightings, and perceptions of value. The more congruent the expectations, weightings, and perceptions of value held by a group of customers, the tighter the segment; the less congruence there is, the stronger the case for further segmentation. This argument is consistent with the thinking behind benefits segmentation, which we will be looking at in chapter 2.

Having identified one or more segments by hypothesising different APV curves, the next questions are which one(s) an airline should serve and where it should position itself in each targeted segment. The first question is answered by deciding upon a strategic position – as a wide-market or niche carrier focusing on differentiation or cost leadership, for example. The second is answered by deciding upon a market position – something that in turn requires service concepts and price platforms to be formulated which distinguish the carrier from competitors in customers' perceptions; a 'price platform' is the walk-up, unrestricted fare for a particular service which, as we will see in chapter 3, provides the foundation for often complex pricing structures. (Strategic positioning and market positioning are therefore closely related, but they are not identical concepts; whereas a carrier's *strategic* position refers to its choice of competitive scope – that

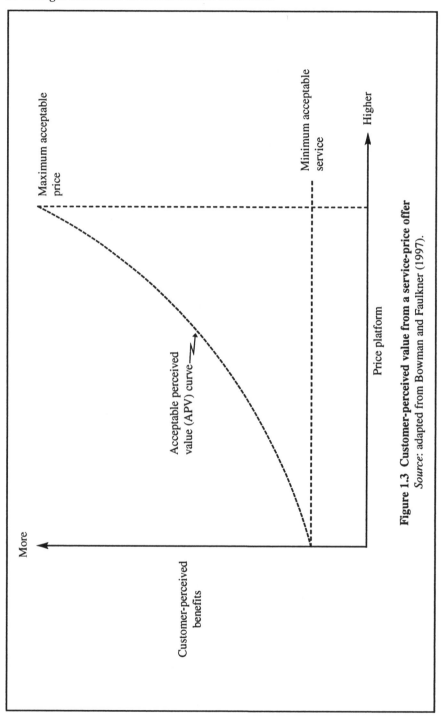

Figure 1.3 Customer-perceived value from a service-price offer
Source: adapted from Bowman and Faulkner (1997).

is, whether in service and/or geographical dimensions it is to be a wide-market or niche differentiator or cost leader – its *market* position is a matter of how its brand is perceived in the minds of targeted customers relative to competing brands.)

Airlines can target a segment by designing a service-price offer that is believed to sit somewhere on that segment's APV curve – perhaps around its mid-point, as carrier A in figure 1.4 has done.

If all the firms in a market are located along the indifference curve, consumers will have little incentive to switch and market shares will be largely stable. One way of shifting market share is to locate away from the curve by offering a new price/benefit trade-off – that is, by making a new service-price offer. However, positions off the curve raise further questions. For example, staying with figure 1.4 and using airline A as a benchmark:

- Airline B is offering fewer benefits at a lower price. The question is whether there is a sub-segment of demand willing to forgo benefits in return for that lower price. If so, which benefits and how much lower price? An example in some US and European short-haul markets might be price-sensitive business travellers willing to forgo the ground and cabin amenities offered by full-service carriers provided there is a low-fare alternative offering high frequencies and reliable schedules.

- Airline C is offering more customer-perceived benefits than airline A and a lower price platform. Provided C can communicate its benefits effectively and further provided that the benefits it is perceived to be offering are sufficient to overcome the switching costs that A might have imposed by creating customer loyalty (whether emotional loyalty to the brand or functional loyalty to its FFP), market share should shift from A to C. The question is whether C's cost structure will enable it to profitably sustain effective delivery of an enhanced benefits package and retain its increased share.

- Airline D is also offering more customer-perceived benefits than A, but unlike C it is charging a price premium. In other words, D is 'differentiating' its product. ('Differentiation' occurs when an airline is able to extract a price premium on the basis of unique or better-delivered benefits; in the absence of a price premium, those benefits might certainly enhance the brand distinctiveness of the airline delivering them, but they would not be a source of 'differentiation' as defined by most economists.) The question in this case is whether there is a sub-segment of demand prepared to pay for the augmented benefits being offered, or whether the airline is 'over-delivering' in the context of the segment concerned. British Airways has regularly introduced innovations into its long-haul business- and first-class cabins, and has

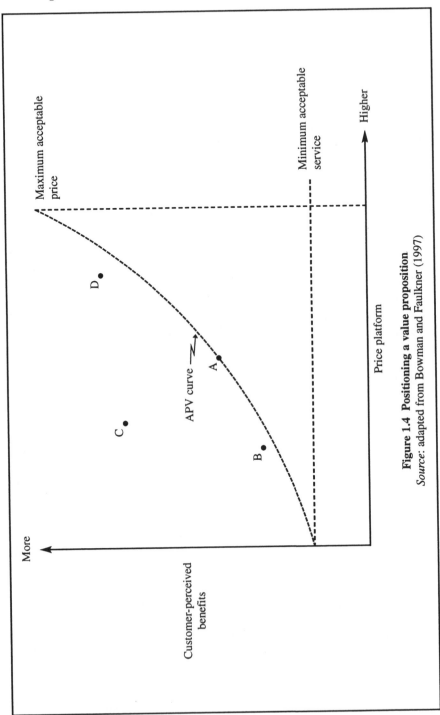

Figure 1.4 Positioning a value proposition
Source: adapted from Bowman and Faulkner (1997)

in some markets been able to price above competitors serving broadly the same segments with less benefit-rich products. However, this strategy does impose an onerous and expensive requirement to be a consistent innovator and first-mover.

Positions right of the APV curve are only sustainable in the long term if there are entry barriers preventing competition from carriers willing to position on or left of the curve, or if the segment is insufficiently profitable to attract such customer-driven competitors.

It should be noted that when talking here about 'customer-perceived benefits', what we are referring to is customers' *expectations* with regard to the benefits they will receive from using a particular service. If those expectations turn out from any customer's perspective not to have been fulfilled during service delivery, there will be a service quality gap. Both service quality and its measurement using gap theory are discussed in Holloway (2002).

All this might sound vague and academic set against the cut-and-thrust of an airline's real-time product design and pricing environment in a highly competitive market. What the analysis does achieve is to underline why both strategic and market positioning need to be based on clearly understood sources of cost advantage and/or benefit advantage relative to identified competitors targeting the same customers in defined markets or market segments.

Cost advantage

Referring back to figure 1.2 (page 26), an airline with a cost advantage has a lower C than its competitors. The critical question is the nature of the customer-perceived benefits B that it is offering and the price P it can charge for them. There are broadly two possibilities.

1. **Benefit parity** An airline offering the same benefits as competitors on the same price platform but off a lower cost base will earn higher profits. (This is what is meant by Porter's (1980) generic strategy of cost leadership; Porter's model describes above-average returns being earned by *the* lowest cost producer charging prices similar to others in the market. Contrary to a widespread misunderstanding, it is a model that hinges on *cost* leadership, not *price* leadership.)
2. **Benefit reduction** In this case, benefits offered are significantly fewer than most competitors are offering, and the price platform is lower in order to compensate. This is the essence of a low-cost/low-fare posit-

ioning strategy. Profits depend upon whether a carrier's lower costs are sufficiently low to sustain its necessarily lower price platform.

Benefit advantage

An airline offering higher customer-perceived benefits (B) may have an advantage – depending on the costs it incurs and the price it is able to charge. Again, there are broadly two possibilities.

1. **Differentiation** If the supplementary benefits offered are sufficiently attractive to customers, the airline might be able to charge a premium price. This is what economists – and Porter's generic strategies model – refer to as 'differentiation'. Perhaps the most extreme example of differentiation is Concorde. The ability to differentiate can support higher production costs; flat-bed and sleeper seats in long-haul business class cabins provide an obvious example insofar as they allow an airline to charge a premium over less attractive 'standard' business class products to compensate for the lower seating densities they impose. If B increases more than C, incremental value will have been created; market forces, through their impact on P, will determine how this is shared between the airline (as profit) and the customer (as consumer surplus). Continuing with the same example, over time competitors will introduce their own upgraded cabins and any price premium is likely to be eroded – either by a general upward movement in competitors' price platforms, or by the innovator having to reduce its platform to compete with upgraded products introduced by carriers which decline to raise prices.

2. **Distinctiveness** If an airline is unable to charge a premium for supplementary benefits, it is not technically 'differentiating' in an economic sense. These benefits may have merit insofar as they help distinguish the airline's offer and perhaps shift sales in its direction, but in the absence of an ability to differentiate (by increasing P) it is evident that any increase in costs (C) incurred in delivering them will reduce profits ($P-C$). Benefit advantage in this case therefore arises from possession of resources and capabilities that contribute to distinctiveness without increasing costs. Box 1.3 explores this further.

Box 1.3: Differentiation or being different?

In order to sell in a competitive market it is necessary to be different from competitors in some way that customers value. But 'being different' is not necessarily the same as what is meant by economists when they talk of '*differentiation*'. *Economists say that two products A and B are 'different-iated' if there is some common price for the two at which consumers prefer, say, B over A; logically then, we can say that in order to get a consumer who prefers B to actually buy A, the price of A will have to be reduced sufficiently to compensate her for forgoing the benefits that drive her pref-erence for B. If the price of A is indeed below the price of B but is not suff-iciently low to convince all consumers to change allegiance, the producer of B is earning a price premium from those who do buy its product and reaping the benefit of differentiation.*

The idea of differentiation, widely popularised by Porter (1980, 1985), in fact goes back to the 1930s. At that time, economists added the concept of 'monopolistic competition' to the microeconomic models of market struct-ure which until then had recognised perfect competition, oligopoly, and monopoly (Chamberlin, 1933; Robinson, 1934). The basic idea of monop-olistic competition is that by differentiating their offers in some way that is valuable to customers, firms gain a degree of freedom to raise prices they would not otherwise have in a perfectly competitive market; in effect, what they do is create a 'mini-monopoly' for the differentiated product.

The perspective on service-price offers taken in this book is somewhat different.

Service *An airline might offer a service that differs from competitors' off-ers in one or more ways which customers value. That difference could lie in functional attributes such as a better schedule or more comfortable cabins on long-haul services, or it might lie in less tangible but arguably more def-ensible emotional (i.e., psycho-social) attributes such as the style and tone of service delivery. (Note that 'attributes' are dimensions of a service offer that generate the benefits customers are buying.)*

- *If customers are willing to pay a premium for this augmented service, we have a case of 'differentiation' as defined by economists. The next questions would then be whether the price premium covers any increm-ental costs – a rough calculation at best, in most circumstances – and how sustainable the competitive advantage on which the differentiation has been built will prove to be over time. Some airlines have been able to charge premia for nonstop services competing against connecting routes, for innovations such as sleeper-seats/flat-bed seats, for sched-ule strength at a dominated hub, and sometimes even for what they consider to be their 'high-quality' brand image. Sustaining such prem-ia on a long-term basis can nonetheless prove challenging.*

- *If customers will not pay a premium in return for functional or psycho-social benefits, other than perhaps temporarily, these benefits are not technically a source of 'differentiation'. They are certainly 'points of*

*difference' (an expression widely used in the brand management liter-
ature), but in this case the airline is not earning 'economic rent' from
the resources or capabilities that make it different – much though it
might like to; it is, nonetheless, giving customers a 'reason to buy' in a
competitive environment hallmarked by product 'sameness' and widespread price-matching.*

*In general, few airlines possess the unique, rare, or costly-to-imitate res-
ources required to sustain either 'differentiation' or 'points of difference'
based on purely functional service attributes. There are exceptions, most
notably those built on possession of critical mass at a hub or in a particular
market; either can lead to the building of a dominant position in customers'
perceptions within a geographical area. But on the whole, it is in respect of
intangible attributes such as culture, service style, and brand image – providing predominantly psycho-social benefits – that sustainable points of
difference can be found.*

Price *This is where we diverge further from the economists' idea of differentiation, because in this book price is treated as part of an overall
service-price value proposition rather than as a reflection of whether or
not an airline has been able successfully to differentiate itself in economists' terms. Take for example a low-cost/low-fare carrier. It might be able
to establish clear points of difference between itself and competitors based
on corporate culture and a positive brand image, as Southwest has done;
but it cannot earn a price premium – that is, 'differentiate' in economists'
terms – because low price is a fundamental purchase criterion in the segment it is targeting. This does not mean that the points of difference built
on corporate culture and brand image are irrelevant, because all other
things being equal – including price and schedule, for example – these give
customers a reason to choose, and remain loyal to, Southwest rather than
another carrier. In other words, although Southwest might for the sake of
argument score equally with the competition on price and on functional
attributes such as frequency and departure timings, the points of difference
it has established by nurturing psycho-social attributes driven by culture
and image give its overall service-price offer a winning edge.*

*In summary, when we talk about price or service 'distinctiveness' in this
book, we are in fact talking about what the brand management literature
refers to as 'points of difference' rather than what economists mean by
'differentiation'. We are talking about design variables in a strategic
service-price offer which give customers a reason to purchase from the
airline concerned rather than from competitors. When the word 'different-*

iation' is used, we mean that an airline is able to command a price premium over direct competitors.

The value chain

Benefit and cost advantages are rooted in an airline's unique resources and capabilities, and reflected in its choice of strategic position; they are operationalised by the activities it chooses to undertake. Activities are conducted within the firm's value chain, which itself is part of a wider value system encompassing also the value chains of upstream suppliers, horizontal partners, downstream distributors, and customers. Porter (1991: 104) has put the argument as follows.

> Competitive advantage results from a firm's ability to perform required activities at a collectively lower cost than rivals, or perform some activities in unique ways that create buyer value and hence allow the firm to command a premium price. The required mix and configuration of activities, in turn, is altered by competitive scope.

Hergert and Morris (1989: 179) explain the microeconomic roots of the value chain.

> The firm is viewed as a collection of discrete but related production functions (activities), where some of them are not freely traded in external markets. These non-traded activities will generate rents for the firms able to perform them and also create entry barriers or cost disadvantages for other firms. Firms perform a variety of tasks in transforming raw materials and primary goods into final products. Although necessary, most of these activities do not distinguish a firm from its rivals. Competitive advantage must be based on those activities in which a firm has proprietary access to scarce resources (e.g., skills, patents, assets, distribution networks, etc.). The first step in strategy formulation is to identify which activities are the actual or potential source of such rents. This is the part of the firm which must be managed. [Anything else is a candidate for outsourcing.]

Returning once again to figure 1.2 (page 26), each activity in an airline's value chain has the potential to augment customer-perceived benefits (B), and each also has the potential to increase the cost (C) that the airline incurs assembling inputs and delivering service. The forces that influence benefits created and costs incurred – called 'activity drivers' – vary across different activities (Besanko et al, 2000). In principle, it is possible to generate value-added analyses which compare the incremental perceived benefit generated by a new activity, or a new way of performing an existing activity, with the cost incurred; in practice, it is often very difficult to isolate the impact that individual activities have on the overall value created by an airline.

What this simple model does nonetheless do is suggest a strategic frame of reference within which to consider airline economics. Many of the concepts introduced in this section, and earlier in the chapter, will be revisited as the book unfolds. In particular, the importance of cost advantage and benefit advantage to strategic and market positioning can be used to anchor the discussion of traffic, yield, output, and costs in Part 2.

iv. The rest of the book

This opening chapter has led us towards several questions, the answers to which help provide a strategic context for the rest of the book.

- What markets/segments are available and which should be served?
- What type of value – what combination of benefits and price platform – do customers in each of these markets/segments expect?
- What strategy-specific resources and capabilities do we have that enable us to deliver the value that targeted customers expect?
- What firm-specific resources and capabilities do we have that enable us to do this better than – and so outperform – competitors targeting the same customers?
- Can we do all this and also make money for our shareholders?

On an operating level, the answer to the last question will depend on how we manage the elements in the following relationship:

TRAFFIC x YIELD > < OUTPUT x UNIT COST
= OPERATING PERFORMANCE (i.e., PROFIT or LOSS)

Part 2 of the book is structured around this relationship, with separate chapters on traffic, yield, output, and cost. Given that capacity management is a critical driver of both revenues and costs, Part 3 contains chapters looking in turn at several of the most important topics in airline capacity management: network management (with separate chapters on design and scheduling); fleet management; and revenue management. Finally, Part 4 wraps up the discussion with a review of some important macro-level performance metrics. Figure 1.5 maps the terrain we will be covering.

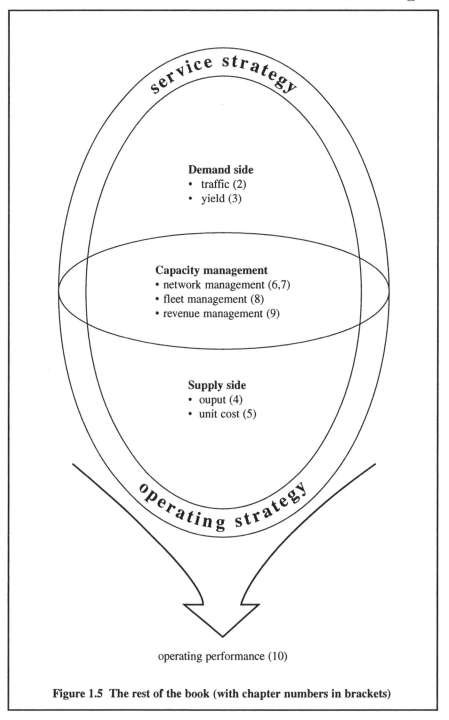

Figure 1.5 The rest of the book (with chapter numbers in brackets)

Implicit in this are both demand-side and supply-side perspectives.

- **Demand side: service strategy and positioning** The fundamental issue here involves deciding which customers to target, understanding what targeted customers expect, and designing value propositions capable of delivering service that meets or exceeds expectations.
- **Supply side: operating strategy and resource advantage** Having designed one or more value propositions, it is then necessary to develop an operating strategy that is both consistent with the customer value to be delivered and able to exploit one or more sources of advantage over competitors.

If there is one core theme running through the book, it is that the revenue and cost sides should always be considered together. In particular, costs must never be endowed with a life of their own, but should be looked at in the context of their contribution to customer value and to revenue.

v. Summary

The message of this chapter is that economics provides us with only one of several alternative lenses through which to look at the organizations we call airlines, at their environments, their objectives, and their decision-making processes, and at the strategies they pursue. Economic analysis is an important element in management decision-making, but it is far from being the only influence.

Focusing in particular on links between economics and strategy, we have seen that according to the resource-based theory of strategy, firms compete by deploying heterogeneous, imperfectly mobile resources. Resources that are rare, difficult for competitors to imitate, and causally ambiguous (i.e., not readily understood by outsiders) allow strategic positions (as *the* cost leader or *a* differentiator, for example) and market positions (relative to competitors as perceived by customers) to be created and sustained; however, over time and in the absence of insurmountable barriers to entry it will be necessary to innovate in order to sustain superior financial performance. A chosen strategic position should be supported by an appropriate underlying resource profile and organizational structure (i.e., by an appropriate value chain). Together, these create the foundations for a competitive strategy built on one or both of cost advantage or benefit advantage (Nickerson et al, 2001).

This link between economics and strategy will be picked up in Part 2 of the book.

Part 2
Operating Performance Drivers

An airline's financial performance over time reflects: choice of strategy; the manner in which resources are allocated and utilised in pursuit of strategy; the methods chosen to finance acquired resources and, in respect of external funding, the terms negotiated; and the extent to which cash flows generated (by ongoing operations, affiliates, and asset sales) are protected against foreign exchange, interest rate, and other risks.

Profit is commonly used to measure financial performance. There are, however, broadly two types of profit.

1. **Economic profit** Whereas accountants define profit as the amount by which revenue exceeds expenditure in a given period, economists also consider opportunity costs attributable to benefits forgone as a result of not employing resources in the next most remunerative activity of corresponding risk to which they could otherwise have been applied; an obvious example is the return on investment expected by a firm's owners. A zero economic (or 'normal') profit means that the firm is exactly covering its accounting costs and also the opportunity costs of the owners' investment; its owners are doing at least as well by leaving their investments where they are as they could by moving them into any alternative venture with the same risk profile.

   In a perfectly competitive market, long-run economic profit is kept at zero by the movement of firms in and out of the industry. Firms earning a negative economic profit should in theory leave the industry; if this causes a drop in output and a rise in equilibrium prices sufficient to allow those remaining to earn a short-run positive economic profit (i.e., a 'supernormal' or 'excess' profit), outsiders will be attracted back and output will again increase – putting downward pressure on the equilibrium price. However, in less than perfectly competitive markets – markets sheltered behind barriers to entry, markets where one producer is dominant, or markets where all or most producers collude – firms might be able to sustain supernormal profits over long periods of time. One interpretation of competitive strategy is that its purpose is to identify or create market imperfections, then sustain the advantages to which

41

they give rise by exploiting or creating barriers to entry. (We will be discussing barriers to entry in chapter 4.)

Shareholder value is an increasingly widely used metric of financial performance which builds on the idea of economic profit. There are several different approaches, some of which are proprietary, but the essence of the concept is to calculate net cash flows generated by a firm and available to stockholders, and to subtract from these the cost of capital; the technique can be used on historic data to evaluate performance, or prospectively (using discounted cash flow analysis) to evaluate alternative strategies or projects. A positive figure suggests that shareholder value is being created, whilst a negative figure implies that it is being destroyed – regardless of what accounts prepared under generally accepted accounting principles (GAAP) might indicate. Although many of the building blocks of both economic profit and shareholder value analysis appear in the following chapters, neither is explicitly referenced. Our interest in this book lies with accounting profit.

2. **Accounting profit** Accountants define profit as the amount by which revenues exceed costs incurred in dealings with external parties other than shareholders over a stated period of time; it is arrived at by following the conventions of double-entry book-keeping, but subject to whatever latitude is permitted by GAAP and other rules in the jurisdiction concerned and also subject within those limits to the practices of given industries and choices made by managers at individual firms – with regard to the period over which fixed assets are to be depreciated, for example. The accounting profits of airlines can be considered at three levels.

   - *After-tax level* After-tax profit is net profit less current taxes.
   - *Net (or pretax) level* Net profit is operating profit adjusted for non-operating items such as debt interest, foreign exchange gains and losses, affiliates' results, investment write-offs or write-backs, and realised losses or gains relative to the book (i.e., depreciated) values of assets (such as aircraft) disposed of during the accounting period.
   - *Operating level* Operating profit is the profit generated by an airline's ongoing air transport operations. (However, it should be noted that some airlines include as operating profit the earnings generated from third-party sales by inhouse units such as maintenance and ground-handling that other airlines, perhaps because these activities are housed in separate subsidiaries, might consider non-operating items.)

It is the operating level with which the present book is concerned, because this is the level at which the fundamental economics of the airline business make themselves most powerfully felt. Performance at the net and after-tax levels depends much more on carrier-specific circumstances and nonoperating policies. The distinction is not always clear-cut; for example, decisions regarding how to finance aircraft will have repercussions at both the operating and net levels: if an aircraft is acquired on an operating lease, rentals – which implicitly include the lessor's depreciation and finance charges – are an operating expense; if the same aircraft were bought with external debt, only depreciation would be charged at the operating level whilst debt interest would be a nonoperating expense. Nonetheless, the operating/nonoperating distinction is important and valid.

Part 2 of the book has been structured around a model of performance at the operating level.

TRAFFIC x YIELD > < OUTPUT x UNIT COST
= OPERATING PERFORMANCE (i.e., PROFIT or LOSS)

Chapters two to five look at traffic, yield, output, and cost respectively.

The airline industry can claim many unique technological achievements. It also has a claim to uniqueness in the economic field: despite a history of expansion well above global gross domestic product (GDP) growth rates, despite impressive productivity gains, despite the cosseting of generally benign governments, and despite the commercial and infrastructural barriers to entry that have arisen in some markets over recent years to dilute the benefits of deregulation and regulatory liberalisation, this is still an industry which in aggregate finds it difficult to earn acceptable profits across the duration of an economic cycle. Historically, and quite apart from the extraordinary impact of 9/11, the reasons for this have been clear enough: output growth has too often run ahead of traffic growth, and burgeoning costs have too frequently been put under pressure by declining yields. The next four chapters outline some of the complexities inherent in managing traffic, yield, output, and costs. They build on chapter 1 by stressing the need for a focused, customer-oriented strategic framework within which to manage these critical variables.

2 Traffic

Markets don't buy services – customers do.
Tom Peters

Chapter overview

Traffic is the first of four elements in the operating performance model around which Part 2 of the book has been structured:

TRAFFIC x YIELD > < OUTPUT x UNIT COST
= OPERATING PERFORMANCE (i.e., PROFIT or LOSS)

'Demand' is the quantity of a product that customers are willing and able to purchase at a particular price over a defined period of time. 'Traffic' is that part of demand for air transport services that has been satisfied by carrying passengers and cargo; it is distinct from demand that has not been satisfied – demand that has been 'spilled', perhaps because space was not available when required and no alternative was acceptable. We will see in Part 3 of the book that 'spill' is a concept critical to network, fleet, and revenue management, and that 'spill models' are used in these functions. Nonetheless, the industry as a whole can only estimate rather than measure spill, and there is a tendency to treat 'demand' and 'traffic' as synonymous; in this book they are kept separate, with traffic treated as a subset of demand.

After first introducing the most common metrics used to measure traffic, this chapter will look at the characteristics of demand for air transport services. Subsequent sections will consider: the identification of available markets; segmentation; and demand forecasting. The chapter will end with a brief look at demand management as a precursor to the discussion of capacity management in Part 3 of the book.

i. Traffic defined

Airline traffic in any given period – in other words, the demand which has been met during that period – is measured by the following metrics.

1. For passengers:
   - total enplanements (or 'boardings'), with one enplanement being the embarkation of a revenue passenger, whether originating, stop-over, connecting or returning;
   - revenue passenger-miles (RPMs) or -kilometres (RPKs), which are distance-weighted measures because they are generated by flying one revenue passenger one mile or kilometre. Thus, a regional airline might enplane the same number of passengers each year as Singapore Airlines, but the latter will generate considerably more RPMs/RPKs because it carries each enplaned passenger much further. This will, in turn, be reflected in its longer average trip length per passenger, which can be calculated by dividing enplanements into RPMs or RPKs.

   Distance-weighted traffic measurements are clearly a function of both traffic volumes and network design. For example, Southwest carried fewer passengers (and had fewer departures) in July 2002 than in July 2001, but RPMs were marginally higher; the rise in RPMs reflected longer average trip-lengths per passenger as transcontinental routes were added to the network, and as the airport 'hassle factor' arising from increased security measures diverted at least some potential customers to surface transport in very short-haul markets. This illustrates the interplay between absolute enplanement numbers and average distance travelled in arriving at traffic figures measured in RPMs; similar considerations apply in respect of other distance-weighted metrics.
2. For freight: freight ton-miles (FTMs) or freight tonne-kilometres (FTKs).
3. For passengers and cargo (including freight) combined: revenue ton-miles (RTMs) or revenue tonne-kilometres (RTKs), which are generated by flying one ton one mile or one tonne one kilometre. Use of an assumed weight per passenger and accompanied baggage (usually in the 90–95 kg range or around 200 pounds) allows passenger traffic to be combined in a single measurement with cargo.

Traffic can be measured for a route (e.g., Tulsa–Dallas), a city-pair market encompassing more than one route (e.g., Tulsa–Dubai), or an entire network – both in respect of individual airlines, groups of airlines (e.g., US majors), or the industry as a whole. An airline's network operating revenue (i.e., the operating revenue earned from carrying traffic across its network) is the product of traffic (e.g., RPMs, RPKs, RTMs, RTKs) and yield (i.e., revenue per RPM, RPK, RTM or RTK); we will look at pricing and yield in the next chapter.

Approximately 75 per cent of US airline operating revenue is generated by passengers, 15 per cent by cargo, and the balance by other transport-related activities; on average, the majors earn around 10 per cent of their revenues from cargo (Air Transport Association, 2001). Elsewhere in the world, cargo's share of RTMs at some combination carriers is relatively large – around or above 50 per cent in the case of several Asian 'majors' and LanChile, and over 40 per cent at Air France, Emirates, KLM, and Lufthansa; however, cargo's share of revenues in each case is substantially smaller – only EVA Air relying on cargo for more than 40 per cent of revenue (although LanChile and China Airlines come close). Despite rapid historical growth, cargo still accounts for only around 15 per cent of global airline revenues on average; high projected growth rates will continue to edge this figure upwards. At present, over half the tonnage shipped globally by air moves in the belly-holds of passenger aircraft (although this figure is substantially lower in US domestic markets because of the preponderance of narrowbodies and the market strength of integrated carriers such as FedEx and UPS).

ii. The drivers and characteristics of air transport demand

Demand drivers

It is useful to consider demand drivers at both the macro- and micro- levels.

Macro-level drivers

The two principal drivers of air transport demand have historically been declining real (i.e., inflation-adjusted) prices and the impact of economic growth.

- Declining real prices (i.e., airfares and cargo rates) through to the 1980s were in large measure attributable to growth in airline productivity brought about by rapidly improving airframe and powerplant technologies. Since then, increased competition and the possibilities opened by IT-enabled business process improvements have contributed significantly to the cost management efforts necessary to support declining real airfares. Airframe and powerplant improvements continue to have a beneficial impact on productivity, but less dramatically so than in the past. In some markets, the expansion of low-fare carriers, with business models radically different from those of longer-established airlines, is now a major stimulus to traffic growth. On the whole, real prices are expected to continue their secular decline – albeit perhaps at a somewhat slower rate than in the past.

- Increases in traffic also correlate closely with growth in global GDP, although both the growth and volatility of air transport demand have been consistently higher than comparable figures for global income. Estimates vary, but some analysts believe that as much as two-thirds to three-quarters of the long-term increase in demand for air transport services can be attributed to global GDP growth.

Micro-level drivers

This chapter opened with a quotation from Tom Peters: 'Markets don't buy services – customers do'. In other words, demand in any market is a reflection of the purchasing behaviour of many individual customers. Neoclassical microeconomic theory recognises two types of individual demand: direct and derived.

1. **Direct demand** comes from individuals who want to consume goods and services which themselves satisfy wants and needs.
2. **Derived demand** applies in respect of 'intermediate' goods and services acquired for their contribution to some other good or service rather than for their own intrinsic worth. Aside from pleasure flights, demand for air transport is just such an intermediate service. It is derived indirectly from the demand for the final service or purpose to which it contributes – notably business meetings, visits to friends or relatives, vacations, trips to and from educational institutions, or the requirement to ship goods rapidly to wherever they are needed.

Because intermediate services such as air transport are not generally wanted for consumption in their own right, demand will depend on:

- demand for the underlying purposes of travel; and
- the costs and benefits they offer relative to alternative intermediate inputs – that is, relative to substitutes. For freight shippers, such alternatives might be truck haulage over short or medium distances and sea, sea-land or sea-air combinations to more distant destinations. For business travellers, electronic media are rapidly becoming viable

intermediate services for satisfying some of their needs to communicate with colleagues, suppliers, and customers. Vacationers on short-haul routes may have alternative intermediate services available in the form of surface transport modes.

Unlike many intermediate products which, as far as consumers are concerned, are submerged into the end-product and only get attention if they contribute to a product failure, air transport services are separable and directly experienced in their own right. This presents opportunities.

1. Airlines are free to design, price, distribute, and promote their products so as to maximise the value provided to consumers in much the same way as if they were indeed dealing with direct demand.
2. They are also free to identify the service being offered with the satisfaction of consumers' ultimate wants and needs. This can be done by promoting a leisure destination, for example, or by bundling air transport services into a vacation package (organized either by an in-house unit or by an external packager).

On the other hand, because the demand for seats or cargo space is a derived demand, an airline could offer service which might in many respects represent excellent customer value but still lose traffic if the end-product – whether business trips or vacations to a particular destination – is for whatever reason losing popularity.

Characteristics of demand

Air transport demand has several important characteristics: it can be strongly influenced by the supply of output; it is prone to marked fluctuations over time; and, in some markets, it is subject to directional imbalances in either the volume or the timing of traffic flows.

The influence of supply

Airline managers have limited control over demand, but using increasingly sophisticated pricing, revenue management, promotional, and loyalty programmes they are able to influence it to a greater extent than has been possible in the past. A more fundamental way to exert influence over demand is through manipulation of supply. 'Supply' in this context means not just raw output, but also the quality of service offered in respect of frequencies, departure and arrival times, seat accessibility, and routings (i.e., nonstop, multi-stop or connecting service). Enhanced supply can stimulate demand. (Note the particular way in which the word 'quality' is used here. When transport economists discuss 'the quality of service' their interest tends primarily to be in the variables listed above. On the other hand, the services management and marketing literatures often measure service quality as the gap between customers' expectations and perceptions of service across a much broader range of benefits – including, for example, punctuality, cabin comfort, the style and tone of service delivery, and brand associations. Use of the word 'quality' in this chapter follows the economists' approach. Later in the book we will broaden the discussion of supply/output to encompass different types of ground and inflight product.)

A good example of the impact that supply can have on demand is provided by the early results of the 1995 United States–Canada open skies bilateral. Prior to this agreement, passenger traffic between the two countries was growing at around three per cent per annum. In the first year of the new agreement – a period during which US carriers still had only limited growth rights at Toronto, Montreal, and Vancouver under negotiated phase-in provisions – traffic expanded by 14 per cent. This acceleration was largely due to the availability of new, nonstop cross-border routes (many of which, incidentally, were made viable by the recent arrival of regional jets such as Air Canada's CRJs).

A different but not unrelated point is that a carrier which expands supply to the extent that it dominates output on a route is widely believed to be able to secure for itself a disproportionately large market share. This is known as the 'S-curve' effect because of the shape of the curve derived from plotting frequencies (on the vertical axis) against market share. (We are assuming here that output dominance arises from offering more, well-timed, departures rather than from flying larger aircraft than competitors.) The rationale is that any wasted time between precisely when a passenger wants to depart and when the scheduled departure nearest to that time allows her to depart detracts from the quality of service being offered. An airline offering the highest frequencies in a market will stand a better chance of having a departure close to the times desired by a greater proportion of potential travellers than will its competitors. It is therefore offering a better quality of service in this important dimension, and so will carry a larger proportion of traffic than its share of aggregate output.

Not all observers accept the existence of this relationship. For example, relatively small competitors with a strong brand image and what is perceived to be a competitive value proposition might be able to retain a market share premium (i.e., a higher percentage share of traffic than of total output offered) without frequency domination – something Virgin quickly achieved over the North Atlantic, for example. Furthermore, some segments of demand are clearly more price-sensitive than time-sensitive. On the whole, however, there is a widespread belief in the 'S-curve' relationship; this sometimes leads competitors to 'overschedule'.

Fluctuations in demand

Demand fluctuations can be cyclical, periodic, and irregular.

Cyclical fluctuations The airline industry's strong secular growth trend has been marred by pronounced cyclicality, due in large measure to the relatively high income-elasticity of demand for air transport services. (We will look at income-elasticity in a moment.) The effect of demand-, and therefore revenue-, cyclicality on airlines' financial performances often tends to be magnified by their generally high short-run operating leverage (i.e., high proportion of fixed to total costs) and financial leverage (i.e., high levels of interest-bearing debt as a percentage of total liabilities plus net worth).

The classic industry demand cycle runs though the following stages.

1. Economic growth begins to slow.
2. Traffic growth rates also gradually slow over the next six to nine months as consumer and business confidence are eroded. Discretionary travel weakens and companies pay closer attention to the number of trips, the number of people travelling, and the class of travel. Airline profits quickly come under pressure because high operating (and financial) leverage continue to generate fixed costs that cannot rapidly be reduced in response to stagnant or declining revenues.
3. Airlines take delivery of aircraft ordered earlier, at the peak of the economic cycle when demand was strong and projections were bullish. Indeed, the turning point in an equipment cycle can usually be called when aircraft deliveries overtake orders and the airframe manufacturers' backlog starts falling. Overcapacity is worsened and, if sufficiently severe, results in significant numbers of aircraft being taken out of service (temporarily when new or young, perhaps permanently if old or obsolescent). Simultaneously, further efforts are made, particularly with regard to labour expenses, to adjust cost structures in line with lower or more slowly growing revenues.
4. The economy bottoms out in the trough of the recession. Traffic might be holding up reasonably well in response to fare wars as airlines struggle to fill surplus capacity which has not been parked, but yields (i.e., revenue per RPM or RTM) remain anaemic.

5. Several months after the economy begins to recover, consumer and business confidence pick up across a broader base, traffic increases, discounts becomes less aggressive and more selective, yields improve somewhat, and load factors rise. However, discretionary travel for leisure or VFR purposes might be slower to rebound than business travel unless discounts and fare sales are maintained to stimulate traffic. (In the aftermath of 9/11, low fares and a weak business environment in fact led to leisure and VFR traffic rebounding more strongly than business traffic, particularly in the United States.)
6. As the economy nears its peak, profits recover first at the operating level and then on a net basis as rising demand and firmer yields combine with cost- and capacity-control measures taken earlier in the cycle. Parked aircraft are brought back into service and orders for new capacity begin to materialise. (The 2001/2002 downturn was different insofar as the advanced ages of many of the parked aircraft meant that a higher proportion than ever before remained permanently grounded.)

(Having described the 'textbook' model, it is worth noting that several of the industry's more serious downturns have been due not to the classic economic or business cycle but to the income effect of external shocks such as the oil crises of the 1970s, the Gulf War, the Asian financial crisis of 1997, and 9/11. These events either caused economic downturns or intensified recessions already underway. In each case, but particularly after 9/11, the impact on traffic and yields was felt more quickly than suggested above.)

In international markets the economies at either end might not be experiencing synchronised economic cycles; any resulting imbalance between the sources of originating traffic will have both marketing and currency exposure implications. This points to one possible advantage of having a geographically dispersed portfolio of international routes, as opposed to a purely domestic system. More generally, a wide network broadens the portfolio of market risks; an airline serving a small number of markets or market segments (particularly a full-service carrier relying on high-yield traffic) will be more adversely affected by a demand downturn in one of them than will a competitor with a better spread of markets to serve.

Given high short-run fixed costs and attendant volume-dependency, the profitability of scheduled airlines in particular is always going to be profoundly sensitive to the effect of economic cycles on their revenue streams. Whilst the overall outlook for global economic growth (using indicators such as GDP, trade, industrial output, etc.) is widely seen as positive, periodic economic downturns will continue to punish overinvestment in capacity, unbridled pursuit of market share, and ill-timed corporate acquisitions made at the top of the cycle; by raising the importance of low prices to consumers, downturns also penalise bloated costs and boost the strategic position of low-fare carriers.

Prior to 9/11 there was already some evidence that lessons painfully learned during the recession of the early 1990s had been taken onboard. A growing number of airlines were reluctant to pursue market share at the expense of shareholder value – and, with one or two exceptions, this was reflected in more carefully considered aircraft orders. Further stability had been added by:

- manufacturers shortening the production cycle and therefore reducing the gap between aircraft order and delivery; and
- operating lessors now large enough to make a significant impact on demand/supply imbalances by shifting capacity away from regions where it is surplus to requirements and towards regions where it is needed.

Nonetheless, because this is still on the whole a growth industry, any given percentage drop in traffic growth implies a larger absolute number than a similar drop would have led to in the past – potentially leading to a correspondingly larger volume of unsold output. The stakes in the capacity management game, and the importance of operational flexibility, are therefore rising.

One final point worth making in this subsection is that the cyclicality of air transport demand has quite frequently been used as a justification for the diversification strategies implemented by a number of airlines and airline holding companies. Often these are strategies of 'related diversification' intended to leverage resources and capabilities in MRO, catering, groundhandling, and other fields related to the core passenger and/or cargo air transportation business. Whilst businesses such as these are themselves exposed to cyclicality in the demand for air transport services, the argument is that they are less exposed than are flying activities and to this extent provide a hedge – albeit an imperfect hedge – to protect corporate revenues in a downturn.

Periodic fluctuations: demand peaking Annual traffic figures conceal pronounced seasonal, weekly, and daily demand peaking. When peaks actually occur in any given market will depend upon the nature of the market concerned, notably whether it is oriented primarily towards business or leisure segments and whether it is short- or long-haul.

- **Seasonal peaking** Seasonal peaks in passenger markets are driven by customs and festivals such as Haj, the eids, Christmas or Thanksgiving, and by vacation practices. Charter (i.e., nonscheduled) carriers serving leisure markets face the most intense seasonal peaking problem. The low-season charter market out of the United Kingdom, for example, is rarely more than one-third of the summer peak. This type of demand fluctuation creates different operational problems from daily or weekly peaks, requiring carriers to employ large numbers of temporary and part-time staff and to work hard each year at deploying surplus aircraft during the low season. Neither are scheduled carriers immune from such seasonal variations in leisure demand; traffic on North Atlantic routes, for example, usually peaks in the summer at twice the level of the February trough. Because scheduled airlines in the US domestic market carry a higher proportion of leisure traffic than most scheduled European airlines (with the exception of Air Malta, Finnair and the low-fare carriers), they also face steep fourth and first quarter down-turns in demand. Indeed, demand peaking is such that many Northern Hemisphere carriers rely on the third (calendar) quarter to make sufficient operating profit and generate sufficient cash to carry them through the other quarters.

  Seasonal peaking also occurs in many airfreight markets, with the pre-Christmas surge, the introduction of each new season's clothing lines, and the seasonal bulge in shipments of different types of fresh foodstuffs out of their production areas being three obvious examples.

- **Weekly peaking** Particularly in short-haul markets, extreme peaking is common on Monday mornings and Friday afternoons/evenings. Traffic in the US domestic system on Fridays is generally around 10 per cent higher than on other weekdays.

- **Daily peaking** Many short-haul business markets have a pronounced morning peak, perhaps a midday mini-peak, and a longer, less-pronounced late-afternoon/early evening peak; the morning and evening peaks are often intensified where day-return business trips are feasible in a particular market. Daily peaking on long-haul flights is usually driven by the effect of time zones, which create preferred departure and arrival 'windows' influenced both by consumer preferences and airport curfews or movement quotas.

The costs of meeting peak demand are high if this entails having capacity lie idle in off-peak periods; capacity-related fixed costs such as lease rentals, depreciation, and insurance have to be charged to the income statement whether or not an aircraft is airborne. The less that aircraft and other assets are used during off-peak periods, the more these and similar fixed costs will have to be recovered from peak-period traffic – perhaps by charging higher fares, or accepting a lower profit, than would be the case were off-peak demand higher. This is a serious management challenge. An airline filling on average, say, 65–70 per cent of the capacity it offers will probably be spilling demand during peak periods and yet still be flying aircraft with less than half their output sold off-peak. The greater the scope of its network – in terms of both numbers and types of destination – and the wider the range of market segments served, the better able an airline should be to spread utilisation of its aircraft and other resources.

Irregular fluctuations Peak/off-peak fluctuations are systemic and reasonably predictable on an average basis. Individual departures, on the other hand, are subject to demand irregularities which are much more difficult to predict. Even if it is known that traffic on a particular departure can be expected to fluctuate by as much as, say, 25 per cent either side of the mean for a given period, managers cannot know with complete confidence what demand will be like on any given flight. Complicating matters further is the fact that random demand variability differs between market segments, with demand from business travellers generally more volatile on a per-departure basis than demand from other segments; this is one reason why cabin planning factors (i.e., target load factors) tend to be lower in business and first class cabins than in coach/economy cabins – the intent being to minimise spill. However, increasingly sophisticated demand analysis tools embedded in revenue management systems are gradually improving predictive capabilities. (We will see in chapter 8 that many full-service European carriers have responded to inter-cabin demand variability by using easily movable curtains or partitions between business and economy classes.)

Summary Demand fluctuations have to be addressed by a combination of pricing and capacity allocation such that load factors and yields are acceptable. An 'acceptable' target load factor is one that is not so low as to waste resources producing unsold output, and not so high as to cause unacceptable demand spill; an 'acceptable' yield on traffic carried is one that generates sufficient revenue to cover costs and either achieve or exceed profit and shareholder value objectives. We will revisit these challenges in subsequent chapters.

Directionality

Pure directionality problems are a characteristic of the airfreight business, whereas directionality on the passenger side is more a matter of timing and is closely connected to the peaking problem.

Freight markets Flows of freight on any given route are rarely balanced in each direction. This could be because of different levels of commercial activity at either end of the route as a result of the two points being at separate stages of the economic cycle. It might be because changing relative strengths of the two currencies concerned (if the market is international) affect consumer buying power; for example, the strength or weakness of the dollar against European currencies is one of the primary determinants of demand directionality in North Atlantic freight markets. Dollar strength also tends to intensify eastbound North Pacific flows, which are anyway strong because of the volume of imports from Asia to the United States; weak westbound yields were cited by United as the reason for withdrawal of its small transpacific freighter fleet in 2000 after only four years in operation.

Another common cause of directionality is the fact that some markets import larger volumes of goods suitable for carriage by air than they export. This is particularly true of countries which import high-value consumer durables or fashion goods but export bulk commodities. For example, while the United States–Latin America market has greater southbound than northbound movement in aggregate, directional flows in and out of different countries vary; Colombia and Chile demand more northbound than southbound capacity, whilst the opposite is true for Argentina and Brazil. On the other side of the world, freighters fly empty from Russia and other CIS countries to Dubai, Sharjah, New Delhi, and certain Chinese cities, but return full of consumer durables.

Passenger markets Demand directionality tends to be much less pronounced in passenger markets because most journeys are return. There are three issues of possible importance, however.

1. There can certainly be short-term mismatches in the directional flows of passenger traffic, which cause peaking at different times in different directions on the same route. For example, more people leave the Middle East in June and July than enter it, while the reverse is true in late August and September. More people fly into a leisure destination such as Las Vegas or Reno on a Friday night than leave it, while on Sunday evenings there will be an outbound flow.

    On routes with a high proportion of day-return business traffic, one end might be a stronger originator of outbound morning flows than the other. Even where outbound morning demand is reasonably balanced, it could be that travellers in one direction generally require an earlier departure – perhaps because ground transfer times at their destination are longer and need to be taken into account when planning the working day (Clark, 2001). Along with maintenance, parking cost, and crew scheduling considerations, these factors will influence where short-haul aircraft are 'stabled' overnight. We will return to this in chapter 7.

2. The economic circumstances at either end of a route, and particularly relative exchange rates if the route is international, can affect which end generates the most outbound traffic. When the dollar is strong, for example, it is likely that more North Atlantic passengers will originate their journeys in the United States than when the dollar is weak. Although directional flows are not in this case unbalanced in the sense that they are in many freight markets, which end of a route is the most significant traffic generator might be important from a marketing perspective: an airline based in a strong outbound market can be expected to have a larger marketing organization there than one based elsewhere, and therefore better access to originating traffic.

3. Extending the last point, demand characteristics at either end of a market might be very different. For example, the LA–London return market (i.e., LA-originating demand) is not the same as the London–LA return market. There is a need for good local knowledge of demand at both ends of any city-pair market.

Directional (or timing) imbalances in passenger flows clearly feed through to load factors. Assume, for instance, high demand for an outbound flight from a hub to a spoke or secondary city at a particular time of day and significantly lower demand for the return flight. Accommodating all the outbound demand implies a low return load factor, whilst operating a smaller aircraft to raise the return load factor will lead to loss of revenue from demand 'spilled' off the outbound leg. This is a problem with several dimensions:

- it is a fleet assignment problem, insofar as we want to operate an aircraft sized to balance the revenue lost from spilled demand on the high-demand flight against the costs of offering too much output for sale on the return leg;
- it is a network management problem insofar as network design which links a spoke or secondary city to more than one hub or other major station can allow aircraft to be flowed across the spoke/secondary city from one hub/major station to another, rather than having to operate a low-demand return leg as part of an out-and-back rotation; and
- it is a pricing and revenue management problem insofar as the price and availability of discounted fares will probably have a significant role to play in raising load factors on low-demand return flights.

Generally, a carrier is successfully managing capacity on a route if it is able to consistently achieve a targeted average load factor which balances the revenue spill inherent in operating aircraft that are too small, against the higher costs and lower yields inherent in operating aircraft that are too large. We will return to this in Part 3 of the book.

iii. Understanding demand

This section will consider the identification and segmentation of available markets. The next section will look at demand forecasting.

Available markets

The global air transport market is comprised of hundreds of thousands of city-pair markets – that is, points of origin and destination between which individual passengers and cargo shipments are transported. An incumbent will of course already be serving a number of city-pair markets. For a potential entrant – that is, either a start-up or an existing airline wanting to expand into new markets – the availability of a market might be constrained by two sets of considerations (Holloway, 2002).

1. **Barriers to entry** A barrier to entry is something that favours incumbents. It might be externally imposed (e.g., government unwillingness to license start-up airlines or grant additional route designations to existing carriers), it might grow over time through force of circumstance (e.g., slot constraints), or it might be deliberately created by an incumbent (e.g., network, brand, or distribution strengths, or a reputation for responding aggressively to new entrants). A barrier will either make entry impossible in a practical sense, or it will leave entrants with higher costs than incumbents. Higher costs suggest not only a weaker competitive position but a greater risk of commercial failure, and this perceived risk in itself is often sufficient to deter entry. Existing airlines, particularly large carriers, generally find it considerably easier to overcome barriers to entry – except, perhaps, regulatory constraints and infrastructural congestion. Not only are they more likely to have the necessary marketing and operational resources, they are also usually betting proportionately less than a start-up or other small carrier on the success of any one route. We will return to this topic in chapter 4, where barriers to entry are discussed again in the context of contestability theory.

2. **Vision** 'Vision', 'mission', and 'purpose' are variously defined in the strategy literature. Whatever the label used and whether articulated or not, strategic decision-makers at most airlines – new or incumbent – will have a sense of what their company is trying to achieve for its stakeholders, particularly its customers, and what it should aspire to achieve in future. From this sense of purpose can be derived a 'strategic description' of the carrier.

Having identified which markets are potentially available and formulated an outline strategy for surmounting any barriers to entry, the next step is to use the current strategic description of the airline as a first-cut filter through which to run market opportunities. One of two conclusions will emerge.

- The market(s) concerned present an opportunity consistent with the current strategic description of the carrier.
- The opportunities presented are not consistent with the strategic description. In this case, a decision will have to be taken as to whether or not a move away from the current description is justified.

Researching the attractiveness of selected available markets

Once it has been decided that an available market is consistent with current strategy or that sufficient justification exists for amending strategy, its attractiveness needs to be assessed.

Market structure To analyse the structure of a market, we can use:

- the neoclassical microeconomic model, which recognises monopolistic, oligopolistic, imperfectly competitive, and perfectly competitive markets. This model will be explored in chapter 4;
- Porter's (1980, 1985) widely adopted five-forces model, which we met in the last chapter. A more finely-grained development of the neoclassical approach (Sinclair and Stabler, 1997), this recognises as key variables in any market's structure the degree of rivalry between existing competitors, the threat of market entry, the threat from substitute products, and the power of buyers and suppliers.

The purpose is to assess the impact of market structure on output and pricing decisions and on likely profitability.

We would also want to consider potential synergies with existing activities, as well as the availability of resources and capabilities appropriate to delivery of what it is that customers in the market expect.

Demand Market size is important. A market may be structurally attractive but too small to justify entry by a carrier with a wide-market strategic position; it might, on the other hand, be attractive to a niche operator. Alongside the size of current and potential demand, a related issue is price-elasticity; a price-elastic market is likely to offer greater opportunities to a low-fare carrier than to a differentiator, simply because it will not respond as favourably to the higher prices that differentiation implies.

Current and potential traffic (RPMs or RTMs) in a market will depend upon economic, political, and social variables, as well as the amount of output produced (ASMs or ATMs) and how it is offered (i.e., nonstop, multistop, or connecting routes); other important factors include the impact of whatever service (including schedule), price, promotional, and advertising stimuli are introduced into the market by competitors as a whole. An entrant needs to consider what effect its arrival – specifically, its output, pricing, advertising, and promotional decisions – will have on demand, what reactions its arrival is likely to provoke from incumbents, and how it might choose to respond to incumbents' reactions. (Game theory can be used to help with this type of strategic assessment; see Besanko et al, 2000, for example.) In the final analysis, managers have to decide what value they are able to bring to customers in the market, how competitors are likely to behave, what revenues can be earned, and whether these revenues will sufficiently exceed service delivery costs. Embedded in this judgement are service and operations management issues that we will be touching upon throughout the book.

Segmentation

I *need* food, I *want* a burger, I *prefer* a Big Mac. I *need* liquid, I *want* a cola, I *prefer* a Coke. I *need* to be in Baltimore, I *want* to fly, I *prefer* Southwest. Looking at the first two of these statements, we can conclude the following: I *need* food and liquid because I am a biological organism that requires these inputs to survive – in other words, I have basic survival needs. I *want* a burger and a cola to satisfy these needs rather than anything else because I am part of a culture that shapes my desires – in other words, I want things that I have been acculturated into wanting. I *prefer* a Big Mac and a Coke because I am an individual, and there is something about these products that appeals to me personally – in other words, I hold expectations that the attributes of these products (whether functional such as taste or emotional such as brand association) will deliver benefits and overall value that at this moment I would prefer to the benefits and value offered by, say, Burger King or Pepsi. Similarly, perhaps I *need* to be in Baltimore because my job (and therefore maybe even the long-term survival of my lifestyle) requires me to be there, I *want* to fly because this will satisfy my need to be there faster than other modes of transport permit, and I *prefer* Southwest because the value being offered – the balance between benefits (both funct-ional and emotional) and price – is at this time more appealing to me than what any other carrier is offering.

At a macro-level, we should understand markets – the actual and potent-ial demand for burgers among the hungry, soda among the thirsty, and air travel among those who are in some specific other place and might need to be in Baltimore. But we also have to understand preferences – why certain people prefer Big Macs, Coke, and Southwest, and how those who do not might be induced to change their preferences. Market segmentation can help.

Segmentation and neoclassical microeconomics

The benchmark model of market structure in the neoclassical tradition, perfect competition, assumes homogeneous intra-industry demand and homogeneous supply. Every industry is assumed to produce a single, commodity product and that is all that consumers demand; if this were not the case, there could be no single industry demand curve and therefore no market-clearing equilibrium price established at the point where such a curve would normally intersect with the industry supply curve. The prob-lem is that when it speaks of 'commodities' the neoclassical tradition does not draw the line at primary products such as oil, wheat, or bauxite, but extends the idea to consumer goods and to services. To speak of a single demand curve for the automobile industry, for example, assumes that dem-and for Chevrolets and Porsches is homogeneous; it is not, and neither is demand for air transport services homogeneous. To speak of a single auto-mobile industry supply curve implies that Chevrolets and Porsches are interchangeable; they are not, and neither are the different types of service that are offered into many air transport markets. Buyers have individual preferences, and most industries develop different products or product var-iants to satisfy different individuals; for convenience, these individuals are grouped into segments – each of which has its own demand curve.

It is the fact that there are many industries in respect of which it is meaningless to speak of a single industry demand curve that led Chamber-lin (1933) to develop the idea of monopolistic competition as an alternative to perfect competition. This idea recognises that some industries do have multiple demand curves. Is air transport one of them? Those who treat the industry's output as a commodity appear to think not; those who spend money on distinguishing their brand images and/or designing differentiated service packages think it is. The view taken in this book is that the answer varies between markets, but on the whole this is *not* a commodity business. Certainly, many air travel purchase decisions are driven by price, and this is one of the hallmarks of a commodity business. As stressed in chapter 1, however, when competitors are matched in terms of price consumers are left making a decision in response to other criteria – an understanding of which can provide the basis for market segmentation; furthermore, there are customers in some markets who are less sensitive to price than to particular service attributes, such as schedule and reliability.

Approaches to segmentation

The competitive strategy literature recognises the importance of market segmentation. It is central to Porter's 'generic' strategies (i.e., differentiation and cost-leadership on either a wide-market or niche basis), whilst resource-based theory argues that firms' heterogeneous resource endowments potentially give each an advantage in serving different segments. Segmentation helps focus the product scope and geographical scope decisions which are implied by an airline's strategic description of itself and which together comprise the 'competitive scope' decision. This decision is perhaps *the* most important driver of airline costs and revenues.

The assumptions underlying market segmentation are that:

- customers are different;
- certain of the differences between them can be used to explain different behaviours, which in turn affect demand and so account for the existence of multiple demand curves within the same market; and
- these differences can be used to isolate within the market as a whole separate groups of customers likely to respond in broadly the same manner to any given marketing initiative.

The purpose of market segmentation is therefore to identify groups of buyers who can be distinguished from other groups on the basis of their different responses to marketing mix variables such as service design, price, choice of distribution channel, and marketing communications mix. This exercise should help managers understand what is being or might in future be bought, by whom, where, when, and why; it can also identify specific competitors and how to out-compete them for segment dominance.

Clearly, any one market can be segmented in a variety of different ways depending on the precise purpose of the exercise. Consider the following.

- **Design of the inflight product** When acquiring and configuring aircraft, demand on the particular routes they will fly has to be segmented by cabin class whenever the carrier concerned is offering multi-class service. Demand for each cabin is an aggregation of demand for the booking classes relevant to that cabin.
- **Pricing and revenue management** Network carriers generally apply multiple booking (or 'fare') classes in every market they serve, each encompassing different tariffs targeted at segments of demand defined by reference to customers' different:
  - price-elasticities (i.e., willingness to pay);
  - time-preferences (i.e., willingness to book in advance and need to travel at specific times); and
  - benefit requirements (i.e., willingness to accept various purchase and usage conditions attached to their reservation, and expectations regarding ground and inflight service attributes).

  Most low-fare airlines use far fewer booking classes, but even when only four or five are being managed, they still represent a limited form of segmentation. We will return to this in chapter 9.
- **Marketing communications** With increasingly fine-grained print, broadcast, and electronic media available, it is becoming possible for those airlines with substantial marketing communications budgets to target narrow segments with focused, relevant messages. These segments may overlap with those used for pricing and product design purposes, but they will not be identical.
- **Distribution** A low-fare airline or the main cabin on a full-service airline might carry a mix of business travellers, independent leisure travellers who chose the airline themselves, others who were influenced by travel agents, travellers on package tours who were not given any choice of carrier, back-packers who bought the lowest fare they could from a consolidator, and people who picked-up last-minute deals on the Internet; each might be targeted with different pricing, marketing communication, and distribution initiatives.

Segments should be as homogenous as possible, large enough to be meaningful, separately measurable, and accessible to marketing programmes. Whether a particular airline's approach to segmentation is rudimentary or sophisticated, it begs five questions whenever a segment is identified: Is it structurally attractive? Is serving it consistent with the carrier's strategic description of itself? Does the carrier have a competitive advantage in serving it? Is that advantage sustainable? Can it be served profitably as well as effectively?

Segments should ideally be comprised of customers who behave similarly in response to the same marketing stimuli – whether price, service design, promotions, or marketing communications. Whilst it is behavioural variables that ultimately matter, managers sometimes need to use descriptive variables instead to isolate segments – variables that do not themselves account for specific purchase behaviours, but which can nonetheless be used as a limited form of proxy. Descriptive characteristics used to profile consumer segments include demographics (gender, age, marital status, etc.), socio-economics (income, education, occupation, etc.), and psychographics (personality, attitudes, lifestyle, etc.); descriptive characteristics used to profile organizational segments include general company characteristics (size, industry, geographic location, structure, etc.), and travel decision-making processes.

For an example of the potential shortcomings of descriptive segmentation variables, however, consider intra-European short-haul markets. Business and discretionary travellers from relatively high socio-economic groups are, at least on some routes, increasingly likely to be found using low-fare airlines. People whose lifestyles might take them to expensive hotels in expensive rental cars when they reach their destination – and people who might use business class on long-haul journeys – can be just as satisfied with the value offered by low-fare carriers as the highly price-sensitive customers that stereotypes would have us believe are the only segment they serve. More generally, people in many parts of the world are now being confronted with so much choice and are becoming so unpredictable in the ways they exercise consumer freedoms that it is increasingly difficult to isolate a single descriptive variable and assert that the individuals described will with some high degree of probability behave in a certain way. This can lead to a polarisation of marketing responses: either define segments increasingly sharply to help fine-tune product, communications, and distribution strategies (the approach of some full-service network carriers), or simply pitch a single value proposition that speaks for itself (the approach of many low-fare carriers). In between is the traditional 'mass marketing' approach of wide-market airlines which like to think they are segmenting their markets by offering separate cabins and a complex fare structure, but which in many cases have very little detailed customer insight.

Encompassing both behavioural and descriptive approaches, four particularly powerful segmentation variables identified by Tapp (1998) are: required customer value, predicted response, lifetime value, and loyalty.

Required customer value The basis for segmentation in this case is the benefits that different types of customer expect and what they are prepared to pay for them. At a strategic level, this is by far the most important demand segmentation variable (Piercy, 1997).

A common proxy for benefits segmentation in the airline industry is purpose of travel, which is discussed in Box 2.1.

Box 2.1: Benefits segmentation by reference to journey purpose

Passenger markets *Journey purpose is still the most widely used proxy for determining customers' expected benefits, and for estimating willingness to pay for those benefits, on the passenger side of the industry. A fundamental distinction has long been drawn between 'business' and 'leisure' traffic. Business travel can be sub-segmented into travel to intra-company meetings, external meetings, or for other purposes such as conferences, training, or as part of an incentive package. A distinction is also sometimes drawn between business travellers employed by large companies, and those who run (or work for) smaller enterprises and so might be somewhat more price-sensitive. Leisure traffic is often sub-segmented into vacation (which could involve independent or inclusive tour sub-segments) and VFR. 'Business' and 'leisure' segments are evidently far from homogeneous. Accordingly, several airlines have moved beyond basic business/leisure segmentation, looking in greater detail at some of the other variables discussed in the main text.*

A third commonly recognised segment is 'personal travel' which, depending on the precise nature of its purpose, might be closer to the business than to the leisure segment in respect of benefits sought (e.g., late booking) and price-elasticity; travel to deal with a family crisis, for example, will be closer to business travel in time- and price-sensitivity than foreseeable journeys such as returning to an educational institution overseas. Whatever the purpose of travel, length of haul is clearly an important additional variable.

As well as benefits sought, journey purpose has been held to provide a good proxy for trip duration, booking pattern, frequency of travel, and both price- and income-elasticity of demand – all of which are important considerations when an airline comes to design a marketing programme. However, demand is more difficult to characterise than this suggests. Weekend breaks, single- or multiple-destination long vacations, a short-haul day-return business trip, a long-haul journey for an urgent meeting with just one client, and an extended marketing visit to the other side of the world planned some considerable time in advance can all be categorised as being either for business or leisure purposes; but in terms of service design, pricing, ticket conditionality, and marketing communications they are each in principle very different.

Journey purpose and choice of cabin *Purpose of travel is a better guide to choice of cabin in some markets than others and at some times of year than others. For example, most occupants of business class cabins on intra-European, intra-Asian, and intercontinental flights tend to be business travellers, whereas on US domestic flights a high proportion of business travellers fly coach – and can fill a significant proportion of coach cabins in certain markets. Some single-class European low-fare carriers are finding that over half the passengers on many of their flights are travelling for business purposes; often these people own or work for small or medium-sized companies rather than large corporations, which still in general tend to favour relationships with network carriers (Mason, 2000, 2001).*

At weekends and during vacation periods, the composition of coach, business, and first class cabins can be expected to change, with leisure and VFR traffic predominant in coach and accounting for a higher proportion of front-cabin loads. FFP redemptions will also tend to be higher at these times in popular vacation markets, putting downward pressure on revenue load factors and on unit revenue (i.e., revenue per ASM).

Freight markets *These have also traditionally been subjected to benefits segmentation – although with journey urgency rather than purpose as the proxy. Commonly identified segments, in increasing order of price-elasticity, include emergency, high value, and routine, with the latter sub-segmented into perishable and non-perishable. (The routine perishable sub-segment, which covers goods that can be physically perishable such as flowers and fresh foodstuffs or economically perishable such as publications and fashion items, is likely to be more price-elastic in the long run than the short run.) Time has long been recognised as a key variable in emergency and routine perishable segments; as airfreight has come to play a greater role in international just-in-time (JIT) logistics systems, time has also become an important segmentation variable in respect of some routine non-perishable goods as well.*

High frequencies, ready space accessibility, late close-out times, a high 'flown-as-booked' rate, rapid transit, priority ground-handling, and in some cases door-to-door service are necessary product attributes in time-sensitive segments. Freight can also be segmented by commodity or by weight, and according to the amount of value added to the basic air shipment product (e.g., pick-up and delivery, simplified documentation, customs clearance, and real-time tracking). However, time-sensitivity and price-sensitivity are arguably the two most important segmentation variables (Herrmann et al, 1998).

Since integrated carriers such as FedEx and UPS – specialising initially in the document and small package segments – began growing rapidly in the 1980s, committed door-to-door delivery times and automated shipment tracking have become increasingly sought-after benefits in cargo markets generally. This is true in many cases irrespective of whether shipments are emergency, routine, high-value, small, or heavy. Allied to this has been an accelerating trend towards considering airfreight expenditures not as a separate line item cost but as just one element of total distribution costs, within the context of which high air shipment charges relative to surface modes need to be balanced against savings in respect of insurance premia and the cost (real or opportunity) of financing a shipment during a long ocean voyage. The 'total distribution cost' concept combines the inventory cost, security, and guaranteed time-to-market benefits of using airfreight in a shipper's logistics chain in order to emphasise that although the transportation element in that chain might be more expensive than competing surface modes, total cost can be lower when saved inventory financing and insurance charges are taken into account. Furthermore, the marketing benefits associated with speed and certainty can be the difference between success and failure in a shipper's marketplace.

The trend towards consideration of 'total distribution cost' within the broader context of an integrated logistics chain has been reinforced by use of JIT inventory management techniques and international sourcing. As a result, cargo products are increasingly being segmented by reference to how time-definite (e.g., next day or second day delivery) and reach-definite (e.g., airport-to-airport or door-to-door) they are. In addition, some carriers have developed niche markets such as the handling and transportation of foodstuffs, flowers, print media, fashion items, and live animals.

Table 2.1 lists some of the advantages and disadvantages of integrated airfreight and traditional line-haul products.

Predicted response The segmentation variable here is the reaction of different customers to variations in the marketing mix (i.e., product design, pricing, promotion, distribution, etc.). One approach might be to:

1. identify the behaviour of interest (e.g., purchase in response to a particular type of marketing stimulus);
2. measure that behaviour for a sample of customers;
3. cluster members of the sample into segments;
4. isolate descriptors that characterise each segment (such as demographic or lifestyle variables or exposure to different types of media); and
5. target marketing initiatives at audiences defined by the relevant descriptors (Rao and Steckel, 1998).

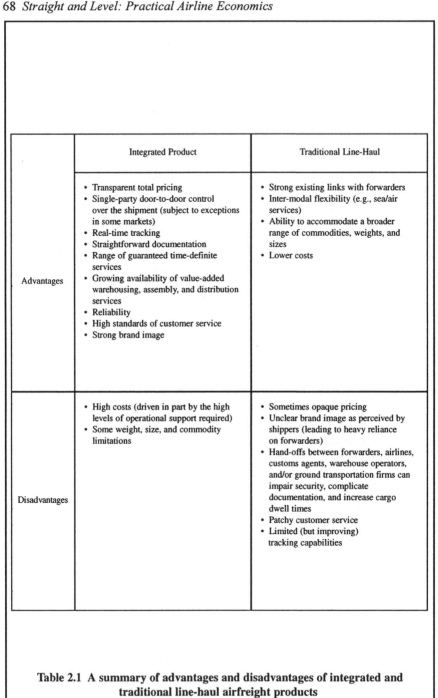

	Integrated Product	Traditional Line-Haul
Advantages	• Transparent total pricing • Single-party door-to-door control over the shipment (subject to exceptions in some markets) • Real-time tracking • Straightforward documentation • Range of guaranteed time-definite services • Growing availability of value-added warehousing, assembly, and distribution services • Reliability • High standards of customer service • Strong brand image	• Strong existing links with forwarders • Inter-modal flexibility (e.g., sea/air services) • Ability to accommodate a broader range of commodities, weights, and sizes • Lower costs
Disadvantages	• High costs (driven in part by the high levels of operational support required) • Some weight, size, and commodity limitations	• Sometimes opaque pricing • Unclear brand image as perceived by shippers (leading to heavy reliance on forwarders) • Hand-offs between forwarders, airlines, customs agents, warehouse operators, and/or ground transportation firms can impair security, complicate documentation, and increase cargo dwell times • Patchy customer service • Limited (but improving) tracking capabilities

Table 2.1 A summary of advantages and disadvantages of integrated and traditional line-haul airfreight products
Source: Virtual Aviation College (www.virtualaviationcollege.org).

As mentioned above, however, identifying appropriate descriptors and predicting behaviour with reasonable confidence are not easy challenges.

Lifetime value Segmentation can be based on the worth of different customers in terms of future revenue and profit potential. This basis for segmentation can usefully be cross-referenced to customer loyalty in order to help understand the potential profitability of different segments and to design relationship management/customer retention programmes (Payne and Frow, 1999). (Most airlines have in fact yet to develop the sophisticated measurement capabilities required for such initiatives, which will anyway be pursued only by larger network carriers.)

Loyalty Garvett and Avery (1998: 572) break traffic down into three customer types.

1. **Occasional flyers** These customers fly seldom and without regular patterns. Purchases are more likely to be stimulated by price than brand loyalty, and even FFP membership might not be relevant to choice of carrier.
2. **Infrequent flyers** These customers fly more often than occasionally and might have more regular travel patterns – perhaps to a particular company site or to visit friends or relations. Again, price may be more important than brand loyalty, although FFP membership can be influential up to a point.
3. **Frequent flyers** These are the relatively few customers whose high frequency of travel mark them out as core drivers of revenue quality in the income statements of carriers to which they are loyal. In the United States, for example, the eight per cent of 'frequent flyers' who take ten or more trips per year account for 40 per cent of total trips taken and, accordingly, for a disproportionately high share of revenue (Air Transport Association, 2001); many of these passengers are travelling on business, although as a whole the proportion of travel for business purposes in the United States has declined from approximately 70 per cent of trips in the 1950s to just under 50 per cent in the 1990s (Bender and Stephenson, 1998).

Although it can be difficult to measure (Tapp, 1998), loyalty is a particularly appealing basis for segmentation given its claimed linkage to profit (Reichheld, 1996; Heskett et al, 1997). There is certainly merit in trying to 'ring-fence' and retain the most loyal and the most valuable customers, relying perhaps on more aggregated approaches to others in the market; indeed, customer retention rate is an important driver of market share and revenue quality. This is expensive stuff, however, so not only must the resources be available to achieve it but there should be reasonable confidence that real payback is likely to flow from the effort in terms of revenue and yield improvement (Holloway, 2002).

Customer loyalty, retention, and defection management are extensively discussed in Holloway (ibid), as are the importance of complaints and service recovery; the economics of the latter are outlined in Box 2.2 below. These are all tools that might be critical to generating future demand, and programmes/procedures to implement them need to be analysed to ensure that they are cost-effective. The attraction of customer loyalty from an airline's perspective is that in its most extreme form it secures a segment of demand for the airline concerned and removes it from competitors' 'scopes'. There are broadly three routes to achieving this:

- genuine brand preference;
- consumer loyalty programmes (notably FFPs); and
- corporate loyalty programmes (corporate FFPs, negotiated deals on prices and condition waivers, and/or end-of-period rebates).

Each should be thought of and analysed as an investment in the sense that resources are committed to customer retention, as a result of which future revenues will flow in over the life of the relationship (ibid); in practice this is relatively rare, with loyalty programme costs often buried in general marketing budgets and neither costs nor benefits rigorously analysed on a market-by-market or segment-by-segment basis. Most programmes track and reward usage (i.e., miles flown and trips taken) rather than the value (in terms of revenue and profit) that each member brings to the airline. Whilst there is most probably a linkage between usage, loyalty, and profit it is ill-understood by the majority of carriers – and some loyal customers might well be unprofitable (Taneja, 2002).

A final point is that the capability to predict customer defection, retention, and loyalty is still not well-developed in most of the industry. (See Ostrowski and O'Brien (1991) for an early study of the issues involved.)

Box 2.2: The economics of complaints and service recovery

Consider figure 2.1. The numbers are purely hypothetical; each airline can use market research to arrive at estimates specific to its own system. The 90/10 split between non-complainants and complainants amongst passengers who encounter service failure is consistent with experiences in the industry as a whole; whilst the repurchase figures are hypothetical (but not necessarily unrealistic), the assumption of only one instance of negative word-of-mouth influence over potential purchasers by customers who choose not to repurchase is conservative (Zeithaml and Bitner, 2000).

Whether or not we accept the actual figures, the message is clear: by not researching customer satisfaction levels to uncover the problems confronted by non-complainants and by not dealing satisfactorily with the complaints that are received, traffic and revenue losses can potentially be very high. Identifying the root causes of recurrent problems and deciding whether and how to remedy them should be treated as an investment project like any other – by doing a discounted cash flow analysis of the relevant costs of remedial action against the 'recapture' of revenue that would otherwise be lost.

There are alternative ways of looking at the same issue. For example, divide an airline's annual operating profit by the annual total of flights flown to derive a profit per flight; then divide profit per flight by the systemwide average one-way fare. The result is an albeit very approximate estimate of the number of passengers per flight that account for the annual operating profit. When Southwest did this calculation in the mid-1990s, it was found that only five customers per flight – aggregating to just three million out of 40 million passengers carried during the 12 months concerned – accounted for an entire year's operating profit (LUV Lines, November 1995). In other words, losing one passenger per flight would in principle have knocked something like 20 per cent off the airline's operating profit that year.

An important challenge to loyalty segmentation is posed by the fact that the nature of the industry's product tends to generate only 'soft' brand loyalty (Crandall, 1995), with price a prominent purchase driver in price-elastic segments and both schedule and punctuality dominant in business segments; airlines have to work very hard to make other service attributes contribute substantially to brand loyalty. In the US domestic market, customers are often willing to switch away from their 'favourite' airline in response to minor differences in price or departure time – especially if they hold multiple FFP memberships (ibid). As was stressed in chapter 1, however, when core purchase criteria such as safety, price, schedule, and/or FFP membership are evenly matched it is essential for airlines to offer 'points of difference' that distinguish them from competitors and provide a basis for loyalty – even if only of the soft, 'other things being equal' variety. Loyalty can be an important driver of both traffic and revenue.

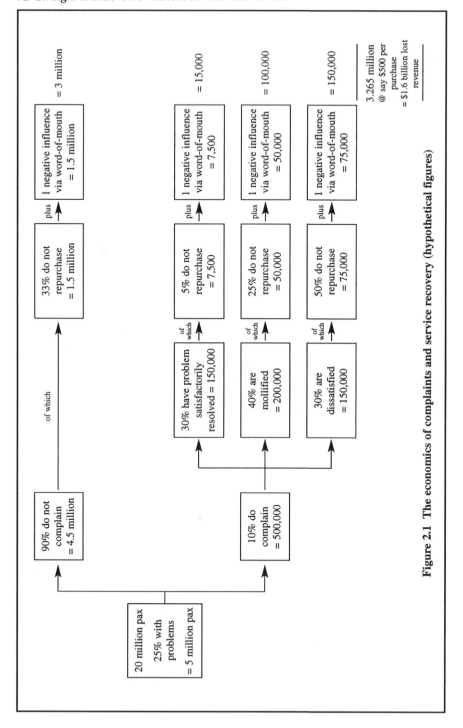

Figure 2.1 The economics of complaints and service recovery (hypothetical figures)

Segmentation in practice

Despite having separate cabins onboard (usually occupied by customers from a mix of different segments – albeit with one perhaps preponderant), and maybe also recognising an 'elite' tier of FFP membership, many carriers still adopt a mass-marketing approach (Zakreski, 1998). On the other hand, some full-service airlines are now identifying and targeting a broader range of more closely defined segments of demand.

Markets are rarely homogeneous. The more sharply that any apparently homogeneous market is brought into focus, the greater the number of differences that can be identified amongst buyers. The more insightful an airline is in segmenting its markets, and the more precisely it can tailor its service design, pricing, marketing communications, and/or service delivery to what it has found out about customers but competitors do not yet know, the more likely it is that segment knowledge – in this context a key organizational resource – will lead to competitive advantage (Holloway, 2002).

Bear in mind the discussion in chapter 1. Segments are not necessarily 'out there' objects; they can also be characterised as the constructions of individual managers' perceptions. Managers whose perceptions of 'reality' take them outside the established industry mindset might unearth segment insights that others have not discovered.

Having said this, segmentation costs money and some airline managements – at low-fare carriers in particular – might take the view that because they are offering a 'one-size-fits-all' service and because the rewards of segmented marketing communications do not repay the costs of segmentation, an undifferentiated approach to marketing is justified. From a product perspective they offer a single service concept targeted at a fairly broad market niche (e.g., cost-conscious travellers who want reliable service with minimal frills). To the extent that they segment their markets (e.g., into business and VFR or leisure segments) they use:

- schedule (e.g., higher frequencies to attract business travellers); and
- revenue management (e.g., higher walk-up than advance-purchase fares – to make late-deciders, who are often business travellers, pay a premium for last-minute access to the seat inventory).

The larger the airline and the more complex its customers' needs and purchase motivations, the more relevant segmentation is likely to be (ibid; Holloway, 1998a).

Traffic mix

The nature of demand an airline chooses (or, perhaps, in less liberal environments is constrained) to serve will be reflected in its traffic mix and will have a profound effect on both its revenue and cost streams.

1. **Revenue side** Choice of markets and market segments drives yield. Traffic mix on a full-service carrier offering more than one class can, if data is available, be broken down into cabin mix and fare mix.
   - *Cabin mix* The distribution of traffic between cabins.
   - *Fare mix* The distribution of traffic travelling on different fares in the same cabin.
2. **Cost side** Choices made regarding which markets and market segments to serve feed through into total cost because they determine product costs, and also because they influence an airline's exposure to the effects of traffic density and demand peaking.
   - *Product costs* Some segments (e.g., most business travellers) are more expensive to serve than others (e.g., most leisure travellers). Business travellers in many markets require, amongst other things:
     - a higher level of ground and inflight amenities (e.g., airport lounges and spacious premium cabins); and
     - a schedule that has relatively high frequencies and is therefore more expensive to deliver than lower-frequency service operated by larger aircraft having, in all probability, lower seat-mile costs. We will return to this in chapters 4 and 7.
     In summary, service design is a significant cost driver.
   - *Traffic density and demand peaking* Traffic density and demand peaking are two important sources of feedback from demand to costs. The higher the traffic density on a route, the more likely it is that a given schedule can be operated by a larger aircraft type (with lower unit costs) than that same schedule would support on a thinner route. The more intense the intra-day and intra-week peaking in particular and the larger the proportion of peak demand that an airline tries to meet, the higher the likelihood that excess off-peak output will have to be sold at a lower yield much closer to the cost of production than might be desirable.

These ideas will be explored in greater detail later in the book.

iv. Demand forecasting

The economics of demand

Market demand is an aggregate of demand for a product across all purchasers involved in the market concerned – whether this is a city-pair market (e.g., Los Angeles–Hong Kong), a regional market (e.g., US domestic), an inter-regional market (e.g., North Pacific), or the global air transport market as a whole. The quantity of a product demanded is a function of (i.e., depends upon) several determinants, notably including: the number of consumers potentially present in the market; income levels and general economic conditions; price, and the price outlook, in respect of the service concerned, its competitors, and available substitutes; the volume and quality of supply (i.e., output offered, whether routings are nonstop, direct, or connecting, and the frequency of service); the prices of complementary services such as hotel accommodation and car rental; consumer tastes and preferences; and the effect of actively managed nonprice marketing mix variables such as distribution, advertising, and promotion.

Demand functions

A statement, usually in tabular form, which relates determinants of demand (i.e., independent variables) at assumed states or levels to a particular quantity of the service demanded (i.e., the dependent variable) is called a 'demand function'. Economists generally express the precise nature of the relationships in algebraic terms. For example,

$$D_a = f(P_a, P_1, P_2....P_n, Y)$$

where demand (D_a) is a function of price (P_a), the prices of other products ($P_1, P_2....P_n$), and income (Y).

Airline managers can in principle create approximate demand functions for individual markets, for segments within each market, and even for individual flights; different departures have different demand functions that ideally need to be understood, although relatively few airlines are equipped to deal with this level of analytical detail and in practice decisions are often based on imperfect and rapidly changing data. Demand functions might include independent variables such as price, personal disposable income (for leisure travellers) or some measure of trade or economic activity at the origin (for business travellers), the tourist or economic potential of the destination, ethnic links between the two catchment areas, and planned advertising and promotional campaigns.

Whilst price and income are usually considered to be the most significant elements in a demand function (Battersby and Oczkowski, 2001), there are certainly other independent variables at work. Service quality can be a particularly important consideration; schedule and punctuality are service attributes that have a critical impact on purchase behaviour in some segments (e.g., business travel) in some markets (notably short- and medium-haul). Leisure segments are somewhat less sensitive to frequency than business segments, and neither have frequencies in most long-haul markets been built to the extent that small variations in schedule will have the same competitive impact that they are capable of having in business-oriented short-haul markets (Clark, 2001).

When demand functions are being created for an individual airline in this way, rather than for the industry as a whole, additional determinant variables will be required to accommodate the impact of competitors' activities – notably their pricing policies, service design initiatives, and advertising expenditures. If we consider demand functions for individual flights, the prices of alternative services – offered both by competitors and by the same airline – will affect demand.

The objective of building a demand function is to find out what impact on demand (and market share) will result from any assumed changes in the independent variables. Construction of accurate, and therefore useful, demand functions nonetheless poses several practical challenges.

1. The assumption that all demand-determining independent variables but the one under consideration can be held constant tends, like much economic theory, to assume away reality.
2. Establishing how each independent variable actually affects demand for passenger or freight services requires a great deal of historical data upon which to perform regression analysis.
3. It has to be assumed that historical relationships between independent and dependent variables are an accurate guide to future relationships. For example, just because a one per cent rise in personal disposable income has led to a two per cent rise in passenger traffic in the past does not mean that it will have the same impact on demand in the future; when air transport markets mature, as they are arguably doing in North America and to a lesser extent in Western Europe, a given level of economic growth tends to generate a weaker demand response than it does in less mature markets.
4. Perhaps the bravest assumption of all is that forecasts of economic and consumer preference variables will themselves prove accurate.

Demand schedules and demand curves

We have seen that a demand function is a statement, in tabular or algebraic form, which relates determinants of demand at assumed states or levels to a particular quantity of the service demanded. The independent variable that gets the most attention is usually price. Again in principle, a table can be constructed which lists a range of alternative passenger fares and freight rates against the number of passengers or the volume of freight that would be carried at each price level in a particular market. This is a 'demand schedule'. (If we were looking simultaneously at more than one market we would probably use yield as a proxy for 'price'.) When price is graphed against the quantity demanded the result is a 'demand curve'. Whereas the demand function specifies the relationship between the quantity of a product demanded and all the independent variables affecting that demand, the demand curve is a graphical expression of the relationship between the quantity demanded and just one of the determinants in the demand function: price. In other words, the demand curve is a graphical expression of the demand schedule. When examining price using a single demand curve, all other determinant variables are held constant; this inevitably assumes away reality, but the demand curve does at least model an important part of that reality.

The usefulness of demand curves to managerial decision-makers actually stems from their simplicity, because they underline the existence of two different sources of changes in demand – which may have very different short-run and strategic implications.

1. **Change in the quantity demanded** This involves only a single de-mand curve, and simply reflects the fact that a rise in price generally decreases the quantity demanded while a reduction in price will cause an increase. The amount by which demand reacts to a given price change will depend upon the price-elasticity of the product concerned. We will look at price-elasticity later in the chapter.
2. **Shift in demand** This involves not a movement up or down a single unchanged demand curve, but the repositioning of the demand curve itself. Repositioning of the curve occurs because of a change in one of the nonprice variables in the demand function such as macroeconomic conditions, consumer preferences or income, or the activities of a major competitor. Such changes alter the demand schedule and, therefore, the position of the demand curve. For example, when an airline invests in a strong brand image and service enhancements it does so with the inten-tion of influencing the preferences of potential passengers and shippers. The objective is to shift the demand curve(s) of the targeted segment(s)

to the right so that either more people are willing to pay an unchanged fare or freight rate, or the fare or rate can be raised without a significant loss of volume.

Airline managers need to be able to distinguish between demand changes resulting from a change in the quantity demanded (i.e., attributable, by definition, to an increase or decrease in price) and those attributable to a shift in demand (perhaps arising from a competitor's marketing initiative). If they are not able to do this, their response to market dynamics might be incorrect. In particular, it is always tempting to boost demand by reducing price along what is assumed to be an unchanged demand curve, whereas what the market could really be signalling is that it wants a completely new service-price offer – which would be reflected in a repositioned demand curve.

Summary

Demand can be understood in terms of the following hierarchy of propensities.

1. **The propensity to travel** We might here distinguish between secular and cyclical effects.
   * *Secular effects* Although growth has slowed compared to the heady rates of expansion in the 1960s, 1970s, and 1980s, global passenger air transport demand is still projected to expand at an annual average rate of five per cent or better over the next two decades (the precise figure depending upon the source of the forecast); air cargo demand is on track to expand at a considerably higher rate. These averages inevitably hide regional variations, with markets in some areas of the world (e.g., US domestic and the North Atlantic) being more mature than others (e.g., intra-Asia, Europe–Asia, the North Pacific, and Latin America). That said, there is some debate regarding how to define a 'mature' market. Graham (2000: 112) identifies three widely used approaches.
     - Maturity evidenced by a declining rate of growth in enplanements or RPMs and RTMs.
     - Maturity evidenced either by declining income-elasticity of demand or, more specifically, by a decline in income-elasticity to unity or below. (We will look at income-elasticity shortly.)
     - Maturity evidenced by declining growth in air transport revenues as a percentage of GDP.

As far as leisure travel is concerned, increasing affluence in many developed and middle-income developing countries is leading people to treat one or more vacations a year as an inviolable component of household expenditure – something not willingly substituted. There is an argument that as markets mature in more developed economies and the number of first-time flyers as a proportion of annual enplanements in these economies diminishes, further substantial demand growth comes to rely more heavily on encouraging increased usage amongst existing customers rather than attracting new customers to the industry; the number of US citizens that has ever flown, for example, rose rapidly in the 1970s but levelled off in the 70–75 per cent range during the mid-1980s (James, 1993). On the other hand, the growth of low-fare carriers might stimulate further demand amongst segments of mature markets that fly irregularly if at all, as well as stimulating incremental demand from customers who already travel reasonably frequently.

Availability of substitutes can also affect the propensity to travel. There has been considerable debate about the impact that price-performance improvements in telecommunications could have on business travel, for example; the consensus seems to be that although some travel on intra-company business might be substituted, the increase in external contacts made possible by the Internet and the technology-enabled globalisation of production processes in many industries will generate a need for more face-to-face meetings than might otherwise have taken place. The precipitous decline in business travel in the US domestic market during 2000/2001 (i.e., even before 9/11) and the accelerating take-up of video-conferencing cast some doubt on this assumption.

In the final analysis, global demographic trends are likely to drive the continuing growth of air transport demand well into the future. Davies (2002) makes a compelling case for the inevitability of demand growth (and the threat of system congestion that this implies) based on widely accepted forecasts for the expansion of the world's population over the next several decades. (In addition to its expansion, there are also foreseeable structural shifts within the world's population that will have a profound impact on demand in many air transport markets. Taneja (2002) explores the implications of current migration patterns as well as the growth in both population and purchasing power in developing countries.)

- *Cyclical effects* During a recession, companies cut back on business travel and individuals reduce leisure travel; in a severe recession such as the early 1990s and 2001/2002 demand might actually fall, but in most cases what has happened is that the rate of demand growth remains positive whilst dropping below the long-term trend-line. (Recessions also induce some of those who do still travel to downgrade to cheaper services – such as first to business or economy/coach class, or from a full-service carrier to a low-fare airline.)

2. **Propensity to travel in a particular market** The demographic and economic characteristics of the origin and its catchment area, the tourist and commercial potential of the destination and its hinterland, trade and ethnic links between the two, and fare levels in relation to the predominant type of traffic will affect demand in a particular market. Market-specific demand can also be influenced by political considerations such as civil unrest or terrorism, and by man-made or natural disasters.

3. **Propensity to travel by air** On long-haul routes, and also over shorter distances in many parts of the world, a decision to travel is a decision to travel by air. Where road and, as in Japan and Western Europe, high-speed rail networks are well-developed, their price and nonprice characteristics will affect demand in competing air transport markets.

4. **Propensity to travel on a specific carrier** Market shares will be influenced by the value being offered. Benefits, including schedule, amenities, brand image, and loyalty programmes, will be weighed against the price and nonprice sacrifices incurred using one carrier rather than another.

These propensities all warrant consideration when demand is being forecast.

Elasticity of demand

Elasticity is a concept used to examine how sensitive demand is to changes in determinant variables such as price, income or advertising expenditure. It is defined as the percentage change in demand in response to a one percentage point change in the value of any chosen independent variable. When we talk about 'demand' in this context we might mean one of four things:

- the global demand for air transport services;
- aggregate demand in a group of markets (e.g., US domestic);
- aggregate demand in a single city-pair market (e.g., Dallas–Houston);
- demand for a particular carrier's service in a city-pair market that has at least one other competitor present (e.g., demand for Continental's services in the Dallas–Houston market). (The significance of at least one

other competitor being present is that the carrier's demand curve and the market demand curve cannot then be the same; we will return to this distinction in a moment.)
We could also segment demand, and consider elasticity, in different cabins.

Our interest here is in the latter two levels of analysis. But before moving on, consider two additional points that arise from the choice of Dallas and Houston as examples.

1. In a short-haul market such as Dallas–Houston, competition can come not only from other airlines, but also from surface transport alternatives – so even were the market served by only one carrier, that airline's demand curve would not be precisely the same as the market demand curve. We will revisit this point shortly in the context of cross-price elasticity of demand.
2. Dallas and Houston are both served by two airports; this adds another dimension to market analysis – albeit one that we will not be exploring further. It needs to be borne in mind that where one or both cities in an O & D market are served by two or more airports, each possible airport pairing within that O & D market might represent a 'sub-market' with its own demand characteristics.

Some independent variables (e.g., income) influence aggregate market demand, some (e.g., price and schedule) can influence both market demand and market shares, whilst others (e.g., the ground and inflight product, and brand loyalty) are more likely to influence market share than aggregate market demand. In the following sections, context should in most cases imply whether we are discussing an elasticity variable affecting market demand, market share or potentially both.

Price-elasticity of demand

Price-elasticity of demand measures the sensitivity of demand to changes in the levels of passenger fares or freight rates, assuming all other determinant variables in the demand function are held constant.

$$\text{Price-elasticity} = \frac{\text{\% Change in quantity demanded}}{\text{\% Change in price}}$$

The relationship is almost always inverse (i.e., price-elasticity is usually negative), which means that the short-run response of consumers to any price increase is to demand less of the service (i.e., traffic falls or grows more slowly than it otherwise would) whilst price decreases tend to stimulate demand. The key issue is the size of these effects.

Price-elasticity is reflected in the steepness of the demand curve for the product concerned. Since an infinitely elastic demand curve is horizontal and a perfectly inelastic curve (i.e., a curve with zero elasticity) is vertical, we can say that the steeper a demand curve is the less elastic it is and vice versa. This is critical to pricing and revenue management, as we will see in chapters 3 and 9.

'Price' might be defined as the yield, average fare, or (least likely) the full fare in a market. However defined, the effect of a price change will depend upon the shape of the demand curve. In figure 2.2, the revenue effect of a price change from P_0 to P_1 will vary depending on whether we are facing demand curve D_A or D_B. In the former case, the price increase will lead to a relatively small demand decline from Q_0 to $Q1_A$, whereas in the latter case the decline to $Q1_B$ is substantially larger; demand curve D_B is therefore more elastic than demand curve D_A.

We can draw the following distinctions.

- **Price-elastic demand** If the percentage change in demand exceeds the percentage change in price that caused it, demand is 'elastic'; this situation might support a price decrease – provided that any decline in margin is at least compensated by growth in (profitable) volume. Because vacationers are generally very sensitive to fare movements, price-elasticity in leisure segments tends to be higher than amongst business travellers. The same is broadly true in respect of VFR segments. Long-haul demand also tends to be more price-elastic than short-haul demand, because any percentage change is likely to represent a smaller absolute dollar amount in the case of short-haul fares.
- **Unitary price-elasticity** In this case, a given percentage change in price leads to the same percentage change in demand.
- **Price-inelastic demand** If the percentage change in demand is less than the percentage change in price, the demand curve is considered 'inelastic'; this would be the preferred situation if prices were to be increased – provided incremental revenue more than compensates for lost sales. Demand from business travellers tends on the whole to be more price-inelastic than demand for leisure and other forms of discretionary travel; also, whereas leisure travellers meet all their own discretionary expenditures, most business travellers receive a 'subsidy' equivalent to their company's marginal rate of tax as a result of the deductions they are able to claim. It does however appear to be the case that since the late 1990s more companies have been taking a proactive stance towards the control of travel expenditures and the implementat-

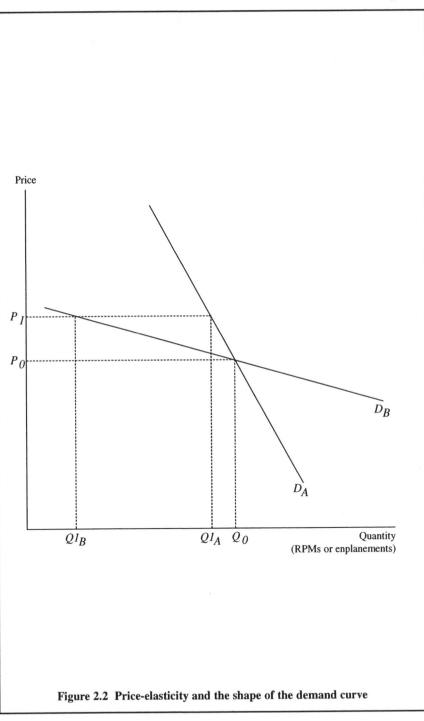

Figure 2.2 Price-elasticity and the shape of the demand curve

ion of travel management programmes, and that business travel dem- and in some markets is becoming somewhat less price-inelastic than has historically been the case. (See Laney (2002) for an overview of US experience in this latter respect.)

Price increases that are not sufficiently large to deter travel might nonetheless lead to a downgrading of the chosen class of travel. Corp- orations in some countries are now also more prepared than in the past to search for low fares and/or negotiate bulk discounts, even at the cost of sacrificing frequent flyer miles. Indeed, the 30 per cent decline in US business travel in 2001 even prior to 9/11 raised questions about wheth- er full-service carriers had pushed their assumptions regarding the price-inelasticity of this segment too far by forcing through multiple fare increases in the face of deteriorating service; for example, DaimlerChrysler was reported to have cut its US travel bill from an annual rate of $100 million to $60 million and to be consciously mak- ing more use of video-conferencing to enable deeper cuts (*Fortune*, 15 October, 2001).

Despite marked price increases in full fares in certain markets (e.g., the US domestic and UK–US markets in the second half of the 1990s), airfares as a whole have on average and in most markets declined in real (i.e., inflation-adjusted) terms over the last several decades. The pattern has been that after deregulation or liberalisation of a market, normal (i.e., 'full' or unrestricted) fares rise steeply whilst the depth and availability of discounts off these fares also both increase; the average fare in the market therefore tends to drop. In fact, falling real airfares – reflected in the long-term de- cline in airlines' real yields (i.e., revenue per RPM or RTM) – may have been responsible for as much as 20 per cent of the growth in passenger traffic experienced by the industry since the 1960s.

In the cargo market certain types of shipment are likely to be less price- sensitive than others. Those which are physically perishable (e.g., flowers), economically perishable (e.g., newspapers or fashion items), high-value (e.g., currency or precious metals), or are needed urgently by the consignee will be less price-elastic than other goods.

Price-elasticity and revenue By providing new service and following its hallmark low-fare strategy, Southwest has been able on average to stimul- ate significant additional **traffic** in new markets rather than having to rely on the diversion of existing traffic from incumbents. In a study of several US markets before and after entry by a low-fare carrier, Perry (1995) found year-on-year average one-way fare decreases ranging from 16 per cent (Reno–Portland) to 82 per cent (Cleveland–Baltimore), and passenger enplanements rising in the range of 58 per cent (Las Vegas–Oakland) to 745 per cent (Cleveland–Baltimore). Of course, what pays the bills in practice is not traffic, but **revenue**. Southwest's entry into a market might well generate a lot of incremental traffic, but because it enters at low prices and forces incumbents' prices down as well the aggregate revenue generated may not actually increase by very much.

Price-elasticity and costs Knowledge of price-elasticity in different segments is clearly necessary to drive pricing and ticket conditionality decisions (although, as already noted, airline managers commonly have to act on imperfect and rapidly changing data). These decisions also affect costs and interact with corporate objectives. For example, whether or not a carrier would find it profitable to cut prices when faced by price-elastic demand will depend upon whether the marginal revenue generated by additional output exceeds marginal costs; a high-cost, full-service carrier might find low prices more difficult to sustain (in the absence of cross-subsidies from other markets) than would a low-fare competitor.

Price-elasticity and competitive strategy Recalling the discussion of cost advantage and benefit advantage in chapter 1, we can make the following generalisations.

- **Cost advantage** A carrier with a sustainable cost advantage will be able to exploit that advantage to its fullest in price-elastic markets. (Of course, the alternative of charging parity prices and so earning higher margins might be open to it, depending upon its choice of strategic position and the level of benefits it is offering relative to competitors.)
- **Benefit advantage** Differentiation on the strength of superior benefits is a strategy likely to be more successful in relatively price-inelastic markets.

Low-fare carriers in particular should be focusing on price-elastic markets that have the potential to grow rapidly in response to the stimulus of low prices. In principle, this should allow them to benefit from improved operating economics as traffic density and their market share both increase. In practice, incumbents might choose to match low fares offered by a new entrant and – by virtue of their size and market presence – absorb much of any traffic growth, so leaving the challenger with little opportunity to expand output unless it is prepared to risk low load factors; the result might be a war of attrition between the low costs of the challenger and the deep pockets of the incumbent. The cards are initially stacked in favour of a large incumbent under these circumstances, but the success of Southwest in the United States and several low-fare operators in Europe and elsewhere suggests that once a well-managed low-fare carrier achieves critical mass it can be difficult for full-service incumbents to compete against.

Determinants of price-elasticity Demand curves can be considered at the industry or market level or, where markets are competitive, at the level of each individual competitor.

- **Industry versus market demand curves** The shape, and therefore the price-elasticity, of the demand curve in respect of any given market will be different from the aggregate industry demand curve. Whereas the industry demand curve is an aggregate encompassing all air transport markets, each separate market will have characteristics of its own which determine price-elasticity. One of the most important characteristics is traffic mix; the high proportion of demand coming from business travellers in markets such as New York–Washington and London (Heathrow)–Frankfurt makes the demand curves for these markets steeper than is the case in respect of more price-elastic markets such as those with, say, Acapulco at one end.

- **Market versus individual airline demand curves** Whenever more than one carrier is present in a market, none of the competitors' individual demand curves will necessarily mirror the market demand curve. Much has to do with pricing behaviour. How the quantity demanded is affected by a change in price initiated by a particular airline in a given market will depend in part upon whether that airline has competitors in the market concerned and, if so, how they react. If all the competitors in a market were to change (i.e., raise or lower) their fares more or less simultaneously, for example, quantity demanded would most probably respond more or less as anticipated by the 'market price-elasticity' as it applies to that market, given its particular traffic mix. On the other hand, were only one of several competitors in a market to change its fares, that carrier would almost certainly be facing price-elasticity of a very much higher order.

  Each carrier's individual demand curve in any market where it faces competition is therefore potentially more elastic (i.e., flatter) than the market demand curve; nonetheless, if an airline expects competitors to match any price change it initiates, market-level elasticity can be used to estimate the revenue impact. One reason airlines spend money on frequent flyer programmes, brand image, advertising, and other sources of distinctiveness is to dampen the elasticity of their own demand curves (particularly amongst high-value customers). In many markets, however, there are segments whose members will respond to these nonprice determinants of demand only if the carrier concerned is at least matching competitors on price.

Price-elasticity is therefore in part a function of the characteristics of demand affecting a particular market, and in part a function of interaction between competitors. In any market, the presence and behaviour of competitors will influence the price-elasticities confronted by individual airlines. Were a new entrant or incumbent to price below competitors in a market heavily dominated by business travellers, for example, the relative price-inelasticity of the market and the importance of nonprice determinants of demand (such as schedule, punctuality or brand loyalty) could justify a more muted price response than were the market dominated by highly price-elastic leisure or VFR travellers; this might particularly be the case if the lower fare were being offered either on a capacity-controlled basis or by a carrier producing a relatively small share of output in the market concerned.

In addition to traffic mix and competitors' behaviour, other determinants of price-elasticity include:

- the availability of substitutes, such as video-conferencing as an alternative to certain types of business trip or other forms of consumer expenditure as an alternative to a holiday. Concerns were raised in the aftermath of 9/11 that in respect of some short-haul US markets the introduction of lengthier security procedures would add an increment to total travel time sufficient to make surface modes more attractive substitutes than they had previously been;
- access to information about alternative services. Technology, particularly GDSs and the Internet, should in principle increase price-elasticity by giving consumers the opportunity to compare alternative offers. Still working in the opposite direction in some markets, however, are overrides and other forms of incentive paid by airlines to get travel agencies to direct business their way. Branding and FFPs are also in part designed to reduce the sensitivity of customers to lower priced, competing offers by building a long-term relationship and fostering consumer loyalty sufficient to curtail a search for alternatives;
- the extent to which a service is considered by the consumer to be a necessity. If a part is required urgently on the other side of the world to keep a multimillion-dollar plant in operation, the price of shipping it by air will be less elastic than if it were non-urgent;
- the proportion of the cost of the end-product which is accounted for by airfares or freight rates. This consideration arises from the fact that demand for air transport is a derived demand. A large absolute increase in

fares would have a greater proportional impact on the overall cost of a short vacation or business trip than on one planned to last considerably longer. Fares are also likely to constitute a higher proportion of expenditure on a VFR trip than on a paid vacation or a business trip, because VFR passengers generally stay with the friends and relations being visited and so spend relatively little on accommodation;

- the proportion of a consumer's disposable income being spent on the service. For example, a large increase in airfares would probably not affect the requirement of an investment banker for periodic transport to a second home in the Caribbean, but it could have a profound effect on the demand for low-end package holidays from Northern Europe to the Mediterranean.

Finally, bear in mind that when discussing price-elasticity we are assuming that nonprice variables, such as the advertising and promotional activities of the particular airline concerned and of its competitors, are being held constant. This is unlikely to be the case.

Problems with price-elasticity estimations There are two cautionary points.

- Elasticities are based on historical traffic data which may have been influenced by variables other than price, yet today's nonprice determinants of demand might be different.
- As we have seen, market elasticities are only a rough guide to the elasticities facing an individual airline wherever there is competition.

Cross-price elasticity of demand

Cross-price elasticity is used to measure how demand for an airline's services varies in response to changes in the prices of other products, which might include products offered by competing airlines or by other industries. The cross-price elasticity of demand for products A and B is the percentage change in the quantity demanded for Product A resulting from a one per cent change in the price of Product B (and vice versa). The two types of product we are concerned with here are 'substitutes' and 'complements'.

- **Substitutes** for business air travel from outside the airline industry will increasingly include various forms of electronic communications media (Roy and Filiatrault, 1998), whilst substitutes for short-haul air transport in some passenger and freight markets are offered by surface modes. Fractional ownership of corporate jets has emerged as a viable substitute as far as a potentially high-revenue segment of some business markets is concerned. In essence, a substitute is any alternative product that can be used by a consumer instead of a particular airline's service. A decline in the price of a substitute may be expected to move demand towards that substitute and away from the airline; in other words, the airline's demand curve will have been shifted to the left. Price movements in the other direction would have an opposite effect. The strength of these demand changes will reflect whether we are dealing with 'close' or 'weak' substitutes – price movements in the former case having a more profound effect on demand. A point not to be overlooked is that virtually any form of entertainment or any consumer durable could in principle be a substitute for leisure travel, particularly if such travel is not part of the main annual vacation that so many people in industrialised (and some medium-income developing) countries now take for granted.

As far as competitors within the airline industry are concerned, customer-driven service design alongside loyalty-generating tools such as brand-building, FFPs, and travel agency commission overrides (TACOs) are intended to reduce cross-price elasticity to the extent that they induce 'loyalty', weaken the substitution value of competitors' products, and – except in the most price-elastic segments – soften the effect on demand of a competitor's price reduction.

- **Complements** These are products which are used together rather than as substitutes for each other. The most obvious example is passenger air transport and hotels. There is an inverse relationship between the demand for a product or service and the price of a complement (or vice versa), such that a major increase in the price of hotels at a particular destination will reduce (or slow the growth of) demand for travel to that destination. The air transport demand curve will shift leftwards. For example, the high cost of food and accommodation in Japan relative to most other countries has drastically curtailed the inbound tourism market whilst, conversely, the strength of the yen has at times been one factor encouraging the growth of outbound tourism to destinations which appear cheaply priced to Japanese vacationers.

  Increased hotel rates in a popular vacation spot (e.g., somewhere in the Mediterranean) might divert package tourists to alternative destinations. Whereas carriers based in the tourists' originating country (e.g., the UK or Germany) would be able to follow the demand by flying vacationers to their newly preferred locations, carriers based in the re-priced destination (e.g., Cyprus) might not have the same network management flexibility. (This is a problem faced by any carrier with a network of limited scope based in a destination which for some reason loses its popularity (e.g., El Al) – a problem not shared to the same extent by wide-market network carriers based in countries from which more diverse traffic flows originate.) Airlines in countries originating traffic can construct a portfolio of outbound routes which might be more resistant to the negative impact of cross-price elasticity than any portfolio of inbound routes. Conversely, of course, inbound route port-folios can be a useful hedge against a downturn in traffic from just one originating source.

Whereas cross-price elasticity for substitutes is positive (i.e., direct) in the sense that an increase in the price of one stimulates demand for the other, cross-price elasticity for complements is negative (i.e., inverse) bec-ause a price increase in one causes demand for the other to decline. Prod-ucts that are unrelated will have zero, or near-zero, cross-price elasticity.

Knowledge of cross-price elasticities is clearly important for the man-agement of pricing and other marketing strategies. For example, an airline with a large portfolio of service concepts might need to look no further than the composition of that portfolio in order to find substitute products. Moving from the front to the rear of the aircraft, each class of service is a potential substitute for another: business for first, unrestricted economy/coach for business, discounted economy/coach for full-fare. An unmatched increase in one airline's business class fare may therefore lead not only to a loss of traffic to competitors, but also to an increase in demand for its own economy/coach product. Before fares are varied, the airline needs to under-stand these elasticities, and possibly to plan the use of nonprice variables such as FFP bonus awards, other promotional activities, or different types of marketing communications to counter them.

A final point about cross-price elasticity is that it can turn an apparent monopolist into an active competitor. For example, an airline holding a monopoly on short-haul domestic routes will not necessarily be able to price or to behave more generally as a pure monopolist would if it faces viable competition from potential substitutes such as surface transport modes; this is the case on some of Air France's domestic trunk routes.

Income-elasticity of demand

Income-elasticity of demand measures the responsiveness of demand to changes in consumers' incomes, assuming all other demand-determining variables (including price) remain constant. A figure in excess of unity would be considered elastic, whilst anything below unity is inelastic.

$$\text{Income elasticity} \ = \ \frac{\% \text{ change in demand}}{\% \text{ change in income}}$$

As economic activity and trade increase, the demand for business air travel and for cargo space will grow. As people's disposable incomes rise, they spend more on nonessential goods and services such as vacations. And in both cases, as prosperity increases people tend to be less sensitive to price and more susceptible to manipulation of nonprice variables in the marketing mix. In a recession, for example, consumers still in the market are often more concerned about price than amenities and brand image, whereas in periods of economic confidence the opposite is likely to be true. Demand changes resulting from variations in income level reflect shifts in the demand curve for air transport services rather than movements along an unchanged demand curve.

Methodological challenges   Inevitably, there are some methodological challenges.

1. As applies to the calculation of any measure of elasticity, it is difficult to isolate the impact on demand of the independent variable – in this case income – when so many other determinants are simultaneously at work. Multiple regression is the tool usually used to accomplish this, but the results are far from perfect.
2. Income-elasticity calculations in leisure markets are complicated by several issues.
    *   *The difficulty of measuring personal income* The ideal measure is real personal disposable income, but in practice per capita GNP or GDP are often used as proxies. The problem with this is that it takes no account of income distribution, which in many developing countries is highly skewed in favour of small elites whose business and leisure travel habits may not be particularly sensitive to changes in income levels. Elsewhere this is less of an issue, and in mature markets predicted growth in GDP or GNP might itself serve as a proxy for traffic growth – that is, income-elasticity of demand might be considered to be unity, with GNP or GDP used as the income measure (Bowles, 1994); American Airlines, for example, uses forecasted US GDP growth as a proxy for traffic growth. Alternative measures are used in some countries: in Britain, an index of consumer expenditure is widely used as an accessible measure of income available to consumers.
    *   *The presence of different sub-segments* Another complication is the difficulty of establishing income-elasticities for the various sub-segments of the leisure market, which encompasses vacationers on package holidays, people travelling independently, and others visiting friends and relations.

- *Intertemporal income effects* Although most studies of tourism demand assume that it depends on current income, there is debate in the literature regarding whether the focus should in fact be one or both of past income or expected future income. Recent developments such as intertemporal choice theory have argued the complexity of real consumer decision processes and, in particular, advanced the idea that current consumption is a function of future income expectations – perhaps moderated to some degree by past experiences (Sinclair and Stabler, 1997).
- *Data reliability* Because leisure air travel is a relatively new form of expenditure it tends to grow rapidly at first and then more slowly as higher income groups reach a point where the law of diminishing marginal utility sets in (i.e., each additional expenditure on travel yields less utility than the last). Income-elasticities in this segment will therefore change over time, raising doubts about the reliability of forecasts based on historical data.

3. GNP and GDP forecasts are still widely used as inputs into demand forecasting models for the business travel segment. However, some analysts – particularly those examining air transport demand out of relatively small economies – prefer to substitute income-elasticity calculations with a measure of 'trade-elasticity', believing trade to have more impact on business travel than any aggregate income figure. Several analysts in the United States have begun in recent years to question whether business travel is, in fact, more dependent upon corporate profits than GDP growth; profits and GDP have historically been quite closely correlated, but in 2002 for the first time they became significantly disconnected and the poor airline revenue environment was more in line with the dire performance of the corporate sector than with the positive, if anaemic, trend in GDP.

4. Where a carrier relies heavily on sixth freedom flow traffic between city-pairs in different foreign countries (e.g., Emirates, KLM, Singapore Airlines), income movements in its domestic economy will not necessarily have as profound an impact on demand as would be the case were it relying entirely on generating traffic to and from its home market.

Conclusions Received wisdom has for many years suggested that income-elasticity of demand for the global airline industry is just over two – meaning, for example, that a 2.5 per cent growth in income will lead to a better than five per cent growth in traffic. This goes a long way towards accounting for the industry's pronounced cyclicality. But behind such a generalisation there are several complications.

- Inevitably, income-elasticity varies depending upon the purpose of travel, with demand from passengers travelling on business being less elastic than demand from leisure travellers. Whereas the income-elasticity of leisure travellers can range between 1.5 and 2.5, for business travellers the figure is likely to be lower. Pindyck and Rubinfeld (2001) cite market – as opposed to individual airline – income-elasticities of 1.2, 1.2, and 1.8 for travellers in first class, unrestricted coach, and discounted coach in the US domestic market.

- Income-elasticities can vary significantly on different routes out of the same point of origin. Partly this reflects the predominant purpose for travelling to a particular destination: income-elasticity of demand would be lower in a business market such as London (Heathrow) to Frankfurt or New York to Washington than in leisure markets such as London to Palma or New York to Las Vegas. It also reflects the length of haul involved, because travelling long distances generally involves a level of expenditure which is less acceptable in difficult economic times than a shorter trip (although in some leisure markets long-haul fares are, in fact, very competitive with short-haul alternatives).

- In addition to these route and purpose variations, it is widely believed that income-elasticity of demand is falling in certain more mature markets, possibly evidencing a decline in marginal utility. This trend seems to be particularly evident in the United States, where using some measures of income the aggregate figure across all segments appears to be approaching unity (which equates to one widespread definition of 'market maturity'), and also to a lesser extent in Western Europe. On the other hand, as wealth percolates down to a burgeoning middle class in many fast-growing Asian countries the income-elasticity of demand for air transport services in this region will remain consistent with that of a growth industry. Even in more mature economies such as the United States and Western Europe, the success of low-fare carriers in making air travel affordable and bringing it within reach of the most price-sensitive segments of potential demand suggests that historical income-elasticity figures will not always be an incontrovertible guide to the future.

- Whereas the income multiplier effect is generally measured by relating global, regional, or national GDP growth to changes in traffic (RPMs or RTMs), what actually pays the bills is revenue rather than traffic. Revenue is a function of traffic and yield, so as well as considering traffic growth in response to income changes we also need to look at the yield being earned on the incremental traffic.

- Whereas global and national GDP growth figures are most widely quoted in real (i.e., inflation-adjusted) terms, airline revenues and yields are generally reported in nominal (i.e., current dollar) terms. Sentance (2001) argues that if nominal airline revenues are deflated to transform them into real revenues, their growth rate relative to growth in real GDP shows a very different pattern from the buoyant historic growth in traffic: real revenues are growing at a rate that is broadly similar to growth in real global GDP – that is, the income multiplier effect we see at work in respect of traffic is not present as far as revenue is concerned. Indeed, in the US domestic market aggregate real revenues (i.e., nominal airline revenues deflated by the US consumer price index) have actually been growing more slowly than real GDP; the picture in high-growth Asian markets, on the other hand, is somewhat brighter.

Approximately 80 per cent of industry-wide traffic growth since the 1960s has been attributable to rising real incomes (although there are indications that income growth might now account for a somewhat lower percentage of traffic growth – perhaps as low as 60 per cent). The global GDP multiplier has been roughly 2.25 over the last three decades; being an average, of course, the figure masks pronounced year-on-year swings. Some observers expect this level of income-elasticity to fall back below two, meaning that each one per cent increase in global GDP will in future generate less than, instead of more than, a two per cent increase in passenger traffic. Others are more sanguine.

Some other elasticities affecting demand

In principle, but subject in practice to measurement difficulties, it is possible to analyse the impact on demand of any independent variable in a demand function. Price and income are simply the most commonly examined (and most important) independent variables, but anything else that affects demand will also have an elasticity associated with it.

When planning their strategies with respect to nonprice elements of the marketing mix, for example, airline managers benefit from an understanding of the impact that changes in each of the elements will have on traffic and revenues. One example is product design: quality of service has an elasticity associated with it such that, say, a change in frequency is likely to affect demand from market segments most concerned with the benefits attached to this particular service attribute – notably business travellers. Box 2.3 amplifies the point.

Box 2.3: The revenue impact of service enhancement

In the final analysis, product upgrades and relaunches are investments which need to be evaluated in terms of the returns anticipated from them relative to costs incurred – much as though they were tangible assets. What can make the mathematics rather difficult is the fact that upgrading 'hard' product features, such as the inflight service environment or the range of amenities offered, may have an unquantifiable but nonetheless positive effect on 'soft' variables, such as employee morale, motivation, and attitudes. This effect broadens the dimensions across which consumers' experiences are being improved and contributes, through enhanced satisfaction, to higher levels of customer retention and to higher revenues.

Whilst variations in service attributes can certainly affect demand, the nature and size of causal relationships have not been widely studied and can be difficult to establish. Research in the United States by the MITRE Corporation, for example, suggests that one per cent improvements in elapsed journey times and on-time performance increase passenger demand by 0.8 per cent and 0.43 per cent respectively (Homan, 2000). The economic reasoning beneath this finding is, first, that time spent travelling carries an opportunity cost that is reduced by shorter journeys and, second, that improved ontime performance reduces consumer uncertainty and so increases the value of the service; both should have a positive effect on demand, reflected in a rightward shift of the carrier's demand curve. If an airline exercises monopoly power (in which case its demand curve is equivalent to the market demand curve), these service enhancements are likely to be reflected in higher prices for the same level of output (Morrison and Winston, 1989); the more competitive the market, the more likely they are to be reflected – at least in the short run – in increased sales (Homan, op cit).

Investment in remedying service failure (i.e., delivery below customers' expectations) also needs to be looked at as expenditure that carries potential revenue implications – in this case future revenue saved. Holloway (2002) discusses service failure at some length. The point as far as the present book is concerned is that each category of recurrent service failure (either across the network or in a specific market) will affect an identifiable number of passengers, a percentage of whom will not repurchase; the cost of remedying the problem by enhancing service design or delivery can therefore be compared against an estimate of revenue preserved. (See Heskett et al (1997: 47-48) for a brief example of some numbers generated by British Airways using this approach.)

Advertising elasticity of demand is another, more widely cited, example. Airline advertising might be targeted at corporate image enhancement, it might be market-specific and so aimed at a particular destination, or it might focus on targeted segments such as business or leisure travellers irrespective of route. In each case, it will be important to know how much additional traffic (and, ideally, revenue) is generated by every dollar of advertising expenditure. A low advertising elasticity of demand would imply that an airline must spend substantial amounts of money to shift a demand curve in the desired direction (i.e., to the right). In this case, there could possibly be more cost-effective alternatives – such as promotional offers targeted directly at FFP members, for example.

The concept of marketing elasticities is closely tied to the distinction drawn by marketers between 'expansible' and 'inexpansible' markets. These models rest at either end of a continuum.

- Expansible markets are sensitive to industry-wide marketing efforts, and within the industry individual market shares will be sensitive to particular airlines' initiatives. In this case, a carrier's revenue forecast will to a considerable extent depend not only on more obvious demand determinants such as price and income levels, but also on how much effort and cash it is prepared to invest in nonprice elements of the marketing mix. Forecast traffic and revenue is therefore an outgrowth of the marketing plan.
- At the other end of the continuum, an inexpansible market offers little more than an opportunity to push on the proverbial 'piece of string': levels of marketing expenditure will have little direct bearing on demand.

Most airline markets are located closer to the expansible than to the inexpansible end of this continuum. One of management's primary tasks is to identify approximately where – that is, to identify the marketing elasticities it faces – and invest accordingly.

A final point which applies to most types of elasticity is that time is inevitably a consideration. The long-run elasticity of any demand-determining independent variable tends to be greater than its short-run elasticity. This is because there is a time-lag between most types of event likely to affect demand and the materialisation of that effect, while information about the event reaches consumers and is processed by them.

Demand modelling

Although the theory of air travel demand is now reasonably well established, relatively few empirical studies of the demand for air travel in specific markets, particularly outside the United States, have been published (Melville, 1998; Battersby and Oczkowski, 2001). Whilst those models that have been developed often differ with regard to the determinants of demand that they incorporate, Jorge-Calderón (1997) has usefully summarised the demand drivers most widely used.

1. **Geo-economic factors** There are two categories.
   - *Activity factors* These describe the demographic, commercial, industrial, and cultural characteristics of origin and destination catchment areas; income and population are the most commonly adopted.
   - *Locational factors* Distance is a key locational factor, but one with a split 'personality'. Demand is generally taken to be negatively associated with increased distance between origin and destination, yet the further apart they are the less inter-modal competition there is and so the greater the share of transportation demand that goes to airlines.

   Several studies of air transport demand have relied on various forms of 'gravity model', using activity and locational determinants.

2. **Service-related factors** In the context of demand modelling, 'service' is usually taken to encompass what are from a customer's perspective the two key aspects of output: quality of the product and price paid.
   - *Quality* The variables most commonly used have been:
     - *Frequency* The argument is that 'time costs money', so the higher the number of departures the less variance there is between preferred and actual departure times, the better the quality of service, and the higher demand is likely to be.
     - *Load factor* High load factors are assumed to be associated with lower seat accessibility (i.e., a lower probability, at any given time a reservation is attempted, of being able to buy a seat in the preferred cabin on the required departure). This increases the risk of 'stochastic delay' (Douglas and Miller, 1974a) arising from the non-availability of space.
     - *Aircraft size and technology* Aircraft size and technology have been found to drive demand insofar as larger aircraft are associated with better inflight comfort, and turbofans are more customer-friendly than props.

   Although evidence with regard to the role of load factors is ambiguous, the other determinants in this category have been shown to be significant (Jorge-Calderón, op cit). On the other hand, Melville (1998) suggests that linking the three in the same model invites multi-collinearity problems, because aircraft size x flight frequency x load factor actually defines demand rather than accounts for it – with the result that using these determinants as independent variables in the demand function simply regresses demand on components of itself (ibid: 316-317).

What is beyond argument is that the dimensions of service quality used in most economists' models of air transport demand are far less extensive than the range of attributes that airline product and brand managers see as influencing customer purchase behaviour (and which are discussed in Holloway, 2002). In part, this is because of the paucity of publicly available information on the impact on demand of 'soft' customer service attributes such as tone and style of service delivery, and even of harder attributes such as cabin configuration, IFE, and IFC facilities; furthermore, some of these attributes might have more impact on individual airlines' market shares and perhaps customer loyalty than on aggregate travel demand. The service quality variable that has in fact received most attention is the time-cost of travel, as reflected in frequencies, routings, and elapsed journey times.

- *Price* As the neoclassical 'law of demand' suggests it should be, demand has been found to be inversely related to price.

References to empirical research developing demand estimation models that use various combinations of these (and other) determinants can be found in Jorge-Calderón (1997: 24-25).

Anecdotally, it appears that although the industry demand function may be reasonably well understood in principle, there are two areas of weakness: first, the precise impact of service attributes on demand has not yet been fully explained; and second, more general demand functions are often, inappropriately, used as proxies for the demand functions of specific individual markets (which may have very different demand characteristics and elasticities). Extending the last point, few empirical studies have endeavoured to model different segments of demand in the markets under consideration; notable exceptions include work on the Australian domestic market by Battersby and Oczkowski (2001).

The role of consumers' attitudes and perceptions is often given scant attention in air transport demand estimation models. Graham (2000), citing Swarbrooke and Horner (1999), distinguishes between factors which make travel feasible (such as economic and social conditions, pricing, schedule, and booking conditions) and factors that influence specific travel decisions (such as an individual consumer's personality, attitude, and perceptions of, for example, different airlines or particular leisure destinations). The latter generally receive more attention in the consumer behaviour, services management, brand management, and general marketing literatures than amongst economists.

Demand forecasting and allocation

Demand forecasting is most commonly used by airlines as part of a two-stage process that also involves demand allocation. Figure 2.3 illustrates the relationship between the two.

Demand forecasting

Whilst forecasts of aggregate demand at global, inter-regional, and intra-regional levels are important, what matters most to airlines is demand in the O & D city-pair markets that are available for them to serve (either alone or in co-operation with other carriers). It is critical that demand is forecast on an O & D basis rather than a route basis because who flies on which routes between a particular origin and a particular destination is a function not just of demand, but also of how airlines design their networks.

When dropping below the global or regional level of analysis, it is important to recall the distinction between a route and a market. Demand on the New York (JFK)-London Heathrow (LHR) route, for example, is driven not only by local traffic but also by traffic originating behind JFK and/or continuing beyond LHR – in other words, by demand in other city-pair markets. Conversely, traffic in the Los Angeles-New York city-pair market might travel on routes originating at any of a number of LA area airports and fly on nonstop routes to any of a number of New York area airports, or it might use routes into and out of intermediate hubs such as Salt Lake City or Denver. The point is that we need to be clear that demand on a route between two airports may be very different from the demand in that same city-pair market – with the difference driven by whether or not the origin and/or destination cities are served by multi-airport systems and, more particularly, by the volume of flow traffic on the route.

Demand forecasts are an amalgam of projections and predictions, tempered by judgement: a projection is an extrapolation of past trends into the future, whilst a prediction depends upon an assumed linkage between these trends and the underlying independent variables in the demand function that shape them – and a further assumption regarding the future development of those variables. By introducing an entirely new source of 'event risk' that is impossible to forecast yet has enormous human and economic consequences for the industry, 9/11 opened the now ever-present threat that

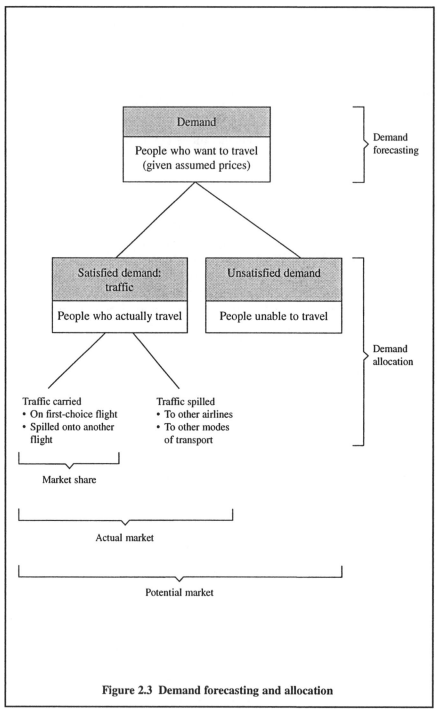

Figure 2.3 Demand forecasting and allocation

a major discontinuity could arise at any time between historical data and current forecasts.

Forecasting can have one or more of several dimensions:

- **temporal**: short-, medium- or long-range;
- **geographical**: global, inter-regional, intra-regional, domestic, and/or city-pair demand at an aggregate level;
- **product-market**: demand in different segments (i.e., for different products) in particular geographical markets.

The uses of forecasting Demand forecasts – along with the market share and traffic forecasts derived from them – are the basis for revenue, cost, profit, and cash flow forecasts, for managing the marketing mix, and for operational planning. The uses to which each type of forecast can be put inevitably vary. For example, short-range forecasts will assist in scheduling and operational planning (i.e., demand allocation, staff rostering, and equipment scheduling), whereas long-range forecasts – particularly as they apply to different geographical levels – will be an essential input into network and fleet planning processes. The most useful are likely to combine more than one dimension, such as medium-term forecasts for business class travel on an airline's short-haul international network.

Forecasts clearly have a profound impact on strategic behaviour. They should drive decisions in respect of competitive (i.e., product and geographical) scope, service concept(s), customer value, positioning, design of ground and inflight service packages (i.e., design of the attributes intended to deliver expected benefits to targeted customers), design of the operating system that will deliver services, and establishment of price platforms for each service package in each market. Some of these ideas were touched upon in chapter 1 when we looked at cost and benefit advantage, the resources underpinning them, and the strategic positions that build upon them. Pricing will be looked at in the next chapter. Holloway (2002) provides a comprehensive discussion of all these topics.

Forecasting methods Choice of forecasting technique should be guided by: the objective(s) of the work; its time horizon; the data, study-time, and resources (financial and human) available; and the risks involved in acting on an incorrect forecast. Data availability in respect of O & D markets can be an issue for start-ups and new entrants in some parts of the world, whereas incumbents have access to historical data; any carrier with sufficiently deep pockets can conduct market research and purchase marketing information data tape (MIDT) data from the GDSs.

The following methods are in common use.

1. **Trend (or time-series) analysis** Trend analyses are widely used for short-term forecasting, particularly at the O & D market level. Although simple and cheap, trend analysis has the major flaw that it addresses only one variable – time – and uses this as a proxy for the real underlying influences on demand. Nonetheless, a good number of market forecasts rely on trend analysis (usually moving averages), supplemented by advance booking data and – particularly in the case of markets critical to a specific airline – perhaps also manual adjustments based on experience and/or market research into travel intentions. (Note that some airlines use advance booking data as more than just a supplement to trend analysis; several plug this data into complex models which project forward bookings some distance into the future, and they use output from these models to guide capacity and pricing decisions and to forecast traffic and yield – sometimes in preference to more macro-level annual or seasonal forecasts (Robertson, 2002)).

2. **Causal analysis** There are two types of causal analysis.
    *   *Econometric modelling* Econometric models are constructed around verifiable statistical relationships between a dependent variable such as passenger enplanements or RPMs and one or more explanatory independent variables such as price, GDP growth or changes in consumer expenditure or personal disposable income. Used to generate global and regional as well as market-specific forecasts and widely considered one of the more sophisticated forecasting techniques available, econometric modelling is always hostage to the precision with which it reflects real-world relationships between dependent and independent variables, to the continuity of those relationships into the future, and to the accuracy of forecasts in respect of future changes affecting the independent variables (i.e., price, GDP, etc.). Until redesigned or recalibrated, econometric models are as exposed as trend analyses to changes in historical data relationships caused by significant discontinuities such as a terrorist incident or deregulation of a major market.
    *   *Gravity models* Referred to earlier in the chapter, these are spatial equilibrium models that work on the assumption that traffic between two points or regions varies directly in response to some economic or demographic measure of their size (particularly where its effect is intensified by ethnic or linguistic links), and inversely in relation to the distance between them (although the impact of intervening geographical barriers can distort this latter assumption). Gravity models tend to be more popular for examining demand in respect of modes other than air transport, although they are certainly used in the airline industry. They are designed more to

examine potential traffic movements in general than to forecast actual demand over a specific period of time.

Long-term forecasting undertaken by the world's larger airlines tends to rely heavily on econometric modelling – particularly when a top-down approach is used to analyse global, inter-regional, and intra-regional markets. ICAO, IATA, and various regional trade associations as well as the major airframe and engine manufacturers also produce aggregate forecasts based on econometric models.

3. **Market research** Market research can be used both for forecasting demand and for looking into the effectiveness of alternative service attributes (e.g., schedule, cabin design, onboard service processes, etc.). The two are closely linked. For demand forecasting purposes, market research can be particularly useful where historical data is unavailable, as in the case of a newly served market, or is erratic or unreliable, as is often true of airfreight demand in thin markets. It can also be used to forecast subjective variables for which time-series data is unavailable, or the effect of particularly radical developments for which there is no precedent in the data. Its usefulness is enhanced when there are relatively few buyers to consider, which is the case in many airfreight markets, and where research into specific planned developments at one end of a market – such as investment in the air transport or hotel/leisure infrastructure – is likely to provide a more accurate guide to the future than historical data. Finally, it can be used to augment other forecasting methods.

4. **Qualitative analysis** Sometimes referred to as 'judgemental' analysis, qualitative methods include scenario analysis, individual expert judgement, brainstorming, group consensus-building, and the Delphi method. These are essentially educated guesses. That they are subjective does not necessarily make them more questionable than 'scientific' forecasting techniques, but their worth in practice will depend upon who is involved and whether action based on what is forecast has the backing of sufficiently powerful interests within the airline concerned. There is in fact an argument that uncertain times subject to unforeseeable and potentially significant discontinuities open the door to insightful judgement wider than periods of routine, 'mechanical' growth.

Returning to figure 2.3, we can see that whatever demand is forecasted to come forward might be left unsatisfied (e.g., at peak periods), or it might be satisfied – either by the airline undertaking the analysis or by a competitor (including, perhaps, a competing mode of transport). Satisfied demand is referred to as 'traffic'. The decisions underlying all this are part of the 'demand allocation' problem.

Demand allocation

How much traffic an airline carries in an O & D market depends upon several variables: the demand coming forward in that market; the volume and nature of output the airline produces in the market; and the volume and nature of output produced by competitors also present in the market. 'Volume and nature' refers to variables such as the size of aircraft used, the schedule, the routing offered (e.g., nonstop, direct, or connecting), and other relevant variables (e.g., price, brand image, inflight service, FFP benefits, and reliability). Decisions regarding aircraft capacity, schedule, and routing represent the core of the demand allocation problem; there are models available to help estimate the impact of these and other decisions on an airline's market share. What is clear is that market share is highly sensitive to how an airline chooses to allocate across its network and schedule the O & D demand available to it. We saw early in the chapter that the volume and quality of supply have an impact on the demand for air transport services; for example, a conveniently timed nonstop in a short-haul market might attract business that an inconveniently timed connecting service would not. Demand allocation decisions can therefore feed back into demand itself.

There are two further points worth noting about demand allocation.

1. Demand spilled from one of an airline's flights could be lost to competitors, or it might be 'recaptured' through allocation to another of the same airline's flights.
2. Demand allocation and fleet planning are closely linked exercises – sometimes still modelled separately, but increasingly integrated into single simulation models. The important thing to remember is that whereas demand arises between O & D points (e.g., Wichita and Munich) it is very often served by more than one flight-leg and by alternative routings (e.g., Wichita–Washington Dulles–Munich, or Wichita–Chicago O'Hare–Munich). How a large network carrier chooses to allocate future demand across its network will strongly influence the fleet optimisation process. We will return to this in Part 3 of the book.

Forecasting approaches: Top-down (macro-level) and bottom-up (microlevel) forecasting

Demand can be forecasted from the top down, or from the bottom up.

1. **Top-down** forecasts are constructed for global or regional passenger and freight markets by generating aggregate industry demand figures;

market share is then forecasted on the basis of historical performance adjusted for any planned output changes or marketing mix initiatives likely to affect consumer preferences – such as new promotions, product launches, or advertising campaigns. Adjustments will also be made to reflect other forecast changes in the commercial environment, particularly the activities of competitors. Figure 2.4 illustrates the process.

2. Forecasts can also be built from the **bottom up** by aggregating figures for different O & D markets. There is a lot to be said in favour of this approach insofar as it is at the individual market level that many short-term operational and marketing decisions have to be taken in practice. Different markets will also tend to have their own individual patterns of intra-day, intra-week, and seasonal demand fluctuations.

   An important benefit of bottom-up forecasting is that because it is more closely aligned with actual operations than the top-down approach, it plugs more readily into detailed fleet planning and assignment decisions. The difficulty is that demand is generally more erratic in individual markets than at a global or systemwide level of aggregation, and so can be reliably forecast only over relatively short periods of time; furthermore, bottom-up forecasting can be a complex, resource-consuming exercise for a large network carrier.

Airlines need O & D market forecasts because they provide critical input for network and fleet planning models as well as scheduling and fleet assignment models. O & D traffic (and revenue) forecasts are in fact the foundation for route and network forecasts.

- **Route forecasts** These depend upon how O & D flows are allocated across a network (a decision that can itself feed back to O & D demand and market share through the impact of network design and scheduling on customers' purchase behaviour). Route forecasts are built by 'un-peeling' O & D demand and layering it onto alternative flight-legs and routes to create a network of nonstop, one-stop, multi-stop, and connecting services, each perhaps serving a number of different markets simultaneously.
- **Network forecasts** Network forecasts are built by aggregating route forecasts.

Iterations can be driven by different price, marketing, competitive, network design, scheduling, and fleet management assumptions.

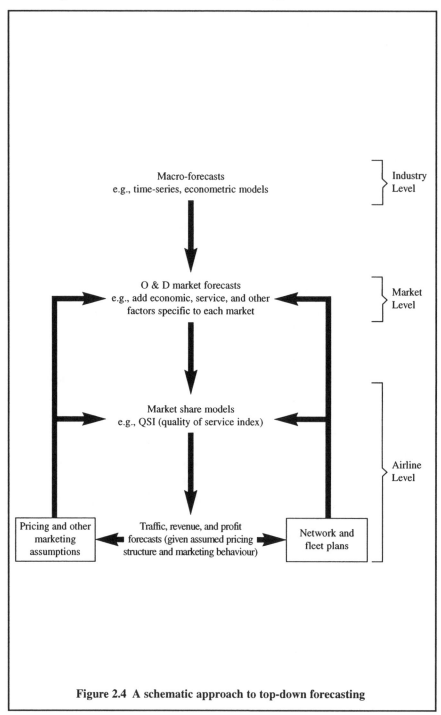

Figure 2.4 A schematic approach to top-down forecasting

The challenge in demand forecasting and allocation

There are several potential pitfalls which turn straightforward theory into rather difficult practice as far as the construction of accurate, and therefore useful, demand functions is concerned.

1. The demand characteristics of markets vary because of the different journey purposes of the traffic which predominates in each. Even in the same market, different economic and other circumstances at either end might argue for separate models of demand to be used to forecast originating traffic (e.g., one for the US–UK market, and one for the UK–US market).
2. Determination of how each independent variable (e.g., price, service benefits, etc.) actually affects demand for passenger or freight service requires a great deal of historical data upon which to perform regression analysis, and it has to be assumed that relationships unearthed in that data will hold into the future. A common complication is that price, income, and other independent variables may be difficult to quantify at the individual market level where the fare structure is complex and other figures are unobtainable, unreliable or out of date. Fares might have to be averaged, with the average weighted to reflect traffic mix, for example; or the yield earned in a market might be used as a proxy for price. Furthermore, there will inevitably be qualitative variables (e.g., crowded airports and aircraft) that are difficult to specify but can nonetheless affect demand.
3. It has to be assumed that when customers make their choices of transport mode and carrier they actually have available perfect information about those of the independent variables specified in the forecasting model that are believed to impact directly upon consumer behaviour (e.g., price and quality of service). The reality could be that consumers are simply unaware of changes in marketing mix or other variables which airlines consider, perhaps correctly in principle, should have a profound impact on purchasing behaviour and hence demand.
4. If we bear in mind the importance of price to demand and the fact that in the United States in particular there are tens of thousands of fare changes daily, the difficulties of forecasting become immediately apparent. Add to this the activities of competitors, demand peaking, random fluctuations, the effects of marketing communications and promotions, and our still imperfect knowledge of consumer choice behaviour and the magnitude of the challenge becomes even more apparent – especially when forecasting at the O & D market level.

5.   It has already been noted that air transport demand is a derived demand because people fly in pursuit of whatever is at the other end of the journey – whether a contract, a suntan or a family member. If the underlying demand falls, say because there are fewer contracts available, suntans come to be associated with ill-health, or family ties weaken as older generations die-out, demand for air services will be affected. The implication is that airlines have to understand and forecast not only the superficially relevant independent variables in their demand functions, but the actual motivations for travel which underlie many of these variables. Such underlying determinants of demand differ from market to market and segment to segment.

6.   Aggregate forecasts also have their problems. The industry's income-elasticity of demand inevitably magnifies any errors in GNP or GDP forecasts. Furthermore, although demand in large markets is generally more stable and easier to forecast than in small markets, a forecasting error of a similar size will obviously be much more significant in the case of a large market. Taking the industry as a whole and depending upon the precise figures involved from year to year, a 50 basis point error in forecasting growth in global RPMs for the forthcoming year could well be equivalent to the entire annual output of a medium-sized carrier. As the industry grows, any given percentage forecasting error inevitably gets larger in absolute terms – something that has serious capacity management implications.

7.   It is vital to remember that a forecast of market demand is not a forecast of what *will* happen. It is a forecast of what will happen if assumptions about how certain independent variables affect demand, and how these variables will themselves change during the forecast period, turn out to be broadly correct. Similarly, market share forecasts are not forecasts of the demand an airline *will* serve. They are forecasts of what could be achieved assuming market forecasts are correct and, in particular, assuming certain decisions are taken with regard to the marketing mix. If elements of the marketing mix are changed (either by the airline or by its competitors), or if customers respond to one or more elements (such as price or advertising initiatives) differently than predicted, market share will not be as forecast. A forecast is not a plan; it is a planning input.

8.   Airlines do not investigate demand functions for individual markets in isolation from an investigation into the costs of meeting forecast demand. Implicit in any cost assumption is a certain level of service consistent with the strategic and market positioning decisions discussed in chapter 1. These simultaneous and iterative studies are plugged into decision models, which could range from the intuitive mental model of

a small airline's chief executive to the computer-based econometric models available to well-resourced carriers. The result shapes competitive behaviour insofar as it determines which markets are entered, which continue to be served and at what levels of service, and which will be exited.

However a forecast is derived, the cost of getting it wrong can be high. In a service industry which is not able to inventory unsold output once it has been produced and yet serves customers – particularly high-yield customers – who in many cases cannot or will not wait if output (i.e., space) is unavailable more or less when required, demand forecasting takes on particular significance. If a forecast undershoots the eventual out-turn, 'cost' manifests itself in forgone goodwill and revenue (i.e., 'spillage' to competitors). If it overshoots, the airline must bear the very real costs of flying unnecessary capacity – of generating too much output – and often, as a result, having to accept weaker than anticipated yields in order to sell the excess and maintain load factors; underutilised resources other than aircraft – call centres, lounges, gates, and the people who staff them, for example – also carry fixed costs that will not be spread across as many units of output as they otherwise might. Capacity costs, many of which are fixed over the short and medium term, are responsible for a high proportion of any scheduled airline's total operating costs.

v. Capacity management: managing demand

Traffic (i.e., output *sold*, measured in RPMs or RTMs) and output *produced* (i.e., supply, measured in ASMs or ATMs) are linked by load factor (i.e., the percentage of output *produced* that has been *sold*). One, passive, way to accommodate rising demand is therefore to accept a rising load factor. The problem with this is that beyond a certain level (which will vary depending upon route characteristics and traffic mix), a high load factor will lead to 'spill' – the loss of traffic and therefore revenue. Many airlines have target load factors keyed-off what they consider to be acceptable 'spill'. It could be argued that a carrier which dominates a route, particularly in terms of frequency, may well find much of any spill going onto its own services rather than those of competitors; on the other hand, no matter how dominant it is on a route, if that route is simply one alternative channel between particular origins and destinations which other carriers could as easily connect over different routes on their own networks, then spill to competitors serving these O & D markets may possibly be high.

We can take two temporal perspectives on demand management: long run and short run.

Long-run demand management

In the long run, the preferred way to grow demand is to understand available markets and their potential, decide which markets and segments to target, understand the preferences and expectations of the customers in these markets and segments, design service-price offers able to provide the value expected, deliver services to specification, monitor customers' perceptions of service, and adjust service design and delivery to take account of identified service failures and changing consumer preferences and expectations. In other words, invest in the product – including, importantly, the people who deliver it – and understand the payback on product investment. This approach is discussed in much greater depth in Holloway (2002); figure 2.5 illustrates it in general terms.

If we think back to the 'perceived customer value' diagram in figure 1.3 (page 30), we can draw the following conclusions.

- Improving the product without raising the price platform moves the offer to the left. Important questions are whether this increases production costs, if so how the incremental costs will be addressed (e.g., by higher productivity), and how (as well as how quickly) competitors might respond.
- If the product is allowed to stand still whilst competitors improve their products, the offer will shift to the right because it embodies lower relative value. A branch of the discipline called evolutionary economics (which we also met in chapter 1) argues that the search for innovative new ways of serving customers is an inevitable dimension of restless, disequilibrating competition, and eventually every competitor must respond in order to stay in the game – unless it is protected by barriers limiting the opportunity for more aggressive competitors to win significant market share. In the short run, of course, downward price adjustments can be made to compensate for product stagnation; in the long run, assuming openly competitive markets, this would at best amount to repositioning in a different (more price-sensitive) segment – and at worst it could be a route to failure.

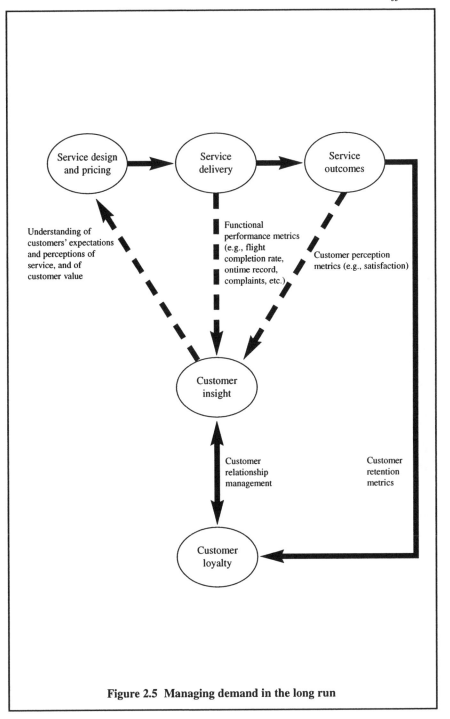

Figure 2.5 Managing demand in the long run

Short-run demand management

Because output is supplied by the plane-load and demand is met by the seat, capacity management in the short-run must rely more heavily on managing demand than managing supply (although, as we will see in chapter 4, there are effective steps that can be taken to manage supply even in the short run). Short-run capacity management utilises demand-side variables such as pricing, promotion, marketing communications, and – in the case of full-service carriers – FFP award variations and also incentives to agents (e.g., TACOs) in order to absorb excess output on particular departures or routes (perhaps pending a 'strategic review' of the schedule or network). The objective is to smooth predictable demand peaks by shifting demand from peak to off-peak periods, stimulate increased demand from segments already served and new demand from segments that might otherwise not travel, and at the same time maximise revenues earned from available output.

Demand which turns out to be greater than forecast, whether during peak or off-peak periods, raises a different set of issues. Even if aircraft are readily available to satisfy unanticipated demand, the additional slots and gates required to use them at congested airports might not be. In regulated commercial environments, the necessary authorities to operate additional frequencies or larger capacity aircraft may not be forthcoming.

vi. Summary

This chapter has distinguished between demand and traffic, and looked at the particular characteristics of demand for air transport services. The importance of understanding and segmenting potentially available markets has been discussed. Demand functions and schedules, elasticity, and modelling have been considered within the context of demand forecasting. Finally, the importance of demand management to wider capacity management efforts, particularly in the short run, has been stressed.

Demand is of course served not by selling the ASMs or ATMs an airline produces, but by delivering a service. The most tangible manifestation of service is a seat on an aircraft but, as is fully explained in Holloway (2002), this is only one dimension of the airline product. What customers buy is a package of attributes which together provide them with a range of benefits. Each package is part of a service-price offer (ibid). The other side of that offer – price – is the subject of the next chapter. Together, service and price drive customer value, as we saw in figure 1.2.

3 Yield

There is a huge difference between 'the best money can buy'
and 'the best value for the dollar'.
Henry Ford

Chapter overview

Yield is the second of the four elements in the operating performance
model around which Part 2 of the book has been structured.

TRAFFIC x **YIELD** > < OUTPUT x UNIT COST
= OPERATING PERFORMANCE (i.e., PROFIT or LOSS)

This chapter will:

- discuss price in the context of the airline industry and introduce different types of passenger fare and cargo rate;
- identify price drivers;
- explain the use of price as both a strategic and a tactical variable; and
- define the concept of yield.

i. Price

Yield – revenue earned per RPM or RPK or per RTM or RTK – is the
element of the operating performance model upon which this chapter will
ultimately focus. But to understand yield we need first to consider pricing,
because it is an airline's passenger fare and cargo rate structures together
with its traffic mix (i.e., the proportions of traffic moving on each fare and
rate basis) that drive system yield.

Price defined

Price is here defined as 'monetary cost to customers'. It is not uncommon in the literature for nonmonetary costs, measured in terms of time or inconvenience for example, to be embodied in the concept of price. The view taken in the present book is that high nonmonetary costs are better treated as low-quality service attributes; in this sense, a multi-stop or connecting service 'costs' more time than a nonstop service and so compares unfavourably on this attribute dimension.

Different perspectives on the role of price

There are several related but separate perspectives on price.

- To an economist, price is a mechanism for bringing supply and demand into balance at a particular level of output. (However, some economists argue that the airline industry is an example of a phenomenon referred to in game theory as an 'empty core' – an oligopolistic market structure unable to arrive at stable equilibrium prices (Button, 1996); the foundation of this inherent instability is the fact that output is supplied in expensive indivisible units such as aircraft whilst demand is much more finely grained and comes forward in most cases one seat at a time. We will return to this in chapter 4.)
- In the accounting model around which this second part of the book has been structured, price – in the form of yield – is one of four elements in what is usually an unbalanced equation, the balancing item being operating profit or loss.
- To a marketer, price is part of a marketing mix along with service design, service personnel and delivery processes, distribution channels, and the marketing communications mix (i.e., advertising, promotion, public relations, etc.); in principle, all the elements of the marketing mix associated with a particular market should be managed in unison so that it can be approached with an integrated service-price offer.

That price and output decisions are closely linked and that price is integral to a complex marketing mix make it rather unrealistic to talk about pricing policy in isolation. Furthermore, price is not only one of the most important threads binding the service concept, marketing communications, and distribution strategy into a single, coherent, strategically positioned offer to the marketplace, it is also a tactical variable in the daily cut-and-thrust of liberalised competitive environments. Nonetheless, for the purpose of discussion we will treat pricing largely as an independent activity.

Responsibility for pricing

Although the two functions need to be closely co-ordinated, at larger air-lines there are usually separate pricing and revenue management departments.

- **Pricing** The purpose of a pricing department is to create and administer the passenger fare and freight rate structures applicable to each market. (Freight rates might in practice be set by a separate cargo department, division or subsidiary.) The pricing function also involves establishing conditions subject to which each fare and rate will be offered (with price and conditions together constituting a 'tariff'), and perhaps deciding on which departures in a given market any particular fare or rate can be sold. Tariff-setting on alliance routes might, where legal, be co-ordinated by the partners.
- **Revenue management** The function of revenue management departments is to allocate the physical space available on each individual flight-leg (augmented by overbooking limits) between the different fare and rate bases available for sale on that leg. (We will see in chapter 9 that there are more advanced revenue management approaches available, but allocation-based methods are still widely used across the industry.) In particular, the purpose of revenue management on the passenger side is to limit the availability of low-yield fares on any departure where unconstrained demand might be expected to fill seats with passengers paying the lowest fares and exclude late-booking passengers prepared to pay more.

At many airlines, a headquarters department is responsible for pricing as well as for the filing and distribution of published tariffs. However, international carriers in particular frequently grant considerable autonomy to local sales offices, which are free within limits both to respond to other airlines' pricing activities and to negotiate unpublished off-tariff deals with targeted agencies at net prices (i.e., prices net of commission) subject to locally agreed conditions. Because of the relatively small number of customers participating in cargo markets (i.e., forwarders, consolidators, and shippers), off-tariff deals are even more common in this sector of the industry.

The fundamental objective of the pricing function is to design a tariff structure for each market that maximises revenue earned from price-inelastic segments of demand, stimulates demand from price-elastic segments to fill space that would otherwise fly empty, and imposes conditions sufficient to limit revenue dilution arising from the diversion of demand from high-yield fare or rate bases targeted at price-inelastic segments to lower fares or rates targeted at more price-elastic segments.

Looking specifically at passenger fares, it can be helpful to treat the full, on-demand, unrestricted fare applied for travel in a particular cabin (economy/coach, business, or first class) in a given market as the strategic 'price platform' for the service concept of which the cabin concerned is a part. Price platforms help define airlines' strategic positioning – as full-service network carriers, low-fare carriers, and so on. From any price platform can be developed a series of lower fares (published and off-tariff) to tap into the price-elasticities of different segments of demand identified by reference to their willingness to pay to travel in the cabin concerned, in the market concerned, at particular times; hence, around 90 per cent of US domestic passengers travel on discounted fares, and the discounts average approximately 70 per cent (Air Transport Association, 2001). In highly competitive markets, these fare structures will be fine-tuned on an ongoing basis; hundreds of thousands of changes are filed every day in the US domestic market, for example. The notion of a 'price platform' is perhaps less applicable to the case of low-fare carriers, whose highest ('walk-up') fares might not in some cases be fully unrestricted, and which offer a relatively small menu of discounts off these fares; the strategic importance of pricing is nonetheless clear insofar as low fares are a defining characteristic of those airlines' service concepts. The functions of price and the role of strategic pricing are further explored in Holloway (2002).

Influence of pricing

Influence on demand

Demand does not just exist; it exists at a price. We saw in chapter 2 that price is one of the most important determinants of demand. It was also shown that there is an elasticity associated with price, as there is with other important independent variables in the demand function; prices influence both traffic generated and the yield earned from that traffic. Liberalisation and deregulation free carriers to manage traffic and yield more proactively than when price structures are imposed by airline cartels and/or governments, and this is what has been happening in a growing number of the world's most significant air transport markets since the late 1970s. Of course, for airline managers to be able to use price as an effective demand management tool, it is necessary that they have some feel for the shape and slope of the demand curves faced by their services at different points in time (e.g., off-peak, shoulder, and peak, or weekdays and weekends, or morning, midday, and late afternoon/early evening). This will allow them to estimate the impact a price change will have on the quantity of service demanded. Complicating the task, however, is the fact that different segments of the market will probably have different demand curves at different times. The need to exploit these differences to maximise revenue underlies the complex tariff structures that most full-service airlines create.

Another complication is the fact that many airline markets tend towards oligopolistic structures, with the result that price changes initiated by any one of the small number of competitors present are likely to be reacted to by the others – leading to shifts in their initial demand curves. (We will look at oligopoly in chapter 4.)

Influence on supply and costs

By influencing demand, price drives revenue. The volume and nature of demand an airline chooses to supply with output in turn drives costs. For example, by offering a tiered fare structure in response to the price-elasticities of people willing to travel only on discounted fares, an airline is not just striving to maximise its own revenues but is also increasing the density of traffic in the markets concerned. This increased density will have two immediate effects on costs.

1. Capacity costs – the costs of generating output by flying aircraft and operating a ground infrastructure – may or may not rise.
    *   They will rise in an absolute sense if additional capacity is required to accommodate the increased traffic. However, unit cost – that is, cost per unit of output produced (e.g., per available seat-mile) – may fall if the higher traffic density allows larger aircraft with lower seat-mile costs to be operated than would otherwise have been the case. We will return to this in chapters 4 and 5.
    *   They will remain largely unchanged if increased traffic can be accommodated within the existing system (e.g., by accepting higher load factors).
2. Traffic costs – the costs of handling and flying passengers – will rise as traffic density increases, irrespective of whether or not capacity has had to be boosted.

Much therefore depends upon how changes in absolute costs and absolute revenues develop in response to increased traffic moving on the discounted fares concerned. This, in turn, will depend upon the structure of the particular carrier's operating system and cost base. We will be looking at both in chapters 4 and 5.

Through the demand it creates, pricing can affect different types of cost.

- **Variable costs** If a pricing initiative generates incremental demand, what will be the extra costs of serving that demand?
- **Fixed costs** Can incremental demand be served by the existing fleet and infrastructure, or must more capacity – and therefore more fixed costs – be added?
- **Unit costs** What will be the impact of higher throughput on unit costs? The answer to this will be shaped by answers to the two preceding questions, by the size of any economies of scale, density, and scope available to a particular airline, and by the precise nature and geography of the incremental demand.

We will be looking at these different types of cost and at economies of scale, density, and scope in chapter 5.

Pricing can have an even more direct and immediate impact on costs. For example, a simple and stable fare structure may contribute to lower distribution costs by reducing sales training requirements, shortening reservations calls (so raising the productivity of reservations staff), and lessening the perceived need amongst passengers to rely on travel agents for current fare information. Simplicity can also help encourage use of Internet distribution channels. On the other hand, price complexity could raise distribution costs both by increasing passengers' reliance on travel agents and, because more enquirers are just shopping around, by ensuring that fewer direct contacts between an airline's own staff and potential customers lead to sales.

Market liberalisation tends to reduce the predictability of fares from the customer's perspective, and can lead to extreme volatility in both fares and the conditions attached to them. The Internet, on the other hand, does mitigate the cost impact of price volatility by making enquiries made through this medium virtually cost-free to the airline concerned.

Influence on profits, market share, and cash flow

We have seen that price is an important driver of both revenues and costs. However, the influence is not proportional. This means that a pricing strategy intended to maximise revenue will not necessarily maximise the difference between revenue and costs – that is, profit. There have been quite a few cases over the last two decades of airlines in financial difficulties pricing to generate cash, with carriers reorganising under the protection of Chapter 11 bankruptcy laws in the United States providing a number of high-profile examples, along with state-subsidised 'flag carriers' elsewhere in the world. What an airline sets out to achieve through its pricing policy with regard to revenue, profitability, market share, and cash flow should be driven by wider corporate and marketing objectives.

Influence on market positioning

Market positioning essentially defines the location of a service relative to competing services as perceived by customers (and is therefore slightly different from 'strategic positioning' which, as we saw in chapter 1, is a supply-side concept used to define an airline's approach to its markets). Price is a vital piece of the information 'jig-saw' assembled by customers. This is true for most products, but especially so for services because their intangibility makes pre-delivery evaluation more subjective (Holloway, 2002). The positioning of a first or business class service, for example, might constrain pricing insofar as it can be highly damaging to the image of a premium product for it to be heavily discounted.

Pricing and market segmentation

We will look at three approaches to pricing: uniform, discriminatory, and differential. The discussion here is oriented primarily to the pricing of passenger fares; freight rates are discussed later in the chapter.

Uniform pricing

Figure 3.1(a) illustrates a uniform pricing structure, which has every buyer paying the same price for a given product; figure 3.1(b) illustrates a situation in which a uniform price is set at $250 – equivalent to the value placed on the service by Consumer 3, but lower than the maximum amounts that consumers 1 and 2 would have been prepared to pay.

In chapter 1 we defined consumer surplus as the value placed by a particular consumer on the benefits received from a service package, less the monetary price paid for that package; in other words, consumer surplus is what a consumer would in principle be prepared to pay for a service less the price actually paid. In figure 3.1(b), Consumer 1 would be prepared to pay $500 for a ticket that is in fact priced at $250 – therefore 'earning' a surplus of $250; similarly, Consumer 2 would have been prepared to pay $400 for the ticket, and so has a surplus of $150. Consumer 3, on the other hand, values the ticket at its market price and so gains no surplus.

On an aggregate level, the surplus from which all consumers as a whole benefit is the shaded area beneath the demand curve and above the market price line at $250. From an airline's perspective, this area represents revenue

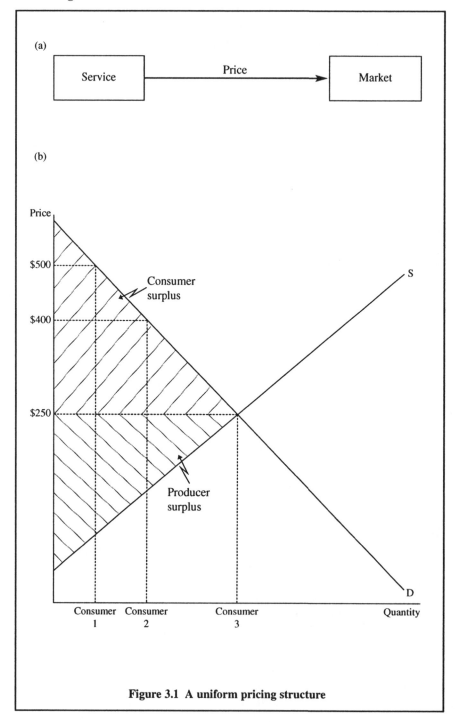

Figure 3.1 A uniform pricing structure

dilution. The shaded area below the market price and above the supply curve is the surplus earned by the producer (attributable to being able to produce the service in question at a cost below the market price).

Although simple and apparently equitable, uniform pricing is rarely a feasible pricing structure. Assuming first that the single price is relatively high, it is likely to leave some consumers still paying less than they would be prepared to pay – that is, paying a lower amount than the value they place on the air transport service bought (so benefiting from a substantial consumer surplus) – and a large number of other, more price-sensitive travellers excluded from the market altogether. When this happens, economies of density are reduced below what they might otherwise have been had more demand been able to come forward, with the result that unit costs will be higher – because of having to operate smaller aircraft with less attractive seat-mile costs, for example. This is likely to cause those who do travel to face higher fares. Furthermore, the high frequencies and wide network coverage particularly valued by the business travellers who will probably constitute a large proportion of those remaining in any market served at a high uniform price might be difficult to support on the basis of the lower level of demand attracted by that single price.

Much depends upon what the single price is. If it is low enough, substantial traffic might indeed be carried. In this case, however, an even higher proportion of passengers would probably be travelling at fares significantly below the value they place on the service, and unless the airline concerned has its production costs well under control profits might prove elusive.

In most cases, airlines use more subtle pricing structures based on market segmentation to redistribute in their own favour those parts of consumer surplus above the market price line in figure 3.1(b) and within the vertical boxes. Most are examples of either discriminatory or differential pricing.

Discriminatory pricing

Price discrimination occurs when buyers of essentially the same service pay different prices which are not attributable to different marginal costs of production; in other words, customers who cost more or less the same to serve are nonetheless paying different prices. In this section of the chapter we will be using class of travel (i.e., onboard cabin and associated ground benefits) as a proxy for 'essentially the same service'; we will see shortly that this is not uncontroversial.

To achieve price discrimination, demand in a market is segmented along two dimensions that are not mutually exclusive.

1. **Passengers' different time-preferences** 'Peak-load pricing' is the term used by economists to describe a peak/off-peak pricing structure. It is in fact less an attempt to capture consumer surplus than to increase economic efficiency by charging consumers who have to travel during peak periods prices that reflect the higher marginal costs of providing service when a system is operating near full capacity (Pindyck and Rubinfeld, 2001). Three features of the airline industry make it a prime candidate for peak-load pricing (Shy, 1995).

   • High intertemporal variations in demand (by time of day, day of week, and season, for example).

   • The requirement to secure production capacity over long periods covering troughs as well as peaks in demand – in other words, to secure sufficient capacity (with all its attendant fixed costs) to meet a substantial proportion of peak demand.

   • The perishability of the product, which prevents airlines from smoothing output by using low-demand periods to produce inventory that can be drawn down during high-demand periods.

   In fact, peak-load pricing linked explicitly to the higher marginal costs of serving peak demand is not a feature of the airline business. The emphasis is generally more on the use of off-peak pricing to shift consumers with weak time-preferences into low-demand periods; in some cabins in some markets (e.g., long-haul business and first class) there is in fact little or no peak/off-peak pricing of any sort.

2. **Passengers' different price-elasticities** The objective of segmenting on the basis of passengers' different willingness to pay for essentially the same service is to ensure that those who value access to the service most highly are charged prices as near as possible to the value they place on the service (i.e., their 'reservation price'), whilst others who value the service less highly are given access to any remaining output at lower fares which reflect their lower willingness to pay. Carriers generally use two variables for tapping into segments that have different price-elasticities.

   • *Identity* Discrimination based on identity often favours passengers by reference to age, military or government employment status, or group membership. These essentially descriptive characteristics are generally a poor proxy for price-elasticity, but they do have the advantage of making the segments concerned easy to target.

   • *Behaviour* Price discrimination based on behaviour is targeted at customers prepared to behave in ways advantageous to the airline, in return for lower prices. The behaviour required usually involves making reservations and paying for travel well in advance of departure, remaining at the destination over a Saturday night (a common restriction in short-haul markets) and/or for minimum and maximum periods, and accepting other conditions that might limit, for example, cancellation and refund, rescheduling, rerouting, open-jaw itineraries, stopovers, endorsement of the ticket for travel on another carrier, and/or interlining.

For a discriminatory pricing structure to be effective in maximising revenue, several requirements have to be met.

1. The market concerned must be divisible into segments that are sufficiently identifiable, large, and distinct in respect of their different price-elasticites, time-preferences, and sensitivities to ticket restrictions to be accessible at reasonable cost. Price discrimination is therefore more likely in markets that have a well-dispersed mix of travellers and a significant traffic volume (Stavins, 1996).
2. Diversion of traffic from high-yield to low-yield fares must be controllable in order to minimise revenue dilution – the purpose of the restrictions mentioned above.
3. Consumers should be neither confused nor alienated by the pricing structure – a requirement that airlines have not, on the whole, been successful in meeting.
4. The incremental cost of administering the fare structure must not exceed the incremental revenue it generates.

In principle, it might be expected that price discrimination is less likely to be evident where a situation close to perfect competition prevails than where there is a monopolist well-informed about consumer preferences and value perceptions – the argument being that where competition is intense, the competitors have insufficient market power to charge prices substantially above marginal cost. In fact, various theoretical studies (e.g., Borenstein, 1985), together with an empirical study of the US domestic airline industry (Stavins, 1996), have argued the contrary: price discrimination increases with competition, and decreases as industry concentration rises. One possible explanation is that although monopolists and oligopolists have relatively little market power over consumers with high price-elasticities, weak time-preferences, and low pain thresholds with regard to ticket conditions, they exercise far more power over consumers – particularly business travellers – who have the opposite demand characteristics (ibid). The source of this market power has been argued to lie in network, schedule, and FFP benefits (ibid). (Note also that whereas in many industries price discrimination is reflected in the higher-than-standard prices paid by consumers over whom market power is exercised, in the airline business it has more typically been manifest in the limited access these consumers are given to discounted fares.)

Price discrimination under a single demand curve We have seen that the primary purposes of a discriminatory price structure are:

- to capture as much consumer surplus as possible from customers present in the market;
- to attract into the market customers whose willingness to pay is low enough that they might otherwise be excluded were a single uniform fare, or a limited range of fares, all that is offered;
- to redirect the demand of customers with weak time-preferences away from peak periods and towards more lightly loaded flights.

To maximise revenue by tapping into the consumer surplus that eludes it under a uniform pricing structure, an airline ideally needs to know each potential customer's 'reservation price' – that is, the maximum that each customer is prepared to pay given the value that he or she places on the service. Because this is clearly not possible, airlines cluster customers into a limited number of segments; members of each segment should have broadly similar price-elasticities. Figure 3.2(a) illustrates the approach, whilst figure 3.2(b) adapts figure 3.1(b) to show how an airline might target three separate segments with three different prices ($250, $400, and $500) in order to expand producer surplus by tapping into consumer surplus.

Price discrimination under different demand curves In fact, each segment in a market has its own demand function and demand curve. Segments which are not too dissimilar in terms of price-elasticity will have similar demand curves (assuming other determinants of demand are broadly the same), but segments that place very different values on a given service will also have very different demand curves. Figure 3.3 illustrates the case of business and leisure segments – the latter price-elastic, the former generally much less so – both travelling in the same cabin but paying different prices; their different price-elasticities are reflected in the shapes of the two demand curves.

Because both segments are served by the same product when they travel in the same cabin, the airline's marginal cost is shown as unchanged between the segments (something which, as we will see shortly, is not a point of view shared by all economists). (The horizontal marginal cost curve is purely illustrative; in practice, marginal cost is likely to vary with output.) If output is set where marginal cost and marginal revenue are equal, as theoretically it should be when profit-maximisation is a corporate objective,

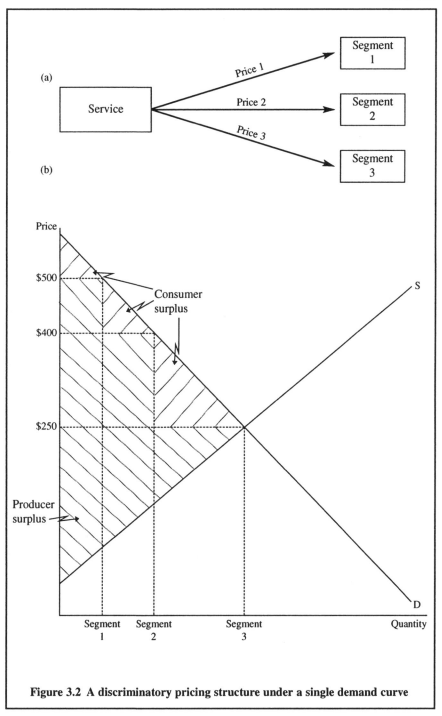

Figure 3.2 A discriminatory pricing structure under a single demand curve

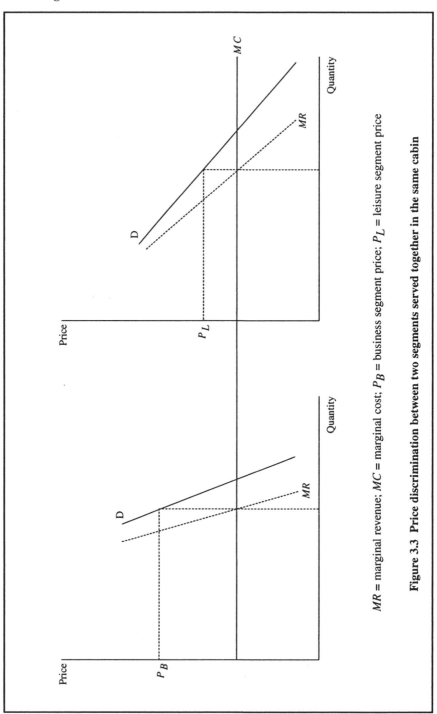

MR = marginal revenue; *MC* = marginal cost; P_B = business segment price; P_L = leisure segment price

Figure 3.3 Price discrimination between two segments served together in the same cabin

the prices that this implies for each segment are different because of the different shapes of their demand curves. (A price above marginal cost suggests that the carrier concerned is able to exert a degree of monopoly power; the impact would be felt more strongly in the business segment because of its relatively inelastic demand curve. We will return to this shortly.)

In fact, introducing the idea that more than one demand function and demand curve exists in respect of different segments travelling in the same cabin is not unproblematic insofar as it raises the question for some economists as to whether the different 'fare products' (i.e., tariffs – combinations of price and booking restrictions) offered to each do not in fact constitute 'differential', rather than 'discriminatory', pricing. The reasons why this might matter are considered next.

Differential pricing

If a market can be segmented by willingness to pay, the question arises as to whether segments can and should be served by different service packages. We have seen that if essentially the same service package is targeted at multiple segments and priced differently for each despite production costs being largely similar, we have a *discriminatory pricing* structure; theoretically, the ultimate goal of discriminatory pricing would be to shift consumer surplus entirely to the producer by having every passenger pay a fare that exactly matches the value he or she places on the service package – something that, as we will see in chapter 9, is the 'Holy Grail' of dynamic revenue management but is still some way off in practice. If, on the other hand, separate service packages are specifically designed and priced for different segments, we have a *differential pricing* structure.

In principle, we can argue that different onboard cabins and associated ground attributes (such as limousine service, valet parking, priority check-in and baggage claim, and/or lounge access) represent different service packages and are differently priced; within each cabin, price differences are the result of discriminatory pricing. This is illustrated in figure 3.4.

In fact, some practitioners and economists disagree with this analysis. Let us reconsider the situation. Differential pricing arises when different prices are charged for different products. If we take the case of a particular flight, everybody on the aircraft is sharing certain service attributes: the airline's network, its schedule (i.e., departure time), its punctuality, its safety, and – perhaps less uniformly – whatever benefits might be derived from its brand image. But there are also product differences to consider.

1. **Between cabins** We have seen that customers travelling in different cabins receive different inflight benefits and, in many cases, different

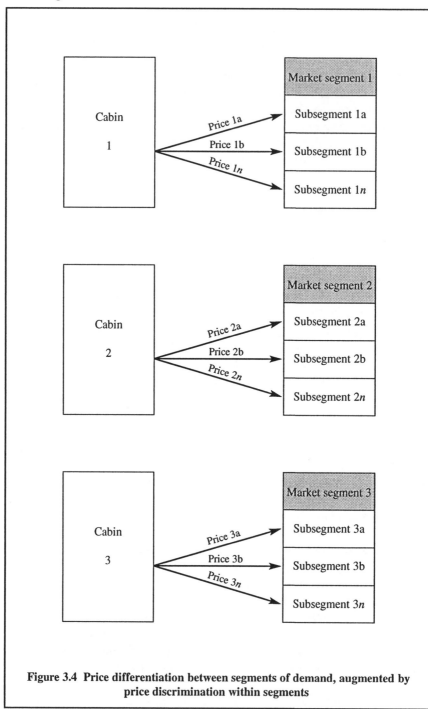

Figure 3.4 Price differentiation between segments of demand, augmented by price discrimination within segments

ground benefits. For these different benefits they pay different prices – a clear example of differential pricing.

2. **Within cabins** Most airlines now use revenue management systems (RMSs) which allocate seats within each cabin (or within the single cabin of a one-class service) to different booking (or 'fare') classes: the highest booking classes (at least on full-service network carriers) usually contain full, on-demand, unrestricted fares, whilst lower booking classes contain discounted fares with progressively tighter restrictions as the depth of the discount increases. The question is whether different fares in the same cabin carrying different booking conditions or usage restrictions represent different products – that is, whether we are dealing with discriminatory or differential pricing.

- *Discriminatory pricing* This view (which was taken in the last section above) accepts that customers travelling on restricted fares can cost less to carry in the same cabin than those travelling on full fares: restrictions on their freedom to reschedule or cancel can save administration and possibly GDS expenses, restrictions on stopovers can save handling costs, restrictions on interlining and on endorsement of the ticket to other carriers can save prorate dilution (which is discussed later in the chapter), and advance payment not only generates early cash flow but also (assuming cancellation restrictions) reduces revenue loss from no-shows. On the whole, however, these passengers are being charged a lower mark-up over marginal cost for essentially the same product compared to full-fare passengers in the same cabin. (Indeed, fares below marginal cost have been widely and persistently sold in some markets.)

- *Differential pricing* This view takes exception to the above argument on two related grounds. First, 'fare products' even within the same cabin are characterised as different; their willingness to pay more shows that high-yield passengers value the flexibility allowed by the fares they purchase. Flexibility is a service attribute, and although people might moan about paying for it, it is a valuable source of product differentiation – and, for the airline, a source of meaningful additional costs. Second, important but often overlooked marginal costs of serving high-yield segments include the cost of operating the large network and high frequencies that customers in these segments demand (Belobaba, 1998b), and the cost (in terms of lower load factors) involved in providing adequate seat-accessibility for passengers booking late or wanting to change itinerary at the last minute.

Developing the latter argument, Botimer (1993) has suggested that each fare represents a different product, defined in part by the flexibility associated with it, and that each has meaningfully different marginal costs of production. Rather than there being just a single demand curve for travel in a given cabin on a particular flight, there are multiple demand functions and demand curves attributable to the multiple segments comprised of people who place different values on different levels of ticket conditionality; importantly, there are also multiple marginal cost curves. According to this argument, the simple models of price discrimination illustrated in figures 3.2 and 3.3 are inappropriate – despite adopting an analytical approach that is widespread in the industry. The practical reason why this might matter is that pricing structures may well not reflect an accurate understanding of the demand curves or the segment elasticities that different prices are designed to tap, and – critically – neither might they reflect the true marginal costs of serving different segments.

Conclusion

The pricing freedom introduced by market deregulation and liberalisation has allowed many carriers to practice much finer and more dynamic price discrimination than was possible under the relatively static and simple price structures associated with most regulated markets. This has led to a reduction in real average fares in many markets as increases in full fares have been outweighed by the wider availability and deeper discounts associated with other fares, and it goes a long way towards accounting for the rapid traffic growth in deregulated and liberalised markets (Pickrell, 1991). Indeed, a significant proportion of the growth in air traffic since the 1960s has been due to price stimulation – a phenomenon reflected in declining real yields. Productivity improvements associated with significant changes in airframe and engine technologies and with business process efficiencies made necessary by intensified competition in liberalised markets have all assisted airlines as a whole in keeping their operating costs sufficiently under control to support declining real yields (although there have been some notable exceptions).

It remains to be seen whether the cost structures of European and North American full-service network carriers in particular can support significant further declines in real yields, or whether the best route to long-run survival for these operators lies in greater consolidation to restrain output growth and competition, together with a revised business model de-emphasising marginally profitable short-haul markets where the challenge of low-fare carriers is most intense. A question mark also hangs over the current pricing structure used by full-service airlines – a structure comprising very high full or unrestricted fares together with a complex web of deeply discounted but heavily restricted fares. In 1992, American tried unsuccessfully to rationalise the US domestic pricing structure by lowering on-demand fares and reducing the number and depth of discounts; most competitors failed to follow, and a damaging fare war resulted. In the wake of 9/11, the future of a business model built around exploiting the price-inelasticity of business travellers and the willingness of others to accept restrictions in return for deep discounts was brought into question as a result of both the reassessment of business travel budgets by corporate customers, and the inexorable growth of Southwest and other low-fare carriers offering consistently low and simple pricing alternatives.

ii. Tariff structures

'Fare structure' is a term encompassing the many different passenger fares that may be offered in a market at any point in time, whilst a 'rate structure' applies to freight traffic. Together with the specific terms and conditions applied to each fare or rate, these structures form 'tariff structures'. A tariff structure should be clear and straightforward enough to be easily understood, particularly by travel agents and others in external distribution channels, and yet also sufficiently layered to tap into the various levels of willingness to pay that exist in different segments; in fact, many tariff structures offered by full-service carriers have over time become complex and arcane. In principle, they should be driven by insight into the service expectations and price-elasticities of different segments of demand; in practice what actually happens is that structures evolve – sometimes haphazardly – in response to incremental market learning (Garvett and Michaels, 1998).

Passenger tariff structures

Pressures shaping passenger tariff structures

Two pressures in particular have contributed to increasingly complex tariff structures and price volatility.

1. Liberalisation and deregulation: airline managers have taken the opportunity to use price proactively as part of both tactical and strategic adjustments to the marketing mix.

2. The use of CRSs and RMSs to micromanage seat availability at different prices: pricing and revenue management have increasingly come to be used together to maximise revenue capture on a departure-by-departure basis. We will return to this in chapter 9.

Each tariff or 'fare basis' in a market can be identified by a fare basis code; depending upon the circumstances in a particular market and the pricing philosophy of the carrier concerned, 30 or more fare bases could be in use across the cabins of a full-service airline on a single departure. To simplify reservations and revenue management, fare bases are usually grouped into one of a small number of booking classes; whether or not a particular fare is available on request therefore depends not only upon whether its conditions (e.g., in respect of advance purchase) can be met, but also upon whether the relevant booking class is open. Variance between fares within a booking class should therefore be minimised, whilst variances between those in different booking classes should be maximised.

On the other hand, less well-resourced airlines or those, such as low-fare carriers, that have less complex strategic positions than full-service network majors, often prefer simple tariff structures that are sufficiently sensitive to tap the different price-elasticities of major segments and sub-segments of demand but at the same time are relatively cheap to manage.

Analysing passenger tariff structures

We have seen that the word 'tariff' refers to a combination of fare and conditions, and that the expression 'tariff structure' refers to the different tariffs available in a particular market. Tariff structures vary between markets, but a typical outline framework applicable to a full-service carrier is illustrated in figure 3.5.

Fares might be published or unpublished.

1. **Published fares** These are fares that are published to the world at large through industry-standard channels, notably the Airline Tariff Publishing Company (ATPCO) and SITA's AIRFARE system. If applicable to international markets and arrived at by resolution at an IATA traffic conference, they might be referred to as 'IATA fares'. They can usually be broken down into 'full' or 'normal' fares and 'special' or 'discounted' fares.

    *   *Normal or full fare* This is the unrestricted, on-demand or walk-up fare charged for travel in a particular cabin (i.e., first, business, or economy/coach) in a market at any given time. (A few carriers have a separate 'premium economy' cabin for full-fare economy

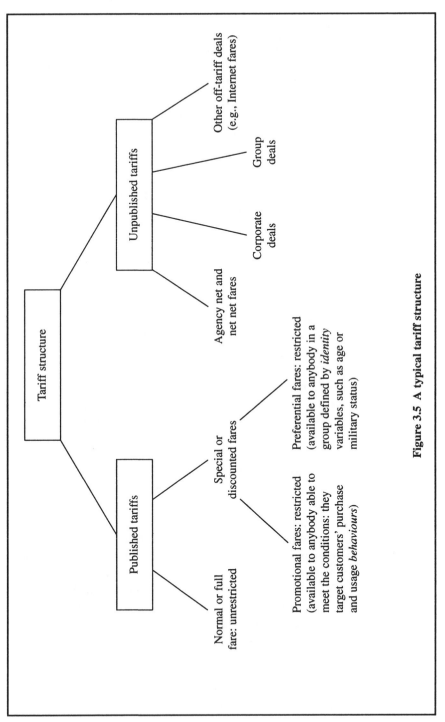

Figure 3.5 A typical tariff structure

class passengers on long-haul routes, keeping the standard economy cabin for others travelling on a range of discounted fares.) We saw in the last chapter that normal fares tend to rise sharply in most markets after liberalisation or deregulation and contribute a disproportionate amount of many full-service carriers' revenue. According to the Business Travel Coalition, at Northwest the 15 per cent of passengers travelling on these fares in the first half of 2001 accounted for 40 per cent of revenue. The normal or full fare can be looked upon as the 'pricing platform' for a carrier's service-price offers in a particular cabin in any given market. It is associated with booking classes such as: R (Concorde); P (long-haul first class) and F (primarily short-/medium-haul first class); J (long-haul business class) and C (primarily short-/medium-haul business class); and Y (coach in the United States and economy elsewhere).

- *Special or discounted fares* These are discounted off the price platform in each cabin and are available in most markets subject to restrictions; they are associated with alphanumeric codes that vary widely from market to market. Airlines commonly break them down into 'promotional' fares available to anybody willing to meet restrictions on booking (e.g., advance purchase) and/or usage (e.g., minimum or maximum stays at destination), and 'preferential' fares available by reference to factors such as age or employment status (e.g., whether retired or in military service). Promotional fares segment the market on the basis of customers' willingness to modify their *behaviour* to suit the airline's cost and revenue management objectives, whilst preferential fares segment on the basis of *identity*. There is no doubting that preferential fares are 'discriminatory' in the economists' sense of the word; as we have seen, whether different promotional fares offered for travel in any one cabin are examples of discriminatory pricing (under one demand curve) or differential pricing (in which case we need to be thinking in terms of several demand curves and different marginal costs of production) is open to debate.

A tiered structure of promotional fares subject to different conditions is now a permanent feature of most markets, and in addition to these it is common for short-term offers to be made to promote a particular service or destination or to offload 'distressed' inventory. Whilst a lot of surplus inventory is distributed through both traditional and online agencies, airlines in some markets commonly initiate their own 'fare sales' (both online and offline), and a few have even branded these short-term promotions (e.g., British Airways' 'World Offers'). Changes in purchase or usage conditions are also often used for competitive purposes alongside changes in price; this happened in the US domestic market when traffic needed stimulating after 9/11, for example.

One final point is that although a primary purpose underlying ticket conditionality is to avoid the revenue dilution that arises when potential full-fare passengers (notably business travellers) trade-down, normal fares in some markets have become so high that a meaningful percentage of business travellers find ways to use discounted fares; in the US domestic market during early 2001, over half of some network carriers' passengers were estimated to be travelling on business yet only around 15 per cent were paying full economy or first class fares (Flint, 2001). This takes us back to the question raised above regarding the long-term sustainability of the current full-service pricing model – at least in US domestic (and mainline intra-European) markets.

2. **Unpublished fares** These are fares offered through specific distribution channels which involve prices (and/or relaxation of ticket conditionality) that are unavailable through general channels. The use of unpublished tariffs owes something to the history of airline pricing and distribution practices.

    *   In some (particularly long-haul international) markets where fares were tightly regulated and airlines themselves were unable to compete openly on price, it became usual for a complex multi-tiered distribution system comprised of different types of agencies (e.g., general sales agents (GSAs), consolidators, and 'bucket shops') to wholesale and retail tickets at 'unpublished' fares. This was the only way of establishing anything close to a market-clearing price structure in many regulated markets, and to the extent that it transferred the risks inherent in price competition to the agencies involved it is a system not without merit from an airline's perspective.

    *   In liberalised markets, however, airlines have the freedom to adopt a more complex structure of published fares and to use RMSs to ration space availability at each of these different fares.

In fact, unpublished fares remain significant in many liberalised and deregulated markets. Figure 3.5 provides some examples.

    *   *Net net fares* These are a feature of several international markets in particular and are notably important in Asia. A 'net' fare in this context is the gross fare for a block of seats sold to an agency (possibly the normal fare or perhaps an IATA group inclusive tour (GIT) fare) less standard commission and any other 'fare adjustment' typically applied in the market concerned; the 'net net fare'

is the net fare less any volume or other incentive (including travel agency commission overrides (TACOs) – volume- or market-share-dependent supplemental incentives) offered by the airline to a particular agency with which it has targeted a special relationship. (The airline might, in addition, offer 'low season', non-volume 'spot incentives'.)

The lower the net net fare available to an agency, the lower the price it is able to charge retail consumers (or the higher the profit margin it can earn). Agencies offered net net fares sometimes subcontract with smaller retail outlets (still referred to in some markets as 'bucket shops') to broaden distribution and help them retain and increase volume incentives available from the airline – although the development of Internet distribution channels is likely to accelerate the erosion of this structure that has already begun in several markets.

- *Other off-tariff arrangements* Corporate (including government) and group deals are broadly self-explanatory. Individually negotiated corporate arrangements, also widely referred to as 'net fares' because they are sold net of agency commissions, might involve a discount off the prevailing published fare and/or a relaxation of booking and usage conditions; in the US market, negotiated 'flat' or fixed-price fares and also pre-paid bulk purchases are common. Alternatively, an end-of-period rebate might be payable by an airline to a corporate client based on actual sales.

  Sometimes fares based on a GIT tariff and intended to be incorporated into a bundled vacation package are sold instead on a seat-only basis. Other increasingly important sources of off-tariff deals include online distributors and airlines' own web-sites, both of which are used to unload seats at prices unavailable through other channels. Some offers made directly by full-service airlines target late-available unsold seats at participating members of their FFPs; not only is this a useful outlet for 'distressed' inventory, but it also provides the opportunity to learn about different customers' responses to different offers – and perhaps to build a deeper brand relationship with customers than can be achieved by using third party distribution channels.

The average fare from a flight, in a market, or across a network is total revenue divided by the number of enplaned passengers. Yield, as we will see later in the chapter, is a distance-weighted metric calculated by dividing RPMs (or RTMs) into total revenue. Because total revenue is a function of the different fares available and the number of customers buying each of them, both average fare and yield will be sensitive to tariff structures.

Conclusion In order to make sense of sometimes highly complex passenger tariff structures, it is helpful to use four analytical dimensions: class of service; time of travel; ticket conditionality; and bundling.

- **Class of service** This dimension corresponds to onboard cabins and associated ground and inflight amenities – or, broadly, to choice of service package.
- **Time of travel** Time-dependency manifests itself in two ways.
  - *Peak-/off-peak pricing* Whilst the use of peak-period surcharges on normal fares is not unknown, neither is it particularly common. Off-peak discounting, most notably in coach/economy cabins, is a widespread feature of the industry.
  - *Inventory allocation* An alternative and widely used approach is to rely on an RMS to allocate most seats on peak departures for high-yielding fares, so limiting the availability of lower fares. This in effect protects more seats for customers who have strong time-preferences that make them willing to pay higher fares to travel on peak departures, and restricts availability for lower-yield demand with weaker time-preferences – spilling the latter onto off-peak departures (or the peak departures of less yield-sensitive competitors).
- **Booking restrictions** We saw earlier in the chapter that in order to target identified segments of demand and/or respond to competitive conditions in particular markets, an airline will offer a range of different fares for travel in each cabin – particularly the economy/coach cabin. Full, on-demand fares (on full-service carriers) are usually unrestricted insofar as they can be used for travel at any time within 12 months, can be rescheduled or rerouted (subject to maximum permitted mileage restrictions), and refunded in full if unused. Fares discounted off the full-fare price platform for travel in a particular cabin in a particular market in order to stimulate demand from price-sensitive segments or sub-segments are, as we saw above, subject to conditions intended to minimise the diversion of price-insensitive, time-sensitive traffic towards low-yield fares. (On some low-fare carriers, all fares are subject to booking and/or usage restrictions and prices vary only in response to the advance booking period.)
- **Bundling** In leisure markets, airfares are commonly bundled together with surface arrangements such as airport transfers, car hire, and accommodation to produce an inclusive product. Most frequently this

bundling is done by tour operators to which airlines sell heavily discounted space.

In some markets, prices charged by network carriers may also reflect the choice of routing – as when an O & D fare is higher for nonstop service than for connecting service over a hub. Whether or not this is the case will often depend upon competitive conditions in the market concerned.

Tariff setting

Domestic markets In the US domestic market, airlines set fares as they wish and file them with fare distributors (notably ATPCO but also SITA), from where they are communicated to participating GDSs and other airlines' CRSs for use in fare construction. Hundreds of thousands of daily amendments pass through these systems. In other domestic markets the level of government intervention in tariff setting varies widely. On public policy grounds, some national authorities (e.g., Malaysia) have imposed price ceilings to maintain low domestic airfares, whereas others keep prices artificially high to protect inefficient national carriers. But on the whole, airlines now have a great deal more pricing freedom than they had in the relatively recent past (e.g., within the European Union (EU), Canada, Australasia, and most Latin American countries).

International markets In many international markets a tariff structure for scheduled services is agreed at semi-annual IATA regional traffic conferences, filed with the appropriate governments as required under the terms of the bilateral air services agreement (ASA) in force between the countries concerned, and then published. As an alternative to multilateral tariff coordination, published fares in a particular market might be arrived at by agreement between carriers designated by the states at either end of that market, or they might be developed and filed by individual airlines; the United States is on the whole unfavourably disposed towards IATA traffic conferences and prefers each carrier (together with its alliance partners, where antitrust immunity has been granted) to establish fares autonomously within the context of whatever ASA applies.

ASAs usually incorporate one of several tariff approval mechanisms. In increasing order of liberalism these are:

- double approval: both governments must approve every filing;
- country of origin: each government approves filings in respect of tariffs outbound from its jurisdiction (one way or return), but has no power to approve or disapprove inbound tariffs;

- double disapproval: both governments must disapprove any filing in order to prevent it coming into effect.

A less common variant is the 'designated carrier' approach, which gives each government the right to approve or disapprove only filings by its own designated carrier(s), irrespective of the country in which travel originates. Separately, some bilaterals allow for automatic approval of tariffs within specified zones around pre-determined reference levels. Different zones might, for example, be defined for first class, business class, full economy/ coach, discount, and deep discount tariffs. Filings outside these zones would be dealt with by the normal method required under the terms of the bilateral concerned (i.e., double approval, country of origin, etc.).

Where open skies bilaterals or agreements having a similar effect have been entered into, either double disapproval or automatic approval might be agreed. The result in the latter case is that neither government has any right to disallow a tariff filing unless – perhaps – it is by some standard determined to be excessively high (and possibly therefore an abuse of dominant position), artificially low (and therefore perhaps predatory), or unreasonably discriminatory.

Tariffs governing nonscheduled services have typically been subject to unilateral state control; many countries continue to ban inbound charters in order to protect their national airlines' scheduled services. However, an increasing number of bilaterals now incorporate clauses in respect of nonscheduled operations, and where this is the case 'country of origin' tariff approval tends to be the rule.

Freight rate structures

Until the early 1980s, international freight rates were largely regulated in much the same way as passenger fares. Nominal competitors agreed rates within the IATA framework and submitted them for rubber-stamping by their governments under the terms of bilateral ASAs. Since then, rates have become a very much more active element in the marketing mix on most international routes and there is now considerable price competition, particularly for the business of shippers and forwarders moving large quantities. Indeed, rates in most major markets are effectively deregulated.

An increasingly complex rate structure evolved during the decades before the 1980s. Box 3.1 summarises this structure.

Box 3.1: The 'traditional' freight rate structure

Subject to some variation between markets, the following structure and terminology came into widespread use.

General cargo or commodity rate *This became the baseline, 'normal' tariff. 'Class rates' are upward or downward adjustments to the general rate in respect of certain categories of goods; an example of an upward adjustment, referred to as an 'exception rate' in the United States, is the carriage of live animals or other shipments that need special handling. The general rate might also be subject to quantity discount, escalating at each of several break-points, to encourage consolidation. Although the situation varies depending upon the level of competition on any given route, only difficult, emergency or very small shipments would move at or close to the general rate. General rates might be agreed at IATA traffic conferences (possibly with different rates applicable depending upon direction of travel).*

Specific commodity rates *These were introduced into various markets and applied to goods relevant to the city-pair concerned, with the objective of countering weak or erratic demand or perhaps just stimulating the market generally – often to help fill burgeoning belly-hold capacity. They are numerous, and are intended specifically to stimulate the use of airfreight by shippers of targeted commodities rather than simply being a figure keyed-off the general rate and adjusted to reflect differential costs. Indeed, specific commodity rates became dominant in some markets, much as discriminatory fares have become in many passenger markets. They proliferated and became extremely complex in their application, both because of wide variations in practice between different markets and because precise definitions of the qualifying commodities have proven cumbersome. Again, weight-breaks usually determine the size of any discounts; minimum charges have tended to be higher than in respect of the general rate. Specific commodity rates have nonetheless contributed substantially to declining cargo yields in some markets.*

Bulk unitisation *Another by-product of the rapidly increasing availability of belly-hold capacity aboard growing numbers of new widebodied aircraft in the 1970s and 1980s was the introduction of lower rates for shipments prepacked onto or into unit load devices (ULDs) – irrespective of the commodity(ies) concerned. The advantage of ULDs for airlines is that they involve lower handling costs because they are ready to load. The usual practice would be to levy a minimum charge per kilo in respect of each* *pallet or container on the assumption that the weight of the shipment is equivalent to a certain 'pivot weight'; if the actual weight turns out to be in excess of the pivot weight, any difference would be charged at a rate more favourable than the general rate. The disadvantage of bulk unitisation was that airlines ceded even more control over their markets to large forwarders able to consolidate shipments from a wide range of shippers and smaller forwarders.*

Contract rates *These increasingly came to be offered to shippers or forwarders able to commit to significant tonnages irrespective of commodity type or ULD usage – although ULDs often benefited from price incentives. In some markets such contract rates were referred to as freight-all-kinds (FAK) rates, but in other cases FAK became simply a term synonymous with the general cargo rate or, indeed, any rate not confined to a specific commodity.*

To this structure might be added special seasonal and promotional rates, higher rates for reserved space on a specific flight, and also ad hoc rates for late-booking shipments on lightly loaded departures.

The traditional rate structure has now been largely superseded in most important markets by a cocktail of 'standard retail' and directly negotiated rates. In addition to the effect of prevailing economic conditions on airfreight demand generally, there are several other structural factors within the industry that are combining to affect pricing.

1. **Downward pressures**
   - In many medium- and long-haul markets, freight rates can be even more volatile than passenger fares where substantial volumes of belly-hold capacity are available on passenger aircraft relative to off-peak demand in the market concerned or relative to the directionality of demand. This is particularly true when widebody twins are operated at a high frequency, and when fifth and sixth freedom carriers with by-product approaches to airfreight costing have to price aggressively to win business from better established third and fourth freedom airlines. (Freedoms of the air and different approaches to costing will be discussed in chapters 4 and 5 respectively.)
   - The negotiation of discounts below 'retail' levels for individual high-volume shippers and forwarders is now widespread. Most airlines still rely heavily on forwarders to generate traffic, and having to deal with this relatively small number of buyers inevitably weak-

ens their control over pricing. The situation is becoming more acute as the forwarding industry consolidates, with close to half the world's airfreight now being shipped by around 12–15 intermediaries.

2. **Upward pressure** A small number of combination carriers (i.e., airlines which fly freight as well as passengers) now offer a range of 'branded' assembly, distribution, and time-definite transportation services in addition to straightforward airport-to-airport haulage; some are offered in partnership with preferred forwarders – the intention being to create a 'virtual' door-to-door network capable of competing with integrated carriers such as FedEx and UPS.

   Integrated carriers offer simple rate structures based on door-to-door service and required transit time. The standard of service provided by these carriers, and particularly their use of time and value-added on the ground rather than the nature of shipped commodities as a basis for pricing (unless special handling is required), have changed customer expectations in many airfreight markets. Some combination carriers and all-cargo airlines have responded, whilst others remain committed to traditional, relatively low-yield, airport-to-airport line-haul services targeted primarily at forwarders.

The payload–volume trade-off

An aspect of the freight pricing challenge not seen on the passenger side of the industry is the need to optimise the payload–volume trade-off such that revenue from available cargo capacity is maximised given the type of aircraft operating a service. Every aircraft has a fixed volumetric capacity for the carriage of freight, and a payload capacity that will vary depending upon the weight of fuel and (where relevant) passengers carried on a particular departure. Clearly, there is no merit in filling (i.e., 'cubing out') available space with a light-weight commodity and then charging shipment on the basis of weight; at the other extreme, neither is there merit in carrying maximum payload in the form of a dense commodity and then charging on the basis of volume. Applying a minimum charge based on assumed weight per unit of cubic capacity (i.e., 'dimensional weight') is one way of managing this trade-off. Generally, airfreight pricing structures have to be designed to maximise revenue by carefully managing charges for weight carried and volume taken-up.

iii. Price drivers

What drives pricing? To help answer this question, it is useful to assume floor and ceiling prices: the floor is set by airline costs, because rational producers do not sell below cost; the ceiling is defined by whatever value customers place on the service being bought. That this is an idealised model of reality is borne out by the following quotation.

> Every thriving businessperson knows that you have to sell a product for more than it costs to make. But there is more to this simple-sounding concept than meets the eye. How should costs be defined? Fully-allocated versus marginal? Short-run versus long run? Tangible versus opportunity? Once this dilemma is addressed, rational pricers learn that the basic rule is true only on average. Prices may be below average costs in off-peak times and significantly above in peak times. Prices may be below average costs for elastic leisure and visiting friends and relations (VFR) passengers and above average for inelastic commercial customers. Customers may pay different amounts based on their relative negotiating leverage.
>
> Thus it becomes clear that pricing occurs in both the world of cost and the world of demand. As a result, skilled pricers will consider cost factors as constraints and demand factors as a primary driver (Garvett and Michaels, 1998: 335).

The fact is that there can be sound competitive reasons for pricing below cost, especially in the short run. The image of a floor and ceiling is nonetheless helpful because it opens the idea of a space within which forces play out to determine how much value created by a service is captured by consumers (as consumer surplus) and how much by the airline providing it.

Costs

On a systemwide basis, there is certainly evidence that costs can feed directly into fares. We see this with fuel surcharges when oil prices spike. Another example came in late 2000 when United followed-up a handsomely rewarding contract for its pilots by increasing unrestricted domestic fares by ten per cent. Using a market-specific frame of reference, however, it is generally true that fares owe more to customers' willingness to pay for what is offered than to the costs of offering it (Smith et al, 1998).

There are in fact plenty of 'disconnects' between airline costs and individual fares.

1. Many airline services are characterised by 'production interrelatedness'. There are two types of production interrelatedness.

   - *By-products* A by-product is output arising unplanned from production of another product. Some carriers argue that this is the case in respect of belly-hold space on passenger services.
     - Many airlines do indeed price belly-hold freight on a by-product basis. They expect revenue to cover direct ground-handling costs, incremental fuel-burn, and freight sales and administration overhead, and beyond this to make a positive contribution to the rest of the airline's income statement – but they do not expect it to cover an allocated share of operating and nonoperating costs not directly attributable to the carriage of freight.
     - Other carriers, particularly those that have spun cargo operations off into separate subsidiaries or profit centres, expect cargo revenues at least to cover fully allocated costs: direct operating costs of a combination flight not specific to cargo (e.g., pilots' salaries and flight despatch costs) might, for example, be allocated between passenger and cargo products on the basis of aircraft volume; corporate overhead could be allocated to cargo products proportionate to their share of direct costs (both specific and allocated).

     Clearly, the use of a by-product approach as a pricing input is likely to lead to lower cargo rates than fully allocated costing – a point that can become particularly knotty when it comes to interlining freight between alliance partners who take different approaches to costing and pricing.

   - *Joint production* A more complex example is joint production of cargo space on a combi aircraft that has both types of capacity on its main deck. Here, output in the two categories is produced deliberately rather than one being a by-product of the other. The complication in this case arises from the opportunity that exists to vary the capacity of each category, unlike belly-hold cargo space which is largely fixed (subject, on some aircraft types, to options to locate galleys and/or sleeping quarters below deck). Another example of joint production arises when passengers travelling from and to a number of different origins and destinations share a particular flight as part of their respective journeys over a hub or other transfer point. And, of course, on any one flight the output associated with different cabins is jointly produced.

   Some airlines use complex cost attribution formulas, whereas others either cannot or choose not to be precise in linking costs to specific fares and freight rates. There is a strong argument that in a network-oriented service business, the further we move away from total cost the further we are venturing into the realm of opinion. This does not mean that efforts to cost the delivery of specific services to specific market segments on specific flight-legs are pointless; what it does suggest is that efforts to argue a tight linkage between these costs and individual fares or freight rates are open to question.

2. When an airline serves a given route with very different aircraft types, each having different seat-mile costs, this is not reflected in fares. Indeed, it might be that off-peak fares are offered for flights which – because of lower demand at the times concerned – are operated by smaller aircraft having higher seat-mile costs than larger aircraft scheduled onto the route at other times to accommodate peak demand. In the freight sector, rates do not distinguish between aircraft used (e.g., passenger, combi or freighter), or the circuity of the route taken between origin and destination, despite very different costs.

3. Passenger fares and freight rates generally taper with distance so that the monetary amount paid per mile for a short journey will tend to be higher than the amount per mile for a significantly longer trip. The reason for this is that aircraft operating costs taper because take-offs and landings, which are expensive activities due to fuel consumption and airport charges respectively, form a much greater proportion of trip costs on short legs than on longer sectors. Long stage-lengths are also often associated with higher aircraft utilisation, producing more output over which to spread fixed and overhead costs. However, fares tend to taper less than costs (presumably in part because of the lack of inter-modal competition on medium- and long-haul routes). Furthermore, the rate at which fares taper is inconsistent across different routes of similar length operated by the same airline using a given aircraft type – with the rate of taper appearing to owe more to the intensity of competition than to airline costs.

4. It is not uncommon for point-to-point services into a hub from a given origin to be more expensive than connecting services from the same origin to a destination beyond the hub. At the time of writing, it is cheaper to buy a return Milan–London–New York business class ticket on British Airways than a return London–New York ticket; it is cheaper to buy a London–Dubai–Bangkok economy class return on Emirates than a London–Dubai return on the same carrier. This type of sixth freedom pricing across international hubs is far from being unusual, and neither is the same phenomenon unknown across US domestic hubs. Even carriers offering services as highly regarded as British Airways and Emirates, and able to sustain relatively high yields in third

and fourth freedom markets, have to respond in many of their sixth freedom markets to the fact that consumers generally value connecting services less than nonstop (or even direct) services – irrespective of the relative costs to the airlines concerned of providing these different types of 'route attribute'.

5. Directional fare differentials exist in a number of long-haul markets. Sometimes these are in part attributable to currency exchange rates, but often they are not. Directional fare differentials (and, incidentally, freight rate differentials) have been particularly marked over the North Pacific, with passengers originating in Asia historically paying more than passengers travelling between the same city-pairs but originating in North America.

Notwithstanding that it was broadly used as the basis for setting US domestic fares prior to deregulation, cost-plus pricing is difficult to apply in practice because there are so many different ways to define the airline 'product' and – as is explained in chapter 5 – so many possible definitions of 'cost' and methods of cost allocation. It is now some way from being the norm, although the smaller an airline is and the more simple its network, the easier a linkage between costs and prices should in principle be to establish. There is anyway an argument that prices should drive costs, rather than the other way around: the sequence (known as 'target costing') is to design service-price offers suitable for the markets and segments being targeted, then get costs down to ensure that forecasted demand can be served profitably.

In the final analysis, customers' willingness to pay for a service is based on the value they place on the package of benefits offered by that service; what it costs the airline concerned to assemble and deliver the package is irrelevant to the customer. How far an airline can eat into consumer surplus by charging a price as close as possible to the value that targeted customers place on the perceived benefits offered by the service concerned will depend upon the degree of 'monopoly power' the carrier is able to exercise.

Monopoly power

An airline does not need to be a pure monopolist (i.e., a sole supplier) to have 'monopoly power' in a market. Many economists define 'monopoly power' as an ability to set price above marginal cost, and they tie this ability into an inverse relationship with the price-elasticity of demand a firm is facing: the less elastic the demand curve, the more monopoly power the firm is likely to have.

Price-elasticity of demand

The price-elasticity of demand faced by any airline is a function of three factors: the price-elasticity of market demand; the number of competitors in the market; and competitive interaction among carriers (Pindyck and Rubinfeld, 2001).

The price-elasticity of market demand We saw in chapter 2 that whether we are dealing with an entire market or a segment of it, the individual demand curve facing any airline serving that market or segment will always be more elastic than the market demand curve (unless the carrier concerned is a pure monopolist, in which case the individual and market demand curves are identical). The price-elasticity of market (or segment) demand places a limit on a carrier's potential monopoly power. The more price-elastic a demand curve, the narrower in general will be the gap between the cost of producing the next unit of output (i.e., the 'marginal cost') and the price that can be charged for it; the narrower this gap, the less monopoly power the carrier can be said to have. If the proportion of total traffic that is travelling for leisure purposes continues to grow as forecast, it can be expected that the generally higher price-elasticity of this segment will contribute to higher aggregate price-elasticity for the industry as well as for many individual O & D markets.

The number of competitors present in the market If we take the global air transport market as a whole, there is a large number of airlines providing output. If instead we look at individual city-pair markets, the number of competitors is invariably much smaller. Just how many airlines are present in any one market will depend upon:

- regulation – whether or not there are route licensing, designation or similar barriers to entry;
- geography – whether the origin and destination are far enough apart to allow for connecting services over one or more intermediate hubs to compete with direct and/or nonstop services (and, if the market is international, what pricing and capacity rights the sixth freedom carriers have with regard to flow traffic); and
- economic attractiveness – whether the density and/or traffic mix appeal to potential entrants.

A persistent issue of debate has been whether or not carriers that dominate 'fortress hubs' are able to charge a 'hub premium' by exerting monopoly power over O & D traffic originating at, or destined for, these hubs. The primary source of this power would be high market share concentration, augmented by the attractiveness of a hub carrier's frequent flyer, corporate discount, and agency incentive programmes given that it serves a far wider range of destinations from the hub than any single competing carrier; as we saw in chapter 2, the effect of these might be to shift the demand curve to the right and so allow a higher price to be charged for a given volume of output. Since the late 1980s various studies have come down on each side of the argument, but there has been no universally agreed conclusion in respect of hub premia (Beyer, 2000).

There is nonetheless intuitive appeal in the view that the higher the concentration ratio in a market, the more monopoly power incumbents are likely to exercise. As markets become progressively more open and competitive, their price-elasticities increase and firms are able to exert less monopoly power. There is therefore a continuum of pricing possibilities dependent in part upon the number of competitors in a market. Neoclassical microeconomics identifies four idealised market structure models along this continuum: perfect competition, monopolistic competition, oligopoly, and monopoly. We will look at these models in the next chapter. What they pay little attention to, however, is behavioural influences on competitive interaction.

Competitive interaction among carriers   Markets dominated by just two full-service carriers are frequently at best arenas of competitive inertia, and at worst of tacit – sometimes even explicit – collusion. Conversely, where one or more low-fare carriers are present in a market they almost invariably have the effect of driving down prices by offering lower fares and/or fewer restrictions than full-service carriers. Clearly, the attitudes and behaviour of other players – rather than just their number – can be a profound influence on the ability of a carrier to exercise monopoly power (in the sense defined above). (This explains the centrality of the 'intensity of competitive rivalry' in Porter's five-forces model of market structure that we met in chapter 1.) Similarly, if two airlines that formerly competed on a route decide to enter into an alliance, it is quite possible that prices will move away from a competitive level and begin to squeeze consumer surplus.

With regard to the last point, however, there are three reasons why an alliance might not in fact lead to higher fares.

- It can be argued that if an alliance results in cost savings compared to the pre-existing situation, the post-alliance exploitation of monopoly power – reflected in prices significantly above (the new) costs – might not inevitably mean that prices are any higher than before the alliance;

in other words, margins will have widened without fares increasing. (Ideally, of course, cost savings should be shared with consumers.)

- In a contestable market freely accessible to potential competitors, excessive profits might – in principle – attract challengers.
- Excessive profits could provoke scrutiny from competition authorities.

With the exception of some remaining state-owned 'flag carriers', the managements of most airlines these days have a reasonable degree of influence, and very often near total control, over the formulation of goals and objectives. These might not necessarily entail setting a profit-maximising price which covers total costs by encompassing variable and fixed costs of the services concerned together with allocated corporate overhead. They could, for example, result in pricing strategies that place fares close to short-run marginal cost in order to expand market share and/or drive out competitors with less financial staying power. If a carrier is in financial difficulties, low prices which are unsustainable in the long run could be justifiable to generate cash.

The behavioural dimension is well illustrated by Northwest's aggressive price-cutting in the spring of 1992 (Gertner, 1993). The crucial driver in this case was management's response to perceived competitive asymmetries. With a relatively weak route network and a poor service image at the time, the only way for Northwest to boost traffic substantially in the teeth of a major recession was seen to be to force an industry price cut so large that at least some of the significant amount of incremental traffic entering the market would inevitably be spilled from stronger competitors onto its own services. Northwest's choice of timing was driven by the fact that summer is the peak period for discretionary travel and that demand from discretionary travellers is more price-elastic and less quality-sensitive than other types of demand.

Product differentiation

Price-elasticity of demand is therefore an important determinant of monopoly power. In addition, there is also the possibility that through innovative service design, the development of a strong brand image, and the nurturing of a loyal customer base a carrier might be able to differentiate its services – thereby creating a quasi-monopoly within the market(s) or segment(s) concerned. In this situation, the airline could possibly sustain a price premium – at least until competitors make a preferable offer; the more price-elastic the segment concerned, the less viable this product strategy will tend to be.

The feasibility of premium pricing is subject to three influences.

- *Economic conditions* It is always easier to charge a premium for a differentiated product or a strong brand image during periods of economic prosperity. What was troubling in some markets during 2000–2001, even before 9/11, was that corporations were taking a much stronger line on travel expenditure even though recession was just a potential threat rather than an established fact.
- *Competition* In due course, 'fast followers' will catch up. British Airways' innovations in long-haul first and business classes during the mid- and late-1990s gave it only short two- or three-year windows over competitors such as Singapore Airlines. The question then is whether any premium price established in a particular market will become the new price platform for the cabin concerned in that market, or whether it will be eroded by competitors charging 'less for more'.
- *Customers' perceptions of value* Customers must feel that the product offers sufficient incremental value to justify a higher price.

Customer value

The ceiling in our simple model of cost drivers is set by customer value. Referring back to chapter 1, where customer value was discussed in a strategic context, we can recall that it has four elements (figure 1.2): perceived benefit offered by a service (in the minds of customers); value created (perceived benefit less all input costs); consumer surplus (perceived benefit less the monetary price paid by customers); and seller's profit (monetary price paid by customers less input costs). The difference between value-based pricing and a cost-plus approach is that the latter starts with costs and then turns to the market, whereas the former looks first to the market – the assumption being that in liberalised or deregulated environments it is the market that decides what can be charged for a given level of service.

A value-based approach to pricing endeavours to pitch price at a level that is above costs and as close as possible to the amount that the customer is willing to pay given her perceptions of the benefits offered by a particular service package. This perception is to a large extent moulded by the manner in which service design and the other marketing mix variables are managed in order to build value in customers' minds. (A product's perceived benefits and the value placed on them by customers are inevitably very difficult to measure with precision; techniques used in some industries include the reservation price method, the attribute rating method, conjoint analysis, and hedonic pricing analysis, all of which are briefly explained in Besanko et al (2000) and are at least touched upon in modern marketing texts. Their use in the airline industry is at an early stage of development.)

Some airlines offer relatively low levels of perceived benefit, but compensate for this with low prices – prices that are nonetheless profitable because of these carriers' low input costs and/or high resource productivity; this is the strategic path chosen by most low-fare airlines and European charter carriers. Others concentrate on maximising perceived benefits, particularly for segments of demand prepared to pay higher prices in return for those benefits; this approach underlies the continuous cycle of product upgrades and relaunches in, for example, long-haul business and first class cabins.

One of management's most important tasks is therefore to decide on the level of service to be offered, and then provide it at a cost lower than the price the market is prepared to pay (bearing in mind that we are here talking averages, because what price the market will pay for a service is variable not only between different segments but across a network and in response to daily, weekly, and seasonal demand peaks in the markets concerned). If competitors can produce a similar service package more cheaply and choose to reflect this in their prices, or if competitors with a lower cost base can profitably offer a better service package at the same price, an airline will find the loyalty of its customers tested.

It is a clever trick, of course, to assess correctly the needs of each targeted segment, design a service that satisfies those needs and is perceived by consumers to meet their expectations, and then pitch the price platform correctly in the context of other marketing mix variables and rather imprecisely estimated elasticities. Nonetheless, there is strong theoretical appeal in value-based pricing insofar as it is keyed off demand, elasticities, and market positioning rather than costs – and the closer an airline can get to charging a fare that equates to the maximum that target customers would be willing to pay, the more of the added value in an air transport service it is capturing for itself.

Conclusion

As markets are progressively freed from tight commercial regulation, prices are increasingly being set by reference to estimations of customer value and in response to the interplay of competitive forces. It is therefore up to airlines to ensure that their costs allow profitable production of the services they choose to deliver at prices customers are prepared to pay. Of course, market structure is clearly an important influence on prices even in liberalised and deregulated markets. Despite all the talk of consolidation and globalisation, the airline industry remains fragmented. Carriers operate in multiple O & D markets that are each differently affected by competition and by the varying demand elasticities of the particular types of traffic that predominate. The same airline's pricing behaviour will therefore not necessarily be consistent between a market dominated by business traffic in which it faces little or no competition (and may therefore have significant 'monopoly power'), and a highly competitive leisure market.

In practice, the management time spent on pricing has often been much less than that spent on other marketing mix variables. This is in part because the industry has a long history of setting prices in a noncompetitive commercial environment which allowed costs (identifiable at a systemwide level, less accurately on a leg- or product-specific basis) to be passed on to customers relatively freely. It is also because much of the information that economists like to assume is available for plugging into pricing models is, in reality, difficult to come by and often of dubious efficacy. More fundamentally, it is very difficult for any airline to assess in monetary terms the benefits and sacrifices embedded in the products being offered to each of its targeted markets and segments – notwithstanding the availability of tools such as discrete choice analysis, conjoint analysis, and quality function deployment (Besanko et al, 2000; Bounds et al, 1994).

Some airlines are nonetheless working on systems designed to predict what different market segments are prepared to pay for specific services at particular times. Several carriers have been developing automated systems able to make pricing decisions that respond to the quality of their services (which might vary from market to market depending upon routing and schedule, for example) relative to what is offered by direct competitors; demand elasticities associated with different service attributes are also factored in. The goal of interactive automation efforts is to encompass product design (including schedule and routing), segment demand elasticities in respect of price and various service attributes, competitors' offers, and both the cost and revenue outcomes of different pricing and distribution alternatives within a single marketing decision support system.

This sort of capability remains a distant prospect for most airlines (and for some – notably low-fare carriers – most probably an irrelevance). It is nonetheless true that in many parts of the world price is becoming an ever more sensitive element in the industry's marketing mix. Price is now both a strategic variable – a platform that helps define the positioning of different services – and a tactical variable used, in conjunction with RMSs, to respond to and help manage short-run demand fluctuations in individual markets.

iv. Tactical pricing

Scheduling and pricing are symbiotic activities – the same coin with different questions on either side depending upon the direction from which it is approached: Given the pricing structure in this market, how much output should be produced and when? Given the schedule we have published for this market, what is the best pricing structure to maximise revenue? This section of the chapter will take the second perspective, looking at how pricing structures can be used to maximise revenue from a given schedule (and therefore setting the scene for consideration of revenue management in chapter 9).

Revenue maximisation is achieved (by pricing and revenue management together) in two ways:

- maximising capture of consumer surplus by ensuring that passengers carried pay fares as close as possible to their reservation prices; and
- broadening the customer base by selling to price-elastic customers who might not otherwise travel (either at all or on the airline concerned) – so raising load factors and reducing the number of seats unsold at departure.

In this section we will deal primarily with the second of these themes: we will look at the use of pricing as a tactical tool under different-shaped demand curves and then at the difficult topic of marginal cost pricing, before turning next to a summary of issues that need to be addressed when introducing and responding to fare changes.

Pricing as a tactical tool

Tactical pricing involves the manipulation of two variables: fares, and the conditions attached to the sale of each fare. We will concentrate on fares.

Price is a valuable tactical tool because it is quicker and easier to change a fare or freight rate than to redesign a product or reorientate a marketing communications programme. Indeed, in the United States most majors have automated pricing systems that identify competitors' price changes as they are filed with ATPCO, apply various algorithms, and in 70–80 per cent of cases decide how to respond without human intervention. Of course, the use of price to manage demand for tactical purposes assumes an airline to have knowledge of the demand curves in different segments of each of the markets that it serves, and knowledge of the elasticities available to be exploited; this is not always the case.

In figure 3.6, a reduction in fare from P_1 to P_2 leads to an increase in the quantity demanded from Q_1 to Q_2; however, the impact on revenue is unfavourable, as is implied by the fact that Area 2 (representing additional revenue earned from the incremental demand) is smaller than Area 1 (which represents revenue lost from existing traffic). In figure 3.7, the slope of the demand curve is considerably more shallow, with the result that the same reduction in fare will lead to a gain in total revenue – as suggested by Area 2 now being larger than Area 1.

If a market is price-elastic (as indicated by a relatively shallow demand curve), total revenues will decline in response to a fare increase and rise in response to a reduction – by amounts that depend on the magnitudes of the fare changes and the degrees of elasticity involved. The problem is that elasticities change over time, and it is today's rather than yesterday's which matter. Furthermore, it is bold to assume too much regarding how accurately any market can be segmented and its elasticities measured. The market research required to uncover such mysteries is anyway very expensive. Relatively few airlines have detailed knowledge of the shapes of the demand curves for their products, or of the various elasticities in their demand functions, across all the many different city-pair markets being served. Nonetheless, this type of information is becoming an increasingly important competitive weapon, especially for full-service network carriers.

Before leaving figures 3.6 and 3.7, we can put them to another illustrative purpose. Thinking back to the discussion of discriminatory pricing above, assume now that two different fares P_1 and P_2 are offered to distinct market segments – so that instead of considering a price change from P_1 to P_2 we are now looking at two quite separate prices. Further assuming that conditions are imposed to prevent passengers willing to pay P_1 buying tickets at P_2 instead, we can make the following observations:

- if only fare P_1 is offered, total revenue will be P_1Q_1;
- if fares P_1 and P_2 are both offered and the targeted segments are kept apart, total revenue increases to $P_1Q_1 + P_2(Q_2-Q_1)$; and
- the higher the price-elasticity (as illustrated in figure 3.6 as opposed to figure 3.7), the greater will be the revenue gain from identifying a more price-sensitive segment and offering to it fare P_2. Also, it becomes more likely that additional segments can be identified, policed, and served at fares above and below P_2, so boosting revenue even further.

These observations lie at the heart of price discrimination, and are therefore central to revenue management – as we will see in chapter 9.

Analysis of this type underpins the complex fare structures that now apply in many air transport markets. A potentially difficult question to

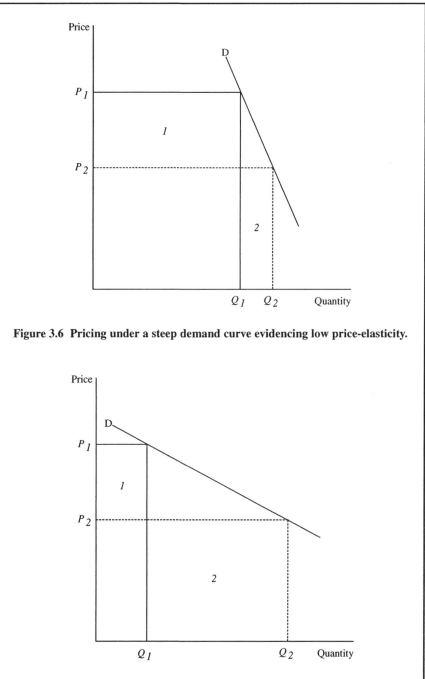

Figure 3.6 Pricing under a steep demand curve evidencing low price-elasticity.

Figure 3.7 Pricing under a shallow demand curve evidencing high price-elasticity

which such structures give rise is how low the lowest discounted fare should be. This leads us to the thorny question of marginal cost pricing.

Marginal cost pricing

Once an airline commits to a schedule, a high proportion of its total costs can be considered fixed and the variable costs of carrying additional passengers on a flight expected to depart with empty seats can seem very low. There is an ever-present temptation in the airline business to argue that once a schedule has been published, the 'marginal' cost of filling an otherwise empty seat is low and therefore justifies low 'marginal cost' pricing of perishable inventory for 'fill-up' purposes. This argument is not incorrect, but it does bring us into the realm of some important definitional issues.

Marginal, fixed, and variable costs

It is important when discussing 'marginal cost pricing' to understand the following distinctions. (We will revisit these topics in chapter 5.)

1. **Output and capacity costs, traffic and traffic costs** For the limited purpose of this discussion, airlines can be said to do two things.
   - They generate output by flying seats; doing this imposes 'capacity costs' – the costs involved in generating output, irrespective of whether or not that output is sold. These costs account for a high proportion of any airline's total costs. 'Marginal cost' is the increase (or decrease) in cost associated with producing one more (or one less) unit of output.
   - Airlines also sell the output they produce. When they do this they carry 'traffic', and traffic imposes 'traffic costs' – such as distribution, handling, catering, and so on. Traffic costs are not insubstantial, but are generally small relative to capacity costs.

   The traditional neoclassical equilibrium models found in most economics textbooks assume that all output produced is sold (at the 'market-clearing price'). In the airline business, however, this is not the case; if it were, load factors would be 100 per cent all of the time. We therefore need to be careful when talking about 'marginal cost' in the airline industry to distinguish between the marginal cost of producing one additional unit of output (which is a 'capacity cost'), and the marginal cost of carrying one additional passenger by selling a unit of output (which is a 'traffic cost'). We also need to distinguish between 'marginal' and 'variable' costs.

2. **Marginal cost** This is an economic concept oriented to the present and the future. Marginal cost can be taken here to be the cost of producing and/or selling an additional unit of output; it is avoidable if that output is not produced or sold. There are two types of marginal cost.

    *   *Short-run marginal cost (SRMC)* If an extra unit of output can be produced within the existing range of capacity (e.g., by improving aircraft utilisation and without adding to the fleet), its SRMC will be very close to the variable costs associated with producing it (e.g., fuel, airport, and ATS charges – but none of the fixed costs that would arise if capacity had to be added). Similarly, the sale of an extra seat on an aircraft already committed to a schedule will carry marginal traffic costs equivalent to the variable traffic costs involved – agency commission, GDS fees and ticketing costs (where applicable), administration, handling and catering costs, for example. If, on the other hand, producing an extra unit of output requires additional capacity or selling an extra unit requires additional output (whether using new or existing capacity), SRMC will in both cases be higher because marginal capacity costs have to be taken into account.

        Crandall (1995) suggests a generalised SRMC figure, depending upon system load factor, in the region of 25 per cent of full costs. The marginal cost involved in adding traffic to a system experiencing low load factors is lower than when high load factors imply that many flights are already facing an overdemand situation and output would need to be increased to accommodate additional traffic. In the latter case, the marginal cost of carrying one more passenger might theoretically encompass not just variable traffic costs, but also the marginal (capacity) costs of adding output to accommodate that passenger.

    *   *Long-run marginal cost (LRMC)* This encompasses SRMC, but also adds one or both of two additional costs: the cost of replacing existing capacity when this becomes necessary in order to maintain service; and the cost of adding capacity to meet future demand growth.

    Whereas SRMC pricing takes no account of future investment needs, LRMC pricing is higher in order to accommodate these requirements. SRMC pricing may distort signals from the market that can otherwise help map out future resource requirements. It is not unknown for airlines facing high demand generated by aggressive discounting to meet it with additional output. However, what might have been sound marginal cost pricing on the original flight may quite possibly represent unattractive, below-cost pricing on the supplementary flight.

3. **Fixed and variable costs** These are concepts met in both economics and accounting; they are oriented to the present and the past.

- *Variable costs* Variable costs increase or decrease in response to changes in the volume of output produced ('variable capacity costs') or sold ('variable traffic costs'). When output is increased within the current range of a system's capacity or when additional sales are made from an existing schedule (i.e., an established commitment of output), variable costs and SRMCs are likely to be very similar. (Low-fare carriers in particular operate with low variable traffic costs whenever they pay no agency commissions or GDS fees, use e-ticketing rather than issuing paper, and offer no free catering.)

- *Fixed costs* Fixed costs are 'backward looking' insofar as they represent an allocation of a share of the costs incurred in acquiring and sustaining fixed assets (such as aircraft, maintenance facilities, ground equipment, etc.) required to generate output. Fixed costs include accounting line items that are either spread arbitrarily over the assumed life of an asset (e.g., depreciation) or charged more or less as paid-for (e.g., hull insurance). They do not vary with output or traffic, as long as output remains within the current capacity range. However, if an increase in output requires additional capacity (e.g., more aircraft), fixed costs will rise because the fixed costs of the new capacity have to be taken into account along with those attributable to existing capacity. Whilst the LRMC concept treats historic costs of acquired capacity as sunk and looks instead at the need for future replacement and expansion, fixed costs arise only once capacity has been acquired.

'Variable cost pricing' of incremental output covers only the variable costs associated with that output (and ideally also makes a contribution to fixed costs). Pricing on the basis of fully allocated costs, on the other hand, covers both variable costs and the share of fixed costs allocated to the output concerned (and should also include a profit margin). Box 3.2 briefly introduces the topic of cost allocation – a topic we will look at again in chapter 5.

Box 3.2: Cost allocation

Once a schedule has been established, the first seat sold on each departure notionally bears all the fixed costs associated with that flight and every other seat bears only variable costs and is therefore ripe for (short-run) marginal cost pricing. Of course, this extreme view is never reflected in pricing practice but it does underline a fundamental question: At what point between selling the first seat and the last seat on a given departure should we treat all fixed costs as fully allocated and so switch comfortably to marginal cost pricing without having to worry further about whether sales cover average total costs? There is no formulaic answer. Everything depends upon the traffic mix and fare structure in markets served by a given flight-leg. If there is plenty of high-yield traffic and a fare structure able to tap into consumer surplus in this segment, then the high contribution (i.e., revenue net of variable costs) made by that traffic will cover fixed costs relatively quickly, and SRMC pricing can be justified in respect of a significant proportion of remaining seats; in markets unsupported by the large contribution margins of high-yield traffic, low-yield sales will have to bear a greater share of the contribution to fixed costs and exceptionally low fares will only be sustainable by a carrier with exceptionally low costs (e.g., low-fare airlines and nonscheduled/charter carriers).

As we will see in chapter 5, it can be argued that there is no such thing as 'the' cost. For example, if each unit of output up to a certain level can be priced to exceed average cost (i.e., (variable costs + fixed costs)/output) and then sold, it might be perfectly rational to argue that 'the' cost of any incremental output is equivalent to its variable costs alone – assuming that fixed costs, which have already been covered in the price of existing output, do not have to be increased. Conversely, we might argue that 'the' cost is the average cost of all output – existing and new. Both perspectives are defensible, but which is the most appropriate will depend upon the nature of the decision for which cost data are required.

When discussing 'marginal cost' pricing in the airline business it is not uncommon for the concepts of marginal, variable, and fixed cost to become intertwined. The fundamental points to remember are as follows.

- Economists recognise welfare benefits in LRMC pricing because it relates future investments in replacement or growth capacity to current users' willingness to pay for that capacity, whilst SRMC pricing offers no input into an evaluation of future requirements. (There is a related point relevant to airlines both as suppliers of output for which demand experiences notable peaks and troughs, and as users of airport and airspace infrastructure which also experiences heavy peaking. Peak-period users of any system place more strain on resources than off-peak users, and therefore contribute more to the eventual need to replace and/or expand existing capacity; this being the case, whilst SRMC pricing of off-peak output can be rational, peak output should always be subjected to LRMC pricing. Although such 'scientific' approaches to pricing are seldom met in practice, airlines do use RMSs to ensure that revenue is maximised from high-demand flights.)

- The perishability of airline seats once the doors close, together with the need to cover the high short-run fixed costs associated with scheduled airline operations, put a great deal of pressure on carriers to sell close to variable cost (which is often referred to in this context as 'marginal cost'). Because marginal revenues even from deeply discounted fares tend to exceed variable traffic costs, additional sales of output produced within a given capacity range will usually make some level of contribution to fixed (capacity and traffic) costs.

- Pricing some sales at little over variable cost fails to cover fixed costs, and so in the long run can only be sustainable if other passengers (i.e., those travelling on higher-yield fares) are paying sufficiently dearly to make up the revenue shortfall. The argument often used to justify deeply discounted fares and so encourage 'fill-up' traffic is that the business they generate is better than empty seats, provided there is a difference between marginal revenue and variable (traffic) costs that can make a 'contribution' – however small – to fixed costs and profits; this is fine as long as these fares are capacity-controlled and there is other, higher-yielding traffic to make a more significant contribution to fixed costs and profits.

- Variable (or 'marginal') cost pricing will seldom cover average costs – because the latter average fixed as well as variable costs. Average cost pricing is helpful in recovering the costs associated with past investments because it includes an allocation of fixed costs, but it does not help arrive at future investment decisions based on consumers' willingness to pay, and neither does it impose the highest prices on those whose pressure on the system actually generates the most need for future investment – that is, peak-period users. Furthermore, charging average cost prices to one set of users is a recipe to do no better than break even unless higher prices are being charged to other users.

- SRMC pricing and variable cost pricing diverge if the output being priced relies on incremental capacity to generate it – because SRMCs would encompass the immediate acquisition costs involved whilst variable costs would not. The use of variable cost pricing not on a fill-up basis but in respect of output produced by incremental capacity is short-sighted from a longer term capacity management perspective. Of course, in practice an airline will not add a frequency or schedule a larger aircraft to accommodate a single passenger. But at some point in time growing demand will force the decision to increase output, and at this point it is important to know whether that demand is coming forward in response to economically sustainable pricing.

- There can sometimes be a tendency to accept as fixed the costs associated with overcapacity, rather than acting to rationalise that capacity
and hopefully underpin firmer prices.

Marginal cost pricing in practice

The apparently low cost of filling an otherwise empty seat makes aggressive pricing attractive at the margin. The problem is that although such agg-
ression might be sound in the short run, it fails to pick up the 'tab' for past
investments or to send accurate signals about future resource requirements.
'Marginal cost pricing' can therefore be an invaluable demand and revenue
management tool, but there are traps associated with its use that require
adherence to the following best practice.

1. Understand the demand curve and, particularly, the price-elasticity of
   any segment at which discounted prices are to be targeted. Where either
   or both detailed statistics or analytical resources are in short supply,
   this is not necessarily straightforward.
2. Control discounting closely.
   - On a tactical level, this means using RMSs to monitor the release
     of space at various discounts and using purchase and usage restrict-
     ions to ensure revenue dilution is minimised.
     - RMSs are critical tools for network carriers wanting to ensure
       that the accessibility of seats on high-demand flights to late-
       booking, full-fare passengers is not inhibited by early release of
       too much space at lower-yielding, discounted fares.
     - 'Revenue dilution' occurs when a passenger travels at a fare
       lower than the highest amount she would otherwise have been
       prepared to pay in order to fly.
   - On a strategic level, control means not letting a surge of traffic in
     response to loosely monitored discounting form a base for output
     expansion. Using discounts selectively to fill scheduled capacity on
     a base-load of higher-yielding passengers might be economically
     justifiable, but building expansion plans on the basis of demand
     from such incremental traffic – which will probably be paying less
     than the airline's long-run average cost – is not.
3. Understand competitors' probable reactions. If competitors have in the
   past acted, or are now signalling an intention to act, in a manner suggesting they will respond in kind to any further discounting within the
   established tariff structure, it is quite possible that a 'fare war' will
   develop. The airlines involved are then likely to fall short of achieving
   their tactical demand management goals and, at the same time, will

probably suffer declining yields. (This links to the discussion of oligopolistic market behaviour in chapter 4, and is a decision area addressed in recent years by game theory.)

Together, the impact of nonscheduled airlines in highly visible markets such as the North Atlantic during the late 1960s, the scheduled airlines' need to fill new widebodies arriving amidst the economic uncertainties of the mid-1970s, and the deregulation of US domestic passenger air transport and then other markets from 1978 onwards set in motion an avalanche of consumer expectations with regard to the availability of discounts off normal or full fares that has yet to lose momentum.

Today, a wide range of discounts is offered by full-service carriers in most truly competitive markets, and even in markets that remain regulated or for some other reason lack intense price competition there are usually discounts available off the fully flexible, on-demand fares applicable for travel in each cabin – either as part of the established fare structure, in conjunction with limited-period promotions, or simply 'under the table'. The pricing structures of low-fare carriers vary, but most are simpler than those offered by full-service airlines and involve: departure-specific peak- and off-peak pricing; discounts off the walk-up fare that diminish at various time thresholds as the day of operation approaches; and – where one-way fares are not quoted, as in fact they usually are – fewer requirements regarding minimum, maximum, and Saturday night stays than full-service carriers have traditionally imposed. (In the challenging market conditions of 2002, a number of full-service airlines (e.g., British Airways, bmi british midland, and several US majors) began responding to low-fare competition on parts of their networks by relaxing conditions – particularly Saturday night stay and return booking requirements – imposed on discount tickets; they also simplified revenue management to base availability of discounts in these markets primarily on customers' willingness to book in advance.)

The only safe conclusion is that discounting – that is, offering a broadly-based structure of fares below the highest fare in each market – is a critical demand and revenue management tool. Discounting down to marginal cost can be justified, but it has pitfalls that need to be understood.

Marginal cost pricing of freight

As we saw above, it is sometimes argued that because combination carriers exist in most cases primarily to serve passengers, belly-hold freight output on passenger aircraft is essentially a 'free' by-product – aside from marketing, documentation, surface transport, warehousing, and handling expenses, and the cost of incremental fuel required. Marginal cost (or 'by-product') pricing is entirely appropriate based on this argument. (Ground-handling, incidentally, accounts for a very much higher proportion of freight trans-portation costs than is the case in respect of passengers.)

The alternative view is that freight capacity made available on passenger flights should bear a share of allocated capacity costs. Airlines relying on freight for a significant proportion of their revenues – particularly carriers that operate freighters – are more likely to cost on a fully allocated basis than those looking on freight as a simple by-product of passenger output; but in either case, the pressure to use something close to marginal cost pricing in order to fill unsold space and to boost load factors and revenues is as real as it is on the passenger side of the industry.

One airline's decisions with regard to its approach to freight pricing can clearly have a profound impact on competition. For many years, several carriers flew freighters from the US West Coast to Australia with high load factors and reasonable yields, onwards to Hong Kong at low load factors and low yields, and then back across the Pacific at high load factors and strong yields. In aggregate, this triangular routing produced acceptable returns to the operators concerned, but local competitors in the Australia-Hong Kong market suffered from the effects of both the incremental output and marginal cost prices brought into that market (Walker, 2002). Multi-lateral deregulation of airfreight markets, a long-running proposal likely to gain momentum as the proportion of cargo carried in freighters (as opposed to the belly-holds of passenger aircraft) increases in the years ahead, would inevitably lead to many more such examples in the future.

Introducing a fare change

Fare changes can be systemwide (e.g., off-peak 'fare sales'), route-specific, or departure-specific – although given the oligopolistic structure and multi-market contact characteristic of the industry, a route-specific change may well ripple, via competitors' reactions, across other parts of a wider net-work. The following considerations apply when initiating a fare change.

- The traffic, revenue, load factor, production cost, and profit changes anticipated given assumed price-elasticities. When prices are reduced, traffic volume should rise: Can this increase be accommodated within the range of existing output (i.e., through higher load factors)? If not, can additional output be produced profitably given the cost base? In either case, will revenue from incremental traffic attracted by the price reductions more than compensate for any revenue forgone by levying the lower price on traffic that would have been carried anyway at the original price? If prices are raised, traffic may fall or it might continue to rise but more slowly than had fares remained unchanged: If traffic falls, will the airline be left with too much capacity bearing high fixed costs? Will the increase in revenue from traffic still carried more than compensate for the loss of revenue from passengers spilled to competitors?

- The traffic and revenue changes anticipated within the carrier's own portfolio of services, given demand interrelatedness within that portfolio and the attendant risk of traffic diversion arising from cross-price elasticities. (We saw in the last chapter that demand interrelatedness arises when an airline has a portfolio of service packages that are possible substitutes for each other.)
- The traffic and revenue impact of competitors' likely reactions – and the carrier's own subsequent response to those reactions. If a carrier is a major player in the market(s) concerned, its price initiatives – particularly reductions – will probably be matched; if it is not, the likely response of any dominant carrier is best judged by reference to past behaviour.

The remainder of this section will look at three contexts within which these considerations might have to be weighed: network context; market entry; and product life cycle.

Tactical pricing in a network context

There are two particularly important issues to highlight here.

1. **Displacement of local traffic by connecting passengers** Any airline carrying a significant number of passengers connecting online over one of its hubs will need to give particular attention to tactical pricing. The reason is that the revenue earned off a passenger carried from origin O to hub H and on to destination D may well be less than the sum of the revenue that could be earned from two 'local' passengers using those same seats to travel from O to H and from H to D respectively. This can happen when passengers in O can choose from competing carriers' hub-and-spoke systems to get them to D, whilst those only travelling to or from fortress hub H are subject to the dominant carrier's market power at that hub. Similar considerations can also arise on a linear multi-stop routing where the sum of local fares for intermediate segments exceeds the end-to-end fare (because of the effect of price tapering). We will look again at these types of situation in chapter 9, when considering revenue management.

2. **Pricing over a hub as a competitive weapon** Depending upon the location of its hub(s), a network carrier might be able to attack price-sensitive segments of a competitor's nonstop markets by offering a range of discounted fares to draw traffic over its hub; to avoid displacing its own local traffic to and from the hub, over which more market power can be exercised, these lower through-fares should be capacity-controlled. Although low fares may not influence time-sensitive, price-insensitive segments, it seems to be the case that price-elastic segments in US domestic markets, for example, treat connecting services as a reasonable substitute for nonstops (Berdy, 1998). (Another possibility might be to boost frequencies on the connecting routes O-H and H-D in order to offer more departures from O to D than the competitor is able to mount with nonstop O-D service; this, of course, requires the reassignment of resources – people, ground equipment, aircraft, gates, and (where relevant) slots – from other network activities, which will have opportunity cost implications. Much depends upon prevailing load factors and system capacity. We will return to this in chapters 6 and 7.)

Tactical pricing for market entry

Pricing for market entry depends heavily upon existing market structure. We will here assume that the market being entered already has one or more incumbents in place.

An airline choosing to enter a market with a similar fare structure to the incumbent(s) will need to offer something else in order to attract traffic – a superior brand image, a more generous FFP (perhaps augmented by bonus awards during the initial promotional period), a wider network, and/or fewer booking conditions at a given fare level. Higher frequencies than incumbents are offering might be required to attract business travellers – but these would be expensive to produce, particularly for a start-up or small carrier, and could lead to excess output in the market.

The case of a small entrant challenging a larger incumbent A small carrier challenging a large incumbent on the basis of lower fares, similar fares but fewer restrictions, or similar fares with better service has essentially three choices.

1. To target relatively low-density 'niche' routes and try to avoid aggravating the incumbent with too many frequencies. This was ValuJet's early approach at Atlanta after start-up in the mid-90s, and it was broadly successful. (Game theorists refer to it as 'the puppy dog ploy'.)

2. To choose relatively dense routes with sufficient volume to allow diversion of enough traffic from incumbents to generate sound operating economics for the aircraft type(s) being put into the market without inevitably provoking a fare war. This was Virgin Atlantic's approach in its early years.
3. To target overpriced and/or underserved markets and rely on price-elasticity to generate increases in traffic volume. This has been the approach of Frontier at Denver, as well as several of the European low-fare carriers.

A challenger sometimes has no alternative other than to price aggressively in order to counter the network and marketing (e.g., FFP, brand, advertising, and general market presence) strengths of a larger incumbent. An unsubsidised entrant choosing to compete on price must have a sustainable cost advantage for the strategy to be viable in the medium and long term.

The case of a large airline challenging a smaller incumbent For the large airline, addition of an extra route may not add greatly to total costs, particularly if underutilised, off-peak capacity can be deployed. Therefore, pricing at little over variable costs can seem a commercially attractive proposition, especially when it generates incremental network feed. However, the same route may account for a significant proportion of the small incumbent's revenues, and therefore not only must it cover variable costs but a substantial contribution to fixed costs also has to be made.

It is seldom advantageous for small incumbents to prolong confrontation with a larger entrant under this type of circumstance unless they have a meaningful cost advantage. Even then, it is quite possible that the resources of the larger carrier (and its greater scope to cross-subsidise from other routes) may better enable it to sustain a protracted fare war.

Stage in the product life-cycle

When an established inflight product has reached maturity and is no longer providing value equivalent to competitors' similarly priced but more recently introduced alternatives there is an argument (often ignored) in favour of downwardly flexible pricing. This might happen, for example, when a competitor raises significantly the standards of inflight comfort, entertainment, and service available in its long-haul business class, as several carriers have done in recent years. Clearly, airlines which do not respond with their own improvements are offering more mature products. Some choose to deal with this by lowering their prices. Others prefer not to respond directly because they perceive themselves as having other advantages, such as a strong brand image, perhaps reinforced by an attractive FFP and network scope; or they might not respond because the innovator has only sufficient capacity to take a small share of the market.

Responding to competitors' pricing

The following considerations apply when responding to a competitor's fare initiative.

- **Identification** Given the thousands of fare changes initiated daily in the US domestic market in particular, the first task is to identify fare changes that matter (i.e., significant changes in significant markets – changes that might shift share in one of the carrier's core markets).
- **Impact evaluation** The next task is to assess the traffic, revenue, and profit impacts the identified changes are likely to have. In a volatile pricing environment, airline managers have to decide quickly which of their competitors' initiatives should be matched.
- **Response evaluation** Some airlines have processes that allow them to respond within hours if necessary, whilst others are more ponderous. In either case, the response must consider very much the same issues that were raised above in the section on initiating a fare change.

We will briefly look at responses in two possible situations: price changes initiated by an existing competitor; and the entry of a new competitor.

Responding to an existing competitor's pricing tactics

If a competitor changes its prices an airline must consider:

- why (e.g., to increase market share, raise load factors, pass on cost increases, generate cash under conditions of financial distress, or stimulate a market-wide price change);
- whether the move is tactical or a strategic commitment; and
- the likely reactions of any other competitors.

It must also consider the alternative responses open to it, the counter-responses each of these might provoke from competitors, and the probable impact on market share and profits under each of the available response and non-response scenarios. Ideally, contingency plans should have been drawn up, because whereas a competitor's action might have been planned over a long period, the time available for reaction is usually short.

Responding to price rises When another carrier raises its fares in an inelastic market, serious consideration should be given to doing the same. Any price advantage gained by failing to respond is likely to be only temporary, because the probability is high that an unmatched fare increase will be reversed once its initiator starts to lose market share. Much depends on the different parties' views of segment price-elasticity and the likely impact on revenue of the new, higher fare.

An airline's strategic position can also be a significant consideration in shaping its price response. Low-fare carriers are in general disinclined to increase fares simply because full-service competitors have raised them.

Responding to price reductions Prices do not fall autonomously; they fall because at least one participant in a market believes it will gain market share by reducing them. Competitors then have to decide whether they want to meet the challenge by matching the reduction. In practice, airlines are often quick to match the introduction of lower fares. Downward pressure on fares is particularly likely under the following conditions (Besanko et al, 2000).

- Where there are large numbers of competitors present, because the larger the number the more likely it is that one will break ranks.
- Where competitors have different costs bases, and those with low costs are committed to low fares as part of their strategic positions and/or believe they can drive high-cost competitors from the market by sacrificing current margins to build market share.
- Where there is excess capacity.
- Where products are perceived as largely undifferentiated and customers have low switching costs.
- Where there are strong exit barriers, such as Chapter 11 bankruptcy pro-tection or the support of state shareholders.

A particularly radical response adopted by a small number of majors has been to introduce a low-cost brand to compete on price with low-fare carriers without diluting the mainline carrier's image or price platforms (e.g., Continental's CALite, the United Shuttle, US Airways' MetroJet, Delta Express, Air Canada's Zip and Tango, and KLM's Buzz and Basiq Air). The disappearance of many of these ventures implies that the strategy of carving a low-cost operation out of a full-service airline is not easy to implement.

A carrier with high market share might instead prefer to exploit its relatively strong position by resisting pressure for widespread discounting, and turn instead to nonprice responses such as improving product quality (e.g., enhanced inflight service), relaxing ticket conditionality, and promoting customer loyalty (e.g., reinforcing brand positioning and/or boosting FFP awards). These responses are not likely to impress the most price-elastic segments, but may have an impact further up the yield structure.

Conclusion Responses to an existing competitor's tactical pricing initiatives should be shaped by the price and value sensitivity of the market(s) affected, the current positioning and life-cycle stages of the product(s) concerned and their significance in the airline's overall product portfolio, the strength and likely objectives of the competitor, and the behaviour of costs in response to volume changes.

Tactical pricing in response to market entry

Much will depend upon the size of the affected market and its significance to the incumbent's overall network, as well as upon the volume of output being offered by the challenger, the number of frequencies operated, the level of fares and the nature of associated restrictions, and the threat potentially posed by the challenger to the incumbent's market share once any inaugural discount period is over.

Response to a limited attack If a market entrant is a start-up or perhaps a minor player it will lack the brand recognition, resources, network scope (and opportunity to cross-subsidise markets), FFP coverage, and strength in agency distribution channels that an incumbent typically possesses; the only competitive dimension open to it is likely to be price. Particularly if the entrant is producing only limited output and the incumbent can offer significant nonprice benefits to customers, existing market shares might not be sufficiently threatened to warrant the revenue dilution likely to follow from a robust response in the tactical pricing arena. On the other hand, complacency can be dangerous; Southwest was once a minor challenger.

Response to a more serious threat An attack on a core market or an attack on the integrity of a network sufficient to erode the flow of connecting traffic over an incumbent's hub is likely to be met by lower fares (and, perhaps, by higher frequencies and aggressive marketing communications). Most airlines try to maintain price leadership if one of their core markets is seriously threatened. However, they might face two potentially troublesome situations.

1. **Where the challenger has significantly lower costs that it is able to sustain** The question in this case is who has the deepest pockets. Whilst full-service carriers have been able to dispose of many of the undercapitalised start-ups that have challenged them, they have had less success dealing with well-resourced low-fare competitors; it is far from clear whether or not the full-service business model can survive in the long term as currently structured in short-haul North American domestic and intra-European markets (or, at least, those markets able to sustain multiple daily services using the 150-seat aircraft favoured by low-fare carriers). Put simply, the problem with this model is that it relies for profits almost entirely on the willingness of business travellers to pay high fares – a willingness sorely tested by the recession that began in 2001 and by the increasing availability of equally reliable but cheaper alternatives.

2. **When a core market priced on the basis of fully allocated costs is attacked by a new competitor using it to absorb surplus capacity and so willing to price closer to marginal cost** A common reaction from relatively sophisticated incumbents attacked in a core market is to offer one or more capacity-controlled discount fares, which should facilitate a counter-attack without unduly diluting the revenue stream. This can be particularly effective where the incumbent has an RMS enabling it to release discounted space on a seat-by-seat basis.

Where a challenger has a more established market presence at one end of a city-pair market than the other, the incumbent might compete more robustly for traffic originating at the challenger's stronger end, relying on its own better-established market presence to counterbalance any price disadvantage in respect of traffic originating at the other end of the market where the challenger is relatively unknown. This was a situation faced by British Midland (now bmi british midland) when it entered UK–Europe markets in the 1990s: British Airways responded more aggressively at the London end of each new route than at the corresponding European end, because British Midland at the time had a much less developed market presence in mainland Europe than in London.

One final point that will be picked up again in chapter 4 is that large incumbents might sometimes feel constrained by the oversight of competition authorities from responding too aggressively to market entry by a small challenger. On the other hand, we will also be noting in chapter 4 that predatory pricing is difficult to prove and has a long history of going unpunished in the airline industry.

Conclusions on tactical pricing

Airlines competing in liberalised or deregulated markets use their pricing freedoms to fine-tune fares as competitive weapons. A common result has been that a growing percentage of markets and a higher percentage of passengers are served by discount and deep discount fares (the latter commonly defined in the United States as fares in excess of 70 per cent below the corresponding full fare). To compensate, however, airlines tend to inflate full fares – with the result that late-booking passengers travelling on business often end up 'subsidising' leisure travellers, and yields remain firmer than they otherwise would despite heavy discounting in price-sensitive segments of the market. (The counter-argument is that deeply discounted fares generate fill-up traffic whose revenues help to limit the rise of full fares and whose presence supports the high frequencies that business travellers in particular value so much.) Of course, whenever prices in one market or segment are cross-subsidised by profits from another, in the absence of barriers to entry an airline may be vulnerable to attack in that high-margin market or segment by a competitor with a lower cost base that does not need to rely on cross-subsidisation (either at all, or to the same extent).

Tactical pricing decisions require knowledge of demand curves, segment elasticities, and competitors' actions and likely reactions. They should be taken with a full understanding of their cost and revenue implications. The availability of information necessary to make informed tactical pricing decisions has therefore become one of the factors critical to success in the contemporary airline industry – certainly as far as the larger full-service network carriers are concerned. However, even if interline markets are ignored, any airline operating a hub-and-spoke system with a significant number of stations served by flights that can be distinguished according to time of departure, day and season of operation, and which serve different segments of demand each with their own demand functions will have a highly complex fare structure – and hundreds of thousands of pricing decisions to make and subsequently amend as both customers and competitors act and react in response to what is on offer. Clearly, pricing on this scale has to mix experience and judgement with effective automation. It also, inevitably, involves decision-making on the basis of volatile and often imperfect information.

v. Yield

Yield defined

Having discussed price in general and what drives it, we now turn to consideration of the average price per (distance-weighted) unit of output sold – that is, per RPM or RTM. This is 'yield', and yield – rather than price – is the component of interest in the context of the operating performance model around which this second part of the book has been structured.

Yield per RTM is the average revenue earned from each ton of payload carried one mile, and similarly yield per RPM is the average revenue generated by carrying one passenger one mile. Yield may be split into: gross yield (i.e., operating revenue/RPMs or RTMs); net yield (i.e., operating revenue net of agency commissions/RPM or RTM); and net net yield (i.e., operating revenue net of commissions, TACOs, and other agency incentives/RPMs or RTMs). In this book, 'yield' refers to gross yield.

Yield can be calculated across the spectrum of an airline's operations, encompassing all the products offered over the entire network. Alternatively, if accounting capabilities permit, it can focus on a particular product – say, first or business class yield systemwide. Or it can be calculated on a market, route, or flight-leg basis – ideally also for each product. (Revenue dilution in any class/cabin – taken here as a proxy for 'product' – can be assessed by calculating actual yield as a percentage of the yield that could have been earned had all tickets in the class/cabin concerned been sold at full fare.)

Any two airlines might generate similar revenue figures whilst having quite dissimilar traffic and yield structures. We will look at the relationship between traffic and yield in chapter 10, but at this point it is worth bearing in mind the following.

1. Traffic and yield tend to trade-off against each other. The extent to which this is the case depends upon the price-elasticity (and, where relevant, the cross-price elasticity) of demand in the market(s) concerned. They also bear different relationships to cost: in the absence of major product upgrades (e.g., better seat accessibility or lower seating densities) or expensive marketing communications programmes, increases in yield can be largely cost-free; increases in traffic (i.e., RPMs and RTMs), whilst not as expensive as increases in output (i.e., ASMs and ATMs), are never cost-free.
2. Because yield is an average of revenue earned per unit of output sold, different airlines will have yield structures which reflect the different source(s) of their revenues – that is, their different traffic mixes. Spe-

cifically, these structures respond to the nature of demand being met in the markets from which revenue is being earned; they need to be related to the costs incurred meeting that demand given the positioning of a particular airline's product(s) within the markets concerned.

- High-yield passengers will often require greater product-related expenditures (notably in respect of higher frequencies and, where they occupy separate cabins, more onboard space) than low-yield passengers.
- Conventional wisdom holds that high yields might to some extent compensate for high costs. This could be true in the short term, but it is not a comfort which is without danger; high-yield traffic can evaporate in a recession, and is at any time vulnerable to a competitor with lower costs able to offer the same or better service standards at lower prices. Furthermore, there is the downward secular trend in industry (real) yields to be concerned about.

3. Low-yield traffic contributes unseen value to high-yield passengers in many markets. It can do this in several ways.

- Low-yield traffic may add density to a route sufficient to enable the use of larger aircraft than high-yield traffic alone can justify. As we will see in chapter 5, any aircraft of a given technological generation is likely to have lower seat-mile (i.e., 'unit') costs than a smaller type. These lower unit costs *might* be reflected in lower high-yield fares than would otherwise have been the case. (However, we will also see that larger aircraft have higher trip costs, so the aggregate revenue earned from incremental low-yield traffic must be sufficient to at least cover these – otherwise, the unit cost advantage will count for little.)
- Corporate overhead that would exist whether or not the incremental low-yield traffic is carried can be spread over a larger output of available seat-miles. This can also contribute to a reduction in unit costs (i.e., cost per ASM).
- The presence of low-yield traffic may permit more frequencies to be mounted than high-yield traffic alone could support (Shaw, 1999).

One certainty that should always be borne in mind is that movements in yield and in profit do not necessarily track each other. It is quite possible for profits to rise at a time when yields are falling and vice versa.

Recent yield trends

In the 1960s, jets replaced propeller-driven aircraft on most trunk routes; in the 1970s, widebodies and turbofans were introduced and average aircraft size increased; in the 1980s and 1990s, commercial liberalisation led to intensified competition in many markets. These events and trends made it possible (in the first two cases) and essential (in the latter case) for airlines to reduce real (i.e., inflation-adjusted) fares over time. This has contributed to an average two per cent per annum decline in real passenger yields across the industry since 1960. Real freight yields, which are generally less than half the passenger yield per ton-mile, have been declining at an average annual rate of three per cent per annum since 1960. In both sectors, the decline in real yields has been a major contributor to the rapid growth in traffic seen over the last several decades.

In addition to the productivity improvements that airlines are still in general passing through to customers, there are three further reasons why yields per RPM will continue their secular downward trend.

1. Price-sensitive leisure travel is growing much more rapidly than business travel.
2. Long-haul journeys, which are generally lower-yielding than short-haul trips, are growing as a proportion of total journeys.
3. Trading down, which has led a growing proportion of business travellers in particular to 'migrate' from premium cabins and – where possible – from unrestricted fares. This trend has been one factor behind decisions taken by several long-haul carriers to eliminate first class and/or introduce 'premium economy' cabins.

These are some of the reasons why costs have come under the strategic 'microscope' in recent years and will have to remain there notwithstanding the cyclical firming in yields that inevitably takes place in some markets from time to time. Unfortunately, real unit costs have in many cases been declining more slowly than yields.

It is worth noting that falling yields do not inevitably imply lower average fares in a given market. For example, assume that a fare between points O and D remains unchanged when the current nonstop service is replaced by a connection routed over hub H. Further assuming that H does not lie directly en route between O and D, the airline carrying passengers from O to D via H is now generating more RPMs to perform the same journey that was previously accomplished nonstop. Given that yield is revenue per RPM and assuming that revenue (i.e., the fare) is unchanged, yield from carrying the existing traffic (i.e., ignoring any additional traffic generated by the network connectivity benefits of hubbing over H) must decline. In the real world, fares and traffic would probably, and costs would certainly, change under this type of circumstance; nonetheless, it illustrates the point. Because it is based on price, numbers of passengers or amounts of freight carried, and the distance of carriage, a change in yield does not always tell the story it might at first appear to be telling.

Comparisons between carriers therefore need to be made with an understanding of the factors that influence yield.

Factors influencing yield

Passenger yields

The following factors affect passenger yields.

1. **Fare structure** The level of normal/full fares and the availability of discounted fares provide the foundation on which yields are built.
2. **Traffic mix** An airline's traffic mix, the proportion of traffic travelling at each different price on offer within the given fare structure in each market, has a fundamental influence on its yield. Traffic mix is a function of three factors.
   • Demand characteristics – for example, the relative proportions of business and leisure traffic.
   • The effectiveness of the carrier's RMS in protecting space on high-demand flights for late-booking, high-yield passengers. (However, we will see in chapter 9 that revenue maximisation and yield maximisation are not synonymous, and that the task of an RMS is to maximise revenue rather than yield – because it is revenue that pays the bills, whereas yield is just a number.)
   • The effectiveness of conditions imposed within the tariff structure to prevent the diversion of passengers from market segments with less elastic demand characteristics (who would have travelled anyway on a higher fare) to products designed for the more price-elastic segment(s) being targeted by discounted fares.
     (A related issue is the extent to which these conditions are applied in practice: either deliberately or in error, it is far from unknown for agencies to sell a fare without applying all the relevant conditions – back-dating ticket validation in order to comply with an advance purchase requirement, for example. This problem is worse in some markets than others, but has been estimated to cost certain carriers as much as three per cent of their potential revenue

(Kale Consultants, cited in Taneja, 2002: 159). Technology is increasingly becoming available to automate the ticket auditing process, thereby broadening its coverage and reducing its cost in comparison with the manual sampling approaches traditionally used.)

These factors are clearly influenced by the manner in which an airline positions its products to tap targeted demand, and the sophistication with which it manages the relationship between product quality, segment price-elasticity, and the release of space. In this sense, yield is to a large extent a reflection of the interaction between product design and pricing activities, because it is these which position a carrier in its markets and shape the traffic mix. However, an airline's control over such variables is never absolute in competitive markets.

Perhaps the starkest contrasts are between the yields earned by charter carriers serving low-yield leisure markets and scheduled airlines operating in higher yielding business markets. Yields earned by European charter carriers are rarely more than half the lowest yield generated by the continent's full-service scheduled airlines, for example.

3. **Length of haul** As already noted, fares per mile are generally lower for long-haul than short-haul routes because unit costs taper as stage-length increases. Other things being equal (which they seldom are, of course), a carrier whose average passenger journey is significantly longer than another carrier's average will probably earn a lower yield. (We look at average journey length here rather than the average stage-length on the airline's network because average stage-length tells us nothing about the volume of traffic carried on flights of different lengths; for example, a predominantly short-haul carrier might have its average stage-length boosted by a few long-haul routes operated at such low frequencies that they carry only a small proportion of total traffic and have little impact on systemwide yield.)

4. **The level of competition** This is clearly critical to yields. The more monopoly power a carrier benefits from, the stronger in general its yields will be. Conversely, increased price competition puts downward pressure on yields. (Nonprice competition, on the other hand, tends to put upward pressure on costs – associated with product improvement or advertising, for example – but may leave yields relatively unscathed.)

5. **Network design** One important variable under this heading is whether we are dealing predominantly with a hub-and-spoke or a point-to-point system. As we saw above, this affects yields insofar as it determines the distance flown in each O & D market; the greater the distance covered in serving a market the lower the yield at any given fare, because the revenue from that fare must be spread over more RPMs. Another variable is the extent to which an airline's network and scheduling lead

it to interline passengers with other carriers; this can influence prorate dilution and therefore yield, and is explored in Box 3.3.

Box 3.3: Prorate dilution

When a passenger buys a ticket from A to B on one airline and then onwards to C on another (whether an alliance partner or not), the fare paid for the entire journey from A to C will normally be less than the sum of local fares from A to B and from B to C. This is because, as noted above, prices generally taper with distance (i.e., the average price paid per mile falls as trip distance rises). The agency issuing the ticket, or the passenger if buying direct, pays the entire fare to the airline used on the first part of the journey, and this airline passes on part of the revenue to the second carrier either through some local arrangement or through the IATA Clearing House. Each carrier therefore experiences 'prorate dilution' as a result of the fact that more could have been earned carrying a local passenger than an interline passenger; the actual cash difference between the local fare and the revenue actually earned is 'prorate absorption'.

The two airlines flying the passenger from A to B and then B to C respectively have to agree on how they will prorate (i.e., divide between themselves) the through-fare bought from A to C. There are two Multilateral Proration Agreements, each open to any scheduled airline; one covers cargo rates, the other deals with passenger fares. In addition, alliance partners (including regionals code-sharing with majors) very often negotiate their own prorate agreements. The following are the most common of the basic approaches used.

1. ***Straight proration*** *This method applies prorate factors based on fares or distance.*
   - Fare prorating *The O & D fare is split according to the percentage of aggregate local fares accounted for by each individual local fare. For example, assume the local fares from A to B and B to C are $100 and $150 respectively whilst the A to C through-fare is $200; if Carrier 1 flies the passenger from A to B it will earn 100/250 x 200 = $80, whilst Carrier 2 flying the passenger from B to C will earn 150/250 x 200 = $120.*
   - Mileage prorating *The calculation is the same, except that miles (or sometimes the square root of miles) flown by each carrier are used instead.*
   Weighted adjustments are commonly applied to take into account the fact that operating costs for a short-haul flight are likely to represent a disproportionately high percentage of aggregate operating costs for

the entire journey. (The reason why this is so will be explained in chapter 5.) Different adjustments are used for cargo and for passengers.

2. ***Prorate factoring with provisos*** *Even after weighting adjustments, mileage prorating in particular can be unfavourable to short-haul operations interlining traffic onto long-haul routes; for example, Lufthansa has very little use for, say, ten per cent of a $400 Bremen-Manchester-New York fare as reward for carrying a passenger from Bremen to Manchester in order to interline onto a transatlantic flight. Fare prorating is somewhat more favourable to the short-haul carrier insofar as the local fare on a short-haul journey is likely to comprise a higher percentage of the O & D fare than short-haul mileage comprises of the total journey length. Nonetheless, it is not uncommon for prorate factors to be used subject to provisos filed by individual airlines requiring either specified percentages of each fare or absolute amounts of money to be 'ring-fenced' before prorating begins.*

Short-haul carriers in particular tend to earn less from interlining passengers than they would from alternative local traffic carried in the same seats; many therefore negotiate interline agreements which specifically give them a more favourable share of any constructed or agreed joint fare. A significant number of domestic operators insist on full or nearly full payment of the local fare as an 'add-on' in preference to prorating; if we look upon such add-ons as deductions from the O & D fare, the result can be serious revenue dilution for international carriers that interline significant volumes of traffic under such arrangements. As an alternative to prorating, some independent regionals in the United States and to a lesser extent elsewhere have signed 'fee-per-departure' or 'fee-per-ASM flown' agreements with their major code-share partners; the regional benefits from improved cash flow predictability, whilst the major gains control over network management (i.e., points served, routing, schedule), pricing, seat inventory, and revenue management.

The fact that a large and growing proportion of the industry's passengers travel on discounted fares which are in most cases only good for use on the issuing carrier has tended to reduce the prorate problem; it has not gone away, however, because the growth of alliances is pushing in the opposite direction by creating networks expressly designed to flow traffic between partners. To the extent that an airline can retain passengers online – clearly an easier prospect for carriers with large networks – prorate dilution will have less of an impact on yields. In the US domestic market, only a very small percentage of passengers interline between unaffiliated carriers.

On the other hand, some African operators with limited networks interline over half their long-haul passengers. This disadvantage is compounded by the severe directional imbalance of fares in many of the markets they serve, with northbound prices often consistently lower than southbound. They are therefore left with little room to negotiate favourable prorates with transatlantic or European domestic airlines in respect of passengers originating from Africa and continuing their onward journeys offline. Directional fare differentials are noticeable elsewhere as well, often as a result of exchange rate effects, and depending upon which end of an O & D market a carrier generates most sales they can magnify or reduce the impact of prorate dilution on revenues denominated in the home currency.

Yields will also suffer if an airline books or carries significant volumes of interline traffic and is inefficient at checking its monthly billings through the IATA Clearing House. This is sometimes a particular problem for those small airlines which, because of the impact of their route structures on the proportion of online to offline revenue ticketed, tend to be net creditors in the clearing system. As far as net debtors are concerned, verifying the accuracy of prorate billing can be burdensome for airlines with thinly stretched resources – but overcharging through incorrect prorate claims is not infrequent and can prove even more burdensome.

Freight yields

In some cases, similar influences also affect freight yields. Although the generalisation might well not hold in a particular market at a particular time, it is often the case that freight yields per RTM are below passenger yields calculated on the same basis. There are several reasons for this.

- Particularly in international markets, a high proportion of freight output is sold in bulk through distribution channels in which buying power is concentrated in the hands of a relatively small number of powerful forwarders.
- The directionality of freight flows, met in chapter 2, leads to weak demand and therefore soft yields in one direction on many routes.
- Output of freight space in most long-haul markets is paced more by the demand for passenger services than by demand from shippers. Long-haul widebodies have significant belly-hold capacity, so when passenger demand and market liberalisation lead to increased frequencies being operated there is an inevitable increase in freight space – whether the market needs it at the time or not.
- Looked at as a whole, airfreight is primarily a medium- and long-haul product – something that is being compounded by the growing proportion of global airfreight accounted for by shipments from Asia to destinations in Europe and the Americas (Taneja, 2002). Long-haul

traffic, as we have seen, tends to generate lower yields than short-haul traffic.

Yields on time-definite express documents and parcels are of course higher than the average for freight as a whole.

vi. Summary

This chapter opened by defining 'price', summarising influences on airline pricing decisions, and considering uniform, discriminatory, and differential pricing, before moving on to look at passenger and freight tariff structures. The degree of monopoly power exerted by a carrier was identified as an important price driver, bracketed by costs on the downside and customer value on the upside. The use of pricing as a tactical tool was considered, with particular attention paid to marginal cost pricing, the introduction of fare changes, and possible responses to competitors' pricing initiatives. Finally, we looked at yield – the element of the operating performance model around which the second part of the book has been structured; we saw that pricing is a fundamental determinant of yield, but that there are also other important influences.

The point has been made several times in the course of the chapter that although an understanding of price theory and the components of yield is critically important, managers often have to make pricing decisions on the basis of imperfect data derived from an intensely volatile competitive environment.

4 Output

An economist's guess is likely to be just as good as anybody else's.
Will Rogers

Chapter summary

Supply of output is the third of four elements in the operating performance model around which Part 2 of the book has been structured:

TRAFFIC x YIELD > < **OUTPUT** x UNIT COST
= OPERATING PERFORMANCE (i.e., PROFIT or LOSS)

This chapter will define supply, look briefly at the economics of supply, and summarise the supply-side characteristics of the airline industry. Market structure and competition policy will be considered. Finally, operating strategy and operations management will be briefly discussed.

i. Definitions

Output

The output produced by an airline is measured by multiplying a unit of seating or payload capacity by distance flown. It can be analysed in respect of a single aircraft, a sub-fleet, or an entire fleet, on a particular route or across a network. Output is measured in:

- available seat-miles (ASMs) or available seat-kilometres (ASKs), each of which represents one seat (irrespective of whether or not it has a passenger on it) carried one mile or kilometre respectively;

181

- available ton-miles (ATMs) or available tonne-kilometres (ATKs), which represent one ton of payload potential (again, irrespective of whether it has been *sold* to passengers or cargo shippers) carried one mile, or one tonne carried one kilometre. Available freight tonnage is calculated by taking the freight volume available on the type concerned after allowing space for passenger baggage and applying an assumed freight density figure. Potential passenger payload is converted to ATMs and ATKs using an assumed weight per passenger and baggage (commonly around 200 pounds or 90–95 kilos).

These measures of output are particularly favoured by airlines with substantial cargo operations. (Cargo is widely defined as freight plus mail plus unaccompanied baggage, and that is the definition used here. ICAO, it should be noted, excludes mail and unaccompanied baggage from its definition of cargo – leaving the word more or less synonymous with 'freight'.) Box 4.1 looks at how cargo output can be produced.

Box 4.1: *Different ways in which cargo output can be produced*

Cargo output is produced by the following types of operation.

1. *Scheduled carriers This category includes 'combination' and all-cargo carriers.*
   - Combination carriers *These are airlines that carry both passengers and freight. They can be further broken-down into three more categories.*
     - *Airlines which despite being active in the freight sector rely primarily on belly-hold capacity, as British Airways does for example.*
     - *Airlines which supplement belly-hold capacity with the use of combis (i.e., aircraft carrying both passengers and cargo on their main deck as well as cargo in their holds).*
     - *Airlines which operate their own freighter fleets, in addition to using belly-hold capacity and perhaps combis as well. This is common amongst the Asian majors, and a few European majors such as Air France and Lufthansa; in North America, Northwest stands out, and in South America LanChile.*
     (Any of these might supplement inhouse capacity by wet-leasing freighters either from time to time or on a long-term basis.)
     The relatively small number of combination carriers operating their own freighters account for approximately half of international freight output if their passenger, combi, and freighter operations

are combined (but much less when the US domestic market is in-cluded, because this is dominated by the integrators).

- Scheduled all-cargo carriers *There are relatively few of these, with Cargolux perhaps the longest-standing sizeable example. A special case is the integrated (i.e., door-to-door) carriers such as FedEx and UPS. These now dominate US domestic freight markets, and although much less significant in non-US markets have been making inroads since the 1990s.*

2. *Nonscheduled (charter) carriers There are large numbers of non-scheduled cargo airlines, some offering general capacity, some specialising in the transportation of certain types of load, and some flying such regular operations on certain routes that they are in effect providing scheduled service. Because aircraft utilisation tends on the whole to be lower than on the scheduled side of the industry, they generally operate older aircraft with lower ownership costs than other sectors might be able to justify; the price they have to pay is higher fuel and maintenance costs – a point we will return to in chapter 8.*

Freighters (scheduled and non-scheduled) are expected to play an increasingly important role over the next two decades, raising their contribution to global cargo output well above the 40 per cent mark (Hatton, 1999). Many of these will be conversions of second-hand passenger aircraft. Separately, a trend that began in the late 1990s saw large forwarders beginning to charter freighters either from scheduled or non-scheduled carriers to operate their own scheduled services, initially across the North Atlantic. Both the number of routes and the volume of output involved are small, but it is a development that could bear watching.

Perhaps the most interesting point to come out of the break-down above takes us back to the comment made in the last chapter regarding the 'disconnect' between airline costs and prices. With so many different types of cargo lift – each having different operating costs – competing in the same markets, and with some combination carriers costing belly-hold space on a by-product basis, linkages between market price and production costs are always going to be tenuous at best.

Capacity, utilisation, and output

This book refers to 'capacity' as a fleet's potential output if fully utilised, and 'output' as the ASMs or ASKs and ATMs or ATKs actually supplied to the market. (RPMs or RPKs and RTMs or RTKs, on the other hand, are a measure of output that has been *sold* – that is, of 'traffic'.) An aircraft or fleet (or any other productive resource) has the *capacity* in principle to produce a finite amount of output if fully utilised (subject to maintenance requirements); the extent to which an aircraft or fleet is in fact *utilised* determines the volume of *output* it produces. Clearly, an airline will in most cases want to get output as close to capacity as possible by maximising utilisation in order to ensure that fixed costs (e.g., depreciation, insurance, lease rentals) are spread over as many units of output as possible and therefore are averaged down. (A notable exception is the short-haul overnight feeder services flown by FedEx and other integrators; these tend to involve low aircraft utilisation, in part because daytime operations are unattractive due to the risk that they might leave aircraft out of position and so disrupt the core high-yield night services. Their output therefore falls well short of theoretical capacity. The answer in this case has to be to use aircraft with very low ownership costs – such as low-cost single turboprops on thin routes, and relatively old passenger conversions on denser routes.)

The problem is, of course, that as far as aircraft are concerned their capacity to produce output over a given period of time is a notional figure rather than an incontrovertible fact. The capacity of any given type of aircraft to produce ASMs (or ATMs) per day or per year will depend to a considerable extent upon the nature of the airline operating system within which it is deployed. In particular, it will depend upon:

- average stage-length – because, other things being equal, longer stage-lengths generally permit more output to be produced in a given time by a given type;
- the nature of the airline's product – because, other things being equal, a full-service product requires longer transit and turnaround times between flight-legs than a 'no-frills' product; and
- network design – because it is generally impossible to extract as much utilisation from a given type operating within a hub-and-spoke network as from the same type flying similar stage-lengths on a point-to-point basis.

For example, a B737 operated by a full-service network carrier will be able to produce less output (i.e., will have less capacity even if efficiently utilised) than one operated by a low-fare point-to-point airline; this is because the nature of the full-service product requires longer turnaround times (e.g., for galley restocking) and schedule buffer time (to allow for air traffic and taxi delays at congested hubs and for delayed connecting passengers to make their transfers). Similarly, a B737 operated by a charter airline serving the Mediterranean from Northern Europe will have more capacity available because it can be – and usually will be – flown day and night during the peak summer period.

Overcapacity, excess output, and spoilage

Particularly when we come to capacity management in Part 3 of the book, we need to distinguish between these three ideas.

1. **Overcapacity** This arises when aircraft are not being as fully utilised as they might, given the nature of a particular airline's operating system. Broadly, it can be equated with having more aircraft than required to produce the amount of output being produced; however, as we will see when looking at network and fleet management in chapters 6–8, the complexities of network design and scheduling and of fleet assignment mean that overcapacity is not necessarily simple to identify in practice. Parked aircraft are the most obvious indicator.
2. **Excess output** This is evident when more output is available than the demand coming forward to purchase it at a given price. Load factor (the percentage of output that has been sold) is a commonly used indicator, and we will be looking at this in chapter 10. However, enough has been said about the peaking characteristics of air transport demand (in chapter 2) and the complexities of pricing (in chapter 3) to make two things very clear.
    *   Although individual flights frequently operate with all their output sold, an entire system never can. Airlines inevitably produce more output than they sell, but the extent to which this unsold output is 'excess' will always be subject to debate. As we will see later in this chapter and in Parts 3 and 4, much depends upon the nature of a particular airline's operating system.
    *   If an operating profit is to be earned, excess output has to be paid for out of the revenue earned from output that has been sold. We will return to the linkage between output and price in a moment, and revisit the point later in the book.
3. **Spoilage** A concept we will meet again in chapter 9 when revenue management is discussed, 'spoilage' occurs where seats fly empty despite there being sufficient demand (at a given price) to have filled them. This can happen, for example, when flights are fully booked, reservation requests are refused, but seats nonetheless remain available at departure because of late cancellations and no-shows; as we will see in chapter 9, overbooking is used to limit spoilage. Excess output and spoilage are therefore similar but distinct concepts; where there is

excess output space flies empty because of insufficient demand at the price(s) offered, whereas spoilage occurs where demand is sufficient to absorb output but for some reason fails to materialise as booked.

It should be noted that although these definitions are technically correct and are adhered to in the present book, it is not uncommon in practice to see 'overcapacity' used as a catch-all for both too much capacity and too much output, and to see 'spoilage' used to refer to empty space at departure regardless of whether or not there ever was demand for it.

Irrespective of what definitions are used, the following critical observation will re-emerge at various points throughout the remainder of the book: whilst it is necessary to maximise resource utilisation (subject to the constraints of each carrier's particular strategic and product positioning) in order to produce as much output as possible over which to spread fixed costs and so average down unit cost, it is also vital to be sure that the incremental output can be sold – and can be sold at a profit. The discussions of cost allocation later in this chapter and in chapter 5 will show how complex the implications of this very obvious statement can be in practice, and Part 3 of the book will explain that it lies at the heart of the airline capacity management challenge.

ii. The economics of supply

This section will look first at the close relationship between output and price, then at the heterogeneity of airline output, and finally at some of the more important supply-side characteristics of the industry. Detailed consideration of costs is held over to the next chapter.

Output and price

'Supply' is the amount of a product that producers are willing and able to make available during a given time period and subject to a given set of determinant (independent) variables. Market supply is the aggregate of each firm's individual supply decisions.

- A *supply function* is a table that relates the current states of various supply-determining independent variables (notably input cost and output price) to a particular quantity of product supplied (the dependent variable).

- A *supply schedule* is a table relating a series of possible prices to the quantity supplied at each price if all other supply-determining variables remain unchanged. In other words, quantity of output supplied (q) is treated here as a function of price (p); we can replace the right-hand side of this general functional equation $q = f(p)$ with a mathematical expression specific to the product concerned – that is, a mathematical expression describing the impact that price changes have been observed to have on the quantity of this particular product supplied in the past. Different values for 'p' can then be substituted to investigate how much output to supply at different price levels.

Focusing here on price, the 'law of supply' states that there is a direct relationship between price and quantity supplied; all other things being equal, if price rises so will the quantity supplied and vice versa. The 'law of demand' that we met in chapter 2 states that as price rises, demand falls; it is these contrary movements up and down demand and supply curves that bring markets into short-run equilibrium. A *supply curve* is a graphical representation of a supply schedule. With price again on the vertical axis and quantity on the horizontal, the curve will be upward-sloping from left to right – illustrating that in most cases 'q' will fall as 'p' declines, and vice versa, assuming all other things remain constant. That 'things' in fact do not always remain constant leads to the following distinction.

- **Change in quantity supplied** This is marked by movement up or down a given supply curve. Everything else that might affect supply – such as falling input costs or the introduction of productivity-enhancing new technology, either of which could hold out the prospect of increased profits and so motivate producers to supply more output – is assumed to remain unchanged.
- **Change in supply** In this case, one of the nonprice determinants of supplier behaviour has shifted the supply curve right or left of its original position and so changed the quantity supplied at each given price. A rightward (or downward) shift in the supply curve increases the quantity that producers are prepared to sell at any given price; an upward or leftward shift implies that producers require a higher price for each unit brought to market (perhaps, for example, because input prices have risen).

The percentage change in output (the dependent variable) that occurs in response to a one per cent change in an independent variable is known as the *elasticity of supply*. The most commonly-used independent variable is price (i.e., the 'price-elasticity of supply'); others include interest rates, wage rates, and non-labour input costs. Supply is generally more elastic in the long run than the short run because most firms face capacity constraints that it takes time to overcome – although the truth of this generalisation depends upon the nature of the product and, in particular, the production process.

Neoclassical theory assumes that profit maximisation is the overriding objective of all business firms. A cost curve illustrates the minimum cost at which a firm can produce each of various amounts of output – but how is the output decision actually arrived at? The level of profit-maximising output will, according to neoclassical theory, be heavily influenced by market structure – to which we will turn in the next section of the chapter.

Regardless of market structure, a profit-maximising firm should nonetheless select the output at which the difference between total revenue and total cost is greatest. This is found where marginal revenue (*MR*) is equal to marginal cost (*MC*). If *MR* exceeds *MC*, profit can be increased by selling more and to achieve this price should be lowered; if *MR* is less than *MC*, profit can be increased by selling less and to achieve this price should be raised; if *MR* and *MC* are equal, profit cannot be increased by raising or lowering output and so both output and price are optimal. In perfectly competitive markets *P*, *MR*, and *MC* are equal. (All standard business economics books will explain the reasoning.)

This is sound economic theory, but there are several 'disconnects' which separate it from the practical world.

1. It is doubtful that decision-makers ever know their marginal costs or, indeed, the details of their demand and supply functions (Bowman and Ambrosini, 1998). (Economists have developed various methods for estimating their way around such problems, but these methods are less than perfect and are anyway beyond the scope of the present discussion.) Analysis is also complicated by the distinction between SRMC and LRMC that we met in the last chapter.
2. As we have seen, airlines inevitably produce excess output (reflected in load factors below 100 per cent). There are two principal reasons.
    *   The sometimes extreme demand peaking experienced by the industry, exacerbated by an inability to inventory output (a point we will look at below), means that any level of capacity capable of meeting a substantial proportion of peak demand will – if reasonably fully utilised at other times – inevitably lead to the production of excess off-peak output.
    *   Some market segments (notably business travellers) are responsible for high levels of random demand variation (on a departure-by-departure basis), yet also require the late availability of space (i.e.,

high 'seat accessibility') to accommodate their last-minute travel purchase behaviours.

This is part of the cost of doing business in the airline industry, but it is something that does not sit comfortably with the structure of traditional economic models.

3. Whilst the idea that output and price are optimised where $P = MR = MC$ might be appropriate to the baseline theoretical model of perfect competition, most airline markets are to a greater or lesser extent 'imperfect'. In imperfect markets firms will try to exploit whatever opportunity they are given (e.g., by a government dispensing route designations in a regulated market) or are able to create (e.g., by building a 'fortress hub') to price above MC. (A price-cost margin (i.e., price - marginal cost/price) of zero is evidence of perfect competition, where $MC = MR = P$; the closer the figure comes to unity, the greater is the monopoly power of the firm concerned.)

4. Price is anyway not necessarily a single, discernible figure; at any one time there can be many different prices charged for essentially similar products in the same marketplace. 'Price' is a highly complex concept in an industry such as the airline business where differential and discriminatory pricing are widespread and output is actively revenue-managed.

5. The last point underlines that even what is meant by 'product' and 'marketplace' is open to question, to the extent that a flight departing from point A en route to point B, which in one sense is itself a 'product' by virtue of its schedule and routing, can also be argued to be offering a number of different products in several different markets: different products might be defined by inflight amenities in the separate cabins or by the various conditions applied to tickets purchased by individual travellers in any one cabin; furthermore, the flight could be carrying not only local passengers travelling from A to B, but also passengers who started their journeys somewhere behind A and/or will continue beyond B – that is, passengers whose journeys constitute purchase decisions made in numerous different city-pair markets.

The assumption made by neoclassical economic models that output – in this case airline output – is homogeneous is therefore open to serious doubt. We will look at this next.

The heterogeneity of airline output

Different airlines produce very different mixes of cargo and passenger output. These can be broken down further into categories such as scheduled passenger, scheduled freight, mail, nonscheduled passenger, and nonscheduled freight output. But there is something more fundamental to consider: although airlines produce ASMs and ATMs, customers each buy a service package comprised of attributes designed to deliver certain benefits. The core of each package is safe, timely transportation for themselves or their goods, but there is much more to any package than just this core (see Holloway, 2002).

Passenger output

'ASM' and 'ATM' are metrics that measure aggregate output but tell us nothing about the nature of that output. General Motors produces X million cars each year and Delta flies Y billion ASMs – but what sort of cars for which markets, and what sort of services delivered on what types of route? If we accept that demand is heterogeneous, as proposed by the theory of monopolistic competition that we will meet later in the chapter and as reflected by the efforts of marketers to divide markets into segments having different demand curves, then supply must also be heterogeneous wherever producers are actually trying to satisfy consumer demand.

In this there are cost implications. One ASM generated by Southwest is pretty much the same as another; any differences in the production costs associated with the output of different ASMs are largely attributable to different stage-lengths (and to a much lesser extent station costs), because the aircraft type and the onboard product are standard across the network. (This is not strictly true given the different series of B737 operated and the slightly higher standard of 'catering' offered on transcontinental routes, but the point holds well enough for the purposes of the present argument.) At American, in contrast, the network output of ASMs is an average that masks considerable differences in the nature – and costs – of the different types of output; because American's fleet contains numerous aircraft types and its service portfolio encompasses much broader geographic and product scope than is the case at Southwest, it is fairly obvious that the larger carrier produces ASMs in many more different ways. The point here is that the raw number of ASMs supplied by an airline tells us only so much. A more complete understanding comes from familiarity with the markets in which it has chosen to generate ASMs and the service(s) it has decided to offer into those markets. Box 4.2 illustrates how American set about designing a product capable of delivering distinctive output into one particular segment: long-haul premium.

Box 4.2: American's 'Flagship Suite'

American Airlines launched a new premium (i.e., long-haul first class) product for its B777 fleet in 2000. This box will briefly describe the concept, the team, the product, and the sequence of events. Its purpose is to link the point made in the main text regarding the heterogeneity of airline output to the practical disciplines involved in designing different service packages for different segments of demand.

The concept *The challenge confronting the design team was to come up with a concept capable not just of matching recent developments in premium cabins introduced by leading competitors, but of setting a new benchmark. The key issue was of course to design something capable of meeting – or ideally outpacing, albeit perhaps only temporarily – the rapidly rising expectations of targeted customers. This was not just a question of identifying a roster of customer preferences, however; anthropomorphic and behavioural differences between national groups had to be taken into account.*

The essence of the task was to design something that would appeal in particular to US customers – the argument being that part of American's positioning in international markets hints at a role as US national 'flag carrier'. Quite aside from questions of taste, important design implications flowing from this decision were the need to accommodate the fact that typical US travellers tend to be larger and also more gregarious than some other nationalities, and are as likely to be travelling in couples or larger groups as they are to be travelling singly (whereas British Airways' premium passengers, for example, have an overwhelmingly single male profile). Practical requirements flowing from these considerations were:

- *to design a 'flying bed' acceptable to the 95th percentile US male – something that would, in fact, be the largest flying bed on offer at the time;*
- *to create an effective, aesthetically pleasing, and space-efficient environment within which passengers can relax, work, and dine;*
- *to maintain a sense of openness in the cabin, whilst providing adequate privacy for customers who want it.*

The team *As would be expected for a project of this complexity, the team was multi-disciplinary and multinational.*

- *Design Acumen (UK), which had previously been responsible for British Airways' revolutionary 'flat-bed' first class seating introduced in 1994, led design of the seat and adjacent furniture.*
- *ETC (US) took responsibility for ergonomic engineering.*
- *Simon Martin Veque Winklestein (US) co-ordinated overall cabin aesthetics.*
- *Other external team members included Bowes Design and Development (UK – full cabin mock-up), Britax Rumbold (UK – seat manufacture), and Total Research Corporation (US – market research).*
- *American Airlines' team members were drawn from programme management, cabin interiors management, and engineering functions (the latter looking in particular at maintenance issues). They reported up to the levels of SVP planning and EVP marketing.*

The product The focal point of cabin redesign was a unique swivel seat intended both to optimise use of each passenger's available space and to facilitate interaction between groups of up to four passengers travelling together. A herringbone pattern combined with the swivel capability was used to maximise utilisation of the cabin cross-section given the 1-2-1 configuration. Specifically, seating offset more than 18° from aircraft centreline is required to have a harness as well as a lap-strap for take-off and landing (which most passengers would prefer not to have), whilst maximum use of cabin floorspace – particularly cabin width – requires fully extended beds to be offset at angles from centreline greater than 18°. The swivel seat, forward-aligned for take-off and landing but adjustable for inflight working, relaxing, dining, and sleeping, was the answer.

In addition to its swivel capability, another critical design first was drop-down arm-rests which transform the 21-inch-wide seat into a bed with maximum 30.5-inch width at the hips where it is needed most. Finally, the design effort also incorporated innovative fold-out workstations and dining tables.

The process American's re-evaluation of its long-haul premium product began in 1996. Market research was conducted during the second half of the year, and the design-build team was finalised by early 1997. Design Acumen began alternative concept presentations to American in March 1997. The preferred option was then developed into a full-size (as yet unstyled) mock-up that was shipped to the United States for design review and ergonomic assessment. Evaluation work looked not only at the seat, but also at the ergonomics of other furniture – one particular issue being that dining and working impose different ergonomic requirements on tables; other issues were the placement of inflight entertainment (IFE) and inflight communications (IFC) hardware, and also the availability of storage space.

A second-round rig was developed to explore the ergonomic lessons learned and to refine design options on the basis of inputs from both customers and professionals. Certification issues then had to be addressed – specifically, 16g testing requirements for the seat, and head-injury clearance relative to adjacent furniture; the high level of seat functionality in particular made engineering a 16g-certifiable seat within realistic time, weight, and cost constraints a significant challenge. Styling also had to be settled.

The final stage was presentation of a complete B777 first class cabin mock-up, with fully functional seats, for sign-off by American, followed by engineering, production, and certification. Press launch came in May 2000, followed by a test and demonstration flight three months later and initial introduction into service a month after that.

Source: adapted from Dryburgh (2000).

(See Holloway (1998b, 2002) for comprehensive discussions of passenger service attributes.)

Cargo output

Airlines differ substantially in the amount of cargo output they generate. A short-haul scheduled passenger carrier competing against well-developed surface modes might carry mail, but is unlikely to need capacity for substantial volumes of freight. As routes become longer, and particularly if they are operated by widebodied aircraft with spacious belly-holds, the output of saleable freight ton-miles increases dramatically.

We can distinguish service concepts such as: airport-to-airport line-haul, primarily serving forwarders; branded time-definite products targeted directly at shippers as much as forwarders; and specialised capabilities in the handling of perishable products, live animals, or outsize loads. Before later starting to diversify, Atlas Air created a niche in the 1990s by leasing out its freighters on an aircraft, crew, maintenance, and insurance (ACMI) basis, with lessees paying rentals, providing traffic rights, and meeting cash operating costs. Finally, some carriers, notably the integrators, are beginning to become multi-modal logistics companies insofar as they offer warehousing, light assembly, and distribution facilities to key accounts – albeit still on a relatively small scale – and in many markets provide fully integrated ground/air services. (Several European carriers also make extensive use of cross-border rail and, particularly, road transport to feed long-haul services, thereby producing ASMs on the ground.)

The four largest cargo markets are: US domestic, North Atlantic, North Pacific, and Far East-Europe. Since the 1980s, virtually the entire US domestic market has been taken over by integrated carriers such as FedEx and UPS, offering high-yield time-definite services. In international markets, although a growing number of combination carriers are now offering time-definite products (some of which are standardised across alliances – as in the case of SkyTeam), many are still primarily engaged in relatively low-yield airport-to-airport line-haul – sometimes on a space-available rather than firm-space basis.

The fundamental issues in respect of cargo output are sales channel design and airline brand visibility amongst shippers. Relatively few carriers have branded cargo operations maintaining significant direct relationships with shippers. Those that do not are essentially offering line-haul products to forwarders and consolidators who can shop around for the cheapest rates because, subject to reliable service, shippers on the whole are not carrier-sensitive. Cargo sales departments at such airlines are filling space, rather than developing markets for their output. To overcome this problem, some carriers are building closer relationships with key forwarders to offer time-definite, 'virtually integrated' door-to-door service in competition with integrated carriers and even, for the largest shippers, an integrated logistics product. This latter trend involves relatively few airlines, however, and it seems likely that over the next few years the integrated carriers will continue to make inroads into high-yield segments of international freight, including heavy freight, markets.

As is the case with the passenger product, cargo services can nonetheless be characterised as being comprised of bundles of attributes targeted at segments of shippers and forwarders with different requirements. A survey of shippers by Mercer Management Consulting suggests that key attributes in order of priority are: reliability; transit times; price; real-time shipment tracking; ease of documentation; guaranteed pick-up/drop-off times; specialised freight-handling capabilities; strong global network; and EDI (Shields, 1998). Cargo output, therefore, need not be a homogeneous block of ATMs; by making explicit service design decisions airlines can pitch their output at specific shipper and forwarder requirements, target specific types of heavy freight and express (document and small parcel) shipment, and position themselves strategically on a continuum stretching from pure capacity provision to value-adding service partner.

The supply-side characteristics of airline service

Heterogeneous though it is, there are certain common characteristics of all airline output that flow directly from the nature of the air transport industry (Rispoli, 1996; Holloway, 2002). The points which follow are framed with reference to the passenger side of the industry, but most can be extended to freight output.

1. It is a feature of airline economics that adding output improves product quality as perceived by customers. This manifests itself in two ways.
    *   Empty airline seats are not necessarily evidence of oversupply – they are also part of a product. Certain types of passenger, notably those travelling on business, tend to book quite close to departure and also to change their travel plans after booking or once a journey has begun. Such passengers usually must pay the highest fares chargeable in the chosen class of travel in order to obtain this flexibility, and the revenue they generate is therefore particularly important for many scheduled airlines. Fully-booked airplanes inhibit such flexibility and, whilst being beneficial to airline revenues in the short term, might have negative long-term repercussions if the brand loyalty of these customers is eroded by frequent inability to make or change bookings at short notice.

        To ensure this does not happen to an unacceptable extent, airlines try to build 'seat accessibility' into their full-fare products (i.e., to build-in a high probability of being able to obtain a booking on the required flight in the preferred class whenever a reservation is attempted); high accessibility is achieved by ensuring seats remain available for this important category of passenger until very close to departure. This means that, particularly in first and business classes, although an airplane might depart with some empty seats there is not necessarily an oversupply problem.
    *   Additional frequencies improve choice of departure time. Frequency competition is a key dynamic in many liberalised markets, especially when the business segment is being targeted; operating smaller aircraft at higher frequencies than before need not inevitably boost aggregate output in a market, but on the whole the recent history of the industry has seen increased frequencies putting upward pressure on output (Wells, 1999).
2. Consumers (i.e., end-users of the service, who may or may not also be the customers who make actual purchase decisions) need to be physically present to receive the core transportation service. This means that

unsold output is lost at the point of production because it cannot be inventoried. Box 4.3 looks at the implications of product perishability.

Box 4.3: Product perishability

Airline seats are perishable. In the case of tangible goods being sold at a price which, in the short run, a producer is not prepared to lower, any output in excess of what the market will absorb at that particular price can in principle be inventoried for later release. Because carriage by air is a service that is produced and consumed at the same time, airline seats and cargo space quite obviously cannot be produced and then placed into inventory for later sale. As we saw when discussing marginal cost pricing in chapter 3, this puts considerable pressure on carriers to lower their prices, often drastically, in order to sell scheduled output remaining unsold as a departure date approaches.

The perishability problem is exacerbated by the demand peaking problem we met in chapter 2. Like nearly all transportation systems, airlines face daily, weekly or seasonal demand peaking (as well as long-term directional imbalances in most freight markets, and short-term imbalances in some passenger flows). Many carriers retain sufficient capacity to meet a significant proportion of all but the highest peak demand. Inevitably what tends to happen is that during peak periods there is an undersupply of output (and a deterioration in seat accessibility) leading to 'spillage' of demand, whilst during off-peak periods there is an oversupply. In principle, the price mechanism should work to dampen these extremes: prices should rise and so reduce demand to match any undersupply, and they should fall in response to oversupply. Indeed, there is widespread peak and off-peak pricing in respect of discounted fares, but aircraft nonetheless still operate at low load factors in off-peak periods.

---

3. We have seen that transportation is an experience derived from a mix of tangible and intangible elements that can be identified as separate service attributes (Holloway, 2002). Different packages of attributes can be assembled pursuant to different service concepts, and this is what makes output heterogeneous; the more service concepts an airline has in its portfolio, the more heterogeneous its output. Different packages have different production costs. (Another effect of intangibility is that the complexity of their price-quality relationship makes services difficult to price.)

4. Because production and consumption of the service can only occur simultaneously, there is a high level of contact between consumers on the one hand and an airline's operational staff, facilities, equipment,

and processes on the other. Interpersonal contacts between consumers and service providers (i.e., an airline's front-line staff) are therefore a significant part of the service experience and are highly significant service attributes. This places the marketing and operations functions into particularly close proximity with each other.

5. Front-line personnel in direct contact with consumers can have a profound impact on the quality of service delivered, but often have little influence over the design of that service.

6. Many airlines have transactional dealings with an overwhelming majority of their customers, but relationship dealings with a relatively small number of frequent (primarily business) travellers who generate a disproportionately high percentage of their revenues.

7. The level of output customisation airlines are able to offer even to their high-value customers is relatively limited, with the result that the style and tone of service delivery are often all that prevent a consumer feeling he or she is being anonymously processed.

8. As well as being people-intensive, airline service is also equipment-intensive and information-intensive, with the result that service delivery depends heavily on the effective management of both people and technology.

9. Airline operations exhibit a great deal of short-run rigidity.

  • Whilst some airlines now manage their fleets much more flexibly than in the past (making late substitutions of different-sized variants within families such as the B737 and A320 series, for example), output (i.e., ASMs and ATMs) remains difficult to adjust on any significant scale over a short period of time – with upper limits imposed by capacity at full utilisation, and lower limits set by the sustainability of fixed costs associated with an underutilised fleet. A countervailing advantage is that because aircraft are mobile, they can be quickly reallocated in response to demand fluctuations in different markets. (We saw in 1991 and, more acutely, in 2001 that airlines willing to take drastic action can in fact make swift and substantial cuts in output; however, unless aircraft that are parked or scrapped are fully depreciated, their ownership costs will remain a burden and a longer-term solution must be found.)

  • As already mentioned, unsold output produced off-peak cannot be inventoried for later sale.

  • It is difficult and expensive to quickly upgrade service quality levels because heavy investments are likely to be needed in facilities and equipment and, particularly, in staff training.

10. The fact that a system comprised of capital equipment and highly trained people has to be in place to offer service on any significant scale

means that fixed costs are high; this in turn puts airlines under pressure to adopt a volume-oriented approach to their business, which then exerts pressure to engage in 'marginal cost pricing' whenever this is what it takes to maintain traffic volume. The impact is often seen in weak yields, particularly when new capacity is added to a market or when the economy turns down.

11. Output decisions in many, albeit a declining number of, international markets remain constrained by the terms of bilateral air services agreements (Holloway, 1998a).

12. In some jurisdictions, competition authorities can influence output decisions which are deemed, for example, to be predatory or an abuse of dominant position.

Picking up on the last point, the next section will discuss market structure using the traditional neoclassical models, and will then briefly touch on competition policy.

iii. Market structure and competition

We saw in the opening chapter that competitive strategy is driven by both internal, firm-specific considerations and by the structure of external markets. The resource-based tradition within strategic management has a strong internal orientation, while the IO tradition – heavily influenced by neoclassical microeconomics – looks primarily to market structure as a driver of strategic conduct and performance. In this section of the chapter we will look at what neoclassical theory has to say about market structure, and relate the models proposed to what is happening in air transport markets. A brief introduction to the evolving role of competition policy will follow.

Determinants of market structure

The neoclassical approach characterises the firm as a technologically driven production function within which inputs are transformed into outputs of goods and services; once an objective function such as profit maximisation has been assigned, the level and price of output can be set and varied in response to changes in input prices, production efficiency, and demand. The precise nature of this interaction will be heavily influenced by the structure of the market in which the firm is operating. Market structure provides a context for management behaviour and so can help explain conduct (i.e., the competitive decisions taken by airline managers) and performance (i.e., how efficient the price and output decisions at which they actually arrive are in allocating scarce resources).

Because a market is comprised of buyers, sellers, and a product, the structure of that market will depend upon the numbers and relative power of buyers and sellers, the defining attributes of the product concerned, and how much information the parties have.

The numbers of buyers and sellers, and their respective power

Most passenger markets have a large number of buyers; airfreight markets have relatively fewer, although rapid growth of the express parcel business is significantly expanding the number. How many sellers are present varies widely between city-pair markets. And here we have the first hint of a truism often overlooked: there is no such thing as *the* air transport market, but instead thousands of individual city-pair markets. In most of these there are substantial numbers of buyers, whereas the numbers of sellers might range upwards from one to quite a few depending upon the regulatory environment and the geography of the market (for example, whether there are competing hubs situated between the origin and destination). Where power lies in a particular market will depend on the impact of any commercial regulations affecting that market, the number of sellers present in it, and the appetite each seller has for real competition. Another variable, to which we will return shortly in the context of contestability theory, is the impact of *potential* market entrants on the supply side. Finally, some competing suppliers might be outside the airline industry – that is, might be producers of substitute products (e.g., videoconferencing).

Ease of market entry, mobility, and exit

Buyers are largely free to enter or leave air transport markets, although some business travellers and freight shippers have less choice in this regard than other users; sellers do not always have the same degree of flexibility. Barriers to entry are characteristics of an industry which place incumbents at an advantage over new entrants. Barriers to mobility are characteristics that limit mobility within an industry insofar as they constrain incumbents wanting to embark on a significant change in strategy. Barriers to exit are industry characteristics which militate against redeployment of assets. We will look at these different barriers later in the chapter.

The extent of product differentiation or distinctiveness

Differentiation exists when one of two or more competing products is perceived by customers to offer differences sufficient to justify payment of a price premium; distinctiveness also arises from perceived differences, but in this case although they might stimulate a preference and a purchase they will not generate a price premium. Either can flow from any of the benefits offered by a particular service package (Holloway, 2002). The purpose of both differentiation (an economic concept) and distinctiveness (a concept drawn from the brand management literature) is to make other products weaker substitutes for the product in question than would otherwise be the case. Substitutes enhance competition; conversely, where a product is differentiated from similar products in a manner which has relevance to buyers, this may constrain competition in the short run – depending upon how competitors react. (Chapter 1 has already explored differences between the concept of 'differentiation' as used by economists and the concept of 'distinctiveness' that is found in the brand management literature.)

Common wisdom these days is that airline seats are commodities. This is debatable. It is certainly true that the number of ways available to make the attributes of a service package truly distinct is limited, and that distinctiveness in the 'hard' attributes derived from facilities and equipment can in many cases be readily imitated. On the other hand, brand image and service style, both underpinned by a strong service culture, are not as easily imitable – and this is often where true distinctiveness lies (ibid). Southwest, for example, has an image and corporate personality which make it stand out; an airline that appears to be selling a commodity service largely on price is in fact selling a distinct combination of service attributes (frequency, schedule, reliability, and service style, for example, as well as the more visible attributes embedded in cabin configuration) – all of which are priced to offer a particular type of customer value reflecting a service concept distinct from any of the concepts offered by, say, American.

The availability and cost of information

This is another important determinant of market structure according to the neoclassical model. The cheaper and more readily accessible information about alternative products and their prices is, the more competitive a market will usually be. Airline CRSs and the remaining GDSs have made it easy and cheap in principle for buyers to tap information about product availability, price, and quality. However, both the architecture of GDSs and the use of booking incentives provided to travel agents by airlines have been documented as introducing distortions into the flow of product information to customers. Various codes of conduct have been adopted in the United States, the European Union, and elsewhere to police the former, whereas the latter remain rife but will decline in impact as a growing proportion of airline reservations are made online. It is worth keeping in mind that those start-ups and small carriers willing to bear GDS fees have an advantage unavailable to minor players in many other industries: ready access to a global, state-of-the-art distribution channel.

Generic models of market structure

The four models of market structure found in neoclassical microeconomic analysis are outlined below, along with some of their implications for the air transport industry.

Perfect competition

The key assumptions of this model are as follows.

- Large numbers of small producers and consumers are present, none of whom is able to influence market price. Producers are therefore 'price-takers' whose individual pricing and output decisions have no impact on market price. None has market power. Indeed, there is no actual *competition* under conditions of perfect competition because by definition no firm can influence the market through its choice of strategic conduct. *Short-run* equilibrium is established by firms varying output in an effort to maximise profitability given their individual cost structures and the price they have to accept for their products.
- All products in the market are homogeneous – that is, perfect substitutes for each other – with the result that no firm can raise its price without losing all of its business. The assumption of product homogeneity means that there is a single market price for the industry's output. According to this model, ASMs produced by flying business class seats from London to Orlando are identical to ASMs produced by flying seats in a charter airline's main (or only) cabin, and consumers do not distinguish between them. In fact, there is no single market for the output of the air transport industry and neither is there a single commoditised output or product; there are thousands of city-pair markets, and in each of these will be separate groups of consumers demanding particular types of output and separate airlines competing to provide these different segments with what they are demanding. There is no

single industry cost curve, and no single market-clearing equilibrium price for air transport services.

- Information is 'perfect' in the sense that it is costless and freely available to all market participants. In fact, consumers do not have perfect information and information-seeking does involve 'search costs'. One purpose of investing in a strong brand image is to reduce consumer uncertainty with regard to service quality and consistency (Holloway, 2002); advertising can help in this regard, as well as providing more specific service information (e.g., regarding destinations served). Also, effective branding can help distinguish an airline and its services – something that is anathema to perfect competition.
- Innovation is entirely exogenous (i.e., from sources external to the market), making firms perforce reactive rather than proactive. The air transport industry in fact has a long history of endogenous (i.e., internally generated) technical and commercial innovation.
- Barriers to entry and exit are absent, allowing perfect mobility in markets for both factor inputs and the product being produced. Similarly, consumers face no switching costs. *Long-run* equilibrium is established by the entry and exit of firms into and out of the industry in response to the presence or absence of opportunities to earn (economic) profit. In fact, there is no shortage of entry barriers in the air transport industry – as we will shortly see.

Bearing on the last point, a key question is whether *actual* market entry is required in order to put downward pressure on equilibrium prices, or whether *threat* of entry is sufficient. Contestability theory argues that the market efficiencies associated with perfect competition can be generated as readily by the credible threat of market entry as by actual entry.

Contestability theory Airline deregulation in the United States was the outcome of three sets of pressures – two academic and one consumerist.

1. A body of research was accumulated during the 1960s and 1970s suggesting that regulation resulted in unnecessarily high service quality (i.e., flight frequencies) and correspondingly low load factors sustained by high fares. (See, for example: Levine, 1965; Jordan, 1970; Kahn, 1971; Keeler, 1972; Douglas and Miller, 1974b.) The particular concern of many leading US economists was that regulation was causing prices to diverge from the welfare-maximising level established by long-run marginal costs (Button, 1993).
2. With the University of Chicago in the vanguard, a view gained momentum that regulation was incompatible with the public interest. The

heart of the problem was thought to be 'regulatory capture': regulated firms, in this case airlines, were argued to have undue influence over regulatory agencies both because these agencies rely on the firms for cost data and also because of the firms' lobbying power.

3. Air travellers were able to see palpable differences between low fares in the deregulated California and Texas intrastate markets and higher prices in federally regulated interstate markets.

A theory sometimes cited as a contributor to the deregulation debate but which was in fact most fully developed in the immediate post-deregulation years and used both as an *ex post* justification (ibid) and as an argument for adopting a relaxed attitude towards the wave of airline mergers in the 1980s was contestability theory (Bain, 1949; Bailey and Panzar, 1981; Baumol et al, 1982). Instead of the large number of *actual* competitors required by the perfect competition model, contestability theory is content with the presence of just a threat of entry from *potential* competitors – all other requirements of the model remaining more or less unchanged. It was argued that under certain conditions many of the benefits of perfectly competitive markets (notably improvements in consumer welfare in respect of price and service quality) could be 'simulated' whenever a plausible competitor was potentially free to attack – if only on a hit-and-run basis – a market in which excessive profits were being made by one or more incumbents.

Hit-and-run entry, it was argued, can be remunerative provided that the entrant is able to establish a sufficiently high price for long enough to permit earnings to at least compensate for the sunk (i.e., irrecoverable) costs arising from entry; the lower these sunk costs are, the more appealing such a strategy could be. This threat alone would then be sufficient to influence prices charged by incumbents, and actual market entry would be unnecessary. In this way, resources would be efficiently allocated, monopoly profits would be unsustainable in the long run, and the industry would produce optimum output at minimum cost.

If contestability theory holds true, it should be possible to identify certain characteristics in a deregulated market (ibid).

1. Active entry and exit affecting both the industry as a whole and individual city-pairs.
2. Pronounced efforts to minimise costs.
3. Absence of sustained supernormal profits.
4. Pricing behaviour that is not primarily driven by the numbers or sizes of actual competitors.

In the post-deregulation United States, the first two predictions have been satisfied only to a limited extent: whilst entry and exit have been active at the industry level and in respect of many domestic city-pair markets, nonregulatory barriers to entry have arisen in some important nonstop markets (e.g., those with a 'fortress hub' at one end); with regard to cost minimisation, this was slow in coming to a number of incumbents. The presence of supernormal profits is difficult to determine because derivation of economic profit from financial accounting presentations is not a straightforward task. Empirical studies have therefore focused largely on airline pricing, and the weight of evidence suggests that contestability – at least in its purest form – is not an adequate predictor of competitive behaviour in deregulated airline markets (Graham et al, 1983; Meyer and Oster, 1984; Bailey et al, 1985; Baumol and Willig, 1986; Moore, 1986; Bailey and Williams, 1988).

On the other hand, Morrison and Winston (1986) have argued that there is support for what they call 'imperfect contestability', if not for 'pure' contestability. Were a market perfectly contestable, fares would be independent of the level of concentration amongst producers; Borenstein (1989) found this not to be the case in the US domestic air transport markets studied, but did find that fares on monopoly routes are reduced – albeit not to competitive levels – when another carrier is already operating at one or both ends of the route. Furthermore, other studies have also found that potential entry constrains fares (Evans and Kessides, 1993). One important consideration, though, is how to identify potential entrants when trying to assess their influence: whilst it is common to assume that airlines already serving both endpoints of a route are potential entrants, there are researchers who consider carriers to be potential entrants only if they are not at a significant disadvantage to the incumbent(s) in generating connecting traffic (Hurdel et al, 1989).

On the whole, it is fair to assume that a majority of observers concur with the findings of Borenstein (1992) and Hurdel et al (op cit) that the impact on ticket prices of the number of *potential* competitors is considerably less significant than the impact of the number of carriers actually operating in a market. In fact, some of the fundamental assumptions underlying contestability theory have come under attack in the literature, most notably the following.

1. **The absence of barriers to entry** A barrier to entry is anything that physically prevents a challenger from entering a market (e.g., lack of traffic rights or slots) or economically disadvantages the new entrant by imposing upon it higher costs than are faced by the incumbent (e.g., economies of scale). We will look at barriers to entry in a moment, but

it is safe to say that few observers now deny that they pose problems in many important air transport markets.

2. **Low sunk costs confronting entrants** Whilst it is true that aircraft are highly mobile and therefore rarely become 'sunk' into a particular market, the same is not true of advertising and route development costs – or of the early post-launch losses often incurred when a new market is entered (Stiglitz, 1994). That said, the size and significance of sunk costs involved in entering a given market will depend upon the identity of the entrant. For example:

   - market entry *might* impose on a large and well-established airline fewer absolute sunk costs than a start-up insofar as it already benefits from a corporate infrastructure with the experience and capacity to launch new routes and, importantly, it may well have an established brand image that is recognised in the market being entered;
   - even if the sunk costs encountered are the same, they are likely to be less significant to an established carrier than to a start-up.

   Airlines certainly do enter routes opportunistically and/or experimentally, but 'hit-and-run' network strategies are nonetheless relatively rare on the scheduled side of the industry as a whole.

3. **Incumbents' inability to respond rapidly to entrants' lower prices** The assumption that incumbents will keep their prices down to avoid provoking potential entry also runs counter to much recent experience. More often an incumbent will price as high as a market will bear, and then respond aggressively to any new entrant that does in fact materialise. Potential entrants now know from their own and others' experiences that in many cases apparent profit opportunities can diminish or disappear the instant they enter, because incumbents have the ability to respond immediately with aggressive capacity-controlled discounting. Certainly, the requirement of the theory that consumers are able to respond more rapidly to an entrant's low prices than is an incumbent, so diverting business almost instantaneously to anybody flying in to attack the incumbent's 'supernormal profits', is unlikely to be met. An incumbent able to lower prices more rapidly than a new entrant is able to establish itself in a market is less likely to be concerned about the dangers of keeping prices high prior to – and under threat of – entry than about keeping costs low, so that it can better sustain a fare war if one were to develop as a result of that threat of entry materialising.

Whatever the perceived merit or shortcoming of contestability theory as a justification for deregulation or liberalisation, there are forces at work in some markets which make it increasingly difficult for potential entrants to turn threat into reality. Even where regulators have backed away, there are other barriers that can inhibit market entry – particularly by start-ups and small carriers, but also by larger airlines as well in some cases. We will look at these shortly.

Conclusion Whilst some financial and commodity markets do approximate the ideal of perfect competition, most – including air transport markets – do not. Few markets are as frictionless as the ideal modelled by perfect competition, and the real use of the model is less as a realistic goal than as a benchmark against which to compare prevailing reality. Perfect competition in fact models an idealised 'limiting case' at the opposite end of the spectrum from monopoly; put simply, what distinguishes the two is whether or not a producer has the power to set prices.

Monopoly

Monopoly is characterised by one seller, high (perhaps insurmountable) barriers to market entry, the non-availability of close substitutes, and a poor flow of information to consumers; a monopolist's demand curve and the market demand curve are identical, whilst there is no supply curve as such.

- A monopolist can set price or output, but not both; the shape of the demand curve it faces is the ultimate constraint. (The law of demand applies as much to monopolists as to other producers.)
- A profit-maximising monopolist will, like other profit-maximisers, set output where marginal revenue is equal to marginal cost; price will be above marginal cost (unlike the situation in a perfectly competitive market where marginal cost, marginal revenue, and price are the same).
- How much a monopolist's price can exceed marginal cost will depend on the market's price-elasticity of demand (i.e., the shape of the demand curve); the more elastic demand is, the closer price will be to marginal cost and the more similar the outcome will be to what would prevail in a competitive market (Pindyck and Rubinfeld, 2001).

Monopolies might be economically efficient in industries with very high fixed costs wherein scale brings to the production process such benefits that average cost can be minimised only by serving the entire market, or where – as in the case of air traffic control – there can only be one provider (circumstances referred to as a 'natural monopoly'). Where unregulated or benignly regulated, however, monopolists tend to offer less and lower quality output at higher prices and subject to higher costs than would otherwise prevail, and 'supernormal' profits are in principle attainable.

Monopoly power Although pure monopoly is relatively rare, it is not unusual for markets to be characterised by relatively few competitors. Where these firms are able to influence price, and in particular sustain a price above marginal cost, they are said to have *monopoly power*. (This observation has already been made in chapter 3, where monopoly power was characterised as one of several possible price drivers.) We will shortly look at market situations that might lead to monopoly power either narrowly within specific niches (e.g., monopolistic competition) or more broadly across an industry (e.g., a collusive oligopoly). The point here is that monopoly (i.e., a single supplier) and monopoly power (i.e., an ability to influence price and earn supernormal profit) are not necessarily synonymous.

Monopolistic competition

The advantage of monopoly power is, as we have seen, the opportunity it confers to pitch prices above marginal costs and prospectively earn supernormal profits. Neoclassical microeconomics proposes models of market structure other than pure monopoly wherein despite several producers being present in the market one or more of them has at least some control over price and is able to charge a price that exceeds marginal cost (Pindyck and Rubinfeld, 2001). We will look first at monopolistic competition, then at oligopoly.

The theory of monopolistic competition was put forward by Chamberlin (1933). The model has less strict defining conditions than perfect competition, notably that products can be perceived by consumers to have important differentiating attributes: competing products are substitutes for each other but not perfect substitutes, so their cross-price elasticities of demand are significant without being infinite. This gives sellers, who must according to the model be large in number, somewhat greater control over prices than in markets with structures closer to perfect competition. Neither will a price change by one firm lead inevitably to a change in price by others, as it would in an oligopolistic market. The extent to which a firm can translate consumers' perceptions of a product's differential advantage into additional profits depends in part upon just how different the product is perceived to be, and in part upon how important the difference is to consumers; in other words, it will depend upon the elasticity of the demand curve that the firm has been able to create by differentiating its product.

Whether monopolistic competition can exist depends on the ability of firms in an industry to differentiate their products, and on the ease of industry entry and exit; the model requires free entry and exit. Whereas in perfectly competitive markets each firm faces its own horizontal demand curve and only the market demand curve is downward sloping, firms under monopolistic competition face downward-sloping individual demand curves; this gives them some monopoly power, but not necessarily free rein to earn substantial profits. Something close to a limited monopoly might be achievable in the short run, but in the long run supernormal profits will be competed away by the arrival of competitors and economic profit will revert to zero. Firms use branding, product design, and other loyalty-generators to 'lengthen' the short run. Indeed, any barrier that prevents or deters market entry by a potential competitor can serve to lengthen the short run.

Monopolistic competition is considered less economically efficient than the ideal of perfect competition because it tends to generate excess capacity, and firms produce at output levels other than those that minimise average costs. On the other hand, monopolistic competition can have the redeeming virtue of offering consumers greater choice insofar as they perceive each producer's offer to be at least somewhat different from other offers. Just how economically inefficient a monopolistically competitive market is relative to the perfect ideal will depend upon the market power of firms within it, which in turn depends upon their number, their attitude towards competition, and how substitutable consumers consider their products to be.

Monopolistic competition and market segmentation   Although it took over two decades and several refinements, the idea of monopolistic competition was perhaps more warmly received amongst marketing practitioners than by traditional neoclassical economists. Alderson (1957) developed from it the idea that firms 'compete for differential advantage' (ibid: 101) in markets where products are not necessarily homogeneous and which can therefore be segmented. 'No-one,' he argues, 'enters business except in the expectation of some degree of differential advantage in serving his customers, and....competition consists of the constant struggle to develop, maintain, or increase such advantages' (ibid: 106).

We can see in this argument, and in the quotation that follows, a significant early step away from the neoclassical assumption of homogeneous firms competing in homogeneous product markets and towards what became the resource-based view – discussed in chapter 1 – that firms apply heterogeneous resources in pursuit of advantage.

> Every business firm occupies a position which is in some respects unique. Its location, the product it sells, its operating methods, or the customers it serves tend to set it off to some degree from every other firm. Each firm competes by making the most of its individuality and its special character. It is constantly seeking to establish some competitive advantage....[because] an advanced method of operation is not enough if all competitors live up to the same high standards. What is important in competition is differential advantage, which

can give a firm an edge over what others in the field are offering (ibid: 101-102).

The vehicle for differential advantage is identification of unserved or poorly served market segments, and the development of service-price offers that will appeal more to constituents of a specific segment than will competing offers. Putting this into the terminology of the resource-based theory of competitive strategy, Hunt (2000: 64) argues that 'firms pursue comparative advantage in resources that will yield marketplace positions of competitive advantage and, thereby, superior financial performance'. (In using the expression 'comparative advantage', he is consciously drawing on international trade theory to help understand sources of *competitive* advantage.) Although rarely acknowledged, there is a striking resemblance between, on the one hand, the notion of differential advantage that grew from seeds sown by Chamberlin in the 1930s, and on the other the idea of competitive advantage popularised in the strategy literature since the late 1970s.

Conclusion The argument has been put forward in recent years that the air transport product has become commoditised – that is, has become a homogenous, undifferentiated product in the sense of the word 'commodity' as used by economists. A very different argument is put forward in Holloway (2002). There is undoubtedly considerable homogenisation of 'hard' or functional product attributes in markets characterised by similar stage-lengths, for example; in any given class of cabin there is often broad similarity between different carriers' products within, say, US domestic markets or intercontinental markets. Nonetheless, functional attributes – particularly in long-haul markets – are not universally the same, and a growing number of carriers are also expending a great deal of effort developing distinctive soft attributes founded on their different corporate cultures, tone and style of service delivery, and brand images.

It is therefore reasonable to characterise at least some air transport markets as monopolistically competitive (Stavins, 1996). The problem is that whilst efforts to make a carrier's service distinctive might generate a brand preference for that carrier when price is broadly comparable with competitors' prices, demand curves in many segments are sufficiently elastic to make premium pricing difficult or impossible to sustain. The real difficulty, however, lies in the long run. To see monopolistic competition in the air transport industry it is necessary to accept contestability theory, because there are few markets in which the defining requirement for a large number of sellers is actually (as opposed to potentially) present, and to take a relaxed view on the impediment posed by barriers to entry – which we will look at below. In a growing number of markets, both propositions are questionable.

Oligopoly

Oligopoly is characterised by few (or few dominant) sellers ('duopoly' being the special case of just two sellers), products which may be either commoditised or differentiated (if only, in the latter case, by heavy advertising), high barriers to entry and exit, and limited consumer access to price, product quality, and cost information. Oligopolistic structures arise not only through internal growth but, characteristically, as a result of mergers and alliances. The airline industry is widely believed to have a strong tendency towards oligopoly.

One of the defining characteristics of oligopolistic markets is the high level of interrelatedness between the actions and reactions of sellers; for example, very frequently a price reduction by one firm will be matched by others – leading, perhaps, to a price war. According to neoclassical theory, a firm's demand curve relates quantity to price, *holding constant all other demand-determining variables*. Thus, its demand curve will 'shift' if the firm lowers its prices in an oligopolistic market because such a change is highly likely to lead to reactive price moves by competitors – in which case other demand-determining variables (i.e., in this case, competitors' prices) are no longer being held constant. This has to be factored into managerial decision-making.

> Managing an oligopolistic firm is complicated because pricing, output, advertising, and investment decisions involve important strategic considerations. Because only a few firms are competing, each firm must carefully consider how its actions will affect its rivals, and how its rivals are likely to react [in response, say, to a price cut intended to stimulate sluggish sales]....These strategic considerations can be complex. When making decisions, each firm must weigh its competitors' reactions, knowing that those competitors will also weigh *its* reactions to *their* decisions. Furthermore, decisions, reactions, reactions to reactions, and so forth are dynamic, evolving over time. When the managers of a firm evaluate the potential consequences of their decisions, they must assume that their competitors are as rational as they are. They must put themselves in their competitors' place and consider how they would react (Pindyck and Rubinfeld, 2001: 429, italics in the original).

Game theory has increasingly been used by economists and strategic management researchers to help understand decision dynamics under oligopolistic and quasi-oligopolistic market structures. The necessity to engage in strategic gaming – that is, to consider how others might react in response to a decision – is characteristic of oligopolistic markets, and sets them apart from the idealised world of perfectly competitive markets where strategic behaviour is irrelevant. The monopoly power held by oligopolists and the profitability of oligopolistic industries depend in large measure upon how players interact when making output and pricing decisions – particularly whether they are prone to co-operate or compete aggressively. Co-operation might, for example, allow firms to charge prices significantly above marginal cost and earn substantial short-run profits whilst at the same time ensuring that entry barriers are kept as high as possible in order to maintain profits in the long run.

Non-co-operative oligopolistic behaviour Nonprice competition – based on product attributes (e.g., network scope, schedule, onboard service), heavy advertising, loyalty schemes or brand image, for example – is common in oligopolistic markets. This is because, as noted above, there is under normal circumstances a considerable amount of price interdependence amongst oligopolists. They generally believe that any price decrease will be matched – causing a decline in profits – and any increase may fail to stick due to competitors' reluctance to follow suit, causing a decline in market share. What they try to do instead, therefore, is shift the demand curve for their products to the right; the objective is to allow more output to be sold at an unchanged price, and although competitors may ultimately react, the response is likely to be less direct or damaging than a response to a price cut. Nonetheless, when rapidly rising output and/or stagnant demand lead to oversupply, price competition can become intense even in oligopolistic markets – particularly where, as in the case of the airline business, the product is perishable.

Although non-co-operative oligopolistic behaviour is perfectly legal in most countries (notwithstanding that it might lead to anticompetitive outcomes and economic inefficiency), oligopolistic market structures are often perceived as being susceptible to price and/or output fixing by producers who either get together openly (sometimes with official blessing) to form a cartel, or collude in secret – the purpose being to create and then benefit from 'monopoly power'.

Co-operative oligopolistic behaviour The objective of acting together is to maintain prices at a level that maximises the aggregate profits of all producers by simulating the behaviour of a monopolist.

Three broad categories of co-operative strategy can be identified: cartelisation; collusion; and strategic alliances. The first and second are illegal in many jurisdictions. Legality aside, the three categories are not mutually exclusive.

- **Cartelisation** Cartels exist where producers formally and openly agree on pricing and/or output levels. Not all producers of a particular product need necessarily be members of a cartel, but if it is to be effective it must embrace producers responsible in aggregate for a significant share of industry output. For a cartel to be successful in driving prices significantly above competitive levels (i.e., significantly above marginal cost), market demand must be relatively inelastic.

  Cartels are illegal in many developed commercial jurisdictions, although some might be explicitly permitted under the terms of a specific exemption to otherwise applicable antitrust/competition laws. Even when they are legal, cartels face two significant challenges: first, getting initial agreement from members perhaps having different cost structures, market projections, and strategic objectives is not necessarily easy; second, the temptation to 'cheat' by lowering price or increasing output to gain market share is ever-present. Only if potential gains from coming together to exert monopoly power unavailable to a member acting individually are sufficiently attractive will the challenges be overcome in the long run. Even then, there remains the question of what impact the pricing and output decisions of non-members might have.

  Cartelisation is not an unfamiliar form of competitive strategy in the airline industry. Until cracks began to appear in the 1970s, the postwar regime governing international air transport – founded on the Chicago system of bilateral air services agreements (ASAs) between governments and multilateral tariff co-ordination amongst airlines – was in essence a cartel.

- **Collusion** Less formal than a cartel, collusive strategies involve airlines co-operating on output and/or pricing decisions. Collusion in its strongest form might involve output restraint in order to keep prices above competitive levels. A weaker case sometimes referred to as 'semi-collusion' might, for example, involve co-operation on prices and competition in output volume (Fershtam and Muller, 1986); the temptation to engage in marginal cost pricing to fill perishable seats makes this type of collusion difficult to sustain in many airline markets, although it can work if demand growth is strong – always assuming that a slower-growing carrier facing loss of market share chooses not to respond by lowering its prices.

  Collusion might be explicit or tacit. Although explicit collusion through open communications is still prevalent in many markets, it is broadly illegal in the United States, the European Union, and several countries with well-developed bodies of competition law (Holloway, 1998a); an exception to this generalisation is the US practice of granting antitrust immunity to alliances between US carriers and partners from countries that have signed open skies bilaterals with the United States.

Tacit collusion exists where output and/or pricing decisions are co-ordinated other than through direct communication; the usual means is through forms of *signalling*, which might be recognised within the industry but not easily spotted by outsiders. Signalling could, for example, involve advance notice of fare or output plans giving time for competitors to indicate how they will react; where competing networks overlap and there is 'multi-market contact', an airline might signal its displeasure at a competitor's initiative in one market by responding aggressively in another, with the intention of getting the initiator to make a connection and reverse the initiative. For instance, the US DOJ reached a settlement in the mid-1990s with ATPCO – a joint venture owned by several carriers and used as an electronic clearing house for current and proposed fares – in respect of allegations that fare postings were often used as a medium for 'negotiation' of prices (Havel, 1997).

Another form of tacit collusion is *parallel conduct*, which can be defined as an implicit understanding that one firm's output and/or pricing decisions will follow those of another irrespective of whether or not such conduct is consistent with what would be expected in a fully competitive market. *Price leadership* – the practice of firms following the price of a tacitly recognised 'leader' – is a particularly common feature of oligopolistic markets; American has sometimes worn this mantle in US domestic markets – although, as the 'value pricing' debacle of 1992 well illustrates, followers cannot always be relied upon to follow, particularly in a difficult market.

Tacit collusion is often a fragile strategy in the long term: first, it is open to cheating; second, any market accessible by a competitor prepared to exploit differentiation or cost advantages will in all likelihood eventually attract just such a competitor. That the airline industry has periodic difficulty balancing output with demand and also faces perennial pressure to dispose of a perishable inventory makes tacit collusion a difficult strategy to maintain; Internet seat auctions, should they spread globally, will probably not make it any easier (unless there is collusion over 'reserve prices'). In principle, the fewer competitors there are in a market, the easier it should be to tacitly collude; much, however, depends upon the attitudes and competitive instincts of the competitors concerned, as the likes of Southwest and Ryanair have shown.

In general, though, the airline industry is still widely held to provide examples of both explicit and tacit collusion, and the lack of competition in first, business, and fully flexible on-demand economy class fares in many liberalised international markets where carriers now have more pricing and output freedom than they have had in the past provides strong circumstantial evidence. Indeed, it can be argued that collusion on pricing is the foundation upon which the postwar international tariff regime has been built and that, although crumbling, it is a foundation that remains broadly in place.

- **Strategic alliances** This type of co-operative strategy exists when firms explicitly and formally collaborate. Their purposes could include collusion on pricing and output decisions where this is legal, but are usually much broader – covering a range of initiatives on both the cost and revenue sides of partners' income statements (Barney, 1997; Dussauge and Garrette, 1995). Whereas collusion tends to be a horizontal strategy within a single industry, strategic alliances can also occur vertically within a value chain and across industry boundaries. They cover forms such as equity and non-equity alliances (e.g., airlines investing in other airlines or airlines entering into long-term supply agreements with third-party maintenance providers), joint ventures (e.g., WOW – a cargo venture initiated by Lufthansa, SAS, and Singapore Airlines), and franchising, for example. Separately incorporated joint ventures are the exception rather than the rule in respect of passenger air transport operations (SAS being a noteworthy example); however, they are becoming increasingly common frameworks for co-operative relationships between airlines and other types of organization (e.g., engine manufacturers in the aftermarket business).

Most horizontal alliances between airlines are based on contractual agreements of one form or another; sometimes a hybrid approach is adopted, wherein certain clearly defined activities are housed in a separately constituted joint venture whilst the rest of the alliance relationship is structured around contract law rather than company law. In economic terms, airlines 'have an incentive to co-operate in strategic alliances when the value of their resources and assets combined is greater than the value of their resources and assets separately' (Barney, 1997: 386). Specific motivations for entering into a strategic alliance include the exploitation of economies of scope or scale, the sharing of costs, the sharing of complementary resources and capabilities, the opportunity to learn from partners, the management of risk and uncertainty, to facilitate legally permissible collusive practices, and to access new markets or segments that otherwise could not be served either at all or cost-effectively. Although alliances between airlines can lead to an increase in monopoly power in inter-hub/inter-gateway markets, the research evidence seems to point to a positive impact on consumer surplus – particularly where the partners' networks are complementary rather than overlapping; this can be attributed to a share of the cost savings that arise from co-operation being passed on to consumers. (Recent empirical support for this generalisation comes from Brueckner and Whalen (1998), and Oum et al (2000); see Pels (2001) for an overview of the evidence.)

An important motivation for many alliances is the overcoming of barriers to market entry. Another motivation may well be to create them. We look at barriers to entry next.

Barriers to entry

According to microeconomic theory, firms in perfectly competitive industries are unable to sustain above-normal returns because these would quickly be competed away by new entrants attracted to the industry. Firms in industries where conditions of monopolistic competition, oligopoly or monopoly prevail are able to earn above-normal returns, but the size and duration of this advantage will depend in part upon the nature of whatever barriers are preventing entrants from moving in immediately.

A barrier to entry is something which favours incumbents already present in a market. As already noted, it might be externally imposed (e.g., government unwillingness to license start-up airlines or grant additional route designations to existing carriers), it might grow over time through force of circumstance (e.g., slot constraints), or it might be deliberately created by an incumbent (e.g., network, brand, or distribution strengths, or a reputation for responding aggressively to new entrants). A barrier will either make entry impossible in a practical sense, or it will leave entrants with higher costs than incumbents. Higher costs suggest not only a weaker competitive position but a greater risk of commercial failure, and this perceived risk in itself is often sufficient to deter entry. It will be recalled that one of the assumptions underlying contestability theory is that the sunk cost of entry is low.

In principle it should be relatively easy to enter the airline industry because some of the largest sunk costs arising in the business – for provision of airport and airway facilities – are met in most countries by government authorities or other parties, and paid for in line with usage (at rates that may fall well below true cost); aircraft can be leased-in and rentals paid out of current revenue; and in a lot of countries many of the services required to run an airline can be outsourced from third parties. Of course, the other – not insubstantial – sunk costs already discussed in the context of contestability theory, notably marketing communications together with any initial operating losses, do have to be funded. Nonetheless, relative to the capital intensity of the industry, it still looks fairly easy on paper to get into the air.

Reasons why this is frequently not the case are listed below. The discussion relates in general to the scheduled passenger side of the business. Cargo and nonscheduled passenger airlines are widely considered to face fewer barriers to entry, and in many cases it is true that these sectors of the industry are more readily contestable. However, if the European passenger charter market is taken as an example, it can be seen that barriers to entry may in fact be quite high. In the United Kingdom and Germany, for instance, a considerable degree of vertical integration has emerged between tour operators, the airlines serving them, and the retail travel agencies which sell their leisure products. This is not an easy market for an independent start-up carrier to penetrate other than on the periphery, supplementing the base-load of business carried by the major groups' inhouse airlines and perhaps also serving smaller tour operators that do not have their own affiliated carriers. Furthermore, the challenge of finding remunerative employment for aircraft during off-peak periods is always present and makes entry into this market segment on any significant scale a high-risk venture.

Similarly, there are parts of the cargo business – notably airport-to-airport line-haul – that are in principle not expensive to enter. But any carrier wanting to compete with the time-definite, door-to-door services offered by integrators such as FedEx and increasingly by committed combination carriers would face heavy, possibly insurmountable, investment requirements.

Returning to our wider consideration of barriers to entry, Bain (1956) identifies three situations that might confront an entrant.

- **Accommodated entry** Entry is accommodated when structural barriers are low and when entry-deterring strategies available to incumbents are likely to be either ineffective or too expensive to sustain.
- **Blockaded entry** Entry is blockaded when barriers exist without incumbents having to act. Barriers in this case will be 'structural'.
- **Deterred entry** Entry is deterred when incumbents successfully engage in 'entry-deterring strategies'.

We will look briefly at structural barriers to entry and at entry-deterring strategies.

Structural barriers to entry These include the following.

- **Government policy** Although many domestic and international air transport markets have been liberalised and in some cases fully deregulated over the last two decades, government policy does still present an effective barrier to entry into a significant number of markets. Box 4.4 reviews the impact of government policy on market entry.

Box 4.4: Government policy and market entry

Constraints imposed by the international regulatory regime Currently in a transitional phase, the regulatory regime governing international air transport services remains rooted in the institutions and practices of the 'Chicago System' – specifically, in the thousands of bilateral air services agreements (ASAs) entered into by pairs of states. Bilaterals impose constraints in respect of traffic rights and airline ownership.

1. Traffic rights *Despite the spread of liberal bilaterals since the late 1970s and the US push for open skies since the early 1990s, there are still many ASAs that stipulate the points in each signatory state that may be served, the maximum output to be made available, the identities of designated carriers, and fare approval mechanisms. The Chicago Convention of 1944 shaped this system by first confirming the principle of state sovereignty over airspace, but then failing to agree on a multilateral disposition of rights to the use of that airspace. The outcome was that freedom to exploit it commercially became a privilege subject to bilateral negotiation within the context of different countries' public policy objectives. One or more of several 'freedoms' might be on the table at any bilateral negotiation (only the first five of which are technically 'freedoms' as defined at Chicago).*

- *First freedom: an overflight privilege.*
- *Second freedom: a privilege permitting technical, non-traffic stops.*
- *Third freedom: a privilege allowing an airline to uplift traffic (passengers and/or cargo) from its home state and transport it to a destination in another state (e.g., Delta flying Atlanta–London).*
- *Fourth freedom: a privilege allowing an airline to uplift traffic from another state and transport it to its home state (e.g., Delta operating London–Atlanta).*
- *Fifth freedom: a privilege allowing an airline to uplift traffic from one foreign state and transport it to another state along a route which originates or terminates in that airline's home state (e.g.,*

Northwest uplifting traffic in Tokyo destined for Seoul on a Los Angeles–Tokyo–Seoul service). A 'change of gauge' might be involved if aircraft of different sizes are used on different sectors. Fifth freedom rights are sometimes restricted to a carrier's own stopover traffic (i.e., 'blind sector' rights). Airlines using fifth (and occasionally also sixth) freedom rights might be required to pay either a 'per passenger' or a 'percentage of revenue' royalty to third and/or fourth freedom carriers.

- *Sixth freedom: a combination of fourth and then third freedom rights resulting in the ability of an airline to uplift traffic from a foreign state and transport it to another foreign state via an intermediate stop – probably involving a change of plane and/or flight number – in its home country (e.g., American carrying traffic from London to Lima over its Miami hub).*

- *Seventh freedom: a privilege granted to an airline permitted to carry traffic between two foreign countries on a route that does not begin or end in its home country (which would be fifth freedom traffic) or make an intermediate stop in its home country (which would be sixth freedom traffic). Seventh freedom privileges are rarely granted for passenger services. (In the early 1990s British Airways received US rights to operate transatlantic flights from a number of mainland European points, but corresponding rights at the European end were unavailable.) The United States now negotiates for the inclusion of seventh freedom cargo rights in its open skies agreements.*

- *Eighth freedom/cabotage: 'cabotage' is a privilege granted to an airline permitting it to carry traffic between two points within a single foreign country. It also is rarely granted. 'Consecutive cabotage' would allow an airline to uplift local (as opposed to 'own stopover') traffic between the first gateway at which a service arrives in the foreign country (e.g., Honolulu) and a subsequent destination in the same country (e.g., Los Angeles) or vice versa. 'Full cabotage' is the operation by an airline of services which originate and terminate wholly within a single foreign country; an alternative to full cabotage that we will look at below would involve the establishment of a locally-incorporated majority- or wholly-owned subsidiary to operate in the foreign country.*

Exchanges of traffic rights (primarily first to fifth freedoms, some sixth freedoms, and very few seventh or eighth freedoms) are enshrined in several thousand bilateral ASAs negotiated between pairs of states.

However, since the late 1980s pressure for fundamental change in the Chicago system has been building as a result of:

- *a shift in public policy priorities in several aeropolitically import-ant countries – specifically, a move away from protecting their air-lines and in favour of promoting economic efficiency, tourism, and consumer interests;*
- *the aggressively liberal thrust of US aeropolitical policy;*
- *the creation of a single aviation market within much of Europe – the European Common Aviation Area (ECAA) – and the more halt-ing development of multilateral liberalisation elsewhere (e.g., parts of Latin America);*
- *pressure from within the industry to be permitted to build global networks; and*
- *the embedding of a broadly liberal multilateral trading regime into non-aviation sectors of the global economy.*

Many observers argue that it is anachronistic to regulate air serv-ices on the basis of a balance of benefits derived by national carriers from serving traffic flowing between their respective states when net-work redesign and increased 'hubbing' by international airlines now frequently lead to diversion of these flows over one or more third coun-tries. Dissatisfaction with the current regulatory regime brings into question what the future might hold. Aside from an unlikely mainten-ance of the status quo, there are two probable thrusts.

- *Further liberalisation of the existing bilateral system. This could take two forms.*
  - Liberalisation of traditional bilaterals *Perhaps as part of a pha-sed move to open skies, restrictive bilaterals will in many cases continue to be relaxed by loosening controls on market access and output (frequency and aircraft size), and by the more widespread use of double disapproval pricing mechanisms.*
  - Open skies bilaterals *Whilst there is no single definition of 'open skies', the influential US interpretation outlined in 1992 (DOT Order 92-8-13) embodied the following elements: open access to all routes between the contracting states and unres-tricted traffic rights (subject to the important exclusion of cab-otage – a highly sensitive area for US airline unions); unrestricted code-sharing; double disapproval pricing; liberal regimes governing nonscheduled and cargo operations; and pro-competitive provisions in related areas such as ground-*

handling (i.e., the right to 'self-handle'), reservations systems, and remittance of foreign currency earnings. Since 1992, the United States has had growing success in securing open skies agreements, and several other countries (e.g., Singapore) have shown a similar inclination. (Interestingly, Dubai has had an open access policy since long before the expression 'open skies' came into vogue.)

- *A second, perhaps more distant, possibility is movement away from the current bilateral regime, replacing it with a multilateral system – in much the same way that agreements covering international trade in most goods and some services have over several decades come to be formulated in multilateral forums. The number of multilateral air transport agreements is certainly growing, but the world is a very long way from seeing an all-encompassing multilateral aviation regime, simply because a majority of states (by number if not necessarily aeropolitical weight) remain committed to maintaining a stronger input into the destiny of 'their' air transport markets than global multilateralisation would afford them. A waypoint is emerging in the form of 'plurilateralism' – the coming together of like-minded states to negotiate liberal agreements that others can join at a later stage. The beginnings of plurilateralism can be seen in agreements such as the one negotiated by the United States, Chile, New Zealand, Brunei, and Singapore, for example, but the big prize in this regard must be the forging of a transatlantic common aviation area encompassing ECAA states, Canada, and the United States. (Forsyth (2001) offers a comprehensive analysis of this alternative.)*

2. Ownership and control of airlines *In addition to traffic rights, the second significant constraint on international market entry imposed by most ASAs is the requirement that each airline designated by a state under the bilateral concerned must be 'substantially owned and effectively controlled' by nationals of that state. There have, in fact, been several occasions on which bilateral partners have chosen to overlook 'national ownership clauses' (e.g., when Aerolineas Argentinas came under Spanish ownership, and – at least temporarily – when Ecuador granted international traffic rights previously held by defunct local carriers Ecuatoriana and Saeta to Chilean, Peruvian, and Salvadorian airlines). On the whole, however, these clauses remain one of two major barriers to the cross-border consolidation of the industry; for example, probable loss of traffic rights between Amsterdam and countries outside the single market of the ECAA was*

seen as a major stumbling block when British Airways first considered acquiring KLM.

(Doganis (2001) provides a concise summary of the evolution of the international regulatory regime.)

Constraints imposed by domestic laws *Many countries retain control over access and other commercial dimensions of their domestic markets. In addition, they place restrictions on the percentage of a locally incorporated airline that may be owned by foreign shareholders. This does not apply within the ECAA, where nationals of other contracting states have 'rights of establishment' in any member state, and there are a handful of other countries that do permit foreign ownership and control of airlines – notably Australia, New Zealand, and several Latin American countries; not being 'substantially owned and effectively controlled' by nationals of the state of incorporation, however, these foreign-owned carriers could have trouble flying outside their home states. (Hence, when Air New Zealand owned Ansett it was necessary to create Ansett International – an Australian majority-owned joint venture – to serve Asian markets.) Alongside national ownership clauses in bilaterals, domestic laws restricting foreign ownership of airlines represent a second major barrier to cross-border consolidation of the industry.*

There was a belief after 9/11 that it would prove a catalyst for the consolidation and restructuring of the industry that many observers had been calling for since the early 1990s, that open skies bilaterals would grow in number, and that national ownership clauses and restrictions on foreign investment would be swept away. Another impetus for change around the same time came from a ruling in 2001 by the European Court of Justice that the Treaty of Rome, which forbids discrimination against EU companies on the basis of nationality, is being violated by ASAs between an EU state and a non-member state which contain a 'nationality clause' and so exclude other EU airlines from the markets concerned; this was seen as a boost to EU ambitions to represent members en bloc in future ASA negotiations. The inevitability of change was and is unquestionable; on the other hand, the Chicago system has survived more or less intact since the 1940s, and the reason for this is that its practices suit significant numbers of states and airlines. If change is inevitable, so is resistance.

Government policy can also affect the supply of airline output in other ways. Restrictions on foreign ownership of airlines might choke-off the supply of foreign investment potentially available for new carriers, thereby constraining the growth of competition. Also, state aid to national 'flag carriers' disadvantages profit-seeking airlines that must compete without subsidy. Finally, enforcement of low domestic fares can make market entry by competitors non-viable.

- **Spatial pre-emption** A structural barrier to entry clearly exists where a potential entrant does not have access to essential production inputs on an equal basis with incumbents. Ultimately, incumbents may be able to extract high economic rents from serving price-inelastic market segments as demand outpaces the supply of these constrained factors. In the airline industry, constraints at certain points in the system and at certain peak times exist in respect of air traffic control capacity, runway slots, gates, stands, baggage-handling facilities, counter space, and even lounges. For example, most of the EU's densest internal routes, which should in principle offer the best opportunities for market entry in competition with incumbent 'national' carriers, have an airport at one or both ends that is congested during peak periods and has insufficient slots available to support the operation of a schedule competitive with existing high-frequency services. This is why much of the post-liberalisation action has come in regional hub-bypass markets and from low-fare carriers using secondary metropolitan airports (e.g., Ryanair), serving secondary destinations, and/or focusing on previously under-served cities (e.g., easyJet at Liverpool).

Supply constraints arise from one or more of poor planning, inadequate funding for necessary expansion, or opposition to growth on environmental grounds. Box 4.5 looks at the issues.

Box 4.5: Infrastructural congestion

Airport access, possibly the greatest long-term challenge to industry growth, is a barrier to entry because essential resources at many of the world's busiest airports remain firmly in the hands of incumbents. There are currently two approaches to runway access.

1. *First-come-first-served This is the approach at uncongested airports, and in the United States even at many congested airports (i.e., airports where at certain times of the day demand for access to runways exceeds throughput capacity given prevailing weather conditions).*
2. *Controlled access There are three approaches in use.*
   - Traffic distribution rules *Certain types of movement (e.g., all-cargo, nonscheduled, or general aviation) are at some airports either excluded or restricted to off-peak periods.*

- Pricing *In a surprisingly small number of cases, pricing has been used to limit access by certain users – usually operators of the smaller regional types (e.g., at London Heathrow).*
- Slot controls *Scheduling committees allocate available slots to applicants, with incumbents' rights 'grandfathered' (subject, per-haps, to some percentage 'use-it-or-lose-it' threshold applied to the previous scheduling season). Scheduling committees are in use at a growing number of airports outside the United States; there is con-siderable debate regarding whether slots are legally owned by in-cumbents, but for the time being the most widespread policy appr-oach is to allow them to be swapped but not (at least openly) exch-anged for cash.*

   In the United States, most airports do not use slots to deal with congestion, and the critical limited-access resources are more of-ten gate and counter space – with gates in particular often held by incumbents on long leases. Slots were introduced several decades ago at New York JFK and La Guardia, Chicago O'Hare, and Washington National under a system somewhat more complex than the IATA procedure – a system which, after 1986 permitted second-ary market sale, purchase, leasing, and mortgaging.

Slot availability at the most congested hubs worldwide is often limited to unattractive times of day, and the chances of an entrant being able to ob-tain sufficient resources – in terms of slots, apron or gate space, counters, and access to other common-user equipment and facilities – to establish competitive frequencies on short-haul routes in particular are poor (alth-ough jetBlue was successful in securing enough slots to make a serious attempt at JFK beginning in 2000).

Slot shortages confronting prospective entrants at key airports can be lessened in one or more of the following ways.

1. **Building new runways at new and existing airports** *Either option is likely to encounter serious community opposition – notably in respect of those airports serving densely populated metropolitan areas where new capacity is most needed.*
2. **Improving the management of aircraft movements** *This option offers considerable scope for the future, using new technologies, improved procedures, better monitoring of surface movements, and restructured airspace.*
3. **Reallocation of available slots** *This has been tried, with mixed results, in both the United States and Europe. The problem is that incumbents generally strive hard to retain their grandfathered slots, and those that*

do become available usually fall far short of what is needed to mount a serious competitive attack – particularly during peak periods.

4. **Forced divestiture of slots** *It is difficult to see majors being compelled to divest significant numbers of slots other than in return for something they want – something such as approval of a potentially anticompetitive alliance. (Even then, as we saw in the case of the American/British Airways alliance, the price might be considered too high.) When a network carrier loses slots, its position is likely to be weakened not just by the arrival in specific markets of the new competitors who take over these slots but also through possible loss of more generalised network synergies vis a vis other network carriers.*

5. **More widespread secondary market trading of slots** *Arguments in favour of this include economic efficiency, whilst arguments against tend to focus on one or both of the windfall benefits accruing to grandfathered carriers and the likelihood of predation by these carriers accumulating unwanted slots simply to exclude new entrants. (See Starkie (1998) for a discussion of the issues.)*

A problem of some significance in the United States is that airlines at several important airports hold long leases on terminals and other facilities which, through 'majority in interest' or 'exclusive use' clauses, give them power to veto capacity expansion. They also have the right to refuse to sublet or, if they do sublet, to charge mark-ups which impose a substantial cost disadvantage on potential competitors; it is not unheard-of for gate subleases to come with surcharges as high as 20–25 per cent.

Another problem area has been **ground-handling**. At many airports outside North America and the United Kingdom ground-handling has traditionally been a monopoly run by the airport authority, by its sole concessionaire, or by the dominant national carrier. This can give rise to a situation where an airline is not only paying high handling charges, but paying them to a direct competitor – that is, the national carrier. Clearly, such circumstances can represent a barrier to market entry – albeit perhaps a minor one relative to some others. It is difficult for any carrier to control the quality of its ground product under these circumstances, and this may affect either or both operational performance (e.g., baggage reclaim time below specifications) or brand image (e.g., poor attitudes on the part of the agent's customer service personnel). Even where an entrant is free to self-handle, unless operations reach sufficient volume it is unlikely to be economic to do so; in the absence of competing handlers, which may be independent companies or other carriers operating into the airport with relatively high frequencies, a small operator might anyway be driven into the arms of rivals. However, handling was significantly liberalised within *the EU in the late 1990s, and competition has also been introduced at airports in several other parts of the world.*

Whereas many barriers to entry can be overcome by new entrants with sufficient resources and strategic skills, congestion at slot-controlled airports is seldom one of them – unless the entrant is a low-fare carrier whose cost base would anyway benefit from using an alternative secondary airport and whose customers do not have a problem with this. That said, there are some rays of hope. Impressive new facilities have been coming on line in Asia (e.g., Hong Kong, Kuala Lumpur, Seoul), and Tokyo has benefited from two new runways. There are even signs of understanding from the UK government that Southeast England needs more than five runways spread around four different airports if it is to retain an air transport infrastructure and a local airline industry competitive with its closest continental rivals.

* **Cost barriers: start-up costs** Significant capital costs are a structural barrier to entry into any industry, particularly when a high proportion represent sunk costs that are irrecoverable should the entrant quickly decide to leave the market. We have already seen that the existing provision of infrastructure and the availability of leased aircraft and outsourced services in principle reduce 'sunk' entry costs into the airline industry. During recessions, there have in the past been pools of skilled labour readily available; given secular skills shortages emerging in some aviation disciplines, this might not be as true in future. Having said all this, initial certification, systems establishment, and provisioning, and also training and marketing costs are not necessarily insubstantial. Any effort to build a sizeable integrated hub will also involve heavy expenditure on resources. Poor risk-adjusted rates of return across the industry as a whole make investment in any new airline a somewhat sporty prospect, and the raising of capital can be correspondingly difficult. Outside the United States, financial markets for such ventures are neither deep nor notably brave; the romantic attractions of the industry are also diminishing. Of course, if an entrant into an individual market is already in the industry, these problems are greatly reduced: it might have the necessary resources and expertise in place, and also be able to benefit more generally from spreading over a large existing output those of its costs that are common to the existing and new services.

  When a start-up or small established airline enters a market with the sort of schedule likely to be necessary to generate credibility amongst customers and distribution channels (assuming it to be relying on agency channels), it is making a commitment which risks proportionately far more of its net worth than a large carrier risks when it launches just one more route. Once the service is running, the larger airline might also feel better able to engage in short-run marginal cost pricing provided there is strategic justification in the context of the network as a whole and that a contribution is being made to fixed costs. A smaller entrant, on the other hand, will need to be covering full costs on most or all of its routes.

- **Cost barriers: production costs** Once operating, any small carrier will face structural cost disadvantages associated with the economics of the industry – notably economies of scale, scope, and density – which in principle make it cheaper for an incumbent to add output than for a small challenger to do the same. Briefly, whereas economies of scale benefit an incumbent when average cost falls as output increases, economies of scope arise where joint production of two or more related services can be achieved at lower unit cost than when both services are produced separately; hub-and-spoke networks, which are designed to produce multiple products in multiple city-pair markets, can generate significant economies of scope. Economies of density arise when it is cheaper for an incumbent to increase output on an existing network than for a challenger to enter the same routes. That life is not always this simple is proven by the success of a handful of low-fare start-ups; broadly, however, any entrant taking on an established network carrier will face substantial structural cost barriers that have to be compensated for by higher resource productivity and, perhaps, lower salaries and benefits.

- **Reputation** A strong brand image supporting a loyal customer base and a dominant market share might be difficult to sell against unless a new entrant is offering something a segment of the market values and is not receiving (e.g., consistently lower prices or more reliable service), and has sufficient inimitable resources to sustain the offer against retaliation. Some new entrants have been successful establishing awareness through public relations rather than paid advertising; the early years of Emirates, Virgin Atlantic, Morris Air (since absorbed by Southwest), jetBlue, and easyJet provide examples. On the whole, however, the requirement for heavy advertising and promotional spending can be a barrier to entry. Furthermore, challengers have to overcome any consumer loyalty from which incumbents might benefit (either in respect of their brand in general or specific unique service attributes in particular); the practical effect of consumer loyalty, whether it reflects 'genuine' commitment or is simply a result of high switching costs imposed by FFPs, is to steepen the incumbent's demand curve.

- **Exit barriers** These are economic, institutional or emotional considerations which keep airlines on one or more routes or in the industry as a
whole when for one reason or another they are earning sub-normal
returns. Shrinking a large airline can anyway be a slow and expensive
process. Where exit barriers are high there tends to be overcapacity,
excess output, and downward pressure on yields. Perversely, exit barriers – such as state aid and US Chapter 11 bankruptcy protection – can
also be barriers to entry when, for example, they sustain in a market
carriers that are in some way being subsidised and so have opportunities to cause market distortions. (See Schnell (2001) for one of the few
studies of exit barriers in the airline industry.)

Entry-deterring strategies An incumbent with a history of responding
vigorously to competitive inroads (e.g., by lowering prices, boosting output
or increasing promotional expenditures) might present enough of a 'credible threat' to deter future entry. (Bear in mind, of course, that it is not airlines which respond, but decision-makers; if one or more key decision-
makers change at an incumbent, so might a potential new entrant's evaluation of the likelihood of a robust response.) Entry-deterring strategies usually involve one or more of the following.

- **Price** The most obvious tactic is to reduce prices in response to entry.
Because air transport is a multi-product industry producing output over
a network, and because start-ups are unlikely to be able to duplicate the
network of a large, well-established incumbent, there is widespread
opportunity to respond to a competitive challenge by engaging in cross-
subsidisation. This could take one or more of several forms. For example, profits from long-haul routes can be used to subsidise aggressive
short-haul pricing; profits attributable to economic rents earned from
local traffic to and from a fortress hub could subsidise more competitive routes; or profits from routes still subject to commercial regulation
of entry, output, and/or pricing could subsidise competition in liberalised markets. Similarly, profits from high-yield fares on one route
could be used to subsidise discounting of coach/economy tickets on the
same or different routes.
- **Output and capacity** An incumbent's capacity to produce output can
be a barrier to entry from two perspectives. First, there is a tendency for
airlines that dominate frequencies in a given market to carry a disproportionately high share of traffic; this is the 'S-curve effect' that we met
in chapter 2. Second, although 'capacity' and 'spare capacity' are not
necessarily the same, the more capacity an incumbent has available in
its system the greater the likelihood that it could redirect some of it to

match, sandwich, or generally swamp a new entrant's frequencies – provided it has sufficiently deep pockets to live with the negative impact on yields and/or load factors that excess output is likely to cause. If the battleground is a hub dominated by the incumbent, it will also have far more flexibility to juggle slots and adjust frequencies in response to entry than the entrant will have to counter the response.

- **Access to distribution channels** Although GDSs are a significant source of costs (for incumbents as well as start-ups), alternative channels over the Internet are available to help surmount this barrier – always provided that the start-up is not targeting a segment which requires agency distribution and GDS access. Where agency distribution is necessary to an entrant's marketing strategy, incumbents can create barriers to entry by encouraging agents to favour them – using allocations of cheap tickets, commission overrides (i.e., sales incentives in addition to standard commissions), or other forms of incentive. Less well-established carriers are likely to have to pay larger overrides or to make a higher proportion of their agency business eligible for overrides.

- **Corporate deals** Large airlines with extensive network coverage are in a strong position to offer corporate deals to significant customers. These could include one or more of price breaks, rebates, free upgrades, or the waiving of conditions normally applied to discounted fares (which itself amounts to a form of price break). Rebates (like overrides) are generally driven by thresholds, applied either to absolute levels of expenditure or to the number of journeys made on a specific group of routes or over the network as a whole. Airlines with large networks emanating from a dominated hub or national market (perhaps augmented by relationships with alliance partners) clearly have more to offer local companies, because any one competitor is likely to be strong – if at all – in only a small number of those markets and so be unable to offer the scope of coverage probably required by a corporation generating trips to a wide range of destinations. As with overrides, to the extent that corporate price breaks and rebates are discontinuous rather than linear – being triggered by attainment of agreed volume thresholds – they offer discounts that are not based on volume economics, and so could be anti-competitive in the sense that they are designed to bind customers to the supplying airline rather than to pass on cost savings.

Conclusion on barriers to entry Dozens of carriers enter the industry each year. It is not difficult to list several that have emerged over the last two decades, survived, and indeed prospered. But in terms of their share of global market output these are not large airlines, either alone or in aggregate. Because this is a network industry comprised of literally thousands of individual city-pair markets, it would be surprising if there were not regular entry and if on occasion entrants did not meet with success – simply because by astutely targeting markets where identified opportunities exist and which they are suited to serve effectively and efficiently, some will inevitably be able to succeed in 'walking between the raindrops'. As a whole, however, this is an industry in which size definitely matters and in which there are some very real barriers standing in the way of challengers wanting to take on established incumbents.

Conclusion with regard to market structure

Many observers believe that the airline industry tends inevitably towards oligopoly. As we have seen, proponents of deregulation in the United States disputed this, using contestability theory to argue that the threat of market entry was sufficient to keep potential oligopolists or even monopolists from exploiting monopoly power in a deregulated environment. They also argued that the absence of substantial economies of scale in the industry removes a fundamental motivation for airline mergers by denying large firms a meaningful cost advantage over small competitors. Consolidation at the industry level and the domination of fortress hubs by individual carriers seem to suggest this is not the case.

The smaller the number of major players left in the industry, the more multi-market contact there is likely to be amongst remaining competitors, and the greater is the danger of tacit collusion – particularly during periods of strong economic growth, when demand is robust. There are, however, two other variables that need to be considered, at least as far as price competition is concerned: behaviour and geography.

Competitive behaviour Actual behaviour in apparently oligopolistic markets will not always be deterministically anti-competitive. There are two reasons for this.

1. The fact that the industry faces significant challenges in managing its capacity (as we will see in Part 3) together with the innate perishability of its output mean that price competition is unlikely ever to disappear.
2. Low-fare carriers in North America, Europe, and a few other parts of the world have successfully staked-out strategic positions in short-/medium-haul and medium-/high-density markets, and where these airlines are present price competition seems likely to remain robust.

Geography The prospects for price competition in markets which for whatever reason fail to attract competing nonstop or through-plane service can still be reasonable where the origin and destination are far enough apart to be connected over two or more competing hubs. This applies in the US domestic market, and also in international markets. If the global industry does, as expected, ultimately consolidate into a small number of alliances – perhaps, some way down the road, followed by cross-border mergers – much will depend upon how actively the resulting networks compete for behind/beyond flow traffic over their respective hubs.

However, intervening hubs are not always in an ideal position when competing against nonstop service.

1. **Short-/medium-haul markets** Intervening hubs are not likely to be competitive against nonstops taking less than, say, two hours because even a conveniently timed hub transfer of 30–40 minutes would increase O & D journey time by a much higher percentage than would be the case were the stage-lengths significantly longer. Price-elastic, non-time-sensitive customers might accept a 25–33 per cent increase in journey time, but business travellers in many cases will not.

2. **Medium-/long-haul markets** Again, few time-sensitive, price-inelastic business travellers will accept a route deviation and hub transfer when a viable, high-frequency nonstop is available. In particular, intervening hubs (e.g., London) are unlikely to provide serious competition in respect of high-yield O & D traffic travelling in another carrier's or alliance's nonstop interhub markets (e.g., Frankfurt–Washington Dulles). This is why high-yield segments of local inter-hub markets have often been 'carved out' of antitrust immunities granted by the US DOT to transatlantic alliances.

   On the other hand, where an O & D market is such a long haul that nonstop service is impossible (e.g., London–Sydney), well-located sixth freedom carriers (e.g., Emirates and Singapore Airlines) can compete with third and fourth freedom through-plane services (e.g., British Airways and Qantas) without imposing a significant time penalty (although the inconvenience of an aircraft change will still dissuade many business travellers).

   A possible constraint in some sixth freedom markets is the question of traffic rights and pricing freedom. Whether or not this is an issue will depend upon the terms of the ASAs negotiated by the intervening (i.e., sixth freedom) state with the origin and destination states; some ASAs specifically address sixth freedom services, some treat them as de facto fifth freedoms and limit them in this way, whilst others ignore them altogether.

   More effective scheduling over sixth freedom hubs has greatly increased the number of service-price choices available to passengers and shippers/forwarders in many international markets. As far as passenger service is concerned, however, it remains broadly true that frequency and routing disadvantages, combined with a lower market profile in originating countries, often restrict sixth freedom carriers to relatively small market shares on long-haul routes. Despite their generally strong images, reasonable frequencies, and stopover possibilities, Emirates, Cathay Pacific, Singapore Airlines, Thai International, and Malaysia Airlines together carry under 30 per cent of total UK-Australia traffic compared with well over half carried by the third and fourth freedom airlines (i.e., Qantas and British Airways). In markets where sixth freedom carriers do not have such strengths, their shares tend to be very much smaller; nonetheless, they do provide valuable competition for price-sensitive traffic.

Commercial liberalisation is allowing hub-based international networks in general, and multi-hub alliances in particular, to reorient the arena of inter-airline competition from the individual route to the network. Nevertheless, what happens on individual routes and in specific markets remains of essential concern to consumers. Competition in the airline industry therefore needs to be considered on three geographical levels: city-to-city; country-to-country; and region-to-region. Sometimes competition can be threatened on just one or two of these levels – as competitors alleged the American/British Airways alliance proposal did in the London–New York and UK–USA markets, but not in the Europe–North America market. Occasionally the threat extends also to inter-regional markets, as has been alleged in respect of American Airlines' position between North and Central America.

The presence of fewer competitors globally and the concentration of higher percentages of global output into fewer hands do not necessarily imply reduced competition, because it is in individual city-pair markets that airlines physically compete for revenue – not in 'the global market'. Furthermore, competition in any marketplace is sometimes as much a reflection of intent as of the raw number of competitors present. On the other hand, at the individual market level global alliances can easily become quasi-monopolies – especially on routes linking their partners' major hubs. Arrangements between alliance partners such as the cost- and revenue-pooling agreements entered into by Lufthansa on the one hand and both Thai and United on the other in respect of routes between their respective hubs at best point towards the anti-competitive potential of alliances, and at worst evoke memories of the pre-deregulation European duopolies.

Whereas some airlines would undoubtedly prefer regulators to limit their oversight to the 'big picture' issue of network-to-network inter-regional competition, it is in consumers' interests for competition law to be applied where it matters most – in O & D city-pair markets.

Competition policy

Commercial regulation of air transport services is generally intended to achieve public policy goals that it is felt would not be realised through the operation of free market forces. It normally focuses on one or more of:

- market access (i.e., route entry and exit);
- output levels (i.e., frequency of service and/or size of aircraft used);
- pricing and conditions of purchase (i.e., tariffs).

Air transport has historically been regulated by industry-specific commercial rules and processes, which in many cases have overridden more generally applicable competition (antitrust) laws that might exist in a particular country. For example, Japan's Civil Aviation Law has precluded application of the country's Anti-Monopoly Law in respect of activities approved by the Ministry of Transport, and the US DOT still has authority to immunise agreements between US and foreign airlines against the application of antitrust laws (Holloway, 1998a). (Indeed, one of the most significant practical benefits flowing from open skies agreements between the United States and others has been the immunity from US antitrust law subsequently granted to alliance partners from the countries involved. Immunity allows considerably more joint capacity planning, fare-setting, inventory and revenue management, and selling than is permissible under a standard marketing alliance or code-sharing agreement without immunity.)

Nonetheless, as liberalisation and deregulation have spread since the late 1970s, general competition laws have come to play an increasingly influential role in several important markets (e.g., US domestic, intra-European, and Australian domestic).

The purpose of competition law

General competition laws in any country which has them are intended in most cases to encourage economic efficiency (i.e., efficient resource allocation) and/or protect consumers by encouraging competition and maintaining a 'level playing field' amongst competitors. Inevitably, many countries have other (often social) items on their agendas as well as or instead of these two; if this were not the case, microeconomic analysis would be the lingua franca of competition policies everywhere and competition laws would be broadly the same – something that is clearly far from being the case (notwithstanding the efforts of the International Competition Network, which is a forum created by several antitrust agencies to promote multilateral co-operation). We can nonetheless generalise that competition laws typically address one or both of the following.

1. **Market structure** The policing of market structure attempts to control alliance formation, mergers, and other forms of consolidation that could lead to market domination.
2. **Market conduct** The policing of conduct addresses areas such as:
    *   abuse of dominant market position (e.g., price fixing, market allocation, and/or output restriction);
    *   predatory pricing;
    *   insistence that entry by a dominant party into one type of exchange relationship (e.g., an interline agreement) should be predicated on the willingness of the other party to enter into another type of relationship (e.g., purchase of the dominant party's ground-handling services);
    *   impediments to the flow of product information to consumers;
    *   interference with competition in downstream markets or distribution channels by practices such as tied selling;
    *   interference with competition in upstream markets, such as vertical integration to obtain control over key resources.

    Competition authorities have also intermittently, and inconsistently, addressed problems arising from the 'spatial pre-emption' of airport slots and gates by grandfathered incumbents.

The issues

Bodies of competition law exist in over 50 countries. These vary in the breadth of their coverage and the diligence with which they are enforced and, as noted above, not all are necessarily applied to the air transport industry. The key issues most address are summarised below.

Abuse of a dominant position There is always a danger that a dominant carrier might deprive consumers of the price and service options from which they would benefit in an open and competitive market. Abuse of a dominant position can be a subtle phenomenon. For example, in 2001 the Swedish competition authority alleged that SAS's EuroBonus FFP distorted competition by strengthening the carrier's 70 per cent domestic market share; the argument was that business travellers were attracted to membership by the carrier's domination of frequencies, and that this in turn exclud-

234 Straight and Level: Practical Airline Economics

ed significant competition and so led to higher prices and lower quality of service than would otherwise exist in what is a liberalised market.

More generally, there is concern that FFPs, corporate deals, and TACOs (particularly those with non-linear reward structures that offer disproportionately higher benefits as successive sales thresholds are crossed) can be used by a locally dominant carrier with a large network to consolidate – and perhaps also abuse – its market dominance and erect effective barriers to entry. (See Hanlon (1999: 50-67) for a full discussion.) These tools can be used by major carriers, alone or within alliance groupings, to reduce cross-price elasticities and so progressively exclude smaller independent competitors from ready access to high-yield traffic – that is, the frequent business travellers who on some networks account for a share of revenues disproportionate to their numbers (ibid). There is also evidence that loyalty programmes allow airlines dominating fortress hubs to extract price premia from local passengers travelling in O & D markets with a hub at one end (Borenstein, 1989) – although agreement on this is less than total (Beyer, 2000). A key question, of course, is how a 'dominant position' should be defined; one argument is that a dominant position exists when a carrier has the power to weaken competition, and that it is being abused when that power is exercised (Kyrou, 2000, following the European Court of Justice).

The other issues listed below could equally apply to a market dominated by one carrier or by a small group of colluding oligopolists.

Market access The question here is who can become a competitor. There are two sub-issues. First, structural barriers to market entry might exist or be created (e.g., airport congestion, or the economies of scope available to carriers having large, integrated networks). Second, predatory strategies could be pursued by incumbents intending to deter competition (or eliminate it if it does materialise). Predation involves forgoing short-run profits in the expectation that this will 'buy' market power and the opportunity to earn greater profits in the long run. It is discussed in Box 4.6.

Box 4.6: Predatory conduct

Predatory pricing is tactical pricing by a dominant carrier at levels which are either below cost or substantially lower than what the market will bear. 'Cost' in this case is usually taken to mean short-run marginal cost (SRMC). Average variable cost (AVC) is sometimes used as a proxy for SRMC, because defining both the marginal unit of output and the cost of that unit can be exceedingly difficult (Areeda and Turner, 1975). In the EU, for example, the European Commission applies a two-tier cost test pursuant to several decisions made by the European Court of Justice:

- *first, a dominant airline setting a fare below AVC would be guilty of abusing its dominant position;*
- *second, even were a dominant airline to price above AVC, its behaviour could be considered an abuse were prices set lower than average total costs and established in the context of a plan to eliminate competition from the market concerned. Going one step further, there is an argument that pricing does not have to be below average total cost to be predatory – the sole criterion for predation being a willingness to accept lower profits than might otherwise be earned in order to deter or eliminate competition (Joskow and Klevorick, 1979).*

However, even an apparently simple concept such as AVC is muddied by the inevitably arbitrary way in which joint costs have to be allocated between products and fare types (e.g., On the basis of cabin floorspace available to each? On the basis of load factor? On the basis of relative service levels?). Thus, whilst determining the AVC for a particular flight is reasonably straightforward, obtaining a meaningful cost figure for different products or fare classes is less easy.

The intent of predatory pricing is often to drive competitors from the market and, presumably, thereafter open the opportunity for prices to be raised again and supernormal profits to be earned. When an airline operates in multiple city-pair markets, cross-subsidisation to support predatory pricing is entirely feasible. Alternatively, the objective might be to deter market entry by using predatory pricing selectively in respect of certain segments of demand; the purpose here would be to demonstrate to potential challengers that their prospective profitability will be limited by lower revenues than might otherwise have been expected from these segments, and possibly also from the market as a whole if such predation is taken as a signal of intent by the incumbent to mount a more wide-ranging price response should entry materialise. (Technically, when the target is a potential entrant rather than an existing competitor, this is a form of what is called 'limit pricing'. Such signalling need not in practice require the introduction of low fares – announcement of an intention to do so, perhaps via a GDS, might be enough to deter market entry. Similarly, if an existing competitor announces fare reductions, a signal can be sent threatening to match such reductions not only in the market concerned but also in other markets where the two compete; this would amount to illegal price collusion in some jurisdictions.)

Predation can be difficult to establish in any industry, but particularly so in the airline business. The facts that airlines generally have high short-run fixed costs and low SRMCs and AVCs, and that their basic transportation product is perishable, make the distinction between marginal cost pricing and predatory pricing largely one of intent. It is not prima facie unreasonable to argue that pricing only slightly above AVC is rational in respect of a flight or a series of flights if revenue generated covers variable costs and makes a contribution to fixed costs; the longer such behaviour persists, however, the less reasonable the argument becomes because it is evident that some motive other than profit maximisation underlies the pricing decision.

There are other complications.

- *A static short-run price-versus-cost analysis ignores the fact that airline pricing decisions are made in a fluid intertemporal context and have outcomes discernible only in the long run.*

- *Even pricing well above AVC can be predatory where the resources required to generate output are retained in a market solely for predatory reasons and despite there being an opportunity cost involved in not moving them to more profitable uses. Predatory intent might in this case be identified in a carrier's willingness to bear economic losses even though accounting results from the operation concerned show a profit (Oster and Strong 2001, citing Comanor and Frech, 1993).*

- *Revenue management systems can be used to disguise predation. Without lowering the deepest discounted fare already offered in a market affected by low-fare entry, an incumbent can engage in predation by aggressively expanding the allocation of seats available to that fare (and perhaps also loosening applicable booking and/or usage restrictions). Distinguishing between predation and well-targeted price competition is, again, not necessarily straightforward for outsiders.*

Often, predation is less readily discernible in prices than in nonprice behaviour. Examples of the latter could include: manipulating GDS displays; dominating slots at congested airports; capacity dumping (i.e., expanding output beyond short-run profit-maximising levels) – which might involve either or both 'swamping' a route with larger aircraft (i.e., 'capacity swamping') or adding frequencies (i.e., 'overscheduling'); 'sandwiching' or 'bracketing' a low-frequency competitor's departures or scheduling away from a competitor's connections (i.e., 'predatory scheduling'); refusing to interline, or imposing discriminatory conditions on access to ground services such as passenger-handling or ramp and maintenance support; monopolisation of traffic feed; monopolisation of access to infrastructure; and predatory use of corporate rebates (including exclusive deals), TACOs (driven by targeted market share increases), and FFP awards (e.g., targeting bonuses at markets challenged by new entrants). One objective of capacity swamping and overscheduling is to benefit from the 'S-curve' effect and maintain a market share premium (Beyer, 1999).

Another form of nonprice predation is 'route overlay' – the duplication by an incumbent of all or a major part of a small challenger's network, as Northwest is alleged to have done to Reno Air in the early 1990s. More subtly, the fact that many airlines compete across networks rather than just in individual city-pairs opens the possibility that predatory behaviour in response to market entry might not be targeted at the city-pair concerned; a carrier threatened by entry in one of its core markets might retaliate – or signal potential retaliation – by adjusting prices, frequencies, aircraft capacities, and/or routings in other markets where the same two airlines compete. These 'network effects' arising from multi-market contact between network carriers can be particularly difficult to uncover and police.

The distinction between fair competition on the one hand and predation on the other is not always easy for the untrained eye to discern. The more liberal or deregulated the market, the more likely predation is to occur and the more important the rigorous application of general competition law becomes. The problem is that the airline business is a network industry which sells highly perishable services and uses mobile assets to produce those services. In circumstances such as these, most bodies of competition law are ill-equipped to distinguish between predation on the one hand and sound marketing or network management on the other. This is why very few allegations of predatory behaviour in the industry have found judicial favour. The complex nature of the industry and the voluminous data required can make it practically impossible to prove unequivocally that an incumbent's actions alone have turned a potentially profitable entry opportunity for a challenger into an unprofitable one (OECD, 1997). Furthermore, the judicial process might outlast the financial endurance of a small or under-capitalised challenger.

Even more difficult to control than overtly predatory behaviour is the latent threat of predation. When a particular carrier builds a reputation for predatory behaviour it might – without having to take any overt action – be able to discourage market entry by more efficient potential competitors who have insufficiently deep pockets to sustain the negative impact on their profits that a predatory response usually implies. The end result of both actual and latent predation is likely to be the same: economic inefficiency and the elimination of price and/or service choices that would otherwise have been available to consumers.

Capacity fixing Continuing our brief review of some of the key issues addressed by competition law, the question in respect of capacity is who determines the level of output in a market, and how. We have noted already that protectionist bilaterals regulate capacity as well as entry in many international markets. Inter-airline 'pooling' agreements between nominally competing carriers have often been used to fix market shares as well as cost and/ or revenue apportionments. Although they appear anti-competitive in intent, there is an argument that some of these arrangements do serve consumers' interests by spreading output to off-peak periods which would otherwise be ignored by carriers interested only in competing for more lucrative peak business. The same argument is now frequently heard to justify joint services or joint scheduling by code-sharing partners. The counter-argument is that such activities deprive consumers of choice and might also artificially restrain market growth. Arguments of this nature need to be assessed on a case-by-case basis.

Tariff fixing The issue here is how the price of output produced is to be determined, and what if any conditions should be attached to tickets sold at various different price levels. Tariff fixing in international markets is an institutionalised part of the Chicago system. Governments have used a variety of methods to intervene in the pricing of domestic air services, but internationally the chosen instrument has been IATA. The Association's semi-annual traffic conferences have historically set fares and conditions, and these are then generally submitted for government approval under the terms of applicable bilateral ASAs. This was the predominant method for establishing prices until the 1970s, and it remains influential in many international markets (although active tariff enforcement by IATA is now a thing of the past). It runs counter to the spirit, if not the letter, of competition laws in most jurisdictions that have them, but in many countries these have either been held not to apply to a government-regulated industry such as air transport or specific industry exemptions have been agreed.

The recent history of these exemptions – in the United States, the European Union, Australia, and several other countries – has seen the tightening of restrictions placed on the definition of circumstances under which airlines and travel agencies are free to collude in respect of IATA tariff coordination. Whilst some degree of tariff co-ordination is essential to maintain the viability of the interline system, the need to police continuing abuses has been well-documented. (See, for example: CAA, 1994; Cotterril, 1997; Holloway, 1998a.)

Distribution The question in this case is how information about output and prices is distributed. For a competitive market to function properly, information on available products and prices must be freely and cheaply accessible to customers. According to neoclassical theory, only if information is openly available and fully incorporated into a price can that price work as an efficient mechanism for co-ordinating supply and demand. The problem is as we have seen that most markets fall short of the assumptions required by the neoclassical model of perfect competition, and one reason is information asymmetries between buyers and sellers. It is not uncommon for sellers to simultaneously work both to overcome and to deepen information asymmetries: brand images are in part a tool used to convey information about what buyers can expect from a purchase and to reduce consumers' uncertainty and search costs; on the other hand, various devices are also used to ensure that information about product availability, price, and quality is presented as favourably as possible relative to competitors' offers.

Potentially predatory practices such as the use of commission overrides, intended to encourage travel agents to channel business to preferred carriers, have already been mentioned. An even stronger concern of competition authorities in the United States and the EU in particular over the last two decades has been the use of GDSs to manipulate markets by biasing information flows. Market power is achievable through a variety of means, including the biasing of screen displays in favour of an owner, and using system data to gain early warning of competitors' marketing initiatives – or to analyse the outcome of initiatives so that counter-attacks can be formulated. These issues remain a threat to competition, but one that has diminished as airline shareholdings in GDSs have been diluted and, in particular, as the availability of Internet booking channels direct into individual airline inventories has grown. The swamping of agents' screen displays by multiple entries for single code-shared flights remains a concern, however, particularly in the United States and other jurisdictions where regulation of the abuse has been less forthcoming than in the EU; we will return to this in chapter 7.

Conclusion

The preceding subsections have barely scratched the surface with regard to the growing importance of competition law. Readers interested in exploring the subject further might want to look at the following texts. Neumann (2001) contains brief summaries of EU competition law and US antitrust law, along with a thorough account of the economic analysis underlying competition policies in general. Havel (1997) has contributed a scholarly review of the US and European airline deregulation and liberalisation experiences, the role of competition law after deregulation or liberalisation, and the need for a transnational approach to the policing of anti-competitive behaviour. Doganis (2001) offers a concise summary of the impact of EU competition law on the process of deregulation within the ECAA.

Arguably the most significant challenge facing decision-makers concerned with the application of competition law to the air transport industry is how to deal with industry consolidation. An important issue in this context is the choice of a geographical frame of reference.

Choosing the correct geographical frame of reference Proponents usually argue in favour of consolidation on two primary grounds.

1. Improved customer service across larger, 'seamless' networks. Competition, it is said, should be considered at the network level rather than the level of individual O & D markets.
2. Cost savings from enhanced efficiency, some of which will be passed on to customers. If after consolidation price-cost margins begin to rise, so the argument goes, this is likely to be due to efficiency gains rather than the exploitation of monopoly power – and it is to everybody's benefit if margins widen whilst prices either fall or rise less rapidly than they otherwise would.

The counter-argument is that it remains important to distinguish between concentration at the industry level (either nationally or globally) and at the market level. In the late 1990s, for example, almost 20 per cent of US domestic passengers were flying on monopoly routes and 46 per cent were flying on duopolies (Transportation Research Board, 1999). This matters because, contrary to the assumptions underlying contestability theory, numerous studies of the US domestic market have confirmed what might be intuitively expected: average prices (adjusted for stage-length) tend to decline as the number of competitors in a market increases (ibid; Stavins, 1996).

Further complicating any analysis along these lines, however, is the fact that 'route' and 'market' are not necessarily synonymous. A city-pair market connecting origin O to destination D might be served by a nonstop route, a multi-stop (same-plane or 'direct') route, and/or by separate routes connecting over one or more airlines' different hubs. One result could be that even though neither the nonstop O-D route nor individual routes to and from each hub are themselves highly competitive, the city-pair market between O and D is. It might therefore be argued that different routes are part of the same market if demand on one is a substitute for demand on the other(s). A lot depends on the impacts that geography and the design of competing networks have on the availability to consumers of alternative routing possibilities. In general, the following types of market are particularly vulnerable to anti-competitive behaviour.

- Markets which at one end serve a hub where the carrier surviving after a merger or acquisition is significantly more dominant than was the case before.

- Markets connecting two hubs, each dominated by a single carrier or by partners in a single alliance.
- Markets in which code-sharing eliminates active competition.
- Thin markets served over a hub by a sizeable network carrier where there is no possibility of rerouting traffic flows over another airline's competing hub or network, in which there is inadequate local traffic to support a competing point-to-point operation, and where the incumbent's network is large enough to offer economies of scope sufficient to exclude existing or potential competitors.

Airlines have an interest in defining markets as widely as possible – making a case, in the extreme, that it is network-versus-network competition that matters rather than what happens on any one route. Whilst this argument has strategic merit, it offers little consolation to consumers in individual markets subject to an abuse of dominant position.

iv. Supplying output: operations and operating strategy

Previous sections of the chapter have looked at airline output through the lens of economics. This section takes a more operational perspective.

Airline output embodies a value proposition made to customers. Some airlines make a single value proposition (e.g., Southwest), whilst others make multiple propositions (e.g., the full-service network majors). Each value proposition should ideally be based on one or more sources of sustainable competitive advantage, and the source(s) of competitive advantage should be fully reflected in operating strategy.

Value chains and processes

The 'value chain' is a concept popularised by Porter (1985) and used to describe all of the activities which come together both within an organization and outside it in order to provide the final customer – the passenger or shipper, in this case – with 'value'. Although the activities through which airlines deliver value to customers must to some extent be common across the industry, individual carriers can nonetheless search for competitive advantage in the value chain. This requires exploitation of whatever proprietary resources an airline might have available to it, and the management of all internal processes and external linkages – whether proprietary or not – in a manner that is coherent in the context of the chosen strategy. (Holloway (2002) discusses value chains, processes, activities, and tasks in greater depth.)

Despite over two decades of interest in value chains, 'the general irrelevance of traditional accounting data for strategic decision-making' remains a significant impediment (Hergert and Morris, 1989: 175). Nonetheless, there is an argument that thinking in terms of a value chain can help understand potential sources of competitive advantage, and the concept does also provide a useful link between competitive strategy on the one hand and operating strategy on the other.

Operations management and operating strategy defined

An operating system is a configuration of processes intended, in the case of an airline, to deliver transportation services (i.e., 'output') to passengers and freight shippers. Operations management is the management of that operating system – management of the processes through which resource inputs are transformed into service outputs. Some authors, such as Slack et al (1998), draw a distinction between resource inputs that are transformed (e.g., materials, information, and customers) and other resources that do the transforming (e.g., facilities, equipment, and staff). Transformation processes therefore use, and in many cases consume, resources; the reasons why they do this, and the rate at which they do it, are 'cost drivers'. We will consider cost drivers in chapter 5.

Following Wild (1989), we can divide the management of any organization's operating system into four components: structure; objectives; strategies; and control.

Operating system structure At the most general level, this is dictated by the nature of the industry concerned – that is, by the nature of the demand being satisfied, of the product being produced to satisfy it, and of the technology used to produce that product. Given that this is not a book specifically addressing operations management, we will make only a few general comments about the structure of operating systems.

1. The fundamental structural driver as regards the operating system of any service business is the fact that there is no separation in time or space between production and consumption of the core service – which, in the case of airlines, is transportation. We can therefore divide a service operating system into the following process categories.
   - **Service delivery system** This includes processes of three types which contribute directly to the delivery of service to customers.

Front-office processes Customers directly experience reservations, check-in, and onboard service processes, for example. In a market-oriented airline, delivery of front-office processes must be designed to meet the expectations of targeted customers.

Back-office processes Customers experience only indirectly aircraft maintenance and deep cleaning processes, for example; because back-office processes do not directly involve external customers, there is often more flexibility in their timing and design than there is in respect of front-office processes.

Hybrid processes These are essentially back-office processes that are witnessed, but not directly experienced, by customers. If passengers remain on an aircraft during a transit stop, for example, they will probably witness cabin cleaning and catering provision – processes that might very well be outsourced by the airline concerned. Interactions between staff during a crew change will also be witnessed.

- **Enabling processes** Critical though they might be to the ability of an airline to deliver service, processes such as strategy-making, budgeting, and even service design are too far removed from actual delivery to be categorised as delivery processes. They nonetheless enable an airline to operate.

2. An airline's operating system – specifically, the design and conduct of processes and their constituent activities – should reflect the effectiveness/efficiency trade-off inherent in its service concept(s). Inevitably, the fact that the customer is present makes effectiveness the key criterion for front-office processes, whereas efficiency can take top billing in respect of back-office and enabling processes; but there is always a balance to be struck – never an either/or choice.

3. There is merit in having as much system flexibility as possible. For example, airframe manufacturers have recognised the need for flexibility by introducing families of aircraft that share type ratings for pilot and engineer licensing purposes and use common components to reduce maintenance costs, allowing airlines to come closer to matching output to short-term fluctuations in demand. We will return to this in chapter 8.

Operations management objectives The objective of operations management is to produce output that has cost as little as possible (i.e., is efficiently produced) consistent with satisfying the expectations of targeted customers (i.e., subject to the constraint of system effectiveness) – and to do this at a profit. What binds effective customer service and efficient resource utilisation together is *productivity*. But not just 'raw' productivity; employees of

a full-service network carrier which emphasises high-quality service are unlikely to be as productive as the staff of a low-fare carrier or a charter airline in terms of ASMs produced per individual, for example. What matters,
however, is the revenue earned per resource unit or per dollar of expenditure. It is clearly nonsense to argue that a flight attendant serving five first
class passengers on a transatlantic flight is less productive than one serving
25 passengers travelling the same sector on deeply discounted fares simply
because the former contributes to 15,000 RPMs (i.e., five passengers multi-
plied by, say, 3,000 miles) whilst the latter contributes to the generation of
75,000 (i.e., 25 × 3,000). Productivity – the link between effectiveness and
efficiency – can only be considered within the context of the type of value
being offered, and the best way of doing that at the macro-level of the airline as a whole is to compare inputs with the revenue, rather than just the
raw output, that they generate. (Of course, at the micro-level of day-to-day
operations management a more traditional input-output approach to productivity monitoring is essential.)

One difficult question is how much slack should be present in an operating system to cover for service disruptions. Slack can be created either by
having extra resource units available, or by using resources at less than
their full capacity (e.g., scheduling an aircraft out of heavy maintenance in
the morning but not putting it back into service until the following evening). Irrgang (2000) suggests target slack in the region of one to three per
cent for aircraft and five per cent for other resources (such as gate capacity). The cost of this spare capacity can readily be calculated (e.g., ownership or leasing costs on one to three per cent of the fleet); the cost of not
having it available will be manifest in more 'irregular operations' – a phenomenon that costs each US major around $500,000 per aircraft per annum
(ibid).

Operations management is the 'engine room' of an airline. A clear understanding of customers and the specification of appropriate service packages will achieve nothing in the absence of an operational capability to deliver what customers expect. The challenge for operations managers in the
airline industry is that customers' expectations are keyed-off not only hard,
'functional' service attributes that can be measured – such as call centre
telephone pick-up times, flight punctuality, and baggage reclaim times –
but also off 'soft' attributes such as the style and tone of service delivery.
This is why a process-oriented, operations-driven approach to the business
is often inadequate in itself – even when selling largely on price; airline op-
ertions managers need to know what *their* customers expect out of *their*
service concept(s). Even in economy/coach, a pile 'em high 'n sell 'em
cheap philosophy reaches its limits amongst demanding consumers as soon
as a better service-price offer comes along.

Operating strategy An airline's operating strategy is the pattern of decisions and actions which establishes the role that the operating system will play in delivering service packages on specification and in such a way that customers' expectations are met. The primary tasks are as follows.

1. Forecasting demand for the type(s) of service an airline has decided to offer in the markets it has chosen to serve (generally over a shorter forecast period than in respect of longer-term fleet and infrastructure capacity planning).
2. Acquiring resources necessary to deliver the output required to meet forecasted demand in targeted markets or segments. Embedded in the acquisition decision will be judgements regarding what is required at a minimum and also how much slack to build into the system – a decision which, again, has to be taken within the context of a deliberate effectiveness/efficiency trade-off.
3. Scheduling resource deployment and usage. In this context it is worth bearing in mind that whilst in a highly integrated operating system such as an airline operational resources (e.g., aircraft, pilots, flight attendants, maintenance facilities) have to be *scheduled* interdependently, it is very often the case that they are *managed* independently (Irrgang, 1995a).
4. Managing demand and supply within the context of current system capacity. In other words, because the system is designed to meet some proportion of peak demand, it is necessary to manage demand and supply subject to that constraint.
5. Monitoring customers' perceptions of service quality against their expectations, and measuring broader system performance against objectives and external benchmarks.
6. Improving system performance – either incrementally or through a major 're-engineering' initiative, and either in response to identified problems or as part of a continuous search for improvement.

Controlling operating system performance The focus of concern is implementation of operating strategies such that required resources are made available in the appropriate quantity, at the appropriate time, and at the appropriate level of quality – with what is 'appropriate' depending upon performance objectives established for the operating system. Defining a plan as a 'statement of intention' and control as the 'analysis of plan outcomes and the making of necessary adjustments', Slack et al (1998: 356) usefully distinguish between three temporal dimensions.

1. **Long-term planning and control** Planning is in the ascendancy over control.
   - Aggregate demand forecasts are used.
   - Different categories of resource requirement are also aggregated.
   - Objectives are largely financial.
2. **Medium-term planning and control** Planning remains important, but control plays an increasing role.
   - Demand forecasts are now partially disaggregated.
   - Resource requirements are more finely determined, and contingency plans are developed.
   - Both financial and operational objectives are established.
3. **Short-term planning and control** The closer in we come, the more operations are being 'controlled' rather than planned, in the sense that operational decisions are taken in response to emerging developments.
   - Forecasts are highly disaggregated, and wherever possible are keyed-off actual demand (e.g., advance bookings and interpretations of what these imply for final demand on each departure).
   - Frequent interventions are made to correct deviations from plan by reassigning and/or rescheduling resources.
   - Operational objectives are very much to the fore (although their financial implications are kept firmly in sight).

We can envisage time-lines which involve fleet and other major resource planning that stretches several years into the future, the development of an outline schedule 12 to 24 months ahead, the subsequent refinement of the schedule followed by resource acquisition and allocation, and finally by control of day-to-day operations. Box 4.7 looks at short-term operations control.

Box 4.7: Operations control

Traditionally, flights have been planned and despatched by different functional areas at each departure station, with nobody taking overall responsibility for what is happening in the network as a whole; aircraft were treated as independent 'batons' handed off from one station to the next. Whilst this remains the case at some airlines, most now use a more co-ordinated approach. Operations control is generally the responsibility of an airline (or 'system') operations control centre (AOCC), charged with co-ordinating large numbers of internal operations units and external service providers. AOCCs are organized and staffed differently in different airlines, but a template for a large carrier suggested by Clarke et al (2000) recognises the following division of responsibilities.

1. **Operations controllers** *Their responsibility is to implement the current flight schedule and manage irregular operations arising from system disruptions. Assisted by increasingly sophisticated decision-support software, these are the people who make the final decisions in respect of operations (albeit in conjunction with other operational departments). They must not only execute the schedule, but also take a proactive position in response to problems as soon as they are identified.*
2. **Online support** *This includes several different groups.*
   - Flight dispatchers *Responsible for flight planning, flight dispatch, and flight following, in a large carrier's AOCC they might be organized by region or by sub-fleet.*
   - Crew schedulers *Responsible for scheduling crews and tracking the location and the legal and contractual duty-time status of individual crew members, they also control the calling up of reserve crews.*
   - Equipment schedulers *This group is responsible for ensuring that aircraft get to the right place at the right time to execute the schedule.*
   - Maintenance operations controllers *Often located in a separate maintenance operations control centre, they are responsible for controlling line maintenance activities and for providing operations controllers with advice regarding the implications of specific malfunctions as they arise.*
   - Customer services liaison *Their responsibility is to maintain information on passenger loads and itineraries, and on cargo loads.*
   - Station operations controllers *Also physically separate from the AOCC, major hubs and gateways will have station operations control centres which control station resources and handling processes.*
3. **Offline support** *These groups support operations controllers in areas such as meteorology, maintenance of the navigation database, flight technical services, route analysis, and operations analysis. Operations analysis is a particularly important support function because it helps improve operational dependability and schedule reliability by identifying resource bottlenecks and process performance shortfalls.*

Most AOCCs also include crisis back-up centres. British Airways' operations control centre, for example, has its Emergency Procedures Information Centre (EPIC) and Operations Control Incident Centre (OCIC). Both

are unmanned areas that can be quickly activated by trained staff in response to certain types of event: EPIC operates in response to an accident
or serious incident involving British Airways or one of the 60-plus other
airlines that have subscribed to use it; OCIC responds to incidents that are
likely to influence the airline's business (Slack et al, 1998).

The temporal span of an AOCC's responsibilities varies from airline to
airline, ranging from two or three days to two or three weeks ahead of any
given day of operation. At many carriers, initial flight schedules are outlined up to two years in advance and finalised for the following season at
semi-annual IATA traffic conferences; US domestic operators tend to final-
ise schedules on a much shorter timescale and vary them more frequently.
Returning to British Airways, scheduling personnel produce a timetable in
response to marketing requirements and in conjunction with operations
personnel; the operations control centre takes responsibility for execution
of the schedule three days ahead of short-haul flights and seven days ahead
of long-haul departures. The performance of the operations control team is
evaluated in terms of the regularity (i.e., completion rate) and on-time departure of flights.

In addition to their AOCCs, some US majors also have ramp co-
ordination centres ('ramp towers') at major hubs. Their responsibilities
tend to fall into the following areas (Irrgang, 2000).

- *Aircraft monitoring* Monitoring aircraft problems, informing passenger services personnel and groups responsible for ramp resources
  that might be unnecessarily tied-up around a delayed aircraft, and
  keeping the AOCC apprised of aircraft status. Ramp co-ordination personnel cannot, however, allocate or re-allocate aircraft.
- *Crew monitoring* Ensuring that crews are checked-in, briefed, and
  transported to their aircraft on time, and keeping the AOCC apprised
  of crew check-in status. Crews cannot be allocated or re-allocated by
  ramp co-ordination personnel.
- *Baggage and cargo loading* Co-ordinating between loading crews and
  the AOCC, particularly with regard to whether and when to load
  standby cargo.
- *Passenger close-out/commercial dispatch* Co-ordinating between
  check-in staff (at counters and, where gate check-ins are permitted, at
  gates) and the AOCC.
- *Catering* Co-ordinating between check-in staff and caterers to ensure
  proper provisioning and, in particular, that standby meals are loaded if
  required.
- *Cleaning* Co-ordinating the work of cleaning crews.

- *Ground support equipment (GSE)* Co-ordinating deployment and effective utilisation of GSE.
- *Gate scheduling* At airports where it is permitted, ramp co-ordination personnel will schedule gates in consideration of passenger flows between connecting flights that would benefit from gate proximity.

One of the greatest challenges confronting any AOCC is recovering from a significant schedule disruption – something that affects up to ten per cent of US domestic operations annually on average (Good, 2000). (In the United States, perhaps as few as 20 per cent of delays are in fact *directly* attributable to weather, traffic congestion, or maintenance issues; the overwhelming majority are attributable to the knock-on effects of *earlier* weather, traffic congestion, or maintenance delays.) Smith (2001: 42-43) describes the challenge as follows.

> The issue....is that you've got a pretty complicated set of flows for aircrew, passengers, and aircraft. When something goes wrong the operations people need to deal with all three of them and there are an awful lot of possible solutions or recovery strategies for each component. If you're looking at a typical US domestic hub with complexes of 40 flights in and 40 flights out, you're talking literally billions of possible solutions out there.

Readers interested in the management of 'irregular operations' are referred to Dudley and Clarke (1998), Clarke et al (2000), and Rogers et al (2000).

Software suppliers are working to integrate decision support tools covering system operations control, maintenance, and airport operations; however, some practitioners doubt that this can be achieved in a way that maps local solutions onto optimal network solutions – at least, not any time soon. More generally, operations researchers within the discipline of management science have developed a variety of widely used models to assist with capacity planning, queue management, resource scheduling, and inventory management under different assumed conditions that are in most cases applicable to some element of airline operations management. There are many texts available in the area, but Fitzsimmons and Fitzsimmons (1998) can be particularly recommended because of its orientation towards service industries.

Balancing process effectiveness and efficiency

Within any value chain, there is always a degree of tension between effectiveness (i.e., satisfying or exceeding customer expectations) and efficiency (i.e., meeting expectations at least cost). Clearly, there is a trade-off to be arrived at (Holloway, 2002).

1. Operating strategy must support an airline's choice of strategic and market positioning by delivering the type of customer value embodied in those positioning choices and in the service-price offers that flow from them. In other words, service delivery needs to be *effective* within its chosen context.

   Operating systems exist to meet the expectations of the particular customers that an airline's services have been designed and developed to serve. Their role is to deliver one or more packages of services to targeted customers, and the only relevant measure of effectiveness is whether or not those customers' service expectations have been met. If expectations have not been met, the problem might lie with the specification developed for the package concerned (in which case service re-design might be called for), or with service delivery; if there is a problem with the operating system that impairs service delivery, this might lie largely outside the airline's control (e.g., weather or traffic congestion) or within it (e.g., underestimating demand, scheduling inadequate resources at peak times, or providing staff with inadequate training or support). What represents 'effective' service delivery will vary as between different attributes in a service package, and between differently positioned packages offering different types of customer value; reliability is certain to be an important criterion in every dimension.

2. Operating strategy must also be capable of delivering desired service outcomes at a cost that is the lowest possible consistent with the particular service concept. That is, output needs to be produced *efficiently* within its particular context.

   There are two levels at which efficiency can be considered.

   • *Network design and schedule planning* A network and a schedule determine the boundaries of resource efficiency. Some networks and schedules (e.g., high-frequency point-to-point) permit more resource efficiency than others (e.g., short-haul hub operations), but – as always – network and schedule design need to be effective in meeting the expectations of whichever customers have been targeted as well as being efficient.

   • *Process design* Given what needs to be done and when in order to deliver a schedule, process design clearly affects how efficiently output is produced – that is, how efficiently resources allotted to each process are used.

This trade-off between effectiveness and efficiency is the essence of operations management (Wild, 1989). The characteristics of most types of services make operations management in a service business such as the airline industry a complex task. This is so because customers' direct experiences of the production processes in which they participate are very much part of the overall service experience, and therefore contribute to the service outcome (i.e., satisfaction or dissatisfaction) just as much as any tangible attribute designed into a service package. Indeed, the style and tone of service delivery are themselves attributes that generate important service benefits. The design of service packages and the processes through which they are delivered are therefore entirely symbiotic; operating and marketing strategies must be tightly co-ordinated, along with human resource strategy – a trio Lovelock (1996) has referred to as the 'services management trinity'.

It is worth at this point revisiting the argument put forward earlier in the chapter that airline output is heterogeneous, and in doing this distinguish between 'output' and 'outcome'.

- **Output** Output is measured in ASMs and ATMs, but these are not common currency. Whether we think in terms of strategy or production cost, a given number of ASMs or ATMs generated by Southwest is not the same type of output as the same numbers generated by American's Flagship Suite.
- **Outcome** The outcome of producing ASMs or ATMs and delivering service to customers is best measured, in the final analysis, using metrics such as customer satisfaction and service quality (see Holloway, 2002). Because they are offering very different value propositions, Southwest and American can both achieve successful outcomes from delivery of two very different types of output.

Some service packages permit considerable efficiency in their delivery – for example, inclusive tour charters operated with high seating densities, load factors, and aircraft utilisation, and low seat accessibility and marketing costs; low-fare scheduled operations also qualify in this regard. Delivery efficiency can be reflected in low prices, leading to a balanced and effective service-price offer providing good value to targeted segments. Other service packages will carry appreciably higher production costs because they do not permit as much efficiency in delivery processes – for example, high-frequency short-haul flights serving business segments with relatively small aircraft, high seat accessibility and marketing costs, and lower seating densities, load factors, and aircraft utilisation. Again, these costs can be reflected in prices – higher in this case, but still allowing a balanced and effective service-price offer to be made. In both cases, intens-ifying competition as markets liberalise encourages airlines to be as effic-ient as possible at achieving required levels of effectiveness – however 'effectiveness' might be defined by particular targeted segments.

The purpose of operating strategy and the task of operations management is to deliver output effectively enough to achieve targeted outcomes, and to do this as efficiently as possible. A production orientation, focused intern-ally on airline requirements rather than externally on customers' expectat-ions, is not the currency of competition in liberalised air transport markets (except perhaps when carriers are forced into 'survival mode', as several were in the aftermath of 9/11); on the other hand, the best marketing progr-amme will yield nothing sustainable if operational processes cannot deliver what customers in targeted segments are expecting. Whereas marketing delivers promises, operations delivers *on* promises (Holloway, 1998b). The fundamental challenge of operating strategy is therefore to get costs into line with prices that targeted customers are prepared to pay in return for the level of service embodied in the airline's service package(s). The correct approach is to identify what the customers in each target segment want, provide it to them at a price they are willing to pay, and then ensure that production costs allow this to be done at a profit. Every service concept implies a particular approach to the management of an airline's cost and revenue streams. Operating strategy must therefore stand on two closely co-ordinated legs.

1. **Revenue strategy** Revenue strategy is driven by an understanding of what targeted customers expect and an appreciation of whether and how a particular airline's resources can be leveraged to deliver service that at least matches these expectations (Grant, 1998). We saw in chapter 1 that some carriers offer relatively low levels of perceived benefit, compensating for this with low prices – prices that are nonethe-less profitable because of low input costs and/or high productivity; this is the strategic path chosen by most low-fare airlines. Others try to maximise perceived benefits, particularly for those segments of dem-and prepared to pay higher prices in return for improved benefits; this approach underlies the continuous cycle of product upgrades and re-launches in long-haul business and first class cabins. It is also found in some short-haul markets.

   These choices about how customer value is to be created in product and geographical markets – the balance of emphasis between benefits and price – help transform a strategic position into the service-price offers that reach individual marketplaces.

2. **Cost management strategy** A strategic position should be supported by a cost structure capable of delivering costs per ASM or ATM (i.e., unit costs) that are low enough to allow profits to be earned given the revenues per ASM or ATM (i.e., unit revenues) implied by that choice of position. One of management's most important tasks is therefore to decide on the level of service to be offered into targeted segments, and then provide it at costs lower than the price that each segment is prepared to pay. In practice, airline costs can be extraordinarily difficult to manage – as we will see in the next chapter.

Figure 4.1 relates these ideas to some of the terrain covered in the opening four chapters

v. Capacity management: the supply side

There are various supply-side options.

• **Fleet management** During the off-peak season, European charter (i.e., nonscheduled) carriers endeavour to lease or sub-lease some of their aircraft to other operators whose seasonal requirements are opposite to their own; they also retain as a core full-time workforce only a relatively small proportion of their peak-season staff complement. Training and heavy maintenance are invariably scheduled for the low season. Scheduled carriers without a varied network comprised of counter-seasonal routes face a different challenge: they can also lease aircraft out and schedule heavy maintenance during the low season (subject to the need to plan a reasonably balanced workflow for inhouse maintenance facilities), but daily and weekly peaks are tougher to accommodate because whilst part-time staff can be employed, aircraft are around to accumulate fixed charges all the time.

An airline wanting to reduce output in the short term can: sell owned aircraft (subject to market conditions) and return leased units (subject to lease return clauses); remove seats from its aircraft (i.e., reduce seating density and therefore cut the output of ASMs generated by any given schedule – as American did in 2001, for example); park aircraft; and/or reduce utilisation of the retained fleet. The more modern a fleet, the more difficult it is to park aircraft or sustain low utilisation; this is because the saving of variable operating costs might well be swamped by high ownership costs which must now be spread over fewer units of output – output that presumably is having to be sold into weak demand and so may itself be generating lower than desirable yields. (On the

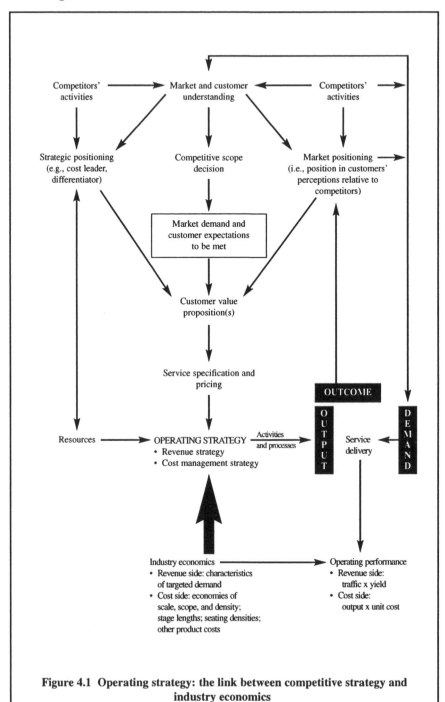

Figure 4.1 Operating strategy: the link between competitive strategy and industry economics

other hand, whereas variable operating costs have to be paid in cash, a significant portion of ownership costs associated with young aircraft will be accounted for by noncash depreciation charges; if revenue is weak and cash-burn is an issue – as was the case for many carriers immediately after 9/11 – it might be justifiable to park even relatively young aircraft and accept a substantial hit to the income statement in order to preserve cash.)

There can be merit in having an age-stratified fleet of owned aircraft supplemented by units under leases with a rolling spread of return options – although the marketing, fuel efficiency, maintenance cost, and residual value implications of retaining older units also have to be considered, as do the relatively high rentals associated with short-term operating leases. We will look at this, and at the output management flexibility contributed by operating families of different-sized variants within the sub-fleet of a type, in chapter 8.

- **Flight scheduling** Because an airline is not a geographically fixed operation serving just one market, it can schedule its available capacity to produce output and meet demand in different markets at different times. Having a balanced portfolio of routes that peak at different times can, assuming the right fleet composition, allow capacity to be shifted in order to offset demand variations. Where this is not possible, airlines facing daily or weekly peaks may use off-peak periods to deploy aircraft onto routes with different demand characteristics from those on their core network. Sometimes such routes are opened specifically to absorb off-peak capacity from these core routes, and if this rationale is used internally to justify marginal cost pricing, charges of capacity dumping are likely to be heard from smaller incumbents.
- **Scheduling other resources** Staff, at call centres and on check-in desks for example, can be scheduled in response to predicted demand on a shift-by-shift basis. Some categories of staff can be cross-trained/multi-skilled (subject to union agreements where applicable); productivity can be raised by having front-line staff do back-office jobs when demand is low, and back-office staff move into the front office when demand is peaking. The use of part-time staff, particularly in customer service positions, is now widespread within the industry; a key issue in respect of part-time customer-contact staff is inevitably whether they can be effectively acculturated – because corporate culture, through the impact it has on the style and tone of service delivery, is a critical variable in any high-contact service business. Finally, the maintenance of equipment, facilities, and staff (i.e., vacations and training) can be scheduled for off-peak periods.

- **Outsourcing** Some inhouse functions and processes can be supplemented during peak periods by the use of external service providers.
- **Increasing customer participation** Internet bookings and automated check-ins are just two examples of how airlines are taking pressure off supply bottlenecks within their service delivery systems by increasing customer participation in certain activities.
- **Making customers wait** Whenever a service delivery system cannot accommodate current demand, customers must wait. In the context of the reservations process, high-yield customers frequently have little tolerance for waiting: this is why many airlines provide dedicated reservations lines for first and business class passengers, and it is also why relatively high seat accessibility is maintained in premium cabins to ensure that late-booking demand is not spilled to competitors. Once inside an airline's service delivery system, waiting takes the form of queues at various points in customers' activity cycles (Holloway, 1998b); what is acceptable here will depend upon customers' expectations – a consideration that should be reflected in the effectiveness/ efficiency trade-off built into design of each service package and the system established to deliver it (Holloway, 2002). Some customers (e.g., those on charter flights) are more likely to tolerate check-in or boarding queues and slow onboard service attributable to low flight attendant ratios, for example, than others (e.g., those travelling first or business class on a long-haul scheduled carrier). (Substantial queues in the check-in and/or security processes that significantly lengthen the total journey time on a short-haul flight might detract from the competitiveness of air transport in markets where surface modes represent viable substitutes.)

Whether or not they are physically in line, any customer waiting for service is in effect queuing. A queue is clearly equivalent to an inventory of physical items insofar as it performs the same function: it is a buffer. Queues mediate between the rate at which customers present themselves for service and the rate at which the service delivery system is able to accommodate them. Waiting within a service delivery system carries economic costs; when internal customers (i.e., other employees) wait for an input the cost is often measurable as lost productivity, and when external customers (i.e., passengers, shippers, or forwarders) have to wait the cost is measurable as reduced satisfaction and possible loss of future revenue – depending upon the length of the wait, customers' prior expectations about the length of wait, and attribution (i.e., where fault is perceived to lie).

One way of dealing with excess output is to reduce capacity and redesign the production process to meet a less ambitious share of peak demand. However, this might well leave little scope for further cuts in output should the need arise without risking a loss of 'critical mass' in market presence terms.

There can also be technical difficulties confronting supply-side efforts to deal with the effects of demand peaking. It might be the case, for example, that service on a route needs to be maintained even during periods when traffic appears not to justify it because some or all of the demand which the underutilised service satisfies is being fed into the wider network and is generating profits that compensate for excess off-peak output on the route itself. Separately, operational requirements affecting staff deployment and aircraft maintenance might militate in favour of a more consistent schedule than market planners feel is justified by demand characteristics alone. Finally, whilst it is one thing to adjust supply on a route to broadly foreseeable fluctuations in demand, it is very difficult to adjust it in response to the significant fluctuations characteristic of some segments (notably business travellers) at the level of the individual departure.

In the short term, it is generally more expensive to adjust supply than to manage demand in order to balance output produced (ASMs, etc.) and output sold (RPMs, etc.). An outline of available approaches to demand management was provided at the end of chapter 2. Together, the management of demand and of supply are the essence of 'capacity management'. In Part 3 of the book, we will be looking in more detail at three specific areas critical to capacity management: network management; fleet management; and revenue management.

vi. Conclusion

Output can be controlled on the following levels.

1. By deciding upon the competitive (i.e., product and geographic) scope of the operation: this was discussed in chapter 1. It will be touched upon again in chapters 6 and 7, when we look at network management.
2. By securing and managing (in particular, scheduling) the capacity to produce output – notably the fleet, the facilities, and the human resources needed: fleet management is the subject of chapter 8.
3. By managing the pricing and release of seats from the 'inventory' created by committing to a schedule: pricing was discussed in chapter 3, and revenue management is the subject of chapter 9.

Before continuing the discussion of capacity management in Part 3 of the book (chapters 6–9), we will look at the remaining supply-side element in the operating performance model around which Part 2 has been structured: unit cost.

5 Unit Costs

All progress is based on a universal innate desire
on the part of every organism to live beyond its income.
Samuel Butler

Chapter overview

The unit cost of output is the last of four elements in the operating performance model around which Part 2 of the book has been structured.

TRAFFIC x YIELD > < OUTPUT x **UNIT COST**
= OPERATING PERFORMANCE (i.e., PROFIT or LOSS)

Unit cost is total operating cost divided by output, and is therefore expressed as cost per ASM (ASK) or ATM (ATK). This chapter will look first at different definitions of cost and approaches to the accounting treatment of costs, and will then briefly review significant airline cost drivers. Finally, broad approaches to cost management within the industry will be discussed. Three critical points to take from the chapter are that:

- most costs are open to a variety of definitions and interpretations;
- passengers do not care about airline costs, but many do care about fares; and
- the purpose of incurring any cost is to generate revenue. It is possible in some markets to make money with a high-cost/high-yield product as well as with a low-cost/low-yield product. From a financial perspective, what matters is how productive each dollar of expenditure is in generating revenue. From a competitive perspective, what matters is how an airline's costs compare with those of competitors targeting the same customers – because a carrier with lower costs can in principle use its advantage to earn higher margins and/or to price aggressively and gain market share.

259

i. Cost defined

Cost data is an important input into most decision-making processes. The problem is that there is often no single number that can be identified as *the* cost of something. Take an aircraft: if it was bought several years ago for $40 million, this is its *historic cost* – something accountants will want to reduce on the balance sheet by taking an annual depreciation charge, but economists will regard as partly *sunk* and therefore to that extent not relevant to future decisions; if it could be sold now (either outright or as part of a sale-and-leaseback) for $25 million, that part of the $40 million historic cost is not yet sunk and any incremental income that could be earned by reinvesting the $25 million more profitably elsewhere represents the *opportunity cost* of not doing so; if a replacement today would cost $55 million, this is its *replacement cost*. Which of these costs is relevant depends on the nature of the decision being taken.

Accountants tend on the whole to be oriented towards current expenditures and revenues, and towards keeping track of how the historical costs of fixed assets such as facilities, ground equipment, and aircraft are amortised or depreciated. They 'account' for what is happening. Economists, on the other hand, are more interested in using costs to assist in making decisions about the future. This orientation towards the future leads economists to recognise several types of cost that have no place in financial accounts. Some of these are briefly reviewed in Box 5.1.

Box 5.1: Avoidable, incremental, sunk, and opportunity costs

Avoidable costs These are costs that can be avoided by a decision not to do something (e.g., to cut, or decide not to launch, a route), to do less of something (e.g., to cut frequency), or to do something in a different way (e.g., to operate a smaller aircraft on a given departure).

Incremental costs These are additional costs that will flow from a decision to do something (e.g., to open a route), to do more of something (e.g., to add frequency), or to do something in a different way (e.g., to operate a larger aircraft on a given departure). Both avoidable costs and incremental costs need to be set against the revenue changes associated with each respective decision.

Sunk costs Any past expenditure that cannot be recovered (e.g., route development costs, or the historical cost of an aircraft in excess of its current secondary market or scrap value) should be treated as a sunk cost; it is not 'relevant' to decisions going forward. Only those elements of past expend-

itures that are 'recoverable' are relevant to current decisions (alongside any new expenditures that might be incurred or avoided as a result of those decisions). Everything pivots on timing. For example, before a decision to enter a new route has been implemented, advertising, route development, and station start-up costs are avoidable; once service has been inaugurated, many of these initial costs are sunk.

Opportunity (or 'economic') cost *This is any cost associated with opportunities forgone by not putting a resource into its highest value alternative use; it is not a cash outgoing, but a recognition of the value existing in opportunities that cannot now be taken up. In practice, opportunity costs are everywhere.*

- *Assume an airline owns a building: for an economist, the cost attributed to whatever activities go on in that building should include the opportunity cost of not putting it to some alternative use – such as renting it out or selling it and redeploying the cash proceeds.*

- *When an airline invests capital in, say, its maintenance, repair and overhaul (MRO) division, the opportunity cost of that capital is the rate of return that could have been earned by investing in an alternative business unit, asset, or project with a similar risk profile.*

- *When a carrier expands business class cabins on a long-haul fleet, it will incur initial expenditures on improved ground and inflight service attributes (such as larger airport lounges, more business class seats, additional galleys and onboard stowage, for example) and perhaps also on hiring and training additional staff; it will also face incrementally higher operating costs (e.g., catering, cabin staff pay, etc.). Beyond this, however, the opportunity cost of the initiative will include any operating profit forgone as a result of choosing to redeploy existing resources (notably cabin floorspace) to the expansion.*

- *Demand spill also represents an opportunity cost. If a passenger takes the last two seats on connecting Phoenix–Dallas and Dallas–New York (LGA) flights, any local Phoenix–Dallas and Dallas–LGA demand trying to book subsequently will be spilled, as will other through Phoenix-LGA passengers and Phoenix-originating passengers wanting to connect to other points beyond Dallas. This spill does not appear in financial accounts, but nonetheless could represent a very real opportunity cost of selling those last remaining seats – depending on the revenues earned from each of the possible sales alternatives.*

We will meet the concept of opportunity cost again when discussing demand spill and revenue management in chapter 9. However, the balance of this chapter is concerned more with the accounting than the economic treatment of costs.

Total operating cost

In the airline industry it is usual to distinguish between operating and non-operating costs; the former are incurred conducting air transport operations, whilst the latter are attributable to activities other than air transport as well as to decisions in respect of how to finance the business. Our concern in this book is with total *operating* costs (TOCs). One approach to analysing them is to look at cost behaviour.

Cost behaviour: fixed and variable elements of total operating cost

'Cost behaviour' refers to the manner in which costs vary in response to managerial action. The action with which we are particularly concerned here is decisions taken with regard to output volume. In this context, the distinction between fixed and variable costs is critical (even though it rarely appears in financial accounts).

1. **Fixed costs** do not vary with changes in output within the capacity range of existing production facilities (notably the fleet).
   - *Committed fixed costs* arise when an airline commits itself to certain expenditures such as the leasing of aircraft, office space, gates, counters, and lounges, for example. In particular, committed fixed costs associated with aircraft (e.g., lease rentals and depreciation) have to be met whether aircraft fly or not – unless they are permanently grounded (in which case either a lease termination payment or a write-off of any undepreciated book value will be chargeable).
   - *Discretionary fixed costs* arise from expenditures that are also not directly connected with output decisions, but which can readily be changed at the airline's discretion. Advertising and (non-mandatory) staff training are two examples. It is therefore not only fixed assets as defined by accountants (e.g., land, buildings, aircraft, ground equipment, etc.) that generate fixed costs; any business bears overhead functions that are neither linked specifically to the ownership or leasing of an asset nor dependent for their cost on the firm's level of output. These are often to some extent discretionary, and so can present ready targets when costs come under scrutiny.

(Fixed costs should not be confused with sunk costs: a sunk cost is a past expenditure that cannot be recovered, whereas a fixed cost is a current or future expenditure that is unconnected to output level.)

2. **Variable costs** do vary with the level of an airline's output. Examples include fuel, landing fees, navigation charges, and flight-hour and cycle-driven maintenance costs. Variable costs move in the same direction as output, but the two do not necessarily change in direct proportion – which is why average cost per unit of output produced tends to be different at different levels of output. The variable costs incurred producing one million ASMs or ATMs will not be twice those incurred producing 500,000, for example; much will hinge upon the operating economics of the network and aircraft involved. The behaviour of variable – and therefore total – costs within a particular operating system will also depend in the short run upon factor productivity and the impact of the law of diminishing returns, and in the long run upon economies of scale and scope; these concepts will be explained later in the chapter.

A decision to outsource ground-handling, catering, or maintenance can be driven by a number of motivations, including a desire both to reduce costs and to make them more transparent. Another critical motivation might be to transform fixed into variable costs. As air transport markets have been deregulated or liberalised they have become more volatile. Airlines accordingly need the flexibility to react to changes in the volume and/or nature of demand more quickly than the heavily integrated, high-overhead architectures of long-established carriers have typically permitted.

The importance of time horizons In time, every fixed cost will ultimately become variable. Economists use the following concepts.

- **The short run** is any period during which the cost of at least one input is fixed.
- **The long run** begins at any point in the future when all costs become variable – in other words, the point at which the firm will be able to free itself from current commitments and entirely reconfigure its operating system. Total cost and total variable cost become the same by definition, because there are no longer any costs that are fixed.

For most firms that are 'going concerns', the long run is an analytical concept rather than an actual point in time – although for small, flexibly configured firms in certain types of (generally non-capital-intensive) industry this need not necessarily be so. From our perspective considering the airline business, there are three important points to stress.

1. The closer in we come along a time-line, the higher the proportion of an airline's costs that is fixed. Whilst output can be curtailed relatively swiftly (as we saw in the aftermath of 9/11), fixed costs associated with the production infrastructure and corporate overhead take time to adjust; it is not necessarily a simple matter to sell aircraft or return them to lessors, lay off or furlough staff, or terminate gate and other facility leases. A high proportion of airline costs is fixed in the short run and difficult to avoid. This is why the rate of cash-burn is so high when an airline's revenue is cut by strike action or other significant system disruptions. In the short run, perhaps as much as 80 per cent of a scheduled carrier's costs can considered fixed (Flint, 2001).

2. As the time-line is stretched, a higher proportion of costs becomes variable or avoidable – that is, a carrier's management has more discretion to reconfigure its operating system and cost structure. For instance, fixed costs associated with owning a fleet of aircraft remain fixed only until such time as the airline is able to adjust the size and/or composition of that fleet. The time required to vary these 'fixed' costs will reflect a number of considerations. If it is intended to add aircraft, a feasible time-frame for achieving this will depend upon the carrier's financial status and the availability of appropriate units from manufacturers, operating lessors, and the secondary market. On the other hand, if the intention is to dispose of aircraft, the time-frame will depend upon the state of the secondary market, manufacturers' willingness to accept trade-ins against future deliveries, and/or the flexibility allowed by lease documentation with regard to early return.

3. The larger and more complex an airline's operating system, the longer the 'long run' is going to be relative to, say, a small, non-unionised start-up that outsources many of its non-flying activities. There is clearly merit in having flexibility to reconfigure production processes as rapidly as possible in response to changing levels of input prices and factor productivity, and also to fluctuations in demand.

Over-focusing on short-term network and fleet analysis can lead to an almost unconscious acceptance of most costs as fixed. The shorter the time-horizon adopted, the more true this is. Conversely, by lengthening an analysis we can unearth more potential flexibility (Frainey, 1999).

Operating leverage One reason why in aggregate the airline industry performs so badly during recessions (and, conversely, benefits strongly during upturns) is that the effects of demand cyclicality are magnified by the high operating and financial leverage from which many carriers suffer. Financial leverage is high when debt and equivalent obligations fund a large proportion of total assets relative to the proportion funded by stockholders; whereas stockholder dividends can be reduced or eliminated, debt interest (a non-operating expense) has to be paid whatever is happening on the revenue side. Operating leverage – which is what we are concerned with here – is high when a large proportion of an airline's short-run total operating cost is fixed; again, fixed costs have to be met regardless of what is happening to revenue. When revenue grows off an unchanged debt and fixed asset base, profits are *leveraged* up; when revenue shrinks, and pending reduction in debt and fixed assets, profits are *leveraged* down.

Most airlines find it difficult to rapidly adjust their fixed costs downward when output begins to run ahead of demand. This can happen where too many new aircraft are delivered relative to prevailing requirements, or when demand growth falls below expectations – two circumstances that frequently coincide. Any downturn in traffic and/or yields could rapidly take an airline's revenue below the level required to meet fixed costs – something that happened to large numbers of carriers in 1991 and, more dramatically, in 2001/2002. At this point, every dollar of additional revenue loss comes straight off the bottom line.

In practice, how high an airline's operating leverage really is depends in part on the time horizon applied, in part on assumptions about the prevailing state of the secondary market for tradable assets (notably aircraft), and in large measure upon the scale of the operations concerned. A small carrier that has outsourced extensively and flies aircraft which are either on short-term leases or are owned but could readily be sold into a currently buoyant secondary market might be shrunk or closed down fairly quickly; the same cannot be said for a large international airline. The industry's 'high' operating leverage is therefore a generalisation which, whilst broadly true, needs to be put into a specific context.

Because financial statements tend not to provide a break-down between fixed and variable costs as such, external analysts generally have to estimate operating leverage by categorising different expenditure line items as either fixed or variable. An alternative is to calculate the 'degree of operating leverage', which is the percentage change in operating profit between two periods divided by the percentage change in sales.

Production functions, cost functions, and the impact of output decisions on costs

Any airline's TOCs reflect the operating characteristics of the industry, the design of that particular carrier's operating system, the prices paid for input resources, and the efficiency with which resources are used; another critical variable will clearly be its level of output. These variables are encapsulated in each firm's production function and cost function, the importance of which is explained in Box 5.2.

Box 5.2: Production functions and cost functions

*An airline's operating system is in economic terms a production process in which inputs – factors of production – are combined to produce output. The quantity that can be produced is a function of the factors of production used and the efficiency with which they are combined; so is the quality of output produced – but, as we saw in chapter 4, much of microeconomic theory treats output as homogeneous. A **production function** is a quantitative statement of the relationship between factor inputs used and the volume of output produced – of the alternative input combinations that can produce a given level of output or, conversely, of the output that can be produced by a given set of factor inputs. The technology available within an industry is the fundamental driver of any production function, but managerial discretion with regard to choice of inputs and how they are deployed is clearly important.*

*If a production function is combined with a schedule of input prices, the result is a **cost function**. A total cost function relates TOCs to output levels, and so helps provide insight into the impact of output changes on costs. One approach is to graph cost on the vertical axis against output on the horizontal and use least-squares regression on historical data to fit a curve that will help describe likely cost movements in response to output changes. Cost functions can also be developed algebraically. Since the mid-1990s, major airlines have been using increasingly sophisticated models to explore both the cost implications of different output decisions and areas where operational efficiency could be improved. (Various generic cost models are also available from industry associations and the principal airframe manufacturers. Although these models are undoubtedly useful, particularly when comparing the operating costs of alternative aircraft types, individual carriers have such different cost structures – attributable to their unique fleets, networks, schedules, labour forces, and operating strategies, for example – that only customised models should be used for profit planning purposes.)*

In addition to TOCs, there are two other important cost concepts to be aware of: average cost and marginal cost.

1. ***Average (or 'unit') cost*** *is, as we saw earlier in the chapter, TOC at a given level of output divided by the number of units of output produced (i.e., ASMs or ATMs, etc.). Average costs are rarely the same at different levels of output.*

   - *In the **short run**, average cost is comprised of average fixed cost and average variable cost. The presence of fixed costs means that short-run total cost can be averaged down by increasing output within the available capacity range. In other words, by fully utilising currently available capacity we can produce more output over which to spread the fixed costs associated with that capacity. What this means in practical terms is that provided additional output generates revenue in excess of variable costs, the addition of output within the existing capacity range can improve the profit potential of all services – both existing and new.*

     Average cost is, however, unlikely to change uniformly. Because TOC seldom varies in direct proportion to output, average cost is not a constant; the short-run average cost (SRAC) curve is often found to have a 'U'-shape when average cost on the vertical axis is graphed against output on the horizontal. The law of diminishing returns in fact tells us that the marginal productivity of variable factor inputs added to a fixed production facility will increase rapidly at first – leading to a marked decline in average cost as TOCs rise less than proportionately with output – and then flatten off and reverse, causing an eventual upturn in average cost.

   - *In the **long run**, the question is whether average cost can be reduced further by adding incremental capacity and generating yet more output over which to average (existing and incremental) fixed costs. The answer will depend upon the shape of the long-run average cost curve (LRAC), which in turn is heavily dependent upon what can theoretically be achieved given the nature of the particular industry's production process. Where average costs fall in response to increases in output beyond the existing capacity range 'economies of scale' are present, and where they rise 'diseconomies' kick-in as capacity grows further. 'Minimum efficient scale' (MES) is achieved where LRACs are at a minimum – that is, at the bottom of the LRAC curve; beyond MES the LRAC curve will be flat or will rise, depending upon the industry concerned.*

     The greater the size of MES relative to total industry output, the smaller is the number of competitors that can simultaneously prod-

uce at MES and the higher the industry's concentration ratio is likely to be. For example, if MES is equivalent to 25 per cent of industry output, there is in principle room for only four competitors producing at minimum LRAC – and the implication of this is that any other competitor in the industry will suffer a cost disadvantage; in practice, of course, other considerations – not the least of which in many industries is the speed of technological change – complicate this simplification. It is nonetheless true that where economies of scale are significant, the larger an industry's dominant firms are likely to be. In particular, industries requiring heavy investment in facilities and equipment carrying high fixed costs tend to benefit more from economies of scale than labour-intensive industries. The presence of economies of scale in the airline business has been a hotly debated topic, and we will return to it later in the chapter.

To summarise, in the short run, firms inherit production process configurations which are likely to be suboptimal for given conditions, with the result that SRACs are inevitably above LRACs. As the time horizon stretches out, it becomes possible to vary progressively more factor inputs. What the firm is faced with, therefore, is a series of SRAC curves – each above the LRAC curve, but touching it at their lowest points. Economies of scale are present where a firm can reduce unit cost by increasing capacity and output; a key issue, of course, is whether the incremental output can be sold at a profit.

2. **Marginal cost** is, as we saw in chapter 3, the change in TOC resulting from a one-unit change in output. When we discuss changes in airline output we are clearly not interested in movements of plus or minus one ASM or ATM at a time; nonetheless, the expression 'marginal cost' is widely used in this context, and we will adopt the same practice here. As long as marginal cost is below average cost, each additional unit of output will reduce average cost; as soon as marginal cost exceeds average cost, each additional unit of output will raise average cost. Of course, whether this matters will depend upon what is happening to marginal revenue (i.e., the revenue earned from each marginal unit of output); in general, there is merit in producing additional output if the revenue it earns exceeds the cost of producing it – an observation that is consistent with the argument of neoclassical microeconomics that profit is maximised at a level of output where marginal cost and marginal revenue are equal.

Each individual airline's cost structure – the relative sizes of different line items and the proportion of fixed and variable costs – will affect the cost impact of output decisions.

The cost impact of output changes

Always subject to a particular airline's cost structure, we can make some general comments about the impact of short-run output changes on total, average, and marginal costs.

Total costs At zero output, TOCs and fixed costs will be the same; there will be no variable costs because there is no output to generate them. At any level of output above zero but still within the range of current capacity, an increase in output will increase total cost by the amount of variable cost incurred in producing that output; fixed costs remain unchanged. As output rises, so do TOCs – unless efficiency can be improved, resulting in a change in the operating system that alters the relationship between output and cost. One objective of the corporate restructurings undertaken by a number of airlines in recent years has been to break their established output/total cost relationships by becoming more efficient. In the past, technology has played an important role in improving this relationship (e.g., improved airframe and, particularly, powerplant technologies); this time around, technology also has a role to play, albeit less dramatic (e.g., improved passenger facilitation), but it is the organization of the value chain and working practices within it that have come under particular scrutiny.

TOCs therefore rise by the amount of any increase in variable costs when output rises within the range of existing capacity. Once existing capacity is fully utilised, further increases in output bring with them additional fixed costs which create a marked step-up in TOCs. Particularly in capital-intensive businesses such as airlines, capacity increases tend to come in indivisible 'lumps', creating marked steps in the cost function. For example, assume a single-aircraft 'fleet'. This aircraft bears fixed costs whether it is flying or not. Further assume that we currently operate it on one rotation a day over a single short-haul route. If the aircraft is capable of operating, say, four rotations a day on this route and we do in fact increase the schedule to four departures in each direction, two things will happen:

- in absolute dollar terms, *fixed costs* remain the same, variable costs (e.g., fuel, airport and ATS charges) rise, and TOCs therefore increase;
- *fixed costs per unit of output* will decline, because unchanged fixed costs are being spread over four times as many ASMs or ATMs (given

four rotations are now operated rather than one). Whether total costs per unit of output (i.e., average or unit cost) also fall will depend upon whether the averaging down of fixed costs is sufficient to outweigh the increase in variable costs; in many cases it will be.

Now assume that we are starting to spill demand and that to meet market needs the requirement is to add a fifth frequency rather than operate a larger aircraft. This additional frequency therefore requires a second aircraft.

1. Although demand comes forward in units of one or more passengers at a time, capacity is added (and output is produced) by significantly larger units – that is, by aircraft. These represent 'indivisibilities' because, much though we might like to, we cannot divide a chosen type into smaller units of capacity to better match output to demand. Indivisibilities occur throughout an operating system, wherever capacity (e.g., stations, gates, simulators, maintenance bays) must be added in larger 'lumps' than demand comes forward to fully utilise it. Supply and demand are fundamentally difficult to match in industries where significant indivisibilities are present. At the level of the individual route there are indivisibilities stemming from: aircraft size; slot and gate allocations; staffing; and infrastructural resources. Potential output is set by constraints imposed by the most limiting of these indivisibilities, and any increase in output beyond that limit will require additional capacity – perhaps a larger aircraft or more gates, for example. Such step-ups in capacity often carry with them significant incremental fixed costs.
2. An expanding airline's total cost function therefore rises in clearly defined steps associated with the addition of fixed costs attributable to each new aircraft (as well as to the addition of other 'lumpy' assets). Clearly, much will depend upon the size of the carrier concerned. Adding an aircraft or a station to the operating system of a small, recently established airline will produce a much more dramatic impact on that carrier's cost function than would adding an aircraft or a station to, say, American's system.

In summary, an airline's current capacity generates certain fixed costs. That capacity will support a range of output from zero to whatever can in theory be produced at full utilisation. Output beyond capacity at full utilisation requires the addition of further capacity, which brings with it additional fixed costs. Because aircraft and some other elements of an airline's operating system are indivisible below certain levels, the additional fixed costs they bring with them are sufficiently significant to cause a marked step-up in aggregate fixed costs and therefore in TOCs. If the new capacity is not at first fully utilised, additional fixed costs per unit of output (i.e., per ASM or ATM, etc.) will be high; as utilisation of the new capacity increases, variable costs associated with ramping up output will rise but fixed costs will be spread over a growing volume of output and so will be averaged down on a per unit basis. This process repeats itself every time existing capacity (e.g., the current fleet) reaches full utilisation and further capacity is added. One possible implication of all this is outlined in Box 5.3.

Box 5.3: Production indivisibilities and the 'empty core'

Production indivisibilities are central to an idea that was mentioned earlier in the book and has been widely discussed over the last few years, at least in academic circles, in respect of the airline industry. The idea of the 'empty core' is that because of production indivisibilities an industry might not be able to sustain an optimal level of supply, but instead has to subject itself to destabilising bouts of undersupply or oversupply – with financial instability the consequence (Telser, 1978).

In simple terms it might be, for example, that one flight is insufficient to meet demand on a route and leads to high fares whilst two flights generate excess output and lead to unsustainably low fares. The outcome in an unregulated market could be constant swings from profit to loss as entrants come and go – perhaps in the extreme leading to withdrawal of service altogether (Hanlon, 1999).

Average cost and marginal cost When output is increased within the range of existing capacity, (short-run) marginal cost is equivalent to the variable costs of this increased output (which is not necessarily the same as saying that it is equivalent to the average variable cost of all output – which might be higher or lower than the marginal cost of new output, depending upon how cost-effectively that new output is produced). If on the other hand production of the marginal output requires extra capacity, fixed costs attributable to that new capacity must be absorbed into marginal cost. For instance, returning to our earlier example of one aircraft flying four rotations on a single route:

- the marginal cost of putting the next passenger into the last available seat on the final departure is equivalent to the variable cost of carrying that passenger (e.g., ticketing and revenue accounting, commissions, ground-handling, catering, and fuel-burn). This is essentially a traffic cost;

- on the other hand, the marginal cost of putting the next passenger onto an extra frequency operated by a newly acquired aircraft – were the airline concerned to be so generous – would be the (much larger) sum of variable and fixed costs associated with acquiring and operating that extra aircraft. This would represent both a traffic *and* a capacity cost.

Simplistic though this example is, it does underline the point that different decisions regarding how to respond to market requirements by allocating output on a route – that is, how to strike a balance between aircraft size and frequency of service – can carry very different cost implications. It also draws out two other points that we met in chapter 3 when marginal cost pricing was discussed.

1. **Looking to the past: the need to recover the full costs of existing capacity** Because of the high fixed costs involved in operating a sizeable scheduled airline, average cost per unit of output (encompassing average fixed as well as average variable costs) will usually be well above short-run marginal cost – which, as we have seen, can closely approximate the increase in variable cost. Product perishability and a widespread perception of low marginal costs exert severe pressures on airlines' pricing discipline – particularly in periods of recession and overcapacity – by tempting them to apply short-run marginal cost pricing, and ignore the need to at least cover average cost if break-even is to be sustained and bettered.

2. **Looking to the future: the need to pay for future capacity expansion** Variable cost and marginal cost should not be confused. Although average variable cost in particular is frequently treated as analogous to marginal cost, there is no reason why the cost of the next unit of output produced should equate to average variable cost (or, indeed, to average total cost). We should therefore be very careful about using the common expression 'marginal cost pricing'. Output within an existing capacity range priced at or near the variable costs of producing it might very well represent *short-run* marginal cost pricing; but if demand pressures suggest that in due course we will have to invest in additional capacity in order to accommodate future demand and yet we nonetheless still choose to price at or near current variable cost, this price takes no account of the long run need to pay for that new capacity.

   For example, a 1992 study of the US domestic system by consulting firm Avitas calculated marginal costs to be approximately 23–28 per cent of TOCs at load factors between 55 and 70 per cent, rising as high as 40 per cent when load factors reach 90 per cent. Any operating system burdened by high fixed costs can have short-run marginal costs well below average cost over a wide range of output, but once pressure to add capacity results in the system incurring more fixed costs, then marginal cost can become substantial. This is why the marginal cost involved in adding traffic to a system experiencing low load factors is lower than when high load factors imply that many flights are already facing an overdemand situation.

ii. Airline cost classification

Operating, nonoperating, direct, and indirect costs

Figure 5.1 illustrates a common approach to airline cost classification. Nonoperating costs, which are not directly related to the transportation of passengers or cargo, can vary so widely between airlines as a result of different corporate activities and financial structures that inter-airline comparisons are often of limited use. Operating costs arise from the production and sale of air transport output (i.e., ASMs, etc.), and can be 'indirect' or 'direct'. Indirect operating costs (IOCs) are independent of the composition or usage of an airline's fleet. Direct operating costs (DOCs) are largely dependent upon the types of aircraft in the fleet and how they are operated, and so would change if the fleet were changed.

A different type of distinction – one that we have already met – is sometimes drawn between the following types of DOC.

1. **Capacity costs** These include:
    *   aircraft-related fixed costs such as insurance, depreciation, calendar-driven maintenance costs, and lease rentals;
    *   leg- (or flight-) specific costs without payload, such as airport and airway charges, variable (i.e., hourly or per cycle) maintenance, basic fuel, and fixed handling charges.
2. **Traffic costs** These are payload-specific costs such as incremental fuel-burn, catering, variable passenger- and cargo-handling charges, and cargo documentation. Travel agencies' commissions and overrides and GDS fees in respect of passengers carried, should also be included.

Capacity costs (i.e., the costs of providing capacity and producing output) are by far the most significant element in any airline's cost structure. Nonetheless, unit costs are to some extent driven by traffic volumes as well: if an airline's load factor were to rise significantly whilst system cap-

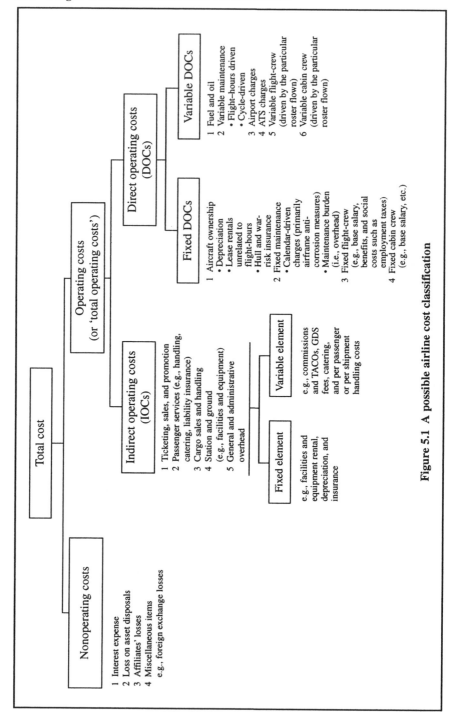

Figure 5.1 A possible airline cost classification

acity and output remained largely unchanged, higher traffic costs would drive up unit cost in the absence of efficiency gains.

For analytical purposes, it is common for cash operating costs to be broken out of DOCs; cash operating costs encompass actual cash outlays arising from the operation of aircraft that would not arise were the aircraft to remain on the ground – such as fuel, airport and ATS charges, and both cycle- and flight-hour-driven maintenance costs. DOCs that do not qualify as cash operating costs include depreciation (a noncash charge), together with cash items such as rentals and hull insurance which are payable annually and do not vary in line with actual operations.

There are four important points to take from this discussion.

1. Different types of airline have different cost structures, and within any airline type each carrier will also vary somewhat in the split between DOCs and IOCs. Very broadly, DOCs might account for as much as 80 per cent of a charter airline's TOCs because of minimal ticketing, sales, distribution, and promotion expenses; for scheduled carriers, the range is more likely to be 45–60 per cent – although much depends on fuel prices at the time, on average stage-lengths, and on labour costs. We will look at the significance of these factors later in the chapter.

2. Whilst figure 5.1 is a representative example, there is no universal agreement on how to allocate costs between direct and indirect categories. Debate does, however, tend to focus on just a few line items. For example, 'cabin crew' and 'airport and en route' are sometimes classified as IOCs, coming under 'passenger services' and 'station and ground' respectively. (In fact, wherever specific airport and en route charges relate to the weight of the aircraft concerned there is a strong case for treating them as DOCs; similarly, cabin crew numbers are arguably better treated as DOCs because they are driven to a significant extent by aircraft type.) Catering is sometimes categorised as a DOC; maintenance burden is frequently classified as an IOC.

3. Many operating costs have both a fixed and a variable element. The shorter the time horizon, the greater the proportion of costs that is fixed. In the very short term, a scheduled carrier that has committed to a timetable is essentially a fixed cost operation. We will return to this point later in the chapter when cost escapability is discussed.

4. Airline costs are driven to a far greater extent by the cost of producing ASMs and ATMs than by the costs of carrying traffic.

For external consumption, airlines generally use a simplified version of the operating/nonoperating cost breakdown in their income statements. Internally, a more analytical approach to cost analysis is required.

Alternative approaches to cost analysis

By function or department

Carriers tend to have different departmental structures, and they can also differ in their choices regarding how to allocate given types of expenditure to different departmental or functional categories. This hinders comparison. It is anyway arguable that aggregating a number of separate activities having different economic characteristics and cost drivers into, say, a flight operations department is not very helpful.

By product

The idea here is that each product should be charged not only with the direct costs that went into producing and delivering it, but also with an allocation of the indirect costs. This approach is referred to as 'absorption costing' because indirect costs are 'absorbed' into product costs.

Airlines produce ASMs (ASKs) and ATMs (ATKs); they measure the part of this output that has been sold as RPMs (RPKs) and RTMs (RTKs). Customers, on the other hand, buy seats or cargo space between many different origins and destinations. Linking costs incurred producing ASMs and ATMs to the cost of carrying a particular passenger or shipment in an O & D city-pair is inevitably going to be difficult. Airlines wanting to cost individual products therefore face two problems: identifying the product and allocating costs.

Identifying the product   There are several different ways to define 'the product' – by geographical region (e.g., regional, domestic, short-haul international, long-haul international), by cabin (e.g., first, business or economy class), and/or by fare type (e.g., full fare, APEX, etc.). Every departure has schedule and routing attributes that make it a product in its own right, in addition to which there may be separate cabins onboard and there will almost certainly be people in each cabin travelling on different fares that carry different restrictions (and so could be characterised as different products); in a hub-based network, there will also be people in each cabin who are travelling in different O & D markets. In the case of cargo, there are other issues – such as whether a shipment is time-definite (and if so whether overnight, two-day, and so on), and whether it requires special handling and/or documentation.

Allocating costs   Having identified separate products, the next challenge is to allocate costs to each. One of the unusual features of the airline industry is that so many different air transportation products are produced by essentially the same operating system within any given carrier. This gives rise to a significant number of joint costs that are not readily separable for allocation to specific types of output.

1. **Separable costs** can be simply allocated to a specific product. For example, catering supplies, flight attendants' salaries, and ticketing costs can readily be allocated to passenger as opposed to cargo products. Ideally they should be allocated to different cabin products (e.g., first, business or economy/coach) and to separate markets – but the fact that this is a network industry in which a given route might serve different O & D markets inevitably complicates matters.
2. **Joint costs** (whether IOCs or DOCs) cannot be so readily allocated. Flight crew costs, for example, can only be allocated arbitrarily between the costs of carrying passengers and those of carrying cargo. Similar problems arise when allocating costs between different passenger products. In chapter 3 we saw how some airlines treat their output of cargo space as a by-product of passenger operations, and so require freight pricing only to cover variable costs, whilst others cost output on a fully allocated basis.

    In summary, costs might be joint across products, such as between passengers and cargo or first and business class; they might be joint across markets, as happens when passengers travelling between different origins and destinations are carried on the same aircraft into or out of a hub; or they might be joint across routes and departures, because the same ground personnel and equipment may service many of both.

It would indeed be helpful for airline managers to be able to walk down an airplane knowing with reasonable certainty what it cost to put each passenger into their seat and serve them whilst they are there. Unfortunately, the more products that an airline produces within a single operating system (first, business, full economy/coach, and several layers of discounted fares within each cabin, for example), the greater the proportion of total costs that could be considered joint (as between passenger and cargo products, for instance), or the higher the ratios of fixed to variable and indirect to direct costs, the more difficult this is to accomplish. As noted in chapter 3, the further any analysis moves away from consideration of total costs, the deeper it is venturing into the realm of opinion.

By route

Route cost calculations require aggregation of the following for each flight-leg operated on the route: variable DOCs (e.g., fuel, airport and airway charges); variable IOCs – notably variable traffic costs such as agency commissions and overrides, GDS fees, catering, and traffic-handling (passenger and cargo); and allocated shares of fixed IOCs and DOCs. The allocation drivers for fixed IOCs are usually route ASMs or ATMs (or perhaps RPMs or RTMs) as a proportion of the systemwide total. Allocation-drivers for fixed DOCs are very often block-times; for example, aircraft ownership costs can be calculated by dividing into each ownership line item (e.g., depreciation, rentals, hull and war-risk insurance, etc.) the annual fleet or subfleet utilisation (in hours) for the type(s) operating the route and arriving at an hourly charge that can then be applied to operations on that route.

Figure 5.2 illustrates how DOCs might be allocated to a particular flight. Box 5.4 summarises the build-up of different flight-leg cost metrics.

Box 5.4: Flight-leg costs

Several different cost figures can be derived in respect of a flight-leg.

- *Trip cost = variable DOCs + variable IOCs (e.g., agency commissions, catering) + an allocation of fixed DOCs + an allocation of fixed IOCs. (Note that depending upon the purpose of analysis, fixed and variable IOCs might be excluded; for example, whilst an allocation for IOCs should be included in an internal analysis of route profitability, they would most likely be excluded if the economics of two alternative aircraft types were being compared as part of a fleet planning exercise.)*
- *Hourly cost = trip cost/block-time in hours.*
  ('Block-time' is the elapsed time from gate to gate or from chock to chock.)
- *Aircraft-mile cost = hourly cost/block-speed in mph.*
  ('Block-speed' is distance flown/block time.)
- *Seat-mile (or 'unit') cost = aircraft-mile cost/available seats or, alternatively, trip cost/ASMs produced.*
  (As we will see in chapter 10, this should be compared with 'unit revenue' – that is, revenue per ASM.)
- *Revenue-mile cost = aircraft-mile cost/seats sold or, alternatively, trip cost/RPMs.*
  (This should be compared with 'yield' – that is, revenue per RPM.)

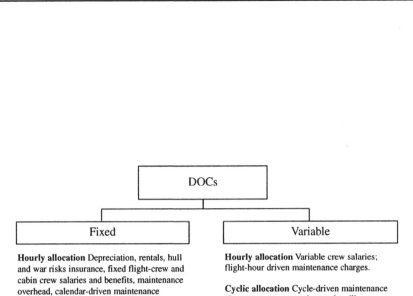

Fixed

Hourly allocation Depreciation, rentals, hull and war risks insurance, fixed flight-crew and cabin crew salaries and benefits, maintenance overhead, calendar-driven maintenance charges.

*****

Alternatively, fixed DOCs can be allocated on the basis of ASMs or ATMs produced by a flight; this calculation requires aggregating fixed DOCs, dividing the sum by system ASMs or ATMs to arrive at a cost per ASM or ATM, and multiplying this by the output of the flight concerned.
(Fixed IOCs can also be allocated in this way.)

Variable

Hourly allocation Variable crew salaries; flight-hour driven maintenance charges.

Cyclic allocation Cycle-driven maintenance charges; passenger and cargo handling.

Load-driven Catering; passenger liability insurance.

Actual expenditure Fuel; ATS charges; airport charges; crew expenses.

Figure 5.2 An approach to the allocation of direct operating costs to a flight

Generally, aircraft-mile and trip costs increase as aircraft size increases – although a modern aircraft might have better economics than a smaller but older type as a result of technological improvements. Conversely, unit cost tends to fall as aircraft size increases because the fixed portion of aircraft-mile and trip costs does not generally grow proportionately with output; again, technological improvements can break this generalisation such that a relatively new type (e.g., the B777) might on certain stage-lengths have better unit costs than an older, larger type (e.g., the B747-400).

The cost of operating in an O & D market served other than by a nonstop route can in principle be calculated by aggregating the costs of operating the connecting routes that serve it. In a hub-and-spoke network, of course, any route into or out of a hub might serve multiple behind/beyond markets; the cost of serving a connecting market must therefore be calculated by allocating a proportional share of route costs. In other words, some of the costs of serving the Phoenix–LGA market over Dallas are borne by markets that are also served by the Phoenix–Dallas and Dallas–LGA routes (e.g., Phoenix–Miami and Albuquerque–LGA markets). The same would apply in a multi-hub system, where the O & D market is connected over two alternative hubs (e.g., Dallas or Chicago on the American Airlines system). Where an O & D market is served over a hub, it is not unusual for the carrier to add a per passenger 'connection cost' for the purpose of internal analysis so that the market bears at least some of the expense of maintaining the hub.

By fleet and sub-fleet

Many airlines also analyse costs by fleet and sub-fleet. This approach can be particularly useful when comparisons between types are being drawn for fleet planning purposes; it is also important to internal benchmarking efforts and can contribute to the fleet assignment process where different types are assigned to routes such that the gap between revenue and operating costs is to be maximised relative to any alternative assignment (given a particular schedule).

By activity

There are profound cost implications inherent in how, as well as which, activities are undertaken to deliver a service. We touched upon the strategic importance of this in chapter 1, and will return to it later in the present chapter when activity systems are discussed. Isolation of individual activities within (perhaps) cross-functional processes allows costs to be classified and managed by reference to the activities that consume them. Activity-based costing (ABC) requires investigation of:

- the resources consumed – man-hours, flight-hours, computer time or materials, for example;
- the activities in which these resources are used – that is, the work they do, such as reservations, ticketing, check-in, transportation, delivering inflight service and so on; and
- the cost drivers underlying each activity.

ABC systems collect costs by activity and then allocate shares of each activity's aggregate cost to products, markets, departures, stations, fleets, individual aircraft, cycles, entire schedules, and other 'cost objects' on the basis of the amount of each activity the cost object consumes. The purpose is not simply to control raw expenditures, but to assist airline managers in making cost-effective decisions by identifying costs with activities and isolating non-value-adding activities. Whereas the traditional approach of allocating costs to departures, products, routes, and fleets can answer the question 'What is happening?', ABC systems dig deeper to answer the question 'Why is this happening?'

British Airways began looking at ABC approaches in the late 1980s, but relatively few carriers have followed. Most do not have management accounting systems aligned with activities. To realign them from their existing, predominantly departmental, focus towards processes that flow through the organization and across functional boundaries is expensive and can be politically sensitive.

By contribution

Any excess of revenue over variable costs is a 'contribution' made by the product, route, department or other profit centre concerned towards coverage of the airline's fixed costs. Figure 5.3 illustrates one possible approach to graphing the contribution margin of a route or an individual departure – that is, the percentage by which it is covering or failing to cover variable costs. By graphing contribution margin against seat factor, yield can be brought into the analysis insofar as it is fairly clear that a high seat factor/negative contribution margin service is suffering from unsustainably low yields; on the other hand, a low seat factor/negative contribution margin service may have a volume problem as well as (or instead of) a yield problem. Either might benefit from a reduction in output – perhaps a smaller aircraft or fewer frequencies.

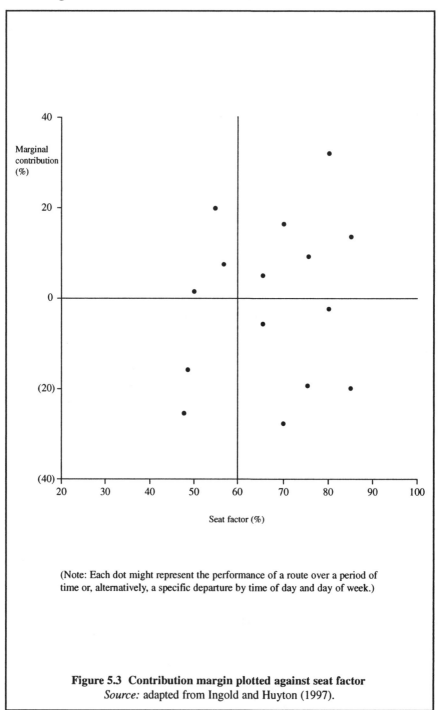

Figure 5.3 Contribution margin plotted against seat factor
Source: adapted from Ingold and Huyton (1997).

Accountants sometimes argue that even a flight that is more than covering its variable operating costs and so making a contribution to fixed costs is ripe for axing if it is not profitable on a fully allocated basis. This begs several questions.

- What else might be done with the aircraft? If given the existing schedule it would be idle when it could otherwise be operating the service under consideration there might well be a case for keeping it in the air, because as long as variable costs are more than covered (in both directions), a positive contribution is made to ownership and other fixed costs that would still be accruing were it on the ground. Not to do so would leave the fixed cost burden on existing services unnecessarily high on a unit output basis. Using this argument, for example, America West in the mid-1990s launched an extremely low-yield night operation out of Las Vegas. If, on the other hand, there are more profitable uses for the aircraft than having it operate the service in question, these opportunity costs need to be considered.
- What impact will dropping the service have on the airline's presence in the affected market(s)? Bearing in mind the 'S-curve' effect mentioned in the last chapter, for example, will reduction in output have a disproportionate effect on sales volume and revenue? Will there be any spillage of high lifetime-value customers who prefer a particular service and use it regularly?
- What will be the impact on network revenue and profit attributable to losing any feed the flight generates?
- Is one of the reasons for its poor contribution margin the fact that the service carries an unusually high share of non-revenue FFP redemptions, and if so what impact might its elimination have on the attractiveness of the FFP? Would allocating a proxy revenue figure to the service be preferable from a system perspective (Baldanza, 1999)?

In the short term, when we can think of aircraft ownership costs as fixed, the answer will probably be that any contribution made by a service to those costs should be accepted unless there are clear opportunity costs involved in not redeploying it. Furthermore, the contribution method of cost analysis can allow new routes some 'breathing space' in which to establish themselves; new routes (if well chosen) generally make a positive contribution quite quickly, but take longer to build sufficient revenue to withstand a full allocation of fixed costs.

At some point, however, an expectation needs to be imposed on all flights that they must cover their fully allocated costs – unless there is some very sound competitive or network justification for cross-subsidising them from flights that are in fact profitable on a fully allocated basis. One just-ification, for example, might be that the internal revenue prorate used does not do justice to the value of, say, a short-haul route which makes a signif-icant contribution to the network as a whole.

Their high operating leverage makes airlines very volume-dependent – under constant pressure to generate revenue in order at least to make a cont-ribution to high fixed costs. Airlines with expensive infrastructures in place to serve the requirements of high-yield passengers can suffer particularly badly whenever traffic growth drops off and/or yields weaken, leaving soft revenues pressing down on a high fixed cost base. The danger in maintain-ing unprofitable services in the long term simply because they are making a positive contribution is that if several competitors adopt a similar approach it will result in sustained overcapacity, excess output, and – in all likelihood – weaker yields than would otherwise be the case. (This is something that has happened during most economic downturns with the notable exception of late 2001, when many carriers moved with historically unprecedented speed to reduce output.)

iii. Cost drivers

Fleet, network, and schedule choices are any airline's fundamental cost drivers. However, this section of the chapter will drill-down deeper to consider cost drivers under the following headings: design and functioning of the operating system; cost of inputs; scale; and learning. Their manage-ment will be addressed in the next section.

Design and functioning of the operating system

We will use the value chain metaphor by considering first the supply chain, then internal operations, and finally distribution. The fundamental point with regard to any operating system is that its design should be driven by two factors.

- **Strategic position** Whatever strategic description of itself an airline has chosen – as an independent regional, a franchised regional, a low-fare carrier, a point-to-point full-service operator, a full-service net-work carrier, a charter airline, an all-cargo airline serving line-haul markets, or an all-cargo carrier offering value-added services, for ex-ample – this position should drive design of the operating system.

- **Market position** Whether an airline has a single service concept (e.g., Southwest) or a multi-service portfolio (e.g., American), the operating system must be configured to deliver each type of service to targeted customers in a manner consistent with the desired positioning of that service relative to competitors in customers' perceptions. This must be done as efficiently as possible given what it takes to be effective in targeted markets (i.e., to at least match customers' expectations).

Holloway (2002) takes a closer look at both topics.

The supply chain

We touched on the vertical scope decision in chapter 1. Start-ups generally rely on external suppliers for a high proportion of input services. Established carriers have also in many cases been outsourcing a growing range of activities. The purpose of supply chain management at any type of airline is to orchestrate suppliers, and perhaps also their suppliers, to deliver cost-effectively whatever the airline requires in order to meet customers' expectations. As discussed in chapter 1, the nature of relationships between airlines and suppliers has changed in recent years; broadly, purchasing has been evolving from a reactive, transactional, administrative procurement function to an activity involving the proactive *management* of a network of suppliers within an integrated supply chain. We will look at these trends later in the chapter when considering cost management.

Internal operations

This subsection briefly considers four aspects of internal operations that have a profound impact on costs: service design; process design; productivity; and fleet structure.

Service design This is a broad field that is fully covered in Holloway (2002). Clearly, the services offered by a carrier reflect its choice of strategic and market position and are a critical driver of unit costs. In other words, an airline's unit costs are strongly influenced by the characteristics of the demand it chooses to serve. The following are important variables.

1. **Network and schedule** Because capacity costs have such a significant impact on TOCs, network design and the schedule flown are absolutely top-tier cost drivers. In deregulated or liberalised environments both need to respond to the requirements of the markets and market segments being targeted.

- *Hub-and-spoke networks* Whilst these are efficient systems for gathering traffic from multiple origins and distributing them to multiple destinations, they can bring heavy fixed costs associated with the facilities, equipment, and staff required to handle the artificial peaks created by each incoming and outgoing bank. The larger the number of daily banks a hub can serve, the more output is produced over which to spread these fixed costs and the lower will be the cost per ASM or ATM imposed by hub infrastructure.

- *Stage-lengths* The further a given type is flown, the higher will be its trip costs because fuel, airway, and possibly crew costs will increase. On the other hand, unit costs (i.e., costs per ASM or ATM) will be lower because more output is being generated over which to spread fixed costs (such as depreciation, insurance, and lease rentals), and because the high variable costs associated with take-off fuel, airport landing charges, and cycle-driven maintenance are also being spread over that larger output of ASMs and ATMs. According to Roberts Roach and Associates, a 500-mile flight-leg was costing Southwest 7.5 cents per ASM in the third quarter of 1998 against fractionally over 6 cents for a 1500-mile sector; corresponding figures for a batch of full-service majors were around 12 cents and 9 cents (Solon, 1999). Looked at another way, we can say that other things being equal it costs less to produce a fixed output of ASMs or ATMs as average stage-length increases.

  There are, however, two caveats. First, most aircraft have an optimal range at which unit costs will be minimised. Second, at some point along its payload-range envelope every aircraft has to begin shedding payload in order to boost range – with potentially negative revenue implications. Nonetheless, it is broadly fair to generalise that longer average stage-lengths are usually associated with higher aircraft and crew utilisation, lower fuel-burn per block-hour, and lower (cycle-driven) maintenance costs (Williams, 2002).

- *Traffic density* This is the volume of traffic carried on a route over a given time period. Deciding how to serve a route requires an airline to make choices with respect to aircraft capacity and frequency – notably whether to offer a small number of flights with a larger aircraft or more frequencies with a smaller aircraft: the larger aircraft will probably have higher trip costs but lower unit costs (because fixed costs are being spread over the larger volume of ASMs its size allows it to produce on any given flight-leg); the smaller aircraft will probably have lower trip costs but higher unit costs. In principle, the market should make this decision; in practice, the presence or absence of competition and the composition of a particular airline's fleet may also be influential – as may the terms of relevant bilateral ASAs if the route concerned is international. Box 5.5 takes a look at economies of density.

Box 5.5: Economies of density

Economies of density are present when unit cost declines as the volume of traffic carried within an unchanged network rises (Graham and Kaplan, 1982; Caves et al, 1984; Bailey et al, 1985). The primary source of economies of density is aircraft size. Large aircraft generally have lower seat-mile costs and higher trip (i.e., aircraft-mile) costs than smaller types of a similar technological generation; major improvements in airframe design and powerplant efficiency from one generation to the next can, however, break this relationship. There are several reasons why increases in trip costs and aircraft size tend not to bear a linear relationship, so accounting for the lower seat-mile costs often associated with larger aircraft: large aircraft do not necessarily burn more fuel per seat-mile than smaller aircraft; they do not require additional pilots; neither, given a specific number of engines and systems, do they demand proportionately more maintenance; up to a point, they can also be both structurally and aerodynamically more efficient; and capital cost per seat tends to decline as aircraft get larger.

Density can increase on a route for one or more of several reasons.

1. *It might grow naturally over time in response to economic and/or demographic developments in the markets served by the route.*
2. *It can be generated by airlines exploiting price-elasticity by offering low fares and attracting both new customers and more sales to existing customers.*
3. *It can be affected by airlines' network design decisions. In particular, by channelling traffic from a spoke city onto a single route into a hub irrespective of ultimate onward destination an airline ensures that the route is much more dense than any nonstop routes from the spoke city to each of those destinations would have been. This allows the carrier to operate larger aircraft with lower unit costs than the spoke city could otherwise have supported (and/or offer more frequencies down the spoke). In multi-hub systems serving double-connect markets, higher traffic densities on inter-hub routes can also support larger aircraft than would otherwise be the case. Where hub-and-spoke network designs are used to re-route traffic flows, economies of density can be traced to unit cost reductions that arise from carrying unchanged*

traffic volumes over a more geographically constrained network which nonetheless serves the same number of points as before.

As density increases on a route, airlines have broadly four choices.

- **Accept higher load factors** Fine in the short run because it leads to a lower cost per passenger (as unchanged aircraft-mile and trip costs are spread over more passengers), ultimately this will lead to unacceptable levels of demand spill. (Although capacity costs are unchanged, traffic costs will rise so there might be upward pressure on unit costs – hopefully more than offset by higher revenue.)
- **Add more seats to existing aircraft** This lowers cost per passenger and also unit cost without substantially affecting trip costs because each flight is generating more RPMs and ASMs from the same trip, but it degrades the inflight product.
- **Use a larger aircraft on some or all departures** This should lower unit costs but will probably increase trip costs, and must always be subject to the caveat that average loads achieved on existing aircraft must be above the break-even load for the larger aircraft given yields on the route concerned.
- **Add frequencies** This generates incremental trip costs but improves the quality of service from the perspective of certain segments of the market, notably business travellers, and so might lead to firmer yields. Around 25 per cent of Ryanair's passengers on routes with one or two frequencies per day tend to be business travellers, for example, but when frequencies increase to three or more the figure can often rise above 50 per cent (Solon, 2001). Ultimately, the 'S-curve' effect we met in chapter 4 could result in higher market share such that both the existing and additional frequencies can be operated by larger aircraft; in this case not only will marketing benefits accrue, but the unit cost declines associated with economies of density will also have been exploited. A lot will depend on the characteristics of demand on any particular route and the activities of competitors.

Economies of density can be an important competitive weapon where it is less expensive for an incumbent to add traffic to an existing route than it is for a new entrant to carry traffic on the same route – say, because the challenger must operate a smaller aircraft (with higher unit costs) given its less established market profile.

*Economies of density should not be confused with **economies of network size**. Whereas economies of density exist when unit cost declines can be attributed to increased volumes of traffic being carried within an unchanged* *network (i.e., with points served held constant), economies of network size exist where unit costs decline as the number of points served increases (i.e., as the network expands geographically). Several academic studies have cast doubt on the existence of economies of network size (Brueckner and Spiller, 1994). Whilst returns to network size are often fairly constant, however, returns to increasing density can be considerable (Button and Stough, 2000).*

- *Frequency* For reasons we will discuss shortly, high frequencies are in general more expensive to produce than low frequencies, all other things being equal. If we assume a route can support four daily rotations with a 90-seater or two with a 180-seater, the former will be more expensive to schedule. Four rotations may appeal to the business segment, of course, so the firmer yields they provide could more than compensate for the higher unit costs of this option – something seen on many routes in North America and Europe, where average aircraft size has trended downwards in the years immediately following deregulation or liberalisation.

- *Aircraft size* We can make two observations in respect of the deployment of large aircraft. First, they can only be used efficiently when the combination of traffic density and product-driven frequency decisions supports their assignment. Second, it is sometimes the case that the larger an aircraft the fewer the routes in a given network on which it can be deployed, and this might harm utilisation; should this happen, hourly charges for fixed ownership costs (such as depreciation, insurance, and so on) will be higher than might otherwise have been the case, with the result that any unit cost advantage these aircraft may have over smaller but better utilised alternatives on the routes they do fly will be eroded.

2. **Scope** Looking at internal operations, we are in the process of considering the cost implications of service design; in addition to network and schedule, another consideration under this heading is competitive scope – a topic first introduced in chapter 1. Economies of (horizontal) scope arise when it is cheaper for a single firm to produce two or more products together than it is for each product to be produced by separate firms. Economies of scope can arise from the sharing of production costs (as when passengers and cargo are carried on the same aircraft) or the sharing of marketing costs (as when general corporate advertising stimulates demand in multiple markets); they can be captured within an organization (as when a carrier extends its network using its own fleet and other resources) or through a market transaction (such as franchising or code-sharing).

290 Straight and Level: Practical Airline Economics

Economists in fact argue about the existence of economies of scope. Some consider them to be nothing more than a facet of intra-organizational linkages (e.g., Porter, 1985: 328). Others believe them to be the very reason why multi-product firms exist – arguing that if single-product firms were more efficient producers, there would not be any multi-product firms (Panzar and Willig, 1981); indeed, they lie at the heart of Prahalad and Hamel's (1990) popular concept of 'core competencies'. Spitz (1998: 492) notes that many research studies point to economies of scope, along with economies of density, as the principal forces driving adoption of hub-and-spoke networks.

The interest here is in economies derived from an airline's choice of competitive scope. Economies of competitive scope are attributable to a shared input which makes joint production of different types of output by a single carrier cheaper than the production of each by separate carriers. Inputs in this context might take the form of specialised and/or indivisible physical assets, service production know-how, opaque and causally ambiguous routines that are ill-understood by competitors (Nelson and Winter, 1982; Holloway, 2002), and marketing assets – most notably a brand name (Douma and Schreuder, 1998). Competitive scope can be divided into two elements, as we saw in chapter 1.

- *Geographic scope* Economies of scope may be evident when unit costs decline as the number of markets (but not necessarily the number of points) being served by an airline increases. For example, by adding a new point-to-point service between two stations already served on other routes, or by fine-tuning a schedule to facilitate an increase in saleable connections over a hub, it might be possible for a carrier to add new markets and new traffic without necessarily increasing fixed station and ground costs. Even if a route is added by introducing a new station to the network, it will usually be cheaper in unit cost terms for a carrier already serving one end of the route – particularly a hub – to introduce service than for a green-field start-up. From another perspective we might argue that the fixed costs of operating a hub are spread across all the markets served over that hub – so the more markets it supports within its existing capacity range, the lower will be the unit costs of output channelled through it.

  To take a broader example, an airline flying only a single route between Tucson and Cincinnati would be constrained by the limited amount of local traffic: it would at best be able to offer only a low-frequency service using relatively small aircraft. Its unit costs would also be adversely affected by the fact that fixed station expenses at Tucson and Cincinnati would be spread only over the relatively small volume of output required to support local traffic. If, however, the route were operated by an airline that hubs at Cincinnati, the Tucson spoke would attract not only local traffic but passengers travelling beyond Cincinnati to other domestic and international points on that carrier's network. This additional traffic would support some combination of larger aircraft and higher frequencies than local traffic alone could justify. The hubbing airline therefore has access to unit cost advantages attributable both to economies of density (gained by operating larger aircraft) and economies of scope (gained by jointly producing on each Tucson-Cincinnati flight output that can be sold as seats in many different markets connecting Tucson with points beyond Cincinnati). Fixed station costs at Tucson and Cincinnati would also be spread across a higher volume of output over a wider range of markets than the single-route operator has available to it.

- *Product scope* Economies of scope can arise when it is cheaper to produce different types of output on a single aircraft than to produce each type in different aircraft. Most obviously, output produced in first, business, and economy/coach class cabins on the same departure can share fixed costs – and, incidentally, benefit from the economies of density derived from operating a larger aircraft than would be required to serve just one type of traffic on a given route. The same argument might also be applied to different 'fare products' in the same cabin – that is, passengers in the same cabin travelling on different fares and subject to different booking and travel restrictions. Whilst it may be cheaper in unit cost terms to offer separate products within the same operating system than to offer each separately, this is not inevitably the case; some, although not all, low-fare and charter airlines sell a single cabin and a limited range of fare-products. Much depends on the choice of strategic position and the particular type of value an airline wants to offer to its customers.

Economies of scope can also be identified in respect of marketing (especially marketing communications, promotions, and distribution) and in various operational support functions such as scheduling (Fitzroy et al, 1998). In areas such as these, however, there remains an unresolved debate about whether we are dealing with economies of scope (evident when unit costs fall as a result of different types of output being jointly produced) or economies of scale (evident when unit costs fall as a result of aggregate output increasing) – a debate that perhaps excites economists more than practitioners.

As with economies of density, a critical point to keep in mind is that economies of scope favour incumbents over new entrants and other small challengers: in essence, this is because the larger an airline's product range and network the greater are its opportunities to benefit from the fact that aggregating separable costs attributable to multiple products with the joint costs attributable to producing them together can sometimes lead to a lower unit cost figure than would be the case were each output produced separately. The advantage might be reinforced by the strength a large network and product range add to loyalty programmes (e.g., FFPs, corporate rebates, and TACOs).

3. **Other aspects of service design** Network and schedule (together with associated choice of aircraft) are, as already noted, the critical cost drivers flowing from service design. There are others, however. Simply put, premium products cost more to produce than basic economy/coach products; clearly, it must be the intention that the revenue per ASM (i.e., unit revenue) earned from these products more than compensates for their higher unit costs. The following are key variables.

- *Seating density* The more seats there are on a given aircraft flying a given leg, the more ASMs will be produced over which to spread fixed costs – and so the lower unit costs will be. The most obvious example of high seating density/low seat-pitch being used to drive down unit costs is seen amongst charter carriers and low-fare airlines. For example, the fact that a B757-200 operated in high-density charter configuration might have 230 seats against 180 in two-class scheduled service immediately reduces the seat-mile costs of the charter carrier by almost one-third compared to a full-service scheduled operator (assuming constant trip costs); this is an extreme comparison between alternatives likely in practice to be pitched at different market segments, but it exemplifies the point. Box 5.6 takes a closer look at seating density.

Box 5.6: Seating density

Seating density is a critical economic variable.

- *Increasing it: reduces passenger comfort and may adversely affect yields if high-yield passengers are lost; takes pressure off load factors (perhaps temporarily); reduces demand spill (perhaps temporarily); raises aircraft seat-mile productivity; and reduces unit cost.*
- *Reducing it: improves passenger comfort, and so may boost yields; puts upward pressure on load factors if demand is already strong (and so is best done either in conjunction with demand weakness or a fare*

increase); could increase spill; reduces aircraft seat-mile productivity; and raises unit costs.

In both cases, the net revenue impact will depend upon how changes in unit revenue and unit cost balance out under the particular circumstances. We can nonetheless generalise that: a carrier positioning itself as a low-fare airline needs high seating density; and if seats are removed by any carrier, higher yields will be needed from the remaining seats to cover forgone revenue (unless load factors are currently so weak that the lost output has little impact on demand spill). For example, removing a single row of 10-across seats from a B747 to give remaining coach/economy passengers no more than an inch of extra pitch may jeopardise several million dollars in revenue: the exact figure will vary, but if we reckon that an average economy/coach load factor of 80 per cent would put eight of these seats into the air with passengers in them for, say, 5,000 hours a year (i.e., around 250 return trips between the US West Coast and Europe) it can be seen how the figures mount up.

Scheduled airlines in particular face difficult compromises between production cost and product specification when deciding on cabin configuration. This is an area that lies at the interface between cost and revenue streams; it has to be driven by the airline's service concept, set within the context of prevailing economic and competitive conditions.

Seating density is in fact part of a multi-faceted service design decision encompassing: how many onboard classes of service to offer; what the appropriate seat pitch and aisle width is for each class, given market conditions; galley requirements (number and size/functionality) – driven by the catering to be provided, the extent to which catering supplies have to be carried outbound for return flights, and the style of service (which could, for example, affect the number of trolleys required); lavatory numbers – driven by the desired passenger/lavatory ratio; and storage requirements – driven by the need to provide closets in premium cabins. Within upper limits established by type certification and lower limits imposed by aircraft economics in the context of yields in the market(s) to be served, it is for airline product planners to decide how to allocate available cabin floorspace; their decisions will certainly have unit cost implications and will probably also affect yields.

- *Service level* The key cost driver in this category is cabin crew ratios. Again, product planners have to establish a level between the legal minimum number of crew required per aircraft type and the economically viable maximum. Most low-fare carriers stick to the legal minimum number. Some full-service carriers use variable staffing formulas to determine the number of flight attendants required for each flight, with an extra crew member being scheduled once passenger numbers rise above a particular threshold. Fine in principle, this can cause service quality problems – particularly when we are talking about mainline narrowbodies which anyway have relatively small crews. First, passengers travelling on a flight carrying a load just below the threshold may experience markedly poorer inflight service than others travelling on the same type carrying a load just above the threshold. Second, a flight booked at just below the threshold close to departure which has more go-shows than no-shows may well depart with one fewer flight attendants than passenger numbers actually require (given the airline's service specification). Finally, a variable staffing formula will always be difficult to implement when crews are working complex integrations for a large network carrier.

- *Other service attributes* Number of check-in desks and their staffing levels, numbers of gate staff, lounge access, catering, IFE, and the entire range of other attributes that might be made available as part of a particular service package all influence output costs. What is appropriate depends upon a finely balanced assessment of market requirements, costs, and the revenues that can be earned. Immediately before the post-9/11 cutbacks, American's market positioning and broad product scope led it to spend an average $8.57 per passenger on catering as against most other full-service US majors in the $4–5 range; Southwest, consistent with its strategic positioning as a low-fare carrier, was spending just 25 cents per passenger.

  IFE is a particularly interesting source of costs insofar as not only does the hardware and software have to be maintained and the content purchased, but with weights of several thousand pounds the interactive systems now available for long-haul widebodies carry a considerable life-cycle fuel-burn penalty. Flat-bed seats in long-haul premium cabins are also heavier than their more simple predecessors, largely because of the weight of electric motors. Service decisions affecting the economics of an operation in fact go down to details such as how often aircraft are deep-cleaned and how frequently seat cushions are changed.

- *Load factor/seat accessibility* Seat accessibility is a measure of the probability that a booking can be made in the desired class on the desired flight at any given point in time before departure. The higher the average load factor on a flight, the lower its seat accessibility is likely to be – certainly close to departure; we will meet this important service attribute again in chapter 9 when discussing revenue management. Although a significant aspect of service design, seat accessibility is fundamentally a revenue-side issue insofar as it is primarily late-booking, high-yield business travellers who benefit from high levels of seat accessibility. There is, however, a cost impact: low load factors generate lower traffic costs than higher loads on the same aircraft type (something that will probably be of little consolation unless the traffic that *is* being carried is generating high yields to compensate).

The purpose of service design and development is to create an offer able to satisfy the expectations of targeted customers. The more demanding these customers, the more expensive delivering service up to their expectations becomes. When recession causes corporate clients to trade-down to economy/coach and reduce overall travel activity, carriers whose strategic position leads them to concentrate heavily on this segment may face the challenge of having high product costs to spread over a weak traffic base – with the result that cost per passenger might rise at the very time when yields are already softening.

Process design Having looked at service design, we will continue this review of the impact internal operations can have on airline costs by considering process design.

National safety regulations have had a significant impact on the organization structures of airlines, particularly in respect of flight operations and maintenance activities; US Federal Aviation Regulations, for example, mandate the existence of certain functions and job titles. It is nonetheless generally fair to say that airlines as a whole have been slow to move towards more process-oriented structures, choosing in many cases to retain a traditional pattern of functional 'silos' (Garvin, 2000).

We saw in the last chapter that one way of approaching an airline's operating system is to characterise it as being comprised of service delivery processes (front- and back-office) and enabling processes. The manner in which processes are designed will clearly have an impact on costs. To get to the heart of process costs, we need to look at their constituent activities.

1. **Activities: a tactical perspective** Two important variables in process design are 'complexity' and 'divergence'.
    *   *Complexity* is a function of the number of activities involved in a given process. The fewer sequences and activities there are, the lower the complexity of a process.

- *Divergence* reflects the degree of latitude allowed for the varying of an activity or the reordering of a sequence. The less latitude permitted, the lower the 'divergence' in a process and the greater the level of standardisation (of activities, policies, and procedures, for example).

Activities generate costs and should also generate (or support the generation of) customer value. Airlines need as far as possible to ensure that the complexity and divergence designed into their processes reflect the chosen strategic position and operating strategy. Both should be as low as possible for a low-fare carrier; a full-service airline might want to introduce a higher level of divergence into its front-office (i.e., customer-contact) processes, although both economic feasibility and possible threats to service consistency may act as constraints. Broadly, it is fair to generalise that complexity tends to be expensive wherever it appears; this is not necessarily a problem provided it contributes to desired customer value and is reflected in the revenue stream.

Each activity in an airline's value chain has its own particular cost drivers – input prices, productivity, scale, and/or scope (i.e., the ability to share costs with other activities), for example. These need to be identified and managed. Always bearing in mind that costs should be considered not just in an absolute sense but in the context of their contribution to customer value and to revenues, there are four broad approaches that can be taken to paring activity costs (Turney, 1991): activity reduction; activity elimination (either absolutely or through outsourcing); activity redesign; and activity sharing (with alliance partners, for example).

2. **Activities: a strategic perspective** Looking on airlines as collections of activities, each influenced by its own cost drivers, implies two general routes to the management of costs for strategic advantage: controlling cost drivers better than competitors; consciously managing the configuration of activities within the vertical chain – taking nothing for granted and being prepared to respond to evolving technologies, customer expectations, and outsourcing opportunities. The key issue is how to manage activities in a strategically coherent manner.

   Porter (1985, 1991, 1996) argues that what distinguishes one company's strategy from another's is its distinctive activity system – what is done, how it is done, and what is not done. Figure 5.4 outlines Southwest's activity system. It illustrates how Porter (1996) uses activity system maps to 'show how a company's strategic position is contained in a set of tailored activities designed to deliver it. In companies with a clear strategic position, a number of higher order strategic themes [the shaded circles] can be identified and implemented through clusters of

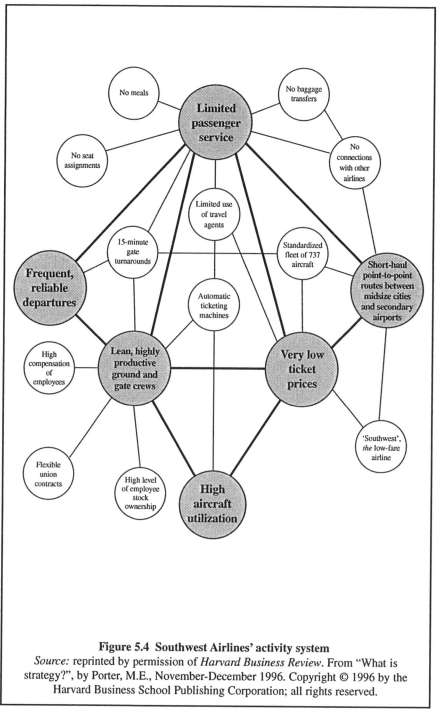

Figure 5.4 Southwest Airlines' activity system

Source: reprinted by permission of *Harvard Business Review*. From "What is strategy?", by Porter, M.E., November-December 1996. Copyright © 1996 by the Harvard Business School Publishing Corporation; all rights reserved.

tightly linked activities' [in the unshaded circles]. This approach resonates with several ideas met earlier in the book: strategy-as-a-theme; consistent management of strategic position through the cost and revenue streams; and the importance of identifying, obtaining or building, and leveraging strategically relevant resources (including skills, organizational routines, and corporate culture).

The following all interact to contribute to Southwest's faster gate turnarounds and high aircraft utilisation, for example:

- its service concept does not include: meals (so there is very little catering provision to be built into ground time); interline or online transfers (so there is no need to hold aircraft for late inbound connections, less chance of bags taking different journeys from their owners, and no prorate dilution); or seat assignment (so boarding processes are quicker);

- its network is oriented towards short-/medium-haul point-to-point routes of a broadly similar length into and out of relatively uncongested airports (notwithstanding the introduction of longer flights beginning in the mid-1990s and also the de facto connections available at some stations as a result of the high frequencies offered to/from different points); and

- it operates a single-type fleet of B737s, which provides great flexibility to the aircraft and crew assignment tasks and also reduces crew training and line maintenance expenditures.

In turn, high aircraft utilisation helps underpin the low fares that distinguish Southwest's service-price offer – an offer that includes reliable, high-frequency service but provides no benefits in respect of meal service, interline baggage transfer, seat assignments, and so on.

Productivity Productivity, the third cost driver we are considering under the heading of internal operations, is the ratio of outputs to inputs (either all inputs aggregated, or just a single category – such as labour). Efficiency is the maximisation of outputs for a given level of inputs. The economic appeal of an operating system that is delivering output both effectively (i.e., in conformity with customers' expectations) and efficiently (given the nature of the output concerned – whether long-haul first class or short-haul low-fare ASMs, for example) is that fixed costs are being spread over as much output as the system can produce given available inputs and also quality requirements.

It is important to remember that whilst high resource productivity is critical to every airline, there are two important caveats.

1. Productivity figures can be deceptive. They are often arrived at by dividing into revenue or output a numerical measure of workforce or asset base (although there are many other ways to calculate productivity). Clearly, productivity can rise if the numerator increases more rapidly than the denominator. Less encouragingly, it can also rise if the numerator edges up only sluggishly or even remains static, whilst at the same time the denominator shrinks; shrinkage could reflect greater efficiency, but it might also result from inadequate investment. A key question is therefore whether productivity improvements built on a shrinking resource base represent a trimming of 'fat' or a seepage of fundamental resources and skills needed to sustain long-term profitability. Bear in mind that:

   - productivity growth and market share decline can go hand-in-hand;
   - similarly, productivity growth and profits can also move in different directions. An airline could increase productivity by raising seat density whilst leaving staff numbers and fleet size unchanged, but if this product deterioration causes high-yield customers to defect and so erodes revenue, it is possible that profits will suffer.

   The moral is that increasing output through higher resource productivity is only half the battle; the other half is selling that incremental output – and selling it at an adequate yield.

2. Passengers are buying a range of experiences when they purchase an air trip. The value they perceive themselves to be getting from their purchase, and its relationship to expectations, should provide a context for productivity improvements; highly productive staff do not inevitably equate to highly satisfied, loyal or profitable customers. For example, cutting cabin crew ratios in business class will raise the productivity of those who remain, but what impact will it have on the perceived experiences of passengers, on their loyalty, and on the carrier's share of the lifetime revenue potentially available from frequent, high-yield travellers?

Whilst productivity matters, therefore, what really matters is how much of the output generated has been sold and at what price. This points to the importance of metrics such as revenue per employee, revenue per dollar of employment cost, revenue per flight-hour (by type), and operating revenue per dollar of operating cost – the last being particularly valuable because it takes into account the effects of outsourcing and code-sharing on employee numbers and flight-hours respectively.

Productivity comparisons between any two airlines or groups of airlines are clearly fraught with danger. The root of the problem is that airline output is not homogeneous (Oum and Yu, 1998). First, different service con-

cepts carry with them very different staffing and resource commitments –
as is most notably underlined by the productivity differences that can be
anticipated between staff serving long-haul premium passengers, and those
working in a low-fare short-haul environment. Second, decisions whether
to outsource or retain inhouse key ancillary functions such as maintenance
and engineering – and, if retained inhouse, whether to bid for significant
volumes of third party work – can have a profound impact on staffing and
resource levels. Third, different network structures, particularly in respect
of average length of haul, also affect certain types of productivity comparison, as do aircraft size, national salary levels, and currency rates of exchange.

Before leaving the topics of productivity and efficiency, we will briefly
look at the critical contribution made to each by high levels of resource
utilisation, and also at its strategic significance.

1. **Utilisation** Utilisation is a measure of the extent to which a resource is
   actively producing output; it can be expressed either in absolute terms
   (e.g., aircraft utilisation in average hours per day or per year), or as a
   percentage of what is possible (e.g., cabin floorspace utilisation as a
   percentage seat factor). All resources – staff, ground equipment, airport
   terminals and gates, simulators, information systems, and distribution
   channels, for example – should be utilised as fully as possible. Of course, the most significant resource we need to be concerned with is likely
   to be aircraft; an airline's production capacity expressed in terms of aircraft seats or cargo space is fixed, but output in terms of ASMs and
   ATMs can nonetheless often be increased by utilising the fleet more
   efficiently. (Aircraft productivity in terms of output ASMs or ATMs
   per annum can be calculated as follows: annual utilisation (block-
   hours) x block-speed (mph) x available payload (seats or tons)).

   Aircraft utilisation in fact has a profound impact on unit costs; high
   utilisation is a fundamental reason why long-haul operators tend to
   have lower unit costs than short-haul operators, and – along with high
   seating densities – it is a critical source of the unit cost advantage that
   low-fare (and European passenger charter) airlines have over full-service network competitors. High utilisation is an objective that carries
   with it some interesting complexities, however.
   • We have already seen that production capacity bears certain fixed
     costs that do not vary with output. If output is low relative to what
     existing capacity is capable of producing, fixed costs per unit of
     output (i.e., per ASM) will be high; as output rises within the range
     of existing capacity, fixed capacity costs are being spread across
     that greater output and so should be falling on a per unit basis. On

the other hand, the same utilisation improvement that puts downward pressure on unit costs by spreading fixed costs over more output also boosts total costs by the amount of the incremental variable costs associated with that additional output. As noted above, a key question is therefore whether additional output can be sold – and sold at prices sufficient to generate incremental revenue in excess of the increase in total costs; this critical point links through to consideration of traffic, yield, and load factors elsewhere in the book.

- From this last point we can draw a significant but often overlooked conclusion: higher utilisation does not *control* costs, but it can reduce their wastage. A production process with a given capacity bears a certain level of fixed costs, attributable to the resources used to create and sustain it. Increasing output within the predetermined capacity does not affect that resource expenditure, it simply results in less of it being wasted on overcapacity. Although it is often viewed as a cost-control mechanism because of its effect on unit cost, the fact is that capacity utilisation is as much a matter of revenue generation as it is of cost control. (Increased utilisation leading to lower average cost might permit lower prices, for example; if demand is sufficiently elastic, lower prices could stimulate sales and – provided incremental costs are at least covered – increase operating profits.) Any consideration of revenue generation in this context inevitably leads back to the topics of product costing and pricing.

- Not only are we faced with deciding whether incremental output generated to boost aircraft utilisation can be sold profitably, we are again confronted with the issue of what is meant by 'profitably'. Accountants may expect each departure to generate a profit after all costs – including fixed as well as variable costs – have been fully allocated. Others might argue that because the manner in which costs should best be allocated across products, markets or routes is something of a mystery – even to accountants – there is no sound basis here on which to make scheduling decisions. They might go on to say that what matters is whether sufficient output on an additional flight can be sold to cover its variable costs and make a contribution to fixed costs. If a flight can make such a contribution, it is usually better to have an aircraft in the air producing output and generating revenue than sitting on the ground – notwithstanding that accountants could characterise the flight as unprofitable on a fully-allocated basis.

Returning to a more general level of discussion, we can say the following about aircraft utilisation.

- The longer the average stage-length operated by a particular type, the higher should be its annual average utilisation because it will spend less of its life on the ground. (Although true at the extremes of intercontinental against short-haul operations, how true this is in the middle ground will depend very much upon network design and scheduling – topics covered in chapters 6 and 7.)

- A given type operated on a point-to-point network should be able to achieve higher utilisation than the same type operated in a hub-and-spoke network because hubs are often congested, causing delays in the air and lengthening taxi times, and because hub scheduling has to allow time for passengers and baggage to make connections from incoming flights before each aircraft can depart again.

2. **The strategic significance of resource utilisation** Maximising resource utilisation is now a critical element in the operating strategies of all well-managed airlines. Taking up the last point above, however, some categories of airline go so far as to build their entire strategic position on a platform of high utilisation.

   - *Low-fare carriers* Low-fare airlines depend upon high cabin floor-space utilisation (i.e., high seating densities/low seat pitches) and high aircraft utilisation to keep their unit costs competitively low. The key to high aircraft utilisation is fast turnarounds facilitated by: avoiding congested hubs (unless, as in the case of easyJet at London Gatwick, access to price-sensitive but nonetheless relatively high-yield business traffic justifies an exception to the rule); minimal provision of catering (which frees-up galley space for extra seating, reduces re-supply times between flight-legs, and saves weight and therefore fuel-burn); quick passenger embarkation procedures (often helped by the absence of seat selection); not carrying belly-hold cargo in narrowbodies; refusing to interline; forgoing online connecting traffic; and having a single-type fleet. At the time of writing, for example, British Airways is configuring B737-300s with 126 seats and achieving a utilisation of 7.1 hours a day; easyJet has 148 seats on the same aircraft and achieves utilisation of 10.7 hours (Mason et al, 2000). Although there are variations in the formula (some low-fare carriers offering two classes of onboard service, for example), a critical part of most low-fare airline strategies is a single-type, single-cabin operating system.

   - *Charter carriers* Those serving European vacation markets in particular also rely on high-density cabin configurations and high aircraft utilisation. With the help of low distribution costs, around-the-clock peak season operations, longer average stage-lengths, and high seating densities, the seat-mile costs of European charter airlines are often up to 30 or 40 per cent lower than those of full-service scheduled carriers operating comparable aircraft on intra-European routes. The advantage is somewhat smaller in long-haul markets, largely because scheduled carriers are able to raise their aircraft utilisation levels closer to those achieved by charter airlines than is possible given the operating patterns required by short-haul scheduled networks. (The operating characteristics of the European charter carriers, together with the fact that they generally fly larger aircraft, also give them a unit cost advantage over the continent's low-fare airlines; however, this advantage is less pronounced if just the scheduled operations/subsidiaries of those charter companies that have them are considered, and the extremely low costs of their pure charter operations are excluded from any comparison.)

- *Cargo carriers* Integrated carriers such as FedEx tend to operate hub-and-spoke systems dependent on overnight short- and medium-haul feed using aircraft that can generate only low levels of utilisation. Accordingly, the high fixed costs of new aircraft are difficult to justify and there is widespread reliance on older models that have lower ownership costs to spread across their relatively low output of ATMs. (Indeed, to support its service guarantees, FedEx has had an empty freighter leaving Portland, Oregon every night for its Memphis hub and tracking close to FedEx departure points in case an AOG situation develops.) On the other hand, expensive newer aircraft such as FedEx's A300-600Fs and MD-11Fs or UPS' B757PFs and B767 freighters require the high levels of utilisation that can be generated by flying longer routes between hubs and major gateways.

Structure of the fleet Having looked at service design, process design, and productivity, the final topic in this review of cost drivers associated with internal operations is fleet structure. As noted above in the context of network design and scheduling, the critical issue with regard to a fleet is its appropriateness to the various payload-range missions expected of it. Subject to this, key cost drivers are as follows.

- **Aircraft age** Older airframes and powerplants generally impose higher DOCs than newer types having a similar mission profile because their higher maintenance costs and fuel consumption outweigh lower ownership costs – although much will depend upon just how old an aircraft is (as this affects maintenance costs), the prevailing level of fuel prices, and how readily manufacturers are prepared to offer discounts off the list prices of new aircraft. In the case of long-haul aircraft, older types can often require intermediate stops that newer models are capable of overflying without a payload penalty.

- **Ownership costs** Newer aircraft generally impose higher ownership costs than older types with a similar mission profile. Larger aircraft tend to be more expensive to own than smaller aircraft. Some airframe-engine combinations are less popular in the secondary market than others, and so can be more expensive to finance. Historically, low-fare start-ups have tended to favour older aircraft with low ownership costs; well-capitalised year-2000 start-up jetBlue, however, chose to launch with new A320s because it considered their reliability and low maintenance costs more important than low ownership costs.

- **Fleet size and composition** Large fleets of a type can benefit from economies of scale – although what is meant by 'large' is a matter of opinion; certainly, a 40-aircraft fleet will benefit from economies unavailable to a two-aircraft fleet, but it is doubtful that operating 150 of a type generates significantly more economies than operating 100. Flight-crew and spares commonality amongst families of the same type (e.g., the Next Generation B737 series and the A320 series) can extend these economies across a range of different aircraft sizes. Conversely, Irrgang (2000: 175) lists the following areas in respect of which inefficiencies can arise from operating too many types: maintenance activities; maintenance inventory; ground equipment; number of pilots required; pilot training and qualification costs; average aircraft utilisation; and reduced flexibility in recovering from schedule disruptions.

- **Aircraft size** We have already seen that larger aircraft are generally cheaper to operate in unit cost (although not in trip cost) terms than smaller aircraft of the same technological generation having a similar mission capability. This advantage is sometimes referred to as 'aircraft economies of scale' (Bailey and Panzar, 1981; Graham et al, 1983; Caves et al, 1984), although the term has fallen from use.

- **Aircraft speed** Because output expressed in either ASMs or ATMs is a function of seats or payload available and distance flown, a faster aircraft will produce more output in a given time than a slower aircraft having the same capacity, allowing fixed ownership costs to be more widely spread and therefore lower on a per unit basis. There might of course be a price paid for this in terms of higher variable costs if the additional speed is reflected in higher fuel-burn – therefore the comparison that matters is between the most economical cruise speeds of different types rather than their maximum speeds.

- **Cabin configurations** Multiple cabin configurations within a fleet or sub-fleet can generate additional expenses which might be unnecessary unless each configuration is specifically designed in response to the demand characteristics of different markets. An example of configuration tailored to demand is the operation of a type configured with both first and business class cabins in addition to economy on routes where there is strong demand from premium passengers, and just business and economy on other routes where first class traffic is thin; Emirates, for instance, uses a two-cabin configuration on some routes served by its B777s and A330s, and three cabins on others, whilst several US majors use different configurations for domestic and international services operated by B767s and B777s.

  In addition to the question of whether or not to tailor the number of cabins on a type to demand on different routes there is the related question of whether to configure a given cabin on a particular type (e.g., the business class cabin) differently for different routes. Clearly, some degree of aircraft assignment flexibility might be lost in either case, even in large sub-fleets – because, in effect, the sub-fleet is being further sub-divided; for example, the decision taken by American in 2002 to switch from two to one cabin configuration on its international B777s was estimated to have led to scheduling efficiencies equivalent to adding two aircraft to the sub-fleet.

Conclusion This subsection has considered four aspects of internal operations that have an impact on costs: service design; process design; productivity; and fleet structure. We will tie these together by summarising the low-fare/low-cost operating model (Doganis, 2001; Lawton, 2002).

1. **Service design**
   - High-frequency service on a predominantly short-haul point-to-point network.
   - Use of secondary airports in preference to major hubs.
   - High-density, single-class cabin configuration.
   - No assigned seating.
   - No catering, or limited provision on a pay-as-you-go basis.
   - Few onboard amenities, and limited airport customer service.
   - A limited range of 'fare products' (i.e., a simple tariff structure, including one-way fares).
   - No FFP.
2. **Process design**
   - Emphasis on direct sales, preferably over the Internet.

- E-ticketing.
- No interlining.
- No hubbing (in the sense that passengers are not sold guaranteed online connections, and baggage is not transferred between flights).
- Lean administrative processes.
- Outsourcing of non-core processes.

3. **Productivity**
   - Maximisation of resource utilisation, especially staff and aircraft (the former reflected in low staff-to-passenger ratios, the latter facilitated by rapid turnarounds).
   - High cabin planning factors (i.e., targeted load factors).

4. **Fleet structure** Standardisation on a single aircraft type (usually in the 150-seat capacity range in high-density configuration).

Other common themes include efforts to produce a simple but reliable product that is recognised as sound value for money, and to be number one or two in market share terms on each route flown. That said, the low-fare model is not uniformly applied. For example: whereas Ryanair adopts a 'bare-bones' approach to customer service, both Southwest and easyJet rely on carefully nurtured corporate cultures to underpin their more user-friendly positioning; AirTran, jetBlue, and Southwest offer loyalty programmes, whereas most low-fare carriers do not; jetBlue provides an inflight product superior to what is offered by most low-fare carriers (and by many full-service airlines); AirTran offers a business class and a regional feeder service, whereas most others offer neither; some serve primary airports (e.g., easyJet and jetBlue), some serve secondary metropolitan airports (e.g., easyJet and Southwest), and some use airports so distant from the metropolitan areas they are serving that those airports might best be described as 'regional' – or, in some cases, 'extremely bucolic' (e.g., Ryanair); several offer assigned seating (e.g., AirTran and jetBlue), but most do not; many have single-type fleets, but easyJet does not. The important point to take from this partial list is that each deviation from the low-fare template carries with it cost (and in some cases also revenue) implications.

Distribution

Having looked at the supply chain and internal operations, distribution provides the third set of cost drivers for consideration under the heading 'design and functioning of the operating system'. Distribution has three purposes: selling – that is, acting as a channel to market; adding value for the customer – in the form of convenience (e.g., time and place utilities when making a purchase) or information (e.g., destination-related advice for leisure travellers, and back-office functionality for business accounts); and building a relationship with customers – something that is difficult to achieve when a channel intermediary is involved.

This subsection will look first at sources of distribution cost, and then at the strategic approaches adopted towards distribution by charter, low-fare, and cargo airlines. Actions taken by carriers to manage distribution costs will be considered later in the chapter.

Primary sources of distribution cost 'Distribution cost' includes commissions, overrides and other incentives paid to travel agencies, GDS fees, the costs of maintaining a sales, reservations, and ticketing infrastructure, and credit card charges. Aside from staffing and other costs that might fall under the heading of a variety of line items (e.g. 'sales and reservations', 'gate and counter'), there are four aspects of airline distribution costs that bear particular consideration: agency commissions, ancillary agency-related expenses, GDS fees, and interline ticketing costs.

1. **Agency commissions** In 1977 just prior to deregulation, 55 per cent of US airline sales were made through travel agencies; by the mid-1990s, consumer uncertainty in the face of constantly changing schedules and prices had driven this figure above 80 per cent. Just a few years later, the growth of Internet bookings and e-ticketing had edged it back down to around 75 per cent. Travel agencies have historically earned commissions in the 8–10 per cent range depending on the market concerned, with additional overrides sometimes being paid by airlines having a weak position in particular markets or by strong carriers wanting to consolidate market share. Box 5.7 looks at commission overrides.

Box 5.7: Travel agency commission overrides

Overrides are often based on the volume of business that an agency books for a carrier, with incentives in addition to the standard commission kicking-in on a sliding scale at defined threshold points specified to encourage stipulated percentage growth over the previous year's business done between the agency and the airline concerned. Alternatively, they may be oriented more specifically to market share by being keyed off comparative sales with respect to other carriers in a particular market. The objective is to induce the agency to favour the carrier with a large share of its revenue base by making it costly in terms of forgone commission to give business to other airlines if to do so would entail missing the next agreed threshold. The initial threshold often triggers a higher commission in respect of the entire volume of business done with the airline during the agreement period to date, whilst subsequent thresholds (some of which could be market-specific) might offer very much higher rewards (in certain North Pacific markets as much as 40 per cent on top of standard commission) – but only in respect of the incremental revenue generated within a specified range of sales. Travel agents in most countries are not obliged to provide information to customers about the override payments received from airlines whose services they are recommending or selling.

There is an argument that because they are nonlinear – and so do not relate rewards for particular volumes of business to the agents' costs of transacting the volumes concerned – overrides are intended primarily to tie agents to particular airlines rather than to reward sales effort. On the other hand, once a carrier having a large market share accounts for a significant proportion of an individual agency's business it becomes steadily more difficult to maintain high percentage annual growth off an already substantial sales base. At this point, it might be argued, override schemes offered by direct competitors could start to look more attractive – particularly if these competitors have a reasonable market presence.

Overrides have come under scrutiny by competition authorities in both the EU and the United States. In 1994, the US DOJ launched an investigation into whether overrides had been used to 'monopolise' traffic at fortress hubs. The debate does not turn on whether overrides in themselves are anticompetitive; they are not, and airlines are free to exercise their commercial judgement in offering them. The point is that where a carrier dominates a hub (or, indeed, a national market for outbound travel) it already generates sufficient volume to make the use of overrides a potent incremental weapon for the exclusion of competitors, either in general or in particular city-pair markets. The argument hinges on how much predatory intent can be ascribed to what in isolation is a justifiable, if expensive, business practice. Undeniably, though, carriers able to combine market presence with access to the real-time competitive information available through analysis of GDS data are in a strong position to employ incentive programmes highly effectively.

Airlines are now generally much more focused in their use of overrides. Programmes are increasingly being assessed by relating their cost to the margin gained from incremental traffic rather than by reference to market share alone.

---

2. **Ancillary agency-related expenses** Commissions and overrides are just two aspects of the costs involved in distributing through agents. There are others. First, major airlines generally have sales forces tasked with telephoning and visiting key agencies. Second, money paid by customers to agencies finds its way to airlines through billing and sett-

lement plans established in each country and takes longer to reach the airline than cash from direct sales. (The equivalent in the United States is the Area Settlement Plan operated by the Airlines Reporting Corporation.) Third, it is not uncommon to incentivise individual agents with mileage awards and prizes, both on an agency basis and as part of a fixed duration, locally targeted sales campaign.

3. **GDS fees** US airlines are paying around $2 billion per annum in GDS fees, and these fees have been increasing at a rate of seven per cent in recent years – much faster than passenger enplanements. The rate of increase is particularly troubling given the dramatic decline in telecommunications and computing costs. Originally charged on the basis of net bookings (i.e., gross bookings less cancellations), GDS pricing structures (particularly in the US domestic market) are now predominantly transaction-based – applying fees to amendments and cancellations as well as bookings. This has not only contributed to rapidly rising fees, it has also left airlines paying for transactions that generate no boarded passengers and therefore no revenue. The problem has been exacerbated by GDSs incentivising agency transaction activity by lowering equipment lease rates in return for high transaction volumes – irrespective of whether the transactions concerned produce revenue for the airlines. Thus, although airlines benefit from the GDSs as a distribution channel, they have little control over the cost of this channel because they have no direct control over agency booking activity. Furthermore, the use of flat-rate fees means that GDS charges are the same irrespective of the class of travel, length of haul or price of the ticket – something that penalises short-haul low-fare carriers in particular and accounts for the unwillingness of many of these airlines to use GDSs. Where fees are charged per segment, as is common, connecting itineraries are especially burdened.

4. **Interline ticketing costs** There are three aspects to this issue.
    *   Traditionally, many carriers have written tickets on their own paper for transportation on another airline's services. Carriers writing such tickets have in the past done so without charge, absorbing the costs involved and benefiting from cash float until billed through the IATA Clearing House. Some airlines write more tickets for others than are written for them, and so are referred to as 'net ticketers'. Strong net ticketers in a number of markets have deemed the float inadequate compensation and, since the early 1990s, have been charging commissions of approximately two or three per cent for tickets written on their paper by agency staff and as much as ten per cent if their own staff are involved.

- As we saw in chapter 3, prorate dilution can be looked upon as a 'cost' insofar as it is likely to reduce the revenue of any carrier interlining passengers with other airlines – again, something that most low-fare carriers refuse to do.
- Prorate payments due (re international itineraries) are netted through the IATA Clearing House, and whilst the system functions efficiently an airline can wait some time to receive revenues in respect of passengers already carried when another airline issued the tickets and received payment (perhaps because that carrier was the first to be used on a multi-airline itinerary). This can have negative cash flow implications. Prorate billings and receipts also need to be checked for accuracy, and this is not a cost-free activity.

Low-fare and charter airlines We have already seen that a major plank in the low-fare/low-cost positioning platform is direct reservations and e-ticketing. Many low-fare carriers (e.g., easyJet) do not use agency channels or GDSs. Those that do (e.g., Southwest) commonly limit the number of GDS listings and the level of functionality they pay for, and/or encourage as much volume as they can through the Internet.

Of course, by cutting themselves off from a potentially important distribution channel capable of 'pushing' sales, low-fare carriers sometimes have to devote disproportionate expenditures to generating 'pull' through public relations (PR) and advertising. Never short of PR exposure, easyJet nonetheless also has to spend heavily on advertising – Mason et al (2000) estimating its spend per UK passenger carried at the end of the 1990s as £2.65 against £0.75 for British Airways; clearly, marketing economies of scale and/or economies of scope also help the larger airline in this instance. Finally, low-fare carriers avoid prorate dilution, cash flow delays, and revenue accounting complications by refusing to interline – something reflected in the fact that easyJet's 17-day collection period is less than half of British Airways' (ibid).

Charter airlines benefit from being able to sell much of their output in bulk to a relatively small number of (often affiliated) tour organisers, and so do not bear either the fixed costs of a large sales and distribution organization or the variable costs attributable to agency commissions and GDS fees. In Northern Europe, many of these carriers are now part of vertically integrated groups incorporating tour organizers and retail travel agencies.

Cargo distribution The problem that many cargo carriers and combination airline cargo divisions face is that they have little direct contact with end consumers of their services – that is, shippers and consignees. The customer in most cases is a forwarder or consolidator which has an interest in shopping around for the cheapest rates it can negotiate; shippers and consignees have little incentive to specify a particular airline, and cargo space is very often commoditised as a result of carriers' invisibility in the airfreight marketing system.

Many airlines simply accept the traditional situation, either paying commissions to forwarders or negotiating cheap net rates for bulk purchases of space and offering a simple airport-to-airport line-haul service. Others have taken a two-pronged approach that has as much to do with the revenue side as the cost side of operating strategy.

1. Building direct relationships with selected high-volume shippers (perhaps on an industry-specific basis), offering value-added services and generally strengthening their brands. This is not a popular approach within the forwarder community.
2. Partnering with key forwarders in an attempt to offer a more coherently priced and branded time-definite door-to-door service than the traditional airfreight product has provided, and in doing this counter the inroads increasingly being made by integrated carriers such as FedEx and DHL in international markets. On the whole, it has to be said that this development is still not widespread and that some airline-forwarder relationships remain ambivalent at best and adversarial at worst.

This concludes our review of the role played by the design and functioning of an airline's operating system as a cost driver – during the course of which we have looked at supply chain management, internal operations, and distribution. The other three cost drivers reviewed in this section of the chapter are input costs, scale, and learning. We turn next to input costs.

Input costs

We have already touched both directly and indirectly on input costs. This sub-section will make some brief comments in respect of the most important of them.

Labour costs

There are several elements driving labour costs.

1. **Staff numbers** Staff are traditionally looked upon as an airline's most significant 'controllable' cost and are therefore in the firing line when times are hard – as in the early 1990s and, more dramatically, in 2001.

2. **Salaries and benefits** On the whole, airline staff are highly paid in comparison with other workers in their local economies, and pilots in particular account for upwards of 30 per cent of labour costs at some carriers. A feature of salaries amongst pilots (and other unionised labour groups) at US majors is 'pattern bargaining' – which means that one airline's generous contractual settlement (e.g., United's pilots' contract in 2000) automatically ratchets up expectations at other carriers. One consequence of the growth of airline alliances will be the spread of cross-border pattern bargaining amongst pilots.

3. **Social costs** Employment taxes and/or compulsory employer payments into state social security and pension programmes represent a substantial proportion of total labour costs in some countries, particularly in Western Europe.

4. **Labour contracts** Most long-established airlines are heavily unionised across all major labour groups (Delta being perhaps the largest exception). The terms of labour contracts can be critical to airline costs not just in respect of the salaries and benefits they confer, but also in respect of restrictions that they might contain in the following areas.

    *   *Job flexibility* Start-ups and also unionised carriers with broadly cooperative labour groups (e.g., Southwest) often benefit from more job flexibility and fewer restrictive working practices than some of their competitors have to contend with. This feeds through to relatively high productivity levels per dollar of human resource expenditure. For example, having flight attendants prepared to undertake light cabin cleaning or dispatchers prepared to help load baggage can contribute to faster turnarounds and, across a large system over a significant span of time, help boost aircraft utilisation. (On a related point, low-fare start-ups have often found it difficult to sustain low pay levels beyond the initial phase of operations without adversely affecting staff morale; in the long term, a low-fare business model demands high staff productivity more than it requires substandard pay. This truism has from time to time been at the root of many of America West's problems.)

    *   *Scope clauses* The expression 'scope clause' can be applied to any union contract that restricts or prohibits the contracting-out of union-controlled work (Jenks, 2001). However, it is an expression most commonly used in respect of pilots' contracts. To protect highly paid jobs, mainline pilots' contracts at most US majors impose a variety of limits on the number, size, and/or output of regional jets operated under code-shares by these carriers' regional partners or subsidiaries – the seat-mile economics of which require that relatively low flight-crew salaries be paid. Some clauses res-

trict either the ASMs or the block-hours that can be flown by regionals under the major's code to a fixed percentage of the ASM or block-hour figures generated by the major (or the major and its regionals combined) over a defined period of time; this structure proved particularly troublesome for affected regionals when majors heavily reduced their mainline flying in 2001/2002. These clauses have had a profound effect on network and fleet management in the United States, and have also affected the design of regional jets sized around the 70–75 seat range where many scope limitations kick in. Network restructuring in the aftermath of 9/11 – specifically, the passing of thin mainline routes to regional operators – put pressure on the sustainability of scope clauses in their established form.

5. **Seniority** Long-established carriers often have more senior and more highly paid workforces than younger competitors (a problem that afflicted TWA, for example). More generally, one of the side-effects of lay-offs and furloughs is that to the extent that it is junior staff who are affected first, average labour cost per head can actually rise; clearly, this has to be offset by productivity growth amongst those who remain. On the other hand, early retirements can lower average labour costs. What happens to unit labour cost (i.e., labour cost per ASM or ATM) as a result of changes to staff numbers will depend upon the relationship between the number of employees affected, the seniority of those employees, the salary levels of retained employees, and the output produced at the revised staffing level.

6. **Training** An airline's approach to non-mandatory training – its accessibility, scope, content, and frequency, for example – will in part be determined by the nature of its service concept(s). A full-service carrier, particularly one with a high-quality brand image, will spend more per head on customer service training than a low-fare carrier.

In mid-2001, labour's percentage of TOCs at US majors stretched from 23 per cent at America West to over 40 per cent at Delta; most carriers were in the 35–40 per cent range. The share of labour costs in TOCs varies not only in response to the factors listed above, but also in response to the sizes of the other expenditure line items that comprise total operating cost. Lower fuel, airport, and airway costs in the United States than elsewhere tend to 'artificially' boost the share of labour costs in US airline TOCs, for example. The strength of a non-US airline's home currency (in which most labour expenses are met) relative to the dollar (in which fuel, and often lease rentals and airport charges are denominated) can also distort the picture – as Japanese carriers have found during periods of strength in the yen.

The absolute cost and productivity of labour are issues of fundamental importance to all carriers because they drive unit labour cost, which in turn contributes substantially to aggregate unit cost. They are of particular concern to those US and European majors whose business model (particularly in short-haul markets) has historically relied upon the high walk-up fares paid by business travellers to accommodate steady upward pressure on labour costs exerted by collective bargaining in what is a highly unionised industry. Widespread resistance to further fare increases from business travellers in some markets – manifested in declining enplanements and growing willingness to use low-fare carriers – began with the economic downturn of 2000 (most notably in the United States), and for the first time placed a serious question mark against the long-term sustainability of the full-service network majors' pricing structures and cost bases.

Fuel costs

At year-2000 consumption levels, every cent per gallon change in fuel prices was worth $200 million per annum either way to US majors. Fuel cost drivers include the following.

1. The age and fuel efficiency of a particular carrier's fleet.
2. The world market price for jet fuel.
3. Network design. It is often the case that fuel costs contribute an increasing proportion of total trip costs as stage-length rises.
4. Regional market price pressures. There are seasonal pressures on fuel prices in certain parts of the world, notably North America and to a considerably lesser extent Northern Europe. Partly this reflects the fact that jet fuel is similar in specification to heating oil; the demand and spot price for heating oil rise in response to severe winter weather, which in extreme cases can lead to the diversion of refining capacity in affected regions away from the production of jet fuel.
5. Local factors at airports on a carrier's network. These can include: the expense of physically supplying particular airports; whether or not there is competition amongst suppliers driving down the costs of both fuel and into-plane services; and the impact of any government taxes or duties. Of particular importance are the costs at a carrier's hub(s) or main base(s) because of the significant proportion of operations they will account for. On the horizon is the possibility that 'green taxes' on fuel will spread, particularly in Europe.

We will look later in the chapter at steps that airlines take to manage fuel costs.

Airport and air traffic service costs

Airlines are estimated to have paid close to $35 billion in airport and air traffic service (ATS) costs in 2000, around 60 per cent of which were airport charges. The principal cost drivers are: airport charges; ground-handling; ATS charges; and delays.

Airport charges These can include charges in respect of: landing (and/or take-off), parking, security, turnaround (e.g., jetway/airbridge and baggage systems), passengers, cargo, lighting, after-hours movements, and perhaps also noise surcharges. The following points are important.

- Airport fees represent a higher proportion of costs on a short-haul than a long-haul flight. Messer (1999) cites 2.6 per cent of trip costs for a B747-400 arriving at Vancouver from Hong Kong, against 7.7 per cent for a B737-100/200 arriving from Calgary. (This is the case notwithstanding the fact that landing and parking charges are still widely based on aircraft weight – London Heathrow being an example of a notable exception which has a combination of flat fee and weight-based pricing that discriminates heavily against regional aircraft.)
- Major carriers in the United States own or hold long-term leases on a considerable amount of the gate and terminal space they use, particularly at their hubs. Airport charges there accordingly relate to a greater extent to the use of runways and taxiways than is the case elsewhere in the world where charges for the use of terminals and gates can be significant. The reverse side of this is that US majors intent on owning terminals have to raise substantial sums to finance this capital expenditure (often in conjunction with revenue bonds issued by the airport authority). Another side-effect of this structure is that through majority-in-interest clauses in their lease agreements, US majors sometimes have a significant influence on whether and on what terms potential competitors can gain access to existing infrastructure and on whether or not airports can expand to accommodate potential competitors.
- Outside the United States and certain UK airports, explicit service-level guarantees are seldom part of an airport-airline relationship. Airlines generally have little control over the quality of service they and their passengers receive from airport operators.
- As more airports around the world are privatised, corporatised, or leased to private operators under long-term concessions, pressures are building not just to increase charges but to change the traditional revenue-side structure of airport operations. Briefly, the 'single-till' approach to pricing traditionally used at many airports nets non-aero-

nautical revenues (e.g., from retail concessions, etc.) off airport costs before levying aeronautical charges sufficient to recover any residual – thereby in effect using landside activities to subsidise airside operations. Since the 1990s airports have been moving to change this structure to a 'dual-till' approach, wherein charges are set separately for aeronautical and non-aeronautical users at levels sufficient to recover from each the costs they impose; a particular bone of contention has been whether the costs of future infrastructure developments should be reflected in current charges. Box 5.8 explores this latter point.

Box 5.8: Infrastructure pricing

Infrastructure constraints occur at particular times because of the demand-peaking characteristics of air transport markets that we met in chapter 2: people want to travel more at some times than others, and airlines want to be able to meet this demand. If we acknowledge that capacity constraints exist in certain airspace and at certain airports at particular times of the day, week, and/or year the question arises as to who benefits from the 'scarcity rents' attributable to excesses of demand over supply. Given that access to airspace and runways is seldom subject to peak pricing (although access to airbridges and other airside facilities might be), it is usually not the infrastructure providers; in fact it is often airlines, which reduce the availability of deeply discounted fares during peak periods and so leverage infrastructure constraints into higher average fares than they would otherwise earn on the flights concerned.

In the United States, airlines do not bear the full cost of producing and operating much of the airport and airway infrastructure they use, and are therefore in effect receiving indirect subsidies; as is true in respect of any subsidised good, demand for access to infrastructure is higher than it would otherwise be. The absence of economic pricing therefore leads to consumption inefficiencies; because producers of infrastructural capacity receive no clear price signals to help them understand the value users put on their facilities, this arrangement also hinders allocative efficiency by obscuring data needed to assess requirements for investment in future capacity (Golaszewski and Ballard, 2001).

Generally, airports are pushing out the envelope on charges – but subject to certain moderating factors. First, although an airport might be a monopoly supplier as far as local O & D traffic is concerned, if it is hosting an airline operating a hub that competes with other hubs for flow traffic it cannot afford to price itself out of the market. Indeed, airports keen to develop as hubs often reduce or waive passenger service charges in respect of transfer traffic. Second, airports – especially smaller airports – competing to attract airlines in general and low-fare carriers in particular sometimes offer very generous pricing structures to bring in business: US airports go to great lengths to attract Southwest, and in Europe Ryanair has become legendary for imposing terms on secondary airports. (Conversely, low-fare carriers may face significant upward pressure on costs after the expiry of initial 'introductory offers' – as easyJet did at London Luton, for example.) Third, several airports (e.g., in Portugal and Belgium) have in the past used bulk discounting and other price breaks (of questionable legality in some cases) to lower costs for their national carriers. Finally, the capping of increases in landing charges as a condition of privatisation at several airports (e.g., those in the UK owned by BAA) has been beneficial to airlines.

Ground-handling There are two aspects to ground-handling: airside and landside. In respect of each, airlines face broadly two situations.

- **No choice** Some airports still have a monopoly supplier of ground-handling services, usually affiliated with the airport itself or the national carrier. This situation is sometimes associated with opaque linkages between pricing and costs, the inability of airlines to select which services in a bundle they wish to purchase, and possibly with inferior quality.
- **Choice** Where a choice of handling alternatives exists, the outsourcing menu might include specialised service providers (e.g., Servisair) and also airlines (perhaps including the national airline or other locally dominant carrier) whose scale of operations at the airport concerned is enough to justify an inhouse handling operation. If a carrier wants to self-handle, it will need both sufficient scale and also access; many airports that allow competitive ground-handling nonetheless limit the number of providers, particularly airside, for practical reasons. Finally, choice might exist in respect of some activities (e.g., line maintenance or catering) but not others (e.g., fuel supply or customer services).

ATS charges Although pricing methods vary, there are broadly two types of charge: en route fees and terminal navigation fees (the latter sometimes included in airport landing fees). The following generalisations apply.

- Because US airway infrastructure is funded by a tax on passenger tickets and revenues, carriers there benefit from the free use of domestic airspace. In Europe and elsewhere there is a system of user charges; these show up as DOCs and so contribute to some of the higher operating costs typical of many European airlines.

- Those countries that do charge fees, which include the vast majority of states, generally use distance flown, aircraft maximum take-off weight (MTOW) or a formula including the two – although a few apply uniform fees. Some grant discounts in respect of domestic flights and also flights that originate or terminate in the country.
- In the absence of consultation, airlines can find themselves confronted with charges keyed-off an ATS cost base over which they have no say. Put crudely, monopoly ATS providers can decide what to spend and then set about recovering costs from the airlines. This was brought home when traffic in 2002 fell below projections and led several European ATS providers to impose stiff (i.e., 20 per cent or more) fee increases on remaining movements in order to achieve their cost recovery objectives. Similarly, there is little incentive for traditionally structured (i.e., government-operated) ATS providers to improve efficiency if the costs of inefficiency can simply be passed on to customers.
- ICAO has in the past rejected long-run marginal cost pricing as a basis for ATS (and airport) charges. Its policy is that costs should be established by dividing estimated charging units (i.e., aircraft transits, adjusted for MTOW, distance covered, services used, etc.) into the cost base – therefore charging on the basis of average cost rather than costs actually imposed by particular users (notably peak-period users). Policy recommendations have since become more flexible, with economic pricing principles (i.e., long-run marginal cost pricing) acceptable subject to cost transparency and consultation with users (ICAO, 2000).
- Regional airlines in Europe are disproportionately affected by price increases because of the greater share of ATS charges on a short flight relative to a medium- or long-haul sector. The threat they face was evident in the Eurocontrol proposal put forward in 2000 to move from a weight- and distance-based charging mechanism to a flat-rate fee structure – something that would not only increase absolute costs for small aircraft by up to 80 per cent, but would leave them paying very much higher per-seat charges than larger aircraft.
- There is (albeit slow and limited) growth in the number of autonomous providers of air traffic services, and in the use of commercial costing and pricing. Experiences in those few countries where this type of development has occurred have been positive for airlines in the sense that fees have often been reduced.
- There are areas of the world where little correlation exists between fees charged and the quality of service. (See Whelan (2000) for a comprehensive review.) In some states, for example, high fees accompany poor air navigation infrastructure. Even where the quality of air

navigation infrastructure is high, as in Western Europe, service actually received by airlines is impaired by widespread peak delays.

Delays Delays add hundreds of millions of dollars to airline operating costs each year as a result of: non-productive fuel consumption; non-productive labour costs; non-productive flight-hour-based maintenance costs; and the handling, accommodating, and rescheduling of affected passengers. Irregular operations caused by serious delays affect resource productivity as aircraft, gates, equipment, people, and other resources have to be reassigned from what, presumably, was an optimal schedule. Also, some of a fleet's apparently high utilisation figure might represent wasted time that could have been used on additional productive revenue service; in the worst case, service delays can mean that an airline needs more aircraft to perform a given schedule than would otherwise be the case. Airport and en route delays are estimated to be costing airlines around $5 billion each year in the United States, and perhaps up to $1 billion more than that in Europe (Kelly, 2001). Lufthansa has estimated that in 2001 its aircraft were in holding patterns an average 38 hours each day, burning around 100,000 tonnes of fuel a year in the process.

Station costs

The sources of station costs are fairly evident – primarily labour costs and ownership charges or rentals in respect of facilities and equipment. Less obvious are the effects that network design and operational decisions can have on the unit cost of station operations.

Network design If a station is served by, say, two routes and one of these is dropped because it is unprofitable, there are two possible side-effects to bear in mind.

1. Pending any reduction in personnel (which might be rapid) and station overhead (which will be slower), and assuming frequencies are not added to the remaining route, station costs per departure will rise – because there are now fewer departures over which to spread fixed costs – and the productivity of station resources will fall.
2. Because it is now having to bear station costs in their entirety rather than sharing them, it is possible that the apparent profitability of the remaining route will deteriorate. This underlines the interconnectedness of network decisions – and might, incidentally, argue for spreading station costs over all routes that benefit from traffic flows originating from each station.

Operational decisions The profitability of a station might, for example, hinge on decisions taken with regard to the aircraft type(s) assigned to serve it (bearing in mind that different types have different operating economics), whether line maintenance is to be outsourced or handled internally, and the extent to which spares inventory will be held locally to support in-house line maintenance.

Maintenance costs

As well as being an important source of airline costs, aircraft maintenance is significant in the contribution it makes to safety, despatch reliability, flight completion rates, schedule integrity, and to the preservation of aircraft residual values. Maintenance is therefore a question of branding and asset management as well as regulatory compliance. The maintenance management objective must be to make the fleet available in an appropriate condition (internally and externally) when and where required to support performance of the schedule, and to do this as cost-effectively as possible.

There is no formulaic answer to the question of whether or not to outsource the MRO function, and both an airline's history and the influence of stakeholders such as unions and politicians can be as strong as any assessment based on transaction cost economics or shareholder value analysis. A growing number of carriers are now using long-term power-by-the-hour and life-cycle maintenance cost agreements with engine OEMs; these allow stable maintenance cost projections and remove the burden associated with investing in engine shop and test facilities, and inventory. Similar long-term outsourcing agreements have also become common in respect of airframe, sub-assembly, component, and avionics maintenance. Nonetheless, that maintenance outsourcing is not a necessary prerequisite for low costs is borne out by the fact that several large and long-established North European charter carriers have extensive inhouse facilities (e.g., Monarch). Clearly, the best decision is the one that keeps as much of an airline's fleet in the air as long as possible and as cheaply as possible, subject to the constraints of safety, regulatory compliance, and required reliability levels.

The following are amongst the most important maintenance cost drivers; most apply whether or not maintenance work is outsourced, although some (notably economies of scale) may vary as between the two options depending upon fleet size. (Note that when leasing aircraft, airlines are normally required to make payments into one or more maintenance reserve accounts in order to provide for the cost of future maintenance; this enforced cash provisioning in effect brings forward these expenditures.)

Fleet age Ageing aircraft cost more to maintain than new models; maintenance costs for older types can be two or three times the equivalent of more modern types designed for similar missions. Factors which affect airframe condition over time include: the number of flight-hours and cycles recorded; whether or not the aircraft has spent significant time on the ground in humid, maritime or desert environments; runway and overnight parking conditions on the network; and maintenance standards (both in general and with particular regard to galleys, lavatories, and cargo holds exposed to spillages of potentially corrosive liquids). The principal threats are corrosion and fatigue, either independently or in conjunction. Powerplant and component maintenance costs also rise with age, particularly in respect of engine rotating parts and hot sections. Another consideration is that a greater proportion of a young fleet is likely still to be under warranty.

Network design There are several maintenance cost drivers under this heading.

1. *Average stage-lengths* Long-haul aircraft can have significantly lower flight-hour maintenance costs than short-haul types (Clark, 2001). They usually have fewer cycle-related costs (including fewer transit and turn-around checks), in addition to which they benefit from higher utilisation over which to spread maintenance burden and they also spend more of their time aloft in dry and relatively stable air.
2. *ETOPS* Rules applied to 'extended-range twin-engine operations' impose a need to increase spares provision to support more demanding minimum equipment list (MEL) requirements on ETOPS flight-legs.
3. *Proximity to maintenance facilities* As far as inhouse maintenance is concerned, costs will be influenced by the number and location of maintenance facilities and how readily they can be accessed (particularly overnight in respect of short-haul aircraft) given aircraft assignments flowing from the carrier's schedule. Airlines located in remote parts of the world suffer additional costs arising from the distance aircraft and components have to travel for outsourced maintenance, and also possibly from the need to hold a larger spares buffer to compensate for being on the end of long supply lines.

Aircraft utilisation High daily utilisation accelerates both scheduled and unscheduled maintenance – particularly in the case of short-haul aircraft operating a lot of cycles. This is, of course, a price worth paying insofar as aircraft do not earn revenue unless they are flying and the more time they spend in the air the greater the amount of output they are generating over which to spread fixed costs (including maintenance burden).

Operational practices Some airlines carefully monitor flight-crew engine handling, particularly during take-off and climb phases, to ensure that operating temperatures are neither higher than they need be nor high for longer than they need be.

Maintenance philosophy Some carriers are much less inclined to delay implementation of service bulletins (SBs) and deferrable airworthiness directives (ADs) than others. The acceptability of non-MEL defects also varies between airlines; some carriers like to fix defects as soon as is practical, whereas others are more prepared to defer items. (If aircraft are leased, of course, lessors will have a voice in whether and when ADs and SBs are terminated.) Finally, some carriers have more of a predilection for undertaking extensive engineering work and modifications on their aircraft than others – British Airways, until relatively recently, being an example.

Maintenance programme design The manner in which required tasks are packaged into maintenance programmes for airframes and engines will affect costs through the impact that design has on the frequency and complexity of each activity. A complicating factor can sometimes be the presence in a fleet of different aircraft of the same type subject to different maintenance programmes because they are owned by different lessors (although if an aircraft is on a medium- or long-term lease it will most probably be integrated into the airline's maintenance programme). Also, the efficiency of maintenance programmes can sometimes be compromised when new aircraft are added to an existing fleet of the same type subject to the same certification requirements as the older models, but with no account being taken of subsequent advances in design, materials, or manufacturing technology since the original models came off the production line.

Maintenance planning Effective maintenance planning balances two considerations.

1. The need to maximise time between checks. It is essential to ensure as far as possible that no scheduled maintenance is undertaken before it needs to be – in other words, that all allowable calendar time, flight-hours, and cycles are fully used and none is wasted by premature checks.
2. The need to balance throughput and maximise utilisation at maintenance facilities. The challenge of scheduling shop visits when aircraft, engines and so on need them, yet also ensuring that maintenance capacity is fully utilised is complicated by the industry's demand peaking –

which means that at certain times of the day, week, and/or year every airline will want as many of its aircraft as possible available for service.

A key challenge in the management of maintenance planning is establishing a critical path for each check given that routine activities will inevitably uncover the need for unscheduled maintenance – some of which might be allowed for in the project plan, some of which might be deferrable and scheduled for subsequent action, but some of which may have to be dealt with immediately and could put pressure on the return-to-service date.

Maintenance input costs There are three primary categories.

1. **Labour costs** On average, 4–5 man-hours of maintenance can be assumed for each jet flight-hour – a figure that has declined by more than half since the early 1990s. Line maintenance costs are practically all accounted for by labour, whilst approximately two-thirds of airframe intermediate and heavy maintenance costs are driven by man-hour rates (Lam, 1995). Only around 10–15 per cent of engine maintenance costs are attributable to direct labour.

   Maintenance man-hour rates vary not only between carriers, but also between different areas of the world. North American hourly rates are generally lower than those in Europe – which means that in order to be competitive, MRO operations such as Lufthansa Technik and Air France Industries need to offer fast, reliable maintenance turnaround/ cycle times and high quality. Man-hour rates in parts of Asia are lower still – which partly explains the growth of joint ventures in the region between airlines (e.g., Singapore Airlines) and original equipment manufacturers (e.g., Rolls Royce).

2. **Material costs** These account for over half of engine and component maintenance costs, but much less in respect of airframes (Lam, 1995). Third-party manufacturers – who compete with OEMs by manufacturing non-proprietary parts subject to PMA (parts manufacturing approval) – are more attractive suppliers in some cases because of their lower prices and better availability; however, PMA parts tend to be available more in respect of mature types than newer models.

3. **Overhead/burden** What is true for the fleet is true for other airline assets, including maintenance facilities: utilisation (of hangars, bays, repair shops, and of maintenance planning, administration, record-keeping, and quality control resources) needs to be as high as possible to generate maximum output over which to spread fixed costs. (Utilisation in this case is a measure of man-hours and facility time that is booked relative to what is available.) Whereas labour rates are a key airframe

maintenance cost driver, the capital costs of facilities are a significant driver in respect of powerplant and avionics maintenance (accounting for over a third of total engine maintenance costs). The high costs of tooling, technical training, and test facilities together with the increasing reliability of equipment (i.e., lower shop visit rates) imply the need for large fleets over which to spread fixed maintenance costs. Even some airlines that have sizeable fleets are now finding it more cost-effective to enter into long-term maintenance agreements with OEMs.

The fact that materials and overhead account for such a high proportion of engine maintenance costs helps keep the role of independent third-party shops much lower in respect of engine overhaul than airframe maintenance: given that engine OEMs have a substantial measure of control over the prices of proprietary materials and benefit from significant economies of scale in the allocation of overhead, independents have only their man-hour costs to compete with – something that OEMs can counter by shifting labour cost disadvantages into mark-ups on their materials.

Productivity Assuming the availability of required facilities, there are three potential influences on maintenance productivity.

1. **The effectiveness of maintenance programme design and maintenance planning** We touched on both of these above.
2. **Labour productivity** This is usually measured by the time taken to perform a given task relative to an established standard. It is likely to be a function of training, work practices, and experience. With regard to the latter, there are maintenance cost learning curves to be exploited as familiarity grows with an aircraft type or a manufacturer's products generally; one advantage of outsourcing – aside from the saving in capital costs associated with investment in hangars, bays, shops, and tooling – is that a smaller airline can benefit from the contractor's experience. More generally, it is common for check intervals to be extended, with the agreement of appropriate airworthiness authorities, after an airline has gained experience with a type.

   Technology is also helping: the digitisation and online provision of maintenance manuals, technical publications, service bulletins, engineering drawings, parts catalogues, and other OEM-provided resources is gradually eliminating time spent by staff updating paper libraries and is also accelerating look-up times and ordering processes; hardened laptops and wearable computers hold out the prospect of bringing higher productivity to the shop-floor and the ramp; and real-time return-to-service updates are helping integrate maintenance operations more closely with other functional areas, most notably aircraft assignment and operations control.

3. **Inventory productivity** Inventory can be categorised as: spare engines; rotables; repairables; expendables (i.e., items discarded after use); and consumables (e.g., oil). Spare engines and rotables are together by far the most significant items in value terms – although an 'aircraft on the ground' (AOG) situation can as easily develop from a stock-out affecting a cheap expendable. Inventory held to support a small fleet may amount to as much as 15–20 per cent of aircraft cost, so there are certainly economies of scale to be exploited by having a large fleet – although estimates of what is meant by 'large' in this context vary. It should also be borne in mind that inventory bears potentially heavy carrying costs – finance, depreciation, warehousing, and insurance – whether used or not. Inventory productivity can be increased by pooling with other carriers, and the availability of spare engines on short-term operating leases can also help reduce inventory costs.

    Introduction of a new type can generate a significant initial provisioning (IP) expense, the size of which will depend upon an airline's bargaining strength and the extent to which it outsources using fixed cost maintenance contracts. Broadly, initial inventory is high as a proportion of total investment in a new fleet until the number of aircraft in that fleet begins to rise; if the powerplant used on the aircraft is already in operation with the airline, this will reduce IP expenses quite considerably. Any fleet build-up after purchase of the first few aircraft dramatically decreases the spares-to-aircraft ratio. A somewhat smaller cost reduction then occurs in later years as the airline uses up any excess parts inventory left over from IP and better manages its purchases of replacement parts, concentrating on those that have demonstrated a relatively high failure rate. Introduction of a mature type usually results in lower initial costs because the airline is able to benefit from the maintenance experiences of other carriers.

Scale Economies of scale are present when unit cost declines as a function of increasing output. Estimates vary, but there is little argument that economies of scale are present in the maintenance business.

1. **Man-hours** The scale of a maintenance facility is generally measured in terms of the bookable man-hours available in a year. The unit cost advantage of a three-million man-hour heavy maintenance shop over one with half this capacity can be as high as 20 per cent.
2. **Inventory** Having already touched upon inventory above, the purpose of this paragraph is to link it explicitly with scale effects. As fleet size

and therefore output of ASMs or ATMs increases, the value – and therefore the inventory cost – of spares needed to support each aircraft (at a given level of confidence with regard to the availability of spares when required) will fall. This is particularly true of rotables, which when held in inventory can support several aircraft as readily as just one; broadly, a six-fold increase in fleet size might require a doubling of the rotables inventory. Overall there is little doubt that the unit costs of supporting a larger fleet are lower than those of supporting a small fleet. There is a rule of thumb that a single-aircraft 'fleet' requires inventory worth as much as 50 per cent of that aircraft's value, dropping to 25 per cent when the fleet grows to ten units, and to ten per cent when it reaches a hundred units. (For mathematical precision in preference to rules of thumb, readers are referred to queuing theory.)

One way for a relatively small carrier to overcome these problems is to outsource in order to exploit economies of scale available to larger airlines, OEMs, or sizeable independent shops.

Aircraft characteristics Very broadly, absolute maintenance costs for aircraft of a similar technology level increase with maximum take-off weight and with engine thrust. Separately, some types have a better reputation for reliability than others, although competitors amongst current generation aircraft are now generally well-matched and highly reliable. With regard to individual aircraft, many carriers closely monitor the fuel consumption and maintenance costs of each 'tail number' to uncover particularly expensive problems as they develop. Another technique sometimes used is to target the known cost drivers on each airframe and engine to bring them under better control.

Market positioning Requirements in respect of cabin and exterior airframe cleanliness will affect deep cleaning frequency and also standards with regard to the acceptability of cabin defects – each of which should be driven by an appreciation of what type of value the airline is trying to deliver to its customers. They will have a direct bearing on maintenance costs.

(Finally, it is worth noting the following distinction in respect of maintenance cost calculations. Block-time is the time from engine start-up at origin to shut-down at the end of the flight-leg; flight-time, on the other hand, is the time from unstick to touch-down (and therefore excludes taxi-out and taxi-in times). Whereas hourly DOCs as a whole are normally calculated per block-hour, it is not unusual for hourly maintenance costs to be expressed per flight-hour. In this case a conversion factor – perhaps based on the experience of the carrier concerned with regard to taxi-times at the particular airports it serves – may need to be applied in order to integrate hourly maintenance cost figures into aggregate hourly DOC figures.)

Ownership costs

Although detailed practices with regard to accounting for leases and owned aircraft vary depending upon generally accepted accounting principles (GAAP) in each airline's home jurisdiction, and will also in many cases be influenced by tax considerations, the following generalisations can be made.

1. **Operating lease rentals** When an airline takes an aircraft on a true operating lease it has use of that aircraft for a relatively small proportion of its economic life, and therefore does not have an economic interest in it beyond current operational use. Operating lease rentals are charged in full as an operating cost on an airline's income statement. (They are in fact fixed DOCs.) The value of the aircraft does not appear on the airline's balance sheet, so depreciation is *not* chargeable.

2. **Economic ownership** When an airline owns an aircraft, or is deemed to have an economic interest in it equivalent in effect to bearing the risks and rewards of ownership, the ownership costs break down as follows.

   - Depreciation is charged as an operating expense (again, a fixed DOC). Within the parameters established by applicable GAAP, an airline can influence depreciation charges by: choice of method (e.g., straight line, declining balance, etc.); choice of depreciation period (with a shorter period front-loading the charges and perhaps reducing near-term taxable income, and so having beneficial cash-flow effects by deferring the payment of tax); and by adjusting assumed residual value (with a smaller residual value increasing depreciation charges over any given number of years). Generally, new narrowbodies are written down to approximately ten per cent over ten or more years, whereas widebodies are commonly depreciated to 10–15 per cent over 15 years or longer; however, policies vary between carriers, depending upon tax issues and the extent to which it is thought desirable to build-up equity in owned aircraft by depreciating them for accounting purposes more rapidly than their cash secondary market value is falling.

   - Interest, whether attributable to debt from general corporate borrowing or from a specific aircraft-related transaction, is not an operating expense but is charged as a nonoperating item.

328 *Straight and Level: Practical Airline Economics*

Operating leases reduce operating income, but in most countries do not appear on an airline's balance sheet. Owned aircraft reduce both operating and nonoperating income (through depreciation and interest respectively), and do appear (net of depreciation) on the balance sheet; because it is a noncash item, adding back the annual depreciation charge to operating income can be a significant 'source' of cash flow in a capital-intensive business such as an airline.

3. **Insurance costs** The principal types of coverage are hull, war risks and allied perils, third-party liability, and passenger liability. Unsurprisingly, the availability of war risks and allied perils coverage was withdrawn subject to the standard seven-day notice period in the immediate aftermath of 9/11, and the costs of all forms of cover spiralled; industry premiums of around $1.25 billion in 2001 more than tripled the following year.

Other input costs

Amongst the many considerations in this catch-all category, we will highlight just two.

Security costs The events of 9/11 imposed heavy additional security costs. At the time of writing it remains to be seen how security requirements will evolve and how the costs of meeting them will be apportioned between passengers, airlines, airports, and governments. The one certainty is that airlines as a whole can expect to spend more rather than less on security in future.

   Even where in principle a security charge is intended to fall ultimately on passengers, the question arises as to whether airlines have sufficient pricing power to pass-on the charge. For example, US carriers as a whole had insufficient pricing power to pass-on a $2.50 per segment security tax imposed by the federal government in late 2001; in the case of Delta, the impact of this tax was a quarter-billion dollar charge to the income statement over 12 months. More generally, even where an airline is able to pass security charges and other government-imposed taxes and levies through to passengers, there could well be an effect on demand – depending upon the price-elasticity of the markets concerned. In late 2002 testimony to Congress, American's CEO noted that a $200 fare for a round-trip journey involving one connection included a 26 per cent ($51.16) tax and fee burden (*Aviation Week & Space Technology*, September 30, 2002: 48).

Administration costs With their lean, flexible, non-bureaucratic structures, both established low-fare carriers and start-ups can be expected to have lower administrative costs (i.e., lower administration cost per ASM or ATM) than full-service airlines with long histories behind them. The latter are often weighed down by inherited overhead, as well as by the complexity of their operations.

Scale

We have already looked at several categories of cost driver: design and functioning of the operating system (encompassing the supply chain, internal operations, and distribution); and input costs (focusing in particular on labour, fuel, airport and ATS charges, maintenance costs, and ownership costs). This section looks at the effect of scale as a cost driver. It starts by addressing the question of growth, and then goes on to define economies of scale and comment on their role in the industry.

Growth

Despite periodic cyclical downturns and the more serious recessions beginning in 1991 and 2001, the airline industry has since World War 2 been a growth industry insofar as both its revenues and traffic have regularly risen by multiples of the growth in global GDP.

The attraction of growth Putting aside what economists refer to as 'agency problems' that arise when airline managers (i.e., 'agents') pursue their own interests at the expense of stockholders (i.e., their 'principals') by pursuing empire-building strategies that fail to create shareholder value, it has been widely assumed in the industry that growth offers several advantages:

- new routes or additional frequencies can stimulate demand;
- passengers prefer nonstop, through-plane, and connecting single-carrier service in that order and prefer same-airline routings, so an extensive network will have broader appeal than a geographically limited route system – an appeal enhanced by FFPs;
- incremental output can be used to discourage or eliminate competitors on a route (although egregious 'capacity dumping' might come under the scrutiny of antitrust/competition authorities in some jurisdictions);
- size can bring powerful benefits at a fortress hub and, more generally, a large carrier is often in a strong position to exercise price leadership in at least some of its markets;

- size should be accompanied by wider brand recognition;
- serving a broad spread of markets can permit cross-subsidisation (although whether this is economically justified is another matter).

It is noticeable that whilst this subsection began by referring to size in terms of traffic and revenue, some of the advantages listed above have more to do with size measured in output terms (i.e., ASMs and ATMs). This leads to a critical caveat surrounding growth that, most notably before the 1990s, has sometimes been overlooked by airline managements.

The caveat Output expansion that is not paced by demand growth will place downward pressure on yields and/or load factors. New capacity comes with fixed costs attached, as we have already seen, so the output it generates not only has to be sold but sold at prices sufficient to more than cover those incremental costs. Having unit production costs that are low relative to those of competitors is only half the battle; the other half is having production costs that are also low relative to the prices at which output can be sold.

One of the attractions of growth in the industry has nonetheless been that in principle it provides an opportunity to average down costs by adding incremental output at a cost lower than the current unit cost. The notion that it is possible to grow out of cost difficulties by averaging down unit costs had a compelling hold on parts of the industry during the 1980s in particular – notably amongst the US 'Big Three'.

This brings us to the question of whether or not economies of scale are present in the airline industry. But before addressing this question we will look briefly at two different but compatible perspectives on economies of scale that are relevant to the discussion: the resource-based perspective and what we might call the 'activity perspective'.

Economies of scale and the resource-based theory of competitive advantage In the neoclassical tradition, the view is that economies of scale are an industry-level phenomenon: there is one 'efficiency frontier' in an industry because all firms share the same production function, and as firms grow they move along this efficiency frontier. Any firm producing at minimum efficient scale (MES) has a unit cost advantage over firms with smaller market shares producing output at sub-optimal levels, or over those producing at greater than optimal scale (and therefore suffering diseconomies). There are two questions: How close to optimum is each firm producing? How many firms producing at optimum output can the industry's demand curve sustain (assuming a profit-maximising equilibrium price)?

Taking a resource-based view of the firm, however, it is possible to argue that because each firm is comprised of a heterogeneous bundle of resources of different type, amount, and quality there is no single production function common to the industry as a whole and therefore no shared efficiency frontier. Instead, each firm has its own efficiency frontier along which it moves as output increases. In other words, firms in the same industry differ significantly from each other in respect of the economies of scale available to them. There are in this view several more questions to be addressed.

1. How close to its own optimum scale, given its unique resource set/ production function, is a firm producing output?
2. What are the relative unit cost implications of each firm's optimum output level – that is, is one firm's optimum output level more cost-efficient than those of competing firms? A firm that has a production function offering greater economies of scale will tend to increase market share because it gains more from increasing size.
3. What are the price implications of all firms producing at their different optimum output levels given the industry's demand curve?
4. How long will advantages derived from firm-specific economies of scale survive before competitors succeed in matching them?

Economies of scale in activities The neoclassical tradition treats firms as 'black boxes' and gives little attention to what happens inside them. But taking a resource-based perspective we can see output as the product of a variety of different activities within a firm, each of which will have different economic characteristics – specifically, different cost drivers and different propensities to exhibit economies of scale. In other words, economies of scale in respect of flight operations (e.g., arising from the size of fleet or number of ASMs produced) will have a very different meaning from economies of scale in maintenance (e.g., arising from size of facilities and bookable man-hours), in call centres, in marketing communications, in the handling of aircraft, passengers, and cargo, and so on throughout other areas of an airline. Assuming MES can be identified, an airline might achieve it in some activities but not in others; one argument in favour of outsourcing, of course, is to access the economies of scale available to large suppliers of maintenance, catering, ground-handling and other services that an airline might not be sufficiently large (in general or at a particular station) to build for itself.

Economies of scale in the airline industry

The presence or absence of economies of scale in the industry has been a hotly debated issue. Early empirical evidence (e.g., Caves (1962) in respect of a regulated market and Levine (1965) in respect of a deregulated market) surfaced doubts about their existence, and this argument was used by the pro-deregulation lobby in the United States to dispel fears regarding the likelihood of consolidation in pursuit of MES. Early post-deregulation studies by Caves et al (1984) and Gillen et al (1985) tended to confirm the absence of economies of scale in the US industry insofar as long-run average costs do not necessarily fall as output of ASMs and ATMs is expanded. However, subsequent studies (e.g., Creel and Farrell, 2001) have found contrary evidence.

Size undoubtedly matters. There are activities in respect of which economies of scale are present – some of which have already been noted: maintenance, catering, ground-handling, etc. There are also economies of scale in flight operations insofar as operating just a handful of a type is usually more expensive in terms of maintenance provisioning and crew training and utilisation than having a more significant fleet. To complicate matters further, there are other activities in respect of which economies are clearly available but it is debatable whether these are economies of scale, scope, or general market presence. (Bear in mind that economies of scale are present when unit costs decline as output of a given product increases, whereas economies of scope are present when unit costs decline as the range of products being produced is increased. Given that there is considerable debate surrounding how to characterise the airline 'product' – by departure, by cabin, or by fare class, for example – it can be seen that drawing a definitional line between economies of scale and scope is difficult as well, perhaps, as somewhat artificial.)

If we look at marketing communications, for example, there is little doubt that a sizeable carrier benefiting from significant brand awareness in its markets and a wide network of routes is likely to reach more potential travellers with any single advertising, PR or promotional initiative than, at the other extreme, a single-route start-up. Advertising economies of scale can arise in media buying (assuming that this is not outsourced) if, for example, an airline's purchasing power is sufficient to negotiate lower rates than a small competitor can arrange. Other economies in advertising, however, could be characterised as either economies of scale or scope.

1. First, larger airlines might be able to spread the inevitable fixed costs associated with any campaign over a more numerous target audience

and so generate a lower unit cost per potential exposure. The same applies to alliance partners choosing to work together on a campaign.

2. Second, if we assume that two campaigns launched by different airlines
    stimulate enquiries from exactly the same number of customers, the
    larger carrier will in all probability be able to serve more of them be-
    cause of its wider network scope and/or deeper schedule. If British
    Airways launches a broad national campaign in the UK and reaches the
    same number of people as a similar campaign from easyJet, the for-
    mer's more extensive geographic and product scope imply that it will
    be offering services that more of these people want to buy.

Finally, as alluded to above, another benefit of size is bargaining strength
vis à vis external suppliers. This, again, is something that technically speaking might or might not be characterised as an economy of scale.

If we look at an airline as a bundle of resources and activities, there is
little doubt that scale, scope, and general size can have a beneficial impact
on unit costs. If, on the other hand, we insist on applying the blunt weapon
that is the neoclassical concept of industry-level economies of scale, we
inevitably come unstuck on the fact that there seems to be no direct correlation between ASMs or ATMs produced and average cost; if there were,
United would have lower costs than Southwest. The following sub-sections
examine some of the complicating factors.

The nature of airline output There are two immediate problems when trying to use raw output figures as a metric against which to compare unit
costs.

1. **Different means of production** A figure of, say, 150,000 ASMs could
    be generated by flying 150 seats for 1,000 miles, 250 seats for 600
    miles, 400 seats for 375 miles, and so on; similarly, 150 seats flown
    1,000 miles could be carried on one 150-seat aircraft, two 75-seat air-
    craft, three 50-seat aircraft, and so on. The economics of generating
    150,000 ASMs of output will be very different in each case and will
    clearly produce very different costs. Decisions will be driven by mark-
    eting as well as cost considerations. For our present purposes the point
    to take from this is that the neoclassical assumption of raw output
    flowing from homogeneous production processes is too simplistic
    given the nature of the airline industry.

2. **Different types of output** Just as production processes are not homo-
    geneous, neither is output. We touched upon one source of hetero-
    geneity above: service frequency. As we saw in chapter 4, there are
    others. ASMs produced by Southwest or Ryanair are not the same as

ASMs produced in American's Flagship Suite – and neither, evidently, are their production costs. Airlines are simply not the homogeneous black boxes with common production functions producing homogeneous output that neoclassical theory would have us believe.

Differences between airlines If we delve into the 'black boxes' of airline production functions, we can see several other differences that are likely to distort comparisons between carriers that try to relate each other's output to unit costs.

1. As noted above, different fleet or network structures inevitably mean that one airline's cost of producing an ASM is seldom precisely the same as another's, and if it is we are dealing with coincidence given the fundamentally different economics of operating different aircraft (e.g., different types, capacities, and ages) over different networks (e.g., different stage-lengths and traffic densities).
2. We have also seen that airlines produce different types and/or mixes of output. At the extremes, services designed to satisfy the expectations of short-haul business travellers are clearly going to be more expensive to produce than medium- or long-haul charter services targeted at the leisure segment.
3. Airlines face different input costs (particularly fuel, airport, and ATS charges) depending upon the scope of their network and, particularly, costs at their hubs and other principal centres of operations.
4. Airlines also differ markedly in their levels of productivity. Some carriers make every unit of expenditure work harder than others, therefore needing less expenditure to pay for a given level of output. (Different regulatory environments can also affect productivity, notably with regard to flight-crew duty-times.)
5. International comparisons are inevitably complicated by currency volatility. Exchange rates can also impact heavily on carriers whose networks give them no or limited sources of dollar revenue with which to meet fuel bills – which are fundamentally dollar-denominated.

Conclusion To the extent that it is rarely twice as expensive to operate two flights as it is to operate one, economies of scale do indeed exist in the industry. However, as far as flight operations are concerned they appear to be limited to a relatively low threshold. Larger economies seem to be derived less from the operation of aircraft themselves than from activities elsewhere in the operating system. Airlines are widely believed to benefit from marketing economies of scale, although there is a semantic question about whether unit cost advantages derived from this source are not in fact economies of scope or perhaps even more general effects of size and market presence. Purchasing economies might also be attributed to either economies of scale or economies of scope.

The competitive implications of economies of scale

We saw in chapter 4 that economies of scale can be a barrier to entry. It is no coincidence that start-up carriers seldom launch complex hubs with large fleets of owned aircraft supported by extensive maintenance facilities; these require heavy capital expenditures that are difficult to fund, and they bear significant fixed costs that a start-up would have insufficient output to absorb (and probably insufficient cash to meet). To go down this route could leave a start-up with a severe unit cost disadvantage.

Instead, start-ups target niches – usually price-elastic point-to-point markets – and outsource potentially capital-intensive activities such as aircraft maintenance. There are exceptions. Emirates, for example, set out to build a sixth-freedom hub at Dubai and to create local aviation-related jobs in areas such as aircraft maintenance; but these are not the rule. It is also true that over time start-ups can grow to the point where they are able to benefit from economies of scale in respect of a wider range of activities; even so, few – particularly amongst low-fare entrants – have yet shown any inclination to take on the fixed costs associated with activities they evidently consider peripheral to the core activities of selling and flying.

Learning

We have seen that economies of scale relate to unit cost declines associated with rising output. A similar but quite distinct phenomenon is 'learning', which is evident when unit cost declines are associated not with single-period increases in output but with cumulative output over time. (Some writers distinguish between 'learning curves', which result from improved human task efficiency, and 'experience curves' that are derived from improved machine efficiency; others use 'experience curves' as the generic umbrella for output-related unit cost declines attributable to human learning and machine efficiency.)

Although any form of human activity should benefit from learning over time, the unit cost advantage of the phenomenon is perhaps more strongly evident in mass production manufacturing industries than in service businesses; indeed, the importance of learning underpinned pursuit of market share and use of tools such as the Boston Box in many manufacturing industries from the late 1960s through the 1980s. That said, there are undoubtedly learning advantages available in areas such as maintenance (Kline, 1999), scheduling, and operations control – although outsourcing can allow relatively new carriers to benefit from the experience of long-established suppliers. It is on the demand side rather than in respect of output that learning may have its most profound effect, however; incumbents with a long market presence should have access to both a broader and a deeper understanding of customers' expectations (Button and Stough, 2000). Customer insight is not always accessed and leveraged, of course.

Summary

This section of the chapter has looked at several categories of cost driver: design and functioning of the operating system; input costs; scale; and finally learning. Table 5.1 illustrates how airline operating costs can be broken down on a line item basis, following the type of reporting structure commonly used in published financial accounts.

It is not enough to identify cost drivers, however; they need to be actively managed.

iv. Cost management

There are two fundamental aspects to cost management:

- first, an airline ought not to be incurring any costs other than those that are essential to the delivery of services as designed to the markets and segment(s) being targeted;
- second, underlying forces which drive the costs necessarily incurred must be understood and, wherever possible, actively managed.

The essence of cost management is to ensure that customers get what they want and are prepared to pay for, and that airlines spend as little as possible providing it to them at a level *consistent with specified quality standards*. Considered in this way, cost management can be a formidable competitive weapon.

Cost management is no easy task, however. To remove just half a cent per ASM from Alaska's unit cost in 2000 would have required knocking $86.5 million off its $1.8 billion TOC figure (i.e., half a cent x number of ASMs performed); $86.5 million was equivalent to the carrier's entire 'depreciation and amortization' line item for the year, and well in excess of

ITEM	Cost structure per ASM (cents)		Difference (cents)	%
	US Airways	Southwest		
Labour and benefits	5.08	2.81	2.27	80.8
Lease and depreciation	1.65	1.02	0.63	61.8
Fuel	1.69	1.38	0.31	22.5
Maintenance materials and outside repairs	0.71	0.65	0.06	9.2
Landing fees and outside services	1.19	0.67	0.52	77.6
Marketing, commissions and food	1.20	0.63	0.57	90.5
Other	0.89	0.53	0.36	67.9
TOTAL	**12.41**	**7.69**	**4.72**	**61.4**

Table 5.1 A line item comparison of US Airways' and Southwest's operating cost structures per ASM in 2000
Source: Morten Beyer & Agnew (*The International Aviation Oracle*, 8, 9, September 2001, p.3).

line items such as 'landing fees and other rentals', 'commissions', and 'food and beverage service'.

This section of the chapter will look first at cost escapability, and then at the thrust of recent airline cost management efforts.

Cost escapability

Costs are the outcome of resource allocation decisions. In the airline business we can think in terms of four levels of decision-making.

1. **Industry entry decisions** A decision to enter the airline industry will entail establishment of a corporate infrastructure which generates general and administrative overheads.
2. **Network design, scheduling, and other product decisions** These generate fixed fleet, crew, maintenance, and station costs, as well as a marketing and service delivery infrastructure carrying its own overhead burden.
3. **Flight-related decisions** Any decision to operate a flight, whether in accordance with a schedule or not, leads to expenditures which are usually classified as variable DOCs. Notable amongst them are fuel, ATS, airport, handling (passenger and ramp), and variable crew and maintenance costs.
4. **Passenger-related decisions** Acceptance of each individual passenger onto a flight with seats available will give rise to costs such as travel agency commission, GDS fees, ticketing, food, and marginal fuel-burn.

Costs are 'escapable' at each level to the extent that they can be avoided by taking an alternative decision: not to form an airline; not to fly the chosen network or schedule; not to operate a particular flight; and not to carry an individual passenger. However, we saw earlier in the chapter that a high proportion of an airline's costs will inevitably be fixed in the short run. Just how escapable costs are in any particular case will depend upon the time-frame under consideration and the cost structure of the airline concerned – specifically, the proportion of total costs that can be considered fixed over the time-frame in question. For example, when Continental announced a 20 per cent cut in its schedule immediately after 9/11, its CEO admitted that TOCs would only drop by ten per cent as a result. Furthermore, when a flight or a route is cut, variable costs will be saved immediately but fixed costs that cannot also be cut right away have to be spread over less output – and this can put upward pressure on unit costs until such time as fixed costs can also be pared. Full-service network carriers offering products that are expensive to produce from complex hubs and carrying significant corporate infrastructures will inevitably be faced with a lower proportion of total costs that can realistically be considered escapable in the short run than will a small competitor offering a no-frills product over a point-to-point network and outsourcing many of its activities.

Managing cost drivers

Grant (1998) has suggested the following approach to value chain analysis of a firm's cost position.

1. Disaggregate the firm into separate activities.
2. Establish the relative importance of each activity to total cost at different output levels. Benchmark costs by activity.
3. Identify each activity's cost drivers. Following Riley (1987), Shank (1989) identifies two categories of cost driver.
   - *Structural drivers* These are attributable to historical and current strategic choices made by management, and include variables such as scale, scope, experience, choice of technology and process, complexity in the range and nature of services offered, and organizational structure.
   - *Executional drivers* These are determinants of a carrier's cost position driven by how efficiently and effectively it is able to manage processes. They include metrics which in some cases are not easy to analyse objectively and are certainly not likely to appear in traditional management accounts – such as workforce commitment, service quality (as in 'cost of quality' analysis), the efficiency of service delivery processes, the effectiveness of brand management efforts, and the management of relationships with customers and suppliers. Some metrics, such as capacity utilisation, can be objectively measured, however.

   The important point to take from this distinction is that raw output is a critical cost driver, but only at an operational level. Strategic decisions regarding the position an airline chooses to occupy in its markets and the type(s) of value its operating system is designed to offer customers are also critical cost drivers – if pursued consistently across the entire range of a carrier's activities.
4. Identify linkages through which the costs of one activity are influenced by the performance of other activities.
5. Identify opportunities for reducing costs – by lowering input costs and/ or improving productivity in respect of key cost drivers, and by impr-

oving both internal and external activity linkages. In some cases, processes might need to be re-engineered and entire businesses restructured.

Following the value chain metaphor adopted earlier in the chapter, the next three subsections will look briefly at cost management efforts being made with regard to: the supply chain; input costs and productivity; and distribution. Process re-engineering and business restructuring will then be considered.

Supply chain management

Current trends in the management of supplier relationships include the following.

1. Centralisation of purchasing to concentrate bargaining power, together with the increased use of consortium purchasing by affiliated carriers and alliance partners (e.g., AirLiance Materials owned jointly by United, Lufthansa, and Air Canada). Consortium purchasing might extend beyond alliances (e.g., the joint purchase of A320 series aircraft by LanChile, TACA, and TAM), and may also extend outside the airline industry in respect of non-aviation supplies. Joint procurement by alliance partners is not always as easy to orchestrate as press releases might suggest, however; sometimes there is a quality issue, and sometimes there is a question of longstanding relationships between member airlines and different suppliers. Neither Aer Lingus nor American availed themselves of **one**world's centralised renegotiation of Frankfurt Airport handling contracts in 2000, for example.
2. The exertion of constant pressure on suppliers to stabilise or reduce costs. Costs of individual purchased items are no longer the sole criterion; more important is total cost within the entire supply chain – including administration, transportation, insurance, and inventory costs.
3. A growing willingness to use innovative approaches such as spares leasing, 'power-by-the-hour' engine leasing or membership of business services swap organizations.
4. Closer attention to suppliers' quality, innovation, customer orientation, and delivery reliability, and a willingness to benchmark supplier performance.
5. Efforts to reduce each carrier's total number of suppliers. At the time of writing, British Airways has a project underway to cut its 8,000-strong supplier base to 2,000 and then build closer relationships with around 150 'partners'. There are two issues here, however. On the one hand, global airlines want global suppliers, and in some supplier industries

(e.g., flight catering) that is what to a still highly circumscribed extent they are beginning to get. On the other hand, large carriers have so many 'production sites' that they are often compelled by circumstances to retain a greater number of vendors than they would ideally want.

6. Willingness to consider long-term, single-source contracts based on relationships with suppliers which – whether correctly or not – are popularly characterised as being driven more by the dynamics of partnership than by traditional vendor-customer relationships. From the airlines' perspectives, cost transparency and predictability are important motivations alongside quality improvement issues. These arrangements require a new set of management skills, many of which are strategic in nature rather than purely transactional.

7. The growth of electronic (B2B) commerce, the primary attractions of which are acceleration of transaction speeds and the stripping out of both inventory and manual processing costs.

Input costs and productivity

Unit costs are influenced by the absolute level of input costs, and by the productivity of inputs used (e.g., ASMs produced per employee). If productivity is rising, it is quite possible for unit costs to decline irrespective of changes in absolute costs. High productivity can go some way towards countering the adverse impact of high input costs, but the ideal is clearly to combine as far as possible both high productivity and low input costs. With the industry's real yields continuing their secular decline in response to increasing competition, the ability to manage input costs and ensure that the resources they buy are used as productively as possible is a critical management discipline.

Input costs Much of the scope for input cost reduction has already been made clear by descriptions of principal cost drivers earlier in the chapter. The following paragraphs provide a short summary of approaches that have been adopted in respect of four critical input costs: labour, fuel, airport charges, and maintenance inventory.

1. **Labour costs** Often cited, somewhat simplistically, as any airline's largest 'controllable cost' – overlooking the impact of unionisation in many countries, the importance to customer service of strong staff morale, and the fact that it is often the youngest, cheapest staff who get laid-off – labour costs are nonetheless usually the first line item to come under scrutiny when times are tough. This is inevitable given that they constitute such high proportions of most airlines' TOCs.

Labour costs can be cut by one or both of a reduction in staff numbers or a reduction in remuneration. Research by Alamdari and Morrell (1998) found that US carriers have shown a greater willingness to cut remuneration (sometimes in return for stock) than European carriers, and that both – but particularly European airlines – have relied heavily on productivity gains in preference to reducing raw labour cost per employee. Some European majors have resisted reductions in staff numbers as a matter of policy, although reductions did occur during the industry recessions that began in 1991 and 2001; US carriers have in general shown more widespread willingness to cut and furlough staff. Elsewhere in the world the picture is mixed, but one broad generalisation is that several Asian airlines have suffered from labour cost inflation since the early 1990s to such an extent that their longstanding cost advantage against carriers from other regions – an advantage which in some cases masked inefficient processes and organizational structures – has been somewhat eroded (Oum and Yu, 2000).

In regulated environments there is limited incentive to keep a tight grip on labour costs because the risk of industrial action is not worth running when costs can readily be passed on to consumers or to government shareholders. This is a major reason why many established airlines entered the post-deregulation era with staff who were overpaid relative to similarly skilled labour groups elsewhere in their economies. That managements still had a propensity to cave-in to union demands as late as 2000 is evidenced by the United pilots' contract that year. Box 5.9 explores the issue further.

Box 5.9: Managing labour costs

There are two considerations in particular that complicate management of airline labour costs.

- *Unionisation On the whole, this is a highly unionised industry populated by groups of specialists, any one of which can close down an airline. When a carrier is grounded, revenue dries-up instantly whilst high fixed costs associated with corporate overhead, aircraft ownership, and stations (e.g., space rentals) burn into cash reserves at a ferocious pace. For this reason, airline managements – with one or two notable, not to say 'infamous', exceptions – have shown a tendency to accede to potentially expensive labour settlements rather than risk shutting down their businesses. Even when strikes have occurred, it has not been unusual for labour to emerge with a favourable settlement. During economic downturns staff reductions and salary freezes or give-backs are widespread, but during upturns the pendulum swings strongly in favour of labour.*

- *Service* Airlines are service businesses, and there is a stream of research in the services management literature that draws explicit linkages between employee satisfaction on the one hand and both customer satisfaction and corporate profits on the other (Heskett et al, 1997; see also Holloway, 2002). Whilst some carriers have a culture and management style that seem to enable them to keep employee satisfaction high and unit costs under firm control (the connection between the two often being high productivity – as in the case of Southwest), many others have a history of combative labour-management relations that inevitably feed through into employee and customer dissatisfaction.

2. **Fuel** Although an increasingly fuel-efficient global fleet has helped since the mid-1980s to make fuel a less significant element in TOCs than was once the case, its price volatility in response to both supply/demand shifts and political events make it a challenging input to manage. Steps taken include the following.

    - *Hedging* For an airline not to hedge or to hedge only partially its fuel requirements is in fact to run a speculative short position. Nonetheless, not every airline chooses to hedge, and even those that do can face challenges: first, it is sometimes crude rather than jet fuel that is hedged, and the price spread between the two may be sufficiently large that even what appears to be a fully hedged position is not; second, less creditworthy airlines might have trouble locating a counterparty for long-term hedges, and any airline may have to cash-collateralise a hedging programme – something that can be a problem for a carrier with poor liquidity; third, a carrier which fully hedges and then subsequently reduces output to well below projections will be left paying for more fuel than required (and then having to resell that surplus on the spot market – perhaps at a lower price).

    - *Purchasing* Some carriers band together to increase their bargaining power by making consortium purchases (although not necessarily within the structure of the broader global alliances). The Internet is increasingly being used to reduce transaction costs, as are software tools which facilitate purchasing, inventory tracking, invoicing, and contract administration.

    - *Operational practices* There is a long list of potential fuel-saving measures available, including: reductions in aircraft empty weight by cleaning, being attentive to the weight of cabin fittings, and perhaps also implementing explicit weight reduction programmes dur-

344 Straight and Level: Practical Airline Economics

ing heavy checks; being attentive to dents and other surface irregularities that can increase airframe drag; stipulating, and by monitoring quick-access data recorders enforcing, economical take-off, initial climb, step-climb, cruise, and descent procedures and usage of reverse thrust (e.g., de-rated take-off and climb, and quick cut-back and clean-up after take-off); selection of suitable alternates to minimise carriage of reserve fuel; use of economic tankering programmes to provide flight-crew with real-time guidance about optimum purchase locations on short-haul rotations; appropriate use of en route redespatch via an intermediate point on long-haul flights to reduce fuel reserves relative to those required for preflight despatch straight through to the final destination; optimising medium- and long-haul routings consistent with day-of-operation weather; monitoring actual fuel-over-destination (FOD) levels to minimise carriage of unnecessary fuel that adds weight and, on long-haul legs, might displace cargo; flying direct routings and visual approaches whenever possible; use of the minimum number of engines for taxiing-in; use of ground power units rather than APUs where possible; monitoring fleet performance to identify individual tail-numbers recording above-average fuel-burn; and regular checking of instrument accuracy (because an under-reading mach-meter will lead to an aircraft being flown faster, and therefore consuming more fuel in the cruise, than intended).

3. **Airport charges** We have already noted that many low-fare airlines gain at least some of their cost advantage over full-service network carriers by flying, wherever possible, to secondary airports that have fewer congestion problems than major hubs and therefore contribute to lower taxi and holding delays and faster turnaround times. These airports also tend to charge lower fees and are in many cases sufficiently keen to attract business that they offer attractive long-term deals.

4. **Maintenance inventory** There is reckoned to be a spares inventory of approximately $35–40 billion worldwide – enough to support over three years of operations. Although a conscious trade-off between despatch reliability and investment in spares (both in an absolute sense and in terms of the stations to which they are distributed) can be an important influence on inventory levels and therefore inventory costs, it is now widely recognised that there are too many spares in the pipeline and airlines have taken steps to address the problem.

   - Some steps taken have acted more to push responsibility for inventory back up the supply chain than to reduce it. These include: sale of surplus inventory; sale-and-leaseback of high-value rotables; sale of entire inventories to parts dealers subject to a long-term inventory management and supply contract; taking inventory either on consignment (i.e., where the supplier retains ownership until use) or on an Internet-enabled just-in-time basis from dispersed supplier inventory hubs; rotables leasing; and flight-hour-driven maintenance agreements.

- Other steps have been taken that in the long run should strip inventory out of the system. These include the reduction of OEM catalogue lead times, and the shortening of repair and overhaul times to put repairables and rotables back into 'live' inventory more quickly; the benefit in the latter case is that items in live inventory can support the fleet whereas items in a shop cannot, so the less time they spend in a shop the fewer of them will be required overall to provide the desired level of support. Some large carriers are allowing other airlines to access their inventories in return for a fixed fee per calendar period or per flight-hour. Finally, a longstanding technique used throughout the industry is spares pooling; the International Airline Technical Pool has been in existence since 1949, and more recently individual groupings of airlines have come together to form inventory pools at outstations.

Productivity Dresner (2002) distinguishes between several different types of measure commonly used to assess airline productivity.

1. **Partial productivity metrics** These include the following.
   - *Labour productivity* e.g., ASMs, ATMs, RSMs, or RTMs per employee.
   - *Flight equipment productivity* e.g., block-hours per day, flight-hours per annum.
   - *Other partial productivity measures* e.g., output per gallon of fuel.
   Although simple to calculate and widely used, partial productivity measures suffer from the fact that they make no allowance for economically rational trade-offs that might be made between different types of input – such as using more labour and less automation (i.e., capital) in a low labour cost but capital-constrained environment.
2. **Gross measures of total productivity** These include the following.
   - *Total factor productivity* This measures total output produced per unit of (total) input. (Morrell (2002a) provides an illustration of how total factor productivity can be calculated.)
   - *Data envelopment analysis* A linear programming technique, this was originally developed as an efficiency metric designed to compare actual inputs and outputs against benchmark criteria est-

ablished by calculating maximum output given a level and mix of inputs (or minimum inputs given a desired level of output). Although theoretically more comprehensive than partial productivity metrics, gross measures of productivity are not without their problems (ibid). First, they are complex to calculate. Second, it is particularly difficult to place an accurate value on input capital. Third, in common with partial productivity metrics they do not take into account the impact on productivity of different operating system structures – notably average stage-length (with short average stage-lengths adversely affecting both labour and aircraft productivity).

3. **Statistical decomposition approach** This attempts to control for carriers' different characteristics – generally by regressing gross productivity scores on variables such as average stage-length, traffic density, various measures of corporate scale, and so on (op cit). Its disadvantage lies in computational complexity (at least relative to partial productivity measures).

Dresner (op cit) concludes that although gross measures and statistical approaches are more comprehensive in their assessment of productivity and the latter in particular should be preferred for inter-firm comparisons, their complexity makes it likely that simpler partial productivity measures will continue in widespread use. He therefore draws attention to studies by Windle and Dresner (1992, 1995) which suggest that RTK and RPK per employee are the partial productivity measures most highly correlated with total factor productivity.

More generally, we have already stressed the importance of getting as much output as possible from airline resources and noted that the nature of the output (i.e., design of the product) and the structure of the operating system delivering it (i.e., network, fleet, and processes) have a profound impact on just what is possible. Steps taken to increase the productivity of aircraft have been mentioned – steps such as accelerating turnaround times and optimising both network design and scheduling. Efforts to improve staff productivity include: outsourcing; the wider use of part-time and seasonal employees; more flexible work-rules and staff multi-skilling (where allowed by union contracts); greater automation of processes (especially back-office processes such as routine purchasing and spares inventory handling, for example); wider use of scheduling models to help assign staff in response to actual requirements (e.g., assignment of check-in staff on the basis of queuing models combining service level requirements and day-of-operation flight loadings, assignment of cabin crews in response to bookings, assignment of baggage handlers in response to projected volumes of loose-loaded baggage on incoming narrowbodies); and having customers participate more actively in service delivery (e.g., Internet booking, self-service check-ins, smart-card airport facilitation). Some carriers targeting high-yield segments have also invested in improved staff training, arguing that consistently high service standards reduce the time that would otherwise be spent on service recovery and so raise productivity. Box 5.10 considers labour productivity.

Box 5.10: Labour productivity

It is often not so much absolute salaries, benefits, and social charges as labour productivity that underlies differences between airlines in respect of unit labour costs (i.e., labour costs per ASM or ATM). Southwest does not on the whole pay its people notably less than other US majors, but their high productivity means that it needs fewer employees to deliver a given volume (and type) of output than would be the case were productivity levels more in line with those of its competitors. Similarly, it is not so much high absolute costs as their relatively low productivity that makes the staff of several European majors more expensive than counterparts at many of the larger US and, particularly, Asian carriers (Hanlon, 1999).

Labour productivity largely depends upon the following.

- *Hours worked per annum.*
- *The efficiency of work processes.*
- *The structure of each particular airline's operations. Some productivity measures – notably the widely favoured ASM or ATM per employee metrics – respond positively to larger aircraft, longer stage-lengths, and scheduling for high frequencies. Large aircraft do not require proportionately more staff to schedule, despatch, operate, and maintain than smaller aircraft; long stage-lengths operated by large aircraft generate more ASMs and ATMs per despatch than short flight-legs operated by small aircraft; high frequencies in principle provide better opportunities to optimise aircraft, crew, and station personnel than low-frequency operations (Doganis, 2001). With regard to productivity expressed in ATMs per employee, carriers generating significant freight revenues tend to benefit from the fact that selling space and handling freight are less labour-intensive than similar operations on the passenger side (ibid).*
- *The extent of outsourcing. Retaining inhouse functions such as catering, maintenance, IT, and ground-handling has little or no bearing on airline output, but does have a significant impact on staff numbers and therefore staff productivity.*

Traditional measures such as ASMs or ATMs per employee or per dollar of labour cost are important, but perhaps less telling than revenue earned per employee or per dollar of labour cost. The latter connect labour cost to the revenue side rather than to another metric (i.e., ASMs or ATMs) on the cost side.

Particularly where directly competing airlines pay broadly the same for their inputs (i.e., labour, fuel, insurance, aircraft, ATS, etc.), any sustainable competitive advantage held by one carrier in respect of unit costs is likely to be attributable to higher input productivity. Important potential sources of higher productivity include labour flexibility (with roots in labour agreements and/or corporate culture) and efficient design of the operating system (i.e., fleet and network structures, resource assignments, processes and activities).

Controlling distribution costs

Particularly since the mid-1990s, airlines have successfully used a broad range of approaches to bring spiralling distribution costs under control.

1. **Commission caps** The traditional agency commission system is fundamentally flawed inasmuch as it is driven by airfares rather than by the amount of work associated with each transaction. Commissions payable to bricks-and-mortar agencies began to come under sustained attack in 1994 when Delta first capped them. Commission capping and reduction have since spread beyond the United States, and both caps and commission rates have been ratcheted down. Commissions payable to Internet agencies have also come under pressure, with some airlines now refusing to pay.

   In 2002, Delta led a further assault on distribution expenses by eliminating base commissions on tickets sold in the United States and Canada. Agency remuneration would henceforth be driven by incentive agreements negotiated with each agency; in other words, incentives that had previously been treated as commission *overrides* were to replace commissions themselves at the heart of sales remuneration.

2. **Transforming the role of agencies** Although their revenues are under pressure and this is leading to consolidation within the industry in some countries, travel agencies will remain important distribution channels for most categories of scheduled airline – notably full-service network carriers. But their role is changing in three important respects.

   - Survivors will have to deliver value-added services to their clients (e.g., corporate travel management services, assembly of leisure travel packages). The trend that has already begun away from a commission-based remuneration structure to a fee-based/transaction-driven model will continue. Airlines increasingly expect passengers to bear the cost of using agencies for the purchase of 'plain vanilla' tickets; agencies in North America, for example, have been charging service fees since early in the post-capping era. (It is worth noting that travel agencies may in the end not even have the 'value-added services' market to themselves. British Airways, for example, has a web-site that allows access to services tailored to the needs of individual corporate customers – including a facility to book on other carriers.)

- Some airlines are building 'preferred supplier' relationships with agencies in key markets, developing joint promotional programmes and making special deals available only through these 'partners'.
- More generally, compensation will be driven by an assessment of the benefits an airline gains from each relationship rather than by the shotgun approach of the traditional commission structure. (Marketing information data tapes – 'MIDTs' – can be purchased for a fee from GDSs by airlines wanting to analyse their share of sales through different agencies.)

3. **Disintermediation** It has been estimated that in 1999 it cost America West $23 to sell a ticket through a bricks-and-mortar agency, $20 through an Internet agency, $13 through its own call centres, and $6 through its web site (Merrill Lynch, 1999). Unspoken though it might be, therefore, a key item on airlines' distribution agendas is to increase the proportion of direct sales. Disintermediation has four threads.

- Encouraging use of airline web sites, so eliminating agency commissions and GDS fees, and reducing call centre workload.
- Using e-ticketing to ensure that once a direct booking has been made there is no need for the customer to get an agency to issue a paper ticket – something that would cost the airline commission and GDS fees notwithstanding the direct booking.
- In the case of full-service airlines, using FFPs, direct marketing, and affinity credit cards to enhance brand loyalty and, over time, develop a direct relationship with their customers.
- Again in the case of full-service airlines, making net fares – that is, fares net of agency commissions and GDS fees – available to preferred customers who book directly.

When no intermediary is involved and payment for a booking is made at or shortly after the time of reservation, the airline concerned also gains a cash-flow benefit compared with using the agency system.

4. **Use of single-carrier fares** One of the most significant features of deregulated markets has been the rapid growth of full fares and the correspondingly high proportion of passengers travelling on discounted fares. Most discounted fares are not good for carriage on another carrier, so eliminating prorate dilution. (Of course, joint fares offered by alliance partners are increasingly weighing in the other direction.)

5. **Controlling GDS fees** One advantage of e-ticketed direct sales is that GDS fees are avoided. The GDSs nonetheless remain a significant element in most full-service airlines' distribution channels. Many carriers have become seriously concerned by the disconnect between GDS costs on the one hand, and passenger revenue on the other. Announcing a review of its pricing paradigm in 2002, Worldspan explicitly recognised the problem inherent in a business model designed to place virtually the entire cost of distribution onto airlines whilst simultaneously incentivising distributors to boost transaction volumes.

   In the meantime, a growing number of carriers are now using GDS billing information data tapes (BIDTs) more carefully to monitor different agencies' booking activities (Arciuolo, 1998) – notably the following.

   - *Passive bookings* These arise when an agency needs to build the passenger name record (PNR) required to track bookings and facilitate ticket issuance through a GDS. Legitimate uses include the ticketing by an agency of both individual and group bookings made directly with an airline. Passive bookings are nonetheless open to abuse; although they are relatively easy to isolate using BIDT audit software, getting GDS vendors to acknowledge abuse and refund fees can be difficult – which is why some US carriers have chosen to hold agencies accountable for invalid bookings.

   - *Multiple bookings* These are reservations made on more than one flight for a single passenger, perhaps as a fall-back in case of a meeting overrun.

   - *Duplicate bookings* These are additional reservations for the same passenger on a single flight, perhaps made in error by an agency. Sometimes two or more agencies will reserve space for a single passenger on the same flight(s) when that passenger has asked for competing price quotes but in the end only accepts one of them. Whilst airlines can and increasingly do pick these up in their own reservations systems, multiple and duplicate bookings made through GDSs remain a source of unproductive fees.

   - *Speculative bookings* Some agencies book space on high-demand flights out of their local hub just in case valued clients have a late need for seats on these departures.

Clearly, the Internet and also e-ticketing have been important developments in airline distribution. Box 5.11 briefly reviews the terrain – a terrain which is inevitably shifting very rapidly.

Box 5.11: B2C channels and e-ticketing

There are at present several different types of B2C web site distributing information and bookings.

1. ***Individual airlines' proprietary sites*** *These essentially reproduce the information and booking services of a telephone call centre, but with the added incentive in some cases of exclusive discount fares (e.g., United's 'E-fares'). New functionality is being added all the time (e.g., mobile access for booking, rebooking, and check-in).*
2. ***GDS-related sites*** *The four large GDSs (Amadeus, Galileo, Sabre, and Worldspan) spawned such notable sites as Travelocity (from Sabre) and Expedia (from Microsoft and Worldspan), and established an early lead with portals, directories, and search engines. Their functionality has spread beyond booking and into the provision of 'value-added' services such as corporate travel management. For many airlines, a feature of several of these sites almost as offensive as having to pay them a booking commission is the fact that some (although not necessarily those named above) actually sell their ability to bias the provision of information to consumers: in return for payments they will undertake to swing market share the way of 'preferred carriers' who pay them or buy banner advertising – by biasing search algorithms and/or introducing biased tie-breakers, for example.*
3. ***Multi-airline portals*** *Orbitz in North America and Opodo in Europe were early examples of fully or partially airline-owned sites, followed by Tabini and Zuji in Asia. One possible motive behind these ventures is to have neutral sites available to put pressure on GDS-related sites to keep their fees down. Another possibility might well be to make some money on an eventual IPO. Both could justify any risk of cannibalising business from each partner's own branded site. Opponents – notably travel agents and consumer groups – argue that a third motive might be the opportunity these sites present for price signalling and other forms of collusion. Whatever the airlines' motivation, both online agencies such as Travelocity and bricks-(or clicks-)-and-mortar agencies are unhappy about the prospect of airlines using either their own sites or multi-carrier portals to distribute exclusive online deals unavailable through non-airline channels (thereby arguably putting competing sites at a disadvantage). (Allaying this concern to some extent, American in*

fact launched its EveryFare Programme in 2002 under which selected bricks-and-mortar agencies in North America are given access to the lowest Internet fares available from the carrier in return for absorbing GDS fees or circumventing the GDSs altogether and booking on American's web site.)

A curiosity about these multi-airline portals is that they are regionally based and cross alliance boundaries – implying to some observers that they have more to do with the battle for control of distribution channels than with delivering to customers the 'seamless service' that alliances like to promise.

4. *Auction sites Priceline pioneered this B2C model when it first invited customers to bid a price for an O & D trip on a certain date and then leave the details – such as choice of airline, routing, and departure time – to the magic of science. The Priceline model, of course, relies on airlines being prepared to give the site access to off-tariff seats. Hotwire is a partially airline-owned competitor. Although it competes with Priceline, Hotwire's business model is slightly different insofar as customers do not bid a price, but instead receive an offer of a fare from the market in which they are interested (also without knowing the carrier, the time, or the routing). The primary purpose of these sites seems to be to dispose of distressed inventory without shouting 'fire-sale' and tarnishing the sellers' expensively cultivated brands.*

5. *Search sites Sites such as FareChase and SideStep were established early in the shift to Internet distribution, their model being to search numerous airline sites for the best fares. The latter, for example, was designed to allow for comparisons with online agencies such as Travelocity and Expedia, and then link through to the chosen airline to close a booking (so bypassing the GDSs).*

6. *Clicks-and-mortar sites These are online initiatives launched by established bricks-and-mortar agencies. Rosenbluth International is just one example – but an interesting one insofar as it was launched with equity participation from British Airways and Continental.*

E-ticketing (sometimes inaccurately referred to as 'ticketless travel') is another development that has become widespread in the United States, Europe, and Japan. It does not necessarily eliminate agents from the distribution channel, but airlines quietly hope that in due course most e-ticketed travel will be booked directly with them – preferably online – rather than through agencies. SITA and IATA established in 2001 that e-ticketing saves airlines around $4 per ticket in US domestic markets, and as much as $8 in international markets. Besides eliminating costs from the need to print, transport, store, protect, issue, and reconcile paper coupons, *e-ticketing also opens opportunities for greater process efficiency where, for example, passengers travelling with hand-baggage only are able to check-in automatically using either smart cards issued to frequent flyers or their own credit cards. (See Eastman (2002) for a comprehensive review of the evolution of e-ticketing.) Many majors now charge a fee for paper tickets where e-ticketing is available (and also for bookings made via their call centres rather than over the Internet).*

Process re-engineering and business restructuring

Process re-engineering Making a large airline smaller in output terms in order to bring down costs does not necessarily change its structure or cost base; business processes may have to be re-engineered as well. This is far more important than simply slashing, say, fleet and payroll. Diet alone cannot transform an elephant into a racehorse.

Business restructuring As markets have been progressively deregulated or liberalised since the late 1970s and increasingly opened to competition, different airlines have responded in a variety of ways – some of which have affected the structure of their businesses.

1. **Organizational form** Some restructuring programmes have focused on organizational form, the purpose usually being to de-layer hierarchies and also in several cases to create strategic business units out of what were previously internal cost centres. The objectives are generally to speed-up decision-making, relocate decisions closer to the customer, and promote a more entrepreneurial and customer-focused mindset.
2. **Network redesign** Surprisingly, several major airlines in the United States left it until the 1990s to start paying close attention to the profitability of individual routes; the result when it came was in some cases network retrenchment (e.g., Northwest), and in others the running down of secondary hubs (e.g., American and Continental).

    Majors in both North America and Europe have for several years now been 'outsourcing' to regional partners thin short-haul routes unsuited to mainline fleet and cost structures. As the 1990s progressed, the arrival of large numbers of regional jets led to expansion of hub catchment areas and the growth of regional airline hubs (e.g., Comair at Cincinnati). The process of handing over marginal mainline routes accelerated rapidly in the aftermath of 9/11.
3. **Low-cost operations** The continued steady expansion of Southwest in the United States and the more rapid growth of European low-fare carriers such as easyJet and Ryanair has provoked a variety of responses

from established network carriers. Some US majors, paced abortively by Continental and USAir and followed by United and Delta (and then USAir again, in its later incarnation as US Airways), established low-cost 'airlines within airlines' or separately branded subsidiaries; Air Canada has done the same. Alitalia, bmi british midland, British Airways, and KLM have tried similar approaches in Europe. Whilst the jury remains out on some of these initiatives at the time of writing, several have already failed from the major airlines' perspectives and been either terminated or spun-off. Their intended sources of savings relative to mainline operations have been: process improvements (e.g., faster turnarounds of a single-type fleet, leading to higher aircraft utilisation than the parent can achieve); lower wage costs and higher staff productivity; and no-frills onboard and ground products. Potential dangers include:

- failure to create a clear sub-brand identity, leading to unfulfilled customer expectations based on the parent's brand positioning;
- failure to offer a distinct value proposition, instead selling merely a de-tuned version of the full-service product;
- the risk of cannibalising the mainline client base; and
- in the case of 'airlines within airlines', as opposed to separately incorporated and externally staffed subsidiaries, difficulties reacculturating staff transferred from the parent.

Japan Airlines and All Nippon have also established small low-cost subsidiaries, primarily designed to use relatively cheap non-Japanese flight- and cabin crews on low-yield medium- and long-haul leisure routes. In 2002, Qantas established Australian Airlines to serve Asian leisure routes, initially into Cairns. The purpose of these and similar ventures elsewhere is not to combat low-fare competition, but to de-link services in low-yield vacation markets from the parents' relatively high cost bases.

4. **Alliances** Alliances have been successfully used to increase traffic densities on existing routes and to extend network scope without the investment that would be necessary to grow internally – assuming, in the case of international markets, that internal growth would have been a permissible option. Although the primary effect of alliances has been felt on the revenue side through network restructuring, there have also been input cost benefits (e.g., joint purchasing and the combining of ticket offices and sales forces) and productivity benefits (e.g., through higher utilisation of both operating and marketing resources arising from joint activities such as ground-handling and marketing communications). Costs have also been saved on a number of international routes by replacing tag-end sectors (such as Amsterdam–Madrid on a

Tokyo–Amsterdam–Madrid route) with code-shared connections. In other words, alliances can have a beneficial impact on costs through the economies of scale, scope, and density they promote; Oum et al (2000) have also found clear productivity improvements attributable to entry into an alliance.

5. **Outsourcing** We have already covered this topic extensively in the present chapter, as well as in chapter 1. Established carriers have been increasingly prepared to use outsourcing to reduce costs where this is feasible and, sometimes more significantly, to transform into variable costs the fixed costs associated with infrastructure supporting what are now considered by some carriers to be noncore activities such as maintenance, catering, and IS/IT provision.

6. **Offshore relocation** There have been two (relatively small-scale) developments under this heading.

   - *Facility relocation* Airlines based in high-cost locations have in a few cases relocated internal back-office functions and activities such as mainframe computer centres, software development, and revenue accounting to cheaper offshore locations. (Carriers that outsource airframe maintenance sometimes also use MRO shops in low man-hour cost environments – notably parts of the Asia-Pacific region.) Facilitated by cheaper and better telecommunications, this is a development that mirrors the migration of some manufacturing industries to low-cost locations.

   - *Offshore staffing* Japanese carriers have, as mentioned above, been particularly noteworthy for their use of overseas-based foreign flight- and cabin crews to reduce costs. Some of the largest US and European long-haul carriers (e.g., United and Lufthansa) have also tapped relatively low-cost foreign-based cabin attendants; inevitably, there has been union opposition in Europe and the United States to any further significant growth of this phenomenon.

Conclusion

Conventional wisdom holds that labour is the only significant 'controllable' cost in an airline – equipment costs, fuel, airport and ATS charges in particular being largely 'uncontrollable'. This is too simplistic. Most costs have a core that is substantially uncontrollable – at least in the short run – and a margin which, if cost drivers are well-understood and properly addressed, can be managed. The real issue is therefore not whether a cost is controllable, but how large the margin of control actually is. For example, to say that labour costs are controllable but fuel costs largely are not misses the point. People and fuel are both necessary to run an airline; the costs of both are manageable at the margin, albeit to different extents, and it is management's responsibility to grasp control and also to optimise the productivity of each unit of expenditure.

We can make the following generalisations about cost management strategies. (Note that this discussion applies in respect of 'normal' market circumstances, rather than extraordinary conditions such as the aftermath of 9/11 when airlines might be more concerned with short-term survival.)

1. A cost management strategy treats costs not so much as absolute numbers that must inevitably be minimised, but as revenue-generators that need to be proactively *managed* within the context of the particular type of value embedded in each service concept. Taking costs in aggregate, by function, and/or by category, a cost management strategy should concern itself not just with their size but with their productivity – that is, the revenue earned per unit of expenditure.

2. Cost management efforts – whether aimed at lowering absolute input costs or raising input productivity – require a framework, and that framework is provided by the customer value being offered to each targeted segment. Cost management cannot be a strategy in itself; it is a fundamental management discipline which becomes a strategy only when linked to a defined revenue generation strategy within the context of a chosen competitive strategy that embodies the airline's strategic position – as a low-fare carrier, a high-quality niche carrier, or a full-service network carrier, for example. Cost structures should not have a life of their own. Their sole purpose is to make possible the delivery of a particular type of customer value. The idea of customer value can therefore be used to help determine which costs should be reduced, which eliminated, and which justifiably increased.

    It can sometimes be useful to think about activities in terms of the following categories.

    *   **Value-adding activities** These contribute directly to why customers make the purchase decisions they do. Consider what the impact on purchase behaviour and/or price would be were an activity to be eliminated or performed to a different standard.

    *   **Enabling activities** These contribute to the maintenance of the business and enable it to serve customers. An example is payroll administration. Many could in principle be outsourced (as, of course, could some value-adding activities).

    *   **Value-destroying activities** These contribute nothing to customer value and nothing to business maintenance. Holding and managing excess parts inventory is an example.

In respect of both value-adding and enabling activities, opportunities might exist for improving efficiency; value-destroying activities need to be eliminated.

3. As well as analysing *which* activities are undertaken and whether they are consistent with the carrier's service concept(s), consideration should also be given to *how* they are undertaken. Airlines each combine inputs differently. An individual airline's cost structure can change dramatically in response not only to changes in the cost behaviour of activities, but also as a result of changes in the way in which activities are configured within the various processes comprising its value chain – that is, as a result of changes in operating strategy.

4. It follows that although 'cost management' frequently involves 'cost cutting', the two are not necessarily synonymous. Cost 'management' implies cutting costs wherever possible but with a purpose, rather than slashing them across the board; sometimes it might even mean increasing them if incremental revenues more than compensate for incremental costs. In other words, the supply side (i.e., production costs) should not be considered in isolation from the demand side (i.e., revenue generation). Short-term cost minimisation and long-term profit maximisation do not inevitably equate, particularly when serving premium segments; the attacks launched on customer value by several US majors during the 1990s suggest that there is an influential body of opinion within the industry which does not share this view.

There are two parts to an income statement: there is a revenue side as well as a cost side. Low costs are a route to profitability, not an end in themselves. The fundamental challenge confronting any business is to get costs into line with prices that customers are prepared to pay for the services being offered – that is to efficiently produce output that is effective in delivering the type of value targeted customers expect. This is easier to write about than to achieve. What is certain is that to have any hope of achieving it in today's market environment it is necessary to approach airlines as systems of activities that need to be managed with strategic consistency (i.e., in accord with a single strategic theme) and as an integrated whole. This links back not only to the discussion of activity systems in the present chapter and in chapter 1, but also to the significance of individual managers' perceptions of their airline, its competitive environment, and its position in that environment (also discussed in the opening chapter).

That cost management is now one of the principal strategic battlegrounds being fought over by competing airlines is beyond doubt. But accountants with sharp pencils – or, indeed, axes – are insufficient. What is necessary is to ingrain cost management into corporate culture. For continuous cost improvement to be ingrained into a corporate culture – something that is far more effective strategically than periodic, often crisis-driven, 'slash-and-burn' cost-cutting exercises – several prerequisites have to be met.

- **Training** Cost management is learned. Educating people about the strategic and competitive importance of cost management is a worthwhile investment. Strategy needs to be widely understood.
- **Participation** People closest to the action are often in the best position to identify cost management opportunities. They need to be consulted and to be involved in decision-making that affects what they do and how they do it.
- **Reinforcement** Changed behaviour needs reinforcing. If the same things are measured and the same performance metrics are used as in the past, new behaviour – specifically, a more thoughtful and proactive approach to cost management – cannot be sustained.

The customer value embedded in an airline's service concept(s) provides a context for cost management. The essence of strategic cost management should be to ensure that customers get what they want and are prepared to pay for and that airlines spend as little as possible, *consistent with targeted quality standards*, providing it to them. Costs are easy to add in a booming market when traffic and revenue are growing rapidly, but they can be difficult and painful to shed when revenue growth slows or turns negative. Furthermore, the high short-run operating leverage faced by most airlines means that even though output can be reduced relatively quickly, costs – particularly fixed costs – are more 'sticky'. A key discipline is therefore never to add *unnecessary* costs – whatever the market is doing.

v. Summary

In this chapter we have identified different types of cost, looked at how airline costs might be classified and analysed, identified key cost drivers, and considered some of the more important cost management initiatives undertaken by the industry. Because the chapter is long and complex, it might be helpful to summarise key headings and sub-headings.

i. Cost defined
Total operating cost
cost behaviour: fixed and variable elements of total operating cost

Production functions, cost functions, and the impact of output decisions on costs
> the cost impact of output changes

ii. Airline cost classification
Operating, nonoperating, direct, and indirect costs
Alternative approaches to cost analysis
> by function or department; by product; by route; by fleet and sub-fleet; by activity; by contribution

iii. Cost drivers
Design and functioning of the operating system
> the supply chain; internal operations (service design, process design, productivity, structure of the fleet); distribution

Input costs
> labour costs; fuel costs; airport and air traffic services costs; station costs; maintenance costs; ownership costs; other input costs

Scale
> growth; economies of scale in the airline industry; the competitive implications of economies of scale

Learning
Summary

iv. Cost management
Cost escapability
Managing cost drivers
> supply chain management; input costs and productivity (labour costs, fuel costs, airport charges, maintenance inventory, productivity); controlling distribution costs; process re-engineering and business restructuring

Conclusion

This chapter concludes Part 2 of the book. We have taken four chapters to look at four elements in a simple model of operating performance.

TRAFFIC x YIELD > < OUTPUT x UNIT COST
= OPERATING PERFORMANCE (i.e., PROFIT or LOSS)

Throughout Part 2 we have highlighted the critical significance of capacity management – of getting traffic and output to an acceptable balance at a yield sufficient to make an operating profit given the unit costs involved in producing the volume and type of output concerned. In Part 3 of the book we will consider three variables at the heart of capacity management: network management (design and scheduling); fleet management; and revenue management.

Part 3
Capacity Management

The fundamental objectives of capacity management are straightforward.

1. To minimise revenue loss from spillage (i.e., producing insufficient output to meet potentially profitable demand).
2. To minimise excess output and spoilage.
3. To maximise resource productivity (consistent with the airline's chosen strategic and market positions, and with the type of value it is offering its customers).

However, we have already seen in the opening chapters some of the reasons why capacity management can be a significant challenge in the airline industry.

1. **Demand instability** The nature of the scheduled airline business is such that carriers have to forecast demand, decide how much and which segments they want to satisfy, commit capacity to the production of output, and then try to sell that output. But forecasting is complicated by four features of the demand for airline output.
    *   Growth in demand is highly cyclical in response to underlying economic fluctuations, the timing and impact of which are notoriously difficult to predict. Compounding this is the industry's tendency to end each economic upswing with an aircraft order backlog equivalent to several years' production, much of which is delivered during the ensuing downturn when demand growth is anyway slowing or possibly even turning negative. The time-lag between order and delivery has been shortened considerably in recent years as a result of manufacturers' efforts and the growth of operating lessors, but it can still magnify the tendency towards periodic overcapacity in an already highly cyclical industry. The most fundamental problem, however, is that particularly on the downside consumers can react to changes in the determinants of demand considerably more quickly than airlines are able to adjust output levels and overhead structures.

361

- Any trend-line of average demand growth conceals the inevitable peaking suffered by most forms of transportation system. European network carriers, for example, can have month-on-month peak-to-trough ratios in the 1.5 to 2.0 range – and considerably higher than this in the case of airlines based in Mediterranean holiday destinations.

- Because traffic – both in aggregate and in larger individual markets – involves sizeable figures, a relatively small forecasting error can be highly disruptive to any projected balance between output and demand. Ignoring circumstances in the immediate aftermath of 9/11, annual global market growth usually generates traffic increases equivalent to adding a mid-size US major to the system each year.

- At the level of the individual departure, traffic can be subject to random fluctuations that are very difficult to predict.

2. **Supply indivisibilities** We saw in chapter 4 that airline capacity and output tend to increase in substantial increments or 'lumps' as routes, frequencies, aircraft, ground infrastructure and so on are added, whilst demand increases in much smaller units (e.g., passenger enplanements). This makes the supply of output and the demand for it fundamentally difficult to match.

3. **Product perishability** We also noted in chapter 4 that because airline output is perishable at the point of production, it cannot be inventoried once produced. Obvious though this is, it deserves restating because it is fundamental to the capacity management challenge.

4. **Liberalisation and deregulation** New freedoms to enter routes and choose the level of output almost inevitably lead to a surge in output. Sometimes this surge is attributable to previously existing demand that had been constrained by commercial regulation. On the other hand, it may also be attributable to belief in the 'S-curve' effect (see chapter 4) and sometimes profitless pursuit of market share; particularly when output is added to a mature, slow-growing market it is very likely that what will happen is that revenues and market share get juggled around and yield-damaging fare wars become endemic. A countervailing consequence of liberalisation is the freedom airlines have to exit unprofitable routes – but this is a freedom many were curiously reluctant to exercise until well into the 1990s, and some state-owned flag carriers even today are not permitted to exploit.

5. **Strategic and tactical dimensions to capacity**
   - The use of capacity to enter a market with the calculated strategic intent of rapidly achieving dominance can throw supply and demand into at least temporary imbalance; this happened when Americ-

an began its aggressive growth strategy in Latin American markets in the early 1990s.
- At a tactical level, demand developments in one region of the world can have an impact on the balance between supply and demand elsewhere; in response to the 1997 Asian economic crisis, for example, several European majors diverted significant amounts of capacity to North Atlantic markets – with the result that yields softened dramatically.
6. **Cargo output as a by-product of passenger capacity planning** The supply of cargo output by combination carriers in medium- and long-haul markets often has more to do with the impact on belly-hold space of planning on the passenger side than it does with underlying demand from freight shippers.

Capacity management requires the matching of resource inputs to the demand for the volume and type of output that an airline's choice of competitive strategy requires it to produce. It can be considered on two levels.

1. **Micro-level** Fleet assignment, the operational scheduling of other resources, optimisation of loads on individual departures, and the management of queues within the service delivery system are primary areas of interest at the micro-level. There are two tasks.
   - *Managing demand in line with output* This requires dextrous use of the marketing mix – particularly price, promotions, and marketing communications – to shave demand peaks and fill troughs. The breaking down of demand into segments is an important part of this challenge for some carriers, because demand curves may very well differ between segments at different times of the day, week or year. The emphasis here is short-term. Price has a particularly significant role to play, as we will see when discussing revenue management in chapter 9.
   - *Matching output to demand* This is fundamentally an operations and human resource management task. The emphasis has in the past been primarily medium- or long-term, with efforts in respect of fleet, facilities, and staff planning particularly important. The advent of analytical tools capable of more accurately forecasting demand by departure and, particularly, the availability of families of different-size aircraft (such as the A320 and B737 series) having similar aircrew type ratings have greatly improved short-term

capacity management opportunities. We will touch on this in chapter 8.

2. **Macro-level** Medium- and long-term fleet and facilities management, within the wider context of strategic network management, is the focus at this level. Network and fleet management are the subjects of the next three chapters.

6 Network Management: Design

If everything seems under control, you're just not going fast enough.
Mario Andretti

Chapter overview

Network management has two elements: design and scheduling.

- Network design addresses two fundamental questions: Which markets do we want to serve – in other words, which markets should we be adding or deleting? What are the financial implications of the route structure used to serve our markets – in other words, what would be the implications of adding or deleting specific routes, and (in the case of multi-hub carriers) of channelling O & D flows in a different way?
- Schedule planning addresses several fundamental questions with regard to individual routes: If a route is to be added, how many flights should be scheduled and when? If an additional frequency is to be added, when should it be scheduled to depart? What will be the financial implications of these decisions, or of any other adjustment to the existing schedule? What are the financial implications of changing the size of aircraft operating particular departures?

The three main sections in this chapter will look at network design, network strategies and tactics, and network outsourcing. Chapter 7 considers scheduling, as well as the interface between network and fleet management. Clearly, answers to the questions above are closely tied to decisions taken in other areas of capacity management – notably fleet management and revenue management. These are the subjects of chapters 8 and 9 respectively.

365

i. Network design

Any airline's network is:

- a key source of brand identity, because its network helps define what type of carrier it is;
- a revenue driver, because network design and scheduling are core service attributes offered to customers;
- a cost driver, because network design and scheduling are critical elements in any airline's cost structure;
- a source of competitive strength or weakness, because a network is something that competitors have to choose whether to confront or avoid; and
- a potential hedge against economic cycles that affect some markets but not others and, if international in scope, against currency fluctuations.

This section of the chapter will review alternative network designs. The first part provides definitions of terms that will be used in both the present discussion and also in the discussion of revenue management in chapter 9, and it also briefly outlines the key variables affecting network economics.

Markets and routes

The words 'market' and 'route' can be synonymous, but often they are not. An O & D *market* exists between a passenger's points of origin and destination. O & D markets can take one of several forms from a network design perspective.

1. Point-to-point markets can exist between:
   - two hubs or gateways (e.g., Dallas and Miami, New York and London);
   - a hub and a secondary or tertiary point (e.g., Dallas and Tucson);
   - two secondary or tertiary points (e.g., Tucson and Albuquerque).
2. Single-hub behind/beyond markets can take one of several forms:
   - secondary or tertiary point to another secondary or tertiary point over a hub (e.g., Tucson–Cincinnati–Hartford);
   - secondary or tertiary point to a hub over another hub (e.g., Tucson–Dallas–Miami);
   - hub to a secondary or tertiary point over another hub (e.g., Dallas–London–Edinburgh).

(Note that in the second and third of these configurations two hubs are involved in the journey, but hubbing only takes place at the intermediate hub whilst the other is either an origin or destination.)

3. Double-hub behind/beyond markets (i.e., 'double-connect' or 'cross-feed' markets) usually involve an origin in a secondary city (e.g., New Orleans or Leipzig) or a tertiary city (e.g., Burlington or Erfurt), transfers at two hubs, and a final destination in another secondary or tertiary city. Most examples are found in multi-hub international alliance structures (e.g., Milwaukee–Detroit–Amsterdam–Stuttgart), although some thinner transcontinental markets in the United States are also served over two hubs.

A *route*, on the other hand, links two points using the same aircraft under the same flight number. It can be operated as either of the following.

1. A nonstop service: this is one flight-leg between start and end-point (e.g., London-Edinburgh).
2. A through- or direct service: in this case there are two or more flight-legs because intermediate stops are made (e.g., Tucson–Cincinnati–New York JFK operated as a through-service by a single aircraft under the same flight number).

If the same flight number is used but a change of aircraft is required at an intermediate point, this is functionally equivalent to two connecting routes being used to serve the market. It might happen, for example, where a single flight number is used for Portland (Oregon)–Cincinnati–New York JFK service but passengers have to change planes in Cincinnati and board an aircraft that originated in Tucson and is operating onwards from Cincinnati to JFK under multiple flight numbers. Flights across US domestic hubs in particular are often through-numbered to improve their GDS display positions; in the above example, the Cincinnati–JFK leg might operate under several flight numbers corresponding to a range of different origins behind Cincinnati, but all except the Tucson-originating same-plane service would require a connection at Cincinnati and so do not in fact offer direct service. (The term 'duplicate leg' is sometimes used to describe an arrangement under which, for technical or commercial reasons, a single leg carries more than one flight number; the same expression can also be used to describe a code-shared flight operated under more than one airline's flight number.)

Any given market might therefore be served in one or more of several ways.

1. **Nonstop route** (e.g., Hong Kong–Los Angeles) 'Route' and 'market' are synonymous for passengers originating in Hong Kong and destined for Los Angeles.
2. **Direct, multi-stop or through-plane route** (e.g., Hong Kong–Tokyo–Los Angeles on the same aircraft operating under the same flight number) Depending upon traffic rights, this route might serve Hong Kong–Tokyo and Tokyo–Los Angeles markets as well as Hong Kong–Los Angeles. (Using terminology we will meet in chapter 9 in the context of revenue management, we can say that the Tokyo–Los Angeles *flight-leg* may carry passengers travelling on Hong Kong–Los Angeles and Tokyo–Los Angeles *segments*.)
3. **Connecting routes** There are several possibilities.
   - *Online connections* These involve an en route change of planes but use a single airline's aircraft. Flight numbers might or might not change:
     - different flight numbers: a change of aircraft at a hub often, although not invariably, involves a change in flight number;
     - same flight number: a single flight-number might be used on two connecting routes. As noted above, this commonly happens in US domestic markets to improve GDS display positions. 'Funnel flights' involving a change of gauge are sometimes used at hubs and international gateways such that an incoming long-haul flight might connect with a short-haul leg operated by a smaller aircraft but under the same flight number.
   - *Code-share connections* These use an airline's designator code on connecting services actually operated by the aircraft of another carrier. (We will discuss code-sharing later in the chapter.)
   - *Interline connections* Increasingly rare, these involve connections between the (non-code-shared) services of two or more different airlines. Passengers might benefit from joint fares negotiated between the carriers for specific markets, and will almost certainly benefit from through-ticketing (although not necessarily through boarding passes issued at the first point of check-in) and from baggage interlining. Most low-fare airlines refuse to interline because of the costs and prorate dilution it involves.

Clearly, whilst any one route can serve one or several markets, any one market might be served by several alternative routes. Each of the different options open to a particular airline for serving the markets available to it carries separate marketing mix implications, because each offers customers a different set of benefits and non-monetary costs (e.g., the shorter elapsed journey times of nonstop flights, the 'seamless' service of online connections, the disadvantages of any change of planes or intermediate stop); it also carries its own different set of operating costs. Box 6.1 looks at one of the implications for competition arising out of the distinction between routes and markets.

Box 6.1: Market competition in the absence of route overlay

Airlines can compete in a market without any route overlay at all. For example, Singapore Airlines serves the London–Sydney market by connecting London–Singapore and Singapore–Sydney routes; Thai International serves the same market by connecting London–Bangkok and Bangkok–Sydney routes. Delta might serve the Buffalo–LA market over Cincinnati, whilst Continental serves it over Cleveland. This is one reason why the immediate competitive impact of a proposed alliance or merger should be considered in terms of market duplication as well as route duplication; mergers and alliances can materially reduce competition in O & D markets even where there is little or no route overlay.

Network economics

In principle, we could visualise a network of 'demand linkages' – that is, lines connecting every city-pair within an airline's accessible service area generating O & D demand. From an individual customer's point of view, it might be preferable if this hypothetical network of demand linkages were duplicated by actual airline service – in other words, by an airline operating a network of nonstops which precisely corresponds to O & D demand. Because the industry's operating economics preclude this, what happens instead is that every carrier has to make network design choices that lead to some O & D markets being served nonstop (in which case demand and network links are indeed congruent), others being served by multi-stop (i.e., direct) or connecting service, and some not being served at all (at least by a single carrier). These choices are in fact the essence of 'network design'.

Within the context established by a particular carrier's strategic description of itself – as a regional, a low-fare point-to-point operator, or a network major, for example – and by the characteristics of the demand being served, and also subject to whatever service obligations or route licensing formalities are imposed by governments, airline managements have more freedom than in the past with regard to how they choose to structure their networks. These choices involve balancing the requirements of different market segments (e.g., for high-frequency nonstop service) against the economics of aircraft operation (which can make high-frequency nonstop service, for example, more expensive to deliver than lower frequencies using larger aircraft).

Network costs are driven in particular by the economies of scope and density, the stage-lengths, and the resource utilisation levels inherent in the design of a network and its accompanying schedule. Revenues reflect in part the quality of service embedded in these same network design and scheduling decisions.

Costs The most significant network cost drivers were highlighted in chapter 5. All are impacted by fleet composition.

1. **Economies of scope** These are in evidence when it is cheaper to produce two products together than to produce each separately. In the context of network design, economies of scope arise when passengers travelling in many different O & D markets are combined for at least part of their journeys on a single aircraft – in other words, when the output produced by a single aircraft flying from point A to point B is sold to passengers originating behind A and/or destined beyond B as well as to passengers in the A-B city-pair market. Economies of scope are accessed by channelling traffic over one or more hubs; they are a significant motivation for building both single-airline and alliance hub-and-spoke systems.

2. **Economies of density** We saw in chapter 5 that these are in evidence when unit cost declines as a result of an increased volume of traffic being carried between points already served. The primary source of economies of density is aircraft size: because increases in trip cost and in aircraft size do not have a linear relationship, larger aircraft generally return lower seat-mile costs (although higher trip costs) than smaller types of a similar technological generation flown on a given flight-leg. One way of exploiting economies of density is to design a network such that traffic flows are channelled onto routes that would otherwise support only smaller aircraft with higher seat-mile costs. Because of the bar-bell double-hub network structure KLM and Northwest designed, for example, behind/beyond traffic flows channelled between hubs at Amsterdam and Detroit support high-frequency service with low seat-mile cost widebodies that the O & D market between these two cities could never support by itself.

3. **Average stage-length** One of any airline's fundamental cost drivers is its average stage-length. This can be calculated in two ways.
   - Average stage-length = total aircraft miles or kilometres flown p.a./ systemwide revenue departures p.a.

- Weighted average stage-length = Σ (length of each sector x flights p.a. on the sector)/systemwide revenue departures p.a.

Other things being equal, unit costs of producing output on long-haul routes are generally lower than is the case on short-haul routes. Conversely, it will cost more to produce a given output of ASMs as average stage-length decreases. Box 6.2 explores this phenomenon.

Box 6.2: The cost impact of average stage-length

The tapering of unit costs as length of haul increases is a fundamental fact of airline economics, and one that can have a particularly influential effect on operating margins because costs generally taper more rapidly than fares.

Longer stage-lengths contribute to lower unit costs for the following reasons.

1. *The time an aircraft spends on the ground for turnarounds or transit stops declines relative to airborne time as average stage-lengths increase. This facilitates higher aircraft and crew utilisation, and hence higher productivity.*
2. *Similarly, average block-speed is higher than on shorter sectors, raising hourly aircraft productivity and so generating more units of output over which to spread fixed operating costs.*
3. *Fuel-burn per mile flown declines the longer an aircraft remains at its optimal, fuel-efficient cruising speed and altitude(s), with the result that fuel costs for a given aircraft with a given payload rise less than proportionately as the length of haul increases.*
4. *Terminal costs decline as a proportion of route costs when stage-lengths increase. The same is true of traffic costs, such as reservations, ticketing, and ground handling. For example, an airline selling 5,000 RPMs will incur lower reservations, ticketing, and handling costs if the sale is generated by carrying one passenger 5,000 miles than if five passengers are each carried on 1,000-mile journeys.*
5. *Cycle-related maintenance costs (e.g., in respect of undercarriage assemblies) do not accumulate as rapidly in respect of long-haul aircraft as they do when shorter flight-legs are being operated.*

In summary, the unit cost of operating a given aircraft with a given payload falls as stage-length increases because the fixed costs associated with each flight are spread over a larger output, and also because the variable costs do not increase proportionately with distance. For example, the cost per ASM for a B747-400 configured with 380 seats falls by around half as stage-length increases from 600 to 6,000 miles. Unit cost improvements are most dramatic as stage-lengths rise from short- to medium-haul. However, they do taper, and as the length of haul becomes extreme, relationships between unit costs and stage-lengths tend towards being linear.

Airlines operating shorter stage-lengths are not necessarily at a disadvantage provided they are able to recover their higher unit costs by earning relatively higher yields than their long-haul counterparts, or compensate with some combination of low input costs and/or high factor productivity. (Bear in mind when looking at the system unit costs of a carrier operating a mixture of short-, medium-, and long-haul stage-lengths – say, United – that these costs have been 'averaged' down by the beneficial impact of operating the long-haul flight-legs; its short-haul unit costs will be much higher than the systemwide average, and therefore probably even more uncompetitive against a low-fare competitor – say, Southwest – than might at first glance appear to be the case.)

Network design and scheduling decisions affect the availability of economies of scope and density and drive average stage-length; they also affect the utilisation of aircraft and of station resources. At the most fundamental level, costs associated with network design hinge upon two decisions taken with regard to how each market should be served.

1. **Nonstop or connecting service** Operating nonstop between two points rather than over a hub has both cost and revenue implications.
   - *Cost* Flying nonstop eliminates the incremental fuel-burn required for take-off and climb-out from the intermediate hub, and may eliminate any route deviation required to reach it; landing at the hub increases maintenance costs because of the additional cycle it involves – something of particular importance in respect of engine and landing-gear maintenance; and stopping will also involve additional airport and handling charges. On the other hand, if flights to the hub are operated by larger aircraft than the nonstop market could support by itself, these aircraft will probably have higher trip costs but lower seat-mile costs than the smaller type that would otherwise have been used.
   - *Revenue* Passengers generally prefer to fly nonstop, and in many cases this preference can be reflected in firmer yields – at least in business and first classes. Furthermore, because nonstop flights save time they can facilitate additional flying – and therefore revenue-earning – opportunities for the aircraft involved. Against this will need to be balanced the fact that operating over a hub and so combining different O & D passengers onto each departure from

the origin should allow higher outbound frequencies and access to a wider range of markets from that city than nonstop service would permit. We will return to these points later.

2. **Capacity versus frequency** There are two variables to consider.

- High-frequency services between two points using relatively small aircraft are generally more expensive to produce (in terms of cost per seat-mile) than lower-frequency services using larger aircraft. The key question (assuming adequate availability of aircraft and, if relevant, traffic rights) is what the market is demanding in respect of frequencies (e.g., at least double-daily long-haul, day-return possibilities short-haul, or connections into multiple complexes throughout the day at a nearby hub), and the extent to which high-yield segments are present in the market and willing to cover the costs of mounting high frequencies.

- As just noted, by channelling over a single hub all the passengers outbound from a spoke city to multiple final destinations it is possible to mount higher frequencies (and/or to use larger aircraft) down the spoke to the hub than would be possible were nonstop services used to link the same origin to each of those same final destinations.

The network product Given a forecast level of demand in a targeted market, therefore, an airline's most basic service decision is whether to serve it with a nonstop, multi-stop, online connecting, interline connecting or code-shared product (or possibly some combination of these), and whether service should be offered at a high frequency – perhaps implying a relatively high unit cost operation with smaller aircraft than might otherwise be used – or at a low frequency, possibly implying a larger aircraft and lower units costs. The choice made will in part reflect the need to balance basic airline economics with the service design requirements that arise from the traffic mix in the markets concerned; the airline's cost structure and market strategy must be weighed against the preferences of target customers and their willingness to pay for different levels of service quality. Fleet mix and, in the case of international routes, the terms of relevant bilaterals will also influence the choices that are made.

Passengers prefer, in order, nonstop, direct, online connecting, and lastly interline routings (Carlton et al, 1980); many markets, of course, do not have the density or mix of traffic to support nonstop service – or at least not the high-frequency nonstop service demanded by the business segment. Airlines nonetheless have to bear these preferences in mind when designing their networks – as well as bearing in mind what competitors are doing. The result of this is that the world's larger carriers, alone or with alliance partners, are now more focused than ever before on their customers' complete journeys – wanting to design networks capable of carrying as many customers as possible all the way, to achieve this seamlessly, and to capture the entire revenue stream from customer itineraries.

In the low-fare sector of the industry, network and schedule can sometimes be key disciminants between apparently similar business models. For example, whereas Ryanair has tended to concentrate on rapid network expansion, easyJet's early years were marked by more attention to network density – that is, to building high frequencies on a relatively tight network. This contrast to some extent reflects the distinction between easyJet's targeting of price-sensitive business travellers (who appreciate high frequencies) in addition to leisure and VFR traffic, on the one hand, and Ryanair's targeting of ultra-price-sensitive segments (Lawton, 2002).

Types of network

Networks can be categorised from both the customers' point of view and from an operational perspective.

Customers' perspectives

There are basically two types of network design from a customer's standpoint.

1. **Connecting/hub-and-spoke** The majority of connecting traffic is channelled over hubs on single-carrier connections, although a significant and growing proportion connects between alliance partners (often on code-shared flights). Interline connections account for a declining share of connecting traffic.
2. **Same-plane/point-to-point service** This can arise in a variety of different circumstances:
   - most low-fare carriers primarily offer point-to-point service (e.g., easyJet), as do a significant number of small- and medium-sized long-haul carriers (e.g., Virgin Atlantic and LanChile);
   - the increased availability of new-generation regional jets, mainline narrowbodies, and ultra-long-haul widebodies having long ranges in the context of their respective markets has allowed network carriers and their affiliates to introduce nonstop hub-bypass services; and
   - even within a hubbed network it is likely that a reasonably high proportion of traffic will be travelling in local O & D markets.

Same-plane/point-to-point service can be either direct (i.e., with an in-termediate stop but no change of planes or flight number) or nonstop. Passengers overwhelmingly prefer nonstop routes.

Operational perspective

From an airline's operational perspective, networks can be categorised as linear, grid, or hub-and spoke.

Linear These are broadly out-and-back operations radiating from a base that does not act as a hub over which traffic is channelled. In the past, many long-haul international carriers operated linear, multi-stop routes, and some still do. Low-frequency services using multi-stop routings with large wide-bodies are often uneconomic, however, because of their relatively low yields (frequencies are insufficient to appeal to business travellers) and high costs (arising from intermediate stops and, more particularly, the inefficient utilisation of aircrews and station resources).

The cost and revenue implications are not always clear-cut. For example, a route from A to B and on to C, combining A-B, A-C, and B-C flows, might attract sufficient traffic to support a larger aircraft with better seat-mile costs than could be supported on separate A-B, A-C, and B-C routes. The downside of the A-B-C route is that because passengers from A to C are being offered a poorer quality service, yield might suffer. Whilst it is possible that such routes can be made to pay if there is substantial freight traffic (perhaps justifying use of combis), the overall trend for long-haul international operations is towards consolidation onto routes that support at least daily nonstop services, with lower frequencies and/or intermediate stops tolerated only where market density and aircraft range constraints make them unavoidable.

Grid These networks generally encompass short- and medium-haul routes focused on several major cities, linking these cities both to each other and to locations in between. Schedules may or may not be co-ordinated over the main cities, but often they are not. The pre-deregulation route structures of several US majors exhibited grid patterns. Another longstanding example has been the domestic network of Indian Airlines, focused on Mumbai, Delhi, Kolkatta, and Chennai. The networks of some low-fare carriers in Europe are also evolving into loose grid patterns (e.g., easyJet at Luton, Amsterdam, Geneva, and Liverpool).

Although sometimes cited as an example of a linear structure, South-west's network has grid characteristics; there is evidence of these in its high levels of station activity – averaging in the 45–50 departures per day range (but with several stations having over 100) – underlining the fact that wherever possible each station is connected to a number of others on the network. When Southwest adds a new station, it quickly builds service to/from several existing online stations and adds sufficient frequencies to allow it to dominate each market; operations are scheduled throughout the day to maximise gate-turns as well as staff and equipment utilisation.

Linking two stations already served from other points (i.e., 'connecting the dots') is cheaper, in both operational and marketing terms, than introducing a new route where the carrier has no established market presence at one end. Advantages include the improvement in station resource utilisation, and also in general market presence (reflected in top-of-mind brand recall) that arise from offering high frequencies to a broad range of different destinations.

Hub-and-spoke Hubs can develop in one or more of three ways.

1. **By design** Since deregulation in the United States, the full-service network majors have consciously developed hubs that interchange traffic between integrated banks of arrivals and departures. Internationally, KLM and Singapore Airlines have been operating sixth freedom hubs for several decades, Emirates successfully set out to do the same in the late 1980s, and many other European and Asian majors now try as far as geography and traffic rights permit to schedule hub arrivals and departures into well-integrated waves.

2. **By frequency growth** Some carriers operate with such high frequencies into and out of key stations that the ready availability of convenient connections in effect simulates a hub operation. This is the case for Southwest at Dallas Love Field, Phoenix, Baltimore, and several other stations that have over 100 departures per day, for example, and is becoming the case for Ryanair at London Stansted. (What distinguishes these stations from classic network hubs is that incoming and outgoing flights are not explicitly scheduled to connect, that scheduling gives precedence to minimising aircraft turnaround times rather than maximising available passenger connections, and that passengers who do choose to connect typically have to collect and re-check their baggage.)

3. **By default** In this case, still exemplified by a number of small- and medium-sized 'flag carriers', traffic might well be fed over the airline's home base but little effort is made to design and schedule a tightly integrated radial network. (Interline connections may or may not be significant.) This type of network, which was also common amongst European majors until the late-1980s, might be characterised as a

'random hub' insofar as connections tend to arise randomly rather than through intent.

Nonstop hub-bypass services, both long- and short-haul, have steadily become more numerous as hub-based network carriers seek competitive advantage by fragmenting network flows both to improve service and pre-empt competitive attacks on spoke cities. Point-to-point service was, of course, a hallmark of networks in the pre-deregulation era, before co-ordinated hubbing came into vogue. However, those services were often channelled through gateway cities (particularly in the case of international flights) or loosely co-ordinated hubs (as distinct from today's tightly integrated hubs), and multi-sector routings were common; this is very different from the current trend favouring development of nonstop routes bypassing gateways and hubs. Technological developments – such as regional jets, variants of mainline narrowbodies with transcontinental range, and ultra-long-haul widebodies – have broadened this opportunity (although its clearest early manifestation in long-haul service came with the 1980s arrival of twinjets on North Atlantic routes bypassing traditional gateways). Carriers doing this are offering customers the benefit of a shorter journey time and avoidance of hub congestion, possibly counter-balanced – at least initially until traffic is built up – by a lower frequency than could be supported on a multi-stop or connecting service. The trade-off for the airline is that, on the one hand, it is gaining better market access but, on the other, it has to forgo economies of scope and density associated with indirect routings over a hub. In many cases, hub-bypass services are interwoven with connecting services to maintain competitive O & D market frequencies.

It is possible to draw a distinction between two types of hub-bypass route.

1. **Secondary city to secondary city** Bypassing hubs altogether, this is most common in regional markets in both North America and Europe, but it is also beginning to be seen in some US domestic mainline markets. When city-pairs at the periphery of a hub-and-spoke network clearly warrant point-to-point service it might be worthwhile for a hubbing airline to pre-empt competition by offering some nonstop flights, so attracting sufficient traffic to discourage competition (unless the competitor has a sustainable price or service advantage to offer), whilst still retaining most of the flow across its hub. Launch costs would be relatively low because both stations are already online from the hub, and the market concerned is already being served.

2. **Hub to secondary city** Bypassing a second hub or gateway, this type of route has become particularly common in long-haul international markets. An example would be Dubai–Manchester, bypassing London.

A closer look at hub-and-spoke networks

Formed by routes radiating from a hub, the heartbeat of these networks is a schedule which maximises the number of feasible connections for incoming passengers whilst keeping their connecting times within some defined and acceptable limit. The following terminology is important.

- **Banks, waves, and complexes** These words describe groups of aircraft/flights that are scheduled to arrive at a hub and then depart again within a given window of time, so allowing passengers to make any of a large number of connections. However, their definitions are not settled. Some authors refer to separate 'complexes' of incoming and departing aircraft, and define two connecting complexes as a 'bank' or 'wave' (Berdy, 2002: 121). Others refer to an incoming 'bank' or 'wave' and an outgoing 'bank' or 'wave' being linked together in a connection 'complex' (Dennis, 1994: 131). This book takes the latter approach – so distinguishing between banks or waves on the one hand and complexes, each comprised of two connecting banks, on the other.
- **Windows** A window is the period from the first arrival in an inbound bank to the last departure in the next outbound bank that schedule planners give themselves to balance schedule connectivity and saleability. The longer a window, the greater will be the number of feasible connections because more flight-pairs (i.e., pairs of arriving and departing flights) exceed MCT (i.e., the 'minimum connecting time' allowable at the airport concerned to transfer between flights); conversely the shorter a window, the tighter connections will be – and the more saleable a schedule becomes if this leads to faster origin-to-destination journey times and therefore more competitive GDS display screen positions.

Defining a hub

The word 'hub' is open to several definitions.

1. The FAA defines as a 'hub' any US airport generating 0.05 per cent or more of national enplanements, but it does not load the term with any scheduling or other operational implications. (Specifically, 0.05–0.249 per cent of enplanements qualifies an airport as a 'small hub', 0.25–

0.999 per cent as a 'medium hub', and one per cent or over as a 'large hub'.)

2. Colloquial, especially journalistic, usage often refers to airports that handle large volumes of traffic and/or are the home bases for particular airlines as being 'hubs', even when inbound and outbound schedules are not co-ordinated. Hubs with little or no schedule co-ordination between inbound and outbound flights, but at which some connections do nonetheless arise from the schedule, are referred to as 'simple' or 'random' hubs.

3. Airlines (including integrators such as FedEx and UPS) generally define a hub as an airport where inbound flights are scheduled to arrive from outlying origins within a short period of time, disembarking passengers (and unloading freight) for transfer to onward flights scheduled to leave shortly afterwards for a wide range of destinations. Hubs of this type – often referred to as 'complex hubs' – act as switching centres, intermediating flows between multiple origins and multiple destinations, as well as contributing O & D traffic of their own. Complex hubs can take several forms.

    •   **Directional** Directional hubs form an hour-glass pattern with, for example, flights from the east connecting with those to the west and vice versa (e.g., Chicago O'Hare, Dallas).
    •   **Omnidirectional hubs** Omnidirectional hubs (e.g., Northwest's at Memphis) have flights coming from/departing to all points of the compass within a single complex.

    (Most flows of traffic through a hub are directional insofar as they pass from one side of the hub to the other. Some local feeder traffic might, however, be nondirectional – such as a short flight taken westwards to a hub in order to connect with a medium- or long-haul flight east.)

Staying with complex hubs, we can distinguish two types of system.

1. **Single-hub systems** Most non-US airlines with hub-and-spoke networks are constrained by the size of their domestic markets and/or by aeropolitical regulations to operate single-hub systems (e.g., Emirates and Singapore Airlines).

2. **Multi-hub systems** These exist in three forms.
    •   The largest US majors have developed multi-hub systems, some of which include several primary and secondary hubs. By connecting spoke cities (e.g., Portland, Oregon) to more than one hub (e.g., Salt Lake City and Cincinnati), it is possible to offer higher frequencies and/or wider timing choices in behind/beyond markets (e.g., Portland–New York JFK) than a single hub might permit. The

relatively long ranges of regional jets and new-generation mainline narrowbodies are allowing hub catchment areas to be extended far more widely than was feasible until the late-1990s, and therefore permitting more multi-hub spoke connections from outlying stations (as well, incidentally, as increasing hub-bypass operations). Integrated carriers have also developed multi-hub domestic systems. The longstanding FedEx hub at Memphis has been supplemented by a secondary hub at Indianapolis, and UPS has a secondary domestic hub at Philadelphia to complement its primary hub at Louisville; both companies have also developed hubs in Europe and Asia.

In any type of multi-hub system, three tasks arise which do not affect single-hub systems: the assignment of spokes to one or more of the alternative hubs; determination of inter-hub linkages (i.e., frequencies and capacities); and the routing of O & D flows through the network (when there are commercially viable alternative paths).

- Some non-US majors have developed limited multi-hub strategies, but with mixed success (e.g., Air France, British Airways, and Lufthansa). Overall, there is little single-airline secondary hubbing outside the United States.

- Global alliances have been actively developing multi-hub systems linking partners' hubs on different continents. Particularly significant have been the North Atlantic 'bar-bell' systems which draw traffic (e.g., from Luxembourg) into a hub on one side of the Atlantic (e.g., Paris CDG), and channel it to a partner's hub on the other side (e.g., Cincinnati) for onward distribution to a final destination (e.g., Omaha). Because of the multi-hub domestic systems operated by their US partners, transatlantic alliances often benefit from multiple bar-bell structures – allowing origins behind Amsterdam to be connected to US secondary points beyond one or more of Detroit, Memphis, and/or Minneapolis, to take the KLM/Northwest network as an example.

Hub quality

The strategic quality of a hub depends on several factors.

Geographic centrality A hub that is geographically central within its defined catchment area can benefit from a balanced spread of primary, secondary, and perhaps also tertiary destinations in opposite quadrants. The more central a hub is to the flows it is serving, the less route deviation it imposes;

deviation can be expensive in terms of additional operating costs and, if O & D journey times are increased to the detriment of GDS display positions, perhaps also in terms of softer yields and forgone revenues.

1. **US hubs** Although some large US hubs clearly channel significant volumes of long-haul international traffic (e.g., Miami), most remain primarily driven by short- and medium-haul domestic flows. Geographic centrality is therefore largely a question of location relative to the flows being targeted (e.g., Northeast–Florida, Midwest–Deep South, southern transcontinental, and northern transcontinental).

2. **European hubs** Most major North European hubs rely heavily on feeding long-haul routes. In part this is because of the historical significance of intercontinental routes to carriers such as Air France, British Airways, KLM, and Lufthansa; it also reflects the fact that a higher proportion of short-haul traffic in Europe than in the United States is carried on routes that are sufficiently dense to accommodate relatively high-frequency nonstop service. Another factor is the structure of the European leisure market: first, a significant proportion of intra-European vacationers are still carried on point-to-point charter services rather than by network carriers; second, the growing short-break market is largely focused on centres that can support nonstop service from most major origins. Nonetheless, flows between secondary European cities are not insignificant, and carriers such as Lufthansa and Swiss which have hubs that are centrally located relative to both north-south and east-west intra-European flows are better positioned to benefit than peripherally-based carriers such as British Airways, Iberia, and SAS.

3. **Asian hubs** Cathay Pacific, Emirates, and Singapore Airlines have consciously exploited the geographic locations of their home bases to build hubs based on sixth freedom flows as well as third and fourth freedom traffic; Korean Air, Malaysia, and Thai have developed similar network strategies.

Particularly in US domestic multi-hub systems it is important to avoid hub clutter – something that has arguably troubled US Airways' hubs at Baltimore, Philadelphia, Pittsburgh, and (in respect of some north-south flows) Charlotte. Internationally, the proximity of Singapore and Bangkok in the context of sixth freedom flows between Europe, the Middle East and Australasia was seen by some observers as a problem when Singapore Airlines joined the Star Alliance – of which Thai International was a founding member.

Strength of feed The economics of hub-and-spoke operations are based largely on the economies of scope and density available to a large, integrated hub-based network and on the fundamental fact that any type of network grows stronger with each connection that is added to it.

We can think in terms of several types of traffic feed.

1. **Regional feed** Perhaps the archetypal example of traffic feed, highly developed in North America and increasingly so in Europe, is provided to major airlines by regional carriers that have fleets and cost structures better suited to short-haul routes linking secondary and tertiary points to a hub. Regionals can offer three particular sources of strategic value: first, traffic feed is valuable to the major if an excess of revenues over costs arises in respect of those passengers who would not otherwise have flown on the major but for the regional connection; second, once feed into a hub has been locked-up, the lack of readily accessible feed for competing services can represent a formidable barrier to entry; third, even if a hub is not dominated, control over a locally important regional might be used to ensure that as far as possible feed is not timed to co-ordinate with a competitor's schedule.

    There is in particular a view that hubs fed by numerous thin spokes can be more resistant to attack from point-to-point, especially low-fare point-to-point, competition than a hub primarily fed by dense routes. The development of 'fortress hubs' in the United States after deregulation was predicated on dominating traffic into and out of a metropolitan airport, and swamping markets within 500 miles of it with high-frequency services to ensure unchallenged regional feed. (The range capabilities and passenger appeal of regional jets pose a threat to this dominance strategy, however, by making even spoke cities close to a hub potentially accessible to another carrier's more distant hub.)

    Feed from regionals has become so important that several US and European majors have either built their own operations internally or, more commonly, acquired their formerly independent regional code-share partners and franchisees. Some implications of this trend are explored in Box 6.3.

Box 6.3: Whether to own or contract for regional feed

American's purchase of Delta Connection carrier Business Express in 1999 deprived Delta of significant volumes of feed in the US Northeast, and helped concentrate minds on the importance to hub viability of controlling regional feed. Whilst internal control of regionals had long been on the agenda for American and Continental, it was only in the late 1990s that

Delta, Air France, British Airways, and KLM, moved to acquire most of their regional affiliates.

On the other hand, an 89-day strike at Comair – one of the Connection carriers that Delta took full control of after its Business Express experience – underlined the risks involved in drawing regional operations too close to the 'gravity fields' of major airlines' flight-crew pay structures. Short stage-lengths and small aircraft make regional airlines expensive operations, and despite their relatively high yields these carriers rely on low salaries and benefits to sustain profitability. The flight-crew costs per ASM of operating a 30- or 50-seater with pilots even at the bottom end of the majors' pay scales are not sustainable. Particularly in the United States, majors have a tough equation to balance.

- *They need to secure regional feed, but purely contractual code-sharing and franchise arrangements might not prove permanent if a regional's ownership changes hands.*
- *Furthermore, inhouse regional operations can make valuable contributions to the corporate bottom line. (The counter-argument, of course, is that balance sheets might benefit from the proceeds of selling-off profitable regional affiliates. This was a major justification for regional spin-offs by Continental and others beginning in 2002.)*
- *Against ownership of regionals is the likelihood that over time any regional controlled by a major will experience upward cost pressures.*
- *In addition, having a portfolio of ownership and contractual relationships with a spread of different code-share partners, perhaps feeding the same hubs down different spokes, in preference to ownership can limit the sort of damage done by the Comair strike at what at the time was a single-feeder hub at Cincinnati. (Delta has been actively pursuing this feed-diversification strategy since 2001.)*

2. **Feed for long-haul international services** Significant international hubs generally rely on either or both regional and short-/medium-haul mainline feed. This is particularly true of European and Asian hubs, as well as a small number of US hubs (e.g., Miami and San Francisco). The presence or absence of feed, and also traffic rights, can have a profound influence on network design at the individual route level. For example, Emirates' extensive feed from the Indian subcontinent into its Dubai hub allows it to operate a daily nonstop Dubai–Birmingham (UK) service tapping ethnic O & D markets; British Airways, on the other hand – confronted by negligible feed behind its small Birmingham hub, thin local Birmingham–Dubai traffic, and no network beyond Dubai – cannot justify operating on the route itself.

3. **Alliance feed** As many as 40 per cent of US passengers flying overseas originate behind international gateways, with the result that foreign carriers lacking an alliance with a strong US partner face an uphill battle accessing this flow traffic. More generally, a key purpose underlying alliance formation is the exchange of traffic between networks. Around $500 million of Delta's approximately $16 billion revenue in 2000 was attributable to alliance flows (Pinkham, 2001). Given the tens of thousands of city-pair markets that multi-hub international alliances can serve 'online', joint network planning and scheduling that allows them to pick-up just a few passengers a week in each can translate into significant revenue gains over a year.

   It is therefore critical that as far as possible a carrier's schedule is timed to exchange traffic with partners' services. For example, airlines will want their international services to arrive at a partner's hub in time to maximise onward connections to a conveniently timed outbound bank, and they will want their return long-haul services to depart after receiving feed from an incoming bank; achieving this given the constraints imposed by time zones, airport curfews, and the need to minimise the turnaround times of long-haul aircraft at partners' hubs is not always easy.

4. **Intermodal feed** For passengers, modal interchanges between air transport and railways have been common in Europe for several decades, and are being both extended and upgraded with the widening of high-speed train services; in the United States, Continental and Amtrak launched an air-rail code-share into Newark in early 2002. Some regional and short-haul mainline flights into hubs that compete against improving rail services will undoubtedly lose local traffic to the point that they are no longer viable even as feeders for long-haul routes; there is therefore the prospect that, particularly in Western Europe, both intermodal feed and straight O & D competition from trains will help release slots at those hubs that are well-connected to the rail network.

   Given the distances some US domestic passengers are prepared to drive in order to access Southwest's low fares, there is an argument that these customers are providing their own intermodal feed. Although this point might sound somewhat semantic, its practical impact is that at a given station Southwest may have a larger surface catchment area than would a full-service carrier charging significantly higher fares. Its traffic volumes at these stations may therefore suffer less from the absence of short-haul regional feed than might otherwise be the case.

   In both Europe and North America, airlines make extensive use of trucks to feed freight onto medium- and long-haul flights. Also on the freight side, several airports around the world (e.g., Seattle-Tacoma and Sharjah) have developed as sea-air transfer points.

Local traffic The amount, mix, yield, and growth potential of the local traffic it can generate to supplement flow traffic is also an important measure of a hub's quality, as is the balance between originating and terminating local traffic (which can affect the directionality of support that day-return passengers travelling to or from the hub provide to the first and last complexes each day). Figures quoted for local traffic as an ideal minimum of total hub traffic range from 25 to 40 per cent. In the US domestic market, Continental's Newark hub relies on local traffic for approximately 70 per cent of its volume, whilst Delta's Cincinnati hub is only around 20 per cent local. Insufficient local traffic was one of the reasons behind withdrawal from some of their secondary hubs by US majors in the 1990s. The potential importance of local traffic to hub profitability is a principal reason why the 'waypoint' concept advanced in the 1990s – the idea of relocating hubs from congested metropolitan airports to newly developed facilities at geographically convenient but lightly populated locations – was still-born.

Most majors like to rely to whatever extent is possible on 'captive', and therefore often reasonably high-yield, local traffic out of hubs which – with one or two notable exceptions such as Chicago O'Hare – they successfully dominate. Absence of strong, high-yield local traffic may leave a hub over-dependent on flow traffic which can in some cases be relatively low-yield business if other airlines are competing to attract it over alternative hubs. One of the reasons for KLM's relatively low yield at various times despite the generally high quality of its product is that its small local market leaves it more reliant on connecting traffic than, for example, British Airways and Lufthansa – both of which are based in major traffic-generating countries.

Hub dominance The scale of a carrier's presence at a hub can be measured in terms of its percentage of aircraft and/or seat departures and – where relevant – its control over slots, gates, and terminal space. A dominant carrier may benefit from the 'S-curve' effect (see chapter 4), economies of scope and density, high station resource utilisation, premium yields from local traffic, local marketing strength, and – at slot-constrained airports – protection behind a significant structural barrier to entry. There is little doubt that hub-and-spoke systems have been an important force behind consolidation in the US domestic market, and are now playing a similar role in the global market.

Expansion capacity Whilst capacity constraints do impose a barrier to entry and so protect incumbents, the lack of terminal space and/or runway slots might be a significant strategic constraint. This can be seen clearly in the comparison between British Airways' problems at London Heathrow and Air France's expansion potential at Paris CDG.

Attractiveness to passengers Hubs are fundamentally attractive because of the range and timing of connections they offer, but where there is little to choose between two competing hubs in this respect it could be that physical factors such as the availability of lounges and other facilities and the design of public spaces might influence choice of airline.

Hub efficiency Particularly when a customer's choice of airline is driven by minimum elapsed journey time, a carrier wanting to attract that passenger to a service which involves connecting over its hub needs to ensure that MCT at the hub is competitive with MCTs at competing hubs. Tight MCTs require airline, suppliers of outsourced services (e.g., catering, handling, etc.), and airport authority to work together in order to sustain an acceptable service level (Nichols and Sala, 2000). This is not only a revenue-side issue; long MCTs at a hub can feed through into less efficient resource utilisation. Important factors can be the ability to use proximate gates to facilitate passenger and baggage transfers over high-volume connections, and the ability to use the same gates for each significant high-frequency market throughout the day (Berdy, 1998). The ideal situation is where an airline can effect all its online and alliance transfers under one roof. This should reduce MCTs compared with multi-terminal operations.

In selecting a site for a new hub, the most critical considerations are geographical location, the economic potential of the catchment area, the availability of uncongested infrastructure or the ability to develop it, the prevailing pattern of service in respect of quality and price, the volume and yield available from local traffic, the co-operativeness of the airport authority, and the costs of operating a station. In the final analysis, what an airline makes of a hub's various qualities will depend to a significant extent on the effectiveness of scheduling; we will look at scheduling in chapter 7.

Hub-and-spoke networks: pros and cons

We will consider these from both airlines' and passengers' perspectives.

Airline perspectives: positive factors There are several.

1. **Connectivity** Hub-and-spoke systems provide better network connectivity, and so wider market coverage, than linear networks. Any given

number of points can be linked over a hub with fewer departures than nonstop or direct services would require. Furthermore, once a hub has been established each additional spoke magnifies the linkage benefits – that is, substantially broadens the range of markets served. Ten spokes could theoretically provide direct service between ten outstations and the hub as well as connecting service between 45 different pairs of out-stations, for example; were the number of spokes to be increased 50 per cent to 15 the number of direct services would also increase 50 per cent to 15, but connecting services would increase 133 per cent to 105. (The formula for this calculation is $n(n-1)/2$, where n is the number of spok-es radiating from a hub.) Good connectivity can underpin greater rev-enue capture from a given area and, assuming feed is online rather than interline, can help reduce prorate dilution compared with what can happen when journeys are interlined.

2. **Load factors** It is generally true that the larger an incoming bank of arrivals, the easier it is to support outgoing flights. A 150-seat aircraft leaving a hub after the arrival of a bank from 25 points, for instance, would need on average to pick up only four passengers from each in-coming flight to achieve a 66.6 per cent load factor (ignoring local traffic); if the bank brought flights from only ten points, ten connecting passengers would be needed from each to achieve the same result. (Of course, what really matters is revenue rather than raw load factors, and this will depend upon the yield earned from each passenger, which is often lower for connecting services than for nonstop routes between the same origin and destination.)

3. **Costs** By channelling passengers from multiple origins to multiple destinations a hub-and-spoke network can address to some extent the production indivisibilities that arise from having to split an airline's output of seat-miles amongst different city-pair markets; hub-and-spoke networks allow more city-pair markets to be served for a given level of output (i.e., ASMs, etc.) than other forms of network. Alternat-ively, fewer legs need be flown to serve a given number of O & D mar-kets.

   • We have already noted that *economies of scope* are generated when it costs less to combine onto one departure down a spoke to a hub passengers wanting to travel beyond that hub to several destinat-ions than it would to provide nonstop or direct services to each of these destinations using smaller aircraft operated at lower frequenc-ies (something which, in thinner markets, might anyway not be feasible).

   • *Economies of density* arise when the combination of traffic onto a spoke allows larger aircraft with lower seat-mile costs to be used

388 *Straight and Level: Practical Airline Economics*

than could otherwise be supported at acceptable load factors – although these economies might be traded-off against higher frequencies using smaller aircraft, depending on the market segments being targeted and the airline's market positioning. Economies of density are essentially 'aircraft economies of scale', with minimum efficient scale dependent upon the stage-length concerned relative to the operating economics of available aircraft.

- *Marketing economies of scale*, particularly information economies, can be exploited when a carrier is able to identify itself strongly with a hub and its hinterland, especially if local distribution channels can be dominated as well. The widespread brand awareness that often attaches to a large carrier can have the effect of curtailing information search by potential customers who simply assume that airline's presence in the market in which they want to travel without further investigating alternatives; challengers have to spend heavily on marketing communications in order to overcome this disadvantage – particularly when it is reinforced by FFP membership and corporate deals.

4. **GDS display priority** Assume a carrier has three services originating in origins O_1, O_2, and O_3. Each uses a separate aircraft to hub H and then a single aircraft (perhaps one of the original three, or perhaps another) from H to destination D. Further assume that the airline markets services from O_1, O_2, and O_3 to D under three different flight numbers. A local passenger enquiring about travel between H and D around the time of the airline's departure on this leg will find the agent's GDS screen displaying three different flight numbers even though the carrier is operating just one aircraft. This use of funnel flights for 'screen padding', which is restricted by codes of conduct in some jurisdictions, can have the effect of pushing competitors' services to the bottom of the important first page of the GDS display from which most agency bookings originate.

5. **Strategy** Also significant for the few carriers with aspirations to play leading roles in the emerging global mega-alliances is the widespread view that such roles are not open to airlines that do not possess a major hub in one of the world's principal traffic-generating regions.

Airline perspectives: negative factors Circumstances vary, but negative factors might include the following.

1. Hub-and-spoke networks require each passenger to be flown a greater distance between origin and destination, and journeys entail the extra costs of landing, ground-handling, and take-off at the hub. The pres-

umption has been that these costs (ignoring additional journey times imposed on passengers) are lower than the costs of providing low-frequency direct or nonstop service in multiple city-pair markets, and are outweighed by the benefits derived from channelling traffic flows over a hub.

2. Average stage-lengths could be reduced by a hub stopover, depending upon network geography; unit production costs generally rise as stage-lengths fall.

3. Hubs can be expensive to build and operate. They require investment in infrastructure; that infrastructure is in essence a production capability offering throughput capacity, and like all forms of capacity it needs to be fully utilised in order to spread fixed costs over the maximum possible amount of output (in this case, flights).

One problem associated with hubbing is that its essence is to concentrate traffic into banks of arrivals and departures. Such self-inflicted peaking, as with all peaking phenomena, comes at a cost in terms of resource utilisation. However, traffic has grown at a handful of the largest hubs to the point that no sooner has the last flight in an outbound bank departed than the first of the next inbound bank is arriving; this situation is referred to as a 'continuous' or 'rolling' hub. American developed Dallas-Fort Worth (DFW) into a 'rolling hub' during the 1990s, for example, with incoming banks as little as 1-1½ hours apart. (In the course of a network-wide capacity reduction programme announced in 2002, it then went one step further by 'de-peaking' the hub – spreading operations more evenly across the day and accepting longer connecting times.) Continuous hubbing removes the disadvantages of self-inflicted peaking by spreading resource utilisation more evenly, and it can also help overcome infrastructure constraints by allocating services from some spoke cities to alternate inbound banks rather than to every complex. (See Berdy (1998) for a discussion of continuous flow networks.)

4. Aircraft may have to spend too long waiting on the ground during each hub turn because passengers need time to connect off arriving flights, and sometimes also because of ground and terminal area congestion; gate utilisation may also be low as a result. Dwell-time at a hub will depend in part on efficiency in allocating aircraft arriving early in an inbound bank to early departures in the connecting outbound bank – something that will in turn depend upon whether the particular type(s) or variant(s) operating early inbound flights are sized correctly to serve early outbound flights.

Dwell-time is likely to increase as flights are added to a bank. Assume 30 arrivals at an average rate of one every 40 seconds, connecting time between last arrival and first departure of 30 minutes (although in reality this is a pairing that might be designed to carry minimal traffic in the O & D market concerned and so be sacrificed to increase efficiency), and an average departure rate of one per minute: the window for the complex is 20 + 30 + 30 = 80 minutes. Assuming we add one incoming and one outgoing flight and maintain the same MCT of 30 minutes, the dwell-time of at least some of the existing aircraft will be increased – albeit by just a few seconds; add more than one flight and magnify the effect across a year's schedule at the hub, and the impact on aircraft utilisation becomes more pronounced.

Another potential source of aircraft utilisation problems is that the need for flights to arrive at and depart from a hub within a fairly narrow time window will mean, in the absence of creative network design and scheduling, that aircraft serving spokes with the shortest flight-times will spend longer periods on the ground at outstations before returning to the hub than will those serving distant points. This clearly involves utilisation and, therefore, unit cost penalties. (We will return to the topic in chapter 7.)

5. Taxiway and terminal area congestion increase unproductive fuel-burn.

6. Difficult choices might be faced with regard to the location of light maintenance activities when aircraft are 'stabled' overnight at outstations in order to offer early departures to the hub. This can particularly affect short-haul aircraft which might otherwise undergo phased checks at night were they at the home base or some other maintenance facility. (A 'phased check' involves the breaking down of intermediate checks into work packages that can be spread over a number of lighter checks performed overnight were the aircraft stabled at a hub with a maintenance facility, but not if it is stabled at an outstation.)

7. Yields from flow traffic in respect of which there might be more competition than local traffic attracts at a dominated hub can sometimes be low. Against this, of course, flow traffic may help exploit economies of density by allowing the use of larger aircraft than could otherwise be supported by local traffic alone. The balance will vary from case to case, but dissatisfaction with low yields from main cabin flow traffic was one reason behind British Airways' downsizing strategy launched in 1999.

8. Ontime performance is vital to the integrity of a hub-and-spoke system, but can be hostage to the weather, technical faults, traffic congestion, and operational inefficiency. A widespread schedule disruption at a hub tends to propagate around a hub-and-spoke system more readily than across a simple, linear system. In a worst-case scenario, enforced holding or diversion of an incoming bank could (if different aircraft are inv-

olved) lead to subsequent complexes backing up on the first – bearing in mind that the last arrivals of an incoming bank and the first arrivals of the next incoming bank might be less than two hours apart at a four-wave hub. (Irrgang (1995a) provides a thorough explanation of the problem.) This was one reason why American chose in 2001 to isolate the Chicago O'Hare hub from the rest of its system.

9. Balancing local and flow traffic to maximise revenue can be difficult. Generally, an airline will earn more revenue from carrying two separate local passengers into and out of a hub than one connecting passenger in the same booking class on the same flights; this is because fares taper with distance, so the two local passengers are each likely to pay more per mile or kilometre than the connecting passenger. Furthermore, it is often – although not invariably – the case that a carrier has more monopoly power over local traffic into and out of its hub than it does over connecting traffic, because connecting traffic might (depending on market geography) have a wide choice of alternative networks available. However, there are two complicating factors.

- First, many carriers unable to sell a high proportion of their seats to local traffic, particularly during off-peak periods, need fill-up flow traffic. (The alternative is to operate smaller aircraft sized more appropriately to the local market and less reliant on flow traffic; if these smaller aircraft have higher seat-mile costs, the product offered must in principle be good enough to sustain the firmer yields now required.)

- Second, it will not always be the case that selling seats to local passengers travelling in a low-yield booking class (e.g., deeply discounted economy/coach) will be optimal from a network revenue standpoint if these seats are no longer available to a higher-yield connecting passenger (e.g., a late-booking, full-fare economy/coach passenger). We will explore this point in chapter 9.

Weighing up the pros and cons of hubbing presents no general rule as to its merits relative to more traditional network designs. Hub-and-spoke networks are effective traffic gatherers and distributors, but they are not necessarily efficient in terms of resource utilisation; as O & D markets become more dense and demand for hub-bypass service grows, neither are these networks necessarily effective in terms of delivering customer satisfaction. Although there have been empirical studies suggesting that hubs contribute to unit cost reductions (McShane and Windle, 1989; Brueckner et al, 1992), the influences putting both upward and downward pressures on hub costs are complicated and intertwined, and may lead to different conclusions in each specific case.

That said, the resource utilisation penalties often associated with hub operations came under particularly critical review in the United States after 9/11. Questions were raised regarding the viability in the changed economic environment of a short-haul business model founded on the twin pillars of:

- full-service hub-based networks; and
- an opaque pricing structure comprising high unrestricted fares targeted at business travellers and very much lower restricted fares intended for leisure/VFR customers – with profitability almost entirely dependent on the former (see McDonald, 2002).

In essence, hubs are able to deliver the network and schedule benefits required by business travellers in particular, but they can be expensive to operate and there is some doubt whether customers as a whole value these benefits sufficiently to cover the costs of delivering them. The best conclusion that can be drawn at present is that the economics of any hub depend upon: points served, demand in local markets with the hub at one end, traffic flows that can be created by channelling O & D demand over the hub, yields available, and how efficiently hub operations are managed.

Passengers' perspectives These vary widely, depending to a large extent upon the impact of network structure on the availability and price of service in those markets in which individual passengers want to travel. Two particular concerns are commonly expressed.

1. **Spoke cities** The concern here is that as hub-and-spoke systems are developed spoke cities frequently lose nonstop service to destinations other than hubs, and that their quality of service suffers as a result. This can be true. On the other hand, there are several counterpoints.
    - First, the channelling of flow traffic over hubs often gives passengers originating in spoke cities access to a wide range of O & D city-pairs – many of which could not support nonstop service from those cities.
    - Second, it is likely that they will benefit from higher frequencies to the hub and onwards to other destinations than nonstop services in individual O & D markets could sustain.
    - Third, as traffic density increases in an O & D market served over a hub, it is possible that direct or nonstop hub-bypass services will be introduced (perhaps to supplement, rather than replace, connecting service).

- Fourth, if connected to different airlines' separate hubs, passengers could benefit from competitive fares to any single destination beyond those hubs.

2. **Hub cities** The primary concern in respect of 'fortress hub' O & D markets in particular is that passengers might have to pay a price premium because of the monopoly power exercised by the dominant carrier (Graham et al, 1983; Bailey et al, 1985; Call and Keeler, 1985; Morrison and Winston, 1987; Borenstein, 1989; Transportation Research Board, 1999; Bamberger and Carlton, 2002). Sources of monopoly power could include co-option of airport facilities, influence over local agency channels, the attractions of the carrier's FFP to passengers based near the hub and so having easy access from there to multiple destinations around its network, and information economies of scale.

    On the other hand, passengers living close to the hub probably benefit from having higher frequencies on offer to more destinations than would otherwise be the case, which leads to several possible advantages: less time is wasted waiting for low-frequency departures or changing planes at another hub, scope exists for day-return trips to a wider range of destinations, and greater opportunities arise to 'earn and burn' FFP awards. Furthermore, hub dominance is sometimes not as overwhelming as cursory analysis might make it appear: dominance of a hub airport is not necessarily the same as dominance of local traffic into and out of the city served by that airport (e.g., Southwest and easy-Jet both use secondary airports to compete with network carriers' nearby hubs in the same metropolitan areas or regions); second, a hub airline's dominance of local enplanements might not be as great as its dominance of aggregate local and connecting enplanements (e.g., British Airways has a much less dominant share of local traffic to and from London Heathrow than of aggregate local and flow traffic); third, dense routes out of a hub might support point-to-point competition, particularly during 'voids' between the hubbing carrier's complexes, so depriving that carrier of some of its monopoly power.

More generally, it seems that hubs are becoming increasingly unpopular, especially with business travellers, because of congestion and delays. Post-9/11 security procedures sometimes add to the problem and threaten MCTs.

ii. Network strategies and tactics

It can be useful to distinguish between network strategies and network tactics.

- **Network strategy** This defines the number and nature of points served (i.e., the mix of primary, secondary, and tertiary points and of city-break, longer vacation, business, and VFR destinations), routes used to serve them, and output (i.e., frequencies and capacities) offered. It is the service proposition on which everything else in an airline should be built insofar as it links directly through to an airline's strategic description of itself – as a full-service global network carrier, as a low-fare point-to-point operator, as a regional, and so on. What represents a 'strong' network will depend upon the competitive strategy and product positioning of the airline concerned. In designing its network Ryanair, for example, looks to points that can be served at relatively low cost (i.e., secondary airports), that will support reasonable frequencies using B737s, and that contain in their catchment areas significant or potentially significant segments of price-sensitive demand – whether from VFR passengers (e.g., UK–Ireland, UK–Italy), leisure (including city-break) passengers, or (in a few cases) business travellers.
- **Network tactics** In liberalised and deregulated competitive environments, networks are both less proprietary and more dynamic than they were when tightly regulated. Rapidly changing competitive environments demand tactical responses – increases or reductions in frequencies, the rerouting of services in particular city-pair markets, and the introduction and elimination of routes.

Whilst network design must remain reasonably consistent for long-term strategic purposes and detailed route patterns have to be broadly fixed for short-term operational purposes, in the medium term networks are likely to be expanded, contracted, and restructured whenever profitability is a corporate objective and an airline is free to design its own route system.

Network strategies

The principal parameters within which network strategies unfold are:

- competitive strategy and product positioning;
- commercial regulation affecting both access to markets and permissible output (i.e., frequencies and capacity) – a constraint that is diminishing in many national and international markets but nonetheless remains an important consideration in others;
- national ownership requirements – which, other than within the EU, Australasia, and a few Latin American countries, preclude foreign control of airlines; and

- infrastructure constraints.

Some carriers are by design point-to-point operators with linear or grid networks; this is particularly true of low-fare airlines, charter carriers, and national carriers whose home bases provide limited hubbing opportunities. Nonetheless, if we look at two apparently similar airlines, it is sometimes possible to identify significantly different network strategies: whereas Ryanair often targets secondary airports (e.g., Frankfurt Hahn), easyJet is more willing to serve major airports (e.g., Nice and Paris Orly) where it believes higher costs can be covered by firmer yields; when first established by KLM uk and British Airways, the network strategies of low-fare carriers Buzz and Go were focused on mainline airports serving price-sensitive segments of the business market (as well as city-break traffic).

Large network carriers and the regionals and/or other affiliates that feed them by definition operate hub-and-spoke networks. In addition, many also operate tag-end flights, 'free flights' (i.e., legs scheduled for otherwise un-utilised aircraft downtime and unconnected to a hub complex), and point-to-point or hub-bypass routes in non-hub markets strong enough to support nonstop service.

Network strategies in different markets

The US domestic market Notwithstanding the consistent and largely point-to-point growth of Southwest and the low-cost 'airline within an airline' initiatives launched by some of the US majors, hubs are a necessary response to the geography of air transport demand in the United States. It is likely that despite ongoing growth in hub-bypass services, hubs will continue to process 70 per cent or more of domestic traffic into the foreseeable future. That said, US majors have for several years been building their non-hub flying by adding point-to-point services – often targeted at 'focus cities', from each of which a number of hub-bypass routes will radiate. Around 20 per cent of American's domestic flying is non-hub, for example (Feldman, 2001). Demand growth in many short- and medium-haul O & D markets that have to date been able to justify only connecting service over a hub is such that nonstop or direct flights are gradually being introduced in more markets either to supplement or to replace hub connections. The payload-range capabilities of new generation regional jets and mainline narrowbodies are helping accelerate this market fragmentation. The preference of some passengers for avoiding large hubs since 9/11 may have added impetus to this pre-existing trend.

The intra-European market Within Europe, hubs cannot be expected to
intermediate traffic flows between primary centres because distances are
generally too short and traffic densities are sufficient to support high-frequency nonstop services. As noted above, infrastructure constraints, the high
costs per seat of operating small regional aircraft at some airports, a growing high-speed rail network, and the significant role of charter carriers in
leisure markets also limit the prospects for intra-European hubbing. Indeed,
infrastructure constraints have been one reason behind the strong growth of
hub-bypass services in Europe.

Given these factors and also the sustained growth of low-fare carriers in
markets supporting at least double-daily service with 150-seaters, it seems
likely that European network carriers' short-haul mainline operations will
focus on feeding their medium- and long-haul networks and serving dense
markets that have sufficient relatively price-insensitive high-yield traffic to
support these airlines' high cost bases. Whilst intra-European hubbing between pairs of secondary and tertiary centres will continue to grow at relatively uncongested primary hubs such as Paris CDG and at secondary hubs
such as Munich, there will be particularly strong growth in non-hub flying
by regionals.

Long-haul international markets With one or two exceptions, most long-
haul international networks tended until the 1980s to be linear in design and
heavily oriented towards one or a small number of primary gateways in
each country. In most countries these gateways were the capital city and/or
significant commercial centres. Since the 1980s several have become hubs
in hub-and-spoke networks; in the United States they have been supplemented by the growth of newer inland hubs, such as Cincinnati and Detroit,
supported by domestic feed. While this process was unfolding, traffic on
the North Atlantic was being fragmented by the growth of flows from gateways or primary hubs at one end (e.g., New York or Washington DC) to
secondary cities (e.g., Nice or Dusseldorf). A much-debated question is the
extent to which this will happen in other long-haul markets – notably those
with points in Asia at one end.

Several types of long-haul international hub can be identified.

1. **Third- and fourth-freedom domestic-international hubs** This is the
    traditional model under which, say, United feeds domestic traffic onto
    its own long-haul services out of Washington Dulles and American
    does the same out of Miami. Conversely, inbound international flows
    channelled over Dulles and Miami are distributed across their respect-
    ive domestic networks.

2. **Fifth freedom hubs** These are relatively rare. They exist where an airline registered in Country 1 and operating one or more routes to Country 2 and beyond to several other countries has traffic rights to carry local traffic between Country 2 and those other countries. Northwest and United gained extensive fifth freedom rights beyond Tokyo, for example, and both developed Narita as an interchange point for traffic from various US origins travelling on to multiple destinations in Asia; flows in the reverse direction are also hubbed over Narita. The availability of long-range B777s and A340s and the opening of transpolar air corridors to serve nonstop hub-bypass routes to South and Southeast Asia from North America will together reduce the significance of Narita as a fifth freedom hub for transpacific traffic, but rights beyond Tokyo nonetheless continue to provide valuable access to intra-Asian routes for the US carriers that hold them.

   Delta inherited from Pan Am a substantial fifth freedom hub at Frankfurt in the early 1990s, but subsequently dismantled it. On a smaller scale, Iberia chose Miami as a change-of-gauge fifth freedom hub, whilst Qantas has used the strategy at Singapore for many years – feeding traffic from points such as Cairns, Townsville, Darwin, and Perth to connect with Singapore–Europe services flown by B747-400s originating in Melbourne or Sydney; in the 1990s, American introduced a cross-connect operation at Sao Paulo, with flights from Dallas, Miami, and New York proceeding onwards to Asuncion, Montevideo, and Rio (the latter destination being domestic from Sao Paulo rather than fifth freedom). On the cargo side, Lufthansa has a number of fifth freedom hubs around the world (e.g., Sharjah), and on a much larger scale FedEx has hubs at Paris CDG and Subic Bay.

3. **Sixth freedom hubs** Sixth freedom hubs exist where a carrier combines fourth and third freedoms to pick up traffic in one foreign country (e.g., Australia) destined for another (e.g., France) and channel it over a hub in its own country (e.g., Dubai). Cathay Pacific, KLM, and to a lesser extent Swissair were operating reasonably well-integrated sixth freedom hubs several decades ago, and in the 1970s Singapore Airlines was amongst the first of a new generation of carriers to develop the strategy further. Emirates followed in the 1980s. A more recent example of what can be achieved is provided by American Airlines' combined domestic-international and sixth freedom (Europe–Latin America) hub at Miami.

   These days, few international carriers of any size fail to make some effort to co-ordinate flows into and out of their 'hubs', but not many are making a real living out of it. This is nonetheless a phenomenon that is continuing to grow and which, in some long-haul O & D markets, is adding a fair amount of spice to price competition.

4. **Interline and alliance hubs** The smooth transfer of passengers between carriers at points where networks meet – facilitated by interline agreements and well-developed IATA procedures – has been a necessary consequence of the postwar Chicago regulatory regime, and has transformed a collection of hundreds of route systems into what is from a passenger's perspective a 'virtual network' of global proportions. Out of this 'interline hubbing', much of which is random rather than tightly co-ordinated, has more recently evolved 'alliance hubbing'. The difference is that either in specific individual markets, across a route-group, or globally, two or more airlines enter into closer marketing ties than those consistent with traditional interline agreements, using one or more of co-ordinated scheduling, code-sharing, joint fares, joint inventory and revenue management, joint promotional activities, mutual recognition of high-value passengers, and shared FFPs to keep passengers 'online'. Box 6.4 takes a closer look at alliance hubbing.

Box 6.4: Alliance hubbing

A scheduled airline's core product is the schedule of departures within its network. If that network can be broadened and/or the schedule can be deepened by incorporating the departures of an alliance partner, the airline has more to offer its customers. No individual airline has – or is likely to develop – a truly global network. A fundamental objective of the handful of emerging global alliances is to extend partners' network reach into as many as possible of the world's major point-to-point markets and, importantly, to gain access to literally tens of thousands of connecting city-pair markets. Alliances might be a carrier's only way into those markets for aeropolitical reasons (e.g., the airline has no traffic rights and is precluded from controlling a foreign carrier that does), for economic reasons (e.g., its fleet and/or cost structure are unsuitable for the markets concerned or those markets will not support competing services), for infrastructural reasons (e.g., slots are unavailable at a desired destination), or for financial reasons (e.g., the airline has insufficient resources to develop new markets on its own). In what may turn out to be a zero-sum game in the end, alliances endeavour to win market share by offering higher frequencies and shorter journey times to more destinations than their competitors.

Network complementarity (i.e., maximisation of unduplicated routes) amongst partners is clearly desirable – from the point of view of reach extension and also because higher complementarity can dilute negative eff-

ects on competition relative to the combining of heavily duplicated networks. Features common to this type of scope extension include:

- *designing networks that tap O & D traffic in major nonstop markets and maximise access to flow traffic in connecting markets unable to support high-frequency nonstop service;*
- *creating multi-hub systems able both to dominate inter-hub markets and to capture flows of traffic originating in secondary or tertiary points behind one hub and destined for secondary and tertiary points beyond another. On inter-hub routes, a relatively high proportion of traffic (over 40 per cent in the case of KLM and Northwest) is likely to be accounted for by double-connecting cross-feed; and*
- *using code-sharing and, in regional markets, franchising to extend network reach and, together with highly integrated scheduling, maximise city-pair connectivity with the objective of capturing and retaining online a high proportion of end-to-end journeys made in targeted market segments.*

The economic and marketing motivations behind international alliances are not dissimilar to those that drive any type of hubbing, with the one difference that they are a vehicle for 'market share gain without balance sheet pain'. They are also a means of coming to terms with the prevailing international aeropolitical regime while politicians ponder just how much of that regime is going to survive.

Conclusion A network carrier's mainline hub-and-spoke and point-to-point operations, alone and in co-operation with partners, might be part of a multi-faceted network strategy using separate operating units and contractual relationships to extend network reach – both broadly across the 'global market', and more narrowly into specific geographical and/or product niches unsuited to the mainline full-service product. As Southwest, Ryanair, easyJet, and European charter carriers have proven, however, hub-and-spoke networks are not the only game in town. Indeed, the argument was widely heard in the aftermath of 9/11 that the cost structures of several US and European majors are such that their short-haul mainline networks will inevitably shrink under pressure from low-fare carriers.

Clearly, network strategy and other aspects of product strategy have to be aligned. A carrier targeting price-sensitive segments, for example, needs low costs and will generally not want to support an expensive hub. A network carrier relying on relatively low-yield transfer traffic (e.g., Emirates and KLM) will need lower cost products (based on either lower input costs or higher productivity) than a carrier oriented more towards premium point-to-point traffic (e.g., British Airways – whose inflight products in premium classes are targeted at high-yield segments but have high unit production costs).

Cargo networks

The overwhelming majority of airlines fly cargo in the belly-holds of pass-enger aircraft, and therefore do not operate separate passenger and cargo networks; scheduling and capacity conflicts can sometimes arise between passengers and cargo, and passenger requirements generally prevail. All-cargo airlines and combination carriers that operate owned and/or wet-leas-ed freighters have more network design and scheduling flexibility; basic network design options – linear, point-to-point, and hub-and-spoke – rem-ain the same, however. With regard to hub-and-spoke systems, it is note-worthy that there is more concentration on the cargo side than on the passenger side of the industry: the top ten cargo hubs account for around two-thirds of cargo movements, whereas the top ten passenger hubs accou-nt for only one-third of passenger movements (Taneja, 2002). The growth of focused cargo alliances is likely to add further momentum to this patt-ern of concentration.

Alliances in fact raise issues of some interest on the cargo side. From a positive perspective, it is the case that provided freight arrives on time, in good condition, and properly documented, neither shippers nor consignees are generally concerned about which alliance partner's aircraft are used and what routing is followed; code-sharing presents fewer service delivery iss-ues than on the passenger side, provided standards of service at customer interfaces are compatible and consistent. Less positively, some alliance members are arguably not as committed to freight as their partners, and this has led in several cases to 'alliances within alliances' such as WOW – the cargo link-up initiated in April 2000 by Star members Lufthansa, SAS, and Singapore Airlines, and subsequently joined from outside Star by Japan Airlines. (SkyTeam is in principle both a cargo and passenger alliance – although, again, Air France and Korean Air appear on the surface to have a much deeper corporate commitment to the cargo business than do several of their partners.)

If airfreight growth outstrips growth in passenger traffic over the next two decades by as significant a margin as forecasts suggest, it is likely that we will see further separation of passenger and freighter operations and therefore the growth of more freight-only networks. Alliance partners will further develop a trend that has already begun by combining their traffic rights to offer round-the-world connections which mirror freight flows. (It is already the case that rather than accept low-volume back-hauls across the

North Pacific from the United States, some Asian carriers route eastbound freighters onwards across the North Atlantic to pick up loads in Europe destined for Asia.) Particularly in noise-sensitive areas such as Europe which also face severe congestion problems at major hubs, it is quite possible that cargo networks will increasingly encompass regional airports – often newly developed or redeveloped and with good surface access – specialising primarily or entirely in handling freight movements.

Network tactics

The interest here is in network design rather than scheduling tactics, which will be discussed in the next chapter. An airline might face a wide range of tactical issues with regard to network design. We will touch on just two of the most common: attacking a hub; and responding to a challenger.

Attacking a hub

There is little doubt that hubs can be a source of significant competitive advantage – notwithstanding concerns about their costs, the downsizing and closure of some secondary hubs in the United States, and the success of a number of point-to-point carriers in some product and geographical markets. The purpose of hub-and-spoke systems is to enlarge the scope of network coverage, and in doing this they can create both operational and marketing barriers to entry. One of their strengths is the ability to consolidate feed down relatively thin spokes onto denser routes between hubs and other major centres. Network flows such as this are arguably more defensible against low-fare entrants than dense linear route patterns; relatively few city-pair markets are sufficiently large to support multiple competitors operating nonstop or direct at commercially viable frequencies and acceptable load factors, and an established hub-based carrier adding one more route to an already substantial network is more likely to be able to sustain service in a thin market than a significantly smaller entrant.

A wide network served with high frequencies over one or more integrated hubs can therefore offer a differentiated product which is difficult and very expensive to compete against. An additional barrier to entry is erected when ownership, franchising, or tight contractual code-sharing agreements lock up most or all of the regional carriers available to feed a hub, leaving any challenger there with insufficient flows to support competitive frequencies at adequate load factors. Once a well-resourced and well-managed airline has established a properly integrated hub-and-spoke network, competitors face an uphill battle breaking into the system. Many choose to avoid head-to-head confrontation. Those that relish a fight can try one or more of the following.

1. Direct entry into dense or potentially dense point-to-point hub markets requiring little or no network feed in order to be viable. Several different approaches have been used.

   - *Full-service* Virgin Atlantic and British Midland in the 1980s and 1990s targeted, respectively, the densest long- and short-haul point-to-point markets out of London in order to compete against British Airways without bearing the full force of its integrated network. This approach will only work where local traffic is sufficiently dense. At the other extreme, one reason why Delta remains unchallenged on transatlantic routes into and out of Cincinnati is that competitors cannot match its feed there, whilst local traffic to and from overseas centres is not sufficiently dense to support point-to-point competition by itself.

   - *Low fares* Low-fare challengers can generate significant new traffic in price-elastic segments (as Southwest and Ryanair have proven), as well as taking market share from incumbents (e.g., easyJet in the London–Nice market). Some low-fare carriers have chosen to tackle hubs head-on; AirTran (in its first incarnation as ValuJet) did this at Atlanta, and Frontier at Denver. Others tackle hubs using secondary metropolitan airports; Southwest has done this at Dallas Love Field, Chicago Midway, and Baltimore, whilst easyJet and Ryanair have done the same in the London area.

2. Introduction of a multi-stop service across the hub being attacked, allowing traffic flows in more than one market to support each other.

3. Draining traffic from one or more spokes by offering either:
   - a routing over the challenger's hub; or
   - nonstop hub-bypass service (which will provide shorter journey times than the incumbent's connecting service but, depending on the aircraft used, will almost certainly support a lower frequency).

4. Linking the challenger's hub (assuming it has one) to the targeted hub so that the competing networks either side of those respective hubs provide a counterweight to each other.

5. Interlining traffic with the hub carrier. This has long been the traditional technique for augmenting an airline network without widening route entry. Some large carriers have tried to reduce their interlining and the interchangeability of unrestricted tickets in order to raise barriers to the entry of actual or potential competitors. Lufthansa, Air France, Aer Lingus and others adopted this tactic in the 1980s and early 1990s against Air Europe, Dan Air, and British Midland. The European Comm-

ission has ruled such behaviour an abuse of dominant market position rather than purely a matter of commercial choice. Nonetheless, the multilateral interline system that grew up after the second world war to create a worldwide 'virtual network' for any carrier irrespective of the scope of its own system, is gradually being narrowed by: online hubbing and passengers' preference for single-carrier connections where connections are necessary; the attractions of FFPs; the spread of code-sharing and of preferential marketing agreements; and the restrictive conditions attached to the discounted tickets on which a high proportion of passengers now travel.

Responding to a challenger

Barkin et al (1995) have suggested the following broad approach for established network carriers responding to a challenge.

1. Understand the challenger's strengths: does it have specific cost or differentiation advantages and, if so, how sustainable are they?
2. Assess the threat to the incumbent's core business(es): for example, will the challenger significantly affect hub traffic flow?
3. Develop specific tactics tailored to the circumstances in each individual market. These will depend upon the incumbent's resources and capabilities, the importance of the particular market concerned in terms of traffic and profits, and the likelihood that the challenger might continue to grow and eventually create difficulties elsewhere in the incumbent's network. We will look briefly at five possible responses to an actual or potential challenge.
   - **Block entry** This could involve one or more of several actions: make entry impossible through, for example, 'spatial pre-emption' of slots, terminal space or route licenses; make entry too expensive by, for instance, reinforcing the loyalty of the existing customer base, making it more expensive to penetrate; make the rewards of entry unattractive or, at best, uncertain by signalling a willingness to lower fares and/or add capacity in response to entry.
   - **Withdraw** This could be acceptable if the route concerned is unprofitable, generating little premium or connecting traffic, if the incumbent has other opportunities to deploy its resources profitably, and if there is no substantial danger that withdrawal would strengthen the challenger for a future assault on another part of the network. On the other hand, many routes operated by network carriers do indeed contribute valuable feed and so, quite frequently, make a positive contribution to network profitability even if not

themselves profitable on a fully allocated basis. In extreme cases, ceding such routes might undermine hub economics to the point that a vicious circle of spoke-cutting is initiated to re-establish network profitability – perhaps ultimately threatening viability of the hub itself. The operational characteristics of a large hub-and-spoke network make downsizing in response to stagnant or declining revenues (whether resulting from competition or a recession) very difficult to effect without causing a disproportionate further loss of traffic. Less dramatic, although also potentially damaging, is the loss of FFP members compelled to rely on other carriers in the vacated market(s).

- **Compete** When a start-up is attacked early and forcefully enough, it might find profitability difficult to establish and therefore access to additional tranches of capital with which to fund expansion less readily available – unless it has the resources of a wealthy corporate or individual shareholder behind it. Whether or not the challenger is a start-up, wherever it enters with low prices fare matching – ideally on a capacity-controlled basis – is the most obvious and widespread response. If a fare-war is the outcome, as often happens, it can be important for the incumbent to have enough capacity available to put into the market and ensure that the challenger does not walk away with a disproportionate share of any incremental traffic stimulated by the competition; this can be an expensive exercise.

  Nonprice responses might include increasing FFP awards, boosting agency incentives, changing schedules, and launching advertising or promotional campaigns. At their most aggressive, these responses could include capacity-dumping, predatory scheduling, and route overlay – the latter involving a major responding to a small low-fare challenger's entry onto one or two of its routes by duplicating most or all of the challenger's network (something Northwest is alleged to have done to Reno Air in the early 1990s). What an incumbent can get away with in terms of competitive response could depend upon the nature of competition law in the jurisdiction concerned, the attitude of the authorities responsible for enforcing it, and the speed of due process.

- **Co-exist** This response might, for example, lead a full-service incumbent to cede most of the price-sensitive segments of local traffic to a low-fare challenger whilst continuing to serve both connecting passengers and higher yielding, predominantly business passengers in the local market. The incumbent may also retain a small slice of the most price-sensitive segment by offering capacity-controlled fill-up fares. Such a response is fine as long as there are sufficient volumes of traffic in each segment to keep both carriers content, and provided business traffic – particularly local rather than connecting business traffic – values the incumbent's service differentiation more highly than the challenger's lower fares.

- **Join forces** A full-service incumbent might decide to forgo bruising fare wars by withdrawing from a market in which it is challenged, whilst at the same time protecting its FFP membership base in that market and also its network coverage by entering into a marketing agreement with the challenger. For this to work: service levels offered by the airlines concerned should not be too far apart, which means that the challenger must in most cases be offering something more than rock-bottom service at rock-bottom prices; and both schedule integration and some degree of operational alignment must be feasible. As with any route withdrawal, the incumbent might later face a renewed challenge elsewhere in its network if the beneficiary continues to grow on the basis of what has been ceded to it, and at some point decides that the potential gains from a more aggressive posture outweigh the advantages of continued co-operation (Holloway, 1998b).

iii. Network outsourcing

The network design process involves not just deciding upon the pattern of routes to be operated but also who will operate them. In the case of low-fare carriers this is generally a non-issue. For network carriers the choice lies between using their own aircraft or outsourcing capacity provision. Many airlines are now extending their marketable networks by entering into code-sharing, blocked-space, franchising and/or wet-lease agreements.

Code-sharing

Code-sharing is by far the most widespread feature of airline alliances – being present in over 70 per cent of cases, whereas shared FFPs are present in only around half, and under 20 per cent cover co-operation in operational functions (Lindquist, 1999). It involves an airline placing its two-letter designator code (e.g., AA, UA, BA) on a flight operated by another carrier. When the operating carrier is a franchised regional, its own code might not be applied to the flight – which is therefore marketed only under the code-sharing major's designator code. Where two (or more) mainline carriers code-share, it would be usual for the operating carrier's designator to be applied alongside that of the code-sharing partner; the flight numbers following each designator may be identical or different. There will usually be at least some degree of schedule alignment between partners, and in many cases this alignment is close. Code-sharing can involve passenger and/or cargo sales on a given flight. The carrier whose aircraft operate the flight is generally known as the 'operating partner', whilst others which simply apply their designators (and possibly contribute some cabin crew) are 'code-sharing partners'. Although the overwhelming majority of code-shares involve just two carriers, intensifying co-operation within the global alliances is leading to more multi-partner code-shares than has been seen in the past.

Code-shares can be either route-specific 'one-off' arrangements or part of a wider marketing relationship which in its most developed form might aim to offer a common service (e.g., KLM and Northwest's World Business Class). These are sometimes referred to as 'naked code-sharing' and 'common product code-sharing' respectively; the latter is still rare.

Code-sharing deals contain many standard elements, but each is nonetheless unique. Where the balance of benefits lies will depend in large measure upon the partners' relative strengths and negotiating skills. Something that often needs particular attention is projection of the code-sharing partner's corporate identity. This might require the presence of that partner's staff and/or signage at different points in the operating partner's service delivery system and be reflected in the phrasing (possibly also the language) of terminal and inflight announcements. Code-sharing partners sometimes place one or two cabin staff onto flights either to establish a visible presence in the aircraft generally, or to identify and serve their own premium passengers in particular. This latter practice raises the following issues.

- **Labour relations** Duty-times, inflight rest procedures on long-haul flights, and whether staff should fly in addition to or instead of the operating partner's cabin attendants will have to be agreed.
- **Service standards** Service levels and procedures are likely to differ between partners until such time as they have a common product to offer consumers.
- **Costs** Additional training is required for the code-sharing partner's staff in respect of service and safety procedures on the operating partner's aircraft.

Types of code-sharing

The following is just one of several possible typologies.

Franchised code-sharing In this case the operator is a franchisee of another carrier, operating under that other airline's brand identity and not using its own designator code. It is primarily a domestic phenomenon within the United States and parts of the EU single market, although British Airways has franchised medium-haul carriers GB Airways and British Mediterranean as well as airlines in Africa. Over time in both North America and Europe, a growing number of franchised regionals have been acquired by their major airline franchisors – in which case they are no longer technically franchisees or code-share partners, but are in fact just separate subsidiaries or divisions of their mainline parents (e.g., British Airways' acquisition and consolidation of several UK-based regionals in 2000, and Delta's acquisition of Comair). We will look at franchising shortly.

Connection (or 'complementary') code-sharing What distinguishes this from code-shared connections between franchisor and franchisee is the fact that the operating partner retains its own designator on the flights concerned alongside that of the code-sharing partner, and retains its own brand identity. Two types of connection code-sharing can be identified.

1. **Non-reciprocal/single-sector code-sharing** It is sometimes the case that whereas domestic or short-haul international flights carry the codes of both the operating partner and a medium- or long-haul code-sharing partner, the connecting medium- or long-haul flight carries only its operator's code. This could happen for one of several reasons.
   - The short-haul carrier may have no presence in medium- or long-haul O & D markets, so its designator code has little marketing value. This situation might arise where a non-affiliated regional feeds a long-haul major with flights that bear both its own code (reflecting presence in its own short-haul markets) and the major's code (to simulate an online connection for the major's long-haul passengers), but sees no benefit in putting its own code on the major's long-haul flights (which the major would probably not allow anyway).
   - The alliance relationship is route-specific or narrowly focused rather than wide-ranging. Before it joined Star, for example, British Midland's domestic services carried the codes of a large number of (often competing) long-haul carriers, whilst the UK carrier (since rebranded as bmi british midland international) did not put its own code on partners' long-haul flights.
   - Non-reciprocal code-sharing can also arise where a wider, more comprehensive alliance is balanced in favour of one of the partners. During much of the period of their relationship in the mid-1990s,

for example, the 'BA' code appeared on a large number of USAir domestic flights whilst the 'US' code did not appear on British Airways' flights.

2. **Reciprocal/through code-sharing** In this case, alliance partners place their respective codes on services connecting beyond one or both of their hubs (or some other interchange point), as when the 'UA' code appears on Lufthansa flights beyond Frankfurt alongside 'LH', for example, or the 'AF' code appears on Delta flights beyond Atlanta alongside 'DL'.

Connection or complementary code-sharing extends the networks of one or both partners. It can cover international-domestic connections or vice versa, international-international connections, or domestic-domestic connections.

Parallel code-sharing There are two principal types.

1. **Sole service** The parties consolidate their services on a route, with only one of them operating flights. This often happens on thin routes unable to support more than one operator at frequencies satisfactory to business travellers.

2. **Dual service** Both partners operate their own flights on a route, but each code-shares on the other's services. The objective here might be to increase the number of frequencies each has available to offer for sale without physically increasing the number of flights.

Conclusion A passenger's itinerary could quite possibly take in each of these different types of code-sharing: a franchised US domestic flight into a United hub, followed by an inter-hub flight to Frankfurt also bearing the UA code but operated by Lufthansa, and then an onward connection on another Lufthansa flight carrying the UA code. From a passenger's point of view the code-sharing typology suggested above – or, indeed, any other – is fairly meaningless; from an airline's point of view, however, it can be analytically useful. From the point of view of competition authorities the distinctions drawn may be critical, as we will see shortly.

Pros and cons of code-sharing from an airline perspective

The primary motivations for code-sharing are as follows.

1. **To broaden network reach** By putting its code on another airline's services, a carrier can gain access to markets that it might otherwise not have access to because:

- it does not have the required traffic rights;
- it does not have the fleet or cost structure necessary to serve the market(s) concerned;
- it has insufficient market presence to mount a sustainable service (perhaps because one end of the market is another carrier's hub and there is insufficient local traffic to support service without the benefit of feed); and/or
- it cannot get access to the slots required to offer sufficient frequencies or appropriate departure times.

2. **To deepen network coverage** Code-sharing might allow a carrier to increase the number of saleable frequencies offered on a route it already serves by placing its code on another airline's services. This could be beneficial where traffic on the route would not support an increase in actual flights, where the code-sharing partner has insufficient aircraft to operate more of its own services, or where airport congestion or lack of traffic rights create barriers to additional frequencies.

3. **To improve the GDS display positions of connecting services** There are two aspects to this.
   - *Online preference* Most connecting passengers have a preference for remaining online, and this is reflected in the priority given by GDS display algorithms to online connections over interline connections in some jurisdictions (e.g., the United States, but not the EU). By taking an existing interline connection and entering into a code-sharing agreement with the other airline, a carrier can turn that connection into a 'virtual online' service and improve its GDS display position. (Even where GDS screen position is not affected, the appearance of online service as far as customers are concerned can provide sufficient revenue-side benefits to justify a code-sharing agreement.)
   - *Screen padding* Code-sharing can also lead to the dual (in the EU) or multiple listing of the same flight under different designator codes and flight numbers, resulting in competitors being pushed further from the top of the first page of screen displays.

4. **To develop alliance strategy** Extending point 3 above, code-sharing is a critical element in the competition between alliances to attract flow traffic (alongside other service attributes such as through-check-in, shared terminals and lounges, cross-recognition of high-value customers, and access to wider FFP benefits).

5. **To contain costs** As well as marketing benefits, code-sharing also has cost-side attractions insofar as it allows carriers to exploit economies of scope and density without increasing output or having to bear the fixed

costs associated with internal/organic growth – thereby holding down production costs and helping support load factors. It can also allow inefficient tag-end sectors to be eliminated.

6. **To safeguard traffic rights** Strong international carriers are sometimes compelled to code-share with a weaker national airline which either does not want, or is unable, to participate in a particular $3^{rd}/4^{th}$ freedom market.

There are potential downsides, however. It is possible for carriers – particularly those operating short-haul routes – to have their yields put under pressure both by prorate deals crafted in favour of the partner competing in lower-yielding (but perhaps more profitable) long-haul markets, and by the periodic fare wars that tend to erupt between larger airlines in competitive markets; on the other hand, independent US regionals selling output to majors on a fee-per-departure or fee-per-ASM basis are protected from both these problems.

There are, in addition, several broader issues in respect of code-sharing. We will look at these next.

Code-sharing: some issues

Competition issues From the competition and consumer welfare angle there are arguments for and against code-sharing. We will look first at several potential competition problems that might arise from code-sharing (Spitz, 1998).

- **Monopoly power** Code-sharing can be anticompetitive where it removes competition or potential competition from a market. Franchised and complementary/connection code-sharing might be anticompetitive if partners able to compete by extending their own networks choose instead to code-share; the threat in parallel code-sharing is that it might remove some or all of an existing competitor's services from a route. Box 6.5 explores this further.
- **Infrastructural barriers to entry** Dominance of hub airport capacity (i.e., slots, gates, and/or terminal space) by an incumbent major and its alliance partners can make market entry with a competitive schedule a practical impossibility for competing carriers and alliances, so denying alternatives to local O & D traffic and allowing the airlines concerned to exercise monopoly power.
- **GDS online preference and display screen padding** As noted above, some GDSs have algorithms which treat code-shared connections as being online, and so give them display preference over interline conn-

ections irrespective of elapsed journey time. (In Europe both the EU and ECAC codes of conduct – the former mandatory, the latter only discretionary – prohibit the favouring of online or code-shared connections; in the United States major GDSs also follow this neutral practice in respect of international, but not necessarily domestic, markets. The situation elsewhere in the world varies.) As was also noted above, another problem is that multiple listings of the same code-shared flights under their different designators can be used to push competing services away from the top of the first GDS display screen. (Again, limits have been placed on such 'screen padding' in Europe.)

Box 6.5: Code-sharing, monopoly power, and alliances

Depending upon market circumstances, code-sharing can be either pro- or anti-competitive. If it allows two carriers to link in order to compete more effectively for flow traffic against another airline or alliance with a larger network or better coverage of certain O & D markets it can be pro-competitive. On the other hand, where carriers code-share simply to reduce the number of operators on a route, the outcome might be anti-competitive. We need to take two perspectives.

1. ***Network competition*** *Code-sharing that extends a network's ability to compete with other networks can be beneficial to flow traffic that as a result has more alternatives from which to choose. On the negative side, the only serious competitive threat faced by the emerging global alliance networks is from the small number of other global alliances; although further shuffling of partners is probable, it is unlikely that the number of global alliances will exceed four – implying that from a network perspective the global market is going to be consolidated into an oligopoly.*
2. ***Market competition*** *What concerns customers, of course, is the level and type of competition in those markets in which they want to travel. Once the alliances have settled down into relative permanence, their impact on competition will depend very much on the dynamics of whatever particular market is being considered and upon the watchfulness of competition authorities.*
   - *Assuming the absence of collusion (arguably something of a stretch given the industry's history), behind/beyond markets should benefit from competition between the different alliance networks trying to attract flow traffic over their respective hubs. Competition will probably be most intense in respect of discretionary traffic moving on discounted fares.*

- *The prospects for local inter-hub traffic are not encouraging. This is particularly true in respect of time-sensitive (primarily business) travellers, who might not look upon a service that involves changing planes at a competing airline's hub (e.g., London) as a viable alternative to a nonstop route (e.g., Frankfurt–Washington).*

- *It can also sometimes happen that a small carrier flying into a large airline's 'fortress hub' and in need of both onward connections to offer arriving passengers and feed to boost outbound traffic has little practical alternative other than to code-share with the dominant carrier – which is the only one able to offer the required range of connections over that hub. Several Latin American carriers serving Miami, for example, have been obliged by circumstances such as these to come to terms with American Airlines' dominance there by code-sharing with what would otherwise have been their primary competitor on international sectors in and out of the gateway.*

In a study of four North Atlantic alliances during the mid-1990s, Oum et al (2000) found that output and consumer surplus were more likely to increase after alliance formation if the partners' networks are complementary and have limited overlap than where routes are congruent or parallel. Where networks are complementary, even inter-hub services are likely to be boosted in order to exploit that complementarity by increasing the double-connect possibilities for cross-feed traffic.

In any international market, much might depend upon the terms of the bilateral air services agreement in force between the countries concerned. A liberal or open-skies bilateral permitting new competitors to enter a market against two former competitors which decide to code-share raises less of a prima facie competition issue than would be the case were the two code-sharers each the sole carrier designated by their respective governments under a highly restrictive, protectionist bilateral. In reality of course, the fact that a market is contestable from a regulatory perspective might not make it economically contestable if one end is slot-constrained (e.g., Frankfurt) or if the origin and destination are hubs dominated by the code-sharers, with both carriers having sufficient network strength at each to make market entry a sporty prospect for competitors (e.g., Paris and Atlanta).

Competition laws are used by the authorities in some countries to ensure that code-share partners continue to compete across those dimensions of the marketing mix that still remain open to competition, but the beneficial impact of such measures is in many cases open to debate.

- *Service design competition in respect of attributes such as safety, routing, schedule, frequency, and the inflight product is removed by definition on any given code-shared flight.*
- *Whilst competition in pricing and marketing communications should still be present unless antitrust immunity has been granted, cynics might question the extent to which airlines that have entered into agreements specifically casting each other as 'partners' will – other than in exceptional circumstances – compete aggressively to unload seats on a shared airplane.*
- *Competition laws are either non-existent or weakly enforced in many countries, and even where they do exist it is still not uncommon for airlines to be specifically exempted. Several transatlantic alliances have been granted antitrust immunity by US authorities keen to use the lure of unfettered alliance relationships between their carriers and US majors to prise open skies agreements from foreign governments. The practical effect of immunity is that the partners are able to co-operate closely on capacity, scheduling, marketing communications, pricing, and revenue management decisions, and to consult with regard to commission levels, net fares, and FFP policies, for example; in other words, they are able to sell jointly out of a shared inventory and, if they wish, share costs and apportion profits. (Some 'carve-outs' have been imposed by the (US) Department of Transportation (DOT) in respect of time-sensitive – that is, full-fare – local traffic in transatlantic inter-hub markets; the result of this is that in those particular market segments the partners have to compete on pricing and promotion, and run their own individual risk of profit and loss.) One advantage of antitrust immunity as far as pricing is concerned is that joint fares can be introduced quickly in response to market changes, rather than having to be formally negotiated case-by-case as arms-length prorate agreements.*

Notwithstanding its potentially negative effects, code-sharing can also have a positive impact on competition and consumer welfare. Code-sharing may add competition to a market in which otherwise only a traditional interline agreement would be competing against one or more established non-stop, direct or online connecting services. Code-sharing can also permit flights to be operated, or frequencies to be increased, on routes which otherwise would not support the same level of service; indeed, the additional supply of output might even stimulate traffic and, perhaps, lead to the eventual entry of new competitors.

Code-sharing may improve other aspects of service quality by facilitating or encouraging, for example:

- integrated scheduling, ideally leading to more connections and/or reduced layovers;
- through check-in and baggage interlining;
- connections to proximate gates within the same terminal buildings at hubs or traffic interchange points;
- shared lounges;
- joint tour products;
- reciprocity between FFPs; and
- lower joint fares resulting from competition between alliances to serve individual city-pair markets over alternative network routings.

Of course, most of the benefits just listed are – or could be – made available through commercial arrangements or interline agreements without the inclusion of code-sharing.

Deception of customers In addition to competition issues, there is also a question regarding whether or not code-shares deceive customers. An airline's designator code on a flight tells a customer what to expect in terms of service quality. Leading airlines spend hundreds of millions of dollars each year designing, branding, and promoting their services to ensure that this is the case. A customer who buys service based on that designator but is instead exposed to a different standard offered by another carrier without being made aware this would happen, has been deceived. Problems most frequently arise when the operating partner offers standards below those marketed by the code-sharing partner. But even where this is not the case, there is still an important matter of principle at stake. A not insignificant additional source of problems is the confusion that can arise when passengers holding tickets bearing the designator of a code-sharing partner do not appreciate that they should be checking-in at the terminal and desks used by the operating partner. Finally, there is scope for confusion in respect of which carrier is liable to consumers should there be an accident or some lesser incident.

Airlines in general argue that code-sharing seems not to be an issue that greatly troubles consumers and, if it were, the marketplace would impose its own sanctions on carriers choosing to enter partnerships with airlines that are significantly weaker in terms of service or safety. They might also argue by analogy that somebody buying, say, Coca Cola in different countries receives essentially the same product irrespective of the fact that each is produced and bottled locally. This analogy could be defensible in the case of common product code-sharing, but such arrangements remain a small minority of total code-sharing deals. Air transport consumers have a right to be concerned with the not inconsiderable chance in many other cases of finding 'tap-water' in the bottle. The particular nature of what is an image-sensitive industry makes this promiscuity with their reputations potentially dangerous for airlines.

The heart of the matter is information, and regulations have been introduced in some jurisdictions (e.g., the EU) mandating that passengers be informed at the time they make their purchases which airline(s) will operate the service(s) they have booked. It is unclear how effective such regulations are.

International regulatory issues When considering international regulatory issues, it can be helpful to distinguish between bilateral code-sharing and third-country code-sharing. For example, Delta putting its DL code on an Air France transatlantic flight to Paris is 'bilateral code-sharing' (because only two countries are involved); on the other hand, putting the DL code onto an Air France international flight beyond Paris (e.g., to Africa or the Middle East) is 'third-country code-sharing'. In the latter case, the third country concerned might take any position ranging from 'no objection' to an outright ban – a position that will depend in general on its aeropolitical policy stance, and in particular on the terms of its bilaterals with the United States and France.

Whilst some governments take a relatively relaxed view on airlines' freedom to enter into code-share agreements, most insist that code-sharing partners must either have existing traffic rights in markets where their codes are displayed for sale or obtain explicit authorisation. The United States takes the latter position (although this is a non-issue for carriers incorporated in countries with which open skies bilaterals have been concluded). The EU has yet to adopt a formal position on intra-EU code-sharing, but it does have the power to review agreements within the context of competition laws.

Elsewhere in the world the regulatory position remains variable and ill-defined. What is generally true, however, is that having initially been considered primarily a marketing device, code-sharing has in recent years moved onto the agendas of bilateral negotiations. A minority of governments now see code-sharing as a quasi-traffic right, arguing that it can provide to designated carriers access in excess of agreed bilateral limitations and to undesignated carriers access into markets which they have no current right to enter. Future bargaining positions could be eroded, according to this view, were foreign carriers to obtain market access through code-sharing without their governments first having to come to the negotiating table and offer something in return. The counter-argument is that the only flights physically operated are those which have been bilaterally agreed by the origin and destination states, and all code-sharing does is channel traffic onto certain of those flights. What matters in practice, however, is less the merit of either argument than the reality that potential bargaining chips are difficult to resist.

Conclusions on code-sharing

Based on their own original research and a partial review of others' findings, Oum et al (2000) have concluded that code-sharing is likely to have beneficial effects on competition, service quality (notably frequencies), and pricing when it involves linkages between two or more complementary networks serving behind-gateway/hub to beyond-gateway/hub markets; they are less sanguine about parallel code-sharing on overlapping routes, particularly those serving inter-hub markets. More generally, we can argue that the competitive impact of code-sharing will depend upon who would have been in the market without it, who is left there because of it, and how intensely any remaining competitors set about competing.

There is as yet no proven general case that global network alliances using extensive code-sharing to compete in open skies environments will inevitably be conducive to consumers' interests. The effect of each of these alliances needs to be considered not within the generalised context usually presented by their proponents, who picture competitive battles being waged between networks across some imprecisely defined global marketplace, but in the context of specific individual markets – assessed in terms of their size, whether real opportunities exist for other network airlines or niche carriers to enter, and the availability of viable alternative routings. In approving the overwhelming majority of applications for code-sharing between US and foreign carriers, the US DOT has found the arrangements to be in the interests of consumers. However questionable some of these judgements might have been in individual cases, consumers' interests were at least ostensibly a major point of reference in the evaluation. Some other governments, in contrast, appear to be more concerned about code-sharing partners posing as holders of traffic rights they have not been awarded than about them posing as the providers of services they do not in fact provide.

As far as the potential for consumer deception is concerned, the case is much clearer. Consumers are exposed to deception unless the partners to a code-share arrangement have essentially merged their products. Point-of-sale disclosure is clearly the answer, but anecdotal evidence suggests that this remains inconsistent. In fairness, the problem appears more often to lie with distributors than with airlines themselves. 'Disclosure' might anyway not always disclose very much – as in the United States, where some reservations media list independently-owned regionals code-sharing with majors not as separately identifiable airlines but under the generic network name of their associated major (e.g., United Express).

Code-sharing is not inevitably to a consumer's disadvantage; few people booking on Delta and finding themselves travelling on Air France should feel mightily aggrieved by differential service levels. The issue here is whether somebody buying 'Coke' from an airline has a right to find 'Coke' in the bottle – irrespective of how good the '7-Up' actually in it might be. In the case of some other alliance relationships, consumers could have much more specific cause for complaint.

Block-spacing and joint services

Blocked-space agreements

Code-sharing is often effected on a 'free-sale' basis, under which the code-sharing partner pays a price for each seat taken from the operating partner's inventory – a price that will vary depending upon the negotiated rate for the cabin concerned. There would be no commitment to take a specific number of seats on each flight. An important point whenever revenue management remains the sole responsibility of the operating partner is agreement on the overbooking policy, mismanagement of which could have negative consequences for the code-sharing partner's reputation.

Alternatively, code-sharing agreements – on passenger and/or cargo services – might involve block-spacing. In a blocked-space arrangement, the code-sharing partner buys an agreed number of seats on the operating partner's flights (at a price below free-sale) and sells them under its own designator from a separate inventory. Arrangements might cover every available class on the flight to provide the purchaser with its required traffic mix, and they might also allow the purchaser to take more than its minimum commitment whenever demand merits or possibly even to give back some unused seats (a 'modified blocked-space' arrangement).

The advantage of blocked-space agreements to the seller is that a proportion of its output is 'underwritten' by guaranteed sales to the partner; this might be sufficient to justify an increase in frequency, which could in turn lead ultimately to a larger market share. Against this is the fact that the sale will be at 'wholesale' prices, which implies that the seller may lose revenue if any of its own 'retail' traffic is spilled or gets displaced into the partner's block. The latter could occur where the partners continue to compete on price and promotion, and also because their respective networks behind the origin and beyond the destination of the code-shared flight might offer different benefits to customers. It can therefore sometimes be the case that there are fewer potential sources of conflict between the partners in a free-sale agreement than in a blocked-space deal.

Blocked-space agreements are a relatively common feature of code-sharing, and can be particularly useful when partners do not have the necessary immunity from competition laws (where applicable) to allow them to manage their seat inventories jointly. (Block-spacing can also arise outside the context of alliance arrangements and code-sharing, of course. For example, a European airline with a service terminating in Singapore might want to secure space for its interline passengers travelling to and from Australia on another carrier's heavily booked flights by entering into blocked-space agreements with that carrier between Singapore and points in Australia and vice versa; as the global alliances continue to extend their reach, however, the need for this type of arrangement is diminishing.)

Joint services

Whereas under a blocked-space agreement each carrier independently manages its own allocated space, revenue management for a joint service is undertaken by one carrier acting for both or by both acting together. Inventories on joint services can be jointly priced and promoted, in which case the partners are not competing against each other. Joint services generally require either a revenue-sharing agreement (based on some level of assumed costs attributed to the operating partner) or a cost- and revenue-sharing agreement.

Some states consider joint services to be essentially the same as code-sharing agreements, whereas others maintain a distinction founded on the fact that partners do not separately bear their own income statement risks. In the latter case they might be frowned upon by competition laws, and this is one reason why antitrust immunity has had to be sought for several of the transatlantic alliances.

Franchising

Franchising involves a substantial carrier with a strong brand (the 'franchisor') licensing to a franchisee (usually for a period of five to ten years) the use of brand identity (e.g., aircraft livery, cabin design, crew uniforms, signage, logos, and brand names), the associated service concept, and aspects of the service delivery system. The franchisor's designator code is applied to franchised services (and the franchisee's usually is not). The franchisee will be a separate corporate entity (with its own air operator's certificate (AOC) or local equivalent) in which the franchisor may or may not hold an equity interest. Freedom with regard to network design and scheduling varies, but the franchisor is likely to want meaningful input if not total control. (Note that this discussion of franchising excludes consideration of operations that are wholly owned subsidiaries or inhouse divisions of a larger carrier, and as such are not franchisees.)

The franchisee typically pays a front-end licensing fee and an ongoing royalty for use of the brand, the sizes of which will to some extent depend on the balance of benefits each party anticipates from the relationship. Franchisees might also either choose or be obliged to use various services provided by the franchisor for which they make separate payments – including possibly brand advertising, training, traffic handling, reservations, sales, inventory control, revenue management, revenue accounting, and management services.

The use of reservations and revenue accounting support is frequently compulsory. These and other services are sometimes provided at a level of sophistication in excess of what is needed by a regional airline and, despite usually being sold 'at cost' and perhaps benefiting from economies of scale, the price could be well in excess of what it would cost the franchisee were the same work to be undertaken inhouse. Distribution costs will also tend to be relatively high because most major airlines (i.e., franchisors) require a presence in all the largest GDSs at the highest levels of functionality available. Finally, it is quite likely that the major will have product standards that impose additional service delivery costs on the franchisee.

Most commonly to date it is corporate brand identities that have been franchised into sub-brands – such as Delta Air Lines into Delta Connection. Franchising does not always involve creation of a sub-brand, however; British Airways franchisees British Mediterranean Airways and GB Airways operate under the corporate master-brand because they offer the same levels of service (i.e., the Club Europe and Euro Traveller sub-brands) as does the mainline operation on short- and medium-haul flights. In contrast, the regional carriers doing business as Delta Connection do not mirror Delta's mainline service offers, and so are separately identified using the 'Connection' sub-brand.

Franchising is essentially a US domestic and intra-EU phenomenon – the principal exceptions at the time of writing being British Airways' franchise agreements mentioned above along with two others in Africa. (Virgin Blue in Australia also qualifies, although it is primarily the Virgin brand-name that is being franchised rather than a service delivery template.) Unlike South Africa and a small number of others (e.g., Australia, New Zealand, and some Latin American states), many countries will not permit franchising where:

- the franchisor is a foreign carrier, because a franchisor could be deemed to have commercial control over a domestic franchisee and most countries' laws forbid foreign control of their airlines; and/or
- the franchisor does not have underlying traffic rights for the route(s) being operated, particularly where only the franchisor's code would be used on the flight(s) concerned.

Cross-border franchising (outside the EU single market and a handful of other countries) therefore potentially falls foul of the restrictions on foreign ownership and control of airlines found in most domestic legal systems and bilateral ASAs (Denton and Dennis, 2000).

Benefits and risks for franchisors

From a franchisor's perspective, franchising can be looked upon as:

- a channel to market (i.e., to markets the franchisor would not otherwise be able to access, either at all or as cost-effectively);
- brand extension; and/or
- network outsourcing.

Franchising is an alliance strategy which can be pursued in conjunction with a franchisor's own operations, those of its subsidiaries, and also in tandem with non-franchise code-sharing agreements. There can be several potential benefits from franchising.

1. In return for little or no additional up-front investment, a franchisor can generate revenue from the licensing of its brand. (Terms vary, but the franchisor might benefit from both an initial lump-sum payment and annual licensing fees.)
2. Depending upon the extent of network complementarity, the franchisor might gain incremental revenue from traffic feed. Any increase in traffic that contributes to higher load factors rather than capacity increases will have a positive impact on revenue per ASM (RASM).
3. Franchisors are able to extend and maintain awareness of their brands in regions where they have no traffic rights or, more usually to date, no ability to offer service given their labour costs and/or fleet structures relative to the demand characteristics of the markets concerned (i.e., price-sensitivity or lack of density); this is typically the case with franchised feeder services, for example, but it can also apply to relatively dense but low-yield leisure routes (e.g., British Airways' franchising of routes to certain leisure destinations in the western Mediterranean).

Awareness of a major brand stimulated by a franchised regional in an area where the major is not strongly represented might translate into brand loyalty when customers from that regional airline's catchment area face a choice between the major and a competitor on medium- or long-haul journeys. This is particularly likely if, as is probable, the franchised regional and the major share an FFP. Franchisors can in this way leverage their systemwide resources and skills to create revenue-generating intangible assets. Nonetheless, brands should in general only be franchised into regions where there is at least a basic pre-existing level of brand equity, and franchising should always be part of a coherent regional strategy.

4. It is possible that franchising on a significant scale could generate sufficient incremental business for some of the franchisor's functional units that their retention inhouse can be justified as an alternative to outsourcing – assuming that outsourcing is under consideration.

In practice, the balance of franchisor benefits between traffic feed (i.e., using a franchisee to operate what would otherwise be uneconomic or inaccessible routes), simple fee generation, and other potential benefits will vary from situation to situation. Much will depend on network synergies.

There are relatively few risks for franchisors.

1. The most obvious is poor franchisee service quality. This can in principle be addressed by carefully crafted service level agreements covering variables such as flight completion rate, ontime performance, and customer satisfaction and complaint levels. Some US franchise agreements based on fee-per-departure or per ASM payments from a major to a regional in fact impose 'holdbacks' from due payments, released once performance criteria are established as having been met.

2. Another risk is the implication for the major's reputation were a franchisee to collapse financially – particularly where a collapse is sudden and leaves passengers stranded.

3. As we saw earlier, a major might also be exposed to a decision by an independently owned franchisee to realign with a competitor, and so perhaps deprive the franchisor of traffic feed and market presence. This concern was one of the reasons why US majors, and subsequently several European majors, began in the 1990s to acquire full control over some or all of their regional franchisees. (Another reason was pursuit of the economies of scale and better integration that could, in principle, be achieved by centralising management of regional operations.) This raises a question mark over the long-run viability of a franchise relationship once the franchisee has become important to the fran-

chisor's network in terms of feed and/or strategy (Denton and Dennis, 2000).
4. Less dramatic but still potentially damaging is the possibility that franchisors might face labour relations problems were franchisees to be perceived by unions as a form of low-cost flight operations outsourcing – which, of course, is what they are. This is seen most clearly in the scope clauses incorporated into pilots' contracts at many US majors.
5. Franchisors rely on franchisees being responsive to any significant shift in fundamental marketing strategy, particularly a shift affecting brand identity.
6. Finally, wherever a franchisee represents a corporate master-brand but offers a diluted product, as opposed to a product separately positioned as a distinct sub-brand, the risk of failing to meet consumers' expectations with regard to brand consistency is very real.

Benefits and risks for franchisees

Benefits Against a background of growing industry concentration, cynics might argue that the outstanding benefit of a franchise from the franchisee's perspective is likely to be survival. However, even carriers whose survival is not in doubt can benefit from association with a strong, well-managed brand.

1. **Revenue-side benefits** Franchisees expect to gain incremental revenue as a result of the marketing communications, sales, and distribution power of their partner, from network synergies (reflected in higher traffic figures and load factors), from a strengthened image (reflected in firmer yields), and from customer loyalty built on strong branding and participation in an attractive FFP. Network growth is also frequently associated with franchise agreements. Franchisees get to provide a respected, usually high-quality product that boosts their market presence (with both customers and travel agents) – and often they get to charge accordingly. Although they sometimes have to pay richly for the privilege, franchisees might also benefit from knowledge transfer in respect of product design, marketing communications, distribution, and revenue management.
   We have seen already that it is increasingly common for independent regionals franchised by major carriers, particularly in North America, to be remunerated on a fee-per-departure or per ASM basis or for a major to enter into a long-term capacity purchase agreement with its regional franchisees; SkyWest, for example, is doing around 90 per cent of its flying on this basis under agreements with Delta and United,

and in 2001 Atlantic Coast signed a ten-year fee-per-departure deal that gave United control over the seat inventory and scheduling of aircraft committed to United Express operations. The advantage to a regional of moving from a revenue-sharing model to a capacity-purchase model akin to wet-leasing is that subject only to whatever control the major might have over capacity, scheduling (i.e., the number of departures), and inventory management, cash flow is reasonably secure throughout the duration of the agreement and both marketing expenses and marketing risks are avoided.

2. **Cost side benefits** Cost savings could be available through joint purchasing and from certain economies of scale in respect of services acquired from the major. Technical assistance can also be valuable.

Risks Against the undoubted benefits and aside from any financial costs attributable to fees, services, and management reporting requirements, franchisees – particularly when they are existing carriers rather than start-ups – must weigh several potential disadvantages.

1. The loss of an independent identity in their markets, which might be irrecoverable were the franchise agreement to be terminated. This problem could in principle be circumvented by a carrier operating only some of its routes as a franchisee, retaining its own brand identity in other markets.
2. The loss of traffic feed from carriers other than the franchisor. This is not a serious problem for most of the franchised regionals in the United States, because many interchange as much as 70 or 80 per cent of their traffic with the major airlines whose brands they license. In Europe and elsewhere, franchisees sometimes depend on a more balanced mix of local traffic, code-share connections with the franchisor, and interline connections – and it is the latter that can be threatened. This problem may be compounded if code-share traffic is subject to a less favourable prorate agreement with the franchisor (and therefore perhaps lower yields) than the agreements negotiated with interline carriers – although in practice most franchisees do benefit from cost-share, cost-plus or modified cost-plus prorate agreements.
3. Yields from local traffic will almost certainly be higher than from any form of transfer traffic – but the key question in this respect, of course, is whether or not the regional can actually survive on local traffic alone in the absence of flow traffic exchanged with the franchisor.
4. There might be times when a franchisee wants to adjust fares but is constrained from doing so.

5. Because franchisors are generally large airlines with slower decision-making processes than are customary at smaller franchisees, gaining approval for initiatives that bear on the product (including network planning) or the brand identity can sometimes be frustrating for a franchisee.

6. There is always a danger that the franchisor might move mainline equipment into markets developed by an independent regional franchisee. United gained a reputation for this type of behaviour in the late 1980s and early 1990s, for example. (Conversely, some franchisors use franchisees' smaller aircraft to provide off-peak service on mainline routes those franchisees could not otherwise serve, and after 9/11 US majors in particular engaged in extensive route transfers to franchisees as well as inhouse regionals.)

7. Franchisees might eventually be pressed by their staff for pay and benefits closer to those available from the franchisor, which could undermine the cost advantages offered by smaller airlines in the thin markets they are usually franchised to serve.

8. Finally, a franchisee can suffer severely if the franchisor's brand runs into difficulties (e.g., a high-profile strike or accident).

Benefits and risks for consumers

When a franchisor franchises and carefully monitors the use of a strong brand, franchising has the potential to offer consumers standards close to those delivered by the franchisor in its own operations – subject always to limitations imposed by equipment type. By offering a well-branded and quality-controlled product, franchising is likely to be better able to meet consumer expectations than is naked code-sharing.

Often, though, the consumer pays handsomely for the benefits offered by high-cost/high-fare branded products, especially in uncontested point-to-point markets (see Denton and Dennis, 2000: 186). Particularly on thin regional routes, the danger that small independent carriers will be overwhelmed by the network strengths of franchised competitors is a very real threat to competition. There has, however, been little outward sign of concern from regulators.

The counter-argument might be that such markets would anyway support no more than one operator or, alternatively, that without network synergies available as a result of the franchise relationship no service at all would be economically feasible. This is particularly true of services linking a secondary or tertiary point to a major's hub: the major itself might not be equipped to provide service, whilst a competitor is unlikely to enter a low-density route into a powerful, non-affiliated hub – leaving a choice between franchised service or no service. On the other hand, were a market in fact able to support competition it is quite possible that entry would be deterred where the sole incumbent is a franchisee of a major brand.

Wet-leasing

Some majors wet-lease aircraft and crews from other airlines both on a short-term basis and, more relevantly to this chapter, as a longer-term capacity solution. Although the lessee usually has more direct operational control than would be the case under a naked code-sharing agreement, branding issues can still arise in passenger operations unless aircraft are painted in its livery and both cabin design and configuration are consistent with the desired brand image. Note that the wet-leasing of foreign-registered aircraft and crews often requires approval from the lessee's regulatory authorities; approval might be time-limited, and conditional on domestic aircraft being unavailable. Some countries have an outright ban on inbound cross-border wet-leasing.

ACMI contracts

Cargo services Under an ACMI contract, a carrier provides additional lift to scheduled airlines on an aircraft, crew, maintenance, and insurance basis – leaving lessees to supply the traffic rights and the loads, and to meet DOCs such as fuel, airport and ATS fees, and handling charges. Aircraft are generally contracted on a multi-year basis at a guaranteed minimum monthly utilisation, which the lessee might be permitted to vary by a few percentage points if required, and subject to a fixed cost per block-hour.

The ACMI lessor is insulated from short-term market risk (because it gets paid throughout the contract period irrespective of load factor), fuel price risk (because this is the lessee's problem), and currency risk (because it can negotiate contracts in the same currency in which most of its costs are denominated – often US dollars). Advantages from the lessee's point of view vary from case to case.

- It might be that a lessee can contract for ACMI lift at rates below the costs it would incur were it to operate its own freighters. (This is most likely to be the case where the lessee can support only a small inhouse freighter fleet; once it grows to the point where a reasonably sized fleet can be justified, ACMI arrangements might either be unnecessary, or useful only to provide temporary supplemental lift – during peak periods or to test a new market, for example.)

- ACMI leases might allow a carrier to tailor output to the needs of an individual route or group of similar routes by making available just one or a small number of a particular aircraft type – a number that it may not be economic to own and operate inhouse.
- ACMI leases can also allow a carrier to expand, either according to a long-term growth plan or in response to a fixed-term contract with a shipper or forwarder, without taking on the ownership risk inherent in further building its own fleet.

Atlas Air became the major cargo ACMI lessor in the 1990s. In response to a marked downturn in demand during the recession that began in late 2000 the carrier launched a fractional wet-lease programme under which lessees could contract for shares of available space on regularly scheduled Atlas flights out of a number of hubs in different parts of the world. It remains to be seen whether this business model will be further developed.

Passenger services ACMI arrangements are also found on the passenger side of the industry. Examples include Qantas' longstanding contract with National Jet Systems on thin domestic routes, and the use of ACMI leases (as well as the lessors' AOCs) by several start-ups during their early years of operations (e.g., easyJet). In a development considered by some to represent first sight of a future in which narrowbodies are used more widely to offer single-class service to premium passengers in thin, long-haul, point-to-point markets (particularly where economy/coach demand is weak), Lufthansa inaugurated in 2002 a trial service between Dusseldorf and Newark using a 48-seat Boing Business Jet wet-leased from PrivatAir.

iv. Summary

This chapter opened by drawing a distinction between markets and routes, before going on to discuss network economics and different types of network – the latter seen from both customers' and carriers' perspectives. Hub-and-spoke networks received particular attention – again, from the perspectives of both passengers and airlines. The second section of the chapter looked at network strategies and tactics, whilst the third discussed different approaches to network outsourcing.

At the beginning of the chapter, the point was made that network management involves both network design and scheduling. Having covered design in the present chapter, we will move on to look at scheduling in the next. The two chapters after that will focus in turn on fleet management and revenue management.

7 Network Management: Scheduling

Remember that time is money.
Benjamin Franklin

Chapter overview

Scheduling choices determine frequencies, departure timings, passenger and aircraft routings and, particularly over hub-based networks, the extent of connections between points served. An airline's schedule is its core service attribute insofar as safe, reliable delivery of a schedule is what satisfies customers' most basic air travel need: the need to be somewhere else by a certain time. Because of its impact on aircraft choice and on the utilisation of equipment, staff, and other resources, a schedule is also – along with network design – a critical cost driver. Scheduling therefore lies at the interface between the revenue and cost sides of an airline's income statement.

This chapter will look at scheduling as a response to demand, to the economics of supply, and to external constraints. It will then consider hub-and-spoke scheduling, and scheduling tactics. The final section will draw together chapters 6 and 7 to consider the interface between network management and fleet management. Fleet management is the subject of chapter 8.

We will begin by considering a typical schedule development process.

i. The schedule development process

Although detailed practices vary, scheduling is in essence a sequential process encompassing the following steps.

1. Decide which markets to serve based on demand forecasts, corporate strategy, and (where relevant) the availability of route licenses or other required forms of designation. (This should have been done as part of a wider marketing planning exercise and will have been the key input into network design.)
2. Take the demand forecast for each targeted market and assume a market share.
3. Decide on the frequencies to be offered, with specific regard to any trade-off between marketing and cost considerations inherent in choices of aircraft size and frequency of operation. This will involve assumptions regarding product quality and target load factors. It will also need to factor-in operational considerations, notably: the payload-range capabilities of potentially suitable aircraft types relative to sector length and traffic density (the latter based on different assumed frequencies); and the capabilities of the airports concerned to accept different types both from a flight operations perspective (e.g., runway length and obstacle clearance) and passenger-handling perspective (e.g., terminal, including counter and gate, capacity).
4. Allocate frequencies to specific timings and routings on the basis of market preferences, network connectivity criteria (including intraline, alliance, and possibly also interline connections), and airport slot availability (where relevant).
5. Establish block-times for each flight-leg.
6. Establish minimum ground times.
7. Calculate hours per annum expected of each aircraft type and factor-in maintenance requirements.
8. Develop aircraft rotations that integrate the schedule and also incorporate maintenance requirements.
9. Consider availability of human and other resources. This will require, in particular, a crew assignment roster that gets as much flying out of pilots as is possible and incurs the lowest feasible expenses in respect of layovers (i.e., allowances and accommodation charges). What is possible with regard to crew assignment will be a function of schedule planning, the location of crew bases, and the terms of duty-time regulations and union contracts.
10. Predict competitors' strategies and reactions.
11. Iterate from 2 to 11.

Clearly, the scheduling/schedule planning function must work closely with the commercial/marketing function, regional sales offices, maintenance planners, flight operations, and station managers. Aside from its cross-functional dimensions, what makes airline scheduling a complicated undertaking is that it involves optimising the allocation of resources to meet demand across a network rather than on a single route. Particularly in a multi-hub network, demand can be served by flowing traffic through a number of alternative channels; the more liberal the regulatory environment, the wider the choices are.

Advance schedules out to two years ahead look at markets on a very general level, expressing demand in terms of RPMs and fleet capacity in terms of ASMs. Unless we are dealing with a start-up, scheduling begins not with a blank sheet of paper but with the current schedule as a foundation and both market and fleet developments as critical new inputs. Many carriers operate a core schedule comprising standard departure times and flight numbers, overlaid by seasonal adjustments; these adjustments might include changes to the size of aircraft operating some of the core services, changes in flight frequencies, and/or the seasonal introduction and deletion of routes.

The closer in we come towards an operational schedule (preparation of which might begin, say, 12 months ahead of introduction), the more influential current schedules become and the more we need to be thinking in terms of specific routings, passenger numbers, marketing communication programmes, fare changes, and equipment types. Scheduling at many carriers is a semi-annual process, with new schedules appearing in spring and autumn; US domestic operations are an exception insofar as some majors introduce new schedules as often as every other month.

The scheduling process cannot be fully automated, but there is no shortage of decision support software to assist: market size and share models; fleet assignment models; spill models; maintenance planning models; passenger routing (or through-assignment) models; GDS display simulation models (to generate market share estimates for inputting into schedule profitability models); and schedule dependability models, which simulate a schedule to detect particular reliability problems (Smith et al, 1998). Each enables solution of different fleet planning, aircraft assignment, routing, and scheduling problems subject to a range of possible constraints. The point to bear in mind is that within the context established by those constraints (e.g., to maximise profits or passenger-miles, to minimise fleet size or operating costs, etc.) they all have broadly the same purpose: to relate output to forecasted demand. What differs is simply the time-scale being applied.

Simulation models allow 'What if?' questions to be posed around fleet mix, schedules, routes, arrival flow management and departure sequencing at banked hubs, and aircraft assignments. Once flight schedules have been established, other models are available to assist with resource scheduling – the allocation of flight crews, ramp personnel and equipment, and check-in, gate, and other customer service staff, for example.

Figure 7.1 illustrates some of the variables that must be considered as part of a schedule development process.

ii. Scheduling: a response to demand

This section will consider scheduling as a response to demand. However, it needs to be kept in mind that routing and scheduling decisions are attributes of the service an airline offers into each of its markets, and as such will themselves have an impact on demand; how significant they are relative to other independent variables, most notably price, will depend upon the characteristics of the demand being served in a particular market (a proxy for which would be its traffic mix).

The theory

An airline's timetable is both a production schedule and the specification of a core service attribute. Because demand is in effect a continuous variable, passengers in each market will have preferred departure times throughout the day. On the other hand, supply is a discrete variable driven by the capacities of specific aircraft departing at specific points in time. A passenger having to take a flight at a time other than when she would prefer to depart will suffer an amount of disutility which depends on just how far apart the actual and preferred departure times are; if this 'schedule delay' (Douglas and Miller, 1974a) is sufficiently severe and alternatives exist, that passenger might be 'spilled' to a competitor offering a better-timed departure. (See Schipper (2001), chapter 7, for an introduction to the economic modelling of frequency choice in air transport markets.)

But passengers care about when they will arrive as well as when they can depart. As far as markets served by nonstop routes are concerned, these two variables are linked almost by definition; when a market is served by two routes connected over a hub, however, schedule delay becomes a function not just of departure frequency from the origin, but also of scheduled transfer times and departure frequency from the hub.

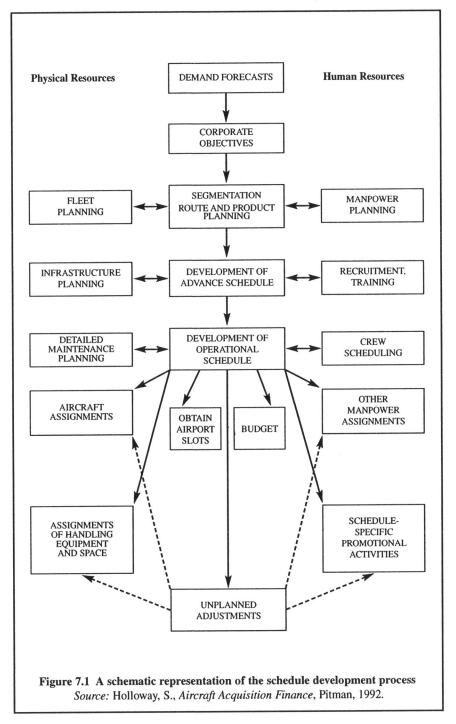

Figure 7.1 A schematic representation of the schedule development process
Source: Holloway, S., *Aircraft Acquisition Finance*, Pitman, 1992.

An airline able to design and deliver a timetable that minimises schedule delay is offering a valuable product feature for which members of those segments of demand that value their time particularly highly, in most cases business travellers, will in many cases be prepared to pay a premium. In addition to routing, which was considered in the last chapter, there are three considerations here: frequency; departure timings; and reliability.

Frequency

The more frequencies an airline offers in a given market, the greater the likelihood that the timing of one of its departures will be close to when a potential passenger wants to travel. Furthermore, an airline operating more flights in a market than its competitor(s) is providing customers who have fully flexible tickets a greater range of rebooking options. Offering more frequencies than competitors may also lead to a better presence high on the first page of GDS displays – which are important in agency channels.

Market preference for higher frequencies was one reason why an historical uptrend in the average size of aircraft in the global fleet came to a halt in the early 1980s, as the effects of deregulation began to take hold in the United States and carriers started competing for market share by operating smaller aircraft at higher frequencies than previously. Deregulation, liberalisation, and the evolution of hub-and-spoke systems have contributed to a tendency to meet growing demand first by raising frequencies, and only as demand thickens further by increasing aircraft size (Boeing, 1997). In some markets, notably the US domestic market, the influence of small differences in departure times on consumer behaviour has provided powerful incentives for airlines to increase frequencies (Crandall, 1995). (The shift towards more price-oriented Internet channels is reducing these incentives.)

Departure timings

Having decided upon frequencies and their general timings, attention also has to be paid to precise timings. In competitive markets, particularly short-haul, adjusting a departure time by just a few minutes can lead to meaningful traffic gains and losses – most notably when fine-tuning has a significant impact on GDS display screen positioning relative to competitors. The shorter the journey, the more sensitive the saleability of a schedule might be to even a minor change in departure time. Assume, for example, that a schedule change affecting a particular daily departure results in the loss of just one passenger and, say, a $400 sale each day: the annual revenue loss would be $146,000. Depending upon the assumed variable costs of carrying those passengers and whether or not commissions would have been payable on sales, the forgone contribution to fixed costs could represent a significant proportion of that figure. Multiplying this across several hundred daily departures, it is clear that the stakes are potentially very high and it is easy to understand why airlines in competitive markets devote so much time to the fine-tuning of departures.

Another point to bear in mind about departure timings is that in a hub-and-spoke network the scheduling of departures into and out of a hub will have an impact on the number and saleability of connections. We will look at hub scheduling in a moment.

Reliability

Having a well-designed schedule with competitive departure timings is only half the battle: the other half is delivering it. Weather and congestion take schedule reliability outside the complete control of any airline, although investment in flight-deck technology (e.g., autoland systems and head-up displays) may be able to reduce weather delays. In Europe, many large airports have slot controls and hourly limits which mean that other than in extreme cases weather conditions have relatively little impact on runway throughput. At most US hubs, in contrast, there are no slot controls to spread demand with the result that peak throughput can be very much lower in poor weather than under favourable conditions.

Other factors affecting reliability include the efficiency of passenger-handling and aircraft turnaround procedures, line maintenance capacity, policies in respect of the holding of line replaceable spares at outstations, and the potentially disruptive unscheduled maintenance requirements often associated with ageing aircraft. The latter concern, together with wider product quality and branding issues, was one reason why year-2000 US start-up jetBlue chose to launch with new A320s rather than older aircraft having lower ownership costs.

Different airlines have different metrics for despatch, en route, and overall schedule reliability. For example, some monitor despatch reliability to the minute whereas others record as on-time any departure up to 15 minutes after the scheduled time. Several carriers place greater emphasis on on-time arrivals, arguing that this is what really matters to customers; there is of course likely to be a close relationship between despatch reliability and on-time arrivals, but just how close this relationship is will depend upon both en route time-keeping and whether scheduled block-times are tight or instead build-in a buffer to absorb delays. Box 7.1 defines three important reliability metrics.

Box 7.1: Basic reliability metrics

Different types of reliability can be targeted and tracked (Friend, 1992).

- *Despatch reliability = 1 – ((delays + cancellations)/total departures).*
- *En route reliability = 1 – ((ground turnbacks + air turnbacks + diversions)/total departures).*
- *Schedule reliability = 1 – schedule interruptions/total departures (where 'schedule interruptions' include delays, cancellations, turnbacks, and diversions).*

Given sufficient resources (e.g., functioning equipment, properly trained and motivated people, adequate spares, and enough time to accomplish required processes), many controllable delays can be eliminated. Some airlines strive to achieve the highest level of reliability they can despite the costs involved, addressing in particular the root causes of persistent delays to particular departures. Others are more prepared to tolerate delays to a certain percentage of flights as an inevitable by-product of the efficiency/ effectiveness trade-off that we saw in chapter 4 lies at the heart of operations management. The latter approach is not without risk in competitive, business-oriented markets. Finally, it is critical that the first departures of the day in a short-haul network keep to schedule, because early morning problems can propagate throughout the day.

In two important respects, however, the seeds of schedule reliability are sown within a schedule itself: block-times and turnaround/transit times.

Scheduled block-times These can vary seasonally on long-haul routes (to take account of winds) and by time of day on short-haul routes (to take account of departures or arrivals occurring at times of particular congestion at the airports concerned). But from a schedule reliability perspective the key issue is how much time to add as a buffer against *unforeseen* delays. By publishing aggressive block-times an airline might hope to benefit competitively from the appearance of faster journeys, but it has less of a buffer within which to absorb delays. Many airlines now allow for some element of delay by publishing longer than necessary block-times; as well as keeping passengers satisfied on individual flights, this approach can also help PR in those few countries where individual carriers' flight completion and punctuality rates are in the public domain. Padding block-times is not without its problems, however.

1. The shorter a flight, the less opportunity there is to recover time lost to a departure delay, yet any meaningful buffer inserted into the schedule to deal with potential delays will represent a more significant percentage of actual block-time than is likely to be the case in respect of a long-haul flight.
2. As noted above, too much buffer time can make a flight appear uncompetitive on GDS displays.
3. Too much buffer time might also lead to ground delays if consistently early arrivals have to wait for assigned gates to become free.

Scheduled turnaround/transit times 'Turn-times' are determined in the first instance by how long it takes to transit or turn around an aircraft of the type likely to be operating each leg at the airports in question, modified by any requirement to allow time for connecting passengers to make transfers and perhaps to await specific high-volume inbound connections before departure. As a contingency buffer, ground times might need to be longer for a given type the longer the block-time of the inbound leg, to reflect the fact that the longer a block-time is – most particularly in medium- and long-haul operations – the higher the chance of delay; the identity of the airport from which an inbound flight departs might also be a consideration if it is prone to delays at the time of day the flight leaves (unless potential delays have been factored into the block-time allowed). Finally, a crew change might lengthen ground time.

By scheduling aggressive turn-times an airline can raise aircraft utilisation, but it has less of a ground-buffer in which to absorb delays – either to the flight concerned (which can have knock-on effects as the aircraft continues its rotation behind schedule) or to inbound connections (which might have less time to link with that aircraft). There are three sub-issues here.

1. Any airline operating a high-activity hub-and-spoke system can face congestion (e.g., on taxiways and aprons) as well as heavy resource loading during peaks of activity at the hub, and yet its product to a large extent stands or falls on achieving high levels of schedule reliability. Hub-and-spoke systems generally require longer turn-times than point-to-point operations in order both to provide a buffer that can help prevent delays propagating across subsequent complexes, and to contribute to the optimisation of connectivity between incoming and outgoing banks. Minimum turn-time for a given type arriving at a hub as part of an inbound bank might therefore be considerably longer than for the same type at an outstation.

2. A number of structural features contribute to the ability of low-fare carriers to build the economics of their operations on fast turn-times and the high aircraft utilisation to which they contribute.

    •   First, these carriers have no need to consider the requirements of connecting passengers because most operate point-to-point services; those that do carry significant volumes of flow traffic (notably Southwest at some of its highest-frequency stations) do not schedule connections as such, but rely instead on high frequencies to simulate a rolling hub.

    •   Second, the complexity of ramp operations is minimised by having a single-type fleet, limited catering, and no need to interline or intraline baggage.

    •   Third, these carriers commonly operate into secondary airports unburdened by congestion.

    •   Fourth, a relatively continuous spread of frequencies throughout the day even at high-volume stations avoids the self-induced peaking, and the need to allow for the resource bottlenecks to which it sometimes leads, that hub-and-spoke carriers have to accommodate.

    Low-fare carriers are nonetheless not immune to delays. A common Ryanair operating pattern therefore schedules aircraft onto four morning flight-legs with 25-minute turnarounds, separated by a one-hour midday 'firebreak' from four afternoon legs also operated with 25-minute turnarounds.

3. Whilst reducing aircraft turn-times can allow a carrier to generate more block-hours and therefore a higher output of ASMs from an unchanged fleet, the question arises whether this incremental output can be sold at prices in excess of variable costs (so making a contribution to fixed costs that would not have been made had utilisation been lower).

To summarise, aggressive timetabled block-times and tight turnarounds increase aircraft utilisation but, unless carefully managed, can threaten both punctuality and schedule integrity. In fact, since the mid-1990s US majors as a whole have been steadily stretching scheduled domestic flight-times to mask the true scale of delays (*Aviation Daily*, 26 July, 2000). The amount of stretching applied can vary, however, even with respect to a given flight-leg. In July 2001 Delta was operating a mix of types on 15 hourly weekday nonstops from Atlanta to Boston; scheduled times ranged from 2 hours 23 minutes to 2 hours 34 minutes for B757s, and from 2 hours 19 minutes to 2 hours 34 minutes for B727s. Schedule stretching is an increasingly common practice in both the United States and Europe.

(Wu and Caves (2000) outline a mathematical model that can be used to optimise the trade-off between aircraft utilisation and turn-time.)

The marketing implications of a schedule

Every feasible schedule is a separate product, with its own saleability. (See Clampett (1998) for a description of software that relates different schedule choices to different yields.)

Passenger markets

The following comments outline a few of the scheduling issues that affect different types of passenger market.

Business segments A schedule targeted at business travellers will be more expensive to produce than one targeting primarily leisure or VFR segments, but the idea is that higher costs should be compensated by firmer yields. To be attractive to business travellers, a schedule needs the following.

1. **Frequent departures** The greater the frequency an airline is able to offer, the better will be its chances of attracting passengers whose requirement is the next available flight and of retaining the loyalty of regular travellers. The economic rationale for this is that business travellers value their time more highly than travellers in other segments, and therefore bear higher costs if forced to wait beyond their preferred departure times. A pronounced relationship generally links frequency share and market share. This is particularly true in short-haul markets, where in respect of flights up to 2–2½ hours in duration frequency has been found to have a very strong influence on demand from business travellers (particularly where multiple FFP memberships are the norm).
2. **Convenient and consistent timings** Efforts should be made to maintain consistency with regard to departure timings (e.g., 1600 daily – rather than 1535 one day, 1610 the next and so on). Although as already noted airlines do fine-tune their timings, there is merit in consistency insofar as regular departures will become familiar to frequent travellers and to agency staff. What represents a convenient timing will vary from market to market, and will also depend upon whether connections are required that lengthen journey times. With regard to short-haul business travel, particularly in potential day-return markets, we can make the following generalisations: at stations where originating traffic predominates, offering the first outbound and last inbound serv-

ices can be competitively advantageous; at stations where traffic originating elsewhere predominates, offering the first inbound and last outbound services might be preferable.

3. **Co-ordinated timings** As far as possible, an airline operating a hub-and-spoke system must ensure the co-ordination of its schedules to minimise waiting time for online transfer traffic and reduce the temptation for passengers to connect onto another (non-allied) carrier.

Leisure and VFR segments A scheduled airline intending to penetrate a leisure or VFR market will benefit from travellers generally being less demanding in their schedule requirements. On the other hand, the fact that leisure and VFR travellers tend to be price-sensitive means that they generate softer yields, so airlines serving them need to develop schedules that are relatively cheap to produce – implying high aircraft utilisation, perhaps larger aircraft operating at lower frequencies than business travellers would require, and high seat factors.

Conclusions regarding distinctions between business, leisure and VFR segments Whilst some markets are clearly business-oriented (e.g., into Frankfurt), some are clearly leisure-oriented (e.g., into Las Vegas), and some are predominantly VFR (e.g., UK-Ireland), the fact is that most scheduled airlines carry a mix of traffic on all but a few of their routes. This means that scheduling has to target the requirements of the predominant segment on a given route – particularly if it is a potentially high-yield segment. Note that a complicating factor in Europe is the important role of highly focused charter airlines operating high-frequency, round-the-clock summer services to Mediterranean leisure destinations; their higher costs keep scheduled carriers out of most of these markets, although low-fare airlines targeting short-break vacationers in particular have entered some of the denser leisure markets in recent years.

Long-haul services On many long-haul routes (particularly North Atlantic, North Pacific, Europe–Asia, and vice versa) the effects of time zones tend to frame relatively narrow windows within which competitors must cluster if they are to schedule feasible and/or desirable arrival times – with feasibility and desirability determined by passenger preferences, airport curfews and quotas, and/or the availability of onward connections.

Eastbound departures from the US East Coast to Europe generally leave in the late afternoon or early evening because any earlier and they would arrive in the middle of the night whilst any later and they would miss the outbound bank of southbound and eastbound medium- and long-haul connections that leave major European hubs in the late morning. Westbound flights to Europe from East and Southeast Asia tend to leave late in the evening in order to avoid curfews at European airports and to catch outbound morning banks for short-haul intra-European connections. These intercontinental timings feed through to the timings of return legs insofar as airlines generally want to boost aircraft utilisation by turning their aircraft around as quickly as possible; where time zones preclude this (e.g., Qantas at London Heathrow), downtime during the day can be used for phased maintenance work or ad hoc charters. (Qantas and British Airways have tried unsuccessfully to obtain regulatory approval for Qantas B747s and crews to operate short intra-European services on behalf of British Airways during the aircraft's daylight downtime at Heathrow.) As demand has grown in some dense international markets such as New York–London and Hong Kong–London, it has become increasingly feasible to schedule morning departures carrying predominantly local traffic that prefers a daylight flight and is not concerned about poor availability of onward connections off an evening arrival. One final point to make about long-haul flights is that they are usually operated by widebodies, which inevitably means that their turn-times are relatively long; figure 7.2 illustrates a transit schedule for a B747 – the timings on which are aggressive but achievable.

Cargo markets

Scheduling is also one of the factors which define an airline's cargo product. Shippers and forwarders often prefer freight to travel at night, particularly in the express segment. This permits late acceptance of outbound shipments; depending upon the time zones being crossed and the urgency of the shipment, it may also facilitate early delivery the next day. Whereas these requirements can be met when all-cargo aircraft are being operated, freight capacity on combis and in the belly-holds of passenger aircraft is usually scheduled to fit the requirements of travellers rather than shippers. Furthermore, where carriers choose to operate short- and medium-haul passenger routes at high frequencies using narrowbodied aircraft into which freight must be loose-loaded, rather than widebodies capable of accommodating unit load devices (ULDs), they will find it very difficult to offer a freight product competitive with surface modes (assuming these to be well-developed in the markets concerned).

Summary

Having designed a network of nonstop, direct, and/or connecting routes with which to serve geographical markets it wants to serve, an airline's

Passengers	Deplaning										
	Transportation										
	Baggage claim										
Crew-operating/F.S.	Deplane										
Baggage	Container offload										
	Container transport										
	Delivery claim belt										
Fuelling	Position, connect										
	Pumping										
	Load verification										
	Disconnect, deposition										
	Engine injection water										
Cargo and mail	Container offload										
	Container transport										
	Bulk compt. offload										
Galley servicing	Main cabin door, 4L										
	Main cabin door, 1R										
	Main cabin door, 2R										
Lavatory servicing	Aft										
	Centre										
	Forward										
Drinking water	Loading										
Cabin cleaning	First-class section										
	Economy section										
	Lounge										
	Flight deck										
Cargo and mail	Container/bulk loading										
Flight service	Aboard										
	Galley/cabin check										
	Receive passengers										
Operating crew	Aboard										
	Aircraft check										
	Engine start										
Baggage	Container transport										
	Container loading										
Weight and balance	Preparation										
	Aboard										
Passengers	Transportation										
	Boarding										

0   5   10   15   20   25   30   35   40   45   50

Time, minutes

Figure 7.2 Gantt chart schedule of transit activities for a B747
Source: Fitzsimmons, J.A. and Fitzsimmons, M.J., *Service Management: Operations, Strategy and Information Technology* (2nd edition), McGraw-Hill, 1998, p.199. Reproduced with permission of The McGraw-Hill Companies.

managers need next to decide how often and at what times each route will be flown. Despite being treated separately here for convenience, network and schedule design decisions cannot in practice be dealt with in isolation from each other or from the aircraft selection and fleet management decisions we will be touching upon in the next chapter; each is an integral part of the capacity management challenge.

For economists, a high level of 'service quality' has typically been associated with high frequencies and consistent departure times. What is meant by 'high' frequency will depend in large measure upon the length of haul involved. Frequency can be a vital competitive factor in short-haul markets generally, and in particular where business travellers represent a significant segment of demand and/or viable competition exists from surface transport.

iii. Scheduling: a response to the economics of supply

We saw in chapter 4 that the heart of operating strategy is the balancing of efficiency (minimum cost) with effectiveness (maximum customer satisfaction); the fulcrum on which this balance is achieved depends upon an airline's choice of markets or segments to serve and its positioning within them. Scheduling is an important part of the trade-off because it has a direct impact on both revenues (being a core part of the airline service offer) and costs (being a key determinant of resource requirements and resource utilisation).

The costs and benefits of using high frequencies to supply output

Frequency is a function of the traffic density and mix on a particular route and how an airline decides to produce output in order to satisfy demand. A given level of output could be offered into a market using the largest aircraft that traffic density will support; alternatively, higher frequencies could be offered using smaller types or variants. Much depends on the characteristics of the demand being satisfied and whether the possibly lower utilisation of the larger aircraft on a particular route can be compensated by deployment elsewhere in the system.

We have already seen that an airline's schedule should ideally be driven by the time-preferences of targeted customers. How strongly time-preferences are held by different customers will affect their elasticities of demand and, as we will see in chapter 9, should be a key input into revenue management processes. Where high frequencies are required by a given market or segment, there are both costs and benefits to consider.

Costs

High frequencies are expensive to produce relative to lower frequencies with larger aircraft. There are two issues here.

1. If acceptable load factors are to be achieved, high frequencies on any route generally require the operation of smaller aircraft than could be sustained were frequencies lower. Although their individual trip costs might be lower, the seat-mile costs of smaller aircraft are generally higher than the seat-mile costs of larger aircraft of a similar technological generation – as we saw in chapter 5. In other words, the cost of supplying 400,000 nonstop ASMs a day between two points 1,000 miles apart will be higher if output is generated by flying 400 seats in four 100-seat departures rather than two 200-seat departures.
2. Departure cost per head will most probably rise as passengers are split into an increasing number of departures, because the fixed handling and despatch costs associated with each flight are being spread over a smaller number of passengers per flight.

Against these costs can be balanced a number of potential benefits.

Benefits

We have seen that the more frequently an airline serves a given route, the more likely it is that it will be able to match a greater proportion of customers' preferred departure times, or at least reduce the implicit time-costs of not matching them. This can provide one or both of two benefits.

1. Because business travellers generally value their time more highly than most leisure travellers, the demand for business travel has historically been sufficiently price-inelastic to permit airlines to build into their tariffs a charge to compensate for the high seat-mile costs and lower load factors that high frequencies imply on all but the most dense routes. Routes with a substantial business travel segment are therefore likely to be able to support the costs of a high-frequency operation.
2. As we saw in chapter 4, the 'S-curve' theory holds that the carrier with most frequencies on a route (assuming a given aircraft size) will attract a higher percentage market share and revenue share than the proportion of total frequencies contributed by its services. The 'S-curve' is derived from a plot of market share as an independent variable against frequency as the dependent variable. Although not universally accepted,

there are reasons why this 'dominance theory' might be borne out in practice.

- Assuming a reasonable spread of departure timings (i.e., effective time-of-day coverage), the carrier with most frequencies could very plausibly come closest to meeting the time-preferences of a greater proportion of total passengers on a route than its frequencies represent as a proportion of total frequencies; this could hold until so many frequencies are offered that customers attribute little or no further value to time savings brought about by another frequency.

- Offering more frequencies than competitors is likely to lead to a position for the airline's services at or close to the top of the first page of GDS displays more often than would be achieved by lower-frequency competitors.

- If an airline offers, say, three return flights on a route each day it is providing nine return products insofar as a passenger departing on any of the three outbound services can return on any of the three inbound services. (These are not necessarily all day-return products, of course.) On the other hand, a competitor offering two return flights has only four products available; by offering just one extra rotation, the first carrier is therefore able to provide nine of the thirteen single-carrier products on offer. High frequencies have generally been held to yield a revenue premium insofar as they attract business travellers who value the flexibility to book and rebook at short notice, and who accordingly tend to purchase relatively high unrestricted or walk-up fares.

Particularly – but not only – in business segments, frequency is one of the most important forms of nonprice competition open to airlines in liberalised or deregulated markets, and pursuit of both network reach and schedule dominance have together been a key motivator behind hub-and-spoke carriers building service at their hubs; similarly, many point-to-point operators commonly strive to build frequency dominance as soon as possible after entering a market. Whilst there will always be exceptions, there is often a strong argument for growing a network in the following order of priority: build frequencies on existing routes; add links between stations already served; add links to new stations.

Resource utilisation

The more that resources are used, the more output they should be able to produce. The more output they produce, the greater is the amount of output over which the fixed costs associated with acquiring and operating each resource can be spread and the lower is the average fixed cost of each unit of output produced. Assuming that incremental output can be sold at a price in excess of the variable costs incurred in producing it, resources need to be utilised as much as possible. Scheduling can help or hinder this effort.

Aircraft utilisation

The task is to keep aircraft in the air as much as possible, and to deploy each type in markets where its profit-earning potential can be maximised. Market liberalisation can assist in two ways.

1. Airline managers are in principle freed to manage networks and schedules to arrive at their own preferred balance between the exigencies of market demand and aircraft utilisation.
2. Pricing freedom allows them to make a range of discounted fare offers in order to achieve acceptable load factors on flights operated by types that would be too large for a route were less pricing flexibility available. (This assumes that the discounted fares are profitable, of course; if they are not, then a smaller type needs to be deployed.)

We have already seen that two linked scheduling decisions in particular can have a profound impact on aircraft utilisation: transit/turnaround times and scheduled block-times. An even more profound issue is the nature of the markets being served. Short-haul markets generally support lower aircraft utilisation than medium- and (particularly) long-haul markets for two reasons: first, short-haul aircraft spend more time on the ground because their flight-legs are by definition shorter; and second, short-haul passengers are often unwilling to fly at night whereas passengers travelling in one or both directions on many long-haul routes have no alternative. There are some caveats here.

- The effect of turn-times can narrow the gap somewhat insofar as transit times for long-haul aircraft are usually an hour or more and turnaround times are longer than that, whilst low-fare short-haul carriers in particular are able to turn aircraft around in 20–30 minutes. The utilisation gap between the two types of operation nonetheless remains significant.
- Carriers able to overnight short-haul aircraft at a maintenance facility can use downtime for phased checks and/or deep cleaning.
- Some short-haul markets do tolerate overnight scheduling if fares are sufficiently low. Most obviously, North European charter carriers operate 24-hour schedules to the Mediterranean and back through the peak

summer season. In the mid-1990s America West began 'Nite Flite' services at Las Vegas. In the late 1990s Cathay Pacific started offering low-fare intra-Asian passenger services at night on flights being operated primarily to move belly-hold freight under contract for DHL.

The fundamental issue with regard to aircraft utilisation is the way in which an airline manages its output in response to the characteristics of demand in the markets being served. Additional frequencies boost aircraft utilisation, but whether or not they are feasible will depend on traffic density and mix: density has to be sufficient to support higher frequencies, and the traffic mix has to generate yields sufficient to support the cost of operating them. (Density and mix are of course linked variables intermediated by the price-elasticity of demand.) In general, higher frequencies provide airlines with more flexibility in aircraft and crew scheduling – the latter subject to regulatory and also often contractual duty-time restrictions – and so facilitate higher utilisation.

Demand peaking also complicates the scheduling task. There might not be enough of the right aircraft available to generate output at peak times, but there will likely be more than enough in off-peak periods. We have seen that the answer to the latter problem could be to boost off-peak utilisation by deploying aircraft onto non-core routes or by adding capacity in existing markets. Whether or not this can be done profitably depends upon how the word 'profitable' is defined, which in turn is in part a function of cost allocation.

High utilisation is neither always feasible nor inevitably essential. Aircraft utilisation tends to decline with age because of increased scheduled and unscheduled maintenance downtime. Also, where sufficient slack exists in a fleet an airline will sometimes schedule new aircraft with lower operating costs more intensively than older models. Conversely, if the nature of an airline's operations leads inexorably to low utilisation, the unit cost problem this implies can be lessened by using older aircraft that are inexpensive to buy and so have relatively low ownership costs. This is why until the downturn of 2001/2002 express carriers had so many long-service narrowbodies in the lightly utilised elements of their fleets, used to serve network spokes just once each night.

Efficient scheduling can have a profound impact on aircraft utilisation – effectively augmenting the fleet without acquiring additional aircraft; incremental output produced by the higher utilisation of existing resources generally comes very much cheaper than that produced by new assets, because the latter bring with them an extra set of fixed costs. On the other hand, overaggressive scheduling affects reported ontime performance and this, as already noted, has led some US carriers in particular to stretch their block-times – the benefit being improved perceptions amongst customers.

Utilisation of resources other than aircraft

An airline's flight schedule drives the scheduling of other resources. Fortunately, there are large numbers of software products now on the market to help even small carriers without their own operations research functions optimise the deployment of human resources. The following represent just a sample of the areas covered (Baldanza and Lipkus, 2000).

1. **Queuing models** Because time spent waiting for service is an important input into customers' perceptions of an airline's overall service package, it is critical that carriers assign resources – specifically, human resources – to processes such as check-in, security screening (where under airline control), and boarding in quantities sufficient to deliver the timeliness of service that targeted customers expect (ibid). We touched on this in chapter 5.

2. **Ground staff manning and rostering models** Again, there is an effectiveness/efficiency trade-off to be arrived at within the context of a particular airline's service concept. For example, the number of baggage-handlers assigned to an inbound narrowbody flight with loose-loaded baggage might be a function of the number of passengers onboard as well as the baggage reclaim time-standards the airline has set. Rostering models are available to help optimise staff assignments subject to shift patterns and labour contract constraints (ibid; Broggio et al, 2000).

3. **Flight-crew scheduling** This is amongst the most challenging of resource scheduling/productivity optimisation tasks because flight-crews are subject to legal and contractual duty-time limits, because their scheduling must also generally reflect intangible quality-of-life requirements, because flight-crew schedules have to be integrated with layover accommodation (the securing of which can also now be automated), and because (in US domestic experience) some ten per cent or more of any schedule can be expected to be disrupted and have to be recovered through 'irregular operations' (Good, 2000). Flight-crew scheduling is nonetheless a particularly critical exercise, because pilots represent such an expensive resource.

   Although some airlines do still use heuristic or manual techniques, optimisation-based solutions are now commonly deployed to solve flight-crew scheduling problems. Butchers et al (2001) and Christou et al (1999) describe solutions developed for Air New Zealand and Delta respectively to address two fundamental crew-scheduling tasks:

- the generation of legally and contractually allowable monthly crew schedules that permit the airline to fly its published flight schedule. Called 'tours of duty' or, in the United States, 'bidlines' or 'lines of time', these are comprised of multiple trips (or 'pairings'), each beginning and ending at a crew base; and

- the allocation (or 'rostering') of crew members to each tour of duty or bidline to create 'lines of work'. This is done either by assignment or, as is common in the United States, by bidding on the basis of seniority.

(See Dillon and Kontogiorgis (1999) for a description of these issues in the context of scheduling reserve flight-crews at US Airways.)

Scheduling also affects the utilisation of maintenance facilities and personnel, as well as station utilisation. With regard to the latter, the higher the number of departures per station, the more output there is over which to spread fixed costs associated with ramp, terminal, and other station resources. On the other hand, those resources themselves – counters, gates, ground equipment, catering facilities, line maintenance capacity, and baggage handling systems for example – also need scheduling to ensure sufficient availability during peak periods. (Whether each of these is the responsibility of the airline, the airport authority, or a third-party service provider will of course vary from station to station.) Peaking is a problem insofar as a given investment in station resources might be adequate to support a certain number of turnarounds spread relatively evenly throughout the day, but not the same number of turnarounds clustered into a small number of complexes.

Generally, however, the higher the number and more even the spread of daily departures, the higher resource utilisation is likely to be; the lower the number and more peaked the pattern of departures, the lower resource utilisation is likely to be. That said, we need to bear in mind that where ground support equipment (GSE) is type-specific, its utilisation is driven not by raw departure figures but by departures of the aircraft type concerned. Box 7.2 looks at gate utilisation.

Box 7.2: Gate utilisation

Depending upon the country and station concerned, an airline might secure gates on an exclusive-use, preferential-use, or common-use basis. An airline owning its own terminals (as at some US hubs) or committing to an exclusive-use gate-lease (again, more common in the United States than elsewhere in the world) will want to monitor gate utilisation using metrics such as daily gate turns (i.e., arrivals and departures) and passenger throughput.

The more complexes per day a hub supports, the larger will be the number of gate turns; at the extreme, a high-volume 'continuous' or 'rolling' hub spreads departures more evenly across the day than other hubs by scheduling complexes more or less back-to-back – so, in principle, opening the possibility of almost continuous gate utilisation. Whether as a result of continuous hubbing or because of high frequencies spread throughout the day on a point-to-point network, the more even the spread of departures and the faster the average turn-time the higher gate utilisation is likely to be; Southwest, for example, achieves eight-to-ten gate turns per day at many of its stations.

An important factor is clearly the nature of an airline's operations. As explained in the main text, the attributes of the products offered by a full-service network carrier (with regard to catering, connections, and seat assignment, for example) mean that its aircraft will inevitably spend longer at the gate than the same type operated by a low-fare carrier. Separately, a gate supporting long-haul services by widebody aircraft that require lengthy periods for deplaning, cleaning, provisioning, and enplaning will support fewer gate turns than the six or more a day that a well-managed rolling hub could support.

We have already noted that scheduling has a distinct impact on gate utilisation as a result of decisions taken by schedule planners regarding whether to go for tight turnarounds or to provide additional time to buffer delays. Clearly, both inbound or outbound delays that cannot be accommodated within the published schedule may affect gate allocation decisions and gate utilisation; as with every other type of resource, a great deal depends upon how much slack (in this case, time and numbers of available gates) has been built into the system – either deliberately to accommodate disruptions, or inadvertently arising from the fact that each gate is an 'indivisibility' that may initially offer more capacity than is required at the precise time it is added to the system.

iv. Scheduling: a response to external constraints

Scheduling is a means of controlling output which interacts closely with characteristics of the demand being served and the costs of serving it. Output is a function not only of capacity management decisions – network and fleet planning, for example – but also decisions governing how that capacity will be deployed. Deployment, though, is constrained by more than a need to balance the characteristics of demand with the costs of supply at an acceptable price. It is also constrained by external considerations such as time zones, curfews, the terms of bilateral ASAs governing international flights, the availability of take-off and landing slots, gate space, and counters at congested airports, and also by competitors' activities.

v. Scheduling a hub-and-spoke network

Scheduling over one or more integrated hubs clearly poses challenges more complicated than those faced in traditional, out-and-back networks. Many can be attributed to the fact that, more so than point-to-point operators, hub-and-spoke carriers design and schedule *routes* but serve *markets*; the schedule established for each route has to take account of the requirements of customers in the various different markets served by that route.

The marketing objective of any hub is to maximise connectivity between points of origin and final destinations, subject to a commercially and operationally acceptable layover between each pair of incoming and outgoing flights. This section will start by looking at the impact of network design and scheduling on the density of traffic on individual routes, and then consider a selection of other hub scheduling issues.

The impact of network design and scheduling on traffic density

It was stressed at the beginning of the last chapter that 'route' and 'market' are not necessarily synonymous; passengers travelling on a particular route (e.g., Dallas–Miami) could have connected from behind (e.g., Albuquerque) and/or be connecting beyond (e.g., to St. Thomas) – and therefore may be travelling in a different O & D city-pair market (e.g., Albuquerque–St. Thomas) to the one served by the route concerned. The way in which a network is designed and scheduled will affect the routing of these flows, and in so doing impact upon traffic densities – and therefore the optimum choice of aircraft – on individual routes. The carrier in the above example might, for instance, also offer an inter-hub route from Dallas to San Juan, together with connections providing a schedule that some Albuquerque–St. Thomas travellers prefer to the routing via Miami.

Hub-and-spoke networks have been developed to manage traffic flows by using hubs to accumulate and distribute passengers (and freight) from and to outlying points. They can affect traffic densities and equipment choice on individual routes in one or all of three ways.

1. We noted above that because flights down a spoke to a hub carry passengers proceeding on to multiple destinations, they have higher densities and can in principle be operated by larger aircraft than point-to-point flights serving each individual market out of the spoke city could support – thereby reducing unit (i.e., seat-mile) costs.

2. Hubs in either single-airline or alliance multi-hub networks can be connected by relatively large aircraft and/or relatively high frequencies to exploit the increased traffic generated by channelling flows between them. Traffic densities between Cincinnati and Salt Lake City and between Cincinnati and Paris CDG are both very much larger than they would be were these not hubs between which double-connect flow traffic is being channelled. Indeed, one of the most important marketing benefits of a multi-hub alliance is that integration of the separate networks often supports higher inter-hub frequencies than would otherwise be the case, and therefore a greater range of departure choices for connecting origins behind one hub to destinations beyond the other.

3. By offering alternative routings and (depending upon scheduling decisions) perhaps more connection opportunities, a multi-hub network may provide a higher level of service than a single hub; on the other hand, it might actually reduce densities on some routes. Taking the example above, availability of a Dallas–San Juan inter-hub connection will divert some Albuquerque–St. Thomas traffic off the Dallas–Miami and Miami–St. Thomas routes and onto the Dallas–San Juan and San Juan–St. Thomas routes. (Whilst Albuquerque–St. Thomas traffic is fairly thin, if we think of traffic flowing between hundreds of origins and hundreds of destinations in thousands of city-pair markets – no matter how thin each might be in itself – the potential impact of route and scheduling decisions on traffic density, aircraft selection, and therefore the economics of individual routes is clearly significant.)

Of course, all that such networks are doing is reorienting traffic flows. The basic decision regarding how to allocate capacity still has to be made within this reoriented framework: higher frequencies with smaller aircraft offering lower individual trip costs and perhaps higher seat-mile costs, or fewer frequencies with larger aircraft whose seat-mile costs will probably be lower and whose individual trip costs will be higher – but whose aggregate trip costs may or may not exceed aggregate trip costs associated with higher-frequency/lower-capacity options.

Schedule saleability can be affected by even minor changes in departure times, and the financial effects of this are leveraged through load factors. For example, if a schedule change results in an increase of just five or ten extra connecting passengers, much of the additional revenue earned should go straight through to the bottom line because of the low marginal costs of carrying them. On the other hand, the same operating leverage effect means that diversion of just a few passengers can turn a series of flights from profit into loss – perhaps because the revised schedule is less attractive than a competitor's schedule, because its GDS display screen position has been compromised, or because it dislocates linkages between flights. Tretheway (1998: 652-653) exemplifies the point.

> Consider the example of a new service from Boston to Vancouver. If the flight is off-peak, perhaps at 3P.M., the carrier must cover the cost solely through origin and destination traffic. But if the flight can arrive during the noon "Asian flight bank," the carrier may be able to win an extra fifty connecting passengers per day. These incremental connects not only generate incremental Boston-Vancouver revenues but also contribute traffic to other flights such as Vancouver-Nagoya, Vancouver-Tokyo, Vancouver-Beijing, Vancouver-Hong Kong, Vancouver-Kuala Lumpur, and so forth. Supposing that the average airfare is $2,000 for a Boston-Asia passenger, then the airline's ability to grow on the peak is worth an additional $100,000 *per day* in incremental system revenue. On an annual basis, this comes to $36 million. A carrier building a hub could find similar incremental peak-period revenues on a range of potential routes. Growth off-peak is expensive (or, more precisely, uneconomic).

Generally speaking, only if there is very strong local traffic, a need to match a competitor's frequencies, and/or a profitable opportunity to raise aircraft utilisation is it justifiable for a hub-and-spoke carrier to operate flights into a hub that are unconnected to a complex.

Some other important hub scheduling issues

Hub scheduling also gives rise to several other issues, the most important of which we will look at in the next few subsections.

Infrastructure congestion

There are three levels on which congestion might make itself felt.

1. **Schedule adjustment** If runway, gate, and/or terminal capacity is constrained at a hub, an airline might have relatively little flexibility to reschedule a particular arrival or departure. (That said, a dominant carrier at a slot-constrained hub – Lufthansa at Frankfurt, for example – should in principle be able to reallocate its slot portfolio more readily

than minor players with smaller portfolios.) When a route serves two slot-constrained hubs, the adjustment challenge is even greater.

2. **Outstation connectivity** It is possible that decisions might have to be taken to exclude certain spoke cities from connection to a capacity-constrained complex, giving them connections instead into alternate complexes. (In fact, depending upon the nature of points served on a network it could be that not every spoke will anyway merit a connection to every complex. A leisure destination might not need connecting to the early and late banks that are so important to business markets and which generate intense peaks, but could well suffice with being connected just to lower volume complexes in the middle of the day. However, this might not apply to destinations serving short-break leisure traffic that needs late-Friday outbound and late-Sunday inbound services.)

3. **Hub development** At its most extreme, an infrastructure constraint might prevent a carrier from developing a fully effective hub at all. The facts that London Heathrow has only two runways and that (until completion of Terminal 5) long- and short-haul passengers are largely segregated into separate terminals on different parts of the airport have been major constraints on British Airways' hubbing; the single runway at London Gatwick is also a constraint on large-scale hubbing. Both situations compare unfavourably with those at some other European hubs, most notably Paris CDG, and at the principal US hubs. (Whereas around 60 per cent of Air France traffic at CDG connects, the figure for British Airways at Heathrow peaked in the mid-90s at approximately 40 per cent and has since declined.)

Hub sequencing

A hub generally serves spokes of different lengths which, depending on the equipment used as well as the stage-lengths involved, dictate different block-times. This can be seen at its most extreme in combined domestic/international hubs, and it raises the question of how most efficiently and effectively to sequence flights in incoming and outgoing banks.

Taking the hypothetical example of a domestic hub, assume that the flight-time from hub H to spoke city A is 70 minutes and from H to spoke city B is 90 minutes. Further assume that both aircraft leave H at approximately the same time and will need to have completed their rotations and be ready to depart H again four hours later as part of a 240-minute hub-repeat cycle. (A hub-repeat cycle is defined by the time between the same points in consecutive complexes (Dennis, 1994) – such as first or last arrival, or first or last departure.) The aircraft serving B will spend 60 minutes (i.e.,

240-90-90) on the ground during the four-hour cycle and so will be reasonably well utilised, whilst the aircraft serving A will spend 100 minutes (i.e., 240-70-70) on the ground and so may have 'slack time' at either or both the hub and the outstation. ('Slack time' is time spent on the ground in excess of what is required to turn an aircraft around.) This simple example points to several issues.

1. **Aircraft utilisation** Short spokes in particular can threaten aircraft utilisation. Answers might include:
   - multi-stop or triangular routings (although these have to be balanced against the product degradation they entail for some passengers); and
   - scheduling short spokes out last and back first to minimise slack time at the outstation (and allocating the incoming aircraft to an early departure in the next outbound bank so that it does not simply spend a long period on the ground at the hub rather than at the outstation).

   Choosing instead to bring the aircraft back off a short spoke significantly ahead of the next inbound bank might be an option as well, but the risk arises that if the spoke city is also connected to another carrier's hub then passengers may choose that carrier should it offer a better aggregate O & D journey time. Even where this is not the case and passengers have no alternative other than to travel via the hub in question, if competing carriers also serve that hub and schedule convenient connections the spoke might simply be feeding those competitors – something that any schedule planning department should in practice be keen to avoid.

   However, the problem is less acute when a short spoke feeds into a rolling or continuous hub. The traffic flows at a sizeable multi-directional rolling hub such as Chicago O'Hare are likely to be sufficient to allow an aircraft turning quickly at a nearby spoke city to return to the hub and feed a significant number of points outbound, even though the lack of a tightly defined complex leaves it unable to feed every potentially feasible destination on the other side of the hub within a commercially acceptable connecting time.

2. **Pacing spokes** The most distant outstation served by a hub (i.e., the one with the longest block-time) is often referred to as a 'pacing spoke'. The longer a pacing spoke, the more scope there is to encounter en route delays and, more significantly, the more it eats into the hub turnaround time between successive inbound and outbound banks. Flights serving the longest spokes therefore tend to be amongst the first to leave in a departing bank and are often amongst the last to arrive off

an inbound bank. This could present connectivity issues, depending upon the precise relationship between out-and-back block-times on the one hand and the length of the hub-repeat cycle on the other. Another option – or in some cases a necessity – might be to connect the longest spoke(s) to alternate inbound banks rather than to every complex. In a multi-hub system the best way forward could be to connect a distant spoke city to alternate inbound banks at more than one hub in order to maintain behind/beyond O & D frequencies.

Looking at hub-sequencing on a more general level, there are several other issues.

- **Last-in first-out** Some observers argue that the last aircraft on an in- bound bank and the first on the connecting outbound bank should be a through-numbered same-plane service that supports good local traffic on both inbound and outbound legs and, importantly, a strong conn- ecting flow – the latter to minimise waiting times for a significant num- ber of passengers (Berdy, 1998). There is a counter-argument that plac- ing high-volume arrivals late on an inbound bank and high-volume departures early on an outbound bank can disrupt an unnecessarily large number of connections in the event of inbound delays – particul- arly delays affecting the high-volume arrival.
- **Widebodies** As far as possible, widebodies should be scheduled to arrive early and depart late in connecting banks to allow time for their slower turnarounds and, especially in the case of international flights, longer passenger facilitation processes.
- **Regional aircraft** Particularly where they are parked on outlying ramps and passengers have to be bussed (as well, perhaps, as making inter-terminal transfers), there can be merit in scheduling regional air- craft to arrive early and depart late in connecting banks (ibid).

Misconnections

Because in a large network not all points that might merit connections can necessarily be linked in a single complex (due to capacity constraints at the hub, for example), decisions often have to be taken in respect of which points are in fact to be connected in each complex. Even where a spoke is fed into an arriving bank, it might not be feasible to schedule that arrival to connect with every departure on the other side of the complex; the over- lapping of inbound and outbound banks (i.e., the scheduling of the first departure for a time that is less than the MCT from the last arrival) might be necessary to overcome infrastructural constraints or to sustain acceptable aircraft utilisation levels. If in order to meet hub efficiency and schedule saleability targets it is inevitable that some flights on an inbound bank cannot deliver the MCT required to connect with some flights on the corresponding outbound bank, these misconnections should only be scheduled in respect of markets with relatively small (and/or low-yield) O & D traffic flows.

In addition, we have already noted that some thin spokes anyway might not support flights connecting into and out of every complex at the hub(s) to which they are linked. This type of timetable asymmetry could affect the opportunity to make day-return trips in short-haul markets, and/or same-day connections in medium- or long-haul markets. One way around the problem might be to pair two thin and reasonably adjacent spokes into a triangular routing (e.g., H-A-B-H for complex 1 outbound and complex 2 inbound, followed by H-B-A-H for complex 2 outbound and complex 3 inbound). On a separate but related point, it is unlikely that medium- and long-haul routes into and out of a mixed domestic/international hub will connect with every complex; some might sustain only daily or double-daily widebody services, and most will face some sort of time zone constraint on scheduling flexibility.

Where to overnight short-haul aircraft

Much depends upon whether a particular short-haul spoke city is predominantly an origin or a destination (or, indeed, whether there is reasonable balance).

Spoke city as origin Where a spoke city is a strong outbound traffic generator, carriers will in many cases want to overnight an aircraft there to provide a competitive early departure that is able to feed the first outbound bank from their hub and – in some short-haul markets – to offer day-return possibilities in the local market between the outstation and the hub; this is a common operating pattern within both Europe and North America, because many secondary and tertiary points on short- and medium-haul networks are more significant originators of outbound traffic than magnets for destination traffic. (The assumption here is that the block-time concerned allows a departure that is both marketable (i.e., not before 0600) and yet early enough to fit into the hub's first inbound bank; some longer short-haul spokes might cause a problem in this regard.) Time zones can also have an influence: westbound first-out departures which cross time zones can benefit from time 'saved', whilst early eastbound departures might be penalised to the point where they arrive at the hub too late to connect with the first outbound bank.

Against the marketing benefits offered by overnighting down a spoke have to be weighed the costs of crew accommodation and allowances, and the fact that aircraft stabled away from a maintenance base are not available for phased checks or deep cleaning. These problems can be avoided if there is a partner based at the spoke city which could operate the first outbound service as a code-share.

Spoke city as destination Some spokes are less likely to originate early-morning traffic than to attract it, either from the hub itself or from origins behind the hub. The fundamental question is where the bulk of this inbound traffic originates. If it largely flows from behind the hub, there might be a strong case for stabling aircraft overnight at originating cities. If it originates primarily at the hub, there could be a case for serving the spoke destination ahead of the first inbound bank (because feed from that bank is not being relied upon), using aircraft stabled overnight at the hub. Another consideration is whether the airline in question has incoming overnight long-haul traffic to feed early-morning short-haul departures from the hub and compensate for a lack of short-haul feed at that hour – something that is often the case at major European hubs, for example.

By choosing to overnight short-haul aircraft at a hub rather than at out-stations a carrier is in effect breaking a complex – leaving an 'orphan' late-night inbound bank without onward connections, and an 'orphan' early-morning outbound bank without short-haul feed. There need to be sound commercial and/or operational reasons for doing this.

Delay propagation

Particularly if it affects departures early in the day, a delay can easily propagate around a highly integrated and tightly scheduled hub-and-spoke network. One approach to dealing with this is building more buffer time into the schedule. For example, in 2001 Northwest put back by 15 minutes the third and fourth complexes at its Memphis hub to allow aircraft more time on the ground at spoke cities between complexes two and three and by doing this provide an opportunity to catch-up with any earlier delays.

Scheduling multi-hub networks

To maximise the connectivity of multi-hub alliance networks it is desirable to schedule partners' networks as a single entity. As far as US airlines are concerned, this is only permissible where antitrust immunity has been granted to the alliance. There are two key variables with regard to both single-airline and alliance multi-hub network scheduling: spoke connect-ions and inter-hub connections.

Spoke connections Fundamental decisions include the selection of the hub(s) to which each spoke city is to be connected and, in the case of conn-ections to more than one hub, the choice of how many complexes at each to connect into. (Note that scheduling simultaneous departures to different hubs could induce a peaking problem at the spoke city, leading to resource utilisation penalties.)

Inter-hub connections There are two types.

1. *Nonstop* Common in both international alliance hubbing and US dom-estic multi-hub systems, these are used both for local traffic and – more particularly in the case of international networks – to channel double-connecting flow traffic between secondary or tertiary points behind one hub and beyond the other. It is important as far as possible to ensure that a departing flight coincides with an outbound bank at the first hub (to ensure it receives good feed from the earlier inbound bank) and arr-ives during an inbound bank at the second hub (to ensure good onward connections on the other side of the complex). Time zones often comp-licate this challenge in respect of long-haul flights; a related scheduling difficulty arises on some long-haul inter-hub routes where one or both of the hubs operate only a small number of daily complexes – so limiting cross-connect possibilities.
2. *Multi-stop* Particularly in US domestic systems, it is not uncommon for an aircraft to leave one hub on a one- or two-stop journey to another hub. By doing this it is serving the intermediate point(s) as part of an outbound bank from the first hub, and an inbound bank to the second hub. This type of aircraft scheduling can help to get around some of the spoke-city slack time (i.e., low aircraft utilisation) problems discussed above, but the potential downside is that it may also contribute to the propagation of delays between hubs – which is why some carriers have chosen to isolate particularly troublesome hubs from the rest of their system when assigning aircraft (e.g., United at Chicago O'Hare). Oper-ating patterns such as this are still relatively uncommon amongst Euro-pean majors, most of which have just a single significant hub.

Generally, the more hubs in a network that are accessible to each origin and destination and the higher the inter-hub frequencies, the more competitive the airline or alliance will be (in terms of frequency and journey time) in double-connect markets. (See Dennis (2000), for example.)

Weekend schedules

Some short-haul operations have weekend schedules significantly different from their weekday schedules to accommodate different patterns of demand, different volumes of traffic, and perhaps also the need to release aircraft for charters. Together, these considerations might require different routing patterns (e.g., replacing nonstops with connecting service), different frequencies, and the assignment of different aircraft types. Short-haul weekend operations can also present a fleet assignment challenge, with the need to link aircraft location on a Friday night into the weekend schedule, and on a Sunday night into the weekday schedule. (See Kontogiorgis and Acharya (1999) for an approach to the solution of this problem.)

The impact of network design and hub scheduling on fleet mix

If we assume that the number of daily complexes at a particular hub is given and that as far as possible it is desirable to have most spokes connected into every bank, then clearly the frequency of service to and from each outstation is also given. If we further assume that a carrier operates, say, four complexes a day at a particular hub, it is fairly unlikely that traffic on each spoke will support four return trips using a single aircraft type; some might support four B757 rotations, some four A320 rotations, some four CRJ200s, and some will require a mix of different types at different times of the day and week. Hub scheduling strategy will therefore superimpose itself on the specific requirements of individual routes to determine an optimal fleet mix – a mix which, incidentally, can benefit greatly from the availability of different-sized variants within families such as the B737, A320, CRJ, and ERJ/Embraer series. We will return to this last point in chapter 8.

vi. Scheduling tactics

What a carrier needs to achieve tactically with its scheduling will depend upon both overall strategy (e.g., whether predominantly hub-based or point-to-point) and the local competitive situation in O & D markets served. A hub-based carrier, for example, will want to ensure that its schedule contributes to hub strength in terms of destinations served, share of departures, and share of slots and/or gates (where relevant), thereby helping create a significant barrier to entry at the hub as well as achieving high levels of network connectivity. For many carriers, frequency domination is a key scheduling objective and we will look at this first. We will also consider the importance of code-sharing and GDS displays in a scheduling context.

An important point to be borne in mind is that whether to improve its own schedule saleability or respond to a competitor's tactics, a carrier operating a tightly integrated multi-hub system (as in the US domestic market) may find it difficult to effect what might on the surface appear to be relatively minor schedule adjustments. A schedule change can, for example, have knock-on effects on the allocation of crews, station resources, maintenance capacity, and perhaps therefore other aircraft, and also on network connectivity.

Frequency domination

We have seen already that the 'S-curve' theory argues a carrier dominating frequencies on a route will benefit from a disproportionately high market share. It is one reason why historically some airline managements have been reluctant to cut output when conditions on a route call for retrenchment, fearing a disproportionate loss of market share. More positively, it can provide a rational argument for exiting routes where there is little prospect of achieving high market share, and instead adding frequencies to routes (preferably high-growth routes) where dominance or at least strong relative market shares are achievable goals. This is true regardless of the length of haul, but on short-haul routes with a significant business segment it is essential to at least match – and preferably dominate – competitors' frequencies. We have already noted that deregulation, liberalisation, and the consequent emergence of hub-and-spoke networks have shaped decisions to serve growing demand, first, by increasing frequencies, and only as demand builds further (or infrastructural congestion requires) by then using larger aircraft.

The classic Southwest scheduling tactic adopted by several low-fare carriers elsewhere in the world is to enter an underserved or badly served, dense or potentially dense, price-elastic point-to-point market with reasonably high initial frequencies, then build rapidly and dominate output whilst at the same time stimulating demand with sustainably low fares. There are actually two types of route to consider in respect of this tactic.

1. **Routes with no alternative intermediate hub** In this case, a competitor cannot engage in frequency competition by combining O & D traffic in the market concerned with traffic in other O & D markets and channelling it over the hub; there is no alternative to competing head-on in the point-to-point nonstop market. With most US majors having

substantially higher short-haul operating costs than Southwest, this is unattractive insofar as their mainline operations are concerned – which is one reason why some decided to launch low-cost operations.

2. **Routes with an alternative intermediate hub** Where they have an intermediate hub available, the power of their hub-and-spoke networks does in principle allow the other US majors to compete with Southwest on frequency. One of the reasons behind Southwest's success, however, is that it only enters routes that other carriers could or do serve over their hubs when these routes will support the addition of high-frequency nonstop or through-plane B737 services so that it need never be outcompeted on frequency; Southwest generally uses low fares and the price-elasticity of unserved or underserved market segments to build traffic to the density required to achieve this – something that incumbents' higher fares had previously failed to do.

Challenging an incumbent on short-haul point-to-point routes

A new entrant onto a route already served by frequent departures will not be offering potential customers a substantial reduction in schedule delay. Nonetheless, entry onto short-haul point-to-point routes serving a significant O & D business segment is likely to be effective only if the entrant comes close to matching the incumbent's frequencies. Even where this is economically and physically possible, it raises potential problems.

- In the short term, while demand is catching up, route entry might lead to excess output and a drop in yields.
- If it is operating aircraft having broadly the same capacity as the incumbent, the entrant will – because of the incumbent's stronger initial market presence – achieve lower load factors. If on the other hand it tries to balance market share and share of capacity offered in order to keep load factors in line with those of incumbents (whilst maintaining approximate parity in frequencies), the entrant will have to operate smaller aircraft; these are likely to have seat-mile cost disadvantages that will need to be outweighed by lower absolute costs and/or higher productivity elsewhere in the operating system.

This is why it is clearly advantageous to target underserved price-elastic markets that have sufficient growth potential to absorb a high proportion of the incremental output brought online by a challenger, and why it is also advantageous for the challenger to have lower costs than the incumbent so that it can profitably sustain the low-fare stimulus and maintain acceptable load factors.

There are few circumstances under which a low-frequency challenge can be sustained against a high-frequency operation. Two possibilities are as follows.

1. Where a hub carrier enters a route primarily to feed one or two of its complexes rather than to tap local O & D traffic.
2. Where a low-frequency entrant offers a distinct benefit not offered by the high-frequency incumbent. Most often this will be a price benefit, and the challenger will position itself – at least publicly – as representing no threat to the incumbent's core business, either because it has no ambition to grow or it is not targeting either potential flow traffic or high-yield local traffic. (This is sometimes referred to in game theory as the 'puppy dog ploy'.) Having watched Delta fall for the ploy when ValuJet started operations out of Atlanta in the early 1990s, it is unlikely that any incumbent would now be sanguine.

Incumbents' responses

Incumbents can use scheduling to fight off market entrants. One approach is to 'overschedule' – that is, oversupply the market and, in all likelihood, weaken yields to the extent that the entrant cannot meet its revenue or profit projections. Entrants can be attacked either by swamping them with new services, matching their frequencies head-to-head, by 'bracketing' or 'sandwiching' them, or by scheduling away from them to avoid the possibility of incoming passengers making a convenient off-line connection. The sustainability of overscheduling will depend upon the extent to which the incumbent is able and willing to cross-subsidise the route in question, and also whether or not the challenger is financially able to sustain low yields.

There is a question as to whether this type of response is in fact commercial or predatory, and care might be needed in some jurisdictions that have actively-enforced competition laws – although, as we saw in chapter 4, predation is notoriously difficult to prove.

GDS displays

So far in the discussion we have looked at the tactical scheduling of 'real' flights. In the battle to ensure marketplace visibility for their offers, some carriers have been using what could be characterised as aggressive techniques to make their schedules appear more competitive than in fact they are. The battleground is usually page one of travel agents' GDS displays. A technique used in North America is to allocate to each service from an outstation to a hub not only its own 'local' flight number, but also several additional flight numbers each tied into an onward flight connecting out of the hub; in this way the single service to the hub receives multiple listings that can push competitors' flights further down the screen – or off the first page altogether. Code-sharing offers similar opportunities where, for example, a single flight is listed separately under each partner's designator codes. (We noted in chapter 6 that, in some parts of the world, codes of conduct do now limit this 'ghosting' and 'screen-padding'.)

Code-sharing

Code-sharing is becoming an increasingly common weapon of choice for network carriers in the battle to design and schedule networks capable of capturing and retaining 'online' more of passengers' entire, end-to-end itineraries.

The essence of network management at a growing number of large airlines is to extend the network and expand the schedule – that is, to add output – whilst taking on as few as possible of the incremental capacity costs that would be required to achieve this through organic growth. Code-sharing, franchising, and block-spacing have become important tactical weapons for use in schedule-building, as well as vehicles through which to pursue wider strategic ambitions.

vii. Interfacing network and fleet management

Although the presence or absence of aircraft with particular payload-range capabilities in an airline's existing fleet does in practice have a profound impact on network management decisions, if we start with a blank sheet of paper it is network management that should drive fleet management.

- **Network design** The design of a network – which markets to serve and which routes to serve them with – reflects a balance between marketing and operational considerations (with the former predominant whenever possible), set within the context of a particular airline's strategic description of itself (as a full-service hub-and-spoke carrier, a regional, a point-to-point operator, or a leisure-oriented charter airline, for example). Network design establishes the broad parameters for fleet selection and management. (Note that if part of a network is relatively insignificant in terms of revenue and profitability yet requires a small subfleet which because of its size is expensive to operate and maintain, there could be an argument for dropping the routes concerned – perhaps instead code-sharing with a carrier that has a fleet and/or cost structure better-suited to serving them.)

- **Scheduling** Having designed a network in response to actual and forecasted demand in O & D markets, scheduling is an attempt to allocate across a range of possible frequencies and timings the output required if the anticipated shares of targeted markets are to be captured. This demand allocation exercise, first discussed in chapter 2, drives requirements for different types and variants of aircraft.

Consider the hypothetical example of an airline serving an O & D market in which an average 400 passengers want to depart the origin each day (given certain assumptions about prices and other demand-determining independent variables).

1. For the airline, the cheapest option (other things, such as aircraft utilisation issues, being equal) would be to operate a single high-density widebody with low seat-mile costs. For passengers, this would pose two problems: first, many prospective passengers will not want to travel at or near the departure time of this single service; second, quite a few will be unwilling to endure a high-density seating configuration.

2. As far as passengers are concerned, if we assume the market has a significant segment comprised of business travellers we might find that on average, say, 160 want to depart between 0630 and 0900, 160 want to depart between 1600 and 1900, and the remaining 80 want to leave at various other times throughout the day. The airline has several alternative options for meeting this demand.

   - It could schedule nonstops – perhaps a single 180-seater or two smaller aircraft – during each of the peak periods, and either a single 120-seater or two regional jets during the day. This would of course be an expensive schedule to mount in terms of both seat-mile and aggregate trip costs, so yields would need to be sufficiently firm to support the costs involved; in such a market yields should be relatively firm provided business travellers are willing to pay in order to have their time-preferences met or approximated by high frequencies – something that can no longer be taken for granted since 9/11. (Of course, the presence of a reliable low-fare carrier in the market offering perhaps three daily B737 departures may well soften yields – and perhaps also stimulate traffic.)

- Bearing passengers' time-preferences in mind, another approach open to a network carrier might (depending upon the geography of the market) be to route some services over a hub in order to thicken departing traffic volumes (by combining traffic headed for other destinations onto the aircraft) and perhaps raise frequencies above the number of nonstops that could be supported by a 400-passenger per day market. Alternatively, the airline could (depending upon the competitive situation) maintain frequencies, but drop the non-stop routing and instead operate larger aircraft to the hub than it can operate in the nonstop market – taking advantage of their better seat-mile costs.

This simple example underlines the complexity of combined network and fleet management. Let us consider another. Assume competitive pressures set a given fare for a journey from Hartford to San Francisco. Further assume that there are three feasible routings open to a particular carrier.

1. Regional feed to New York LGA, connecting with a transcontinental widebody.
2. Mainline jet feed to Chicago O'Hare, connecting with a narrowbody.
3. Nonstop hub-bypass service using a narrowbody.

An airline might, for the sake of argument, design its network to incorporate one or more of these options. Because each involves different production costs for the output being sold and for competitive reasons these costs cannot be reflected in the fare (ignoring the possibility that a premium *might* be earned on the nonstop route), profits will differ between routing alternatives. Further complicating the issue, as we will see in chapter 9, is the fact that carrying passengers on two-leg itineraries over New York and Chicago involves opportunity costs insofar as they occupy seats that could have been occupied by passengers – perhaps higher-revenue passengers – travelling either in the local markets or in other Hartford O & D markets (e.g., Hartford–New Orleans via either New York or Chicago).

Whilst the exigencies of network management should be highly influential on fleet management decisions it is, as noted above, inevitable that at least in the short run the composition of a particular carrier's fleet will have a strong influence on network design and scheduling. Influence also flows in this same direction when radically new aircraft or variants appear on the market. Box 7.3 looks at two examples.

Box 7.3: Two examples of the influence of aircraft technology on network design

Long-haul markets: Airbus and Boeing perspectives *Put simply, Airbus has been arguing since the early 1990s that demand for very large aircraft will be spurred by strong inter-hub traffic growth and by worsening slot constraints at major hubs and gateways. This was the thinking behind launch of the A380. Boeing, on the other hand, argues that inter-hub traffic growth can be accommodated by existing large types until well into the second decade of the century, with the odd stretch here and there, and that the real action lies in ultra-long-haul 250–350-seaters overflying major hubs – that is, in 'market fragmentation'. The main arena for this fragment-ation will be the North Pacific, following on some 20 years after the same phenomenon saw established North Atlantic gateways to some extent by-passed by newly arrived twin-jets such as the A310 and B767.*

The success of many of the transpolar and North Pacific airways opened since the beginning of the decade, and which assist market fragmentation by facilitating ultra-long-haul routes bypassing established hubs and gate-ways, has depended on ETOPS approval insofar as the B777 is being wid-ely used on these routes. The ETOPS philosophy that emerged in the 1980s as part of a process intended to permit twins to fly optimum North Atlantic routings was essentially predicated on the development of certification and operating criteria that would allow these aircraft to operate at least as safely as trijets and quads flying the same routes. To achieve this, intense focus was brought to bear on identifying, understanding, and resolving powerplant reliability issues in particular, and this effort has had a benef-icial impact on powerplant reliability across the industry.

There is now some debate between US and European regulators, motiv-ated it seems as much by commercial as operational considerations, reg-arding whether ETOPS rules should be superseded by a new generation of LROPS (long-range operations) regulations – the argument being that twins are now sufficiently reliable to justify refocusing on the dangers to all aircraft specific to ultra-long flights over inhospitable terrain and oceans.

Regional markets: the RJ phenomenon *Technological developments are continuing to have a strong impact on regional airline networks. Specific-ally, the introduction of regional jets (RJs) allows carriers to:*

- *widen hub catchment areas by serving spoke outstations that turbo-props cannot reach, so helping hubs to develop new markets and raid other hubs' hinterlands over 1,000 miles away. This type of 'hub cap-ture' can sometimes penetrate close to a competitor's hub and have potentially important competitive implications – as, for example, where customers at a spoke city have a choice between 200 miles in a turbo-prop to the nearest hub or 500 miles to an alternative (but, in terms of total O & D journey times, equally convenient) hub on an RJ;*

- *replace either similar gauge or smaller turboprops on regional spokes;*
- *replace mainline aircraft operated at unsatisfactory load factors;*
- *supplement majors' mainline fleets and improve their service by operating RJs on trunk routes at off-peak hours;*
- *develop longer hub-bypass routes than turboprops have the range to fly. This strategy, which is particularly common in Europe, can protect spoke cities from other carriers' 'hub capture' efforts;*
- *help build secondary hubs, something for which RJs have been used by both Air France and Lufthansa at Lyon and Munich respectively, for example; and*
- *compete in other niche markets.*

(It needs to be borne in mind, that the acquisition and deployment of RJs are, at the time of writing, still severely constrained in the United States by the scope clauses in most US majors' mainline pilots' contracts.)

---

viii. Summary

After first looking at a typical schedule development process, we discussed scheduling as a response to several influences: demand, the economics of supply, and various external constraints – such as time zones, airport curfews, slot availability, and so on. We then considered issues associated with scheduling a hub-and-spoke network, before next looking at alternative scheduling tactics. The chapter ended by exploring the interface between network management (design and scheduling) on the one hand, and fleet management on the other.

Notably in the United States, the period after 9/11 saw hubs come under intense scrutiny because the high costs of operating them (relative to offering point-to-point services) were no longer being underwritten by high-yield business travellers in the new, profoundly weakened revenue environment. At the time of writing, some observers are questioning the continued viability of hub-and-spoke systems generally, and in particular the scheduling of arrival and departure banks into tight time windows. It is too early to perform 'last rites' on hub systems, however.

1. **Hubs will survive** There are two principal reasons.

- First, despite the ongoing growth of hub-bypass operations there will continue to be many relatively thin markets connecting secondary and tertiary points which can only be served by hubbing, because nonstop service (at a marketable frequency) is uneconomic.
- Second, too much has been invested by majors in their hubs to walk away from them. Less emotionally and more pertinently, because the network majors as a whole will have difficulty getting their short-haul unit costs down to the levels achieved by low-fare competitors they need sources of differentiation in order to generate the higher RASMs that their higher CASMs make essential. Hubs will continue to offer a connectivity benefit for which some market segments are prepared to pay.

2. **Hubs will have to become more efficient** We have seen that one of the primary sources of cost in a hub operation is the adverse impact that self-induced peaking has on resource utilisation. We have also seen that some majors have addressed this problem by de-peaking their busiest hubs (e.g., American at Chicago O'Hare and Dallas-Fort Worth). De-peaking gives precedence to the maximisation of aircraft and hub resource utilisation over the minimisation of mean and median passenger connection times; instead of arrivals and departures being bunched into a number of complexes operating within tightly constrained time windows, they are spread more evenly throughout the day – the benefit to the airline being higher resource utilisation, and the cost to the passenger being that connection times are generally lengthened. The position can be summarised as follows.

- De-peaking was *necessitated* at several US hubs after 9/11 by a precipitous decline in the high-yield traffic relied upon under the post-deregulation network carrier business model to support the high cost of hub operations.
- De-peaking was *facilitated* by the increased willingness of consumers (particularly in US domestic markets) to accept longer elapsed journey times (attributable largely to longer hub transits) in return for the lower fares now being demanded. It has also been facilitated (again, notably in US domestic markets) by the growing significance of Internet distribution relative to traditional agency channels: whereas GDS screen position, in part reflecting elapsed journey times, can be an important driver of consumer purchase behaviour when agencies are used, Internet channels tend to be somewhat more price-oriented. (This is not to say that journey times are now unimportant – just that their weighting relative to price has become weaker in the post-9/11 US revenue environment.)

De-peaking is not the answer at every hub. First, it is easier to de-peak a mega-hub than a secondary hub; de-peaking a relatively small hub with just a few daily complexes can risk depriving it of critical mass in terms of marketable connections. Second, several international hubs outside the United States were not undermined by soft revenues to quite the same extent as was the case in respect of US domestic hubs. Even where de-peaking is either infeasible or unwarranted, however, the majority of hub-and-spoke carriers have put a great deal of effort into raising hub efficiency – and scheduling is clearly central to such initiatives.

There is tension within any airline's operating strategy between the requirements to be as efficient as possible in order to minimise costs, and to be as effective as possible in satisfying customers' expectations (although it is true that this tension is perhaps somewhat less pronounced in the case of low-fare carriers than full-service airlines offering premium products). Scheduling, given its direct impact on both costs and revenues, is arguably the most sensitive interface between the needs of consumers and airlines.

Scheduling also lies at the nexus of network and fleet management insofar as it is critical to two linked, but distinct, processes (Clark, 2001).

- **Demand allocation** This is a broadly strategic process that increasingly relies on simulation models to analyse alternatives for distributing aggregate O & D demand around different feasible network patterns given alternative schedules (i.e., mixes of aircraft capacities and frequencies) and assumptions with regard to passengers' routing preferences (themselves perhaps influenced by routing-driven price variations).
- **Fleet optimisation** This is a broadly operational process concerned with how to deploy a given fleet most efficiently in the context of a given schedule.

The further out in time a demand allocation model runs, the more acceptable it is to aggregate supply and demand in terms of ASMs and RPMs; the closer in we bring the model towards an operational time-frame, the more we need to be thinking in terms of seat and passenger numbers and aircraft types and variants. In the medium-term (say, around three years), there will be overlap insofar as certain operational issues (e.g., heavy maintenance) will need factoring into what nonetheless remains a fairly generalised demand allocation model.

Demand allocation and fleet management are therefore closely linked. It is to fleet management that we turn next.

8 Fleet Management

There are three routes to disaster: gambling is the quickest, sex is the most
enjoyable and technology the most certain.

Georges Pompidou

Chapter overview

Having considered network management over the last two chapters, we
turn next to a second topic central to managing capacity: fleet management.
Traditionally, fleet *planning* has focused on aircraft acquisition. Many large
airlines now take a broader view, with fleet *management* encompassing:

- aircraft acquisition and financing;
- tactical fleet management;
- asset value maintenance; and
- trading.

This chapter will follow that four-part approach, but will concentrate on
acquisition and on tactical fleet management.

i. Aircraft acquisition and financing

An airline is in principle a portfolio of resources – some tangible, many
intangible – brought together to pursue a corporate mission or purpose. In
the same vein, a fleet is a portfolio assembled to fulfil a number of payload-
range missions. The primary objective of fleet planning is to equate production capacity (and the output that capacity is able to produce if efficiently

utilised) with forecast demand, given certain price and other marketing assumptions. There are two fundamental reasons for acquiring aircraft.

1. **Replacement of existing capacity** It might be necessary to replace part of the current fleet because of high operating costs, unacceptable noise or emissions, limited remaining structural life, inadequate passenger appeal, type rationalisation, or an ongoing fleet rollover policy intended to maintain a low average fleet age. The task is to find an aircraft capable of performing a largely unchanged mission more effectively and/or efficiently than the aircraft to be replaced.
2. **Capacity growth** Because the demand for air transport services is on the whole continuing to grow, the need to replace ageing aircraft that are becoming expensive to operate or environmentally unsound is often interlaced with the need to increase capacity. Incremental capacity might be needed for one or both of two purposes.
    *   *Growth within the existing network* Aircraft acquisition could be necessary to accommodate traffic growth arising from either or both an expanding market or improved market share. Growing demand can in principle be met by using larger aircraft and maintaining frequencies, by operating more of the same aircraft at higher frequencies, or by some combination of the two. (It can also be met by raising utilisation, increasing seating densities, and/or accepting higher load factors in respect of the existing fleet, by code-sharing, or by wet-leasing aircraft and crews from another carrier.)
    *   *New missions* Capacity might be needed to satisfy new mission requirements beyond the capability of the existing fleet, such as the introduction of ultra-long-haul services.

An 'absorption ratio' can be calculated for an individual airline or, indeed, for a group of airlines (e.g., US majors) or the industry as a whole. This is the ratio of outstanding orders (aircraft units or number of seats) to the existing fleet, net of planned disposals or retirements. When projected absorption runs well ahead of forecast demand growth, questions need to be asked. For example, assuming annual passenger demand growth of five per cent and fleet retirements equivalent to three per cent of current capacity, we might expect fleet augmentation of around eight per cent per annum. If this percentage or its equivalent 'orders-to-fleet' ratio is substantially exceeded, there might be an overcapacity situation developing. (On the other hand, it should be borne in mind that at a macro-level demand growth is usually measured in RPMs – which can be produced by aircraft of many different sizes, and therefore numbers, flying many different alternative stage-lengths – whilst purchases and retirements are measured in discrete aircraft or, less usually, seat numbers. So, for example, a single-airline or industry-wide shift to higher frequencies using aircraft similar in size or smaller than aircraft already operated might raise aircraft acquisition numbers without necessarily threatening overcapacity.)

There are at least three reasons why fleet planning should be treated not as a separate, isolated or occasional exercise, but as an ongoing process intimately linked to marketing planning.

1. **Changes in the marketplace** A fleet can only ever be optimised to serve one particular set of markets at one particular point in time; as existing markets change in size and/or structure and as markets are added or deleted, the fleet will become sub-optimal. Fleet planning is therefore a continuous process of reassessment.

2. **Changes in corporate priorities** Fleets and networks are managed within the wider context provided by decisions about which markets and segments to serve, and how to serve them. If, for example, an airline decides to change its market position by offering higher frequencies and/or an improved inflight product this could well have an impact on its optimum fleet. Similarly, when British Airways decided in the late 1990s to de-emphasise low-yield flow traffic and concentrate on premium traffic (particularly in point-to-point markets), this had an immediate impact on its projected fleet mix – with future requirements shifting from B747-400s to B777s, and from B757s to the A320 series.

3. **Strategic commitment** A significant fleet acquisition or restructuring also has a strategic impact beyond its direct effect on future costs, revenues, and cash flows. This is usually discussed in the strategic management literature under the heading of 'commitment', and it is outlined in Box 8.1. After that, we will begin looking at aircraft evaluation criteria.

Box 8.1: Commitment

Strategic commitments are decisions to acquire and deploy resources that have a long-term impact and are difficult and/or expensive to reverse. They have a direct economic influence through their effect on revenues and costs, but they can also have an indirect impact through their effect on competitors' behaviour and therefore on market equilibrium.

A competitor faced with a visible, understandable, and credible (i.e., largely irrevocable) commitment is likely to adjust its own tactical and/or strategic behaviour in some way. A decision by a carrier to increase capacity by a significant amount might deter new entrants, but could also in-

tensify price competition amongst incumbents. Game theory (augmented by simulation models) has been increasingly used to help understand the impact of strategic commitments on market rivalry and how, in turn, the nature and intensity of market rivalry influences commitment decisions.

Strategic commitments can induce competitors or potential competitors to behave less aggressively, or they might alternatively lead to intensified competition. Managers would do well to look at what their competitors actually do, rather than what they say. For example, when a new entrant's managers say they have no intention of challenging incumbents' core markets but nonetheless commit to rapid fleet expansion, it is the strategic commitment rather than the words that matter. Ryanair and easyJet, on the other hand, make no secret of their strategies: they intend mounting a sustained challenge to European full-service carriers in their short-haul mainline markets, and they are making the commitments in aircraft required to implement this challenge.

Airlines clearly need as much flexibility in their fleets as they can get. A good start is shorter lead-times on purchase and customising decisions for new aircraft, even at the top of ordering cycles. In particular, many carriers want greater flexibility in determining variants and even types when they enter into long-term purchase contracts – the idea being in some cases to project seat requirements, but leave until as late as possible the final specification of units into which those seats will be broken down. Airframe manufacturers and their suppliers have in fact worked hard to improve flexibility by shortening order lead times – the average having dropped from close to five years in the mid-1980s to a little over a year by the late 1990s (Clark (2001), citing *Airclaims* data).

Another source of flexibility is the use of purchase options (including 'rolling options') which, depending upon market circumstances, manufacturers quite frequently price far below their real value. The growth of operating leasing has also added flexibility; although operating leases rarely run for less than three to five years and frequently have lives well in excess of this, the lessee usually has an option after a certain period to pay an early termination penalty and return the aircraft.

Aircraft evaluation: passenger aircraft

The intention here is to highlight some of the principal issues that arise in the course of comparative evaluations. Readers interested in a more detailed explanation of fleet planning should refer to Clark (2001).

The people involved

In any airline, various people will want to have their say in fleet planning decisions. Sometimes the influences are balanced. On other occasions discussion might be oriented towards the interests of operations personnel concerned primarily about aircraft performance and maintainability, marketing personnel preoccupied with product design, or finance people focused on operating costs and the appeal of the different types to financiers (or alternatively the willingness of respective manufacturers, and possibly their export credit agencies, to provide finance or credit support). Political factors sometimes come into play, and government interference in the decision-making processes of national carriers is not uncommon.

Collation of airline-specific data

The type of data required will include the following.

- **Network data** Markets to be served and the route patterns and frequencies flown to serve them. This data flags payload requirements.
- **Route data** Flight-legs to be operated and alternate airports for each destination; stage-lengths; reserve fuel requirements; en route meteorological assumptions; and turnaround times. This data flags likely speed and range requirements.
- **Airport data** Runway lengths, slopes, and construction; obstacle clearance; elevation; average and extreme meteorological conditions; taxiway and apron widths and load-bearing capabilities; dimensions of parking spaces on the ramp and at gates; and terminal infrastructure and handling capacities. This data flags the need for specific capability requirements, such as good hot-and-high performance.
- **Current fleet** When considering new types an airline will often benchmark its analysis against types with similar mission capabilities that it currently operates.
- **Product requirements** Passenger service requirements by class are derived from marketing decisions in respect of service attributes such as seat pitch and width, aisle width, bin sizes, entertainment and communication systems, and provision and location of galleys and lavatories. Cabin cross-section can affect passengers' overall perceptions of spaciousness, the feasible seating configuration across each row (which itself affects both passenger perceptions and, on widebodies, the efficiency of meal service in the main cabin), and the scope for different galley, lavatory, storage, and crew rest-area options. (The ability to operate ultra-long-haul flight-legs depends upon the provision of crew

rest-areas which, if located below the main deck rather than in a cabin ceiling void, may displace revenue payload.) Through their impact on frequencies and seat accessibility targets, product requirements will also affect the capacities of aircraft needed to operate a given route network. (Seat accessibility will be discussed in the next chapter.) Finally, in many regional markets passengers are increasingly unwilling to accept turboprop service when jet alternatives are available.

Carriers with significant freight businesses will in addition have specific freight-related requirements in respect of belly-hold capacities and cross-sections, and container compatibility with other types in the current fleet that will be retained into the foreseeable future.

Marketing analysis

Despite significant cuts in delivery lead-times, and despite the growing contribution of operating lessors to improving fleet flexibility, airlines still must make their strategic fleet acquisition decisions on the basis of forecasts that run an uncomfortable distance into the future. Three types of forecast in particular have to be used.

- **Demand forecasts** Demand can be forecast by region, by O & D market, and by segment. A common approach is to forecast aggregate growth, then focus down onto individual markets and segments.
- **Traffic forecasts** 'Traffic' is the share of demand that a particular airline forecasts it will carry given price and other marketing assumptions.
- **Revenue forecasts** Both demand and traffic forecasts are driven by a wide range of assumptions, one of which is average yield (i.e., revenue per RPM). Revenue management systems can be a valuable source of information on current yields. Revenue models link traffic forecasts to variables such as fare structures, freight rates, discounting, prorate dilution, and agency commissions.

Clark (2001) identifies two complementary approaches to the building of forecasts: macro and micro.

1. **Macro- or top-down approach** This combines a forecast of the RPMs that a network and rough-cut schedule will generate (given certain marketing assumptions) with a target load factor, to arrive at a figure for the ASMs that the fleet must be able to produce each year in the forecast period if it is to accommodate forecasted traffic at that targeted load factor. In the case of a large airline, this exercise might be broken down into a number of sub-networks each containing different traffic

densities and stage-lengths (e.g., short-haul mainline, medium-haul, intercontinental, and regional); even a small airline might be broken-down into sub-networks if one or two of its routes have particularly strong characteristics that distinguish them from others in the network.

A forecasted requirement for output growth on a network or ident-ified sub-networks could, if relatively small, be met by improving util-isation of current capacity – through revised scheduling or increased seating density, for example. Alternatively, it might point to a need for additional aircraft – particularly if some of the existing fleet will have to be retired for operational or marketing reasons.

2. **Micro- or bottom-up approach** Using this approach, a demand alloc-ation model is calibrated to explain the link between consumer behav-iour variables and traffic on specific flight-legs and segments in the current network, and then used to forecast future traffic on a flight-leg and segment-specific basis. It is first assumed that traffic will continue to flow on existing flights over existing routes unconstrained by load factor considerations (i.e., irrespective of available capacity); the next step would then be to arrive at a required number of seats by adjusting for acceptable load factors; finally, consideration of frequency, routing, and seat accessibility issues would lead from a raw seat number to several different potential aircraft sizes.

Clark (ibid) points out that despite their undoubted appeal, demand allocation models have several drawbacks:

- beyond a relatively short time horizon (say, three years), the causal relationships in historical data upon which they are calibrated can be upset by market changes attributable to demand volatility and/or competitive action;

- although flight- and segment-specific data is widely available, most carriers do not have the O & D demand data that models really need (although it can be accessed through MIDTs bought from the GDSs); and

- the data acquisition and processing required place a heavy burden on the resources of small airlines, yet if their quality is not good the output of these models will be suspect.

(For a refresher on the distinction between flight-legs, segments and O & D journeys consider a passenger travelling on Royal Brunei from Dubai to Brisbane using a London–Brunei service that stops in Dubai and Singapore, then connecting with a Brunei–Brisbane nonstop: this passenger travels on three *flight-legs* (Dubai–Singapore, Singapore–Brunei, and Brunei–Brisbane), on the Dubai–Singapore–Brunei *segment* of the London–Brunei through-service, and in the Dubai–Brisbane O & D *market*.)

Consideration of airline-specific data and marketing data together should lead the fleet planning team to a broad, preliminary conclusion with regard to candidate aircraft and the approximate numbers likely to be required. The more varied a carrier's network in terms of traffic densities and stage-lengths, the more likely it is that the theoretically optimal fleet composition will contain more types than is going to be desirable once operating cost considerations are brought into the analysis; compromises and trade-offs are inevitable.

As we saw in the last chapter, a particularly important trade-off revolves around how to produce output on each route – the trade-off between aircraft capacity and frequency. A route might have sufficient traffic to support relatively large aircraft, but the marketing requirement to offer high frequencies in order to feed other routes or to provide higher quality service to business travellers could argue in favour of smaller aircraft with less attractive seat-mile costs. Box 8.2 briefly revisits the critical topic of demand spill; we will meet it again in chapter 9.

Box 8.2: Demand spill

Assume a single aircraft operates a route. As demand and traffic grow over time, it eventually becomes too small and begins to spill demand. One of two decisions can be taken to reduce or eliminate spill.

1. **Use a larger aircraft at the same frequency** *Provided that average revenue on each departure of the existing type is sufficient to at least cover the break-even point for the larger type, this is a viable option. As demand continues to grow, however, even this larger type might eventually need supplementing.*

2. **Add frequencies** *Adding one or more frequencies, operated either by the type currently used or by a smaller type, improves the product and so might lead to firmer yields if the route concerned carries traffic that appreciates the improvement; higher frequencies could also stimulate demand. The problem is that until traffic builds sufficiently to achieve satisfactory load factors on the additional frequencies, the incremental costs of operating them might penalise profitability.*

The smaller an aircraft serving a route, the sooner demand growth is likely to lead to spill. Models have been developed (notably by airframe manufacturers) to help arrive at frequency/capacity trade-offs given demand conditions in both directions on a route. The fact that demand in both directions has to be considered is clearly important.

·   *At what point should a move to a larger aircraft be made? The answer depends on two primary considerations.*

1.   *The capacity/frequency trade-off required by demand, competition, and product design requirements in the market(s) concerned.*
2.   *Average load factor and yield on the existing departures.*
   •   *Load factor: in principle, we might shift to a larger aircraft if we do not want to add frequencies **and** the load factor achieved on the current aircraft exceeds break-even load factor on the larger aircraft (given known route operating costs and assumed pricing).*
   •   *Yield: rather than adding output, we might take pressure off load factors on the existing aircraft by firming yield (i.e., raising prices and/or allocating less space to low-yield fares).*

Linear multi-stop routes can pose particular complications when trying to resolve these issues. For example, take a Royal Brunei flight operating London–Dubai–Singapore–Brunei. The Dubai–Singapore leg carries traffic in the London–Brunei, London–Singapore, Dubai–Singapore, and Dubai–Brunei markets as well as traffic originating in London and Dubai and connecting over Brunei to points in Australia; each of these markets has very different demand characteristics.

Aircraft size (and, of course, chosen seating configuration) inevitably has a strong impact on earnings. Spill models can be used to estimate, under different assumed demand conditions, the number of passengers likely to be spilled off the smaller of any two aircraft under consideration. The value of lost revenue must at the very least be offset by lower acquisition and/or operating costs in the case of the smaller aircraft. However, not all spillage will necessarily be lost to the carrier because of the 'recapture' effect whereby a passenger unable to be accommodated on one flight might be booked instead on another service operated by the same airline. This recapture effect is strongest where the carrier has a high frequency on the route concerned and/or can rely on brand loyalty, possibly attributable to a frequent flyer programme. Conversely, in an integrated network oriented towards online connections over a hub, spill on one leg of a passenger's multi-leg itinerary might lose the carrier that entire itinerary, even if there is space available on the other legs.

There are also profit profiling models available which relate monetary profits to route density (passengers per week, say) so that the profit impact of choosing aircraft of significantly different sizes can be evaluated over a range of traffic forecasts. What they generally show is that:

- smaller aircraft, requiring fewer passengers to break even (given an assumed pricing structure and traffic mix), are more profitable until a certain point, at which they start to spill passengers;
- thereafter, assuming no larger aircraft is available in the fleet, an additional frequency has to be added. This has two contrasting effects:
  - pending market growth, the second frequency will quite possibly average a load factor below break-even. This reflects the cost indivisibilities associated with adding capacity in aircraft-sized units when demand changes only by one passenger at a time;
  - if the journey duration is below 2½ hours (where, other considerations such as FFPs being equal, frequency has a compelling impact on consumer choice – particularly in the business segment), the extra flight may attract further traffic;
- exactly the same irregular profit growth pattern occurs in respect of the larger aircraft, except that the fixed costs associated with adding one, then perhaps ultimately more, additional aircraft are larger and kick-in at higher levels;
- as a market continues to grow, the gap between the (higher) number of small aircraft and the (lower) number of large aircraft will also grow, and the lower seat-mile costs of the latter will begin to assert themselves over the lower trip and aircraft-mile costs (together with any fleet-size economies) associated with the former. The result is that beyond a certain point the larger aircraft could gain and sustain a profitability advantage over smaller aircraft in serving a given number of passengers. A point is arrived at where the marketing benefits achieved by adding frequencies are outweighed by the cost savings of operating current frequencies with a larger aircraft;
- a larger aircraft should *never* be put onto a service until the average passenger load achieved on the existing aircraft exceeds the load required for that larger aircraft to break even on the route concerned (assuming unchanged revenue).

Conclusion Demand growth tends over time to thicken traffic on most routes. Aside from accepting higher load factors and/or raising seating densities, it can be met in one or more of three primary ways: adding larger aircraft; adding frequencies; and/or 'fragmenting' the markets served by a particular route – that is, by replacing a direct/multi-stop or connecting service with a nonstop service (which therefore diverts traffic from the existing route(s)). Decisions about how demand is to be served and traffic allocated are therefore in many ways as important to fleet planning as forecasts of demand itself.

Technical analysis

Technical analyses, which generally follow the ATA 100 coding formulated by the Air Transport Association in the United States to facilitate description of aircraft components and systems, will consider:

* structures and flight controls;
* mechanical systems;
* avionics and instrumentation systems; and
* propulsion systems.

The systems of different aircraft are compared by ranking them in respect of attributes describing their design objectives, overall safety, reliability, redundancy, maintainability, simplicity, use of proven technology, and effects on the airline's existing equipment and personnel infrastructure. Fleet planners will also want answers to a variety of questions related to aerodynamics, stability and control, interior noise, exterior noise and emissions, and certification criteria. The *structural efficiency* of an aircraft (i.e., payload relative to weight) is an important cost-related issue which is increasingly being addressed by the use of composite materials.

Performance analysis

'Performance' refers to the capabilities and limitations of an airplane in different phases of flight. It is outlined in each aircraft's performance manual and can be illustrated by expressing graphically a number of relationships – the most widely recognised of which is perhaps the payload-range diagram. Performance analysis involves looking at maximum take-off weight (MTOW) and its various components, payload capabilities at different ranges, and range capabilities with different payloads to gain a sense of the aircraft's performance and economics in the context of the airline's present and likely future networks. A carrier might be looking for a type optimised for a specific group of its routes having particular stage-lengths and payload requirements, or it might be more interested in the flexibility to operate an aircraft profitably across a number of different mission profiles.

In addition to more general analyses, performance will often also be evaluated, using the airline's standard procedures, at a limiting airport and on a limiting route within the network that are subject to abnormally demanding operational requirements. Separately, some short-haul operators wanting to maximise aircraft utilisation by keeping turnaround and transit times to a minimum will be interested in the ability of a type to operate multiple sectors without refuelling – so much so that an aircraft's 'range' in this sense can be an important input into evaluation exercises even though the routes served might each fall well within its performance capabilities. (Clark (2001) looks in detail at performance evaluation and is an excellent source of information on the subject.)

Cost analysis

This subsection distinguishes between capital and operating costs (DOCs). In fact, capital cost feeds through into DOCs through 'cost of ownership' line items such as depreciation and/or lease rentals (which are fixed DOCs). Furthermore, what really matters is the cost of acquiring and operating an aircraft across its entire life cycle, and it is therefore life-cycle costs as a whole that need to be the focus of analysis. At a growing number of air-lines, shareholder value is the framework used for this analysis: the acquis-ition and operation of an aircraft must be seen to add shareholder value through its impact on either or both revenues and costs.

The most important point to bear in mind is that whilst an aircraft's cap-ital and operating costs are critical, they are – like any costs an airline might incur – relatively meaningless figures outside the context of revenue generated. With regard to aircraft, we need to look at the revenue they can generate (and therefore at their service design implications in respect of variables such as the onboard product and also frequency/capacity trade-offs on the airline's network) in order to assess whether their life-cycle costs are acceptable.

Capital costs Different manufacturers break down their prices in different ways, but most will include the following elements.

Airframe price (including engine nacelles) at standard specification
+   engines (the price of which will be separately negotiated where there is a choice of powerplant)
+   options (which might include standard options, customised options, seller-furnished equipment (SFE), and buyer-furnished equipment (BFE) and could, if not already certified for the type, entail addit-ional certification costs)
=   AIRCRAFT CONTRACT PRICE
+   price escalation per agreed inflation formula (something many large airlines will no longer accept – a few now even being able to negotiate a clause entitling them to a price reduction if another buy-er obtains a better price from the manufacturer during a defined period after contract signing)

- negotiated discount and/or the value of credit notes from the OEM(s) already held by the airline and/or any fleet integration assistance (i.e., financial support from a manufacturer to smooth the integration of its aircraft into the fleet of an airline currently operating a competitor's products, and perhaps provided in preference to offering a larger discount which might then serve as a benchmark in future price negotiations with the same airline or with other carriers)
+ change orders initiated by the airline after contract signing
= FLYAWAY PRICE
+ product support (i.e., training of engineers/mechanics and aircrew, initial provisioning with spares, and the cost of any type-specific ground support equipment)
= TOTAL INVESTMENT
÷ number of seats on the type in the airline's configuration
= TOTAL INVESTMENT PER SEAT

Price per seat has trended upwards with each successive generation of aircraft technology that has been introduced. The reasons have been general price inflation in the global economy, and the constantly improving levels of technology and performance incorporated into new types (Trevett, 1999). However, airlines – particularly carriers with strong bargaining positions – are no longer willing to accept ever-increasing capital costs for new generations of aircraft performing essentially the same missions as those they replace unless there are palpable benefits in terms of firmer yields or, more usually, lower DOCs. Aircraft are simply revenue-generating resources, and carriers are increasingly insisting on a linkage between capital cost and their potential contribution to shareholder value. OEMs and their suppliers have, on the whole, responded well to this new pricing environment for their products. The A380 in particular looks set to offer a highly competitive cost per seat, based on the assumptions used in table 8.1.

Direct operating costs We saw in chapter 5 that DOCs are operating costs that are dependent upon the type of aircraft being flown. They have two elements: fixed and variable. Certain variable DOCs, notably fuel-burn, crew costs, and en route charges, are sensitive to the stage-length chosen for a DOC analysis. Standard formulae have been developed by aircraft manufacturers and airline trade associations to assist with DOC forecasting. However, care has to be taken to ensure their underlying assumptions are compatible with a particular airline's network, fleet size, and operating environment.

Aircraft	Average List Price ($ millions)	Maximum Seats	Cost per Seat ($ thousands)
A318-100	42	130	323
A319-100	49	145	338
A320-200	54	179	302
A321-200	66	220	300
A310-300	87	280	311
A300-600R	110	375	293
A330-200	129	405	319
A330-300	143	440	325
A340-300	154	440	350
A340-500	167	440	380
A340-600	178	485	367
A380	251	854	294
Narrowbodies	(Total of averages) 211	(Total of maximums) 674	(Average) 313
Widebodies	(Total of averages) 968	(Total of maximums) 2865	(Average) 338
Jumbo	(A380) 251	(A380) 854	(Actual) 294
Total	(Total of averages) 1430	(Total of maximums) 4393	(Average) 326

Aircraft	Average List Price ($ millions)	Maximum Seats	Cost per Seat ($ thousands)
B717	37	125	296
B737-600	45	132	341
B737-700	51	149	342
B737-800	61	189	323
B737-900	64	189	339
B747-400	197	610	323
B757-200	77	231	333
B757-300	85	279	305
B767-200ER	106	255	416
B767-300ER	121	375	323
B767-400ER	132	375	352
B777-200	162	440	368
B777-200ER	191	440	434
B777-200LR	200	440	455
B777-300	190	550	345
B777-300ER	217	550	395
Narrowbodies	(Total of averages) 420	(Total of maximums) 1294	(Average) 325
Widebodies	(Total of averages) 1319	(Total of maximums) 3425	(Average) 385
Jumbo	(B747-400) 197	(B747-400) 610	(Actual) 323
Total	(Total of averages) 1936	(Total of maximums) 5329	(Average) 363

Table 8.1 A selection of aircraft list prices per seat

Source: Morten Beyer & Agnew (adapted from *The International Aviation Oracle*, 8, 9, September 2001, p.16).

Notes: 1. 'Average list price' is calculated as (highest + lowest)/2. (List prices are not necessarily the actual prices paid by purchasers.)
2. 'Maximum seats' refers to the maximum certificated seating capacities of each aircraft (whereas actual seating configurations vary between operators).

DOCs incurred by alternative aircraft flying a given stage-length selected for an evaluation (because it is either representative or particularly challenging within the context of the carrier's network) can be examined using many different criteria. The following are perhaps most critical.

1. Aircraft-mile and trip costs – which are, respectively, the cost per mile and the cost for the trip as a whole.
   - With dollars on the vertical axis and distance on the horizontal, the curve graphing this relationship for any given aircraft slopes downwards (as stage-length increases) and then levels off.
   - Aircraft-mile and trip costs are generally higher for any given type than for a smaller type of the same technological generation.
2. Seat-mile (or 'unit') costs. These generally decline as aircraft capacity increases. (Airlines with substantial freight businesses will also want to look at the cost per ATM as well as per ASM.)

(Because aircraft-mile and seat-mile costs vary depending upon stage-length selected and larger airlines operate any one type over many different stage-lengths, it is not unusual to use cost per block-hour as another basis for comparison.)

As noted earlier, carriers commonly benchmark cost analyses against types in their present fleet used for the mission under consideration. Figure 8.1 provides a simple illustration of what the results of this exercise might look like. Relative to the base model, aircraft A offers savings on both ASM and trip costs, whilst aircraft B offers substantial ASM savings but a higher trip cost. The reason for this could be that aircraft B is larger than both aircraft A and the base model – raising questions about whether or not the additional output it generates can be sold profitably given projected demand on the routes it will fly. This analysis can be undertaken for each route, for a typical route, or for a number of core routes – depending on the size of the airline involved.

Box 8.3 looks at the elements of seat-mile cost.

Box 8.3: Seat-mile costs

Cost per seat-mile (or seat-kilometre) is attributable to absolute input costs and aircraft productivity. Aircraft productivity is here defined as ASMs per hour or other period of time. Two key drivers of aircraft productivity are capacity and block-speed.

- ***Capacity*** *The larger an aircraft, the more output (ASMs or ATMs) it will produce per hour of flight at any given speed (because it is carry-*

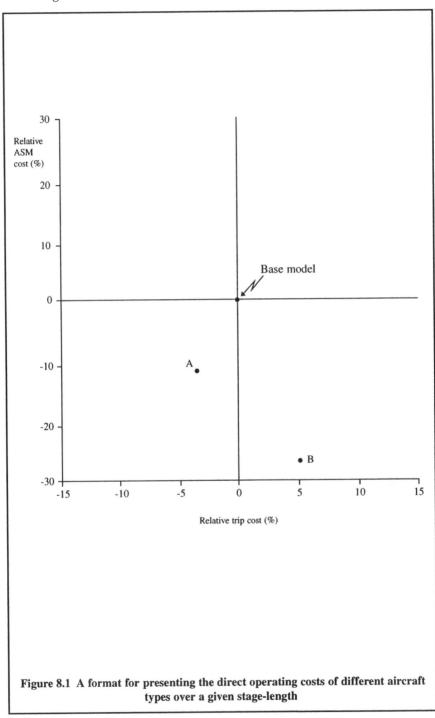

Figure 8.1 A format for presenting the direct operating costs of different aircraft types over a given stage-length

ing more seats and cargo capacity over the same distance as a smaller aircraft – assuming comparable block-speeds).

- **Block-speed** *The faster an aircraft, the more output it will produce per hour of flight assuming a given capacity (because it is carrying the same number of seats and amount of cargo capacity over a longer distance than a slower aircraft).*

The potential hourly productivity of an aircraft flying a given stage-length is therefore a function of payload capacity and block-speed. It feeds through to unit costs because the more output an aircraft produces each hour, the more output there is over which to spread hourly-charged DOCs. Unit cost curves vary between types, but they are generally 'U-shaped' when cost per ASM (on the vertical axis) is graphed against range (on the horizontal). This reflects a unit cost decline as range and hourly productivity increase until the point is reached where payload must be sacrificed to obtain further range, and productivity suffers. (This point is equivalent to 'range at maximum payload' in a payload-range diagram.) An aircraft can be said to be optimised for the point at which its unit cost curve bottoms-out; an interesting question is how steep the sides of the 'U' are – because this gives some idea of the flexibility the aircraft offers for serving sub-optimal stage-lengths.

Both seat-mile costs on the one hand and aircraft-mile and trip costs on the other are important considerations in any cost analysis, and they have to be traded-off very cautiously. It is not axiomatic that airlines should always choose aircraft with the lowest seat-mile costs.

- In some short-haul and/or business markets frequency is such an important consideration that it largely drives choice of aircraft; in cases such as this, trip costs can be a more powerful factor than seat-mile costs.
- Second, depending upon a particular airline's network structure, it is possible that smaller aircraft will provide greater assignment flexibility – in which case their lower hourly productivity might be more than compensated by the higher utilisation they are able to achieve than larger aircraft suited to only a handful of routes. It all depends upon network design and scheduling. We will look at aircraft assignment in the next section of the chapter.

The ideal objective, therefore, is to select a fleet of aircraft that is not only sized to suit the network it has to serve, but also combines the right mix of seat-mile and aircraft-mile cost characteristics to serve it economically. Small carriers might be able to undertake the required analysis on a route-specific basis, but larger airlines will have to aggregate routes into sub-networks differentiated by stage-lengths and demand characteristics.

Although aircraft technology is moving forward rapidly, the profile is one of 'high-speed incrementalism' rather than quantum leaps. Notwithstanding the relative maturity of current airframe and powerplant design, significant step-ups in productivity on a scale similar to those produced by the introduction of jet engines, widebodies, and then efficient high-bypass turbofans are on the agenda rather than on the horizon. Operating cost improvements will largely come from increased levels of commonality built into their product ranges by manufacturers, and from incremental improvements in fuel-efficiency, maintainability, reliability, structural life, and weight.

Powerplant analysis

Particularly where there is a choice of engine suppliers for an airframe and therefore heightened price competition between powerplant manufacturers, the percentage of an initial investment in airframe and engines combined that is accounted for by the engines can be as low as 20 per cent (Golaszewski and Klein, 1998). On the other hand, fuel and engine maintenance are such significant elements in DOCs that the percentage of typical life-cycle costs accounted for by powerplants can exceed 50 per cent (ibid).

Engine evaluation involves consideration of technical issues, analysis of any differences in aircraft performance attributable to alternative engines on a given airframe, and an economic analysis of individual airframe/engine combinations. There are many different technical metrics that engineers use to assess powerplants, amongst the most significant of which in respect of turbofans are *thrust, specific fuel consumption* (i.e., the quantity of fuel required to provide one pound of thrust for one hour under stated conditions), *fuel-burn* given an assumed payload-range mission, *exhaust gas temperature margin* (i.e., the amount by which an engine's maximum turbine temperature exceeds its operating temperature), and the *thrust-to-weight ratio*. An aircraft's fuel-efficiency is a function of: aerodynamic efficiency (i.e., lift-to-drag ratio); propulsive efficiency (i.e., fuel-burn); and structural efficiency (i.e., structural weight as a percentage of MTOW). Each carrier will of course want to be certain that an engine has sufficient thrust to accommodate the most challenging take-off conditions that the type concerned will confront in its system. Noise and emissions levels are also now critical evaluation parameters.

At a very general level of analysis, two important issues are commercial productivity and maintenance variables.

- **Commercial productivity** An airline will want to know how many ASMs or ATMs each airframe/engine combination will deliver per gallon, pound or kilo of fuel consumed on routes that it will typically serve and assuming a seating configuration appropriate to marketing requirements: stage-lengths can be plotted (on the vertical axis) against ASMs or ATMs generated per unit of fuel consumption. This is arguably a more useful metric than block fuel consumption.

- **Maintenance variables** Noise and fuel-burn were the key parameters for powerplant evaluation in the 1980s, after which reliability came into sharper focus. These days, airlines are requiring low fuel-burn, noise, and emissions along with high reliability – the latter reflected in better technical despatch reliability, reduced maintenance requirements, and lower shop-visit rates (and therefore longer on-wing times); improvements in maintainability and on-wing replacement of modules are also expected. Maintenance cost is a significant element in any engine's life-cycle cost, but it will vary between operators depending upon network structure (i.e., engine usage) and institutional factors (i.e., whether maintenance is outsourced or undertaken inhouse).

   Powerplant families built around common cores are very much in vogue, and as in the airframe manufacturing business a great deal of development now comes from derivatives rather than brand new models. As with airframe 'families', engine families reduce spares and maintenance training costs when an airline operates several derivatives of the same type – perhaps used on different airframes (e.g., the CFM56 on A320s and A340-200/300s). It is, however, noteworthy that as airlines increasingly outsource powerplant maintenance they may become less concerned about commonality; British Airways, for example, operates B777s with both GE90s and Rolls Royce Trents.

The improved operational capabilities and productivity of current generation aircraft are largely attributable to powerplant developments. Not only has the thrust available continued to grow towards and over the 100,000lb threshold, but thrust-to-weight ratios, specific fuel consumption, reliability, maintainability, and environmental impact have all improved as well. The sources of these improvements have been a combination of higher bypass ratios, improved thermal efficiency, more advanced materials, and better design of components and modules. (See Pickett (2002) for a comprehensive review of the aircraft engine selection process.)

Avionics

Some avionics systems (e.g., flight management, display, and engine control and monitoring systems) come 'bundled' with the aircraft as 'seller-furnished equipment' (SFE), whereas others are buyer-furnished; buyer-furnished avionics might either be essential (e.g., a basic level of CNS equipment) or discretionary (e.g., head-up displays). As with other technologies, airlines have become increasingly value-conscious in their assessment of buyer-furnished avionics applications. The key issue is whether the cost of equipment is outweighed by improved safety, higher revenues (e.g., resulting from a reputation amongst high-yield travellers for good on-time performance in low-visibility winter conditions), or reduced operating costs. (Head-up displays (HUDs), for example, are available as both factory-fitted options and retrofits, and can be used either as an alternative to autoland where this is unavailable or as a back-up to installed autoland systems; Kanellis (1999) provides an interesting analysis of a HUD investment decision.) Again, life-cycle costs – rather than capital or operating costs alone – are the key issue; flight-hour maintenance cost agreements entered into with avionics OEMs are providing airlines with added certainty in this respect.

Since the early 1990s the trend has been towards integrated modular avionics, and away from sub-modular line-replaceable units (LRUs). The ultimate goal of integration must be to tie together the delivery of capabilities in the following areas (Mineck, 1995: 613): all-weather landing; terrain avoidance; reduction in runway incursions; improved traffic flow; heightened traffic awareness; better insight into atmospheric conditions; safe reductions in aircraft separation; and improved monitoring of aircraft systems status. (Nickum (2002) outlines an economic model that has been developed to evaluate avionics purchases.)

One advantage that avionics suppliers have over powerplant OEMs is that whereas developments in materials sciences and propulsion technologies are not always cheap or easy to apply to older airframes, new avionics developments able to justify themselves financially can often be retrofitted. If a decision is made to forgo a factory-fitted avionics option, there might still be a possibility of retrofitting an upgraded version at some later time. (Developments in options pricing theory within the field of finance now allow this type of flexibility to be priced as a 'real option' – although there is little evidence that many airlines yet do this.) On the other hand, the growing functional integration of each successive generation's airframes, flight control systems, and avionics – together with the increasing integration of avionics packages themselves – may limit future avionics choices insofar as a greater range of applications will become standard equipment rather than an option.

Options and customisation

Although more complex typologies can be used, the basic breakdown is as follows.

- **Standard specification** This is the base aircraft, or perhaps a high gross weight version subject to additional certification and purchase costs. There will be some latitude for customisation to a particular airline's requirements in minor respects. (Note that glass cockpits may be helpful insofar as displays can be customised by adapting software rather than changing hardware – although this in itself is not cost-free.)
- **Seller-furnished equipment (SFE)** These are 'catalogue options' supplied by the manufacturer. Some represent equipment or subsystems that have to be bought from one supplier or another (e.g., lavatories and overhead stowage) and which might therefore come as ready-certificated 'catalogue options', whilst others might not have to be bought at all (e.g., non-essential avionics). At the time of writing, one widebody comes with over 100 alternative lavatory options.
- **Buyer-furnished equipment (BFE)** Major items in this category include seats, galleys, entertainment systems, and perhaps also communications and navigation equipment. Choice of BFE can make several thousand pounds' difference to the weight of a long-haul type operated by one carrier compared with the weight of the same type operated by another carrier – with obvious life-cycle fuel-burn implications.

Options add to the cost of new aircraft – as much as 10–20 per cent according to a former CEO of United who was amongst those pushing hard in the late 1990s for greater standardisation, but considerably less in the view of OEMs. Options cost serious money not simply because of the manufacturing inefficiencies and costs to which they give rise, but also because everything going onto an aircraft requires certification; certifying multiple options is more expensive than certifying a single standard item.

There has been intermittent pressure from airlines to cut the scope of customisation and option availability in order both to reduce aircraft purchase prices and to remove a complication from secondary market trading. Manufacturers have to an extent responded – Boeing, for example, having moved from full customisation to a set of pre-defined interior configurations (referred to as 'standard selection interiors'). The problem is that few full-service airlines – particularly amongst those serving long-haul business travellers – can resist the urge to customise wherever possible in order to distinguish their brand identities. That said, the argument in favour of standardising equipment that passengers do not see is compelling insofar as standardisation can contribute significant cost reductions. Alliances should in principle advance this process and, with their claims of seamless service, extend it into visible areas of the cabin that can be used to establish a common brand platform. Clearly, the case for standardisation of freighters is overwhelming. There has been some, but relatively little, progress towards standardised buys within alliances.

The growing significance of a small number of major operating lessors is a source of additional pressure towards standardisation, but even here if an airline is prepared to commit ahead of ordering to a long enough lease, customisation is likely to be on the table.

Customer support analysis

Initial provisioning Initial provisioning (IP) with spares and ground support equipment must be programmed to correspond with the rate of aircraft deliveries. Typical questions are: What has to be acquired to optimise inventory costs against target despatch reliability and what expenditures will this require? Can spares be taken on consignment rather than purchased outright? What are the assumed hours/cycles upon which IP estimates are based, and are they realistic? What has been the price history of spares in recent years, and how readily are they available from legitimate sources other than OEMs? What sort of reputations do the manufacturer and its suppliers have for responsiveness to urgent requirements? Is credit available? Must foreign currency be paid out before orders are shipped (a particularly important issue for airlines in some developing countries)?

Airlines are now analysing IP requirements – and, indeed, inventory policies in general – more carefully than at any time in the past. Whilst despatch reliability and service levels have to be maintained, efforts are being made to exploit both new opportunities for closer working relationships with suppliers and the reliability of express delivery services to cut inventory costs. Much depends on an airline's operating profile (notably forecast hours and cycles) and the location of its network relative to suppliers' distribution centres.

Training and technical support The *training package* will cover aircrew (initial conversion training) and engineers. *Technical support* should cover the following.

- **Technical publications** to ATA 100 specification standards (typically over 30 titles) will be supplied in negotiable quantities.
- **Field service** may involve the secondment of technical representatives to an airline operating a substantial fleet of a particular type.
- **Operations support** may run to the provision of line training captains and route proving assistance, together with updates of technical data, airworthiness directives, and service bulletins.

Warranties and guarantees These will be given by the airframe manufacturer, engine manufacturer, and other equipment vendors. They should cover, inter alia, design, materials, workmanship, service life, component reliability, repair turnaround, despatch reliability, maintenance cost, maximum parts cost, spares buyback, shop visit rate, cost per brake landing, fuel-burn deterioration, etc. Aircraft weight and performance undertakings (particularly for launch orders) should comprise, inter alia:

- weight-related guarantees: manufacturer's empty weight; operating weight empty; payload;
- field performance guarantees: take-off distance; landing distance; take-off weight and landing weight achievable at given airports under pre-specified operating conditions; and
- en route performance guarantees: all-engine and engine-out rates of climb; single-engine ceiling (for twins); cruise-specific air range; mission payload; payload-range performance.

Some of these guarantees might come with an allowable fixed or percentage margin of exceedance, but others (e.g., field performance) often will not. Compliance with margin allowances could be tested by reference to an approved document or by a field test under approved conditions. Settlement of disputes, after any contractual 'time to cure', could be by rejection of the aircraft (normally short-term, with late delivery compensation payable), lump-sum compensation, measured compensation based on an identifiable economic impact during a stated performance shortfall period (e.g., restricted payload on given routes), or product improvement at the manufacturer's expense.

Whereas large airlines will often have airframe and engine manufacturers' representatives attached to their engineering departments, small carriers risk finding themselves being ignored. For this reason they should ensure that in the *Product Support Agreement* the manufacturers undertake to despatch qualified support personnel several times each year to discuss any problems that have arisen. In the final analysis, airlines should enquire with other, similar, operators regarding their product support experiences. Also, it is too easy to focus on the airframe or powerplants and lose sight of the fact that there is much more to an aircraft; support will be required from component manufacturers as well, raising questions about the nature of contractual relationships with this type of OEM and their regional support infrastructures.

Finally, smaller airlines in regions remote from the main manufacturing and support centres, particularly those with a thinly spread technical infrastructure, need to ask themselves some searching questions about their own ability to support complex, new equipment without being entirely dependent on outside assistance to keep it flying on a day-to-day basis.

The fleet commonality issue

'Commonality' refers to the presence in an airline's fleet of a family of airframe derivatives (e.g., the B737-600/700/800/900 series and the A318/319/320/321 series) and/or engine derivatives (e.g., the PW4000 series and the Rolls Royce Trent series).

Airframe families The 'family' concept extends not just to variants of the same type such as the B737 and A320 series and the various regional jet families, but also to different but closely related types such as the A330/340 and the B757/767. It offers several potential advantages.

1. **Aircraft assignment flexibility** Traditionally, airlines have adjusted their deployment of different types and variants at the beginning of each timetable period or season – although some carriers have insufficient flexibility within their fleets to adjust even to seasonal fluctuations in demand, other than by changing frequencies and concentrating heavy maintenance during slack periods. In principle, having two or more variants of a single family available within the sub-fleet of a particular type can provide flexibility to adjust capacity to demand right up to the day of operation. In practice, it is not clear how widely this flexibility is used other than when timetables are changed. As much as anything else, a large network carrier with a complex flight schedule and aircraft routing pattern may find it difficult to make unforced late changes to aircraft assignments without this having a knock-on effect on the rest of the day's flight programme and perhaps also on maintenance schedules; carriers operating less complex out-and-back assignment patterns have more opportunity to exploit fleet flexibility. We will look at aircraft assignment below.
2. **Aircrew training and rostering flexibility** These have two aspects.

- *Common type ratings* A significant advantage of the family concept is that aircrew operating, say, the Next Generation B737 series can be common type-rated to fly any variant. (The same is also true of the B757/767, A320, and A330/340 series, as well as several regional jet families.) Common type rating allows the aircraft assignment flexibility provided by having variants with different payload-range capabilities in a single sub-fleet of a type to be complemented by the flexibility to roster pilots to fly any of these variants.
- *Cross-crew qualification (CCQ)* Airbus has developed CCQ, which leverages common design concepts and cockpit configurations between types, to reduce the transition from the A320 series to the A330/340 series from a multi-week conversion course to a much shorter period of 'differences training'. As a result of CCQ, Airbus has been able to offer the prospect of 'Mixed Fleet Flying' (MFF), where pilots can be scheduled to fly any aircraft in the two series. At the time of writing around 30 airlines use CCQ, and about a third of that number have adopted MFF.

The benefits of this flexibility are argued to come from lower training costs than would otherwise be incurred by pilots converting between aircraft with different payload-range capabilities, and cost savings from reduced pilot numbers – the latter attributable to having a single pool of pilots from which to draw for routine rostering and to cover late crew and aircraft changes, rather than a larger number of smaller, less flexible pools supporting a broader range of types. How significant these benefits are will depend upon the size of an airline's fleet and the nature of its route network; airlines with large sub-fleets of a single variant will tend to gain somewhat less benefit than others.

3. **Inventory and type-specific ground support equipment (GSE)** Families benefiting from extensive spares and GSE commonality can offer lower investment and inventory carrying costs than the alternative of having to support several types, each with fewer aircraft in the sub-fleet. This is true both at maintenance bases and also at outstations.
   - *Capital expenditures* One advantage of fleet standardisation is that the capital expenditure required for each aircraft added to a fleet of the same type diminishes (ignoring inflation) because expenditure on parts inventory, spare engines, type-specific GSE, and training pursuant to the acquisition is lower than would be the case were a new type to be introduced. (This is one reason why manufacturers sometimes have to price aggressively or offer generous 'fleet integration' finance in order to get airlines to switch allegiance.) The family concept extends these benefits.

- *Operating costs* Inventory costs include insurance, handling, storage, and depreciation. If having a family of aircraft in a sub-fleet increases the number of aircraft in that sub-fleet to the point that a particular item of inventory is able to support more aircraft than it otherwise would, this will contribute to lower inventory costs compared to the alternative of having more types and smaller sub-fleets in the overall fleet.

The Embraer 170/190 series provide a good example: there is 95 per cent commonality between the 170 and 175 and between the 190 and 195, whilst commonality between the 170/175 and the 190/195 runs close to 90 per cent.

4. **Training and rostering of maintenance personnel** At a general level, because maintenance personnel become familiar over time with the design concepts and maintenance procedures associated with a particular manufacturer's aircraft there will inevitably be a learning curve to climb if a new manufacturer's products are introduced into a fleet. Extending the argument, personnel familiar with a particular type are likely to be more efficient dealing with variants of that type than switching periodically to different types. Aside from any efficiency gains that might arise, commonality is argued to offer training and scheduling benefits in respect of maintenance personnel that are similar to those offered in respect of pilots.

In essence, commonality within a family can raise the productivity of aircraft, crews, and maintenance inventories whilst also allowing the airline to fine-tune supply to demand on a departure-by-departure basis. It allows airlines to balance the need for fleet rationalisation (i.e., the minimum number of types) against the need for fleet flexibility (i.e., the maximum network-relevant payload-range capability spread). That said, how significant the benefits of commonality are will vary from airline to airline. In particular, whilst small carriers can benefit from economies of scale associated with being able to build a reasonably-sized fleet out of relatively small numbers of different variants, the largest carriers – particularly the US and European majors – generally have numbers of aircraft, pilots, and maintenance personnel so large and schedule integrations so complex that the benefits of commonality are perhaps fewer than a small operator might experience. Another potential problem is that shrinking a type in order to complete the lower-capacity end of a family might sometimes impose weight penalties as a result of design having been optimised for the larger base model; this can lead to higher operating costs that may erode some of the benefits of commonality.

On the horizon is the possibility that in future fleet commonality issues may be viewed not just from the perspective of the airline making the immediate decision, but with one eye on the aircraft acquisition strategies of alliance partners. Clearly, though, alliances must be close and have a solid prospect of survival well into the future for this to be a powerful consideration. Not only should a chosen type be appropriate for similar missions in partners' networks, but to reap the full benefits of manufacturing cost savings the carriers concerned must be prepared to agree on common options packages. The distance to be travelled in this regard is illustrated by the facts that at the time of writing **one**world members operate 18 aircraft types and 22 airframe/engine combinations, whilst Star members operate 22 types and 26 combinations. (A related point is that the two alliances boast 13 and 25 B747 cabin configurations respectively.) It is perhaps ironic that one of the earliest examples of alliance purchasing involved a substantial Airbus order from Qualiflyer partners Swissair, Sabena, and Austrian – shortly after which Austrian left to join Star and, some time later, the other two collapsed.

Powerplant families It has already been noted that derivatives of common powerplants are used not only within airframe families such as the A320 and B737 series, but also on different types such as the A320 and A340 or the B767 and B747. As with airframe commonality, there are inventory, maintenance infrastructure, and personnel training and scheduling benefits to be gained from powerplant commonality. On the other hand, power-by-the-hour and life-cycle maintenance cost agreements can be used to shift the burden of a mixed engine inventory onto OEMs (or even third-party MRO shops) which have enough volume in each engine type to pass through to the airline some of the benefits arising from economies of scale. Commonality might still offer cost savings in respect of line maintenance if this continues to be handled inhouse.

Other considerations

Amongst the additional considerations likely to enter into a fleet planning exercise are the following.

1. The timing of a manufacturer's available delivery positions relative to need and/or planned phase-out of current aircraft.
2. The availability of offset deals.
3. The availability of vendor financing or financial support (possibly including trade-ins against current aircraft, integration funding to support

the inevitably higher costs of introducing a new type into the fleet, and/ or concessions on prepayments prior to delivery).

4. Cargo container compatibility (e.g., Airbus widebodies can accommodate side-by-side in their belly-holds the LD-3 containers used on B747s, whereas the B767 cannot – requiring LD-2s instead).

5. The ease with which loose-loaded baggage can be loaded and offloaded to facilitate efficient narrowbody turnarounds. More generally, turnaround times can be a significant consideration in respect of aircraft operated on high-frequency short-haul networks. The Embraer 170/190 series come with a guaranteed 20-minute turnaround time attributable in large measure to a 2 x 2 seating configuration and, in particular, to the related fact that these are long aircraft for their capacity and so can accommodate the simultaneous positioning of all required GSE.

6. Whether a carrier has a single-type or single-manufacturer fleet policy. One of Southwest's many sources of cost advantage over other US majors has been its single-type fleet of B737s (albeit mixed between classics and 'Next Generation' series). Several other US majors have made long-term commitments to Boeing. On the other hand, some carriers prefer not to be over-reliant on a single supplier. A key issue is whether on a life-cycle basis DOC savings derived from commonality are outweighed by capital cost savings attributable to price competition between manufacturers; easyJet decided that they were when in 2002 it ordered A319s for its previously all-Boeing fleet.

7. The growth potential of the type (i.e., scope for weight increases and development of derivatives).

8. Projected residual values (RVs). Some airframe-engine combinations have better RVs than competing models designed for similar missions, and this can affect financiers' appetite to take on their asset risk, as well as the long-term preservation of the airline's capital (if the aircraft are to be owned rather than leased). Key factors affecting RV aside from the operating characteristics of an airframe-engine combination are the number of units in the global fleet and both the number and regional spread of operators; the more popular a type and the wider it is spread across different markets around the world, the easier it should in principle be to remarket and the less RV risk it should pose for financiers. (Given the nature of these criteria, it will be interesting to see how RV estimates develop for the A380.)

Another variable affecting RV is how early in a type's production run the aircraft concerned will have left the factory. Because later aircraft benefit from weight reductions and various other enhancements, it is often the case that they maintain RVs better than aircraft produced significantly earlier in the production run.

9. Confidence in the manufacturer to abide by its undertakings.

The question of confidence in the future of the manufacturer is something brought sharply into focus by the demise of Fokker, the takeover of McDonnell Douglas, and the withdrawal of Saab and BAE Systems from commercial airframe assembly. When a manufacturer leaves its markets, long-term product support may or may not be thrown into question; experience to date in this regard has not been particularly bad, although periodic parts shortages were reportedly one reason behind American's decision taken in 2002 to begin retiring its F100 fleet. More problematic for affected operators are the impacts on both the secondary market value of the current fleet and on future fleet development plans – problems faced by British European (now 'flybe'), which was in the process of re-fleeting around the RJX when BAE cancelled the programme in 2001.

Pricing and economic analysis

Every aircraft acquired should be capable of contributing positively to shareholder value. The fundamental variables that determine whether or not this can be achieved are price, operating revenues and costs, and RV.

Price Few airlines pay the 'sticker price'. Launch orders, bulk buys, and orders from strategically important customers in particular attract sometimes substantial discounts. When alternative engines are available on an airframe, heavy discounts off engine list price are also likely to be available, and this can clearly have a profound impact on total aircraft price. Another consideration is product substitutability: although competing manufacturers produce closely matched types and variants for most payload-range missions, one manufacturer's product might sometimes be better-suited to a particular airline's network and demand characteristics. If this is not the case and competing products are essentially substitutes for each other, pricing is likely to be finer. All of this needs to be set against general market conditions. When backlogs are low, there are 'white tails' in storage, and demand is weak, manufacturers are clearly going to be more accommodating with regard to price than in a tight market. Some carriers (e.g., easyJet, Ryanair, and Qantas) have proven particularly adept at benefiting from soft prices in a buyers' market.

On the whole, it is fair to say that pricing has more to do with what purchasers will bear than with manufacturing cost. What a purchaser will bear has to be capped below the economic value of a particular aircraft operated on its specific route network – irrespective of current market conditions. There is no deterministic reason why the amount an airline is prepared to pay for an aircraft, established after analysing future cash flows based on what it considers to be realistic assumptions, should bear any relationship to the manufacturer's cost of building that aircraft and allocating overheads to each unit produced. Of course, manufacturers should hope that it does – otherwise they have got their costing wrong. From an airline's perspective, the driver in price negotiations must be the economic value of the airplane to that particular carrier and not some target discount off the manufacturer's sticker price.

Economic analysis Any aircraft's *output* productivity (i.e., ASMs, ATMs) is primarily a function of its payload capacity, speed, and utilisation; consideration of *economic* productivity requires further assumptions to be made regarding load factor and yield. A choice of aircraft will be driven by many different considerations, but in principle the chosen type should generate more cash than it will absorb over the study period and yield a positive net present value (NPV) and acceptable internal rate of return (IRR). In simple terms, cash flows are projected and then discounted back to present value:

	Present value (PV) of cash operating revenues over the assumed ownership period
Less	PV of cash operating expenses over the assumed ownership period
Plus	PV of residual value of the aircraft (and remaining spares and equipment) at the end of the ownership period
Less	Initial investment (in the airframe and engines, spares, ground equipment, maintenance tooling, training, and fleet integration)
=	NET PRESENT VALUE (at the assumed discount rate)

(Discounted cash flow techniques are in fact not without their shortcomings; Stonier (2001) reviews some of these and discusses the potential for use of real options in fleet planning decisions.)

Much the same analysis applies whether a prospective purchase is new or used. If either a new or used aircraft is being bought to replace an existing aircraft rather than to accommodate demand growth, the analysis should take into account any resale proceeds attributable to selling the existing aircraft and should focus in particular on the NPV of incremental changes to operating revenues and costs attributable to the replacement decision. Clearly, the purpose of any economic analysis should not be just to compare alternative acquisitions; another important comparison to be made is between these alternatives and the current (baseline) case – the alternative of retaining the existing fleet, possibly after some form of cabin, flight-deck, and/or powerplant upgrade.

Outcomes will of course be sensitive to forecasts in respect of revenue drivers (e.g., demand, market share, load factors, and yields) and cost drivers (e.g., fuel and labour costs), and also to the assumed discount rate. Forecasts and assumptions will therefore have to be varied as part of a sensitivity analysis to establish how robust the conclusions are under different operating and interest rate scenarios. Manufacturers frequently assist by providing route suitability and comparative cost studies, but these are sales documents and as such need to be treated cautiously.

Finally, it should be borne in mind that whilst all airlines face constraints on the availability of investment funds, carriers in some countries have to do their budgeting not only under a capital rationing constraint but also under a foreign exchange rationing constraint; they must therefore analyse foreign currency cash flows as well as total cash flows. Whilst this problem is often at its most serious for carriers in developing countries, most non-US airlines face a natural short-dollar position attributable to dollar-denominated expenditures on aircraft acquisition and on fuel purchases (set against revenues that tend to be heavily weighted towards their home currencies); hedging can help, but the life of most hedging instruments and techniques is short compared to the life of a new-build aircraft.

Contracting

Once a purchase has been finalised in principle, the next step will be signature of a letter of intent that briefly outlines the airline's agreement with the manufacturer but makes the signing of a firm contract conditional on production of an acceptable customised specification, price, and delivery schedule, together with other required documentation, within an agreed time period.

Deposits will usually be payable on signature of the letter of intent or memorandum of understanding, but these may be quite small – depending upon the prevailing market situation, whether discounts off sticker price are applied as a reduction to all advance payments or are front-loaded to eliminate early payments, and on whether the airline is holding any credit notes from the airframe or engine manufacturer. Further payments will usually be due on signing a contract, and in instalments thereafter with the balance due on delivery. The present value of an aircraft's purchase cost can be materially affected by variations in the amount and timing of progress payments.

Aircraft acceptance criteria will be specified in the contract. Large carriers frequently have engineers resident at the manufacturer's facility, at least for the duration of a delivery programme, to monitor construction and accept delivery.

Aircraft evaluation: cargo capabilities

Passenger aircraft

Despite continued growth in the freighter fleet, a significant proportion of airfreight still moves in the belly-holds of passenger aircraft. An airframe design, particularly a widebody, might be optimised for passengers or specifically for a passenger/cargo mix. This can be an important consideration for a carrier earning a substantial proportion of its revenues from cargo. Aircraft belly-hold volumes and overall payload capacities need to be considered, and a determination arrived at as to which is most significant from the point of view of the particular airline's network. (Interestingly, because of the volume of passenger baggage it is required to accommodate, the baseline A380-800 in passenger configuration actually has less cargo capacity than a B747-400.)

Freighters and combis

There are several additional considerations to be borne in mind with regard to all-cargo and combi aircraft (the latter being aircraft that carry both passengers and cargo on their main deck).

- **Design density** Freighters are limited in respect of volumetric capacity as well as payload (i.e., weight). Design density is that density which combines the full use of volumetric capacity with the highest payload feasible. (The 'density' of cargo is weight/volume, expressed in pounds per cubic feet.) It is important that on any individual route an aircraft does not 'cube (or 'bulk') out' too far ahead of the payload at which it would 'weight out'. If the density of freight actually carried is below the design density for the aircraft concerned, payload capacity will be left unutilised; this can be a particular problem for some narrowbodied freighters. Manufacturers might base their economic studies on average freight densities closer to the design density (i.e., higher) than many airlines will actually come across in practice, because this obviously raises the payload output of their aircraft.
- **Access door dimensions** These affect the ease with which containers, pallets, and outsize shipments of different dimensions can be loaded.
- **Fuselage cross-section** This governs the size of containers which can be accommodated and the volume of space above standard containers, once loaded, available for payload 'make-up'.
- **Weights** Cargo doors, strengthened floors, and onboard handling equipment carry significant weight penalties.

The cargo traffic mix on a particular airline's network can be a critical criterion when considering the relative importance of an aircraft's volumetric and weight capacities. More generally, whilst a small package carrier would in most cases be more concerned about volume considerations than payload, for a line-haul carrier specialising in heavy freight it is tonnage over different flight-legs on its particular network that is likely to be more significant.

Although Boeing and Airbus offer factory-built freighter versions of several of their models, over three-quarters of the freighters currently in operation are converted passenger aircraft whose value had dropped sufficiently to make conversion a sound economic prospect. Under normal market conditions, the value of a passenger aircraft might be expected to drop into the range where cargo conversion becomes economic once it is 12–15 years old; during deep recessions, as in 2001/2002, the number of parked or underutilised aircraft can put such downward pressure on values that conversion of younger aircraft (with more attractive operating costs) becomes economic – at least for those with faith in a rapid cargo market upturn.

The conversion market is increasingly dominated by airframe manufacturers, who not only have more comprehensive documentation and analyses on their models than do third-party shops but also have an interest in taking aircraft out of passenger service to stimulate replacement orders. (An exception in the latter regard was the B747-400, for which Boeing was originally in no hurry to see a conversion programme build momentum as long as orders for new-build freighter variants represented a significant proportion of total factory orders for the type.)

As many as 70 per cent of the additions to the global freighter fleet over the next 20 years or so are likely to come from passenger conversions, largely because the generally lower utilisation of cargo aircraft than similar types in passenger operation makes the economics of conversion more compelling than the purchase of a new freighter for all but a relatively small number of cargo networks. Unless the DOCs for a new-build are sufficiently below those of a converted older aircraft, the high ownership cost of a factory-built freighter will very often overwhelm the acquisition plus conversion costs of an older aircraft. Sometimes, however, the greater payload-range capabilities – and therefore also productivity advantage – of newer models (such as the B747-400F) give it a marketing advantage over conversions (of, say, B747-200s); despatch reliability can also weigh in favour of newer aircraft. Cargolux is one example of a carrier that found B747-400Fs preferable to -200 conversions for its markets – their better payload-range capabilities and utilisation potential, and lower DOCs, outweighing higher capital costs.

Aircraft evaluation: used aircraft

It is quite possible for as many used aircraft to change hands in a year as are delivered new (Trevett, 1999). Much the same economic analysis needs to be applied whether a proposed aircraft purchase involves new or used units. There are several arguments advanced in favour of new aircraft.

1. **Costs** Although used aircraft are cheaper in terms of capital costs, their cash DOCs (i.e., excluding ownership costs) tend to be higher than those of newer aircraft designed for similar missions. There are several reasons for this.
    *   Aircraft performance declines as the airframe ages because surface deterioration increases drag.
    *   Weight gradually rises over time as a result of engineering modifications, the accumulation of moisture, the accretion of dirt in places not readily washed, and (at least between heavy checks) the addition of paint layers. Furthermore, later line numbers of any aircraft type are sometimes lighter than aircraft produced earlier in the production run as experience allows initially conservative design margins to be relaxed.
    *   The specific fuel consumption of engines tends to increase as they age, and more modern engines are anyway designed for improved consumption compared with their predecessors. A steeply rising fuel price can be the single most important factor weighing against the purchase (or retention) of older aircraft.
    *   Maintenance costs, particularly in respect of unscheduled maintenance, rise as airframes and engines age. Two related issues might be the detrimental impact on customer satisfaction and yields that can arise from poor despatch reliability, and the less responsive after-market support from OEMs than would be expected during warranty periods.
    Thus, older aircraft become less attractive to operate as fuel and maintenance costs rise. Added to this are environmental pressures on noise and emissions in a number of countries. During periods when these pressures are not too intense, airline managements can be sorely tempted to retain fully depreciated older aircraft rather than face the high capital costs of replacing them. Many low-cost/no-frills start-ups have also been launched on the relatively lower ownership costs of old aircraft. Conversely, there are carriers which roll their fleets regularly for both financial and marketing reasons, whilst amongst start-ups we have already noted that jetBlue launched with new A320s.

2. **Passenger preference** Although if asked most passengers would probably opt for new aircraft over old, the reality is that relatively few have any accurate idea how old an aircraft is and arrive at judgements based on standards of external and interior appearance. Several airlines nonetheless perceive a virtuous circle linking assumed passenger preference to fleet management strategy: a premium brand image leads to a sound base of high-yield traffic, leading in turn to strong cash flow that is enhanced by the favourable operating economics of newer aircraft, by the stronger secondary market values of young models traded out of the fleet on a regular rollover cycle, and by the tax shelter available from a policy of depreciating new purchases rapidly over a brief period of ownership and therefore deferring cash outflows to tax authorities. Singapore Airlines is the most widely quoted practitioner in this regard; EVA Air has a 12-year age limit on its fleet. Of course, the virtuous circle can be broken by a prolonged cyclical downturn in aircraft secondary market values.

3. **Finance** Depending upon an airline's particular circumstances and also prevailing market conditions, it can on occasion be easier to arrange financing for new aircraft than for a secondary market purchase. Financially weak airlines reliant on export credits and/or support from manufacturers may find themselves in this position, for example.

There is nonetheless sometimes an argument that the nature of markets served by a carrier – particularly a start-up or a relatively small airline operating thin routes at low frequencies – might make the economics of older aircraft more attractive. Any airline flying new aircraft will need to maximise utilisation in order to spread high ownership costs (such as depreciation or operating lease rentals) across as much output of ASMs and ATMs as possible and keep downward pressure on unit costs. If high utilisation is difficult to generate because a carrier serves relatively few markets at relatively low frequencies, it might well make sense to accept the higher operating costs of older aircraft in order to reduce the burden of high ownership costs.

With regard to freighters, the secular decline in real freight yields makes high ownership costs associated with the sticker prices of new aircraft a serious burden which all but a few airlines seem unwilling to bear. Whilst several Asian operators, a few European airlines, and some of the integrated carriers have the demand base and network structures to accept high ownership costs in order to benefit from the operating cost and range advantages of new models, many others are content to rely on converted passenger aircraft.

Aircraft finance

Aircraft can be acquired from an airline's internal funds or a mix of internal funds and debt; alternatively, they can be acquired using one of a wide range of available lease structures – a key defining feature of which is the percentage of its economic life over which the airline has use of the aircraft. Export credit financing and support from manufacturers can also play a role. This is what is generally referred to as 'the financing decision'. It is typical in both corporate finance textbooks and the practice of many airlines to separate the investment decision (Which aircraft should be acquired?) from the financing decision (How should the aircraft be financed?). Unfortunately, different financing alternatives available in respect of competing aircraft can sometimes have a profound impact on the NPVs of cash flows arising from different choices. (See Stonier (1998) for an explanation of the various methods available to model interactions between investment and financing decisions.)

Aircraft are resources that are expensive to acquire and introduce into service, long-lived, and subject to cycles in secondary market values that might be broadly predictable as to onset but less so as to depth or duration. This makes them a particularly risky class of asset. Risk can be reduced by maintaining financial flexibility around the core fleet – something that accounts for the growing role of operating lessors, whose portfolios are now being driven as much by the strategic requirements of large and financially sound carriers as by the lack of financing alternatives available to smaller or less stable airlines.

Fleet acquisition is an investment decision which, like all other investment decisions, depends for its efficacy on assumptions made with regard to future revenues and costs. Considerable effort might go into making these assumptions as robust as possible, and 'sophisticated' discounting techniques can be used to evaluate cash flows. But in the final analysis airlines are investing hundreds of millions of dollars based on forecasts of demand, and assumptions about input costs, utilisation, yields, and seating densities, as far into the future as 10 to 15 years. Many cannot forecast these variables with sufficient accuracy over periods considerably shorter than this.

Such uncertainty argues for the use of a two-pronged approach to fleet acquisition and financing: a core fleet of owned aircraft (assuming the airline starts with this sort of financial strength), and the balance on flexible leases permitting either their retention for a secondary period or their return to lessors on short notice and with minimal exposure to asset value risk (i.e., to the risk that the aircraft will be worth less than any contractually required early-termination payment).

Buying-in capacity on the strength of demand which fails to materialise to the extent anticipated can be very expensive, and the risk argues strongly in favour of an airline expanding its core fleet gradually, leasing at the margins, timing lease expiries to coincide with new deliveries into the core fleet, and negotiating leases with both extension and early termination rights. This type of flexibility carries its own costs – but rarely are these as punishing as overinvestment in an inappropriately sized or structured fleet, locked in place by inflexible funding arrangements. Inevitably, though, it tends to be creditworthy airlines that can negotiate the most flexible arrangements with financiers.

Readers interested in more comprehensive coverage of airline and aircraft financing should refer to Holloway (1992) and Morrell (2002b).

ii. Tactical fleet management

This section of the chapter will look at tactical fleet management from two perspectives: aircraft assignment and routing, and cabin floorspace flexibility.

Aircraft assignment and routing

An airline with a fleet of given size, composition, and maintenance requirements and with an established schedule to meet faces what are referred to in the literature as 'the aircraft assignment problem' and 'the aircraft routing problem'. We touched on these in chapter 7 as well as earlier in the present chapter, and saw that fleet assignment modelling is in many respects an operational extension of the longer term and more 'strategic' modelling of future fleet requirements: scheduling, fleet planning, and aircraft assignment are closely related elements of the wider capacity management challenge.

Once a base schedule has been established and evaluated by a schedule profitability model, the next step is to assign available aircraft types to the scheduled flights. The objective of a fleet assignment model is to maximise the 'contribution' of the given schedule by maximising the gap between revenue capture and DOCs – subject to operational constraints. Fleet assignment models are commonly based on spill models that estimate how much demand will be turned away given the use of a particular aircraft on a particular departure – the objective being to minimise the sum of DOCs and spill costs (Belobaba and Farkas, 1999). Some of these models have shortcomings.

- While most will net estimates of no-shows off forecasts of unconstrained demand, few make allowance for the impact of revenue management policies in respect of overbooking and with regard to the effect on spill of different booking limits imposed on each applicable booking class. A related point is that the use of revenue management systems (RMSs) results in different local passengers having different revenue values. (These concepts will all be discussed in chapter 9.)
- There is also the problem of connecting passengers. Traditional fleet assignment approaches have been leg-based, intended to respond to traffic and revenue forecasts for each leg and assuming passenger demand to be independent on each flight-leg. This approach ignores the fact that limiting output on one flight-leg could reduce traffic on connecting flight-legs (ibid; Jacobs et al, 2001).
- Some fleet assignment models assume that demand during each season or period is stable on a per-departure basis, and that airlines will maintain fleet assignments throughout each schedule season or period such that the same departure every day is operated by the same type. In fact, at the level of the individual departure demand can be quite volatile.

Schedule profitability and fleet assignment models tend still to be run in iterative sequences. The ultimate goal is to integrate scheduling, fleet assignment, aircraft routing, maintenance planning, and perhaps also crew assignment into a single model capable of producing one optimal solution.

Aircraft assignment is therefore part of a time-line of different activities.

1. Some months in advance (perhaps 3–6 in domestic markets, but closer to 12 in many international markets) a schedule is fixed (subject perhaps to possible late adjustments), flights are advertised in distribution channels, and early – usually low-yield – bookings begin to load.
2. Once a schedule has been built and published, weekly rotations of generic aircraft are created to match aircraft types (sub-fleets) to scheduled flight-legs and through-services in a minimum-cost *assignment* that is feasible given the number of aircraft in the sub-fleets of each type operated by the airline; the turn-times of different types at each station have to be allowed for, and the availability of adequate pilot duty-time in aggregate per type also needs to be considered. 'Minimum-cost' in this sense refers both to aircraft operating costs and to the opportunity costs of spilled passengers attributable to offering insufficient output relative to demand.

   One additional issue often encountered is the need to balance directionality on a route at specific times of day. An aircraft large enough to accommodate a high proportion of demand going into a major business centre during the morning peak might very well be too large for demand on the return leg. One answer could be to use a smaller aircraft and accept spill; another could be to allocate very few seats to low-yield (or FFP redemption) booking classes inbound, and far more on the outbound leg.

3. The next step is to design sequences of flights ('lines of flying') to be flown by specific aircraft, taking account of the maintenance requirements of each. This is the *aircraft routing problem*.

4. By this stage, crew scheduling will also need to be addressed by creating pairings and individual rosters.

5. Actual demand in respect of any particular departure will inevitably fluctuate around the average, sometimes quite widely. Throughout the booking cycle an RMS should monitor demand and release space on the assigned aircraft at different fares – a process that will be discussed in chapter 9. Marketing communications and promotional initiatives might also be used to help fine-tune demand.

6. Most carriers rework initial fleet assignment and routing solutions in response to changing commercial and operational circumstances right up to the day of operations. (See Jarrah et al (2000) for an example of practice at United.) If close to the departure date (which might mean a few hours to a few days, depending on fleet and network circumstances) it is apparent that the assigned aircraft is either too large or too small for demand coming forward at the prices being asked, an aircraft swap might be considered. The objective of aircraft reassignment and the tailoring of output to actual demand is to provide support to load factors and/or yields and also to reduce trip costs if the aircraft originally assigned is too large, or provide better seat accessibility or boost revenues if it is too small.

    Two forms of swap are possible.

    - *Between different types* Aircraft types vary with regard to their mission flexibility. The greater the spread of payload-range mission profiles a type can operate economically, the more flexible it is.

    - *Between different variants* Both carriers operating only one or two types and airlines with a broader fleet mix can benefit from having families of related models such as the A320 series or the B737 series. As discussed earlier in the chapter, these benefits extend beyond the capacity management flexibility in which we are interested here; other advantages include elimination of the additional line maintenance and equipment costs often attributable to operating multiple types into any one outstation.

The ability to swap aircraft with different capacities on or close to the day of operation is referred to as 'dynamic fleet management' (DFM) or 'demand-driven despatch' (D^3).

Dynamic fleet management

The scope an airline has to engage in DFM is dependent on two variables (Clark, 2000, 2001).

1. **Network structure** A short-haul out-and-back assignment pattern which rotates aircraft regularly through a hub or main operating base is more conducive to late reassignments than either a long-haul linear or a grid structure that commits each aircraft to a particular pattern as soon as it departs the first airport. Not only do short-haul out-and-back routings assist in efforts to match output to demand, they can also help isolate schedule disruptions at a single hub or base – whereas assignments that route aircraft out of one hub and via outlying stations to another can propagate delays across an entire multi-hub system; in 2002, SAS adopted out-and-back routings on its intra-Scandinavian operations from Copenhagen, Oslo, and Stockholm in order to boost aircraft utilisation and assignment flexibility, and also to limit delay propagation between the three centres.
2. **Fleet structure** Aircraft swaps presuppose a fleet of different-sized aircraft – ideally including aircraft from 'families' which share operational characteristics that allow aircraft to be substituted close to departure with minimal impact on crew and other resource scheduling.

Even when an airline has a sufficiently varied fleet, there are nonetheless several potential obstacles to late reassignment.

1. **Replacing an assigned aircraft with a smaller aircraft** This can raise a number of issues.
   - Passengers might perceive a smaller aircraft (e.g., a narrowbody substituted for a widebody, or a regional aircraft substituted for a mainline narrowbody) as a less attractive service environment.
   - Some of the cabin crew originally scheduled for the larger aircraft might be left unutilised.
   - Cargo may have to be offloaded.
   - Depending upon the nature of its network, an airline might find the larger aircraft that is being replaced difficult to reassign profitably. Carriers with a small number of aircraft that are significantly larger than the rest of their fleet and which have few routes sufficiently

dense to support these aircraft can sometimes, for this reason, find it difficult to maintain satisfactory utilisation levels.

2. **Replacing an assigned aircraft with a larger aircraft** This may also pose problems.
   - The destination airport clearly has to be able to accommodate the larger aircraft (in terms of runway length and loading, and terminal capacity, for example).
   - Additional cabin crew may need to be available.

3. **Replacing any type with another** Whenever aircraft are reassigned, the maintenance requirements of the tail numbers involved need to be considered, as do the downline implications of having them out of position. Other issues also arise, one of which – as we will see in the next chapter – is that changes in available seat inventories will have to be communicated to the reservations system, RMS, and external distribution channels (notably GDSs). When the swap is between different types rather than within a single-type family, the following factors need to be kept in mind.
   - Pilot rosters will be affected: pilots must be legally and contractually available to fly the swapped-in aircraft on the routing concerned, and the downline effect of their use on this routing should not harm crew utilisation.
   - The availability of line replaceable spares and suitably qualified line maintenance engineers at destination airports might be a consideration if the substitute type is seldom operated on the route concerned.
   - Reassignment might be constrained where the types involved have markedly different block-speeds on the flight-leg if this is sufficient to materially threaten schedule integrity (including the sequencing of flights in and out of a banked hub).
   - Flexibility can also be constrained on some routes where the range of the substitute aircraft is inadequate given the payload it is being assigned to carry. (This applies within families of a type as well as between types.)

In practice, swapping aircraft within a sizeable and tightly integrated schedule is never going to be straightforward, if only because of its downline implications. It is particularly important that the capacity of the swapped-in aircraft is suitably sized not only for the flight under consideration, but also for booked loads on return or onward flight-legs.

The extent to which an airline actually needs to resort to DFM depends in part on the traffic mix served by a particular route insofar as leisure demand is less randomly volatile than demand from the business segment and

generally comes forward well ahead of departure – although this generalisation is now less true in North American domestic and intra-European
short-break markets than was typically the case before 2001/2002. DFM
comes into its own in particular when the swapping-in of a larger aircraft
(or variant) than originally scheduled enables a carrier to accommodate an
unanticipated late surge in high-yield, time-sensitive bookings.

Before leaving fleet assignment flexibility and turning to the topic of
floorspace flexibility, a final point needs to be made with regard to the additional tactical fleet management flexibility that charter/nonscheduled carriers have over scheduled network operators. The latter certainly add and
delete seasonal routes and also seasonally adjust frequencies and aircraft
types on year-round routes – although their ability to do this depends in
large measure on network and fleet structures. In future, seasonal swaps
between alliance partners will become more common, provided they can
agree on acceptable cabin configurations. Charter carriers, on the other
hand, sometimes have the flexibility to reorient the bulk of their fleets; for
example, Canadian charter airlines have historically concentrated on North
Atlantic leisure markets in the northern summer and Florida, the Caribbean,
and Latin America during the winter vacation season. (Desrosiers et al
(2000) describe the implications of this for Air Transat's aircraft routing,
crew pairing, and work assignment tasks.)

Floorspace flexibility

Capacity management is concerned not only with the number and types of
aircraft in a fleet, but also with how their floorspace is configured. Floorspace within each unit is the real production capacity derived from operating aircraft, and how it is configured can have a significant impact both on
output and yield. We will look at just three examples.

1. Rapid cabin reconfiguration has been practised for a number of years
    on short-haul aircraft in Europe, such that by moving a curtain or light-
    weight rigid partition the size of a narrowbody business class cabin can
    be increased or reduced. Seat pitch remains the same as in the economy
    cabin. Such flexibility is valuable, both because it allows the accomm-
    odation of peak early morning and late afternoon business class dem-
    and on any given route, and because it also facilitates deployment of
    aircraft on a range of sectors with entirely different traffic mixes.

    Convertible (also referred to as 'variable geometry') seats are incr-
    easingly used to reduce the number of passengers across each row in
    business class without forgoing the flexibility to reconfigure into econ-

omy class density as required, but these are generally heavier than standard economy class seats. Perhaps more importantly, they suffer from marketing disadvantages when competitors offer fixed and less dense business class seating configurations. For example, the flexibility to reconfigure a row from 3 x 3 economy to 2 x 3 or even 2 x 2 business class seating is a valuable capacity management tool, but if the competition is offering a fixed 2 x 2 business class layout – possibly with greater seat pitch and recline as well – there is a clear trade-off in product quality. Conversely, poor business class seat pitches and widths are on some routes increasingly exposed to the value propositions put forward by low-fare carriers. Convertible seats nonetheless remain in widespread use in intra-European business classes.

2. The far higher standard of seating comfort and access to other amenities required in business class on long-haul flights has generally precluded short-run floor-plan flexibility. One particular problem – increasingly met as well on the short-haul aircraft of full-service carriers – is that seats are now very frequently wired to entertainment and communications systems. Another problem is the difficulty of relocating galleys and lavatories on long-haul aircraft. Boeing has addressed the latter challenge with the 'flex zone' concept; pioneered on the B777, these zones allow galleys and lavatories to be relocated to pre-engineered areas in the cabin as part of a relatively short reconfiguration process. There is a weight penalty, of course, but the marketing flexibility in respect of seasonal demand fluctuations on a given route or reassignment of an aircraft to a different type of route with a different traffic mix can be significant.

3. One obvious way to adjust the output of ASMs produced by any given amount of flying is to change seating density.

   • *Raising densities* Most commonly this involves reducing seat pitch, although it could be done by replacing some galley or storage space with seats. Each aircraft is certified for a maximum number of seats; full-service scheduled carriers will very rarely approach this maximum (other than on some high-density Japanese domestic services), but single-class charter and low-fare operators come much closer. The addition of seats may require more cabin crew.

   • *Reducing densities* There have been two service design developments that have led to lower densities on some airlines. First, a number of carriers have been extending the seat pitches available to their long-haul business class passengers; an early example was British Airways' introduction of flat-bed seats in 2000/2001. Second, at around the same time several US carriers took seat rows out of some or all of their aircraft to give additional seat pitch either to every coach seat (e.g., American) or to high-yield passengers and high-value frequent flyers provided with an intermediate product in the front rows of coach (e.g., United).

Changing seating density is a relatively cheap and easy way in which to adjust output, but it is not without its engineering costs and neither should it be done without first giving consideration to the impact it has on the inflight product, customer satisfaction, and future revenues.

The common thread running through each of the past few paragraphs has been that greater flexibility in the use of cabin floorspace and the reduction of set-up times can be an important capacity management tool. Aside from the special case of intra-European business classes with convertible seats and easily movable partitions or curtains separating them from the economy cabin, floorspace flexibility is not a flight-by-flight option.

Before leaving this section, Box 8.4 looks at the flexibility offered by mixed passenger/cargo operations using convertible, quick-change (QC), and combi aircraft.

Box 8.4: Convertible, quick-change, and combi aircraft

Convertibles Aircraft convertible between passenger and all-cargo configurations can be useful for smaller airlines serving passenger markets that experience extreme peaking (e.g., transatlantic leisure markets during the northern summer) and wanting to deploy at least part of their fleets into cargo markets that peak at different times (e.g., pre-Christmas). Martinair has used this approach successfully for many years. A particular type of convertible narrowbody sometimes encountered is the QC model.

QCs Aircraft designed for rapid conversion between passenger and freight operations first appeared in the 1960s, but subsequently fell from favour. In France, Aeropostale (succeeded by Europe Airpost) continued to operate a largely QC B737 fleet, allowing its core night postal operations to be supplemented by daytime passenger services flown on behalf of Air France; more recently, Lufthansa converted a number of B737-300s to QC configuration. In both cases the changeover process was designed to effect installation or removal of palletised passenger seats in under an hour. (The same time-frame applies to the B737-700QC, whereas the -700 convertible requires around five hours to remove or install passenger seats.) Virgin Blue announced in 2002 that it was considering the use of QCs for night airfreight operations and daytime passenger service back-up. Relatively few aircraft have QC capability, and all are inevitably short-haul narrowbodies.

Combis These aircraft carry both passengers and cargo on their main decks. *They are inherently flexible insofar as they can be used to develop new routes or to offer higher frequencies on existing routes than would be sustainable by an aircraft of similar size having broadly the same DOCs but relying just on passenger traffic (perhaps supplemented by belly-hold cargo). One approach might be to enter new routes that have freight dem-and sufficient to justify the use of combis able to deliver revenues fairly rapidly from freight traffic whilst the passenger market is being penetrated. For combis to be useful, either adequate freight demand has to be present on the route concerned or that route must be part of a network within which cargo flows can be redirected towards it; if neither is the case, a smaller (passenger) aircraft is the only alternative.*

Combis have fallen from favour somewhat in recent years, primarily for the following reasons.

- *Stringent cargo compartment fire regulations introduced following an accident in the mid-1980s have imposed an additional weight and therefore cost penalty.*
- *The schedule requirements of passengers and shippers are sometimes difficult to reconcile. (This is, of course, a problem also confronted in respect of freight carried in the belly-holds of passenger aircraft; how serious an issue it is will depend upon the mix – and therefore service requirements – of freight traffic on individual routes.)*
- *The emphasis airframe manufacturers have placed on the development of derivatives since the 1980s has meant that airlines have a wide range of mission capabilities from which to choose in respect of avail-able passenger aircraft, and so have less need for combis to develop new passenger routes or niches.*

Combis nonetheless remain important to some carriers (e.g., EVA Air and KLM). Recent developments have focused on cutting down the time taken to adjust main-deck configurations to different mixes of passengers and freight.

Although convertibles, QCs, and combis all offer capacity management flexibility, this comes with a cost: there is a weight penalty attributable to strengthened floors, access doors, additional onboard equipment necessary for handling freight, and (in combis) fire suppression capabilities. An airline must be confident that it has sufficient freight traffic at adequate yields to justify the higher than necessary DOCs these aircraft will be generating whenever they are only (or, in combis, also) carrying passeng-ers; the by-product costing and marginal-cost pricing of freight are (or at least should be) out of the question.

Conclusion

The aircraft available for assignment within a network have a profound effect on profitability because the seat-mile and aircraft-mile costs, as well as the marketing implications, of types in different size categories vary considerably. What airlines with more than one type or variant in their fleet need to be doing is matching aircraft to flight-legs with a view not to optimising individual flight assignments, but to maximising network profitability. Tactical fleet management is a key ingredient of cost-conscious, market-oriented capacity management.

iii. Maintenance of asset value

Maintaining the secondary market value of aircraft is an important element of fleet management, whether they are leased or owned. If they are leased, lessors will in most cases insist on strictly defined maintenance, insurance, and return conditions and will have a right to inspect the aircraft and their documentation at specified times; if they are owned, the airline has an interest in monitoring their value to maximise proceeds from eventual sale (including sale-and-leaseback).

There are two elements to the maintenance of aircraft value.

1. **Maintenance, repair, and overhaul** Aircraft are maintained according to a maintenance programme established by the airline under the guidance of OEM recommendations, modified by the airline's operational circumstances and experience, and approved by airworthiness authorities in the country of registration. Beyond the requirements of the maintenance programme, actions will also be taken in response to airworthiness directives (ADs) issued by airworthiness authorities, mandatory service bulletins (SBs) issued by OEMs, and perhaps also discretionary SBs. Two aircraft that are both in compliance with their respective maintenance requirements might have very different maintenance conditions as a result of: programme design; the assiduousness with which work has been completed; the extent to which ADs and mandatory SBs allowing time for termination have in fact been terminated; whether optional SBs have been actioned; and whether attention is paid to non-safety-critical and cosmetic work or there is a culture of inattention or deferral.
2. **Insurance** In the present context we can ignore the otherwise critical area of liability insurance and highlight two types of coverage vital to the maintenance of an airline's investment in its fleet.

- *Hull insurance* This protects the insured airline (or lessor) against loss or damage to the airframe, engines (excluding mechanical breakdown), and spares, up to the limits of the policy. Hull policies can be placed on the basis of: insured value – essentially the market value of the aircraft at the time of loss; agreed value – a schedule of figures agreed at the inception of the policy tied not to market value, but to the amounts outstanding from time to time on loans secured on the aircraft; or casualty value/stipulated loss value – a figure in excess of the aircraft's acquisition cost that its operating lessor owner might insist on to take into account the interruption of lease payments attributable to total loss of the aircraft (Margo and Houghton, 1999).

- *War and allied perils insurance* This covers losses attributable to acts of war, terrorism, hijacking, civil commotion, sabotage, and similar defined events that are excluded from hull and liability policies. As was vividly illustrated in both 1990 and 2001, these policies have traditionally been amendable (e.g., with regard to geographical coverage) or cancellable by insurers at very short notice. (At the time of writing it seems unlikely that the commercial insurance industry will in the foreseeable future be prepared to resume provision of full war risk cover on the same basis as applied before 9/11; various industry mutual arrangements have been launched, with governments in some cases providing last-resort cover.)

iv. Aircraft trading

An important part of the fleet management process is to keep analysing and questioning fleet structure.

- Are any aircraft in the current fleet surplus to requirements? If so, should they be sold or returned to lessors, leased or sub-leased out or traded-in against purchases? If not, do secondary market prices – and the airline's balance sheet ratios (e.g., financial leverage), cash and tax positions, and/or credit rating – make sale-and-leasebacks advisable?
- Are additional aircraft needed and, if so, what should be their mission capabilities? Should they be new or is there merit in buying in the secondary market?
- Should the fleet be restructured, but without increasing the number of either seats or units above those offered by the current fleet?

Aircraft trading is a technically complex area into which we will not delve deeply. The important point is that large airlines in particular need to keep the size and composition of their fleets under constant review in the context of current and projected commercial requirements, the current availability and prices of new and used aircraft, the operating costs associated with alternative types, and the market values of owned aircraft relative to their book values on the balance sheet. An airline might, for example, decide to lock-in the market value of an aircraft currently in high demand, and perhaps also take a profit if this exceeds the book value to which the aircraft has been depreciated on the carrier's balance sheet, by selling it in the secondary market; if the unit is not yet surplus to requirements, a sale-and-leaseback might be negotiated.

The argument is now often heard that competencies required to operate aircraft in revenue service are not the same as those required to own and manage them, and that it is in the airlines' interest to change the industry's business model. Strands of this argument can be seen in the increasing share of the global fleet owned by operating lessors (just under 30 per cent and rising), as well as in the growing propensity of carriers to outsource maintenance, inventory management, and other aircraft-related services. The industry is nonetheless still a long way from the vision put forward by some observers of 'one-stop-shop' asset management specialists which own and manage aircraft and spares – perhaps rotating them between carriers in response to even short-term fluctuations in demand. The aftermath of 9/11 did, however, underline something that has been evident since the early 1990s: considered across an entire economic cycle, asset managers with well-diversified portfolios of aircraft and airline risk frequently offer more acceptable credit profiles to financial markets than individual airlines are able to offer by themselves.

Other than in the depths of an industry recession, there is usually an active secondary market in aircraft being bought and sold and leased-in and -out by airlines. The final subsection of the chapter reviews the topic of aircraft appraisal.

Aircraft appraisal

There are two fundamental sets of distinctions that need to be drawn.

1. **Type of appraisal** We can distinguish between the following.
   - *Desktop appraisal* The appraiser relies on information supplied rather than on a physical inspection of the aircraft, and estimates either a current value or a future value. A current value may ass-

ume 'half-life' (i.e., the airframe is half-way between major checks (e.g., D-checks) and its engines are in average condition given stated hours and cycles), or it may be 'full maintenance' (i.e., reflect known deviations from half-life assumptions).

- *Physical inspection* A 'full appraisal' requires physical inspection and a detailed report on the aircraft concerned.

2. **Purpose of appraisal** Appraisals can be conducted for any one of several reasons, and appraised value of the same aircraft can be different depending upon the appraisal purpose. The most common type is a 'fair market value appraisal', which reflects a willing seller/willing buyer transaction under current market conditions. This figure might differ from an appraisal for insurance purposes and neither would it necessarily reflect the aircraft's value-in-use to a particular airline – the latter being dependent upon the carrier's ability to generate a positive net cash flow from the aircraft.

Other commonly encountered valuation bases are lease-encumbered value, distress value, and future base value. The lease-encumbered (or 'securitised') value of an aircraft should be higher than the value without a lease attached, although this will depend upon the creditworthiness of the lessee and the remaining tenor of the lease (particularly the remaining non-cancellable period); value will be driven by the NPV of future lease rentals and the projected end-of-lease RV of the aircraft. Distress value might be below current market value because there is a market perception that the sale is taking place under abnormal circumstances – such as the pressure or threat of bankruptcy, for example. An aircraft's 'base value' – its intrinsic value in revenue service, around which market value will fluctuate subject to short-term pressures – can be projected (usually as a relatively stable curve) from the present time to the end of its useful economic life, and future base value is represented by a point on that curve at some future time as estimated from the present; as an aircraft reaches the end of its life the value of installed engines becomes increasingly dominant in base value estimations, and ultimately it will be worth more for parting-out – particularly if a popular, widely operated type – than in service.

The fair market value of an aircraft arrived at after a full appraisal will reflect a wide range of variables: prevailing market conditions; type-specific considerations; and aircraft-specific considerations.

Prevailing market conditions

The fair market value of any aircraft will be heavily influenced by current economic and industry conditions, near-term traffic projections, airline profits and cash flows, and supply and demand conditions in the used aircraft market generally.

Type-specific considerations

There are a number of considerations that might affect the value of a type, with 'type' here meaning airframe/engine combination.

1. The ubiquity of the type is important. Some have had relatively little market acceptance (e.g., the MD-11 in passenger configuration). Where acceptance is not an issue, types operated by a large number of carriers spread over a broad geographic range tend to be more 'liquid' in the secondary market than types operated by a small number of carriers; the reason is that there are so many potential acquirers or lessees operating across such a diversified spread of regions that one or more of these regions should be performing relatively well economically at any given time. (Fair market value is in fact a 'global figure' which takes no account of regional differences in earnings capability at a particular time.) The number and geographical distribution of airlines operating each airframe-engine combination can often be more important than the absolute numbers of each combination produced. Generally, narrow-bodies are more easily remarketed than widebodies.

    Even when an airframe is ubiquitous, however, idiosyncratic engine choices can undercut values. The classic example was the Pratt and Whitney-powered DC-10-40, and a more current example is the Rolls Royce-powered B767.
2. Where alternative engines exist for a given airframe, one might be more appealing than its competitor(s) for technical reasons. Technical characteristics that distinguish one engine from another could include thrust (which affects MTOW), specific fuel consumption, life-cycle maintenance costs, spares pricing, noise, or emissions.
3. Certain types might be affected by regulatory requirements or the threat of future regulatory requirements – in respect of noise, emissions, or mandatory maintenance work – that can reduce their value.
4. High gross weight versions of a type can often command higher prices to reflect their broader range of mission capabilities. However, to be able to justify the higher purchase and operating costs of a heavier

model, an airline needs to operate stage-lengths that require its better payload-range capabilities.

An important input into any appraisal that combines the effects of prevailing market conditions with type-specific considerations is information available in respect of recent secondary market transactions involving the type.

Aircraft-specific considerations

This is obviously a very complex and technical area. Broadly, the following aspects specific to the individual aircraft being appraised are important.

1. **Age** The younger an aircraft is, the longer it has ahead of it as a value-generating asset. However, the year-of-build factor needs to be adjusted to reflect whether the particular unit is above or below industry average for its age in terms of hours and cycles flown. Generally, aircraft can be expected to lose around 50 per cent of their initial sticker price over the first 8-10 years in service; after that, value stabilises over the next 10–15 years.
2. **Line number** A slightly different consideration, but one still related to age, is the point in a type's production run at which the aircraft concerned was built. Later models often benefit from improvements driven by the early in-service experience of their predecessors, from weight-savings as design margins are reduced on the back of accumulated operational and manufacturing experience, and from engine refinements.
3. **Maintenance condition** In most cases, aircraft that have been well-maintained will be worth more than similar units with a less impressive maintenance background; the weaker the market, the more true this is likely to be because there will be fewer purchasers willing to accept either the known fact or the risk of high maintenance expenditures. The extent of compliance with ADs and SBs will also be an issue, as might be the recency of the last heavy check and the compatibility of the maintenance programme with programmes of prospective purchasers.
4. **Documentation** It is not sufficient that maintenance condition is good. It is just as important that the requisite documentation is in place (ideally in English) to prove the fact and to allow the origins of components to be traced.
5. **Cabin configuration, options, and BFE** Idiosyncratic decisions in these areas might affect appraised value insofar as prospective purchasers may not be prepared to pay for options or BFE they do not want, or

might make a downward price adjustment to accommodate the cost of reconfiguring the cabin.

6. **Appearance** If only because the external and internal appearance of an aircraft can serve as a proxy to help evaluate the care with which it has been maintained, presentation can have an impact on appraised value. In the worst cases, poor appearance that might have no effect on airworthiness could require meaningful expenditures that a purchaser will net out of the price it is willing to pay for the aircraft.

7. **Scope for conversion** We have already noted that as aircraft age, their declining capital cost might make them candidates for conversion from passenger to cargo use – provided the type is suitable for conversion and the OEM or some third party has obtained a supplemental type certificate (STC) for a conversion programme. The existence of a technically successful conversion programme for the type and demand from integrated carriers and other cargo airlines can help underpin the value of individual aircraft once they cross the 12–15 year age threshold.

Aircraft appraisal is a highly technical business, but it is also an art. There is never one figure that represents *the* value of a particular aircraft.

v. Summary

This chapter has recognised four elements to fleet management: aircraft acquisition and financing; tactical fleet management; maintenance of asset value; and trading. It has shown how fleet management meshes tightly with network design and scheduling. The next chapter will look at the final aspect of capacity management being covered in this part of the book: revenue management.

9 Revenue Management

Managing is like holding a dove in your hand. Squeeze too tight, you'll kill it.
Open your hand too much, you let it go.
Tommy Lasorda

Chapter overview

This chapter will:

- define and identify the objectives of revenue management;
- outline the circumstances that favour deployment of a revenue management system (RMS);
- describe the essential differences between leg- and segment-based revenue management on the one hand and origin and destination (O & D) itinerary management on the other;
- identify the critical components of an RMS; and
- highlight differences between the revenue management of passenger and freight traffic.

i. Revenue management defined

We saw in Part 2 of the book that an airline's operating performance is the result not of one factor alone, but of a complex series of interactions between output decisions (ASMs and ATMs produced), the cost arising from those decisions (unit costs per ASM or ATM), the volume of output that is actually sold (RPMs and RTMs), and the yield earned from output sold (i.e., revenue per RPM or RTM). The fact that the fixed costs involved in operating a schedule – largely capacity-driven rather than traffic-driven – represent such a high proportion of total costs defines the core revenue management task: having scheduled a given level of output on each flight-

521

leg, accepted the fixed costs associated with producing that output over a specific period of future time, and – however temporarily – settled on tariff structures for the one or more markets served by each flight-leg, the challenge is to maximise revenue earned from the output produced. (The fact that output is delivered by *flight-legs* whilst prices and revenue relate to *markets* is an anomaly that will be looked at later in the chapter when O & D revenue management is discussed.)

1. The first step towards tapping into demand is for the pricing department to create a fare structure in each market consistent with the airline's market positioning – that is, consistent with the targeted traffic mix – and responsive to the characteristics of demand in that market with regard to willingness to pay (i.e., price-elasticity) and willingness to pay for space on a particular departure (i.e., time-preference). Some airlines have large numbers of 'fare bases' in each market they serve whilst others, notably low-fare carriers, limit themselves to just a handful of fares defined by reference to the advance booking period required and perhaps also by whether travel is peak or off-peak.

2. The second, and in practice closely related, step (at least as far as the current generation of RMSs is concerned) is for the revenue management department to assign fare bases into a smaller number of booking classes (or 'fare classes'), allocate the seat inventory on future departures amongst those classes, and then to manage that inventory until departure. The object is to sell 'the right inventory unit to the right type of customer, at the right time, and for the right price' (Kimes, 1997: 3). Put another way, the purpose of *seat inventory control* is to arrive at a revenue-maximising solution to the problem that by accepting too many low-yield reservation requests on high-demand flights an airline may sacrifice later-booking higher-yield sales, yet by rejecting too many low-yield requests it is possible that seats will be left unfilled at departure (Belobaba, 1987). In the largest airlines, seat inventory control requires the management of millions of seats over periods of up to and beyond 300 days into the future. This is the process we will be looking at in the present chapter.

Before going on, we need to revisit a definitional distinction drawn earlier in the book.

- Some observers use the term 'revenue management' to encompass both of the two steps described above, and refer to the second step as 'yield management' (Smith et al, 2001).

- Others use the term 'revenue management' to describe just the second process (in preference to the older term 'yield management'), and keep it distinct from pricing (McGill and Van Ryzin, 1999). This is the approach adopted here.

However defined, pricing and seat inventory control are often now much more closely integrated than in the past – some airlines even integrating them fully. No longer is pricing just accepted as a given which precedes and stands separately from seat inventory control. Figure 9.1 illustrates how revenue management and pricing relate to each other within the context of revenue and profit planning.

Figure 9.2 illustrates the relationship between fare basis, booking class, and cabin.

- **Fare bases** These are tariffs which combine a price and, in the case of discounted fares, a set of purchase and/or usage conditions (such as advance purchase and refund restrictions). They each represent an offer being made at a particular time to different segments of demand in the market concerned, with segments defined by cabin preference, price-sensitivity, time-preference, and willingness or ability to accept various conditions. The purpose of conditions is to act as a 'fence', preventing the diversion of potentially high-yield customers towards lower fares. Fare bases are the building blocks of the fare structure in a city-pair market, and each 'fare + restrictions' combination can be characterised as a 'fare product'.
- **Booking (or fare) classes** Each fare basis is grouped into one of a smaller number of booking classes in order to simplify the management of seat inventories within CRSs. The fare bases in each booking class should have broadly similar values and booking restrictions; ideally, the variances between fare-bases within each booking class should be minimised and the differences between booking classes should be maximised. It is the job of the revenue management department to allocate available capacity between booking classes with a view to maximising revenue. The fare ranges established for each booking class will differ, and should be set so that the classes are reasonably evenly loaded in terms of allocated seats – although demand conditions on a given route often make this infeasible. Table 9.1 provides a hypothetical illustration of a possible outcome once fare bases have been incorporated into booking classes.
- **Cabins** The physical capacity of each cabin onboard a departure is fixed (other than on certain intra-European flights with movable curtains or partitions separating business and economy classes). In an

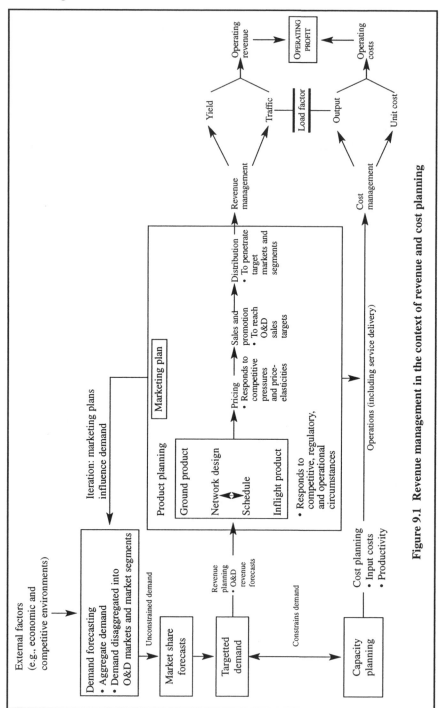

Figure 9.1 Revenue management in the context of revenue and cost planning

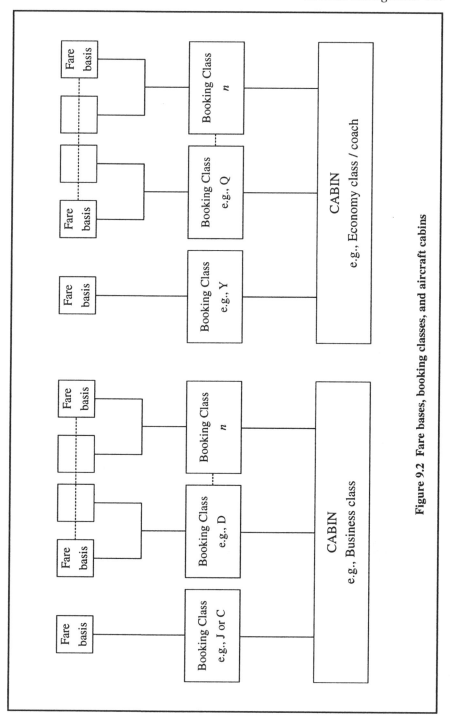

Figure 9.2 Fare bases, booking classes, and aircraft cabins

Booking class:	Empty seats	X	G	L	V	H	B	Y	J
Ticket price range	-	0	$100-199	$200-399	$400-599	$600-799	$800-999	$1,000-1,999	$2,000+
Average fare	-	0	$162.45	$324.90	$541.20	$758.10	$974.70	$1,624.50	$2,707.50
Passengers	8 empty	19	34	23	23	49	23	15	18
Load factor	4%	9%	16%	11%	11%	23%	11%	7%	8%
Revenue	-	0	$5,523	$7,473	$12,448	$37,147	$22,418	$24,368	$48,735
Average advance purchase (days)	-	-	65	46	35	32	26	14	12

Table 9.1 Typical booking data
Source: Boeing (figures are hypothetical).

allocation-based RMS, the seats available in each cabin are allocated to a booking class relevant to that cabin and then sold on whatever fare basis an eligible customer requests.

Revenue management is the practice of controlling the availability of seats for sale at different fares and subject to different conditions, with a view to maximising revenue. What airlines really want to maximise is profit or shareholder value, but because their short-run capacity costs are fixed and the variable (traffic) costs associated with each additional passenger are relatively small we can take revenue maximisation as a good short-run proxy for profit maximisation (or, indeed, for the maximisation of contribution – a concept discussed in chapter 5).

Revenue management objectives

The objective of passenger revenue management is to maximise the revenue earned from each departure given the constraints imposed by cabin capacity and the applicable fare structure. This implies maximisation of revenue per ASM or ATM *produced*, rather than maximisation of yield (i.e., revenue per RPM or RTM, which in effect means per ASM or ATM *sold*); neither is maximisation of load factor in itself the objective – although it might in fact be a by-product of effective revenue management.

- **Yield maximisation** The goal of RMSs is to maximise the revenue earned from each seat flown and therefore from each flight. To achieve this it is necessary to sell as many seats as possible and at the same time maximise the yield from each seat sold; this is not the same as maximising the yield from a flight (or, indeed, from an entire system). Assume for example that a carrier has two seats remaining on a 3,000-mile flight just about to depart, one in business class for sale at $1,000 and one deeply discounted at $300. Yield from the former would be 33.3 cents per RPM (i.e., $1,000/(1 passenger x 3,000 miles)), whilst the yield from the latter would be ten cents. Assuming that average yield from passengers already booked for the flight is less than 33.3 cents but above ten cents per RPM, acceptance of the business class passenger would increase yield from the flight; clearly, accepting the passenger paying a deeply discounted fare would reduce average yield (even though it would increase revenue from the flight as a whole). A (flight) yield maximisation objective would therefore suggest denying space to the extra coach/economy passenger even though the seat would then fly empty and the airline would forgo $300 revenue –

something that is obviously unsound. The objective should be to maximise yield not by departure, but in the sense that every seat actually
sold is sold for the highest yield that can be earned from it; if that yield
is only a few cents, then this is better than having the seat fly empty
even if these few cents have the effect of lowering average yield for the
flight as a whole. The important point to remember is that airlines bank
revenue, not yield.

- **Load factor maximisation** Maximisation of revenue and maximisation
  of load factor may well amount to the same thing on a low-demand
  flight; on a high-demand flight, however, high load factor is a given
  and the challenge becomes one of ensuring that space is released to the
  highest-yield demand that is 'bidding' for it. Maximising load factor is
  therefore an objective of revenue management systems, but not in isolation. Load factors can generally be maximised by selling inventory
  early in a flight's booking cycle at rock-bottom prices, but this will not
  maximise the revenue that flight could earn; what an RMS tries to achieve is to ensure that each seat is occupied by a passenger willing to
  pay as much as or more than anybody else in order to occupy it. We
  will be returning to this point in the next section of the chapter.

The fundamental objective of a revenue management system is therefore
not to maximise yield or load factor, although an airline will certainly want
to monitor yield in the context of its product positioning and desired traffic
mix and to maximise load factor in order to minimise 'spoilage' of unsold
seats for which there is demand. (Recall that if seats are unsold because
there is insufficient demand we refer to 'excess output', whereas if they are
unsold despite there being demand for them we refer to 'spoilage'. Spoilage
can arise, for example, when booking limits for a discounted class are set
too low – providing higher-yield classes with more protection than they
need given the demand that actually comes forward, and so closing out the
discounted booking class too early.) The primary objective of revenue management is to maximise unit revenue from a given schedule – that is, to
maximise revenue per ASM or ATM produced (i.e., RASM or RATM).
This is done by balancing average price and capacity utilisation (Weatherford and Bodily, 1992). On a low-demand flight it can be achieved by maximising load factor; on a high-demand flight it can be achieved only by
ensuring as far as possible that space is released to the highest-yield dem-
and coming forward – that is, by ensuring that each seat is sold to the
person willing to pay most to sit in it.

Conditions appropriate for revenue management

Revenue management is a useful tool for airlines because it works best under circumstances widely found in the industry (Kimes, 1997; Herrmann et al, 1998).

- **Fixed capacity carrying high fixed costs** In the short run, an airline's capacity is fixed by the potential output of its fleet at full utilisation, and the output it actually produces from this capacity is broadly fixed by published schedules. The high short-run fixed costs associated with a scheduled airline's infrastructure impose pressure to maximise output over which to spread those costs, and to sell that output rather than allow space to fly empty.
- **Perishable output** The inability to inventory output after production means that any seats or cargo space unsold at departure will be lost.
- **Segmentable demand** The demand for airline services can be segmented in many different ways, as we saw in chapter 2, but for revenue management purposes the two most important segmentation variables are willingness to pay (i.e., price-elasticity) and willingness to pay to be on one flight rather than another (i.e., time-preference).
- **Demand peaking** The fact that air transport demand is variable by time of day, day of week, and/or season allows airlines to use price to redirect less time-sensitive/more price-elastic demand to off-peak and other low-demand flights, and to allocate a greater proportion of space on peak or high-demand flights to time-sensitive/price-elastic segments willing to pay the most to travel on those flights.
- **Low marginal production and sales costs and high marginal revenue** We saw in chapter 5 that short-run marginal costs are generally considered to be low in the airline business (although in reality they are not always as low as they might appear). Their low marginal costs and high marginal revenues, together with the ability to segment markets by willingness to pay, provide airlines with the opportunity to offer a tiered pricing structure capable of maximising revenue from price-inelastic segments whilst also stimulating demand from more price-elastic segments.
- **Reservations system** Revenue management only works when output is sold in advance by a reservations system able to discriminate between purchasers.
- **Data availability** The most sophisticated approaches to revenue management require an ability to forecast demand by segment and by departure. This calls for a great deal of historical sales data against which to calibrate forecasting and decision-support models. (The availability

of historical data is not an issue for airlines which open the entire inventory on each flight for sale at a given price, then ratchet-up the price of remaining seats as various date thresholds (such as 21, 14, and 7 days) are passed; some low-fare carriers use this simple time-dependent approach, whilst others do use RMSs to protect inventory for late-booking passengers paying 'walk-up' fares. In 2002, several full-service carriers – including British Airways, for example – also began using a simplified time-dependent pricing model in some of their short-haul markets to improve price transparency and simplify revenue management.)

ii. Approaches to revenue management

The heart of the revenue management problem for any airline is whether to accept or reject a booking request. With thousands of booking requests per second entering every large reservations system, it is not yet possible to assess each on its individual merits in real-time; instead, it is assessed relative to specified 'control limits' that are updated from time to time in the light of emerging experience.

We will look first at the simple base-case example of uniform pricing, and then move on to consider how flight-legs, segments, and increasingly networks are controlled by opening and closing the system to different booking requests.

Uniform pricing

The simplest pricing strategy is to apply a single fare; there is no need for revenue management, because we do not have multiple booking classes amongst which to allocate the available seats. The flaws in this approach were discussed in chapter 3: depending upon the level at which the single price is pitched, some consumers will travel on fares well below the maximum they would have been prepared to pay (and so retain significant amounts of 'consumer surplus' – revenue that is lost to the airline), whilst more price-elastic consumers might be excluded by a price that is higher than they are willing to pay.

Figure 9.3 illustrates uniform pricing under two extreme scenarios. In both cases, area 1 represents revenue lost to consumers who would have been prepared to pay higher fares (i.e., consumer surplus), whilst area 2 represents revenue lost because some potential consumers are unwilling to

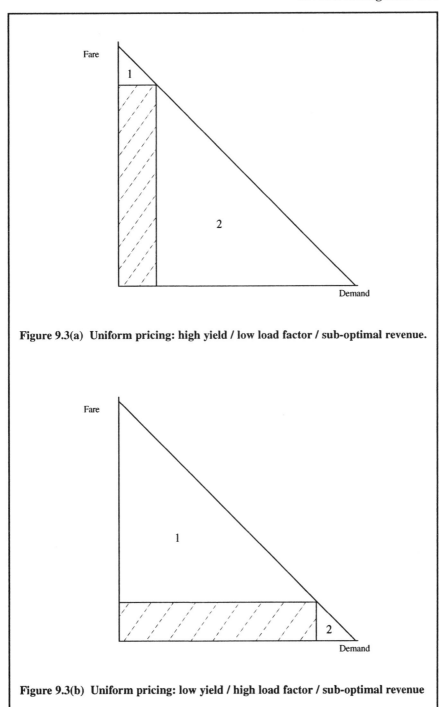

Figure 9.3(a) Uniform pricing: high yield / low load factor / sub-optimal revenue.

Figure 9.3(b) Uniform pricing: low yield / high load factor / sub-optimal revenue

pay the single fare; areas 1 and 2 together represent unaddressed revenue that a revenue management system can tap into.

Revenue-managing a flight-leg: leg-based control

We saw in chapter 3 that to maximise revenue by tapping into the consumer surplus left untouched by uniform pricing, the airline ideally needs to know how much each passenger would be prepared to pay in order to travel. In figure 9.4, we assume that every potential consumer divulges the maximum (or 'reservation') price that he or she is prepared to pay for the service package in question; we are, in effect, thinking of the demand curve as a slope on which each consumer can be lined-up in descending order of reservation price.

Suppose the service package is sold at a single price of $600. Consumers A to D will buy, and will each benefit from a consumer surplus; consumer A will benefit from a surplus of $800 (i.e., $1400–600), B from one of $600, and so on. Consumer E will buy, but will not benefit from any consumer surplus; consumers F and G will not buy, because they do not value the service at $600 – a figure that is above their 'reservation prices'. If the airline were to eat into the consumer surplus (the area above the $600 price line and below the demand curve) by raising price, it would drive E, then D, then C out of the market – losing their revenue despite them being willing to buy *at a price*. Alternatively, by lowering the single price in order to target F and G, the airline will cede consumer surplus (i.e., potential revenue) to the others (and perhaps create an overdemand situation). Obviously, it is preferable for consumer surplus to be accessed by having every potential buyer pay a price as close as possible to their reservation price, and this is illustrated by the vertical boxes in figure 9.4.

Each flight departure offers finite capacity, of course. Assume we are flying only a six-seater so there is insufficient space for all seven of our potential consumers. Further assume that we know each consumer's reservation price and are able to sell to each at these respective prices. Clearly, we do not want to sell space to G until we are reasonably confident that the same space cannot be sold to one of the others at a higher price; if only six including G eventually want to travel, then selling space to G is better than having an empty seat; but selling space to G, then to B, C, D, E, and F only to find that the day before departure A wants to travel but cannot get a seat is sub-optimal from a revenue maximisation standpoint. Revenue management systems should help prevent this happening; specifically, they should protect space for late-booking, high-yield passengers – a capability that translates into the service attribute called 'seat accessibility'. This is evid-

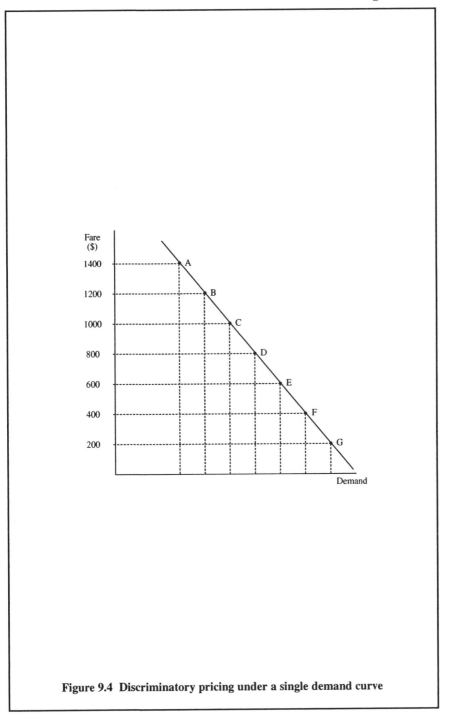

Figure 9.4 Discriminatory pricing under a single demand curve

ently easier to achieve in a larger aircraft than a six-seater, insofar as sales can be made well in advance of departure to a number of low-yield purchasers such as G whilst still protecting seats for those willing to pay more and coming forward at a later time. Seat accessibility is discussed in Box 9.1.

Box 9.1: Seat accessibility

Accessibility is measured by the probability that a seat will be available in the preferred cabin and booking class on a chosen flight at any given point in time when a booking is requested. High accessibility is achieved when a seat can readily be booked close to departure, although what is meant by 'high' and 'close to' is not uniformly defined. Any attempt to penetrate the business segment in a fully competitive market requires good seat accessibility to facilitate late bookings, rescheduling, and rerouting. It is a less important product feature as far as many leisure travellers are concerned, because (other than in the short-break segment) they tend to make their bookings much further in advance; this is one reason why higher load factors can be achieved on predominantly leisure-oriented routes than in business markets.

Airlines protecting seats for late-bookers run a risk that seats they could have sold earlier will become 'spoilage'. High accessibility requires empty seats, and the closer to departure that seats remain empty and available the greater is the likelihood that a flight will leave with unsold space. This is an expensive service attribute, particularly if a high accessibility policy is maintained during peak periods (so possibly worsening off-peak overcapacity). Always assuming that unsold output is not excessive, it can to some extent be considered a cost of doing business. The business being done is the offering of a high-accessibility product to late-booking passengers; in principle, the cost incurred should be absorbed by the higher fares those passengers must pay by virtue of being unable to meet advance booking requirements imposed on lower-priced tickets.

Overbooking can help. Nonetheless, high accessibility tends to be associated with downward pressure on achieved load factors. Looked at another way, movements in average load factor can serve as a useful proxy to evaluate the 'quality of service' on offer; a high average load factor may imply increased 'spillage' of passengers wanting, but unable, to make reservations. In the final analysis, accessibility and load factors will reflect:

- *first, an airline's marketing strategy – the characteristics of the market segments it chooses to serve and how it sets about serving them; and*

- *second, what competitors are themselves doing to offer high accessib-ility to the segments demanding it.*

Taking another simplified example, an airline operating a 170-seat flight could, for the sake of argument, fill it well in advance by offering $125 fares. This would generate up to $21,250 in revenue, but it would also remove seats from the inventory for which later-booking passengers would have been prepared to pay more. If, instead, the airline offers five fares (with varying restrictions attached) such that 15 seats are available at $350, 25 seats at $275, 40 seats at $250, 50 seats at $175, and only 40 seats at $125, then (ignoring any connecting or interline traffic) its potential reven-ue rises to $35,875.

Differential and discriminatory pricing revisited

As a practical matter, an airline cannot know every potential customer's reservation price. What happens therefore is that the pricing department segments the market by willingness to pay, creates a fare basis for each segment, and then ring-fences all but the full, on-demand fare with condit-ions designed to restrict 'revenue dilution' (i.e., high-yield, price-inelastic customers buying lower fares designed to exploit the elasticities of more price-elastic segments). In principle, every fare basis should be designed to exploit the targeted segment's price-elasticity with a view to generating just the amount of demand required to achieve high load factors, maximum rev-enue, and a traffic mix consistent with the carrier's market positioning; in practice, life is rarely as precise as this.

When a market is segmented, the question arises as to whether segments should be served by significantly different service packages. In chapter 3, it was argued that if a service package is designed for a specific segment of demand and priced above other packages, we have *differential pricing* (e.g., long-haul first class); if, on the other hand, essentially the same product is targeted at multiple segments travelling within the same cabin but priced differently for each segment despite production costs being the same we have *discriminatory pricing*. We also saw in chapter 3 that there has been some debate about whether customers travelling in the same cabin on diff-erent tariffs (i.e., combinations of fare and conditions) are the subjects of 'discriminatory' or 'differential' pricing; Box 9.2 examines the distinction.

Box 9.2: What's in a name?

Revenue management involves charging different fares to different passengers in the same cabin. To stop demand within any one cabin gravi-

tating to the lowest-yielding fare available, progressively tougher booking and usage conditions are applied as we move from the unrestricted, on-demand 'full' fare towards the most deeply discounted and heavily restricted fare; these restrictions vary by market, but commonly include one or more of advance booking requirements, minimum and maximum stays, Saturday night stays, stopover and open-jaw restrictions, rebooking and/or cancellation restrictions or charges, bans on interlining and endorsement of the ticket to another carrier, and refund restrictions. (Gale and Holmes (1993) argue that advance purchase requirements are the category of restriction likely to contribute most to profit maximisation; in the downturn of 2001/2002, some European and US full-service carriers in fact began lifting a number of the other conditions that had typically been applied to discounted fares in short-haul markets – notably Saturday night stays – and relying more heavily on advance purchase requirements to limit migration of potentially high-yield business travellers to cheaper fares.)

There is some debate in the literature regarding whether the imposition of different purchase and/or usage conditions for travel within the same cabin represents differential or discriminatory pricing. Whilst there are several technical issues of interest to economists embedded in this debate, it also hinges to some extent on airlines' sensitivity to use of the word 'discriminatory' in respect of their pricing practices; not only does it sound bad, but unjustifiable and arbitrary price discrimination is illegal in several jurisdictions that have well-developed bodies of commercial law.

1. *Pricing differences between cabins*
    *   *Some observers see the quality differentials inherent in different onboard classes as 'relatively minor' (Button and Stough, 2000: 31), and argue that higher production costs in business and first class cabins are to an extent mitigated by economies of scope.*
    *   *An alternative view is that production costs are sufficiently different – particularly on medium- and long-haul services – that pricing distinctions between cabins can be treated as examples of differential pricing, whilst distinctions within cabins are examples of discriminatory pricing. Differential pricing provides price platforms for each cabin (i.e., the full, unrestricted fare), whilst discriminatory pricing is used tactically to manage revenue earned from each individual cabin – particularly, but not exclusively, from the economy/coach cabin – by selling space in the same cabin to different customers at different prices.*
2. *Pricing differences within cabins*
    *   *As just noted, there is a widely held opinion that the practice of charging different fares to passengers travelling in the same cabin*

is an example of 'discriminatory pricing' (Kimes, 1997) – because consumers are being charged different prices for what is essentially the same product with the same production costs.

- *On the other hand, if we look upon ticket conditions which restrict passengers' booking and/or travelling behaviour as 'negative service attributes', it can be argued that an unrestricted full fare (i.e., one in respect of which no restrictions are applied) is a substantially different product from a highly restricted discount fare; significantly, it has 'flexibility' as a product attribute that is unavailable to restricted fare classes. Many academics and practitioners use this argument to categorise within-cabin price segmentation as 'differential pricing' (Belobaba, 1998b).*

  The argument is that fully flexible 'fare products' do not cost 'essentially the same' as low-yield fare products. On a relatively trivial level, processing costs arise in respect of unrestricted fares when there are schedule changes, reroutings, and cancellations that would not be permissible in respect of restricted tickets; handling costs arise from stopovers (which are freely allowed in the case of unrestricted tickets, subject only to the maximum permitted mileage stipulated for the market concerned). These tickets are also more exposed to prorate dilution wherever interlining is allowable. More significantly, some economists argue that the real cost of providing flexibility to make reservations late in the booking cycle and to make short-notice itinerary changes actually arises from two capacity variables: the provision of high seat accessibility (i.e., protecting seats for late-bookers and perhaps therefore achieving lower load factors than might otherwise have been the case); and the provision of a high-frequency schedule to offer wide booking and rebooking options.

Whilst some economists do therefore characterise within-cabin pricing differences as examples of differential pricing, a widespread view nonetheless remains that such differences represent discriminatory pricing. The reason why this matters is that discriminatory pricing assumes a single demand function and demand curve, whilst differential pricing models assume multiple demand functions and demand curves – one for each 'fare product', in fact; optimal capacity and revenue management decisions cannot be made if we are working on incorrect demand curve assumptions. In chapter 2 it was noted that in a dynamic marketplace, demand curves will frequently shift as a result of changes in nonprice determinants of demand. A change in one independent variable that leads to a rightward shift in the demand curve (e.g., a successful advertising campaign, a favourably received inflight product upgrade, an increase in consumers' incomes, a decrease in the prices of complementary products such as destination hotels, or increases in competitors' fares) can enable a carrier to sell higher volumes at the same price or to sell the same volume at a higher average price; in the former case capacity might have to be added (bringing with it incremental costs that need to be considered), whereas the latter case might simply involve reallocating inventory away from low-yield fare classes and expanding allocations for high-yield fare classes. If we reverse any of the examples above and assume a leftward shift in the demand curve, the response might be to downgauge the aircraft used in the market concerned (if this is an option given fleet composition) or reallocate inventory in favour of low-yield fare classes. Clearly, managing or responding to changes in such variables is complicated by uncertainty over how many demand curves we are actually dealing with.

Many revenue management models still assume a single demand curve, along which the quantity demanded varies in response to price. As yet, the debate remains unresolved. On the other hand, Belobaba and Farkas (1999: 220) note that, 'The use of a single demand density to represent total demand for a single departure does not account for the different fare class demands or their corresponding fare values. Yet, it is a fundamental assumption of [yield management] systems that different demand densities exist for each fare class offered.'

The revenue management process

The revenue management process, as it is still widely practised, can be broken down into three elements: allocation of inventory; overbooking; and management of inventory.

Initial allocation of seats Assume that the pricing department has designed a fare structure for, say, the Edinburgh-London Heathrow (LHR) market, grouped the different fares into booking (or fare) classes applicable to each of the different aircraft cabins (i.e., 'base compartments') being offered, and attached conditions to the purchase of anything other than unrestricted, on-demand, 'full' fares in order to prevent revenue dilution. The task of the revenue management department is then to allocate available seats on each departure to the booking classes applicable to that departure. The process of allocating seats to booking classes with a view to maximising revenue is sometimes referred to as 'fare-mix optimisation'; it is based on forecast demand and targeted average fare for each booking class (the latter being a function of the fares included in each booking class and the number of seats sold at each of those fares). Booking limits are established to set a ceiling on the number of bookings that will be accepted in each class, and this 'protects' remaining seats in the cabin for sale in progressively higher-yield booking classes.

Algorithms are used which calculate the revenue consequences of allocating the next seat to a given booking class relative to the alternative of protecting it for the next (higher-yield) booking class, using historical data as a basis for forecasting the probability that a request for a fare in that higher-yield booking class will be received in the time remaining prior to departure. This probability will vary market to market, by season, by day of week, and by departure. (See Belobaba (1989) for an explanation of the logic involved in the context of his widely adopted and modified EMSR (expected marginal seat revenue) model. Broadly, what an EMSR model does is calculate a probability distribution for demand in each booking class and multiply the average fare in that booking class on the flight-leg concerned by the probability that demand will subsequently come forward, thereby arriving at an expected marginal revenue figure for each incremental seat; this figure can then be used to establish 'protection levels' or booking limits. The latter are calculated for each subordinate class by subtracting seats protected in all higher classes from the number of seats remaining physically available in the cabin concerned.) Another statistic of interest here is the probability that the passenger being denied access to the next available seat will be prepared to pay for a higher fare from another booking class in order to travel on the preferred flight (i.e., a 'sell-up').

The allocation process uses dynamic programming, with the objective function being revenue maximisation and constraints being set by the capacity of each cabin and stochastic forecasts of demand for each fare; forecasts (and initial booking limits) are based on historical analysis of traffic carried at different fares (i.e., the disaggregated demand distribution) on this particular departure adjusted for any known circumstances that might impact the forecast, such as a major sporting or cultural event. (Use of the word 'dynamic' to describe programming models means that the solutions they suggest with regard to establishment of booking limits will be amended over time on the basis of evolving demand experience from the opening of the flight through until departure; 'static' models, on the other hand, treat the booking period as a single time interval and establish booking limits only once at the beginning of that period.)

In addition to the booking limits established for the allocation of inventory to booking classes, 'authorisation levels' may be set to control the number of seats released through different distribution channels or in specified geographical regions.

The allocation problem therefore incorporates four sub-problems.

1. **How to ensure that the highest booking class is not sold out ahead of lower-yield booking classes** Reservation requests can follow one of several 'arrival patterns': requests for low fares might arrive before requests for high fares (as when leisure or VFR segments book well in advance), requests might arrive in a sequence corresponding to the booking classes, or – more likely – arrivals could be 'interspersed' (i.e., follow no particular pattern relative to booking classes). This sub-problem is addressed by 'nesting'. There are three generic types: serial (or linear), parallel, and hybrid.

   • *Serial (or linear) nesting* This is the term used to describe a hierarchical structure of booking classes which makes all seats in lower ('subordinate') classes available to each higher (or 'prime') class. Even when a booking class is sold out to its initial allocation, it can (assuming it is not the lowest class) take available seats from a subordinate class (applicable to the same aircraft cabin or 'base compartment') in response to a booking request that would otherwise be denied. The booking limit for a prime class always therefore includes inventory allocated to subordinate classes – the result being that a prime booking class can never be closed when a subordinate class remains open.

   On the other hand, subordinate classes that have sold out can only access availability in a higher class once it has become clear from comparisons of actual against historical booking data that the higher class is unlikely to need all of its initial allocation – a decision that is more likely to be taken, if at all, relatively close to departure. In this way, seats in the higher class(es) are 'protected' by booking limits imposed on subordinate classes. Some systems also impose a 'control limit policy' that places an upper limit on the number of seats that can be sold in each booking class (or group of booking classes) at different points in time prior to departure.

   In periods of strong systemwide demand or in respect of specific high-demand flights, airlines might assume that there is a higher than normal probability of late-booking, full-fare passengers coming forward and so may choose to lengthen the advance-purchase restrictions on the lowest-yield booking classes as well as reducing seat allocations to these classes. Both tactics force low-yield passengers out of the market, onto a lower-demand flight, or into a higher booking class on the requested flight (or perhaps 'spill' them to a competitor that is less yield-sensitive).

   • *Parallel nesting* Each subordinate booking class is nested only into the highest class for the cabin concerned (e.g., Y). Thus, the prime class can draw on the inventory of all subordinate classes, but those subordinate classes are partitioned insofar as they are not nested with each other and none can draw on the inventory of another.

- *Hybrid nesting* This combines features of parallel and serial nesting insofar as there is partitioning of some low-yield booking classes from each other, but nesting of these and intermediate classes into the full-fare booking class – which has access to all subordinate classes.

Serial nesting has clear advantages over parallel and hybrid nesting, although there are occasions when the latter can be useful. Weyer (1998), for example, suggests that they might be used to protect inventory for travel wholesalers or for 'retail' promotions.

Figure 9.5 provides a conceptual illustration of serial, parallel, and hybrid nesting, and table 9.2 uses hypothetical data to show what serial and hybrid nesting imply in terms of the availability of seats in progressively higher booking classes; note that in figure 9.5 the initial allocations incorporate overbooking – a subject we will look at shortly. An interesting question is whether or not demand for fares in one booking class on a given departure is statistically independent of demand for fares in other booking classes. There is a broadly-held view that in fact it is not (Hopperstad, 1994).

2. **Whether to re-open closed booking classes** A booking class might be closed because the seats allocated to it have been sold, or the closure might be time-determined – as when the advance purchase requirements restricting the fare bases in the class can no longer be met. If sales have not developed as forecast and close to departure there is a significant number of unsold seats in the same cabin allocated to booking classes higher than the one that has been closed, one approach would be to re-open the lower-yield class (perhaps relaxing purchase restrictions) and use price to stimulate demand. The problem with this is that if done too frequently as a matter of policy, customers come to expect late-availability of cheap fares; this not only affects booking behaviour, but it could lead to the diversion to discounted fares of some late-booking and potentially high-yield passengers who would travel anyway on the departure concerned (Zhao and Zheng, 2001). (Web sites offering 'last-minute' availability pose a similar problem.)

3. **How to control group bookings** A 'group booking' involves the sale of a significant number of seats for the same itinerary to a group of people travelling together at a rate negotiated by the group organiser with airline staff. (A 'batch booking' or 'multiple booking', on the other hand, involves several passengers travelling together on the same itinerary whose reservation requests arrive at the same time but through normal distribution channels and without any separate negotiation.)

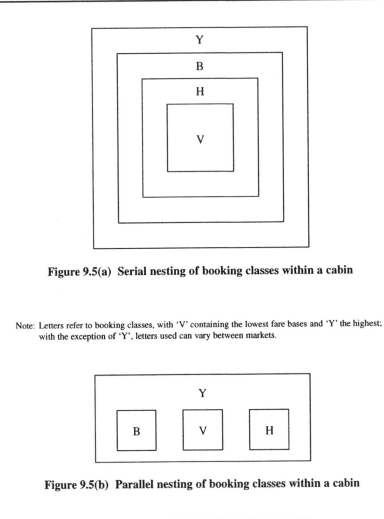

Figure 9.5(a) Serial nesting of booking classes within a cabin

Note: Letters refer to booking classes, with 'V' containing the lowest fare bases and 'Y' the highest; with the exception of 'Y', letters used can vary between markets.

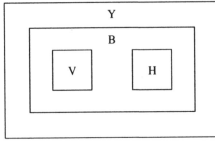

Figure 9.5(b) Parallel nesting of booking classes within a cabin

Figure 9.5(c) Hybrid nesting of booking classes within a cabin

Booking Classes	Forecast demand (constrained)	Serial nesting			Hybrid nesting		
		Initial seat allocation (including overbooking)	Nested booking limits	Seats protected from access by subordinate (but not higher) booking classes	Initial seat allocation (including overbooking)	Nested booking limits	Seats protected from access by subordinate (but not higher) booking classes
Y	21	27	137	27	27	137	27
B	41	45	110	45	45	110	45
H	33	38	65	38	38	38	38
V	25	27	27		27	27	
	120	137			137		

Table 9.2 Nested booking limits for a 120–seat departure

The proportion of a scheduled airline's traffic attributable to groups will be driven to a large extent by its geographical scope – specifically, how significant popular leisure, exhibition, incentive, and conference destinations are within its overall network. Groups usually book early in a flight's booking cycle, generate 'churn' as a result of cancellations and additions to the party, and produce low yields. Fares negotiated by travel agencies, tour operators or other travel organisers with an airline's group sales desk or department will depend upon the booking status of legs on the requested itinerary at the time of booking, the size of the group, number of complimentary seats requested, expected attrition rate for the group concerned, estimated revenue displacement, and the nature of any ongoing business relationship that might exist. Sales departments whose performance and therefore planning are driven by load factors rather than quality of revenue can sometimes be in conflict with revenue managers – particularly when sales targets are established over extended periods of time, making them insensitive to the departure-specific concerns of revenue management. However, the growing trend amongst airlines to reward sales efforts on the basis of revenue rather than volume is helping improve group control. (Yuen (1998) provides insight into how an airline might maximise the revenue potential of groups by redefining the internal processes used to evaluate group requests and by utilising group revenue management software.)

4. **How to deal with misconnections, no-shows, and late cancellations**
A 'misconnection' is a passenger who fails to board a flight because of the cancellation or late arrival of an incoming flight. A 'no-show' is a passenger who fails to board a flight for any reason other than a missed connection, and who does not cancel the reservation. No-shows (and late cancellations) might result from a decision not to travel or from either multiple bookings (i.e., bookings held on more than one flight as a fall-back) or duplicate bookings (perhaps made in error by an agency) that the airline has failed to pick up in its CRS. More sinister sources of no-shows can be: speculative bookings by agencies claiming inventory without having a specific passenger, but wanting to have space on popular departures from the local hub to offer to any late-booking high-value clients; and possibly even abusive bookings by agencies trying to benefit from incentives offered by GDSs in return for high and rising transaction volumes. We met some of these phenomena in chapter 5 when discussing airlines' GDS costs. (There is also a small sub-group of no-shows and late cancellations called 'defections', comprised of passengers with endorsable or refundable tickets who show up for a flight, find it has been delayed, and switch to another carrier; to predict

this type of 'defection' it is necessary to forecast the probability of departure delays.)

One way to improve the quality of bookings (i.e., reduce no-shows) is to impose ticketing time limits (TTLs) – the theory being that ticketed reservations are more likely to result in boarded passengers than unticketed bookings. TTLs also offer the added advantage to new entrants onto a route that they provide some degree of control over no-shows in the absence of historical traffic data on which to base reliable overbooking models. The problem is, of course, that TTLs are difficult to enforce in unrestricted booking classes because even a ticketed passenger will be able to reschedule or obtain a refund. Another problem is that when an agency allows a TTL to expire on a flight that is still open and then rebooks, the airline has to pay additional GDS fees in respect of the rollover.

The fundamental answer to the no-show and late cancellation problems for airlines that do not take non-refundable payments at or shortly after entering a reservation is overallocation and overbooking – that is, to allocate more seats to booking classes in aggregate than are physically available on the aircraft (particularly to booking classes that do not bear heavy rescheduling or cancellation penalties), and sell up to these limits.

Overbooking In 2000, Lufthansa had around 5.5 million no-shows, and overbooking is estimated to have allowed close to a million customers to travel who would otherwise have been denied space. Overbooking to avoid 'spoilage' attributable to misconnections, no-shows, and late cancellations is an essential element in revenue management. They pose related but distinct problems.

- **Misconnections and no-shows** The problem posed by no-shows and misconnections is that their non-arrival is only known so close to departure that unless there are standby passengers waiting to go, seats fly empty. Part of any initial over-allocation of seats (i.e., overbooking limit) might need to be retained on high-demand flights right up to departure to account for no-shows.
- **Late cancellations** Overbookings also accommodate the situation where a flight is sold out ahead of departure, but subsequent cancellations release space which – but for overbooking limits that enable the acceptance of reservations even after cabin (or booking class) capacity has been sold-out – would fly empty. Some RMSs allow cancellations to be put back into inventory, but as departure date approaches and overbooking limits are ratcheted down towards cabin (or booking class)

capacity, cancelled seats are progressively eliminated from inventory – in effect, 'eating into' the overbooked inventory in order to get it down to zero by the time of departure.

Overbooking limits are commonly set by optimisation models designed to minimise two sets of costs.

- **Spoilage costs** If a booking class is closed by the sale of a refundable or rebookable ticket to a passenger who fails to turn up and that seat could have been sold later in the booking cycle, there has been 'spoilage'. Overbooking is a particularly important capacity management tool insofar as booking classes containing fully flexible and refundable fares are concerned, because this is where no-shows are likely to be the highest. The higher the proportion of an airline's fares sold on a non-cancellable, non-refundable basis the lower its no-show rate will be. Ryanair, for example, does not overbook because reservations are paid for in advance and are non-refundable; no-shows – currently running at around ten per cent of reservations – can, however, rebook on payment of a fee. (Note that prices charged by low-fare carriers in some markets are so low that their non-refundability may not be a particularly strong deterrent to no-shows.)

  Another consideration is load factor. The higher the load factor on a flight, the greater is the likelihood that no-shows will have displaced potential customers who tried and were unable to make a reservation. Generally, the lower an airline's break-even load factor, the easier it is to adopt a conservative overbooking policy. Airlines facing low yields and high break-even load factors have an incentive to overbook more aggressively – although, as noted, less so if they place tight restrictions on cancellation and refunds.

- **Denied boarding costs** Depending upon airline policy and the jurisdiction concerned, an airline 'bumping' passengers could incur compensation costs (e.g., cash or vouchers for future flights – although the latter are often heavily conditioned), administration costs arising from rebooking, and perhaps meal and accommodation costs; particularly in high-value, time-sensitive segments of demand, sometimes the most troublesome cost is loss of customer goodwill. The most unpredictable behaviour comes from holders of fully refundable tickets, yet these are likely to be a full-service airline's highest-value customers and the ones it least wants to anger by aggressively overbooking. (Ticketed but un-booked 'go-shows' without a reservation – either because they did not make one or because there was a reservations process failure – are also most likely to be in high-value segments.) Overbooking limits must therefore take particular account of demand variability in high-yield segments, but they cannot be too aggressive if an image-damaging denied boarding problem is to be avoided; caution in this regard may, of course, lead to lower achieved load factors in high-yield booking classes – something that could be argued to represent a product cost and be reflected in the fares that are charged.

A good RMS will disaggregate no-show, go-show, and cancellation patterns and set overbooking limits appropriate to each departure. By doing this it is not only minimising costs (including forgone revenue), but also enhancing seat accessibility because it permits customers to book and travel on flights of their choice which might otherwise have been shown as 'sold-out' at the time reservations were attempted. Overbooking policy nonetheless needs to be carefully monitored. Because limits are based on averages for each departure, there will be many occasions on which the number of no-shows falls below the mean. A denied-boarding problem could develop if overbooking limits are fixed too close to that mean or, over time, a change in the average goes unnoticed. Having said this, some level of denied boarding is inevitable if overbooking limits are being used to their full potential. It is therefore important that compensation packages are designed to be sufficiently attractive to ensure that as many denied boardings as possible are voluntary rather than involuntary; in practice, airlines as a whole have not been particularly good at handling the denied boarding problem, and some have resisted even the very basic compensation requirements mandated in those few jurisdictions – notably the United States and the EU – where they have been imposed.

Management of booking classes Having decided the initial allocation of physical seats to booking classes and the creation of 'virtual seats' by overbooking, the next task in the revenue management process is to manage allocations through to the day of operation. As we have seen, each booking class on a flight is subject to an initial booking limit that allocates to it a proportion of seats in the relevant base compartment (e.g., the coach/economy or business class cabin) and also incorporates an overbooking limit. As seats are sold, a 'booking curve' or 'booking profile' develops – a plot of reservations against time. Various points above and below the booking curve might be set to trigger the automatic opening and closing of booking classes. If actual sales take the booking curve for a class significantly away from the forecast curve, the flight will be flagged for a revenue manager's attention pursuant to whatever 'booking policy' has been established. Some systems compare actual with historical data, calculate final sale probabilities under different sets of pricing assumptions, and flag individual flights for attention if any of the probabilities fall outside a pre-set range. Another approach is to monitor the booking class closing rate – the rate at which low-yield booking classes are being closed to sale. (Older, less automated approaches rely not on automatic flagging but on revenue managers manually checking flights at specified 'read-points' in the booking cycle to verify that bookings are evolving as predicted.)

The original booking (including overbooking) limits might therefore be varied if demand on a particular flight fails to develop according to forecast. As noted above, serial nesting permits seats from subordinate booking classes to be made available when a higher booking class sells more quickly than expected; it ensures that all seats allocated to booking classes below a given class are counted in the inventory available to that class (assuming they are in the same cabin), so that no booking class can ever be sold out ahead of a subordinate class. Conversely, if at some point in time prior to departure it becomes statistically probable that the originally forecast demand in a higher booking class will not materialise, seats from that class might be released into subordinate classes. Where demand is slow to materialise, low-yield booking classes might be expanded. If demand is stronger than expected, low-yield booking classes might be closed at levels below initial allocation and high-yield classes expanded; offers might also be opened on alternative, lightly loaded flights to redirect the more price-elastic segments whilst at the same time minimising spillage to competitors. As departure date approaches, the task becomes more challenging because the demand coming forward is likely to be relatively price-inelastic. If late in the booking cycle either too much space remains even for late-booking, high-yield passengers to fill or too little space remains to accommodate them, a swap to a better-sized aircraft type or variant might be the preferred option if feasible.

At a handful of carriers each flight has a business plan. An important part of this is a sales plan generated by capacity management software capable of analysing multivariate historical data and adjusting for known seasonal influences and specific sports, cultural or other types of event likely to affect demand. Once a business plan has been accepted – probably several months ahead of departure – sales are monitored automatically, with human intervention only required if the booking trend develops abnormally relative to expectations. As the departure date approaches, capacity managers generally play a more active role in releasing seats and accepting or amending the system's reallocation recommendations. Amendments might be based on an intuitive reading of the current competitive environment, or they could arise from pressures exerted by other departments such as sales or scheduling which have their own agendas.

Summary

The core competencies of a full-service carrier's RMS are its ability to block adequate space for high-yield traffic and avoid having airplanes full of people travelling on the deepest discounts, yet at the same time to exploit the price-elasticities of more price-sensitive travellers to stimulate 'fill-up' traffic. This involves 'layering' demand on each flight. The highest prices should be charged to those over whom the airline has market power. This could include, for example, traffic originating in or destined for a dominated hub, and consumers who value schedule convenience and other premium product features. Remaining seats can be released at multiple lower prices in such a way that revenue capture will be maximised given the traffic mix potentially available on the departure concerned. In essence, revenue management is based on cross-segmenting the market in terms of:

- the quality of service being sought;
- segment price-elasticities and time-preferences; and
- the ability and willingness of different customers to accept varying levels of conditionality on their tickets.

To the extent that aircraft are operated with fixed first and/or business class cabins (i.e., partitions are not easily moveable and seating configurations are markedly different from economy/coach class), revenue management must in the short run be applied to each separate cabin. The more floorspace flexibility available, the more flexibly an RMS can operate.

Allocation-based RMSs which control inventory on the basis of individual flight-legs remain in widespread use, and contribute sometimes substantial dollar amounts of revenue enhancement (Smith et al, 1992); revenue gains in excess of five per cent have been cited (Belobaba and Wilson, 1997). However, many do still suffer from an inability to properly control flow traffic in a complex network.

Revenue-managing a flight segment: segment control

The last section looked at revenue-managing a flight-leg, and in the course of that discussion a number of approaches and concepts were introduced that are also relevant to the revenue management of flight segments and hub-based networks – which are covered in this and the following section respectively. The present section considers the revenue management of segments; note that we are talking here about *flight* segments rather than market segments. Travel on a flight segment can be synonymous with travel on a single flight-leg or – more relevant here – it can refer to travel on more than one flight-leg on a route operated under the same flight number as a direct/multi-stop/through service. For example, a London Heathrow (LHR)–Bangkok (BKK)–Sydney (SYD) through-service has three segments and two flight-legs: the LHR–BKK and LHR–SYD segments both flow over the LHR–BKK flight-leg, and the LHR–SYD and BKK–SYD segments flow over the BKK–SYD flight-leg. Broadly, we can say that aircraft operate flight-legs whilst passengers travel on segments; sometimes the two are synonymous, and sometimes they are not. Capacity in a segment-controlled system can be allocated to booking classes on each segment based on forecasted segment traffic, and the booking classes can be nested as under flight-leg control.

Allocation-based RMSs have now in many cases been adapted to accommodate demand from both through- and local traffic on multi-leg flights operated under the same flight number. For example, a 'segment closed indicator' (SCI) in a reservations control system might close a booking class for the LHR–BKK segment, but leave it open for traffic in the LHR–SYD segment. The system in effect arrives at a judgement that given the current booking profile, there is a higher probability of maximising revenue by selling each incremental seat in that booking class to LHR–SYD traffic than to LHR–BKK and BKK–SYD local traffic. What segment control cannot take into account is the value of an LHR–BKK passenger who wants to connect at BKK with a flight on the same carrier to, say, Perth.

There might, on the other hand, be circumstances where it makes sense to allocate a higher proportion of seats to high-yield local traffic than to through- or connecting traffic on a flight-leg that also serves multi-stop and connecting markets. Particularly in short- and medium-haul markets, it may be possible to extract a price 'premium' for nonstop service in the O & D market served by that flight-leg, whereas through- and flow traffic is being offered less valuable service and so cannot sustain a premium.

Clearly, segment control is more complex than revenue-managing a single nonstop flight because decisions have to be taken regarding the probability and value of demand developing in several different markets served by the same flight (e.g., the LHR–BKK, LHR–SYD, and BKK–SYD markets). The challenge becomes more complex still when we move from considering the revenue management of a single flight-leg or a simple multi-stop flight with multiple segments to consider the revenue management of a network of connecting flights.

Revenue-managing a hub-based network: O & D itinerary control

The scope of the challenge

Any flight in a network designed to channel traffic over one or more hubs will be carrying passengers whose different O & D itineraries may have very different revenue implications. For example, if a low-yield booking class on an Edinburgh–LHR flight is sold-out, booking class control would refuse a request for space in that class from a potential connecting passenger wanting to travel from Edinburgh over LHR to Sydney – thereby depriving the network of much more revenue than a local Edinburgh–LHR passenger who may just the moment before have taken the last available seat in that class. (The 'network opportunity cost' of selling a seat to a local passenger who consequently blocks subsequent sales to passengers on longer itineraries is sometimes referred to as 'beyond displacement cost'.) The O & D fare control problem is therefore a matter of how to take into account all possible passenger itineraries at all fares available between every O & D city-pair served by the network. This problem remains too large for current systems to handle, but pursuit of a solution has nonetheless led to the development since the early 1990s of increasingly sophisticated network-oriented RMSs.

We have seen that inventory can be controlled by leg (i.e., flight), by segment (which may cover more than one leg if there is a direct routing as opposed to a nonstop or connecting route), or by passenger itinerary (i.e., with regard to different passengers' origins and destinations across the network as a whole). Leg- and segment-control fail to take account of 'network effects' – the fact that sale of a seat on a single leg might close-off the opportunity to sell any of a number of O & D itineraries across the network that need that seat; this problem has become particularly acute with the growth of hub-and-spoke networks since the early 1980s. On any leg or segment carrying a significant amount of flow traffic connecting from origins behind or to destinations beyond, there are two issues that need to be addressed by an RMS: interline and online connecting traffic.

Interline traffic If our Edinburgh–LHR leg channels traffic onto other carriers, particularly long-haul carriers, the need to prorate the O & D fares paid by connecting passengers (i.e., to share the revenue with the other carrier(s) involved) will mean that the yield earned from these passengers will be lower than the yield that would have been earned by carrying any displaced local traffic in the same booking class. (As noted in chapter 3, this is because fares taper with distance; the fact that the fare per mile drops as the length of a journey increases means that the O & D fare from Edinburgh to Tokyo via LHR will be less than the aggregate of local Edinburgh–LHR and LHR–Tokyo fares booked in the same class.) The revenue situation would be even worse if an interline passenger displaces a potential long-haul *online* connection.

There are two mutually compatible ways to deal with this problem. The first is by negotiating favourable prorate terms – something that will be easier to achieve when the carrier concerned feeds a preponderance of traffic to the other rather than receives feed (and needs the feed received to maintain load factors and/or frequencies); if specially promoted joint fares and/or code-sharing are part of the equation, the dynamics of the negotiation may be very different from the case of a more arms-length relationship. The second approach is to have an RMS able to exercise itinerary (or 'journey') control – that is, accept or reject a booking request on the basis of its revenue implications for the network as a whole.

Online connecting traffic This is where network O & D inventory control really comes into its own for airlines operating networks designed to channel flow traffic over integrated hubs. For example, reconsider the case where we sell the last available seat in the lowest booking class on the Edinburgh–LHR departure to a local passenger and then have to deny space to a passenger who wants to connect at LHR for Sydney but has been 'blocked' from doing so by the local sale. Clearly, it can sometimes be advantageous to hold space back for online connecting traffic: one way of doing this is a technique called 'virtual nesting', which we will look at shortly. But how much space should be allocated? On an aggregate level, the answer is straightforward. We might, for example, establish that on average over, say, six months or a year approximately 30 per cent of Edinburgh–LHR passengers in each booking class on the departure concerned connect over London – so in principle we should protect up to 30 per cent of seats for flow traffic (the exact figure depending upon an assessment of the relative merit from a network revenue perspective of flow traffic in low-yield booking classes against local traffic in high-yield classes). We might also discover that over the same period on average two per cent of passengers on the Edinburgh–LHR flight travel onwards to Sydney.

The problem with these averages, however, is that not only can we have little confidence that on a departure-specific basis 30 per cent of passengers originating in Edinburgh will actually connect, we most certainly cannot argue that on any given departure two per cent will be on their way to Sydney. This latter difficulty is sometimes referred to in the context of a flow network as 'the small numbers problem' – a problem attributable to the impact of random fluctuations on small booking entities, such as Edinburgh–Sydney traffic per flight. Alliances further complicate the small-numbers problem. Whilst British Airways might, for the sake of argument, be able to arrive at a satisfactory formula for predicting Edinburgh–Sydney traffic, it will never be able to predict demand on specific flights for lightly-travelled itineraries such as Edinburgh–Sydney connecting onto Qantas for Broken Hill; the problem is that as global alliances expand and begin to move towards joint inventory management, the revenue attributable to 'rare itineraries' (McGill and Van Ryzin, 1999) is becoming quite substantial in aggregate.

But what should we do if on a particular Edinburgh–LHR flight we have one seat remaining in a booking class that is protected for connecting traffic and a passenger bound for Cairo requests space in that class? Should the request be accepted, or should space be held in case another passenger headed for Sydney (or Tokyo, or LA, or somewhere else that generates more revenue than Cairo) appears? Dealing with this aspect of the small numbers problem is at the cutting edge of revenue management. Broadly, the answer is to plumb historical data to identify the probability that a more revenue-rich passenger will come forward, and in this way develop an 'opportunity cost' figure which must be exceeded by the Cairo fare if that last seat is to be released. This is the heart of bid-price O & D revenue management, which we will look at shortly.

RMS developments

O & D inventory control has been developed in an effort to overcome the weaknesses of leg- and segment controls and maximise revenue from combined local and connecting traffic. O & D systems need to be capable of doing three things in particular (Belobaba, 1998a).

1. Giving preference to higher-revenue connecting traffic, even if that traffic generates lower yields (i.e., revenue per RPM) than local traffic.
2. Denying space to connecting passengers where the revenue they would generate is lower than the aggregate revenue earned from the local passengers on each leg who might otherwise be occupying the seats concerned, and there is a high probability that these seats will ultimately be sold to local passengers.
3. Identifying 'bottleneck' routes on which insufficient capacity leads frequently to the denial of space for behind/beyond itineraries (as well as for local traffic).

The focus of revenue management is moving steadily from leg- and segment-control to journey-/itinerary-control. Particularly as their hubs become more capacity-constrained in the years ahead, many large international airlines will want to have control over passengers' entire itineraries rather than single legs or segments. This is a complex undertaking. Consider an airline that operates just three flight-legs: Omaha–Chicago, Chicago–London, and Chicago–Frankfurt. There are five possible itineraries that need to be considered when releasing space: Omaha–Chicago, Omaha–London, Omaha–Frankfurt, Chicago–London, and Chicago–Frankfurt. Multiply this by perhaps eight booking classes and then set it in the context of a real network the size of, say, American's and the scale of the challenge becomes clear.

Furthermore, we might also want to have control over release of space oriented not just to demand and revenue, but to the source of demand. These and other considerations are discussed in Box 9.3.

Box 9.3: Commercial considerations and revenue management

Booking requests might need to be evaluated not only by reference to their revenue value, but also in the light of wider commercial issues (Yuen and Irrgang, 1998: 322-323).

1. *Sales strategy*
   - *Biases can be established in favour of a particular route – perhaps a new route on which market share is being built. More generally, a region might be targeted for priority by a marketing department wanting to build market share in originating traffic.*
   - *Certain distribution channels might be favoured – an agency with which a relationship is being established or which is already a 'preferred supplier', for example, or a direct channel which avoids commission and GDS costs.*
   - *The lowest-yield booking class(es) in markets with heavy ethnic traffic might be released only to agencies specialising in those market segments to avoid diversion from other segments of demand (Garvett and Michaels, 1998).*
   - *Some carriers use a point-of-sale control technique known as 'hub complex optimisation' to simulate network inventory control using leg- or segment-based data (Narayanan and Yuen, 1998). This involves allocating seats in each booking class into and out of a hub for sale in specific geographical areas. The idea is to try to ensure that demand from high-yield local traffic is not spilled by selling too much space to low-yield flow traffic; this is done by using historical data to impute the nature of itineraries booked in each geographical area of the network (or possibly through specific distribution channels in each area), and then allocating invent-*

ory in such a way that these average booking patterns can be used to generate the desired traffic mix.

2. **Currency issues**
   - *Biases in favour of itineraries requested from points of sale offering prices and/or exchange rates favourable to the airline can be introduced. Because of competitive circumstances, exchange rate differentials, or country-of-origin pricing mechanisms in bilateral ASAs, fares for round-trip journeys between two points could be lower if a journey originates at one point rather than the other, so a carrier might prefer to sell at the higher-fare end.*
   - *Separately, some developing countries insist that outward remittances are held for long periods in central bank queues awaiting foreign exchange, so carriers might want to limit the volume of local currency sales made in such countries.*

3. **Pricing strategy** *Biases in favour of itineraries encompassing markets in which a pricing initiative has been launched can be used to support competitive activity in these markets. (Because the O & D inventory control that we will be discussing shortly is market- rather than leg- or segment-oriented, it is better able to achieve this than leg- or segment-level controls.)*

4. **Revenue quality** *Biases can be introduced in favour of high-value individual and corporate accounts – assuming the airline has a database of high-value customers and estimates of their lifetime value. Forms of bias could include protecting last-seat availability for late-booking high-value customers, or re-opening a booking class to accommodate a high-value customer who might otherwise be spilled – the latter sacrificing short-term economic benefit for long-term goodwill. (For this to happen, seamless connectivity between external booking channels such as GDSs on the one hand and the airline's own CRS on the other is critical: booking requests will have to be referred through to the airline's CRS for real-time approval or denial, because no carrier is likely to let external parties interface directly with its customer database.)*

Summary The requirement for journey control in the context of a hub-and-spoke system raises complex issues. The benefits of releasing space to local traffic to and from the hub have to be weighed against the benefits of selling the same space to passengers with connecting itineraries; furthermore, each different connecting itinerary will have its own specific costs and revenues to be considered. The impact on an airline's profitability will therefore differ depending upon whether it releases a seat to a local passenger travelling only as far as the hub, to a connecting passenger proceeding onwards down a short-haul spoke, or to a passenger connecting onto a long-haul spoke. In addition, sale to a connecting passenger of the last seat from Origin 'O' to the hub and then the last seat from the hub to Destination 'D' might prevent future sale of *two* connecting tickets: from O to the hub and on to any other final destination (the first leg now being full), and from any other origin to the hub and on to D (the second leg now being full).

Leg- and segment-based O & D revenue management

On any flight into a large banked hub it is likely that a significant percentage of the passengers will be local and that, as we saw above, the balance will in many cases be spread so thinly across a wide range of onward connections that there are severe limits on the confidence that can be placed in the probability of demand existing for one particular behind/beyond itinerary on any one particular inbound flight. Compounding this problem is the fact that many airlines continue to store booking data by flight-leg, segment, and booking class, and therefore do not have data organised in such a way that forecasts by itinerary and booking class can be generated. Another problem has been the continuing reliance on booking classes themselves; even had optimal network flow solutions been developed in the past to account for the thousands of different possible itineraries on a large hub-based network, they would still have had to be mapped into a small number of controllable booking classes for space allocation purposes. This situation has been changing (McGill and Van Ryzin, 1999).

The first step on the migratory path of airlines moving from allocation-based RMSs towards network O & D inventory control is a compromise approach. Two techniques have been used to enhance revenue capture by developing the existing leg- and segment-based models rather than moving to pure O & D inventory control: virtual nesting and fare stratification (Belobaba, 1998a).

Virtual nesting This approach to O & D inventory control distinguishes between fares in different markets on the basis of the dollar revenue each generates for the network as a whole. Whilst booking classes can be managed only on a leg- or segment-basis, virtual nesting can capture the network implications of accepting or rejecting a space request. Virtual nesting involves clustering the many different O & D fares available on a single flight-leg or segment into a number of virtual 'buckets' (or 'value classes') based on the revenue value of booking classes. A booking limit is set for each bucket on the flight-leg concerned. Every request for space triggers the indexing of the fare relevant to the O & D itinerary concerned into a bucket determined by the total revenue the journey would generate for the carrier, and a sale is made only if seats from that bucket are available on the flight(s) requested. The buckets are 'virtual' in the sense that they do not correspond to any one booking class; each bucket has many different booking classes from many different possible O & D itineraries mapped into it (Smith et al, 1998).

It is the buckets, which are nested (often serially), that are used to control inventory rather than actual booking classes. The clustering of fares into buckets is accomplished by dynamic programming models designed to minimise revenue variances within buckets and maximise separation between buckets. The outcome could be, for example, that a high-yield local passenger might be in the same revenue class as a connecting passenger travelling on a deeply discounted fare.

Returning to the Edinburgh–LHR example, it is likely that high-yield fares for long-haul connecting itineraries will be indexed into the highest value bucket because of the revenue they generate; high-yield fares for local traffic will most probably go into a lower bucket, but one that may be higher than the bucket(s) containing fares used by low-yield connecting traffic (depending, of course, on the revenue associated with the particular itinerary concerned), and low-yield local traffic will be in one of the lowest buckets. Because the buckets are nested, those supporting itineraries that generate the richest revenues have more inventory available to them in any cabin than the lower priority buckets – which therefore get closed-out more quickly.

These are, of course, generalisations, and the clustering process will depend greatly on the O & D itineraries forecast to be served on the leg concerned, the fare structures in these markets, and the algorithms used. One conclusion we can draw is that although it is an improvement on leg and segment control, virtual nesting will not optimise network revenue (Weatherford and Bodily, 1992); this is because it is still essentially an allocation-based system. At a practical level, there are also difficulties involved in mapping value classes (or 'revenue classes') into existing reservations and distribution systems.

Fare stratification An alternative to virtual nesting designed to overcome the mapping problems associated with that technique is 'fare stratification'. This retains existing booking classes but, instead of incorporating into them only the fares available on a given flight-leg, each will contain fares in any market served by that leg which generate revenue within certain bands. For example, the full unrestricted Edinburgh–LHR fare would no longer be a Y fare but would fall into a lower booking class – a class that would also include other itineraries/fares for travel beyond LHR which generate revenue within the same band. Only high-yield long-haul (economy class) connecting itineraries might appear as Y fares out of Edinburgh. Fares are therefore assigned to booking classes on the basis of their revenue implications for the system as a whole rather than their fare type and yield in the local market, and space is allocated accordingly (Belobaba, 2002).

Conclusion Both virtual nesting and fare stratification provide opportunities to enhance revenues compared to simpler allocation-based methods, but neither taps into the full potential of network revenue. There remain two potential problems: first, allocations to each bucket still have to be predetermined for each flight and so are forecast-driven rather than demand-driven; second, whilst a connecting itinerary can be given priority over a local journey provided it generates sufficient revenue, there is no absolute guarantee that the connecting itinerary will not be given priority over two or more local journeys on the same legs that together would have generated more revenue. (For example, a request for space on the basis of a £400 Edinburgh–Rome fare might be given preference over both a £200 Edinburgh–LHR fare and a £300 LHR–Rome fare simply because £400 is a higher revenue figure than either of the local revenue figures for each of the two flight-legs – even though the aggregate of the local fares exceeds £400.) What is needed is real-time evaluation of the opportunity cost (in terms of network revenue displacement) of accepting particular booking requests at a given time; ideally, each booking request should be evaluated not only in terms of the revenue it brings to the airline, but in terms of revenue net of whatever alternative revenue is lost by displacing passengers that might subsequently have come forward (or 'bid') for the same space. This is a capability that is under evolutionary development.

Leg-based 'bid price' (or opportunity cost) control

What is ideally required in order to optimise network revenue is not just to accept itineraries offering the richest revenue, but those offering the richest revenue net of upline and downline displacement costs – that is, after taking into account future revenue displaced by accepting a requested reservation. One way of achieving this is to establish a 'bid price' for each remaining seat on a flight equivalent to the revenue that seat is expected to generate from future bookings as departure approaches, provided it is not sold now; if the fare for the requested itinerary exceeds the bid price release of space can be authorised, but if not the seat will be held open. A method that has been developed to move revenue management practice in this direction is 'continuous nesting'.

Continuous nesting Continuous nesting (or 'bid price control') is an alternative to traditional allocation-driven leg-based, segment-based, and virtual nesting controls. A request for space on a flight is judged against two criteria (Vinod, 1995).

- **Physical availability** This is determined by the type of aircraft that has been assigned to operate the flight and by the overbooking limits set for each base compartment (i.e., for the first, business, and economy/coach cabins).
- **Financial availability** This is a question of whether the fare being requested exceeds the current 'bid price' for the next seat to be sold in the base compartment concerned. If it does, the booking request will be accepted, but if not it will be denied.

A bid price (also 'hurdle price' or 'displacement cost') is the opportunity cost of demand that might yet come forward but would be displaced by accepting the request in hand. At a somewhat simplistic level, it is possible to generate a 'bid price' by using the spill tables produced by Airbus and Boeing – or by some airlines, based on their own experiences – which estimate the probability of selling another seat given a flight's load factor; this probability can then be applied to an estimate of the highest displaced fare that could have been earned from that marginal seat to create an expected value or opportunity cost figure. In fact, a bid price is a constantly changing figure driven by what historical data and the pattern of demand as it is actually emerging lead an RMS to predict could be earned if the requested seat were held open for longer. Thus, if there is a high probability that a remaining seat will generate more revenue by being held back for a connecting itinerary than being retained for local traffic, this will be reflected in a higher bid price than local traffic would be willing to bear.

Multi-leg itineraries are easily dealt with by summing the current bid prices for each leg to determine the aggregate bid price, which then constitutes the minimum acceptable fare (MAF) for the requested O & D itinerary. Any fares in the market that exceed the current MAF and carry conditions that can be met are open for sale. For example, if the bid prices for a Portland–Cincinnati leg were $200 and for a Cincinnati–Paris CDG leg $350, the current MAF for Portland–CDG would be $550; valid reservation requests for fares in excess of $550 would be accepted. Every sale and cancellation will lead to an increase or decrease in the bid price by an amount determined by the 'bid price gradient' (i.e., the steepness of the booking curve that plots bookings against time) for the flight(s) concerned.

Continuous nesting attempts to establish a *continuous* relationship between the MAF in a cabin on a particular leg and evolving demand across the network, whereas the 'lumpy' nature of traditional allocation-based methods at best approximates this relationship at the various points in time when decisions are taken to open and close different booking classes. Availability is not prestored in booking class allocations (although over-booking allocations do still need to be established for each cabin); financial availability is instead recalculated each time space is requested.

The ultimate objective of continuous nesting and similar initiatives should be to dispense with booking classes and buckets, and to establish a bid price for each marginal seat on every flight-leg equivalent to the opportunity cost to the network as a whole of releasing that seat for sale. Challenges exist, however.

Challenges confronting network bid price O & D control Clearly, applying bid pricing not just to the last seat on a single flight but to seat inventories covering every departure with historically high load factors across a major network is a considerable task. There are, in addition, some specific issues that need to be addressed by bid price O & D systems.

- Group and batch bookings complicate analysis insofar as it seems unlikely that the displacement cost applicable to sale of the first seat in a group or batch will be the same as for the second and subsequent seats.
- Whilst the hardware available is up to the job and software is becoming more capable all the time, relatively few airlines have the data required for building network forecasting models in the right form. The best that many can do with reasonable accuracy is estimate the local traffic that might be displaced by a multi-leg itinerary; the ability to estimate not just the potential displacement of local traffic but also the revenue from alternative connecting traffic that might be displaced across the network by accepting a particular multi-leg itinerary remains elusive. The bid price heuristic described above is being adopted by the still relatively few carriers that have invested in developing itinerary-, rather than just leg- and segment-, based data.
- Another issue concerns connectivity between an airline's CRS and any GDSs used to distribute its services. Airlines manage seat inventory in their CRSs, which may be either inhouse or hosted in a partitioned area of an external system (perhaps another airline's CRS or a GDS). As we have seen, many CRSs are capable of managing inventory only by flight-leg and segment, and so are not geared to implement continuous nesting and O & D itinerary control. Even an airline that has adapted its CRS to accommodate O & D inventory control can have problems implementing it if a significant proportion of bookings come through GDSs or other airlines' CRSs. The reason is that external channels will simply show availability by booking class on each leg and will sell against this availability notwithstanding that the airline's own CRS will be

evaluating each booking request by reference to its economic value rather than simple availability; in other words, an airline might be able to exercise O & D (or itinerary) control over internal bookings received at its own counters, offices, call centres, and web sites but not over booking requests made through external channels. Cases could arise where a booking request made directly to the carrier would be rejected, but the same request would be accepted if channelled through the agency system via a GDS.

The answer is what is sometimes called 'seamless availability' or 'seamless connectivity'. This is the highest level of participation a carrier can negotiate with a GDS, and it requires excellent communications between GDS and CRS (assuming the CRS not to be co-hosted in the GDS concerned, in which case speed of communications should not be an issue). First agreed by several US majors in the mid-1990s, seamless connectivity allows each booking request into a GDS to be relayed instantly to the participating carrier's CRS, which then immediately accepts or rejects it on the basis of value rather than availability (Belobaba, 1998a).

- A final point worth noting is that the rapid growth of code-sharing has further complicated O & D revenue management because an international customer's itinerary is increasingly likely to draw on the seat inventories of two or more alliance partners. One of the most important advantages flowing from the 'immunisation' of international alliances involving US carriers is that their members are protected from antitrust action in respect of output, schedule, and pricing co-ordination. In other words, they are free to create, price, promote, and revenue-manage what amounts to a single seat inventory even though output continues to be produced by the separate partners.

This is a fast-moving field at the cutting edge of airline automation, but a note of realism is required: a majority of the world's airlines have yet to implement anything other than basic RMSs – some, in fact, still have no revenue management capability at all – and carriers primarily serving point-to-point traffic arguably have a limited need for this type of technology. Many low-fare airlines, for example, revenue-manage only flight-legs or (less frequently) segments and do this simply by allocating inventory to a small number of booking classes, each of which represents a single fare basis, selling the cheapest fares first, and then progressively closing each class and moving to a higher-yield booking class as departure date approaches; the closing of classes is both demand- and date-driven insofar as high demand might close a 14-day advance purchase fare further out than 14 days. An even simpler approach sometimes encountered is the management of bookings entirely by reference to date of purchase such that, say, only four fares might be offered depending on whether purchased more than 28 days, 14–27 days, 7–13 days, or fewer than 7 days prior to departure; conditions – in respect of cancellation or rebooking, for example – may be the same irrespective of date of purchase.

Large network airlines carrying significant volumes of connecting traffic and the smaller airlines feeding them are playing in a very different competitive environment, however, and will need to keep pace with developments in the field. At the very least, network carriers should be looking to exert O & D revenue control over flights with high average load factors and heavy connecting traffic.

iii. RMS components

Many large airlines continue to develop RMSs inhouse. There are also several off-the-shelf products targeted at small- and medium-sized carriers, regionals, and cargo airlines; particularly in the case of cargo airlines, some degree of customisation is required to make these systems effective (Herrmann et al, 1998). This section of the chapter will look at three topics: technology, people, and adjuncts to an RMS.

Technology

There are several critical elements in an RMS.

1. A database for each departure comprising historical records of booking build-up curves, cancellations, no-shows, go-shows, achieved load factors, and spilled demand, each disaggregated by booking class and – ideally – itinerary.
2. A capability to track advance bookings up to 12 months ahead of departure, and to break-down an analysis of emerging trends in the same categories listed in point 1 above to facilitate comparison.
3. Decision support software. Smith et al (2001) identify several types of model used in RMSs.
   - *Forecasting models* are used to predict future demand, cancellations, no-shows, and go-shows, and they underpin three types of decision: overbooking; management of seat inventories – specifically, the availability of seats at discounted fares; and itinerary control. Most RMS forecasts are relatively short-term, going out from

the next day into the 120–180-day range; clearly, their accuracy increases as departure date approaches.

In allocation-based systems, the purpose is to guide establishment of (allocation) limits for each booking class, the setting of overbooking limits, and the shifting of inventory between booking classes within each cabin as demand for a particular leg or segment gradually comes forward over time. The more sophisticated stochastic network optimisation models emerging for O & D itinerary control search all possible combinations of fare and market (including nonstop, direct/multi-stop, and online connecting markets) to derive revenue-maximising bid prices for guiding release of space. Competition for seats amongst passengers flowing between multiple origins and destinations on high-demand flights and travelling in multiple fare classes, together with the inherent uncertainties involved in predicting air transport demand generally, call for a stochastic optimisation approach (ibid). It is so difficult to forecast across a complex network demand disaggregated into O & D markets served and booking classes purchased (i.e., the small numbers problem) that probabilities have to be used for modelling rather than more deterministic approaches.

Generally, this component of an RMS is referred to as 'seat inventory control'. It is hampered by continuing constraints on the ability of many airlines to accurately forecast demand at a sufficiently disaggregated level (i.e., market, route, cabin, booking class, and departure); other functional areas are somewhat less sensitive than revenue management to relatively minor forecasting inaccuracies.

- *Overbooking models* are used to set a limit on the aggregate number of reservations that can be accepted (a limit in excess of physical capacity).
- *Fare management models* are used to time the closing of low-yield booking classes in order to protect space for later-booking, higher-yield passengers.
- *Traffic models* are used to determine the optimum mix of local, through-, and connecting traffic to maximise revenue-capture.

4. A CRS to manage availability and record bookings. Particularly for O & D journey control, it is essential that GDSs apply the same inventory control logic as the airline's inhouse CRS and that agencies accessing inventory through GDSs receive true last-seat availability on their displays: any 'itinerary class' where market fare exceeds the 'itinerary' bid price/MAF should show as available. Because in dynamic competitive environments fares change frequently, it is critical that the RMS

has real-time access to the carrier's fares database showing all publish-ed fares currently applicable as well as unpublished net net fares nego-tiated with individual agencies. Current fare details need to be instantly accessible to the carrier's CRS. In respect of published fares filed elect-ronically in industry-standard databases such as ATPCO and SITA, this is generally not an issue; unpublished net net deals negotiated by far-flung sales offices can be more of a problem for international carriers unless the salesforce has access to a fully automated system and fares are relayed instantly back to the head office fares database (Yuen and Irrgang, 1998).

Note that an airline will not want competitors to know via a GDS precisely how many seats it is offering in each booking class. Availab-ility shown in the GDSs is therefore capped at a low level (e.g., seven), even though in reality there might be many more seats available for sale; only when the remaining number of seats drops below seven will the figure change. This is illustrated in table 9.3.

5. A revenue integrity system. An aspect of revenue management that has gained attention in recent years and been the subject of significant software developments, 'revenue integrity' is a question of ensuring as far as possible that the revenue anticipated from accepting a reservation does actually materialise. An important part of this effort involves 'flight firming', which is largely a matter of verifying that bookings are ticketed and paid for, conditions are observed, no-shows are minim-ised, and any booked connecting flights are cancelled as soon as a passenger is confirmed as a no-show at the first point of departure. The purpose is to release for sale seats that would otherwise fly empty.

An interesting question is what to do about partial cancellation of a multi-segment itinerary. In order to maximise revenue from available seats on all the segments requested, a carrier might only confirm space for a booking on the basis that each segment is 'married' to the others as a single set. Where such 'married segment control' is imposed, any subsequent alteration to the booking on one segment might cause the airline to withdraw confirmation on the other segments and require a rebooking of the entire itinerary – something which may or may not at that time be possible, depending upon how demand has developed since the original reservation was made.

6. A performance benchmarking system should be in place, covering at least the following indicators (tracked against same-carrier historical data and – where known – competitors' performances):
   - unsold seats, or the reciprocal of the achieved seat factor, on each route;
   - seat factor against market share;

Booking class	Seat allocation	Add overbooking	Seat inventory	Booking limits	Bookings	CRS: seats available	GDS: seats available
Situation 1: Bookings = 0							
Y	10	2	12	114	0	114	7
B	20	2	22	102	0	102	7
H	30	4	34	80	0	80	7
V	40	6	46	46	0	46	7
	100	14	114			[114]	
Situation 2: V class bookings = 43							
Y			Numbers unchanged		0	71	7
B					0	59	7
H					0	37	7
V					43	3	3
					43	[71]	
Situation 3: V class bookings = 43; H class bookings = 36							
Y			Numbers unchanged		0	35	7
B					0	23	7
H					36	1	1
V					43	1	1
					79	[35]	

Table 9.3 Seat inventory versus seat availability (under serial nesting)
Source: Boeing (2001). (Figures are hypothetical.)

- dilution costs (discount percentage) in each market;
- revenue per ASM (i.e., RASM);
- yield (i.e., revenue per RPM);
- denied boardings (i.e., oversales) per thousand boarded passengers, against industry average;
- revenue share of each market (or route group – such as UK–USA), against output share;
- closing rates of the different booking classes;
- estimated demand spill; and
- accuracy of demand, no-show, and go-show forecasts.

The complexity of any large RMS can be gauged by considering a single allocation-based system managing 200 daily departures, each averaging 160 seats; these 32,000 seats, augmented by overbooking, may be allocated among eight booking classes and each departure might (particularly in medium- and long-haul international markets) be managed for up to a year ahead. In fact, none will be actively managed, beyond making initial allocations, until much closer to departure date – but the scale of the task remains considerable. If we double the number of daily departures and introduce virtual or continuous nesting, the scope of the challenge is magnified. Not all airlines need this amount of analytical power, of course – low-fare carriers operating point-to-point networks being the obvious example. On the other hand, network carriers trying to compete against others with cutting edge RMSs but not possessing this type of management tool themselves risk diluting their revenue by releasing too many discounted seats – possibly with the result that their own late-booking, full-fare passengers will be spilled to airlines better able to control allocation and release of their inventory.

People

A central component of any RMS is a team of revenue managers who have a sound understanding of their markets, as well as up-to-date knowledge of both their airline's marketing objectives and competitors' activities. Critically, these people need the proactive support of a senior management team whose members look upon revenue management as a philosophy – a framework within which to integrate product, network, fleet, marketing, and operational planning – rather than as just a tool.

In addition to experience, sound judgement, and technical skills, revenue managers need to be able to co-operate smoothly with other departments.

Managing the release of inventory across multiple distribution channels is not a simple task, and revenue managers sometimes enter the arena long after decisions critical to flight profitability have been made elsewhere – by sales teams, for example.

The internal organization of a revenue management department might also affect revenues. A department organized by route-group, market, or region can sometimes generate sub-optimal decisions for the network as a whole if units protect inventory to optimise their own revenue or profitability rather than network performance.

Other components in the system

It is not uncommon in large airlines for scheduling, sales (including group sales), pricing, marketing communications, and revenue management functions to operate in a less than fully co-ordinated way. Revenue management should in fact be looked at not as an isolated technical task, but as part of an integrated marketing effort.

1. **Pricing** Pricing and revenue management departments need to co-operate. For example, one possible response to declining load factors on a flight-leg might be to offer promotional fares in one or more of the markets served by that leg; this type of price stimulus can only be effective if adequate space is allocated to the booking class concerned.
2. **Advertising and promotion** When several flights to the same destination are showing similarly unfavourable projections, steps might be taken to promote either or both the flights and the destination. Again, this type of initiative works only if adequate space is allocated to appropriate booking classes.
3. **FFP management** Space allocated for award redemption can be varied in response to forecasted demand on a series of flights. (Redemption conditions and award rates can also be varied either seasonally or as part of limited-period promotions in particular targeted markets.)
4. **Sales activities** There are several types of sales activity that can have a significant impact on revenue management.
   - *Group sales* We have already seen that group sales can complicate the revenue management task.
   - *Corporate deals* When a carrier's sales department does a deal with a corporate client, there are several possible approaches. The most straightforward is a negotiated discount off the full, unrestricted fare for travel in one or more cabins; the discount might be across-the-board, or it might vary from market to market depending upon

load factors and the airline's marketing objectives. Alternatively, a volume-driven rebate might be assessed at the end of a specific period, such as a year. Another approach is to agree to sell low fares to the client – perhaps the lowest available in each market – but waive conditions normally attached to the fare-bases concerned and make space available from higher booking classes if necessary to ensure that the negotiated price advantage is not compromised by restricted availability in the low-yield booking class. Arrangements such as this inevitably complicate revenue management.

- *Agency incentives* Although most carriers are accelerating disintermediation efforts, agency sales remain important in many markets. They are not infrequently encouraged by incentive programmes targeted at individual agents and at their agencies. Commission overrides to reward agencies contributing to achievement of agreed volume, market share, or revenue targets are an expensive, but still widespread, example. Some airlines offer awards to individual agents based on their sales figures. Both agency and individual incentives can be targeted at particular markets, routes, departures, and/or booking classes. These activities need to be co-ordinated with revenue management.

- *Fare reporting* Slow reporting of unpublished net net fares negotiated with travel agencies can hinder revenue managers' inventory allocation efforts.

- *Sales team remuneration* The task of revenue managers can be complicated where sales teams rewarded on the basis of volume respond to declining load factors by taking a more aggressive stance in negotiating off-tariff net net fares, group deals, and corporate rates.

Revenue management should not be seen as a stand-alone function, but should be integrated with pricing, marketing communications, promotional, and sales activities. This is not always the case. Amongst airlines that do in fact pursue integration, many do so on a flight-by-flight basis; a few have in recent years been moving towards a more comprehensive approach to network profit optimisation.

Ultimately, simulation will be widely used to evaluate proposed changes in every element of a marketing programme in terms of consumer acceptance and revenue impact. This will represent a major advance on current 'what if', single-event analyses. Neural networks will be used to make booking request accept/reject decisions not on the basis of forecasts derived from historical booking profiles alone, but on the basis of unfolding knowledge about what customers are willing to pay for a particular service at a particular point in time given product differences and prevailing economic and competitive circumstances at that time. In due course, customer databases will become part of the revenue management system with a view to giving preferential access to high-lifetime-value customers; the beginnings of this approach are already evident in the access some premium-tier FFP members are given to 'fully-booked' flights.

It will not be easy for a full-service network carrier without cutting-edge RMS capabilities to compete effectively in a dynamic, liberalised marketplace against competitors able to pinpoint accurately the precise sources of their revenues and to plug this information into a fully integrated, largely real-time marketing programme – something that remains beyond the grasp of most carriers but is clearly on the horizon.

iv. Conclusion

'Yield management' is a misnomer. Booking classes with different yields are certainly being managed, but the objective of any yield or revenue management system is to maximise revenue – ideally, in the case of full-service network carriers, on a network basis rather than by individual leg or segment. What matters is whether an airline's total revenues exceed its total costs: if costs are well-managed and are below revenues that are being maximised given current capacity constraints, declining yield need not in itself be a problem. Yield and profit are quite capable of moving in opposite directions; indeed, real (i.e., inflation-adjusted) yield has been in secular decline across the industry as a whole for several decades. It is revenue that really matters, and one reason for this is the powerful leverage effect that relatively small amounts of incremental revenue can have on airline profits.

Claims have been made that a good, basic RMS can boost revenues by substantial amounts – a figure of $1 billion per annum having been rumoured in respect of one US major in the late 1990s. Unpublished Boeing figures in respect of an Asian carrier suggest that a 0.2 cent increase in average yield would have added $15.3 million to gross revenue, and an extra $1,500 earned on just half of its departures would have added $16.4 million. The point made by these figures is that RMSs need earn only small increments to have a significant impact on operating profits. Benefits come in particular from yield enhancement derived from protecting space in high-yield booking classes. The beauty of yield enhancement is that much of any increment goes directly to the bottom line (after deduction of any additional agency commission), whereas increases in traffic generate traffic-related costs. Certainly, a lower percentage increase in yields will

have the same impact on profits as much greater increases in sales or decreases in any cost line item.

If an RMS also allows an airline to carry relatively low-yield traffic
which would not have been carried had a simple, uniform fare been charged
in each class and only the most inelastic market segments been targeted,
this traffic will quite probably permit more frequencies to be flown on a
larger network than would otherwise have been the case. Service quality
will therefore be improved for all market segments, but particularly for
high-yielding business travellers who value frequency. If the extra traffic is
sufficiently profitable to justify use of larger aircraft than could have been
supported by the smaller traffic base provided by inelastic segments alone,
the lower seat-mile costs of these aircraft might lead to fare levels lower
than they would otherwise have been – again benefiting consumers.

RMSs can also help impose management discipline. Traffic is tangible
and clearly visible at departure time whereas, in the absence of an RMS,
revenues and yields are known only days or weeks later and profits come to
light even further into the future. This can encourage overattention to
market share and a tendency towards the marginal cost pricing of ever-
perishable seats. An RMS, on the other hand, is interested first in maximising revenues and only secondarily in maximising load factors – and in this
sense imposes discipline on the release of space.

RMSs are important for most airlines and vital for network carriers,
particularly when the competition has them. Nonetheless, they need to be
treated with caution.

1. RMS models are driven by historical data. As soon as something significant changes, such as a massive fare sale by a competitor or the entry
   of an aggressive challenger, past booking profiles may no longer be
   such an accurate guide to future demand. (This problem is being addressed by research into 'passenger choice modelling', which uses causal
   models to enhance simulation capabilities, and by the development of
   'neural nets' capable of learning in response to events.)
2. RMSs do not necessarily eliminate the generic airline industry marginal
   cost pricing dilemma. An RMS can only do so much to counterbalance
   poor product design or delivery and bad scheduling. In particular, if too
   much output is scheduled, RMSs cannot fill it – this is the job of pricing and other marketing functions, pending a review of the schedule.
   These systems are, in fact, most valuable when used to control flights
   that have consistently high load factors. They make money for airlines
   only when demand exceeds supply, and in the Northern Hemisphere
   this is most likely to happen on an aggregate level in the third calendar
   quarter (and possibly either side of Thanksgiving in the US domestic

market and Christmas in a variety of other markets). When supply exceeds demand, what is needed is less capacity and/or a pricing initiative.

3. It is not unknown for overallocation of seats to low-yield booking classes to generate traffic volumes which appear to justify an increase in frequency or gauge (i.e., aircraft size) on a particular route. Insight and discipline are necessary to avoid an interlinked, and possibly unprofitable, upward spiral in output (with its attendant costs) and downward spiral in yield.

4. Some observers argue that RMSs encourage oversegmentation of markets, perhaps even harming yields in the process. Interestingly, it was American Airlines, whose affiliates had been at the cutting edge of RMS technology, which took the lead (unsuccessfully, as it turned out) in trying to simplify the US domestic fare structure in 1992.

5. As noted above, it is possible for an RMS to be undermined by incentive schemes that reward sales personnel on the basis of the volume rather than the profitability of their activity.

6. Large airlines may house scheduling, pricing, and revenue management in different departments, and staff each area with people having different professional backgrounds and time-scale orientations. Conflicts can arise when reactions to evolving patterns of demand are different. For example, high achieved load factors on a particular departure might encourage scheduling to increase output, pricing to eliminate low fares, and revenue management to reduce allocations to low-yield booking classes; together, these reactions could lead to higher operating costs (attributable to increased output) and lower load factors (attributable to a combination of increased output and the impact of higher average fares on demand), but with an uncertain impact on revenue (dependent upon the price-elasticity of demand in the market(s) concerned). We have already seen that there is a need for scheduling, pricing, and revenue management efforts to be closely co-ordinated; in practice, organizational structure and incompatible information systems continue to prevent this at some carriers.

7. To date, Internet seat auctions have largely been used to dispose of distressed inventory. If this changes and carriers start on any significant scale to use auctions as a regular pricing mechanism, the underlying bases on which RMSs work will have to change insofar as real-time knowledge of consumer behaviour and price-elasticities across much smaller segments of demand will become a critical adjunct to the historical records and forecasting models that currently underpin these systems. Revenue management will become an even more dynamic discipline than it already is, and further downward pressure on average yields can be expected (Doganis, 2001).

In the final analysis, any airplane can be filled by offering seats at low enough prices to attract demand and by making their availability widely known. RMSs cannot create demand which is profitable in the long term if people are unwilling to pay the prices necessary to ensure profitability, given the nature of the products being offered and a particular airline's cost base. Revenue maximisation might approximate profit maximisation in the short term, but it is less likely to do so in the long term. In other words, RMSs need to be deployed in a 'long-term context' defined by an acceptable balance between output, traffic, and price. That balance should in turn be set within a strategic context defined by the airline's service concept(s) – the type of value it is offering its customers and the positioning of its service-price offer(s).

v. Managing freight revenues

The objective when revenue-managing freight is the same as the objective when revenue-managing passengers: to maximise the revenue earned from each unit of available output. The revenue relationships are also the same: on the passenger side, revenue is driven by RPMs (i.e., output sold) x yield (i.e., revenue per RPM); on the freight side, revenue is driven by FTMs (i.e., output sold) x yield (i.e., revenue per FTM).

However, the revenue management of freight is a less well-developed science than passenger revenue management. This has been due in part to business strategies strongly oriented towards load factors, but also in part to some very real practical issues:

- the much shorter booking cycles for freight than passengers;
- the multi-dimensional nature of each freight shipment (i.e., volume, weight, urgency, and perhaps also place in a sequential series of shipments), compared to the homogeneity of passenger bookings;
- the fact that cargo space is not as fungible as passenger seat inventories – in respect of particularly heavy shipments needing a specific onboard container or pallet location, for example;
- the application of regulations governing carriage of certain (notably dangerous) goods;
- the widespread use of negotiated rates;
- the fact that precise availability of belly-hold space on a given passenger flight might not be known until very close to departure if the aircraft concerned is operating at the extreme of its payload-range

performance and there is a chance that under certain weather conditions freight might be offloaded to accommodate a full passenger load;

- the fact that whereas on the passenger side low-yield traffic tends to book well in advance, so closing out lower booking classes and forcing later reservations into higher-yield booking classes, excess output of cargo space on many medium- and long-haul routes (primarily in the belly-holds of passenger widebodies) has contributed to the reverse situation where ad hoc late sales are often made at lower-than-contract rates (Herrmann et al, 1998); and

- lack of the same precise inventory management tools that passenger CRSs provide.

A further complicating factor is that there is more scope for service customisation in respect of freight than passenger transportation, in part because there are fewer customers and their specific requirements for value-added services can often be clearly understood in advance of shipment – requirements for special handling of particular types of goods or special facilitation procedures, for example. In those cases where carriers, or carriers and forwarders together, have integrated themselves into the logistics system of a particular customer, individual commercial relationships may be sufficiently important to supersede the more transactional biases of a revenue management system.

Nonetheless, progress is being made in developing more sophisticated freight revenue management tools. For example, considerable work has been done on the use of routing algorithms: requests for space trigger a search of capacities on alternative routes the shipment could take through the particular carrier's network, and controls on the pricing and release of space are established in this context (Rao, 2000). The foundations of progress are the fundamentally similar principles that underlie all forms of revenue management: demand segmentation; forecasting by market segment; capacity allocation; overbooking; and a commitment to maximising revenues rather than load factors on high-demand flights and to optimising revenues across the network rather than by leg, segment, or geographic region.

Ideally, the revenue management of freight and passengers should be integrated by combination carriers to the point that in those relatively few cases where the value of the lowest yielding freight forecast to materialise on a payload-constrained departure exceeds the value of the lowest-yielding passengers it is space for the latter that is closed out. Average freight yields on most routes are, however, consistently lower than passenger yields (per RTM) – so in most cases it will be freight rather than passengers that gets bumped when payload is an issue. That said, introduction of branded, time-definite freight products by a growing number of airlines in recent years requires that carriers serious about their positioning in these market segments have to be careful when prioritising freight for shipment. A few airlines now even give their cargo divisions or subsidiaries sufficient autonomy to buy space on other carriers if this is what it takes to provide reliable service and meet high-yield customers' expectations.

Finally, in the case of some types of aircraft operating certain routes, standby cargo can on occasion be used as a revenue management tool to utilise payload capacity left unused by passengers. Particularly on widebodies, even an achieved 80 or 90 per cent seat factor may leave several thousand pounds of payload potential available for the late loading of standby cargo after passenger close-out.

vi. Conclusion to Part 3 of the book: the importance of 'spill'

Figure 9.6 outlines many of the relationships between different activities that have been discussed in the book. In particular, it isolates the role of the three capacity management tools we have been looking at in Part 3 – network management, fleet management, and revenue management – in the process that runs from design of one or more service concept(s) through to the delivery of differently priced service packages to customers. Of course, this is an idealised view of reality. In practice, it is not uncommon in large airlines for product planning, scheduling, sales (including group and cargo sales), pricing, and revenue management functions to operate in a less than fully co-ordinated way. Efforts to improve the effectiveness of linkages between internal processes can clearly bring significant potential benefits to the revenue side, as well as the cost side, of an airline's income statement. The metric by which to judge improved co-ordination should be revenue contribution (i.e., revenue minus variable DOCs): whereas pricing and revenue management decisions can be evaluated by looking at revenue alone, scheduling decisions have to bear in mind the operating cost implications of assigning different aircraft types to a given route – hence the need to take variable DOCs into account (Jacobs et al, 2001). (Belobaba and Wilson (1997) describe the results of a simulation experiment that clearly illustrates the positive revenue implications of linking revenue management to scheduling decisions.)

Deciding how to make money out of delivering output into available markets is an iterative process that encompasses the following steps.

- Forecasting demand and projecting market share in available city-pair markets.

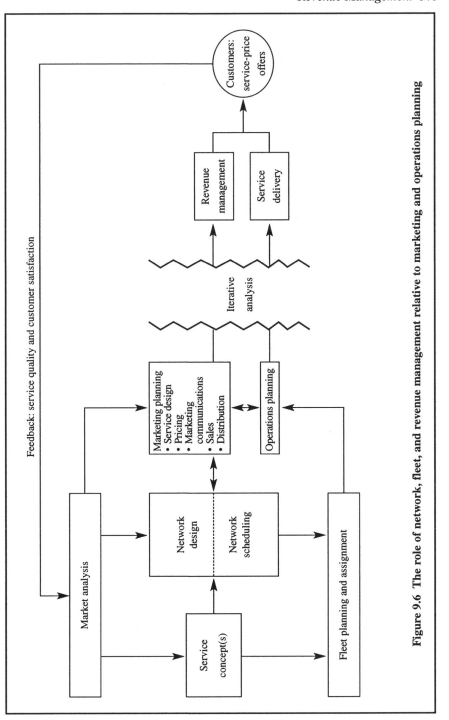

Figure 9.6 The role of network, fleet, and revenue management relative to marketing and operations planning

- Allocating demand to flight-legs and segments according to a first-cut network design and schedule plan.
- Estimating the revenues attributable to each flight-leg given pricing and traffic mix assumptions.
- Assigning optimal aircraft types to each leg, balancing operating costs against revenue and spill to arrive at a profit-maximising outcome. (The models used to achieve this are similar to those used for fleet planning and aircraft routing.)
- Measuring network performance, and in particular ensuring that each decision to add or drop a leg or segment or to change the schedule on retained flights enhances shareholder value. (In fact, relatively few airlines yet have the capability to assess the full network impact of individual route and schedule decisions using real-time demand or cost, including opportunity cost, information.)

The concept that unites pricing, network, fleet, and revenue management and lies at the heart of capacity management is 'spill'. Spill is demand that is unsatisfied because an airline has insufficient space in a given booking class, cabin, or airplane. It is the difference between *unconstrained demand* (i.e., the number of passengers that would book if there were no limits on the capacities of cabins and booking classes) and *constrained demand* (i.e., the number of passengers that actually book). Demand can be spilled from one departure to another within an airline's schedule (referred to as 'recapture'), or it can be spilled to competitors. The latter is evidently of more concern because not only is current cash revenue lost, but goodwill costs (equivalent in the worst case to the NPV of a spilled customer's lifetime value) could be incurred if a customer denied a booking defects permanently to a competitor. The problem is that airlines do not track denied reservation requests once a booking class has been closed; in other words, they can track whether or not a booking limit has been reached but they have no records with which to calculate the 'demand factor', which is the ratio of demand to capacity for a given booking class or flight.

Demand for air travel is generally assumed to have what statisticians refer to as a 'normal distribution'. However, the shape of demand distributions very often varies between cabins. Because demand for space in business and first class cabins comes predominantly from the business segment and this segment generates demand that is more prone to random fluctuations and therefore more difficult to predict on a departure-by-departure basis, its demand distribution (as illustrated in figure 9.7(b)) tends to be relatively flat as a result of a wider dispersion of observations around the mean. Because economy/coach cabins often carry more discretionary travellers whose purchase behaviour is less prone to random fluctuations, demand (assuming a given fare structure) is more heavily clustered around the mean. Generally, less traffic will be spilled if we target a high load factor (i.e., a high 'cabin planning factor') when the demand curve is relatively tightly dispersed around the mean (as in figure 9.7(a)) than when it is more widely dispersed.

(See Clark (2001) for an explanation of how to calculate spill both in general and in particular market segments, and how to use the calculations to assist in determining appropriate aircraft size, cabin configuration, and cabin load factors.)

Accurate estimates of spill and spill costs are important to fleet and network management generally, but are particularly critical to fleet management processes in order to ensure that flights are operated by aircraft with optimal capacities. Belobaba and Farkas (1999) comprehensively explain the linkages between RMSs and spill estimates – linkages that hinge on the impact of overbooking and of booking limits on spill, and on the potential use of RMS booking data to improve spill forecasting. Booking limits affect both the aggregate number of passengers spilled and their fare mix – so driving spill costs: spill models should relate unconstrained demand and aircraft capacity in order to estimate the expected number of spilled passengers, and then calculate spill costs as the product of that number and the average fare of spilled passengers (ibid).

From an economic perspective, spill is inevitable; it is in almost all cases not viable to sustain the costs of meeting unconstrained demand (i.e., all demand coming forward) when it peaks, and then tolerating low load factors (i.e., poor cabin floorspace utilisation) at other times. Instead, a balance needs to be struck between on the one hand revenue forgone from spilled demand, and on the other the cost of underutilised resources. What adds piquancy to this analysis is that the demand most likely to be spilled at certain times (e.g., weekday peaks) comes from late-booking, high-yield travellers; this is why RMSs can be so critical because they are able to protect at least some level of seat accessibility for high-yield market segments.

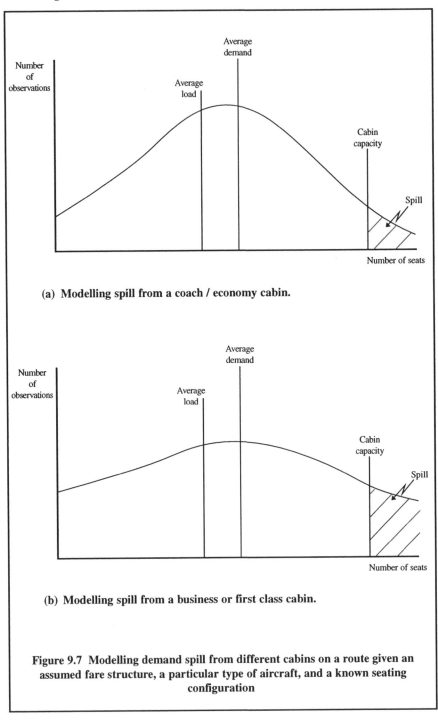

(a) **Modelling spill from a coach / economy cabin.**

(b) **Modelling spill from a business or first class cabin.**

Figure 9.7 Modelling demand spill from different cabins on a route given an assumed fare structure, a particular type of aircraft, and a known seating configuration

Part 4
Operating Performance

High market share is in principle no bad thing, but an important question is how it has been acquired. Specifically, has it been bought or earned? Airlines *buy* market share by pricing at levels which, given their costs, cannot generate and sustain acceptable profits. Conversely, they *earn* market share by making service-price offers (i.e., putting forward value propositions) that are both appealing to customers and rational in the context of their cost bases. For example, since being established in the early 1970s Southwest has grown steadily to the point where it is now a highly significant player in the US domestic market, but it has not bought market share; it has focused instead on keeping costs low enough to enable low fares to be profitably sustained over time, and in doing this has both stimulated and captured demand.

Industry downturns can present a particularly intense challenge to airline managements needing to balance the four elements in the operating performance model around which Part 2 of this book is structured: traffic, yield, output, and unit cost. Whether a cyclical downturn is more strongly reflected in figures for traffic or yield will depend in part upon the pricing decisions airlines choose to take in response to weakening demand. History suggests that in a 'regular' cyclical downturn it is likely that yields will soften as pricing becomes more aggressive in an attempt to maintain traffic, load factors, and market share; when there is a major exogenous shock as in 1990/1991 and 2001, both traffic and yield will suffer and output cuts will be essential.

Whenever significant output cuts are in fact made, they will eventually come up against a gradual recovery in demand. This situation confronts airlines with broadly two options for a return to profitability.

1. Hold output at the new level for as long as possible and then increase it only gradually, let rising demand bump up against constrained output (i.e., let load factors rise), and consolidate yields by reducing the availability of deep discounts.

2.   Respond to returning demand by reinstating output as quickly as possible – with the likely result that traffic will bounce back more rapidly, but yields will take longer to recover.

From an industry-wide perspective, the first option would generally have more merit; from the perspective of individual carriers – particularly carriers giving a high priority to market share – the second option might be tempting. An important attraction in the second option is that providing reinstated output can be sold at prices above marginal cost, the incremental revenue it earns will at least make a contribution to the fixed costs that continue to accrue irrespective of whether or not aircraft are flying. Chapter 10 brings together the principal issues and metrics underlying this type of decision.

10 Strategy, Economics, and Operating Performance

Recession is when you tighten your belt. Depression is when you no longer have a belt to tighten. When you've lost your trousers, you're in the airline business.

Adam Thomson

Chapter overview

The purpose of this chapter is not to list operational performance metrics, but to bring together at a macro-level the economic fundamentals discussed in previous chapters. The opening section will discuss operating performance in general; the main body of the chapter will look at relationships between unit revenue (revenue per ASM or RASM), unit cost (cost per ASM or CASM), yield (revenue per RPM), and load factor (traffic as a percentage of output).

i. Operating performance

Figure 10.1 illustrates a sample of the pressures on airline cost and revenue streams that determine operating performance. At this level of analysis, airlines are not materially different from other businesses: to improve operating performance it is necessary to boost revenue by selling more output and/or earning more from each sale, and to reduce costs by lowering input expenditures, raising productivity, and better matching supply to demand – all the while retaining focus on customers' expectations relative to the value being offered to them. Complicating matters are typical issues such as price-, income-, and cross-price elasticity which influence the profitability of pricing and output decisions. The purpose should be neither to maximise revenue nor minimise costs, but to maximise the surplus of revenue over cost; the precise nature of the relationship between revenues and costs – for

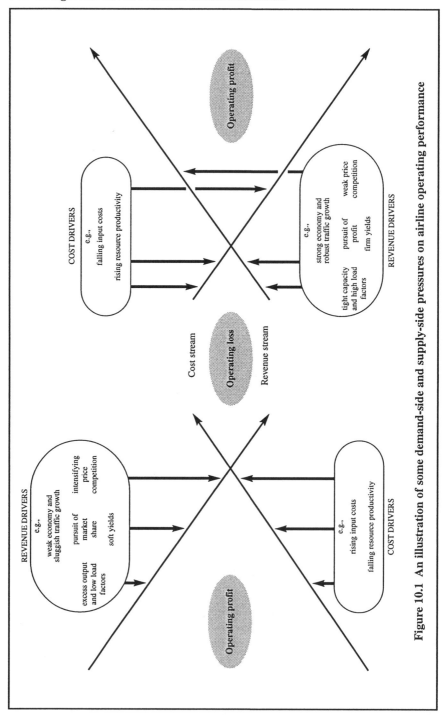

Figure 10.1 An illustration of some demand-side and supply-side pressures on airline operating performance

example, high-yield/high-cost or low-yield/low-cost – will depend to a large extent upon brand positioning and competitive strategy.

If, however, we dig a little deeper the picture becomes more complex. Whereas operating revenue is generated in O & D markets, direct operating costs (DOCs) – which represent a substantial element of most airlines' total operating costs – are generated by individual flight-legs (i.e., by fleet, network design, and scheduling decisions). Total operating costs therefore depend heavily upon how an airline chooses to serve each market – with nonstop, multi-stop or connecting flights, and at high or low frequencies, for example.

Despite the analytical importance of these (and many other) lower level metrics, management decision-making is often now more closely attuned to the needs of the network as a whole. Berdy (2002: 126) puts it as follows.

> Some airlines now focus on integrating the functions of scheduling, pricing, cost control, and yield management in the interests of network profit optimization rather than managing similar parameters on a flight-by-flight basis.
>
> Evaluating networks as a whole always produces system results that are decidedly different from the old technique of summing the results of a series of individual route forecasts. This is especially true if the network model contains logic that evaluates passenger and revenue flow when segments are added or deleted and flows are subsequently diverted to other flights, segments, or competitors. Experiments on routes and schedules are performed in a computer-simulated environment before being tested in the real world. Systems now model the effects of changes simultaneously as part of the schedule development process....[Another] example is the focus on the fleet optimization process. Airlines with multiple fleet types are using sophisticated computer models to make the optimal match between fleet type and individual flights, with the goal of optimizing network profitability rather than route performance.

We can nonetheless make two broad generalisations.

- The profitability of a market will depend in part upon the cost and revenue implications of the type of service offered (i.e., nonstop, direct or connecting). As we have already seen, some markets are served by all three types – each with different costs that are not necessarily reflected in different fares when prices are competitively set.
- The profitability of a flight-leg or a route will depend not only upon the DOCs each generates, but also upon how indirect operating costs (IOCs) are allocated. (For example, IOCs might be allocated by reference to ASMs or ATMs flown on the leg or route as a percentage of network ASMs or ATMs, or by reference to leg or route DOCs as a

percentage of system DOCs.) For network carriers (as opposed to predominantly 'point-to-point' low-fare operators), another issue is how revenues from the various behind/beyond O & D markets each leg or route might serve are internally prorated.

Managers will, of course, want to drill down much further into their cost and revenue streams than this. They will want the capability to make decisions based on profitability or contribution analyses by product, customer type, flight number, hub, country and/or region, distribution channel, and – where relevant – operator (i.e., mainline, affiliate, or code-share partner) – as well as by flight-leg, route, and O & D market. As noted, these lower-level metrics will inevitably be affected by the choice and consistency in usage of internal revenue and cost allocation methods.

Returning to a more general level of analysis, it is clear that the crux of an airline's operating performance is the relationship it achieves between RASM and CASM (or 'unit cost'). The next section will look at this relationship, revisit yield, and discuss load factor.

ii. Unit cost, unit revenue, yield, and load factor

In Part 2 of the book we disaggregated the revenue and cost streams by looking at the following relationship:

TRAFFIC x YIELD > < OUTPUT x UNIT COST
= OPERATING PERFORMANCE (i.e., profit or loss)

Part 3 looked at capacity management – which is a matter of bringing output produced (i.e., 'output') and output sold (i.e., 'traffic') into reasonable balance (always bearing in mind that whereas airlines *produce* ASMs and ATMs by operating flight-legs, they *sell* seats offered in O & D markets). Figure 10.2 recasts these relationships and highlights four metrics that lie at the heart of airline operating performance (at least at a macro-level of analysis): CASM, RASM, yield, and load factor.

Unit cost and unit revenue

Irrespective of how we choose to build up an airline's cost and revenue streams (by flight-leg, route, O & D market, cabin, region, and so on), the ultimate measure of operating performance is whether or not RASM (i.e.,

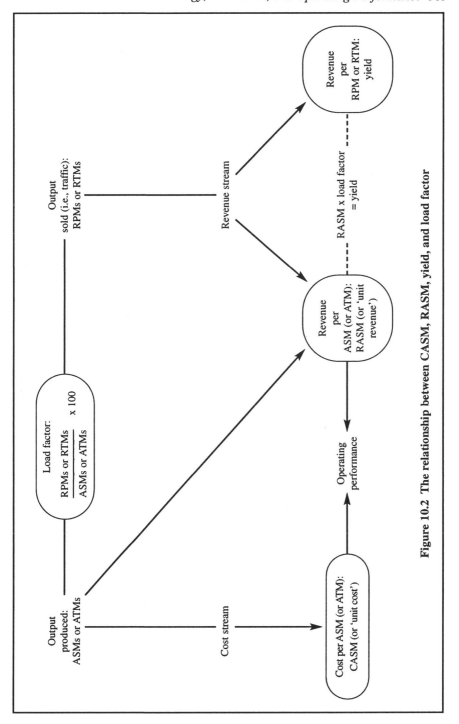

Figure 10.2 The relationship between CASM, RASM, yield, and load factor

revenue per unit of output *produced*) exceeds CASM (i.e., the cost of producing each unit of output).

1. **CASM** Improving CASM requires absolute input costs to be lowered and/or productivity to be raised.
2. **RASM** Improving RASM requires generating more revenue from the same level of production (i.e., output), or the same revenue from a reduced level of production. At any given level of output, it is possible to improve revenue and therefore RASM either by improving yield and holding load factor (i.e., sales) steady or by improving load factor (i.e., increasing sales) while holding yields steady. The following points are important in this context.
   - Increasing either yield or load factor without reducing the other will be a challenge unless the markets concerned are firm and relatively price-inelastic. It is generally difficult to increase load factor and yield simultaneously; for this to be achieved, it must usually be against the background of either a strong market or significant cuts in output.
   - Raising load factors within the current output range should not be expensive, but it will entail incremental traffic costs (arising from the delivery of ground and inflight service to additional passengers), incremental distribution costs (in respect of sales through agency channels), and perhaps higher marketing communication costs (to stimulate the incremental sales).
   - Higher yields are also likely to have little impact on the cost side unless they arise from a product upgrade that is expensive in capital and/or operating cost terms. Again, firmer yields might lead to higher distribution costs.

Conversely, if a positive margin between RASM and CASM is to be maintained in the face of either declining yield or declining load factor, the other metric must move upwards.

- **Declining yield** Achieved load factor must rise. High price-elasticity in the market(s) concerned might help. (The revenue effect of a one point increase in load factor at a given yield is: yield x 0.01 x ASMs.)
- **Declining load factor** Yield must rise. This is likely to be difficult to achieve if poor load factors are indicative of carrier-specific or industry-wide demand softness and excess output. (The revenue impact of a tenth of a cent rise in yield at a given traffic level is: 0.10 x RPMs.)

Unit costs, unit revenues, and output

Growing output Growing output can put downward pressure on unit costs, provided increased variable costs arising from the higher production level are outweighed by the beneficial impact of having more ASMs over which to spread fixed costs. The important question, of course, is whether the additional output also places so much downward pressure on yields that RASM declines faster than CASM and erodes operating profit. Assisted by the industry's long history as a growth business and fuelled by the apparently compelling attraction of market share to its managers, many airlines have tried in the past to grow their way out of cost problems.

Very generally, we can say the following.

- Raising output within a carrier's current capacity range is often sensible because it allows broadly unchanged fixed costs to be spread over more units of output (i.e., ASMs or ATMs); the key question is whether and at what price the incremental output can be sold – specifically, whether incremental RASM exceeds incremental variable CASM (which will rise) net of incremental fixed CASM (which should fall).
- If, on the other hand, incremental output is generated not just within the existing capacity range but by adding further capacity with its own fixed costs, the challenge is greater. Because of the indivisibilities encountered in the industry – the fact that demand increases by one seat or passenger at a time per market whereas capacity increases by one aircraft (or gate or route, etc.) at a time – new capacity often brings with it more incremental output than demand is able to absorb in the short run. This can lead to softer yields as price is used to maintain load factors in the face of higher output. Not only is CASM adversely affected by higher fixed costs (albeit still being spread over higher output), but RASM might also be negatively affected by weaker yields.

Shrinking output Although shrinking output should lead to an almost instant reduction in variable DOCs, an equally important issue is how quickly the structure of the operating system can be adjusted to bring about matching reductions in fixed DOCs and IOCs. If adjustment is slow and overhead remains at levels high enough to support previous output figures but above current needs, shrinking output can put upward pressure on unit costs; if only because it is unusual for a substantial carrier to be able to shed overhead as quickly as it can reduce frequencies or withdraw from routes, it is possible that the beneficial impact on unit costs brought about by reductions in variable DOCs may be counterbalanced in the short run by the fact that there are now fewer ASMs or ATMs over which to spread fixed costs.

There are broadly two reasons why a carrier might shrink output.

1. In response to an industry downturn or carrier-specific difficulties.
2. As part of a strategic reorientation intended to underpin or boost yield.

The first of these is exemplified by American's substantial capacity reduction initiated in the third quarter of 2001. The second was the path chosen by British Airways when in the late 1990s it decided to downsize capacity and output, upgrade its products, and focus more strongly on high-yield market segments. The dangers in this strategy are that high yields might be difficult to maintain in the face of a weak economy and/or competitors' upgraded products, and that costs associated with a relatively narrower system (notably smaller aircraft and perhaps reduced economies of scope) and an expensive product might put upward pressure on CASMs. Clearly, a high-yield strategy needs to be supported by a clear focus on costs just as much as does a low-fare strategy, albeit to different ends.

Inter-airline comparisons: revex ratio, cost productivity, and operating margin

Taking up the last point, it is evident that an airline's RASM and CASM need to be managed within some strategic context. Comparing different airlines' unit revenues and unit costs can be informative up to a point, particularly when the comparisons encompass direct competitors, but given that these figures are not adjusted to take into account each carrier's average stage-lengths, product strategies or brand positioning they tell at best only half the story of relative operating performances. The following can help fill-in the gaps.

1. **Revex (or 'operating') ratio** This is defined as: (operating revenue/operating cost) x 100. One hundred per cent indicates a break-even result at the operating level, whilst a figure in excess of that is indicative of an operating profit. (Revex ratios can in principle be calculated at several different levels. For example: an airline as a whole; an individual flight-leg, route or market; a cabin or a fare type (e.g., PEX or APEX) in a particular market. The finer-grained an analysis becomes, the more subjective the outcome will arguably be because of the alternative approaches available for internally prorating revenues and allocating costs to the different objects of analysis.)
2. **Cost productivity** Although the terminology adopted here is not settled, one possible definition is as follows: operating revenue/operating cost. This is simply a recast version of the revex ratio, intended to

find out how productive in monetary terms each dollar of operating expenditure is in generating revenue (whereas revex describes revenue as a percentage of cost).

3. **Operating margin** This is calculated as: (operating profit/operating revenue) x 100.

Comparing RASM and CASM figures for, say, Singapore Airlines and Southwest would tell us relatively little because these are very different types of airline, operating in different markets, and pursuing different competitive strategies. The above calculations, on the other hand, form an arguably better basis for comparison. Taking figures for 2000, Singapore Airlines had a revex of 115 per cent and an operating margin of 12.80 per cent. Southwest's revex was 122.14 per cent and its operating margin was 18.11 per cent, suggesting a somewhat better operating performance. Such ratios and the figures on which they are based should nonetheless be taken as broad descriptions of much more complex realities; only by digging down into the two airlines' cost and revenue streams can a rich understanding be gained in respect of what was driving these different but very creditable operating performances.

Conclusion

It is common for managements to set target CASM figures. Whilst this is sound, CASM in itself means relatively little unless related to assumed RASM. What needs to be done is to target an operating margin, assume RASM based on market conditions and the carrier's brand positioning and product offering(s), and derive a CASM target. Operating margin requirements should be driven both by stakeholders' expectations and by the re-investment needs of what is a capital-hungry industry.

In fact, with the exception of brief periods such as the mid- to late-1990s, the airline industry as a whole has historically been unable to sustain acceptable profits. Too often, output has been so high that sufficient demand could only be stimulated by lowering prices to levels inadequate to generate satisfactory operating – let alone net – profits given prevailing cost structures.

Yield

Yield – revenue per unit of output sold (i.e., per RPM or RTM) – is a highly significant metric, but it is by definition just the mathematical outcome of two even more fundamental metrics: output sold and revenue earned. When comparing revenue with cost, RASM is a more useful unit of analysis than yield because RASM and CASM have the same denominator (i.e., ASMs); since the denominator in the yield calculation is RPMs (or RTMs), yield cannot be directly compared with unit cost unless an adjustment is made for load factor. (An alternative is to compare yield with cost per RPM – something that is simple enough to calculate, but which adds little to the more usual CASM versus RASM comparison.)

Yield is nonetheless an important tool to help gain an understanding of the interplay between price and traffic figures when accounting for revenue performance in different parts of an airline's system. Figure 10.3 illustrates a simple revenue build-up approach.

For 40 years, real (i.e., inflation-adjusted) yields across the industry as a whole have been in decline, and the price stimulus to which this has given rise accounts for a significant proportion of the traffic growth achieved during these decades. However, this is not to say that nominal (i.e., current dollar) yields reported in airline financial statements are invariably in decline, or even that real yields cannot rise periodically under certain market circumstances. Very broadly, the following generalisations apply.

1. Yields will soften when:
   - traffic growth is flat and/or insufficient to absorb output growth, and low prices are used to sustain load factors;
   - one or more carriers decides to lower prices either to stimulate the market generally or to increase market share, and competitors match on a significant scale.
2. Yields will remain firm or harden when:
   - load factors are already high and output is growing no faster than traffic;
   - traffic growth is outstripping growth in output;
   - no significant competitor feels it necessary to use price either to stimulate the market further or to build market share.

Note that changes in yield (or, indeed, average fares) can result not just from price adjustments, but also from amending allocations to different booking classes in an RMS. Shifting inventory from high-yield to low-yield booking classes or buckets can result in lower yield, whilst reallocation in the opposite direction will harden yield (providing that the increased allocations are sold). The fact that traffic, load factor, and revenue as well as yield will each be affected by these types of adjustment illustrates once again how intimately connected these variables are – all within the context of available output.

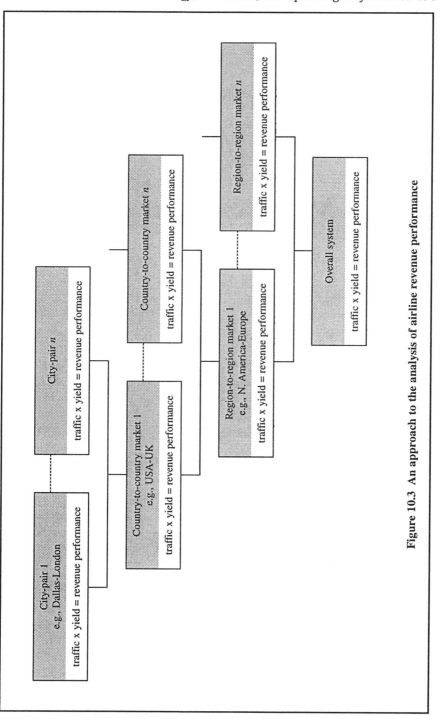

Figure 10.3 An approach to the analysis of airline revenue performance

Yield and unit costs

The higher an airline's unit cost, the more reliant it is on firm yields. Several full-service network carriers – United and US Airways, for example – found their high costs 'beached above the water-line' in 2002 when revenues and yields came under downward pressure as a result of weak demand for full-fare tickets from business travellers. This, in essence, is what led several observers at the time to conclude that these airlines' short-haul business model – a model featuring high production costs underpinned by high full fares paid by a relatively small proportion of passengers travelling frequently on business – was in need of radical overhaul (particularly in markets where low-fare carriers were, or were likely to become, part of the competitive equation).

Load factor

Load factor measures the percentage of an airline's output that has been sold. Several different metrics are used.

1. **Passenger load factors** There are two calculations in common use.
    - *Seat factor* This is the percentage of the seats available on a flight or series of flights that has been sold (with 'sold' also referring to FFP redemptions as well as revenue enplanements). It is not a distance-weighted measurement.
    - *Distance-weighted passenger load factor* This is what is commonly meant when the expressions 'load factor' or 'passenger load factor' are used, and it is calculated as RPMs/ASMs x 100.
    The two approaches can lead to dramatically different figures. Consider a two-leg flight operated by a 200-seat aircraft: the first leg is 500 miles and is flown with 80 per cent of seats occupied (i.e., 160), whilst the second leg is 3,000 miles and is flown with 40 per cent of seats occupied (i.e., 80).
    - Distance-weighted passenger load factor is (80,000+240,000 RPMs)/(100,000+600,000 ASMs) x 100 = 46 per cent.
    - Seat factor for the flight is (80+40)/2 = 60 per cent. (An alternative path to the same figure is (160+80)/(200+200).) In practice, this figure can be useful at the level of individual departures – with regard to aircraft assignment decisions, for example – but, as Box 10.1 suggests, there are pitfalls when it comes to averaging figures across a broader system. In the latter case, distance-weighted measures are preferable.

(It is also worth noting that average stage-length and the average distance flown by passengers are different. Average stage-length is (500+ 3,000 unduplicated route-miles)/2 departures = 1,750 miles. The average distance flown by passengers is (80,000+240,000 RPMs)/(160+80 passengers) = 1,333 miles. The moral is that averages can be analytically useful as long as sight is not lost of the fact that they do not describe anything real. On a systemwide level, the same moral can be applied to CASM, RASM, yield, and load factor as well as average stage-length and passenger journey.)

2. **Cargo load factors** Load factors on all-cargo flights can also be measured in the same way: as (payload capacity sold/payload capacity available) x 100, or on a distance-weighted basis as (RTMs/ATMs) x 100.

3. **Overall (or 'weight') load factor** These calculations account for both passengers and cargo by assuming a standard weight for passengers and their baggage (often around 90–95 kilos or 200 pounds), and comb-ining this with cargo tonnage. As in point 2 above, this can be done on a non-distance-weighted or a distance-weighted basis. When looking at individual flights or series of flights, the former approach can be useful, whereas network analyses and comparisons tend to adopt the distance-weighted metric.

Box 10.1: The pitfalls of averaging

If one flight between two points is operated by a 400-seat aircraft at a 60 per cent seat factor and another is flown by a 100-seater at 80 per cent, the average seat factor is not 70 per cent; it is (240+80)/(400+100) or 64 per cent. In fact, whenever looking at anything other than a single departure (or a series of departures on the same route using aircraft with the same seating capacity), it is normally safer to calculate load factor as aggregate RPMs expressed as a percentage of aggregate ASMs.

Similar traps lie in the calculation of yield and unit cost. For example, if first class yield (i.e., revenue per RPM) on a service is $1,000/1,000 RPMs or $1 per RPM and economy class yield is $50,000/200,000 RPMs or 25 cents per RPM, the route yield is not the arithmetic mean of 100 cents and 25 cents. It is $51,000/201,000 or 25.4 cents per RPM. The same type of calculation needs to be applied when averaging unit costs across cabins.

Clearly, if we start with an airline's aggregate RPM figure and divide it by aggregate ASMs to calculate load factor, if we start with total revenue and divide it by aggregate RPMs to calculate yield, or if we start with total operating cost and divide it by aggregate ASMs to calculate unit cost there should not be a problem. It is usually only when calculating averages from the bottom up – by building from figures for individual routes and cabin classes – that problems sometimes arise.

The inclusion of cargo in a load factor calculation adds a number of complications.

1. Cargo payload has two facets: weight and volume. Whereas most transportation modes are more concerned with weight carried as a percentage of payload capacity available, we saw in chapter 8 that aircraft frequently 'cube-out' before they 'weight-out' (i.e., the volume of space available for carriage of cargo is filled before the weight of cargo loaded reaches the maximum that could be uplifted). The result is that an aircraft departing absolutely full in volume terms might well have a weight load factor considerably below 100 per cent. The extent to which this matters will depend upon the yield per pound being earned. High-volume cargo which 'wastes' payload capacity (as well as high-density cargo which 'wastes' volume capacity) should, ideally, be priced to offer attractive yields in compensation.

2. As far as combination carriers (uplifting both passengers and cargo) are concerned, the same flight may have different load factors depending upon which calculation is used. For example:

   • assume that an aircraft with a payload capacity of 20 tons on a particular flight-leg actually carries passengers and cargo weighing 10 tons: its overall load factor is $(10/20) \times 100 = 50$ per cent;

   • if on the same flight the aircraft were configured with 130 seats of which 85 were sold (the rest of the payload being cargo), the seat factor would be $(85/130) \times 100 = 65.4$ per cent.

   Although the example is hypothetical, it does illustrate an important point: overall (or weight) load factors are often lower than passenger load factors. In 2000, for example, members of the US Air Transport Association recorded an average 72.4 per cent seat factor, but only a 58.5 per cent weight load factor. This type of disparity arises because the management of cargo capacity is constrained by the need to trade-off payload weight against payload volume, and because the heavy directional imbalances in freight flows tend to put downward pressure on cargo load factors when they are averaged across a route network. (In the case of the US domestic system the disparity also owes much to the fact that combination carriers have conceded most of the freight market to integrated carriers and, increasingly, time-definite trucking services.)

3. On some (particularly long-haul) flight-legs, combination carriers can have difficulty maximising cargo load factor because they do not know

how much cargo capacity is available until after passenger close-out (i.e., until after the passenger load has been finalised – something that might not happen until a few minutes before departure). This argues for having standby cargo ready to be loaded at the last moment when final passenger payload calculations reveal how much, if any, additional cargo can be carried.

Achieved load factors

Average load factors for the industry conceal marked variations between different types of airline, with regional carriers at the lower end of the spectrum and charter airlines generally achieving far higher load factors than scheduled carriers. The average for any individual airline masks variations between different markets and cabins (with economy/coach generally achieving higher load factors because customers tend to book further in advance and expect lower levels of seat accessibility than is the case in premium cabins); it also conceals pronounced daily, weekly and – in particular – seasonal variations. An average annual passenger load factor of, say, 65 per cent or more will conceal full flights and spilled demand during peak periods, as well as load factors perhaps as low as 40 per cent or worse on midday Tuesday departures in February (a common low point for many North American domestic and intra-European scheduled flights). Furthermore, a year-round system load factor of 65 per cent would encompass much more dispersion around the mean (i.e., a flatter distribution curve and therefore greater spill) than would be the case were the same figure to apply either to a single route or a single month.

Aside from general economic conditions and pricing decisions, achieved load factors are driven to a considerable extent by the following.

1. **Traffic mix** The higher the proportion of business travellers carried by an airline, the lower its average seat factor is likely to be because:
   - demand for business travel has a random element that makes forecasting on a departure-by-departure basis relatively challenging and means that if adequate seat accessibility is to be maintained there is going to be inevitable downward pressure on load factors;
   - high frequencies demanded by business travellers tend to result in lower average load factors than would be achieved were the same output generated by larger aircraft operated at lower frequencies.

   The more a carrier relies on advance-booking leisure and VFR traffic, the higher its load factor should be as a result of the higher predictability of booking profiles. (The downside, of course, will be relatively low yields.)

2. **Payment policies** A closely related point is that a carrier taking non-refundable payments at the time of reservation, as most low-fare carriers do throughout the aircraft and full-service carriers do in respect of deeply discounted economy/coach fares, is likely to have relatively fewer no-shows and a relatively higher seat factor than one selling a higher proportion of tickets on a fully flexible basis.

3. **Commercial success** The success of product design, pricing, promotions, marketing communications, distribution, and service delivery will clearly influence current load factors – as will the relative success of competitors' efforts.

4. **Revenue management** The effectiveness of an RMS in minimising spoilage will influence load factors.

Achieved load factors are in part a measure of the success or otherwise of an airline's capacity management efforts. As we have already seen, these efforts are hindered by the fact that whilst demand fluctuates in units of single seat-departures in different O & D markets and is volatile, supply can only be produced in units equivalent to the capacity of whichever aircraft type is available to operate the flight-legs and routes designed to serve targeted O & D markets and is broadly fixed in the short run. Furthermore, the requirements to maintain both a high flight completion rate and the integrity of network connections and aircraft and crew assignments might preclude a scheduled passenger carrier from cancelling a significant number of its lightly loaded flights.

The influence of demand characteristics on load factors Achieved load factor will depend to a large extent upon the market segments an airline serves. We have seen that load factors will generally be lower in respect of business travellers than the leisure and VFR segments; a carrier's premium cabins can therefore be expected to return lower load factors than the main cabin (although in the US domestic market FFP redemptions and upgrades tend to alter this picture), and business-oriented routes as a whole will often have lower load factors than leisure or ethnic/VFR routes. High-yield products such as those sold to first, business, and full-fare coach passengers generally have high seat accessibility built-in as an important product attribute. (Recall that seat accessibility is measured as the probability of being able to make a reservation successfully at a chosen point in time prior to departure. Late-booking business travellers who are consistently unable either to find a seat in the required class or to change their itineraries at short notice are, in the absence of overriding brand loyalty, likely to be spilled to any competing carrier offering a similar service level, convenient departures, and higher seat accessibility.)

The problem with high seat accessibility is that it puts downward pressure on achieved seat factors. At extreme ends of the accessibility-load factor 'continuum' are markets dominated by business travellers requiring high accessibility and having average seat factors in the mid-50 to mid-60 per cent range (or perhaps somewhat higher during economic upturns, as in the second half of the 1990s), and leisure markets in which the combination of a very low accessibility requirement and stiff cancellation or rebooking conditions can generate load factors over 90 per cent (e.g., many European charter markets). High seat accessibility is an expensive product attribute the cost of which is, in principle, reflected in the higher prices charged to customers who value it.

One final point with regard to the relationship between demand characteristics and load factors is that although demand from leisure and VFR segments is more price- and income-elastic than business demand, it is less volatile on a departure-by-departure basis – which implies that distributions around the mean are less pronounced and that an average load factor is likely to be more representative of the generality of achieved load factors than would be the case in respect of the business segment. The fact that demand amongst business travellers is volatile and that achieved load factors (by flight) show more extreme distributions around any mean figure imply that demand spill will be encountered at a lower average load factor than would be the case with a tighter distribution of achieved load factors around the mean (Clark, 2001).

The implications of high load factors Depending upon prevailing market circumstances, it is often the case that load factor and yield trade off against each other: unless demand is particularly strong and output growth is under firm control, it is likely that raising yield will put downward pressure on load factors, and reducing yield will boost load factor. Two relatively recent developments are assisting airlines in managing this trade-off.

1. On high-demand flights, RMSs can help increase yield without lowering load factor.
   - Even when an aircraft departs with a few empty seats, to the extent that these are the result of late cancellations or no-shows together having exceeded go-shows it is likely that potential customers will have been turned away at some point in the booking cycle. The use of overbooking models based on departure-specific historical data helps raise load factor by reducing this spoilage.
   - RMSs are designed to ensure, as far as possible, that the yield from each seat sold (although not necessarily from each flight taken as a whole) is maximised.

2. On low-demand flights, Internet distribution channels and seat auct-
    ions, alongside more general 'fare sales' and the use of consolidators,
    are used to dispose of 'distressed inventory' and raise load factors.

Airline managers will generally want to arrive at a capacity plan with target load factors that strike a balance between the costs (i.e., forgone revenues) of turning passengers away and the costs (i.e., operating costs) of
meeting all the peak demand coming forward and seriously oversupplying
the market at other times. In principle, they will want load factors to be
high – provided this does not require them to give away more in yield than
their cost base can tolerate. High load factors might sometimes be a
'double-edged sword', however.

- On the positive side, because approximately two-thirds of an airline's
  costs can be directly related to the operation of aircraft and are independent of the number of passengers carried (Wells, 1999), higher load
  factors generate lower average costs per passenger or per passenger-
  mile than would be the case were the same output of ASMs being produced but a lower load factor being achieved. If we assume a flight-leg
  DOC total of $20,000 for a 160-seater, the cost per passenger (without
  adjusting for changes in traffic costs) would be $167 at a 75 per cent
  load factor, rising to $179 at 70 per cent.
  However, what really matters is how the average cost per passenger
  compares with the average fare per passenger (metrics that are not very
  meaningful in the case of global network carriers unless disaggregated
  into component route groups (e.g., regional, mainline, domestic, long-
  haul international, etc.), but which can be informative in respect of
  single-class short-haul carriers); also of interest is how average cost per
  RPM stacks-up against yield (i.e., average revenue per RPM). If yields
  are falling faster than costs, it might well be load factors that have to
  take up the slack in order to keep RASM ahead of CASM. (Note that
  RASM can be calculated as yield x load factor, as well as rev-
  enue/ASM.)
- On the negative side, we have already seen that high load factors can
  imply unacceptable levels of spill and, accordingly, forgone revenue.
  (We noted in the last chapter that spill is usually less than 100 per cent
  of unaccommodated demand because some passengers will be booked
  onto earlier or later flights on the same carrier, and so 'recaptured' rather than lost to a competitor.) At the operational level, high load factors
  can lead to slower turnarounds – perhaps impacting on aircraft, gate,
  and staff utilisation and even schedule reliability. This is a problem
  Southwest identified and addressed in the late 1990s, for example.

Conclusion Load factors measure the percentage of output produced that has been sold. From an operating performance perspective this is important, but not as important as whether the revenue earned from sold output (i.e., RPMs and RTMs) is sufficient to cover the costs of producing total output – both sold and unsold (i.e., ASMs and ATMs). We therefore need to dig deeper by comparing achieved load factor with break-even load factor.

Break-even load factor

Achieved load factor is important, but in itself tells us nothing about operating performance until we relate it to break-even load factor (BELF). It is quite possible for an airline to achieve a higher load factor than a competitor but return a weaker operating performance (i.e., a lower operating profit or an operating loss), because the two have different BELFs.

Break-even load factor is the load factor at which costs and revenues are equal. It can be calculated at the level of net costs (including nonoperating items such as debt interest) and total revenue (i.e., operating and nonoperating), at the level of total operating costs (TOCs) and operating revenue, or at the level of DOCs and operating revenue. Our focus here is on break-even at the level of TOCs and operating revenue. The calculation of operating break-even is therefore as follows.

BELF = (TOCs/ASMs or ATMs)/(operating revenue/RPMs or RTMs)

A simplified version of the same calculation is (CASM/yield) x 100.

(At break-even, CASM and RASM are equal. However, it is worth keeping in mind that a carrier with high financial leverage – that is, high interest-bearing debt relative to shareholders' equity or net worth – could achieve a load factor in excess of operating break-even and so make an operating profit, yet still return a net loss because the positive operating result is insufficient to cover debt interest and other nonoperating expenses net of any nonoperating revenue. This has historically been a common occurrence amongst airlines during and immediately after periods of weak economic growth when profits have been poor and balance sheets have become over-leveraged by heavy borrowing.)

Break-even load factor can be calculated for a network as a whole or for individual flight-legs. In the case of individual flight-legs, however, a performance below fully allocated break-even (i.e., break-even calculated on the basis that all fixed costs and overhead are fully allocated to the flight) might not be critical if variable costs are being covered, a contribution is being made to fixed costs, and/or traffic profitable to the network as a whole is being carried. (This was explained in chapter 5.) At the system level, on the other hand, BELF is a critical benchmark that needs to be beaten.

The following additional points are important.

1. Any calculation of BELF is inevitably based on assumed unit costs and yields. An airline reaches break-even when it is selling enough output at a given yield to cover the fixed and variable costs of producing not only the output sold but also the portion of output that remains unsold (i.e., empty seats and cargo space on departed aircraft). We can therefore generalise that falling costs and/or rising yield will lower BELF, whilst rising costs and/or falling yield will raise it; we might also anticipate that introducing significant additional output could initially place upward pressure on BELF insofar as the incremental fixed costs associated with it (e.g., aircraft ownership costs) have a more or less immediate impact, whilst achieving higher load factors or firmer yields to compensate may not initially be easy given the boost to output (unless, of course, increases in output are timed to lag demand). The problem with using BELF as a management tool, therefore, is that it represents a moving target: neither prices, costs, their relationship nor their behaviour in response to output changes are constant over time. Nonetheless, BELF can be a critical input into product and route decisions.

2. If we move below the system level to calculate BELF in respect of an individual cabin or flight-leg, the analysis is inevitably hostage to choices regarding cost allocation and internal revenue proration.

3. We saw in chapter 5 that, at least in the short run, scheduled airlines suffer from high operating leverage – that is, high fixed costs as a proportion of total costs. What the word 'leverage' in this expression implies in practice is that once break-even is breached on either the upside or the downside, the impact of changes in revenue on operating profit are relatively greater than would be the case in a less leveraged industry. In the case of airlines this means that apparently quite small differences between achieved load factor and BELF can have a significant impact on operating results; whenever an airline is operating close to BELF, the sale of just one or two extra or fewer seats per departure can make a profound difference to systemwide operating performance.

4. An airline's BELF will be heavily influenced by its traffic mix. Break-even load factor for carriers on the North Atlantic can range from over 90 per cent in coach/economy to 40 per cent or even less in the premium cabins. At times some airlines have trouble more than breaking even on low-yield traffic but nonetheless use it to boost density and permit the operation of larger aircraft with lower seat-mile costs than high-yield traffic alone could sustain, relying on the high-yield traffic

for most or all of their operating profit. This is fine as long as high-yield traffic remains robust.

However, the interplay between traffic mix and BELF is not as straightforward as high-yield/low-BELF and low-yield/high-BELF. Ryanair appears to have its costs so firmly under control at the time of writing that its BELF is in the low 50 per cent range despite low yields and low average fares, whereas the figures for most full-service European majors are either side of the 70 per cent mark – which is not very different from the figures for some of the better-managed European charter airlines. Even before 9/11, a combination of expensive labour settlements and a precipitous decline in high-yield business traffic brought United's BELF close to 80 per cent – considerably higher than the US industry average, which prior to 9/11 had been running under 70 per cent for several years (figure 10.4).

5.   Freight revenue also needs to be taken into account when calculating BELF. One approach that is commonly used is to deduct freight revenue from operating costs (including costs attributable to the carriage of freight) in order to arrive at an adjusted BELF.

Conclusion   Because airlines each have different unit costs and yields, every carrier inevitably has a different BELF. Two incontrovertible facts are that a relatively high achieved load factor does not guarantee operating profits, and neither does a relatively low achieved load factor guarantee operating losses (as many regionals regularly prove). To take just one possible example of why this might be so, it is fairly obvious that if a fleet or sub-fleet is insufficiently utilised in terms of its aggregate time in the air – in other words, if it is not producing all the output it is capable of producing – even the sale of a high percentage of this unsatisfactory level of output (i.e., achievement of a high load factor) will not necessarily generate an operating profit. As we have seen at various points in the book, airlines generally have high short-run fixed costs which require that:

•   as much output as possible is produced over which fixed costs can be averaged (i.e., capacity utilisation should be high);
•   as much of this output as possible is sold (i.e., achieved load factors should be high); and
•   the output sold is sold at prices that exceed the cost of producing both sold and unsold output (i.e., BELF should be managed as low as possible and achieved load factor should be as far as possible above it). Even a good load factor achieved on well-utilised aircraft will be inadequate if aggressive pricing and/or high costs leave BELF at a higher level.

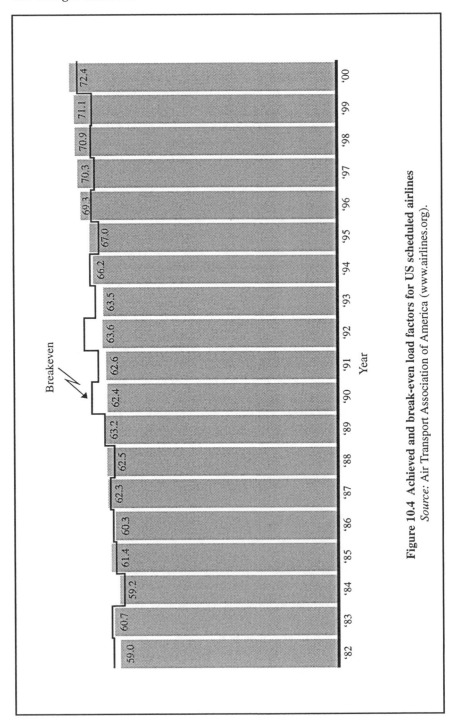

Figure 10.4 Achieved and break-even load factors for US scheduled airlines
Source: Air Transport Association of America (www.airlines.org).

Clearly, there is a close relationship between yield, unit cost, BELF, and achieved load factor.

1. **Yield** Strategic and market positioning provide the framework. Within this framework, how much influence an airline has over its yield depends in large measure upon the prevailing price-elasticity(ies) of demand for the particular product(s) it is offering, and on the level of competition in its markets.
   - If yield rises whilst unit cost remains unchanged, BELF will fall (i.e., improve).
   - If yield falls whilst unit cost remains unchanged, BELF will rise (i.e., deteriorate).
   - The higher the yield on a route or network, the lower will be its BELF at any given unit cost level.
   - When yield softens, unit cost must also be reduced if BELF is not to rise.
2. **Unit cost** As we saw in chapter 5, unit cost will be a function of absolute input costs and productivity – both of which will be affected by a carrier's network and fleet structure, and by the nature of the product(s) it offers.
   - If unit cost rises whilst yield remains unchanged, BELF will rise.
   - If unit cost falls whilst yield remains unchanged, BELF will fall.
   - The lower the unit cost of operating a route or network, the lower will be the carrier's BELF at any given level of yield.
   - If unit cost rises, yield must be improved if BELF is not to rise.
3. **Achieved and break-even load factors**
   - A moderate achieved load factor might be acceptable if BELF is sufficiently low – as when, for example, a high-yield (and therefore presumably high-accessibility) product is being offered.
   - A high achieved load factor will not necessarily be enough to ensure acceptable operating performance if BELF is high – as when, for example, unit costs are high or yield is low.
   - If achieved load factor rises whilst yield and unit cost (and therefore BELF) remain constant, operating performance will improve (and vice versa).

iii. Concluding comment

Part 1 of the book briefly provided a strategic context within which to consider industry economics. Part 2 was structured around the relationship between operating revenue (traffic x yield) and operating cost (output x unit cost). Part 3 looked at several topics central to capacity management, the fundamental objective of which is to bring the relationship between revenue and cost into profitable juxtaposition.

Operating revenues can change because of changes in traffic and/or changes in the yield earned from carrying traffic. Operating costs can change because of changes in output and/or changes in the unit cost of producing output. When the two sides of this relationship balance, achieved and break-even load factors (at the operating level) will be identical. When one variable changes without a compensating change in another, achieved and break-even load factors will go their separate ways – the direction of which will quickly feed through to operating performance because of the industry's high short-run operating leverage.

Volatility in the constituent parts of each of these elements – the most significant of which have been discussed at various points throughout the book – accounts for the roller-coaster ride in airline operating performance. Drawing from the present book and from Holloway (2002), there is a strong argument that three of the most fundamental variables in any service business are employee satisfaction, customer satisfaction, and cash flow. Managing all three to acceptably high levels in the complex and volatile environment of an airline is not a straightforward challenge.

References

Air Transport Association (2001), *Annual Report*, Washington DC.

Alamdari, F.E. and Morrell, P. (1998), 'Airline Franchising: Brand Extension or Outsourcing High-Cost Routes?', in Butler, G.F. and Keller, M.R. (eds), *Handbook of Airline Marketing*, McGraw-Hill, New York.

Alderson, W. (1957), *Marketing Behaviour and Executive Action*, Irwin, Homewood IL.

Arciuolo, F. (1998), 'The Role of Technology in Airline Product Distribution', in Butler, G.F. and Keller, M.R. (eds), *Handbook of Airline Marketing*, McGraw-Hill, New York.

Areeda, P. and Turner, D. (1975), 'Predatory Prices and Related Practices Under Section 2 of the Sherman Act', *Harvard Law Review*, 88, 4, 697-783.

Bailey, E.E. and Panzar, J.C. (1981), 'The Contestability of Airline Markets During the Transition to Deregulation', *Law and Contemporary Problems*, 44, Winter, 125-145.

Bailey, E.E. and Williams, J.R. (1988), 'Sources of Economic Rent in the Deregulated Airline Industry', *The Journal of Law and Economics*, 31, April, 173-202.

Bailey, E.E., Graham, D.R., and Kaplan, D.P. (1985), *Deregulating the Airlines*, MIT Press, Cambridge MA.

Bain, J.S. (1949), 'A Note on Pricing in Monopoly and Oligopoly', *American Economic Review*, 39, March, 448-464.

Bain, J.S. (1956), *Barriers to New Competition*, Harvard University Press, Cambridge MA.

Bain, J.S. (1968), *Industrial Organization* (2nd edition), Wiley, New York.

Baker, C. (2002), 'Fuel for Thought', *Airline Business*, January, 52-54.

Baldanza, B.B. (1999), 'Measuring Airline Profitability', in Butler, G.F. and Keller, M.R. (eds), *Handbook of Airline Finance*, McGraw-Hill, New York.

Baldanza, B.B. and Lipkus, L.S. (2000), 'Fundamentals of Airport Operations Staffing and Quality Assurance Measurement', in Butler, G.F. and Keller, M.R. (eds), *Handbook of Airline Operations*, McGraw-Hill, New York.

Bamburger, G.E. and Carlton, D.W. (2002), 'Airline Networks and Fares,' in Jenkins, D. (ed), *Handbook of Airline Economics* (2nd edition), McGraw-Hill, New York.

Barkin, T.I., Hertzell, O.S., and Young, S.J. (1995), 'Facing Low-cost Competitors: Lessons for US Airlines', *The McKinsey Quarterly*, 4, 86-99.

Barney, J.B. (1986a), 'Organizational Culture: Can it be a Source of Sustained Competitive Advantage?', *Academy of Management Review*, 11, 3, 656-665.

Barney, J.B. (1986b), 'Strategic Factor Markets: Expectations, Luck, and Business Strategy', *Management Science*, 32, 3, 1231-1241.

Barney, J.B. (1991), 'Firm Resources and Sustained Competitive Advantage', *Journal of Management*, 17, 1, 99-120.

Barney, J.B. (1997), *Gaining and Sustaining Competitive Advantage*, Addison-Wesley, Reading MA.

Barney, J.B. and Ouchi, W.G. (1986), *Organizational Economics*, Jossey-Bass, San Francisco CA.

Barry, D. and Elmes, M. (1997), 'Strategy Retold: Toward a Narrative View of Strategic Discourse', *Academy of Management Review*, 22, 2, 429-452.

Battersby, B. and Oczkowski, E. (2001), 'An Econometric Analysis of the Demand for Domestic Air Travel in Australia', *International Journal of Transport Economics*, 28, 2, 193-204.

Baumol, W. J. (1959), *Business Behaviour, Value, and Growth*, Macmillan, New York.

Baumol, W.J. (1982), 'Contestable Markets: An Uprising in the Theory of Industry Structure', *American Economic Review*, 72, 1-15.

Baumol, W.J. and Willig, R.D. (1986), *Contestability: Developments Since the Book*, Research Paper 86-01, New York University, New York.

Baumol, W.J., Panzar, J.C., and Willig, R.D. (1982), *Contestable Markets and the Theory of Industrial Structure*, Harcourt, Brace, Jovanovich, New York.

Bazerman, M. (1998), *Judgement in Managerial Decision-Making* (4th edition), Wiley, New York.

Belobaba, P.P. (1987), 'Airline Yield Management – An Overview of Seat Inventory Control', *Transportation Science*, 21, 63-73.

Belobaba, P.P. (1989), 'Application of a Probabilistic Decision Model to Airline Seat Inventory Control', *Operations Research*, 37, 183-197.

Belobaba, P.P. (1998a), 'The Evolution of Airline Yield Management: Fare Class to Origin-Destination Seat Inventory Control', in Butler, G.F. and Keller, M.R. (eds), *Handbook of Airline Marketing*, McGraw-Hill, New York.

Belobaba, P.P. (1998b), 'Airline Differential Pricing for Effective Yield Management', in Butler, G.F. and Keller, M.R. (eds), *Handbook of Airline Marketing*, McGraw-Hill, New York.

Belobaba, P.P. (2002), 'Airline Network Revenue Management: Recent Developments and State of the Practice', in Jenkins, D. (ed), *Handbook of Airline Economics* (2nd edition), McGraw-Hill, New York.

Belobaba, P.P. and Farkas, A. (1999), 'Yield Management Impacts on Airline Spill Estimation', *Transportation Science*, 33, 2, May, 217-232.

Belobaba, P.P. and Wilson, J.L. (1997), 'Impacts of Yield Management in Competing Airline Markets', *Journal of Air Transport Management*, 3, 3-9.

Bender, A.R. and Stephenson, F.J. (1998), 'Contemporary Issues Affecting the Demand for Business Air Travel in the United States', *Journal of Air Transport Management*, 4, 99-109.

Berdy, P. (1998), 'Developing Effective Route Networks', in Butler, G.F. and Keller, M.R. (eds), *Handbook of Airline Marketing*, McGraw-Hill, New York.

Berdy, P. (2002), 'Developing Effective Route Networks', in Jenkins, D. (ed), *Handbook of Airline Economics* (2nd edition), McGraw-Hill, New York.

Besanko, D., Dranove, D., and Shanley, M. (2000), *Economics of Strategy* (2nd edition), Wiley, New York.

Beyer, B. (1999), 'Competitive Practices Under Pressure', *The Avmark Aviation Economist*, September, 1-2.

Beyer, B. (2000), 'Premium Hub Fares: Reality or Myth?', *The Avmark Aviation Economist*, May, 14-16.

Boeing (1997), *Current Market Outlook 1997*, Boeing Commercial Airplane Group, Seattle WA.

Boeing (2001), 'Revenue and Yield Management', presentation by Richard Lonsdale to the Euromoney *European School of Aircraft Economics*, Vinkeveen, Netherlands, 24-27 September.

Bogner, W.C. and Thomas, H. (1996), 'From Skills to Competences: The "Playout" of Resource Bundles Across Firms', in Heene, A. and Sanchez, R. (eds.), *Competence-based Strategic Management*, Wiley, Chichester.

Borenstein, S. (1985), 'Price Discrimination in Free-Entry Markets', *RAND Journal of Economics*, 16, Autumn, 380-397.

Borenstein, S. (1989), 'Hubs and High Fares: Dominance and Market Power in the U.S. Airline Industry', *RAND Journal of Economics*, 20, Autumn, 344-365.

Borenstein, S. (1992), 'The Evolution of US Airline Competition', *Journal of Economic Perspectives*, 6, Spring, 82-88.

Botimer, T.C. (1993), 'Airline Pricing and Fare Product Differentiation', Ph.D. dissertation, Massachusetts Institute of Technology.

Bounds, G., Yorks, L., Adams, M., and Ranney, G. (1994), *Beyond Total Quality Management*, McGraw-Hill, New York.

Bowles, R. (1994), 'Air Travel: A Growth or Mature Industry?', *Canadian Aviation Forecast Conference Proceedings*, 69-73, Transport Canada.

Bowman, C. and Ambrosini, V. (1998), 'Value Creation Versus Value Capture: Towards A Coherent Definition of Value in Strategy – An Exploratory Study', *Working Paper SWP 14/98*, Cranfield School of Management.

Bowman, C. and Faulkner, D. (1997), *Competitive and Corporate Strategy*, Irwin, London.

Broggio, G., Falcomatà, S., Paoletti, B., Felici, G., and Gentile, C. (2000), 'An Optimization Framework for Ground Staff Roster Management Using Integer

608 Straight and Level: Practical Airline Economics

Programming', in Butler, G.F. and Keller, M.R. (eds), *Handbook of Airline Operations*, McGraw-Hill, New York.

Brueckner, J.K. and Spiller, P.T. (1994), 'Economics of Traffic Density in the Deregulated Airline Industry', *Journal of Law and Economics*, 37, 2, 379-391.

Brueckner, J.K. and Whalen, W.T. (1998), *The Price Effects of International Airline Alliances*, Unpublished paper, University of Illinois at Urbana-Champaign.

Brueckner, J.K., Dyer, N.J., and Spiller, P.T. (1992), 'Fare Determination in Airline Hub-and-Spoke Networks', *RAND Journal Of Economics*, 23, 3, Autumn, 309-333.

Butchers, E.R., Day, P.R., Goldie, A.P., Miller, S., Meyer, J.A., Ryan, D.M., Scott, A.C., and Wallace, C.A. (2001), 'Optimized Crew Scheduling at Air New Zealand', *Interfaces*, 31, 1, January-February, 30-56.

Button, K.J. (1993), *Transport Economics* (2nd edition), Edward Elgar, Cheltenham.

Button, K.J. (1996), 'Liberalizing European Aviation: Is There an Empty Core Problem?', *Journal of Transport Economics and Policy*, 30, 275-291.

Button, K.J. and Stough, R. (2000), *Air Transport Networks*, Edward Elgar, Cheltenham.

CAA (1994), *Airline Competition on European Long-Haul Routes*, CAP 639, London.

Call, G.D. and Keeler, T.E. (1985), 'Airline Deregulation, Fares, and Market Behaviour: Some Empirical Evidence', in Daugherty, A.H. (ed), *Analytical Studies in Transport Economics*, Cambridge University Press, Cambridge, England.

Carlton, D.W., Landes, W.M., and Posner, R.A. (1980), 'Benefits and Costs of Airline Mergers: A Case Study', *Bell Journal of Economics and Management Science*, Spring 1980, 11, 65-83.

Caves, D.W. (1962), *Air Transport and its Regulators*, Harvard University Press, Cambridge MA.

Caves, D.W., Christensen, L.R., and Tretheway, M.W. (1984), 'Economies of Density Versus Economies of Scale: Why Trunk and Local Service Airline Costs Differ', *Rand Journal of Economics*, 15, 4, 471-489.

Chamberlin, E.H. (1933), *The Theory of Monopolistic Competition*, Harvard University Press, Cambridge MA.

Chandler, A.D. (1962), *Strategy and Structure*, MIT Press, Cambridge MA.

Christou, I.T., Zakarian, A., Liu, J.M., and Carter, H. (1999), 'A Two-Phase Genetic Algorithm for Large-Scale Bidline-Generation Problems at Delta Air Lines', *Interfaces*, 19, 5, September-October, 51-65.

Clampett, S. (1998), 'Airflite: Developing a Premium Product', *Flight Scheduling Journal*, Sabre, Dallas TX.

Clark, P. (2000), 'Dynamic Fleet Management', in Butler, G.F. and Keller, M.R. (eds), *Handbook of Airline Operations*, McGraw-Hill, New York.

Clark, P. (2001), *Buying the Big Jets: Fleet Planning for Airlines*, Ashgate, Aldershot.

Clarke, M.D.D., Lettovský, L., and Smith, B.C. (2000), 'The Development of the Airline Operations Control Center', in Butler, G.F. and Keller, M.R. (eds), *Handbook of Airline Operations*, McGraw-Hill, New York.

Comanor, W.S. and Frech, H.E. III (1993), 'Predatory Pricing and the Meaning of Intent', *Antitrust Bulletin*, 38, 2, Summer, 293-308.

Cotterril, R.M. (1997), 'Open Skies, Competition, and Airline Alliances', presentation to the Smi conference *Managing & Rationalising Market-led Airline Alliances*, London, 27–28th January.

Crandall, R.L. (1995), 'The Unique US Airline Industry', in Jenkins, D. (ed), *Handbook of Airline Economics*, McGraw-Hill, New York.

Creel, M. and Farrell, M. (2001), 'Economies of Scale in the U.S. Airline Industry After Deregulation: A Fourier Series Approximation', *Transportation Research*, Part E, 321-336.

Cyert, R.M. and March, J.G. (1963), *A Behavioural Theory of the Firm*, Prentice-Hall, Englewood Cliffs NJ.

Damodaran, A. (2001), *Corporate Finance: Theory and Practice* (2nd edition), Wiley, New York.

Davies, R.E.G. (2002), 'Air Transport Directions in the 21st Century (The Lessons of History)', in Jenkins, D. (ed), *Handbook of Airline Economics* (2nd edition), McGraw-Hill, New York.

Dennis, N. (1994), 'Scheduling Strategies for Airline Hub Operations', *Journal of Air Transport Management*, 1994, 1, 131-144.

Dennis, N. (2000), 'Scheduling Issues and Network Strategies for International Airline Alliances', *Journal of Air Transport Management*, 6, 75-85.

Denton, N. and Dennis, N. (2000), 'Airline Franchising in Europe: Benefits and Disbenefits to Airlines and Consumers', *Journal of Air Transport Management*, 6, 179-190.

Desrosiers, J., Lasry, A., McInnis, D., Solomon, M.M., and Soumis, F. (2000), 'Air Transat Uses ALTITUDE to Manage Its Aircraft Routing, Crew Pairing, and Work Assignment', *Interfaces*, 30, 2, March–April, 41-53.

Dillon, J.E. and Kontogiorgis, S. (1999), 'US Airways Optimizes the Scheduling of Reserve Flight Crews', *Interfaces*, 29, 5, September–October, 123-131.

Doganis, R.S. (2001), *The Airline Business in the 21st Century*, Routledge, London.

Douglas, G.W. and Miller, J.C. (1974a), *Economic Regulation of Domestic Air Transport: Theory and Policy*, The Brookings Institution, Washington D.C.

Douglas, G.W. and Miller, J.C. (1974b), 'Quality Competition, Industrial Equilibrium, and Efficiency in the Price-Constrained Airline Market', *American Economic Review*, 64, 657-669.

Douma, S. and Schreuder, H. (1998), *Economic Approaches to Organizations* (2nd edition), Prentice Hall, Harlow.

Dresner, M. (2002), 'Metrics in the Airline Industry', in Jenkins, D. (ed), *Handbook of Airline Economics* (2nd edition), McGraw-Hill, New York.

Dryburgh, I. (2000), 'First Revolution', *Aircraft Interiors*, September, 18-22.

Dudley, M. and Clarke, D. (1998), 'Irregular Airline Operations: A Review of The State-of-the-Practice in Airline Operations Control Centres', *Journal of Air Transport Management*, 4, 67-76.

Dussauge, R. and Garrette, B. (1995), 'Determinants of Success in International Strategic Alliances: Evidence from the Global Aerospace Industry', *Journal of International Business Studies*, 26, 505-530.

Eastman, R. (2002), 'Ticketless Travel, or the Evolution of E-Tickets', in Jenkins, D. (ed), *Handbook of Airline Economics* (2nd edition), McGraw-Hill, New York.

Evans, W.N. and Kessides, I.N. (1993), 'Structure, Conduct, and Performance in the Deregulated Airline Industry', *Southern Economic Journal*, 59, 450-467.

Fabrycky, W.J., Thuesen, G.J., and Verma, D. (1998), *Economic Decision Analysis* (3rd edition), Prentice-Hall, Upper Saddle River NJ.

Falkenburg, A. (1996), 'Marketing and the Wealth of Firms', *Journal of Macro-marketing*, 16, Spring, 4-24.

Feldman, J. (2001), 'Connecting the Dots', *Air Transport World*, October, 48-52.

Fershtam, C. and Muller, E. (1986), 'Capital Investment and Price Agreement in Semi-Collusive Oligopolies', *RAND Journal of Economics*, 17, 214-226.

Fitzroy, F.R., Acs, Z.J., and Gerlowski, D.A. (1998), *Management and Economics of Organization*, Prentice-Hall, Hemel Hempstead.

Fitzsimmons, J.A. and Fitzsimmons, M.J. (1998), *Service Management: Operations, Strategy, and Information Technology* (2nd edition), McGraw-Hill, New York.

Flint, P. (2001), 'Hard Times', *Air Transport World*, November, 23-27.

Forsyth, P. (2001), 'Promoting Trade in Airline Services', *Journal of Air Transport Management*, 7, 43-50.

Foss, N.J. (1997), 'Resources and Strategy: A Brief Overview of Themes and Contributions', in Foss, N.J. (ed), *Resources, Firms, and Strategies*, Oxford University Press, Oxford.

Frainey, W.M. (1999), 'Network Profitability Analysis', in Butler, G.F. and Keller, M.R. (eds), *Handbook of Airline Finance*, McGraw-Hill, New York.

Friend, C.H. (1992), *Aircraft Maintenance Management*, Longman, Harlow.

Gale, I.L. and Holmes, T.J. (1993), 'Advance-Purchase Discounts and Monopoly Allocation of Capacity', *American Economic Review*, 83, March, 135-146.

Garvett, D.S. and Avery, A. (1998), 'Frequent Traveler Programs', in Butler, G.F. and Keller, M.R. (eds), *Handbook of Airline Marketing*, McGraw-Hill, New York.

Garvett, D.S. and Michaels, L. (1998), 'Price Parrying: A Direction for Quick, Decisive, and Profit-Maximizing Pricing', in Butler, G.F. and Keller, M.R. (eds), *Handbook of Airline Marketing*, McGraw-Hill, New York.

Garvin, M.R. Jr. (2000), 'Service Delivery System: A Regional Airline Perspective', in Butler, G.F. and Keller, M.R. (eds), *Handbook of Airline Operations*, McGraw-Hill, New York.

Gertner, R. (1993), *The Role of Firm Asymmetries for Tacit Collusion in Markets With Immediate Competitive Responses*, Working Paper, University of Chicago.

Ghemawat, P. (1991), *Commitment: The Dynamic of Strategy*, The Free Press, New York.

Gillen, D., Oum, T., and Tretheway, M. (1985), *Airline Cost and Performance: Implications for Public and Industry Policies*, Centre for Transportation Studies, University of British Columbia, Vancouver.

Golaszewski, R.S. and Ballard, B.D. (2001), 'Aviation Demand and Capacity: Do Current Institutions Promote an Efficient Balance?', in Butler, G.F. and Keller, M.R. (eds), *Handbook of Airline Strategy*, McGraw-Hill, New York.

Golaszewski, R.S and Klein, F.J. (1998), 'Airline and Manufacturer Issues in Marketing Large Commercial Aircraft', in Butler, G.F. and Keller, M.R. (eds), *Handbook of Airline Marketing*, McGraw-Hill, New York.

Good, W. (2000), 'Flight Crew Scheduling Update: The Strategic Management of Airline Intellectual Capital and Core Competencies', in Butler, G.F. and Keller, M.R. (eds), *Handbook of Airline Operations*, McGraw-Hill, New York.

Graham, A. (2000), 'Demand for Leisure Air Travel and Limits to Growth', *Journal of Air Transport Management*, 6, 109-118.

Graham, D.R. and Kaplan, D.P. (1982), 'Airline Deregulation is Working', *Regulation*, 6, 26-32.

Graham, D.R., Kaplan, D.P., and Sibley, D.S. (1983), 'Efficiency and Competition in the Airline Industry', *The Bell Journal of Economics*, 14, 118-138.

Granovetter, M. (1985), 'Economic Action and Social Structure: The Problem of Embeddedness', *American Journal of Sociology*, 91, 3, 481-510.

Grant, R.M. (1998), *Contemporary Strategy Analysis,* Blackwell, Malden MA.

Hanlon, P. (1999), *Global Airlines: Competition in a Transnational Industry* (2nd edition), Butterworth-Heinemann, Oxford.

Hatton, R. (1999), 'Complexities of Air Cargo vis-à-vis Air Finance: The Economics of Wide-Body Freighter Aircraft', in Butler, G.F. and Keller, M.R. (eds), *Handbook of Airline Finance*, McGraw-Hill, New York.

Havel, B.F. (1997), *In Search of Open Skies*, Kluwer, The Hague.

Hergert, M. and Morris, D. (1989), 'Accounting Data for Value Chain Analysis', *Strategic Management Journal*, 10, 175-188.

Herrmann, N., Müller, M., and Crux, A. (1998), 'Pricing and Revenue Management Can Reshape Your Competitive Position in Today's Air Cargo Business', in Butler, G.F. and Keller, M.R. (eds), *Handbook of Airline Marketing*, McGraw-Hill, New York.

Heskett, J.L, Jones, T.O., Loveman, G.W., Sasser, W.E. Jr., and Schlesinger, L.A. (1994), 'Putting The Service-Profit Chain to Work', *Harvard Business Review*, March–April, 164-174.

Heskett, J.L., Sasser, W.E. Jr., and Schlesinger, L.A. (1997), *The Service-Profit Chain*, The Free Press, New York.

Holloway, S. (1992), *Aircraft Acquisition Finance*, Pitman, London.

Holloway, S. (1998a), *Changing Planes: A Strategic Management Perspective on an Industry in Transition (Vol. 1: Situation Analysis)*, Ashgate, Aldershot.

Holloway, S. (1998b), *Changing Planes: A Strategic Management Perspective on an Industry in Transition (Vol. 2: Strategic Choice, Implementation, and Outcome)*, Ashgate, Aldershot.

Holloway, S. (2002), *Airlines: Managing to Make Money*, Ashgate, Aldershot.

Homan, A.C. (2000), 'The Effect of Changes in Flight Time and On-Time Performance on Commercial Air Transport Demand', in Butler, G.F. and Keller, M.R. (eds), *Handbook of Airline Operations*, McGraw-Hill, New York.

Hopperstad, C. (1994), 'The Application of Path Preference and Stochastic Demand Modelling to Market Based Forecasting', in *AGIFORS Reservations and Yield Management Study Group Proceedings*, Hong Kong.

Hunt, S.D. (2000), *A General Theory of Competition: Resources, Competencies, Productivity, Economic Growth*, Sage, Thousand Oaks CA.

Hurdel, G.J., Johnson, R.L., Joskow, A.S., Werden, G.J., and Williams, M.A. (1989), 'Concentration, Potential Entry, and Performance in the Airline Industry', *Journal of Industrial Economics*, December, 38, 119-139.

ICAO (2000), 'Report of the Conference on the Economics of Airports and Air Navigation Services – Air Transport Infrastructure for the 21st Century', Montreal, 19-28 June.

Ingold, A. and Huyton, J.R. (1997), 'Yield Management and the Airline Industry', in Yeoman, I. and Ingold, A. (eds), *Yield Management: Strategies for the Service Industries*, Cassell, London.

Irrgang, M.E. (1995a), 'Airline Irregular Operations', in Jenkins, D. (ed), *Handbook of Airline Economics*, McGraw-Hill, New York.

Irrgang, M.E. (1995b), 'Fuel Conservation', in Jenkins, D. (ed), *Handbook of Airline Economics*, McGraw-Hill, New York.

Irrgang, M.E. (2000), 'Airline Operational Efficiency', in Butler, G.F. and Keller, M.R. (eds), *Handbook of Airline Operations*, McGraw-Hill, New York.

Jacobs, T.L., Ratliff, R.M., and Smith, B.C. (2001), 'The Importance of Integrating Airline Scheduling, Pricing, and Yield Management Activities', in Butler, G.F. and Keller, M.R. (eds), *Handbook of Airline Strategy*, McGraw-Hill, New York.

James, G. (1993), 'US Commercial Aviation: A Growth or Mature Industry', *18th FAA Aviation Forecast Conference Proceedings*, FAA-APO 93-2, 182-202.

Jarrah, A.I., Goodstein, J., and Narasimhan, R. (2000), 'An Efficient Airline Re-Fleeting Model for the Incremental Modification of Planned Fleet Assignments', *Transportation Science*, 34, 4, November, 349-363.

Jenks, C.B. (2001), 'Global Alliances: Three Strategically Key Evolutionary Uncertainties', in Butler, G.F. and Keller, M.R. (eds), *Handbook of Airline Strategy*, McGraw-Hill, New York.

Jordan, W.A. (1970), *Airline Regulation in America: Effects and Imperfections*, Johns Hopkins University Press, Baltimore MD.

Jorge-Calderón, J.D. (1997), 'A Demand Model for Scheduled Airline Services on International European Routes', *Journal of Air Transport Management*, 3, 1, 23-35.

Joskow, P.L. and Klevorick, A.K. (1979), 'A Framework for Analyzing Predatory Pricing Policy', *Yale Law Journal*, 89, 2, 213-270.

Kahn, A.E. (1971), *The Economics of Regulation*, Wiley, New York.

Kanellis, G.R. (1999), 'A Method for Evaluating and Selecting Avionics Equipment for Commercial Aircraft: The Head-up Guidance System (HGS®) Example', in Butler, G.F. and Keller, M.R. (eds), *Handbook of Airline Finance*, McGraw-Hill, New York.

Keeler, T.E. (1972), 'Airline Regulation and Market Performance', *Bell Journal of Economics and Management*, 3, 399-414.

Kelly, T. (2001), 'A Strategic Challenge: Delivering Airspace Capacity', in Butler, G.F. and Keller, M.R. (eds), *Handbook of Airline Strategy*, McGraw-Hill, New York.

Kimes, S.E. (1997), 'Yield Management: An Overview', in Yeoman, I. and Ingold, A. (eds), *Yield Management: Strategies for the Service Industries*, Cassell, London.

Kline, R. (1999), 'Managing Aircraft Costs Through Passenger Value Management', in Butler, G.F. and Keller, M.R. (eds), *Handbook of Airline Finance*, McGraw-Hill, New York.

Kontogiorgis, S. and Acharya, S. (1999), 'US Airways Automates Its Weekend Fleet Assignment', *Interfaces*, 29, 3, May–June, 52-62.

Kyrou, D. (2000), *Lobbying the European Commission: The Case of Air Transport*, Ashgate, Aldershot.

Lam, M. (1995), 'An Introduction to Airline Maintenance', in Jenkins, D. (ed), *Handbook of Airline Economics*, McGraw-Hill, New York.

Laney, E. (2002), 'The Evolution of Corporate Travel Management: Reacting to the Stresses and Strains of Airline Economics', in Jenkins, D. (ed), *Handbook of Airline Economics* (2nd edition), McGraw-Hill, New York.

Lawton, T.C. (2002), *Cleared for Take-Off: Structure and Strategy in the Low Fare Airline Business*, Ashgate, Aldershot.

Levine, M.E. (1965), 'Is Regulation Necessary? California Air Transportation and National Regulatory Policy', *Yale Law Journal*, 74, 1416-1485.

Levine, M.E. (1987), 'Airline Competition in Deregulated Markets Theory, Firm Strategy, and Public Policy', *Yale Law Journal*, 4, 393-484.

Lindquist, J. (1999), 'Overview of Alliance Development in the Airline Industry', paper presented at the *Maximising ROI of Airline Alliances* conference, Paris, 7-8 July, Institute of Marketing Research.

Lovelock, C. (1996), *Services Marketing* (3rd edition), Prentice Hall, Upper Saddle River NJ.

Margo, R.D. and Houghton, A.T. (1999), 'The Role of Insurance in Aviation', in Butler, G.F. and Keller, M.R., *Handbook of Airline Finance*, McGraw-Hill, New York.

Mason, E.S. (1939), 'Price and Production Policies of Large Scale Enterprises', *American Economic Review*, 29, 61-74.

Mason, K.J. (2000), 'The Propensity of Business Travellers to Use Low-Cost Airlines', *Journal of Transport Geography*, 8, 2, 107-119.

Mason, K.J. (2001), 'Marketing Low-Cost Airline Services to Business Travellers', *Journal of Air Transport Management*, 7, 103-109.

Mason, K.J., Whelan, C., and Williams, G. (2000), *Europe's Low Cost Airlines: An Analysis of the Economics and Operating Characteristics of Europe's Charter and Low Cost Scheduled Carriers*, Cranfield University, Air Transport Group Research Report 7, January.

McDonald, M. (2002), 'Endangered Species?', *Air Transport World*, June, 34-38.

McGill, J.I. and Van Ryzin, G.J. (1999), 'Revenue Management: Research Overview and Prospects', *Transportation Science*, 33, 2, May, 233-256.

McShane, S. and Windle, R.J. (1989), 'The Implications of Hub-and-Spoke Routeings for Airline Costs and Competitiveness', *Logistics and Transportation Review*, 25, 3, September, 209-230.

Melville, J.A. (1998), 'An empirical Model of the Demand for International Air Travel,' *International Journal of Transport Economics*, 25, 3, 313-322.

Merrill Lynch (1999), *e-Commerce: Virtually Here.*

Messer, R. (1999), 'Pricing Aeronautical Fees at Private Airports', in Butler, G.F. and Keller, M.R. (eds), *Handbook of Airline Finance*, McGraw-Hill, New York.

Meyer, J.R. and Oster, C.V. (1984), *Deregulation and The New Airline Entrepreneurs*, MIT Press, Boston MA.

Mineck, D.W. (1995), 'Satellite-Based Navigation and Communications: The Impact Upon World Airline Operations', in Jenkins, D. (ed), *Handbook of Airline Economics*, McGraw-Hill, New York.

Mintzberg, H. (1989), *Mintzberg on Management: Inside Our Strange World of Organizations*, Free Press, New York.

Moore, T.G. (1986), 'US Airline Deregulation: Its Effects on Passengers, Capital, and Labour', *Journal of Law and Economics*, 29, 1-28.

Morrell, P. (2002a), 'Capital Productivity and the Role of Capital Intensity in Airline Labour Productivity', in Jenkins, D. (ed), *Handbook of Airline Economics* (2nd edition), McGraw-Hill, New York.

Morrell, P. (2002b), *Airline Finance* (2nd edition), Ashgate, Aldershot.

Morrison, S.A. and Winston, C. (1986), *The Economic Effects of Airline Deregulation*, The Brookings Institution, Washington DC.

Morrison, S.A. and Winston, C. (1987), 'Empirical Implications and Tests of the Contestability Hypothesis', *Journal of Law and Economics*, April, 30, 53-66.

Morrison, S.A. and Winston, C. (1989), 'Enhancing the Performance of the Deregulated Air Transportation System', *Brookings Papers on Economic Activity*, 61-112.

Narayanan, P.R. and Yuen, B.B. (1998), 'Point of Sale: An Alternative Form of O & D Control', in Butler, G.F. and Keller, M.R. (eds), *Handbook of Airline Marketing*, McGraw-Hill, New York.

Nelson, R.R., and Winter, S.G. (1982), *An Evolutionary Theory of Economic Change*, Belknap Press, Cambridge MA.

Neumann, M. (2001), *Competition Policy: History, Theory and Practice*, Edward Elgar, Cheltenham.

Nichols, W.K. and Sala, S. (2000), 'Minimizing Connecting Times: A Must for Airline Competitiveness', in Butler, G.F. and Keller, M.R. (eds), *Handbook of Airline Operations*, McGraw-Hill, New York.

Nickerson, J.A., Hamilton, B.H., and Wada, T. (2001), 'Market Position, Resource Profile, and Governance: Linking Porter and Williamson in the Context of International Courier and Small Package Services in Japan', *Strategic Management Journal*, 22, 251-273.

Nickum, J.D. (2002), 'Airline Considerations in Avionics Equipage Decisions', in Jenkins, D. (ed), *Handbook of Airline Economics* (2nd edition), McGraw-Hill, New York.

OECD (1997), *The Future of International Air Transport Policy: Responding to Global Change*, Paris.

Oster, C.V. and Strong, J.S. (2001), 'Competition and Antitrust Policy', in Butler, G.F. and Keller, M.R., (eds) *Handbook of Airline Strategy*, McGraw-Hill, New York.

Ostrowski, P.L. and O'Brien, T.V. (1991), *Predicting Customer Loyalty for Airline Passengers*, Department of Marketing, Northern Illinois University, June.

Oum, T.H. and Park, J.H. (1997), 'Airline Alliances: Current Status, Policy Issues, and Future Directions', *Journal of Air Transport Management*, 3, 133-144.

Oum, T.H., Park, J.H., and Zhang, A. (2000), *Globalization and Strategic Alliances*, Pergamon, Oxford.

Oum, T.H. and Yu, C. (1998), *Winning Airlines: Productivity and Cost Competitiveness of the World's Major Airlines*, Kluwer Academic Press, Boston MA.

Oum, T.H. and Yu, C. (2000), *Shaping Air Transport in Asia Pacific*, Ashgate, Aldershot.

Panzar, J.C. and Willig, R.D. (1981), 'Economies of Scope', *American Economic Association, Papers and Proceedings*, May, 268-272.

Payne, A. and Frow, P. (1999), 'Developing a Segmented Service Strategy: Improving Measurement in Relationship Marketing', *Journal of Marketing Management*, 15, 797-818.

Pels, E. (2001), 'A Note on Airline Alliances', *Journal of Air Transport Management*, 7, 3-7.

Penrose, E.T. (1959), *Theory of the Growth of the Firm*, Basil Blackwell, London.

Perry, L.J. (1995), 'The Response of Major Airlines to Low-Cost Airlines', in Jenkins, D. (ed), *Handbook of Airline Economics*, McGraw-Hill, New York.

Pickett, D.C. (2002), 'The Aircraft Engine Selection Process', in Jenkins, D. (ed), *Handbook of Airline Economics* (2nd edition), McGraw-Hill, New York.

Pickrell, D. (1991), 'The Regulation and Deregulation of US Airlines', in Button, K.J. (ed), *Airline Deregulation: International Experiences*, David Fulton, London.

Piercy, N. (1997), *Market-Led Strategic Change* (2nd edition), Butterworth-Heinemann, Oxford.

Pilling, M. (2001), 'Flights of Fancy', *Airline Business*, January.

Pindyck, R.S. and Rubinfeld, D.L. (2001), *Microeconomics* (5th edition), Prentice-Hall, Upper Saddle River NJ.

Pinkham, R. (2001), 'Bringing Delta Home', *Airline Business*, March.

Porter, M.E. (1980), *Competitive Strategy*, The Free Press, New York.

Porter, M.E. (1985), *Competitive Advantage*, The Free Press, New York.

Porter, M.E. (1991), 'Towards a Dynamic Theory of Strategy', *Strategic Management Journal*, 12, Winter, Special Edition, 95-117.

Porter, M.E. (1996), 'What is Strategy?', *Harvard Business Review*, November-December, 61-78.

Prahalad, C.K. and Hamel, G. (1990), 'The Core Competence of the Corporation', *Harvard Business Review*, May-June, 79-91.

Rao, B.V. (2000), 'An Origin-Destination Model for Cargo Revenue-Mix Optimization', presentation to the *AGIFORS Cargo Study Group*, Louisville KY.

Rao, V.R. and Steckel, J.H. (1998), *Analysis for Strategic Marketing*, Addison-Wesley, New York.

Reichheld, F.F. (1996), *The Loyalty Effect*, Harvard Business School Press, Boston MA.

Riley, D. (1987), 'Competitive Cost Based Investment Strategies for Industrial Companies', *Manufacturing Issues*, Booz, Allen, Hamilton, New York.

Rispoli, M. (1996), 'Competitive Analysis and Competence-Based Strategies in the Hotel Industry', in Sanchez, R., Heene, A., and Thomas, H. (eds), *Dynamics of Competence-Based Competition: Theory and Practice in the New Strategic Management*, Pergamon, Oxford.

Robertson, R. (2002), University of New South Wales, private correspondence.

Robinson, J. (1934), 'What is Perfect Competition?', *Quarterly Journal of Economics*, 49, 104-120.

Rogers, W.H., Allen, J.A., and Hoyme, K.P. (2000), 'The Airline Operations Center Dilemma: Solving "Day-of-Operation" Disruptions With Greater Economic Efficiency', in Butler, G.F. and Keller, M.R. (eds), *Handbook of Airline Operations*, McGraw-Hill, New York.

Rothbard, M. (1962), *Man, Economy, and State*, Van Nostrand, Princeton NJ.

Roy, J. and Filiatrault, P. (1998), 'The Impact of New Business Practices and Information Technologies on Business Air Travel Demand', *Journal of Air Transport Management*, 4, 77-86.

Rumelt, R.P. (1984), 'Towards a Strategic Theory of the Firm', in Lamb, R. (ed), *Competitive Strategic Management*, Prentice-Hall, Englewood Cliffs NJ.

Schipper, Y. (2001), *Environmental Costs and Liberalization in European Air Transport: A Welfare Economic Analysis*, Edward Elgar, Cheltenham.

Schmalensee, R. (1985), 'Do Markets Differ Much?', *American Economic Review*, 75, 3, 341-350.

Schnell, M.C.A. (2001), 'Managerial Perception of Barriers to Route Exit: Evidence from Europe's Civil Aviation Markets', *Journal of Air Transport Management*, 7, 95-102.

Scott, W.R. (1995), *Institutions and Organizations*, Sage, Thousand Oaks CA.

Selznick, P. (1957), *Leadership in Administration: A Sociological Interpretation*, Harper & Row, New York.

Sentance, A. (2001), 'Living With Slower Growth', *Airline Business*, July, 76-78.

Shank, J.K. (1989), 'Strategic Cost Management: New Wine or Just New Bottles?', *Journal of Management Accounting Research*, 1, Fall, 47-65.

Shaw, S. (1999), *Airline Marketing and Management* (4th edition), Ashgate, Aldershot UK.

Shields, M. (1998), 'The Changing Cargo Business', in Butler, G.F. and Keller, M.R. (eds), *Handbook of Airline Marketing*, McGraw-Hill, New York.

Shy, O. (1995), *Industrial Organization: Theory and Applications*, MIT Press, Cambridge MA.

Simon, H.A. (1960), 'Corporate Decision-making: An Empirical Study', *Journal of Applied Psychology*, 53, 1-13.

Sinclair, M.T. and Stabler, M. (1997), *The Economics of Tourism*, Routledge, London.

Slack, N., Chambers, S., Harland, C., Harrison, A., and Johnston, R. (1998), *Operations Management* (2nd edition), Pitman, London.

Smith, K.G., Grimm, C.M., Gannon, M.J., and Chen, M. (1991), 'Organizational Information Processing, Competitive Responses and Performance in the US Domestic Airline Industry', *Academy of Management Journal*, 34, 60-85.

Smith, B.C., Leimkuhler, J.F., and Darrow, R.M. (1992), 'Yield Management at American Airlines', *Interfaces*, 22, 8-31.

Smith, B.C., Barlow, J., and Vinod, B. (1998), 'Airline Planning and Marketing Decision Support: A Review of Current Practices and Future Trends', in Butler, G.F. and Keller, M.R. (eds), *Handbook of Airline Marketing*, McGraw-Hill, New York.

Smith, B.C., Günther, D.P., Rao, B.V., and Ratliff, R.M. (2001), 'E-Commerce and Operations Research in Airline Planning, Marketing, and Distribution', *Interfaces*, 31, 2, March–April, 37-55.

Solon, D. (1999), 'A Formula for Profitability', *The Avmark Aviation Economist*, March.

Solon, D. (2001), 'Cut-price Carriers Shrug Off Worldwide Slowdown Jitters', *The Avmark Aviation Economist*, June, 2-4.

Spitz, W.H. (1998), 'International Code Sharing', in Butler, G.F. and Keller, M.R. (eds), *Handbook of Airline Marketing*, McGraw-Hill, New York.

Starkie, D. (1998), 'Allocating Slots: A Role for the Market?', *Journal of Air Transport Management*, 4, 111-116.

Stavins, J. (1996), *Price Discrimination in the Airline Market: The Effect of Market Concentration*, Federal Reserve Bank of Boston, Boston MA.

Stiglitz, J.E. (1994), *Whither Socialism?*, MIT Press, Cambridge MA.

Stonier, J.E. (1998), 'Marketing from a Manufacturer's Perspective: Issues in Quantifying the Economic Benefits of New Aircraft, and Making the Correct Financing Decision', in Butler, G.F. and Keller, M.R. (eds), *Handbook of Airline Marketing*, McGraw-Hill, New York.

Stonier, J. E. (2001), 'Airline Fleet Planning, Financing, and Hedging Decisions Under Conditions of Uncertainty', in Butler, G.F. and Keller, M.R. (eds), *Handbook of Airline Strategy*, McGraw-Hill, New York.

Swarbrooke, J. and Horner, S. (1999), *Consumer Behaviour in Tourism*, Butterworth-Heinemann, Oxford.

Taneja, N.K. (2002), *Driving Airline Business Strategies Through Emerging Technology*, Ashgate, Aldershot.

Tapp, A. (1998), *Principles of Direct & Database Marketing*, Pitman, London.

Telser, L.G. (1978), *Economic Theory and the Core*, University of Chicago Press, Chicago IL.

Transportation Research Board (1999), *Entry and Competition in the U.S. Airline Industry*, Special Report 255, National Academy Press, Washington DC.

Tretheway, M.W. (1998), 'Airport Marketing: An Oxymoron', in Butler, G.F. and Keller, M.R. (eds), *Handbook of Airline Marketing*, McGraw-Hill, New York.

Trevett, J. (1999), 'New vs Old', *Aircraft Economics*, 44, July–August, 39-41.

Trott, P. (1998), *Innovation Management & New Product Development*, Pitman, London.

Turney, P.B.B. (1991), 'How Activity-Based Costing Helps Reduce Cost', *Journal of Cost Management*, Winter, 29-35.

Varoufakis, Y. (1998), *Foundations of Economics*, Routledge, London.

Vinod, B. (1995), 'Origin-and-Destination Yield Management', in Jenkins, D. (ed), *Handbook of Airline Economics*, McGraw-Hill, New York.

Walker, S., (2002), Virtual Aviation College, private correspondence.

Weatherford, L.R. and Bodily, S.E. (1992), 'A Taxonomy and Research Overview of Perishable Asset Revenue Management: Yield Management, Overbooking, and Pricing', *Operations Research*, 40, 5, September-October, 831-844.

Wells, A.T. (1999), *Air Transportation: A Management Perspective* (4th edition), Wadsworth, Belmont CA.

Wernerfelt, B. (1984), 'A Resource-Based View of the Firm', *Strategic Management Journal*, 5, 2.

Weyer, T. (1998), 'Keeping Yield Management Under Control', *Aviation Strategy*, May, 16-19.

Whelan, C. (2000), 'Air Navigation Charges: Worldwide Benchmarking of Fees', *The Avmark Aviation Economist*, March, 10-17.

Wild, R. (1989), *Production and Operations Management* (4th edition), Cassell, London.

Williams, G. (2002), *Airline Competition: Deregulation's Mixed Legacy*, Ashgate, Aldershot.

Windle, R.J. and Dresner, M.E. (1992), 'Partial Productivity Measures and Total Factor Productivity in the Air Transport Industry: Limitations and Uses', *Transportation Research –A*, 26A, 6, 435-445.

Windle, R.J. and Dresner, M.E. (1995), 'A Note on Productivity Comparisons Between Air Carriers', *The Logistics and Transportation Review*, 31, 2, 125-134.

Wu, C-L. and Caves, R.E. (2000), 'Aircraft Operational Costs and Turnaround Efficiency at Airports', *Journal of Air Transport Management*, 6, 201-208.

Yuen, B.B. (1998), 'Group Revenue Management', in Butler, G.F. and Keller, M.R. (eds), *Handbook of Airline Marketing*, McGraw-Hill, New York.

Yuen, B.B. and Irrgang, M.E. (1998), 'The New Generation of Revenue Management: A Network Perspective', in Butler, G.F. and Keller, M.R. (eds), *Handbook of Airline Marketing*, McGraw-Hill, New York.

Zakreski, E. (1998), 'Beyond Frequent Flyers: Knowing Customers as a Foundation for Airline Growth', in Butler, G.F. and Keller, M.R. (eds), *Handbook of Airline Marketing*, McGraw-Hill, New York.

Zeithaml, V.A. and Bitner, M.J. (2000), *Services Marketing: Integrating Customer Focus Across the Firm* (2nd edition), McGraw-Hill, New York.

Zhao, W. and Zheng, Y-S. (2001), 'A Dynamic Model for Airline Seat Allocation With Passenger Diversion and No-Shows', *Transportation Science*, 35, 1, February, 80-98.

Zou, S. and Cavusgil, S.T. (1996), 'Global Strategy: A Review and an Integrated Conceptual Framework', *European Journal of Marketing*, 30, 1, 52-69.

Index